Liao Architecture

Liao
Architecture

Nancy Shatzman Steinhardt

University of Hawai'i Press

Honolulu

02 01 00 99 98 97   5 4 3 2 1

LIBRARY OF CONGRESS CATALOGING-IN-PUBLICATION DATA

Steinhardt, Nancy Shatzman.
Liao architecture / Nancy Shatzman Steinhardt.
p. cm.
Includes bibliographical references and index.
ISBN 0–8248–1843–1 (alk. paper)
1. Monasteries, Buddhist — China — Liao River Region.
2. Building, Wooden — China — Liao River Region.
3. Sepulchral monuments — China — Liao River Region.
4. Architecture — China — Sung-Yüan dynasties, 960–
1368.   I. Title.
NA6046.L5S74   1997
726′.7843′095182 — dc21   97–3096
                                            CIP

Publication of this book has been assisted by grants
from the following organizations:

Chiang Ching-kuo Foundation for
International Scholarly Exchange

Furthermore, the publication program
of the J. M. Kaplan Fund

Millard Meiss Publication Fund Committee of the
College Art Association

MM

Design by Christine Taylor
Composition and production by
Wilsted & Taylor Publishing Services

To my mother, Miriam Levin Shatzman,

and

the memory of my father,

Ben Shatzman (1915–1993)

Contents

List of Maps and Tables

Preface

MY INTRODUCTION TO LIAO architecture was not remarkable. Like most graduate students of East Asian art since the 1940s, at some point during my first year of graduate school (in my case 1974), I came across the two volumes of plates entitled *Ryō-Kin jidai no kenchiku to sono Butsuzō* (Liao-Jin period architecture and its sculpture) and the two-volume *Tombs and Mural Paintings: Ch'ing-ling* while looking for something else in the folio stacks of the library. Every one of the wooden halls and brick pagodas and each of the reconstituted wall paintings pictured in these books seemed intrinsically interesting. Yet neither the buildings nor the tombs came up in lectures or seminars or associated readings.

In the twenty years that have passed since that initial encounter, countless new monuments from every province and region, and every time period, have led to reevaluation and rewriting of the history of Chinese art. Liao (947–1125) architecture, wall paintings, and artifacts have been as numerous as those of any other period. Still, Liao material rarely finds a place even in the post-1980s history of Chinese art.

There are reasons for the lacuna. Ever since the collapse of the Liao dynasty in 1125 there have been obstacles to its study. Liao is the first of three dynasties who ruled in China in succession between the tenth century and 1368 that often are referred to in the West as "conquest dynasties" and in China as "barbarian dynasties." Either name marks the separation of these groups from the perceived mainstream of Chinese civilization. In China, in addition, the shame of foreign occupation in the tenth through fourteenth centuries is underscored by the fact that the eastern half of Liao territory was that part of the Asian continent from which the non-Chinese Manchu dynasty known as Qing (1644–1911) emerged. Furthermore, materials concerning the homeland of the last non-Chinese dynasty—the geographic region known in the first half of this century as Manchuria—have been most extensively studied and published by Japanese scholars during the occupation in the 1920s and 1930s. Thus it became not just unpopular, but unpatriotic, to conduct research on any material (tenth to fourteenth century or seventeenth to nineteenth century) that had first come to light through these Japanese archaeological teams.

It was not until 1986 that I entered a Liao building. Again my introduction was the standard one for an art historian of China: I visited Datong where I saw what remained at the Huayan and Shanhua monasteries. The Liao-period sutra library and two main halls were splendid—yet seen just a day after my first experience at the rock-cut caves of Yun'gang, and the same day I saw Sima Jinlong's fifth-century lacquer screen, I did not leave Datong with an urge to write a book about Liao architecture. From Datong I went on to Ying county, and it was there, as I walked along the outer and inner rings of columns of the various levels of the nearly 70-meter-high timber pagoda, that I began to think about what must have been required to put this building or those from Datong together and what it might have meant for them to stand along China's

"barbarian-occupied" northern fringe in the eleventh century. I also sought some kind of link between what I had seen at Datong and what was in front of me, for the timber pagoda had been erected less than twenty years after the sutra library and only 85 kilometers to the south.

There were, of course, other motivations for writing this book. One was a research interest in Chinese architecture in general. In the fall of 1986 I began to reread the secondary Chinese literature about Liao architecture. This literature comprised two main groups. The earlier works were written mainly in the 1930s by a newly formed Society for Research in Chinese Architecture whose membership was primarily Western- and Japanese-trained architects who became China's first architectural historians. The later literature has been written after 1949—after the dispersal of the society—by some of the society's members and, by the 1980s and 1990s, by their Chinese students. Having seen several Liao buildings by the time I began reading, I felt it was fitting that a Liao-period pavilion and gate were the subjects of the first monograph on Chinese architecture. In this article of 1932 and those of the next decade about Liao structures I came across statements like "I felt the aura of somberness and grandeur" [as I stood before a Liao building]; or "I was moved by the power of the architecture"; or "artistically, this is the best building in China." Such had been my own feelings when I stood in front of the same buildings, and I was gratified to find similar personal sentiments in print. I determined at that point to figure out why the wooden buildings of non-Chinese patronage in northeastern China had elicited such remarks.

The next summer, 1987, I returned to China and followed the 1930s itineraries of several members of the Society for Research in Chinese Architecture. They had sought the old buildings that survived among those named in local records; I sought to determine how the Liao buildings they had first described had fared a half-century of war and political turmoil. It was on the same trip that I first saw a temple complex of Song, the Chinese dynasty contemporary to Liao to its south. This experience convinced me that the unique contribution of Liao to Chinese architecture could only be understood through a discussion of the general issues of tenth-through twelfth-century Chinese architecture. That period's architecture, and the wooden architecture of the non-Chinese Jin dynasty (1125–1234) that succeeded Liao, became the parameters of timber-frame architecture discussed in the first part of this book.

In 1989 I began to explore the Liao funerary tradition. It was through my research on tombs and tomb decoration that I came to understand, as I explain in Parts Two and Three of this book, important purposes of Liao timber architecture. Thus a book that began as a monograph on fourteen wooden halls, and grew to a study of Chinese architecture from the tenth through thirteenth centuries, has come to include funerary architecture as well.

It was not until 1992 and 1993 that I received permission to see Liao architecture in Inner Mongolia and Liaoning. By the summer of 1993 I had seen all but one of the nine extant Liao wooden buildings and twenty-odd brick pagodas. I had walked in all sixteen *zhou* (prefectures) of North China that were Liao's at the zenith of their empire; I had stood in their "ancestral *zhou*" and had touched pieces of the outer walls or other ruins at all five Liao capitals; and I had seen numerous Liao treasures in the museums of prefectures and towns of Inner Mongolia and Liaoning. The monuments and objects, especially against the backdrop of the Mongolian grasslands, have not ceased to make me wonder about the circumstances of their construction by seminomads in the tenth, or eleventh, or twelfth century. Through the years of research and writing, it has remained the inherent visual power of the monuments and my own curiosity about their makers, Qidan tribesmen who confederated into the Liao empire, that have made every day of this study rewarding.

My next motivation for writing this book was my previous research experience. Few art historians or sinologists begin as Liao specialists. I am no exception. Like others, I have moved from the study of one seminomadic conquest dynasty to another. In my case, the move was back several centuries from research on the art and architecture of the thirteenth-to-fourteenth-century Mongols. Although the territory of China and North Asia where Liao wooden buildings survive is smaller than the scope of the Mongolian empire, the study of Liao architecture was more challenging to initiate. The Liao period offers no counterparts to Marco Polo and Friars William of Rubruck or Odoric of Pordenone whose Western-style descriptions of the life and architectural spaces of the Mongols have led scholars into the Yuan period. Writings about the Liao come primarily from Song Chinese scholars. No portraits of Liao khans hang in museums. There is neither an Inner nor Outer Qidania where one can be certain to meet descendants of the Liao khans. No university courses are offered in the language of the Qidan. In fact, although the Liao wrote with two scripts, neither has been completely deciphered. The Mongols were important to this study, however—not only because aspects of the acculturation of that seminomadic group, including their use of architecture, in the process of empire formation could be informative in the study of the Liao, but also because the majority of the Liao empire eventually fell to the Mongols and much of the Liao portion of the Mongolian empire eventually fell to the Manchus. Thus, in some cases, Liao buildings have been preserved in Mongolian or Manchu packaging.

In some ways the study of Liao buildings has more to offer than that of their Mongolian counterparts. Whereas to this day no burial site of a Mongolian emperor of China and only about twenty nonimperial Yuan-period tombs have been excavated, the tomb sites of all but the last Liao emperor are known, as are those of members of the imperial consort clan. Excavated nonimperial Liao tombs number close to 300, more than 40 with wall paintings. Of this huge group, no single plan is standard and the mural programs are as complex as any subterranean ones known from Chinese tombs.

My final motivation for writing this book was the nature of the documentation about Liao buildings. The timber buildings exhibit a range of wooden joinery techniques: some are the only extant examples of a type described in an architectural treatise; many are examples of the most eminent standards the Chinese building tradition offers. The literary documentation has included primarily stele inscriptions and descriptions in local records. Through them, detailed histories of the buildings and their patrons in this seemingly remote part of Asia have come to life.

Research for this book, especially the site-by-site trips to the eastern and western Inner Mongolian Autonomous Region and through Liaoning, was expensive. Without generous support from the following organizations neither the trips nor the writing could ever have been accomplished. I thank the Graham Foundation for Advanced Studies in the Fine Arts, the American Council of Learned Societies, the Getty Grant Program, the National Endowment for the Humanities, the American Philosophical Society, the Asian Cultural Council, and the Research Foundation of the University of Pennsylvania for funding specific components of this project between 1987 and 1996.

Since I became interested in the Liao in the mid-1980s, Denis Twitchett, Frederick Mote, Marilyn L. Gridley, and Hok-lam Chan have willingly answered questions and been gracious sounding boards for my thoughts. Professors Mote, Gridley, and Chan, as well as Victor Mair and Tracy Miller, have read this manuscript at different stages. Their contributions are indicated throughout the notes. A grant from the Northeast Asia Council of the Association for Asian Studies that was matched by the School of Arts and Sciences made it possible for the University of Pennsylvania to have a Liao Seminar during the spring semester of 1992. Participants in that seminar, Denis Twitchett, Morris Rossabi, Yvgeni Lubo-Lesnichenko, Pamela K. Crossley, and Marilyn L. Gridley, were influential stimuli for this work. So too were discussions about Liao architecture with the late Alexander Soper and with Lothar Ledderöse. Chinese colleagues have been a continuous source of help in China—not only through correspondence but also, occasionally, by sending me a copy of a publication so obscure that I had no hope of getting it in the United States. Among the many who have helped I thank, in particular, Xu Pingfang and Ying Zhaojin and, in Japan, Tanaka Tan. In addition, I am ever grateful to the numerous drivers, local guides, monks, and villagers who led me across farmland and grassland, opened local museums, and gave me permission to photograph.

From the beginning of this project, I was determined to include an extensive photographic record of Liao architecture and related material. The laborious task of transforming my slides and photographs from a variety of sources, some of them of very poor quality, into their present form was accomplished by H. Fred Schoch and Francine Sarin of the Museum of Archaeology and Anthropology, University of Pennsylvania. I thank them for their continued willingness to reshoot and reprint and for their good cheer. At the University of Hawai'i Press, I am grateful for the production help, including some tedious layout work, that brought this book to completion. Most of all I thank Patricia Crosby, editor and by now good friend, and Cheri Dunn for their enthusiasm about this book and commitment to it at every stage. In addition, I want to express my appreciation to copy editor Don Yoder for his meticulous reading of this manuscript and to Jeffrey Klein and Chang Che-chia for help with computerization of portions of the text.

The first summer I saw Liao architecture I was the mother of two preschoolers. By the time I wrote the last page of this manuscript I had one child in middle school, two in elementary school, and an infant. Each research trip, and each night or weekend I worked, required sacrifice on their parts. Without that sacrifice, without Paul's taking time from his work so that I could do mine, and without my parents' continued willingness to be here while I was in Asia, all that follows could not have been finished.

Liao Architecture

MAP 1. Major Sites of the Liao and Song Empires. [Drawn by Andrew K. Y. Leung]

1

Introduction

THE LIAO RIVER RUNS SOUTHWARD from the meeting point of Liaoning and Jilin provinces and the Inner Mongolian Autonomous Region (Inner Mongolia), cutting Liaoning province in half and emptying into the Bohai Sea. Eastward into this point flows the West Liao River, across nearly 500 kilometers of Inner Mongolia. Together the two Liao Rivers serve the modern cities of Liaoning and Inner Mongolia—Shenyang, Liaoyang, Jinzhou, Fuxin, Chaoyang, and Chifeng—and the smaller towns and banners (*qi*) of the region such as Faku, Beipiao, Tongliao, Aohanqi, and Naimanqi. In the other direction, some 200 kilometers east of the rivers, are Tonghua and Changchun in Jilin province (Map 1). It was this region and points northward, the area watered by these two rivers, and the rivers Laoha, Jiaolai, and Eastern Liao, that the founder and shapers of what was to become the Liao dynasty claimed as their homeland: Shira-müren (literally, "yellow river," but more generally a reference to the river and grasslands that encompass it). The exotically named locale was rendered famously remote in pictures published by Torii Ryūzō in the 1930s. It remains largely unchanged since that time (figs. 1 and 2).

FIGURE 1. Shira-müren grasslands with pagoda in distance, Inner Mongolia, ca. 1930. [After Torii, *Ryō no bunka*, vol. 2, pl. 97]

FIGURE 2. Shira-müren grasslands with pagoda in distance, Inner Mongolia, 1992. [Steinhardt photograph]

TABLE 1. Liao Emperors

Name	Temple Name	Reign Dates	Tomb Site
(Yelü) Abaoji	Taizu	907–926	Zuling, Zuzhou
(Yelü) Deguang	Taizong	927–947	Huailing, Huaizhou
(Yelü) Yuan	Shizong	947–951	Xianling, Xianzhou
(Yelü) Jing	Muzong	951–969	Fengling, Huaizhou
(Yelü) Xian	Jingzong	969–982	Qianling, Qianzhou
(Yelü) Longxu	Shengzong	982–1031	Yongqingling, Qingzhou
(Yelü) Zongzhen	Xingxong	1031–1055	Yongxingling, Qingzhou
(Yelü) Hongji	Daozong	1055–1101	Yongfuling, Qingzhou
(Yelü) Yanxu	Tianzuo	1101–1125 (d. ca. 1128)	none recorded

Source: Cambridge History, vol. 6, p. xxi.

A SHORT ACCOUNT OF THE LIAO

Who exactly these pastoral nomads were is still a subject of discussion. By the tenth century they called themselves Qidan (Khitan/Kitan),[1] a name used in Chinese historical texts by the fourth century.[2] The fourth-century predecessors of the Qidan were members of one of the Xianbei tribes, the most famous branch of which established the Northern Wei dynasty (386–534).[3] While northern peoples formed new states along China's northern fringe and to its north, the Qidan seem to have been vassals of the most powerful ones: the Northern Wei, the Northern Qi beginning in 553, and the Tujue Turks beginning in 586. For most of the seventh century the Qidan were a tributary group of the Tang empire (618–906). Successful and less successful attempts at breaking with Tang resulted in an eventual vassalage relationship with the Uyghurs in the second half of the eighth century. After the fall of the Uyghur empire in 840, the Qidan and their neighbors, the Xi and Shiwei, again allied themselves with Tang. The details of the Tang–Qidan(–Xi–Shiwei) alliance are uncertain, but by the second half of the ninth century the Tang were far from the supreme Asian power they had been a century earlier. Coincident with the fall of Tang in 906 was the rise of a man of the Yila branch of the Qidan who would come to be known as (Yelü) Abaoji (872–926), founder of what was to become the Liao dynasty (see Table 1).

Another Northeast Asian group whose fate was intimately connected to the Qidan in the seventh, eighth, and ninth centuries was the Bohai (Parhae).[4] Occupying most of Heilongjiang and Jilin and parts of Korea, much of this former Tang tributary state, and for a short time an independent empire, fell to Liao control. At its zenith the Liao empire would extend from these Bohai lands across Inner Mongolia into the Mongolian People's Republic and the Gobi Desert and southward into sixteen prefectures (*zhou*) of Shanxi and Hebei provinces of China.[5] Somewhere in these lands of tenth-century Northeast or North Asia the Qidan

FIGURE 3. Wall remains from Liao Shangjing (Balinzuoqi).
[Steinhardt photograph]

saw architecture of sedentary life. Those buildings provided them with visual images of an Asian empire.

From what we know about the predynastic Qidan, their brand of pastoral nomadism did not include permanent residences or tombs. It is believed that the pre-tenth-century Qidan lived in portable dwellings. Unlike other North Asian seminomads such as the peoples of the Russian steppe, the Qidan did not even build a permanent architecture of death. They left corpses to rot on the limbs of trees.[6] Although the Qidan worshiped the sun, as well as gods associated with natural features, mountains, and spirits of the dead, there is no clear record that the predynastic Qidan performed ceremonies to them inside buildings.[7] By modern definitions, the Qidan were shamanistic.[8]

Yet in 918, just twelve years after the final collapse of Tang and nearly thirty years before the official establishment of the Liao empire, Abaoji had a walled city built at Linhuang (today Lindong or Balinzuoqi) about 200 kilometers north of the modern city Chifeng. Immediately upon its founding it became a city of adjacent north and south walled enclosures (fig. 3) with an exterior perimeter of about 13.5 kilometers (fig. 4). The northern city, known as Huangcheng (imperial city), had a palace area named Longmeigong, residence for Qidan wives, concubines, and officials, monasteries, and military barracks, all within a ward system.[9] Formed along strict perpendicular street lines, this first capital of Qidan seminomads bore an impressive resemblance to a Chinese city. Its impressiveness is only slightly tempered by the fact that it was constructed on the ruins of a Bohai capital the Qidan had conquered.[10] Whoever the builders, Abaoji had decidedly cast his lot with the age-old symbols of the Chinese empire and Chinese rulership: a walled city with a palace inside it. The archetype of this design was the plan of the Sui-Tang (586–906) capital, Daxing-Chang'an, implemented by others aspiring to Chinese-style rulership in Japan and Korea, as well as by the Bohai.[11]

For the Mongols, too, the city with its palace became a symbol of their aspirations of Chinese-style kingship.[12] Yet even though Chinggis Khan had seen urban centers throughout Asia, including Bukhara, Samarkand, Gurganj, Balkh, Nishapur, and Bamiyan, and the Jin (1126–1234) capital beneath today's Beijing, it was not until the generation of Chinggis' sons that Mongolian khans began to build walled cities with palace areas for holding court and for enclosing their portable-tent residences.[13] For Abaoji, Liao counterpart of Chinggis, the decision to have a walled capital was immediate. In 902, five years before Abaoji was proclaimed khan, a city called Longhua with a monastery (si) in it was built by Qidan patronage in the region of the Shira-müren. For laborers the ruler used resettled Chinese prisoners from northern Shanxi province, thus guaranteeing that a Chinese-style city could be constructed. Longhua was followed in rapid succession by scores of cities built by Abaoji or his relatives in the first two decades of the tenth century.[14]

South of Huangcheng at the first Qidan capital

was Hancheng, "city of the Han (Chinese)," a name that expressed the ideology of formal separation of the non-Qidan population from the ruling clan. This first capital also housed many races other than the Han, including Bohai and Uyghurs. The concept of coexistent but separate Qidan and non-Qidan walled cities inside the capital would persist when the Qidan moved south and built their second capital. For the Qidan, the walls of sedentarism had the purpose of self-segregation as well as protection.

Balinzuoqi (former Shangjing) today bears little evidence of a city with a complex palace area in its northern half. The images are still those published by Torii Ryūzō: a weathered, now headless, monumental Buddhist sculpture rising on the grassland (fig. 5) and brick-faced, eight-sided pagodas, the only survivors of their original monasteries, beacons of the expanse of the former Liao empire (see fig. 2). The solitary statue has been identified as the bodhisattva Guanyin, perhaps one of the earliest white-robed versions, perhaps a personal favorite of Abaoji's successor for its military associations.[15]

About seventy years after the establishment of this first and northernmost capital, Shangjing, a wooden pavilion was constructed around a 16-meter image of the bodhisattva Guanyin in Ji county of Hebei province, about 500 kilometers to the south (fig. 6). It was already the reign of the sixth of eventually nine Liao rulers, the last four of whom would rule a total of 143 years. The earliest extant wooden building in Liao territory had been constructed only eighteen years earlier, in 966. By the end of the turmoil of six changes of ruler and the concurrent struggles not just about who would rule but to what extent he and his government would follow Chinese-style sedentarism as opposed to the ways of the steppe, the direction of Liao imperialism was clarified. It was, especially in territory south of the upper capital, to be in form and appearance seden-

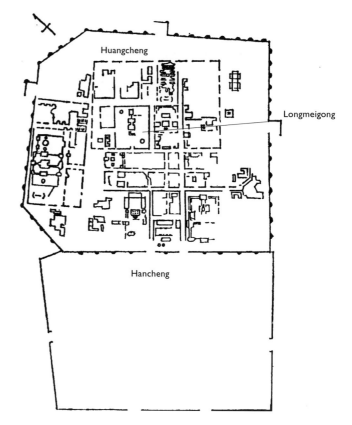

FIGURE 4. Plan of Liao Shangjing (Balinzuoqi). [After *Linhuang shiji*, p. 25]

FIGURE 5. Guanyin (?), tenth century, Liao Shangjing. [Steinhardt photograph]

tary. Once the direction was set, the Liao empire, which adopted the name Liao only in 947, would undertake a program of monumental construction the likes of which had never been seen at China's northern border. The wooden pavilion around the bodhisattva Guanyin in northern Hebei was only the beginning.

Yet artistically, the nativity of the patrons of Liao art and architecture never completely vanishes. The comparison between the stone statue out-of-doors and the clay statue in a Chinese-style hall (see figs. 5 and 6) is typical of the duality that characterized the commingling of nomadism and sedentarism in Liao society long after the formative century of Liao imperialism according to Chinese models.[16]

Some insight into what this transformation process from Qidan to Liao must have entailed is of-

fered by information about death and burial practice during the first two Qidan reigns. Certainly death is the occasion when people tend to examine their own culture and ideology most seriously, and it may be the one occasion when they are willing to compare its possibilities with those of competing ideologies. Attention to what happens to posthumous remains was particularly significant, for instance, to certain groups of North Asian seminomads on the Siberian steppe in the seventh and sixth centuries B.C. who, as far as is known, had no permanent dwellings for life but created elaborate ones for the afterlife.[17]

The meanings of life, death, kingship, and power came to a head upon Abaoji's death in 926. Although ten years earlier the leader had arranged for his eldest son, Bei, to be his undisputed successor, by the time Abaoji died Bei had gained a reputation as an aesthete. In fact, one of the few paintings on silk of Qidan that is believed to bear some resemblance to them is attributed in a Yuan-period colophon to this son, Yelü Bei (900–937), as a painter known as Li Zanhua, the name presented to him by the Later Tang emperor.[18] As Bei could not amass enough support to become the second ruler of the Qidan, the former Bohai territory became his fief until 930 when he fled south to China, living there for seven years until he was murdered.[19]

Bei's fate was very much tied to a decision made by his mother upon her husband's demise. The widowed Empress Yingtian decided to break with native Qidan and more generally North Asian custom and not join the 300 souls who accompanied the deceased ruler into his tomb. She offered instead to cut off her hand and bury it with Abaoji, saving the rest of herself, the story goes, for regency while raising her young sons.[20] It was during this period of "regency" that the extremely powerful woman secured succession for a younger son, Deguang (902–947), who became the second emperor, Taizong.[21]

Apocryphal as the story may be, it emphasizes the confrontation of value systems and resulting compromises, and the way that pragmatism and politics can be justified in their names, as seminomads prepare themselves for rule of an Asian empire that can compete with China. In every aspect of life, even the most private, the pastoralist nomad's thought process had to determine what of his upbringing to retain, what to abandon, or how an accommodation between them could be made. Again one is impressed with the speed of this transformation: even before the dynasty called Liao existed, subterranean burial in imperial style was under way.[22]

Concerning Empress Yingtian's decision, one wonders just how her detached hand might have been interred. It seems unlikely that it was unceremoniously placed in Abaoji's tomb. Perhaps it was encased in the handpiece of a burial garment like the one excavated at Haoqianying (fig. 7 and see fig. 289). One would assume that the container for the clan leader's empress was made of the finest material available and by the best craftsmen, probably Chinese or perhaps Korean—but in what style? What decoration or symbols might have been on it?

This combination—sedentary East Asian craftsmen but Liao taste—might describe a crown in the Museum of Fine Arts, Boston (fig. 8). When the crown came to the museum in 1940 it was a piece of flattened, gilded silver believed to be Korean of the Koguryŏ period.[23] The identification of the Boston piece as Liao came about with the excavation of a gilt-silver headgear from a Liao tomb in Jianping county, Liaoning.[24] The Liao date still does not rule out Korean manufacture. Nor, we shall see, is architecture of the Korean peninsula without its role in the formation of a Liao tradition. More than its materials or manufacture, the crown is a profound symbol of kingship according to sedentary ways. Whereas sacrificial burial or even amputation at the wrist to avoid it might mark a barbaric act associated

FIGURE 6. Guanyin, ca. 984 or Tang with repair in 984, Guanyin Pavilion, Dule Monastery, Jixian, Hebei.
[After *Ancient Chinese Architecture*, p. 82]

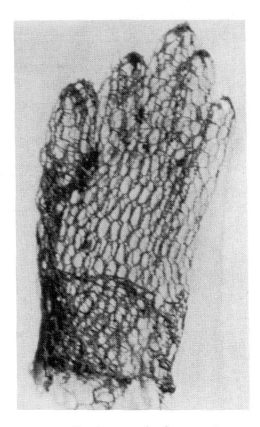

FIGURE 7. Handcover made of copper-wire netting, excavated at Haoqianying Tomb 6, Chayouqianqi, Inner Mongolia. [After Lu and Du (*Wenwu* 1983, no. 9), pl. 1, 4]

with the predynastic Qidan, the crown represents the accession of emperorship, which occurred upon the transfer to the third ruler of what was thenceforth known as the Liao dynasty.

A comparison as informative of the competing ideologies represented by the two monumental Buddhist images (see figs. 5 and 6) is one between the crown in Boston and another equally famous example of Liao metalwork in the United States: the death mask in the Museum of Archaeology and Anthropology, University of Pennsylvania (fig. 9). When the death mask was acquired and first published, its function was certain, but its suggested provenance varied. Once again, both curators in Western museums and eminent Japanese archaeologists suggested Koguryŏ as a possible source. Again it would be excavation that would provide the evidence to confirm that the University Museum mask was Liao.[25]

A death mask, in fact, is associated with the burial of Abaoji's successor, Deguang. Describing the preparation of the second ruler's body for interment, Southern Song author Wen Weijian wrote that when Deguang died far from his intended burial site, his body was cut open and the abdomen, intestines, and stomach were removed. After washing, his body was stuffed with fragrant herbs, salt, and alum. Next it was sewn up with five-colored string. Then the skin was pricked with sharply pointed reeds in order to drain all blood and other bodily fluids. His face was covered with a gold and silver mask, and copper wire was wound around his hands and feet. According to Wen, the Chinese referred to Deguang's remains as "imperial dried meat" (*di ba*).[26] We shall see in Part Two that the encasement of corporeal remains in metal was fairly widespread among Qidan royalty. It will be shown to be an example of the retention of a seminomadic custom beneath the facade of a Chinese tomb.

Besides city building and burial practice, another

FIGURE 8. Gilt-silver headgear, Liao period. [Courtesy of Museum of Fine Arts, Boston]

major aspect of the transformation from Qidan to Liao is symbolized by a second object ascribed to Liao in the University of Pennsylvania Museum (fig. 10).[27] The Buddhist faith, its architecture, and its statuary offered powerful means through which rulers and subjects could be transformed into new cultural identities. Buddhist art and architecture— from tricolor *luohan* (monks; Chinese for the Sanskrit "*arhat*") to wooden temples to house them— represented the highest artistic capabilities of East Asia at the time. The nationality of the craftsmen (Chinese, Korean, or others) is not so much an issue as the desire of Qidan patrons to be surrounded by these images and their structures.

The themes represented by the three objects— kingship by the crown, native ritual by the death mask, and imported religion by the *luohan*—and the sources of them for the Qidan are themes addressed by every Liao building discussed in this book. The wooden buildings number fourteen plus three that were sufficiently altered by the next dynasty in North China, Jin (1125–1234), that they are as well labeled Jin (or Liao-Jin). The ingenuity of timber joinery in Liao architecture is such that the bracket sets in just one of these buildings are more diverse (fifty-four different formations) than the total number of corbel bracket types known from any other dynasty. Liao tombs number several hundred,

FIGURE 9. Death mask, bronze, Liao period. [Courtesy of Museum of Archaeology and Anthropology, University of Pennsylvania]

pagodas in the scores. Similarly, tombs and their wall paintings, and pagodas and the imagery sculpted on their exteriors, are as complicated as any that came before or after them in China. Through architecture and its decoration, this book will examine how and why a group of seminomads on the fringe of sedentary society came to worship statues in temple complexes, to bury themselves in multichamber brick tombs, and to visualize their Buddhist world in relief sculpture on pagodas in tenth-century Northeast Asia. What follows, then, are case studies: in borrowing, transfer, adoption, adaptation, and absorption of forms and symbols,

both with and without retention of their meanings; in collaboration and assimilation of taste; and in the confrontation of native and nonnative built environments in the formation of an architectural tradition called Liao.

Liao architecture does not follow an obvious chronological progression of styles. One can see a benchmark upon the accession of sixth emperor Shengzong in 982—a division not only between the short and long reign periods, but also between the absence and presence of timber architecture. (Timber construction certainly occurred between the reign of Abaoji and the Shengzong reign. Yet evidence for it is confined to one building and literary descriptions of palaces and monasteries.) In funerary architecture the division occurs in the mid-eleventh century, after which the octagonal tomb chamber with two side niches becomes the most common plan.

In 919, the year after Abaoji established his upper capital at Linhuang (today Balinzuoqi), he set up his eastern capital, Dongjing (initially called Dongpingjun), about 500 kilometers southeast at the site of the former Bohai capital, Liaoyang. It was still seven years until the official date of the Liao takeover of Bohai lands (926) that came to be known as Dongdan (Eastern [Qi]dan). Clearly, Abaoji had been persuaded at Shangjing of the potential of a walled city as a power base for his anticipated conquest of sedentary people to the south.

Also a capital of adjacent northern and southern walled areas (here called *ben-* [native] and *Hancheng*), the physical remains of the second major city of Abaoji is today only a pagoda on the Manchurian plain whose present form has the date 1161–1189 with evidence of later restoration (fig. 11).[28] A theoretical reconstruction of the unexcavated capital based on texts suggests that the northern city was occupied primarily by a palace-city *(gongcheng)*

FIGURE 10. *Luohan*, tricolor-glazed ceramic, Liao period. [Courtesy of Museum of Archaeology and Anthropology, University of Pennsylvania]

surrounded on three sides by a city with government offices (*huangcheng*) and that Hancheng was a city of monasteries and markets (fig. 12).[29]

No specific buildings are associated with Abaoji's successor Deguang (Taizong). He is credited with seeing to fruition his father's vision of conquest into China. The emperor Taizong led a successful invasion into northern Shanxi in 936. He continued his pursuit of the Chinese eastward across Hebei and south into Henan. In 947, Deguang entered the city of Bianliang (today Kaifeng) without resistance.[30] Almost immediately the Qidan ran into practical problems in their attempt to maintain this Chinese city, and later the same year Deguang returned north to "avoid the summer heat."[31] It was on this return home that he died suddenly, making it possible for Chinese to observe and describe the treatment of his corporeal remains. In terms of the history of Qidan art, the several months inside the Chinese capital in Henan were significant. The city was looted by the troops and subsequently books, maps, astronomical charts, instruments, carriages, ritual implements, and the Confucian classics engraved in stone were transported to Shangjing. So too were thousands of artisans, astronomers, diviners, and palace women.[32] Pieces of the Chinese palace halls thus became available for reuse in the Qidan cities, and southern artisans were available for repairs and new construction or decoration.

Another event in the history of Chinese and Liao architecture occurred in the last year of Deguang's reign: the southern Liao capital, Nanjing (also known as Yanjing), was established beneath what is today Beijing. That city has been mapped and described in detail, and evidence for the locations and names of some of its halls is more reliable than for the upper or eastern capitals (fig. 13).[33] Yet like the eastern capital at modern Liaoyang, only one Liao building, dated to the reign of the last Liao emperor in the twelfth century, stands there today. It is the

FIGURE 11 (top). White Pagoda, Liao Dongjing (Liaoyang), twelfth century with later restoration. [Steinhardt photograph]
FIGURE 12 (above). Theoretical reconstruction of Liao Dongjing. [After Ye Dasong, *Zhongguo jianzhu shi*, vol. 2, p. 451]

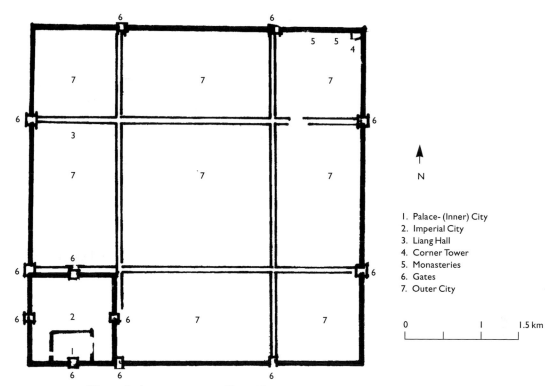

FIGURE 13. Theoretical reconstruction of Liao Nanjing. [After Steinhardt, *Chinese Imperial City Planning*, p. 126; courtesy of University of Hawai'i Press]

1. Palace- (Inner) City
2. Imperial City
3. Liang Hall
4. Corner Tower
5. Monasteries
6. Gates
7. Outer City

brick pagoda of Tianning Monastery, by the 1980s part of a record factory (fig. 14). In the Western Hills of Beijing, Liao-period pagodas are among the many at Jietaisi and Tanzhesi (fig. 15).[34] By the establishment of the third Liao capital, only two Liao rulers had been buried. Abaoji was laid to rest at Zuling (ancestral royal tomb) in a mountainous region west of the ancestral prefecture, Zuzhou.[35] Taizong was buried 30 kilometers northwest at Huailing in Huaizhou.

The third Liao reign, that of Shizong, son of Abaoji's eldest son Bei, was short. Emperor Shizong was assassinated in 951 after only four years in power and was buried in Xianling. Neither capital nor monument is associated with him. He is credited

with the official implementation of northern and southern administrative divisions of his empire: the northern was more heavily populated by Qidan, who ran its government and wore Qidan dress; the southern contained a Chinese population in excess of 5 million.[36] In the first year of his reign the name Liao became the official name of the dynasty.

Taizong's eldest son, Jing, succeeded Shizong as Emperor Muzong. He reigned for eighteen years until he was assassinated in 969. The earliest extant Liao wooden building, Mañjuśrī Hall of Geyuan Monastery, was built three years before his death in Laiyuan, Hebei province. Like his father, Muzong was buried at Huaizhou.

The first years of the fifth Liao reign, that of Jing-

FIGURE 14 (right). Tianningsi Pagoda, Beijing. [Steinhardt photograph]
FIGURE 15 (below). Pagodas, Tanzhesi, Beijing. [Steinhardt photograph]

zong, saw the consolidation and expansion of Song power. By 976, only two remnants survived of what had in earlier decades of the tenth century been five dynasties and ten kingdoms. With the fall of Wuyue to Song in 978, only the Northern Han remained south of Liao territory but outside the Song empire. Despite Liao efforts to intervene, the Song conquered the last northern Shanxi state in 979. Northern Han (951–979) is one of the tenth-century dynasties from which a wooden Buddhist hall survives. It is Ten Thousand Buddhas Hall, from Zhenguo Monastery near Pingyao, built three years before Mañjuśrī Hall of Geyuan Monastery.

By the time of Jingzong's death in 982, it was clear that Song-Liao relations were to be tense. Each was a power with whom the other could not avoid reckoning. In addition, both the Xi Xia (Tanguts) in North Asia, centered around the Ningxia Hui Autonomous Region and including part of Qinghai and Gansu provinces, and the Jin, in present Jilin and Heilongjiang, were beginning to pose threats to Liao. When Jingzong died suddenly in 982, an eleven-year-old was left as successor. Jingzong's widow, Dowager Empress Chengtian, came into a position not unlike that of Abaoji's widow Yingtian.[37]

The reign of the sixth Liao emperor, Longxu (Shengzong), was to endure almost fifty years. It was the first of three reign periods during which the majority of Liao wooden architecture was constructed. Shengzong's was also the earliest of the three most splendid Liao imperial tombs, popularly known together as "Qingling."

During the initial decades of the Shengzong reign, government was almost exclusively in the hands of the empress dowager. To ensure her position, Chengtian made the sort of unprecedented interpretation of Qidan ritual that Yingtian had made in her decision to avoid sacrificial burial.

Once in 984 and twice in 986 she partook of the ritual known as *zaisheng* ("rebirth"), a ceremony that involved recreating the birth of a ruler amid a group of newly erected tents or buildings that contained tablets and images of past emperors. The key rite was performed through surrogates for the boy, his mother, a midwife, the emperor, and old men.[38] Eighty years into Qidan imperialism, the royal family still had not relinquished the ways of their chieftain days on the Shira-müren grasslands. In some of the most symbolic rites of life and death, they never would.

Chengtian chose able ministers to help her. Two of them were Chinese from Ji prefecture of northern Hebei. The older, Shi Fang (920–994), was the first recipient of the *jinshi* degree under Qidan rule. A younger man, Han Derang (941–1011), was also from Jizhou. His family had had ties with the royal Qidan since the capture of his grandfather, Han Zhigu, who subsequently had become a member of Empress Yingtian's household. Han Zhigu had aided Abaoji in establishing Chinese-style cities. Han Derang's father, Han Kuangsi, had been the director of Abaoji's ancestral temple. Kuangsi became viceroy of Shangjing and eventually of Nanjing, a post inherited by his son Derang under Emperor Jingzong. The Guanyin Pavilion of 984 and a later funerary pagoda in the same prefecture were erected through Han family patronage. The most massive Liao wooden hall that survives, at Fengguo Monastery in Jixian, Liaoning, was also built during Shengzong's reign.

In 1007 Shengzong designated a central Liao capital—Zhongjing, at Dadingfu, today Ningcheng—in Inner Mongolia near the Liaoning border. Its plan combined what had become standard for Liao capital cities, adjacent northern and southern walled enclosures, with the foremost identifying feature of the Tang-style capital: an enclosed

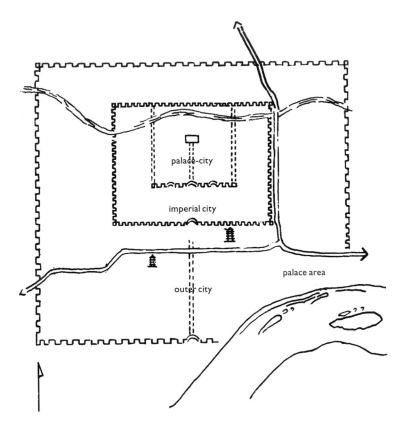

FIGURE 16. Plan of Liao Zhongjing. [After *Liao Zhongjing jianjie,* inside back cover]

palace-city along the center of the northern wall (fig. 16). Yet at Liao Zhongjing each walled area had its own palace sector. The artisans of Zhongjing had been transferred from the southern capital and Ji prefecture, and it has been claimed that the buildings were modeled after those from the Song capital at Bianliang.[39] Pieces of the city wall (fig. 17) and several Liao pagodas (see fig. 360) can still be seen among the ruins of the Liao central capital. A hall to three bodhisattvas, built at Guangji Monastery in Baodi prefecture, Hebei, in 1025, survived from Shengzong's reign until the Sino-Japanese War.

The event of Shengzong's reign that had the most profound effect on Liao policy and Song-Liao relations was the signing of the Shanyuan Treaty in January 1005. Other major accomplishments with which his reign (or Chengtian's regency) are credited are the regular offering of examinations whereby official positions could be attained, more systematic record keeping, the codification of a Chinese-style legal code, the promulgation of the first Liao calendar, significantly improved roads, and an increased minting and use of coins. By the last years of Shengzong's reign, however, the limitations of Liao power were already becoming apparent. The Qidan suffered a crushing defeat at the hands of the Korean state Koryŏ. They managed to withstand a rebellion of the Bohai people in 1029, but at great cost.[40]

The accession of the seventh Liao ruler, Emperor Xingzong, was not as smooth as his father's. Xingzong's adoptive mother and Shengzong's chief wife, Qitian, was robbed of her anticipated role as empress dowager by banishment and eventual suicide orchestrated by the new fifteen-year-old emperor's birth mother, a concubine named Noujin (Empress Qin'ai). Three years later, in 1034, Xingzong caught Noujin in a plot to replace him with her own brother. Noujin was exiled to Qingzhou, site of Shengzong's mausoleum, and Xingzong took over his empire. He would have to walk a line between the two mothers' relatives for the rest of his life, but the one to whom he had true allegiance seems to have been made clear through an architectural project initiated at the time of Xingzong's death by his son and successor.

During Xingzong's reign the last of the five Liao capitals, the western capital at present Datong, was officially established in 1044. Although no portions of its walls survive and its plan has never been reconstructed, clearly it was a focus of imperial Qidan attention. Four Liao and three Liao-Jin buildings and nearly thirty Liao Buddhist statues survived at Huayan or Shanhua monasteries in present Datong until the 1930s (figs. 18 and 119). In addition portraits of Xingzong's successor were donated in 1062.[41] Liao power was not to extend much farther west in China. Just 200 kilometers away was the border with the Xi Xia kingdom. From the proclamation of the Xi Xia empire in 1038 (perhaps it was not coincidence the Liao built the Sutra Repository at Huayansi that year) through the remainder of Qidan rule, this kingdom was to be a persistent threat to Liao and Song power.[42]

Another Buddhist hall in northern Hebei survives from the Xingzong reign. The Main Hall of

FIGURE 17. Wall remains from Liao Zhongjing. [Steinhardt photograph]

FIGURE 18. Shanhuasi, Datong, Shanxi. [After "Shanhua Temple: A Historic Site in Shanxi," Beijing Slide Studio, no. 1]

FIGURE 19. White Pagoda, Qingzhou, Inner Mongolia, Liao period. [After Takeshima, *Ryō-Kin jidai no kenchiku*, vol. 2, pl. 8]

Kaishan Monastery was erected in Xincheng in 1033. Finally, a number of brick-faced pagodas have dates from the reign of Xingzong. One, the four-sided pagoda in Chaoyang, is believed to be a Tang pagoda that was refaced in 1042 (see figs. 365 and 366). A second is the White Pagoda, dated 1047–1049, in Qingzhou (fig. 19).[43]

Xingzong died suddenly in 1055 and was succeeded without incident by his son Hongji (Emperor Daozong). The following year the most spectacular Liao timber monument, the Timber Pagoda at Yingxian (fig. 20), was built by the new emperor at the site of his grandmother's (father's adoptive mother's) family home. Although it is the only wooden building that can be definitely dated to his reign, there are many brick-faced pagodas. One in Zhuo county, Hebei, dates from 1079 and one nearby from 1092 (fig. 21), and the octagonal pagodas of Jinzhou are from 1057.[44] Much of the mass production of sutras in stone near Yunju Monastery Pagoda in Fangshan also occurred during the Daozong reign (fig. 22).[45]

By the year of Daozong's death, 1101, one might have foreseen the Liao would not endure. Already in the 1060s and 1070s, the chancellor Yelü Yixin had posed a threat to the empire. He orchestrated the execution of the empress and her son, the heir apparent, Prince Jun. Then came a series of natural disasters—earthquakes, floods, and famines. The year 1092 brought a war with the Zubu people that lasted until just after Daozong's death the same year. The Emperor Daozong was buried with his father and grandfather in Qingzhou.

The last Liao emperor, Tianzuo, was not awarded royal burial. Three wooden buildings and several pagodas were constructed during his reign. Halls dedicated to two Buddhas and a bodhisattva were built at Kaiyuan Monastery in Yi prefecture, Hebei, between 1101 and 1105. Two pagodas at Yunjusi in Fangshan might be dated to 1117. Perhaps even then

FIGURE 20 (left). Yingxian Muta,
Yingxian, Shanxi, 1056.
[Steinhardt photograph]
FIGURE 21 (below). Liao-period
pagodas, Zhuoxian, Hebei.
[Steinhardt photograph]

FIGURE 22. Stone tablets inscribed with Buddhist sutras, Yunjusi, Fangshan, Hebei, Liao dynasty. [Steinhardt photograph]

it was unknown how serious a threat had been posed five years earlier in 1112 when a bold Nüzhen (Jurchen) chieftain named Aguda had refused to dance in symbolic submission to Liao at the First Fish Feast on a bank of the Sungari River in modern Heilongjiang.[46] Sparing the defiant Nüzhen at the advice of one of his ministers, Tianzuo lost his empire to him in 1125. A remnant of the Qidan made their way westward and established an empire known as Western Liao, or Qarā-Khitāy, that extended westward from the old Xi Xia kingdom to Transoxiana, incorporating famous Central Asian cities like Qoço, (Gaochang), Beshbaliq, Kashgar, and Samarkand. The Western Liao finally succumbed to the Mongols.

LIAO ARCHITECTURE,
ITS RESEARCHERS, ITS BIBLIOGRAPHY

As I explained in the preface, the initial motivation for writing this book was the buildings themselves. The research data on these buildings turned out to be equally extraordinary, but structure by structure extremely limited. Although different parts of the

book rely heavily on certain sources, the whole book could not have come together without all of them.

Undoubtedly others who stood before Liao wooden halls or brick pagodas realized the inherent significance of this material and its importance for the explication of medieval and later Chinese architecture. Yet each of the most prolific ones, all to be introduced here, was limited in ways that by the 1980s when I began this research had ceased to be obstacles. None of my predecessors in the study of Liao, for instance, had the opportunity to see as many buildings as I have. Those who saw wooden structures never saw tombs; those who entered tombs perhaps also photographed pagodas, but could not venture far enough south to study timber-frame halls. Sometimes the stumbling blocks were political, especially during wartime, other times they were caused by nationalism.

These comments are made for only one purpose. I want to say at the outset that I have sought secondary sources by authors of every East Asian nationality regardless of political circumstances or the times during which they were written. Further, I have relied on those who are most accurate, whatever their personal attitude toward China or Japan or Korea or North Asian peoples might have been. To be blunt: many of those who conducted literary or archaeological research on Northeast Asia and the Qidan harbored an innate dislike for the Liao, for North Asian peoples, or for the country in which they were engaged in research. In the 1980s and 1990s, I have been able to cross boundaries that limited fieldwork fifty or sixty years ago.

The Liao left few records about themselves. Those who tell us the most about the Qidan were either their enemies (the Song) or their conquerors. The two most important primary sources for this book are the *Qidanguo zhi* (Record of the Qidan state), completed around 1247 by a Song scholar, and the official dynastic history of Liao, *Liaoshi*, traditionally ascribed to Tuotuo (1313–1355), a minister at the Mongolian court.

The next important period of scholarship about Liao architecture was the Manchu dynasty, Qing. Although many of the authors were Chinese, the sponsorship of these publications at court was by a dynasty that traced its cultural roots to territory that had been the Liao empire. The Qing literary works consulted for this study are primarily local records, *difang zhi*, of the sixteen *zhou* where Liao buildings survive. Studies of the Beijing region like *Rixia jiuwen kao* (Research on day-by-day events)—completed in 1744 based on *Rixia jiuwen* of Zhu Yizun (1629–1709) and his son—and *Shuntianfu zhi* (Record of Shuntian prefecture)—compiled under several chief editors, including Miao Quansun, and published in the 1880s—have also been particularly helpful for architecture in northern Hebei.

A more important role of the Qing for the study of Liao architecture was their revival of Qidan monasteries for their own worship. Without exception, every monastery with Liao wooden architecture bears signs of Jin, Yuan, Ming, or Qing additions or restoration. Although sometimes it is frustrating to see what the Qing restorers did, and to realize that it is impossible to know what a building or site looked like in the eleventh century because it was a living monastery in the eighteenth, it was the Qing concern for these monasteries that prevented deterioration or destruction.[47]

Turning to twentieth-century scholarship, for historical background this book has relied most heavily on the following research: Karl Wittfogel and Feng Chia-sheng, *History of Chinese Society: Liao*; Yao Congwu, *Dongbeishi luncong*; Chen Shu's various books, but in particular *Qidan shehui jingji shi gao* and *Liao-Jin shi lunji*; Denis Twitchett's chapters on Liao in *The Cambridge History of China*; and various writings of Herbert Franke.[48]

Except for local records, the history of Liao architecture, like the history of Chinese architecture in general, has been written exclusively in the twentieth century. It begins with three articles by French missionary Joseph Mullie that appeared in *T'oung Pao* in 1922 and 1933. The first, entitled "Les anciennes villes de l'empire des grands Leao au royaume Mongol de Bārin," remains the major Western contribution to the study of Liao architecture or archaeology. It is primarily a geographic study, however, based on what must have been an arduous and exciting journey through the former Shira-müren plain. Mullie's map and accompanying descriptions were the basis of later Western discussion of Liao geography, including Wittfogel and Feng's. Unfortunately, the combination of Mullie's use of the French romanization for the transcription of Chinese, and his French renderings of local Mongolian names of the sites under discussion, make his article difficult to use, even with Chinese characters.

In his 1933 article, Mullie published a geographic study of the Raole River and an article based on inscriptions he found at the three tombs of Liao emperors in Qingzhou. Mullie's introduction of the tomb site was to be superseded almost immediately by the work of Japanese archaeologist Torii Ryūzō, one of the leaders of Japanese exploration teams in Manchuria under Japanese occupation. Although Mullie's research was known to the Japanese team, it is not clear if the French scholar was aware of Torii because he did not refer to Torii's four articles on wall paintings from these tombs published in 1931.[49] Torii published information about the tombs and the first Liao capital, Shangjing, in his monumental four-volume *Ryō no bunka* (Liao culture) of 1936.

While Torii was conducting archaeological reconnaissance of the Shira-müren region, events that would shape not only the study of Liao architecture but the modern study of Chinese architectural history were occurring in the former Liao southern capital (still in Chinese hands). In 1929, Liang Sicheng (Ssu-ch'eng) (1901–1972) and his wife Lin Huiyin (Whei-yin) (1903–1954), the most influential of the first group of Western-trained architectural historians, returned to China.[50] At just the same time, the former Qing scholar-official Zhu Qiqian (1872–1962), credited with the rediscovery of the Song architectural manual *Yingzao fashi* and author of major studies of the history of Beijing based on texts, had founded the Society for Research in Chinese Architecture. Zhu appointed Liang director, at which point the society's key mission became the identification and recovery of old buildings and the study of them according to the current methodology, including documentary history, employed by the newly burgeoning field of architectural history in the West.[51] The Western model for this study was coursework at the University of Pennsylvania, where Liang, Lin, and at least thirteen other Chinese students, using Boxer Indemnity funds to pay their tuition, had studied architecture between the years 1918 and 1930. Paul Crèt was one of Liang's teachers and Louis Kahn was his classmate. Another methodology came from Japan, where Liu Dunzhen (Tun-tseng), who joined the group in 1932, had received his university training. In addition to Liang, Lin, and Liu, two of their students, Mo Zongjiang and Chen Mingda, helped in the work of the Society for Research in Chinese Architecture. These five people remain giants in the Chinese contribution to the study of Liao architecture.[52]

The routine of the group was to search through *difang zhi* (local records) of the various regions of China; to go to the regions and seek the buildings listed in either the *guji* (historical relics) or *siyuan* (["living"] monasteries) sections; to ask about and search out other old buildings; to measure, photograph, and study the buildings detail by detail, including copying any stele or other inscriptions; and then to return to their offices to make publishable drawings and write their reports. The writing stage always included an investigation of how closely construction might follow building details in the *Yingzao fashi*.

The society's first trip directed by Liang Sicheng was to a Liao monastery named Dulesi. Thus his initial publication about "old architecture" in China was the detailed description and analysis of the second- and third-oldest Liao buildings, the Front Gate and Guanyin Pavilion of Dule Monastery, both dated 984. Liang's publication of another Liao building, Sandashi Hall of Guangji Monastery, came out the same year; his monumental study of seven Liao-Jin-period buildings at Datong was published in 1934. Meanwhile, Liu Dunzhen was investigating early architecture to the south. The only published research on three Liao buildings at Kaiyuan Monastery in Hebei is found in Liu's work on architecture in western Hebei of 1935.

In 1937, Beijing fell to the Japanese and Liang went into exile in Sichuan, where he stayed for the duration of the war. Only six volumes, several issues each, of the *Bulletin of the Society for Research in Chinese Architecture* were published before Liang went south. The final volume was published in handwritten form and is preserved in only a few libraries. Liang and his team continued writing up their fieldnotes and conducted some site work in Sichuan and Yunnan during their years in the southwest, but much of the work of these several years has survived only as fieldnotes in architectural institutes in China.

In just nine years (1932 to 1941), the Society for Research in Chinese Architecture conducted research in more than 200 counties of fifteen provinces.[53]

The subsequent study of Liao and other premodern architecture of China would not have been possible without their groundbreaking work. Of the fifteen Liao-Jin buildings first studied and published by Liang and Lin—all but two of the total now known—five were lost during the war with Japan and a sixth was completely rebuilt in 1953. In other words, had Liang and his colleagues not ventured into the Chinese countryside in the 1930s, the study of Liao architecture after 1950 would be based on about two-thirds of the material investigated here.

The loss of one-third of the buildings extant fifty years ago is only part of the effect of the war and its political aftermath on all subsequent research on Liao architecture. The military conflict between China and Japan that placed Liao remains half in the territory of Japanese occupation and half in Chinese hands during the crucial years right after Liang and his group returned to China has remained so deep-rooted that even now some Chinese scholars decline use of Japanese publications about Liao sites; often they are not even available in China. Thus the stigma of Japanese domination was added to material that would always be a reminder of North Asian domination of China in both the tenth to fourteenth centuries (Liao originals, Jin restoration, occasional Mongolian restoration) and the seventeenth through the nineteenth centuries (Manchu China).

After the war, Liang Sicheng too would be cast into the political net, drawing him away from scholarly work. Upon the founding of the People's Republic in 1949 and for most of his years thereafter, Liang would play a dominant role in the reconstruction and revitalization of the physical city Beijing. He would as well be remembered by colleagues outside of China for his years in the United States, including the unique Chinese participation in the architectural planning committee of the United Nations. Although Liang continued to teach at Qinghua (Tsinghua) University in Beijing in the 1950s and 1960s, the study of Liao and other old architecture was left to his students.

A few Westerners in China during the years of Liang's work in the Society for Research in Chinese Architecture and up to the war should be noted. The photographs in Ernst Boerschmann's several books on Chinese architecture include Liao buildings, some of which have since been lost or restored.[54] Similar in its photographic, rather than documentary, value are the two major studies of the architecture of Beijing and a volume on Chinese architecture written by Osvald Sirén in the 1920s.[55] More scholarly investigation of Chinese architecture was undertaken by Gustav Ecke. Ecke began research on Chinese pagodas in 1923. In that year he was invited to Amoy (Xiamen) University, Fujian, and he thereupon initiated research on the thirteenth-century twin pagodas in the provincial capital, Fuzhou.[56] From there he moved to Beijing where he worked with Liang, Liu, and others during the early years of the Society for Research in Chinese Architecture. According to Ecke's widow, Tseng Yuho, the German scholar felt that due to his experience with pagoda architecture in the southeast it was most logical to apply that fieldwork to a study of pagodas of the same time period in North China. He proceeded to measure and draw stone by stone and piece by piece every pagoda he saw in Shanxi and Hebei provinces, employing the methodology of his European education in art and architectural history (see fig. 360). The majority of his finds turned out to be from the Liao period. The Sino-Japanese War halted Professor Ecke's fieldwork. When he departed from Beijing in 1948 he left his unfinished work and unpublished drawings behind. (It is not clear whether they were deposited in an institute or left with a person.) They have never been recovered. Gustav Ecke's research after the China years dealt with the Chinese minor arts, furniture, and eventually painting. In addition to a book, *The Twin Pagodas of Zayton* (1935), he published three major studies of northern pagodas, including the ones in Zhuo county (fig. 21), and the only Western account of the society's research.[57]

The only other foreigner conducting research on architecture in China before and during the first years of the war was Alexander C. Soper. As a Princeton graduate student he had seen issues of the *Bulletin of the Society for Research in Chinese Architecture* that his art history professor George Rowley had brought back with him from China in 1933 or 1934. Soper embarked upon a study of East Asian architecture in Japan in the fall of 1935, but by the time his research took him to China, so much of the country was under Japanese occupation or otherwise blocked from foreign travel that he was permitted only one month of travel in the spring of 1938. Thus he saw buildings only in northern Shanxi, northern Hebei, and Liaoning—as it turned out, the heart of former Liao territory.[58] The results of the travel restrictions meant that much of Alexander Soper's visual image of Chinese architecture was Liao architecture. His architecture chapters for *The Art and Architecture of China* remain standard literature in the field.

Otherwise, the fieldwork and scholarship on Liao architecture in the 1930s and 1940s, and publications even into the 1970s, were dominated by the work of Japanese archaeologists who had had access to former Manchuria and the vicinity of Beijing in the decades before and during the war. Alongside Torii Ryūzō's four volumes of 1936 (*Ryō no bunka*) was Sekino Tadashi and Takeshima Takuichi's *Ryō-Kin jidai no kenchiku to sono Butsuzō* (Liao-Jin architecture and its Buddhist sculpture), published as two volumes of plates in 1925 with an accompanying text in 1944. The plates remain an unsur-passed photographic record of Liao pagodas. The volume of text, although section by section sometimes less extensive than Liang, Lin, or Liu's articles in the *Bulletin of the Society for Research in Chinese Architecture,* was at that time the best book on Liao architecture and has been outdated only because new material has become available, especially in the last twenty years or so. Sekino is also one of two archaeologists responsible for the five-volume study of Chinese Buddhist monuments (*Shina Bukkyō shiseki*), many of which have also since been lost.[59] His scholarly work includes studies of Chinese art and archaeology from as early as the first millennium B.C.

The other major Japanese publication that resulted from the years of occupation was Tamura Jitsuzō and Kobayashi Yukio's study of the three royal tombs known as Qingling; subtitled in English, *Tombs and Mural Paintings of Ch'ing-ling,* it was not published until 1953. Twenty-four years later Tamura updated the material in that monograph by a more general study of Liao wall painting incorporating material excavated by the Chinese in the intervening years.[60]

By 1977, of course, excavation of Liao tombs was well under way. By now they are so numerous that no study, including this one, should be considered comprehensive. The shortcomings of Chinese publications about the excavations, however, are characteristic of inherent problems of the Liao material—problems more deep-seated than the standard obstacles such as reckless speed of excavation and casual documentation. First, the majority of material is in Inner Mongolia and Liaoning, under the jurisdiction of provincial archaeological institutes. Limited funding, more so than for Beijing, for example, leads to publications without illustrations or in short-lived local-university journals that rarely reach the West. Other times, a researcher in the Cultural Relics Bureau of one province simply cannot cross the line to work on, or even to see, material in a different province. The greatest problem, however, is that the political scars of Japanese occupation are so deep that scholarly publications from those years are rarely consulted in post–People's Republic research.

Whereas most tombs were not opened until after 1949, there have been different stumbling blocks for the study of timber architecture. Some of the society's research that could not be published due to wartime conditions was held up from publication long afterward because it was deemed politically not worth printing. Chen Mingda's extensive work on Ying county's Timber Pagoda, for instance, research for which was conducted sixty years ago, was distributed internally in the 1960s; but *Yingxian Muta*, the only monograph on a Chinese wooden building, was not published until 1980. Chen's

study of the *Yingzao fashi*, based on research initiated in his years with Liang in the society, was not published until 1981. The existence of Geyuan Monastery's Liao hall was announced in a two-page article in 1960; the only study of it was published nineteen years later. The Main Hall of Kaishan Monastery was published in a short article in 1957 and, currently a storage facility, has not been discussed in print since.

Much has changed since 1980, however. Most important has been publication of the collected papers, including many articles from *Bulletin of the Society for Research in Chinese Architecture*, of Liang Sicheng and Liu Dunzhen.[61] Included in these are occasional notes and revisions by their students. What follows, then, builds on the work of all those mentioned here. It could not have been done without them.

The Timber Frame Tradition

I

FIGURE 23. Guanyin Pavilion viewed from Shanmen, Dulesi, Jixian, Hebei, 984. [After *Ancient Chinese Architecture*, p. 80]

2

Dulesi

THERE IS NO PLACE but Dule Monastery to begin a study of Liao architecture. It was with the discovery of its two wooden Liao buildings in 1931—the oldest known timber structures in China when they were found—that Liang Sicheng and other members of the Society for Research in Chinese Architecture began their piece-by-piece investigation of traditional Chinese timber frames.[1] After sixty-five more years of searching, studying, reading, and chance finds, Dulesi's Liao pavilion and gate remain among the twenty-or-so oldest wooden Chinese buildings. One really begins here, however, because the overpowering visual and aes-

thetic impact of Dulesi's Liao architectural core has preserved its preeminence (fig. 23) even as other buildings in China have come forth one by one to predate it.

Liang Sicheng commenced his study of Dulesi by articulating for a Chinese audience the meaning of phrases like "measured drawing" or "site plan" that he had learned during his study of Western architecture in the United States from 1924 to 1928.[2] The Dulesi article remains a model for an investigation of premodern Chinese architecture. Yet in the opening line of the introduction to Dulesi and the study of Chinese buildings more generally, the

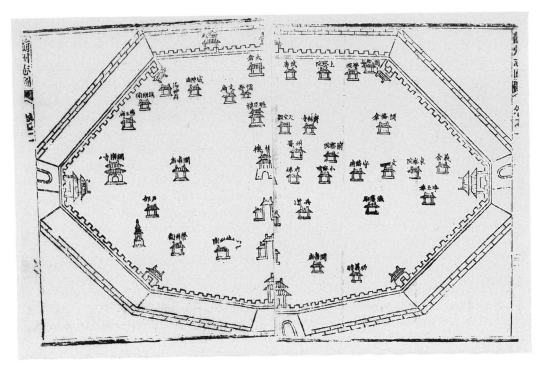

FIGURE 24. "Jizhou city past." [*Jizhou zhi*, pp. 54–55]

power of the monument seems to have prevailed upon Liang to abandon his technical agenda and write, "Hearing one thousand times is not as good as seeing once."[3] Nearly sixty years later, Liang's contemporary, Chen Mingda, called the Liao pavilion of Dulesi "artistically number one" among China's architecture.[4]

As much is known about Dulesi's history as is known about any other Liao monastery except possibly Fogongsi, home of the Timber Pagoda (see fig. 20) in Ying county, Shanxi. The wealth of information must be due partly to its location. Some 90 kilometers from the city Beijing, during the Qing dynasty the site was within the same prefecture, Shuntianfu, as the national capital. During the Qing heyday of compilations of past records, therefore, information about Jixian, county of Dulesi,

and its monuments was gathered and found its way into massive collections of materials relevant to Beijing such as *Rixia jiuwen* (Records of daily life) and *Shuntianfu zhi* (Record of Shuntian prefecture). The survival of data is fortunate, for corroborative evidence about what might be observed from actual contact with the architecture is otherwise available only through local records—in this case in compiled information about Ji county (Jixian; formerly Jizhou [prefecture]), stelae inscriptions, and informants. The Ji records by and large duplicate the nationally sponsored publications about the capital city—in some cases local records became the source for the Qing court compilers in Beijing, but in other instances Beijing publications predate the local sources. It is impossible to determine how many of the stelae, including some quoted by Liang

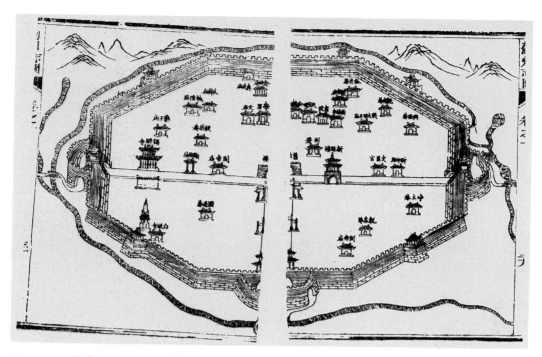

FIGURE 25. "Jizhou city present" (1831). [*Jizhou zhi*, pp. 58–59]

Sicheng, have survived. As for informants, "old-timers" as Liang refers to them, their anecdotes of the 1930s based on stories from their late-nineteenth-century childhoods in Ji county confirm primarily that the monastery was a powerful and integral part of life in this prefectural town.

The same fact is conveyed by maps entitled "Jizhou city past" and "Jizhou city present" published in *Jizhou zhi* in 1831. According to the map of the earlier city, in pre-Qing times one of walled town's three multilevel buildings stood at Dulesi. The second, based on its position in the center of the town at a crossroads implied by four cardinally located gates, must have been a bell tower (fig. 24).[5] The third multistory structure in Jizhou was a pagoda located in the southwest corner near the town wall. By the mid-nineteenth century it appears to have

gained prominence, for it is labeled "Baitasi" (White Pagoda Monastery) in the later diagram of the town (fig. 25). By this time the main east-west thoroughfare in Jizhou also is noted. The relation between pavilion and pagoda will be discussed later in the chapter.

HISTORY OF DULE MONASTERY

The earliest references to the town where Dulesi stands are from the Han dynasty (206 B.C.–A.D. 220), when it was Yuyangjun (commandery).[6] In the *kaiyuan* period (713–742) of the Tang dynasty the town became Jizhou. After the fall of the Tang in the early tenth century, Jizhou was taken by Shi Jin, one of the military generals during the Five Dynasties period (906–960) trying to amalgamate disparate parts of the former empire into a reunited

China. The unity that would occur was not to include Ji. It would be among the sixteen prefectures in northern Hebei and Shanxi that came to the Qidan from the state of Jin even before the fall of the last of the five dynasties. Officially it was awarded to Liao by the treaty signed with Song in 1005. Prior to this period, however, sometime during the Tang dynasty (618–906), a monastery had stood at the Dulesi site.

The fact that a monastery existed under Tang is reported in the local record of Panshan, *Panshan zhi*, which survives in seventeenth- and eighteenth-century editions and is recounted from that source in *Rixia jiuwen*. "We do not know," the text goes, "when the monastery was established, but it was repaired in Liao times."[7] The implication is that destruction occurred during the Five Dynasties military struggles.

A tidbit about the monastery's name came to Liang Sicheng from one of his old-timers who claimed that Dule, literally "solitary joy," was a reference to An Lushan, also known as An Dule.[8] An Lushan was a man of Soghdian and Turkic descent who at this spot had rallied troops to follow him in a rebellion that forced the Tang court into temporary exile in the 750s. By personality, according to Liang's source, An was a loner who celebrated his joys in private. An Lushan is associated with other monasteries in the Beijing vicinity and northern Hebei as well.[9] In the context of Liao history, "Lushansi" could have been a positive reference to a scion of Chinese history who had seen to the overthrow of imperial China. The second possibility, more mundane, is that the monastery was named for the Dule River, which runs northwest of the Ji city walls. It is not certain, however, if this waterway was known as Dule in Liao times.

The Liao building history begins with information from a lost stele whose inscription survives. Known as Liu Cheng Stele and dated to the first summer moon of 986, it is named for its author who, the stele tells us, was a member of the Hanlin Academy of scholars but who has no biography in the Chinese dynastic histories.[10] According to the stele inscription, *shangfu* Qinwang (the Prince of Qin with the honorific title *shangfu*) ordered the monk Tanzhen to repair the pavilion to the bodhisattva Guanyin and its bodhisattva image in the tenth moon of 984. The Prince of Qin was first identified in secondary literature as Yelü Nugua, a grandson of the Liao founder Abaoji.[11] This identity of imperial patronage is appealing because it would seem to justify the magnificence of the Guanyin Pavilion and heighten expectations of the grandeur of the lost portions of the Liao monastery.

In fact, the Prince of Qin was not the emperor's relative. Rather, he was an official of Chinese descent and a member of one of the most powerful nonimperial families in Liao history. Karl Wittfogel and Feng Chia-sheng correctly identified *shangfu* Qinwang as Han Kuangsi.[12] In 1985, Su Bai recounted the fascinating relationship between the Chinese official and the monument.[13] In the eleventh moon of 979, Han Kuangsi was still the Prince of Yan. By the seventh moon of 985, however, he had received the fief of Qin and the honorific title *shangfu*. Conflicting dates in funerary inscriptions and emperors' biographies in the *Liaoshi* relate that the title was received by the eleventh moon of 981 or posthumously (within several years after Han Kuangsi's death in the twelfth moon of 982). Certainly the dates are close enough to the rebuilding of Dulesi in 984 recorded in the stele inscription to strongly underscore the ties between this man, the pavilion, and, as it turns out, his descendants for almost two more centuries.

Han Kuangsi was a native of Yutian, Jizhou. His ancestors' ties to the county can be traced back two generations. When the territory fell into Qidan hands, Han's grandfather became a member of the household of Abaoji's wife, Yingtian. His father rose to the position of *shangshu ling* (president of the secretariat). Han himself was a favorite of the widow Yingtian and was placed in charge of Abaoji's ancestral temple. Eventually he oversaw the affairs of the Shangjing and Nanjing circuits and, the *Liaoshi* records, had his own "fortified city."[14]

Su Bai has reconstructed the Han family lineage and provided documentation of the continued ties between Han Kuangsi's five sons and their descendants and the imperial households of Liao and even Jin through the year 1175.[15] Su has also published funerary inscriptions of the family Han that record not only repairs at Dulesi by Han Kuangsi but continued patronage of the monastery located in the region of his birth by his descendants, even though Han family members spread far enough from Ji county that the remains of Han descendants were not always returned to the ancestral home for burial. For those who were buried in the county, their relation will be shown to have been not just with Dule Monastery but with a white pagoda to the south, the same one, it will be suggested here, illustrated in *Jizhou zhi* (see figs. 24 and 25).

After the time of association with the Han family, the next recorded events in the monastery's history are repairs during the late Ming and Qing periods. The first of these is recorded in "Dulesi Dabeige ji" (Record of Great Compassion Pavilion of Dule Monastery) written by Wang Yubi, the man who supervised the repairs.[16] According to this Kangxi-period (1662–1722) source, Wang had received his *jinshi* degree in 1595. Sometime thereafter he came to Ji county as *duxiang* (supervisor of rations). His stele inscription records several facts about Dulesi's history. Although one might assume repairs to have occurred during the last 600 years, we are told only that the repairs of the 980s had long since decayed, implying that his was the first repair since the tenth century. Furthermore, the passage about repairs of

the 980s mentions only painting and decoration, suggesting the work to have been more superficial than structural. Wang also tells us that his supervision was a continuation of work initiated by one Ke Gong about whom we know nothing. This inscription is the only instance in which a pavilion at Dulesi is called Dabeige. Since Dabei is a reference to Guanyin, it is assumed to be an alternate name for Guanyinge. If it was the name used in the Liao period, a further significance of the appellation will become clear in our discussion of the tenth-century Song monastery Longxingsi.[17]

The second repair stele preserved in full is "Xiu Dulesi ji" (Record of repair of Dulesi), dated 1658, which refers to the pavilion as "Guanyinge." During the more than sixty years between the two stelae, the time of Ming-Qing transition, the Ji prefectural city suffered devastation three different times. On each occasion this monastery and Taxiasi (Monastery at the Foot of the Pagoda) were safe havens for the local population.[18] Taxiasi does not appear in either of the Jizhou maps. The mention of a pagoda in its name may be a reference to the white pagoda and its monastery, but one cannot prove this.

It must have been in the aftermath of the city's devastation that the official Huang Huashan stopped at Dulesi while passing through the county. Huang was amazed by the terrible state of what he saw. A monk named Chunshan apologetically came out to greet him. One thing led to another and eventually to repair of the Guanyin Pavilion and front gate through donations of both local officials and passersby. Since the two Liao halls are mentioned specifically in the 1658 stele, one can probably assume some structural repairs at that time.

The next repair occurred in 1753 under the Qianlong emperor who "restored" so many of China's old buildings according to the broadest definition of

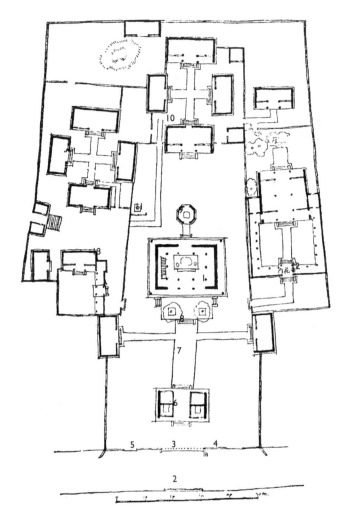

FIGURE 26. Plan of Dulesi in 1932. [After *Liang Sicheng wenji*, vol. 1, p. 48]

the term. In the case of Dulesi, the plan was altered. A *zhaobi* (freestanding wall opposite the entrance) was added, thereby cutting the natural approach to the front gate, and an entire precinct was constructed in the east. Any old buildings that may have stood there would have been destroyed. One assumes the symmetrical courtyard on the west was added at the same time, although at least one of the building groups in it appeared to Liang Sicheng to be Ming period (fig. 26).[19] Four exterior poles to help support the falling roof eaves of Guanyin Pavilion's upper story were also part of these eighteenth-century repairs.

An old-timer told Liang a story associated with the mid-eighteenth-century restoration. When a laborer took a meal break an old man came up and the worker offered him a bite. "It's short on *yán*," he said. This was a play on words, for "*yán*" means both roof eaves and salt. Actually, an allusion was being made to the semilegendary master-builder of China, Lu Ban,[20] who is reported to have lengthened the short eaves of Chinese architecture. The preservation of widely projecting roof eaves—in contrast to the widespread Qing-style changes that during the Qianlong-period restoration would be expected to have included shortened eaves—is attributed to this comment.[21]

It was again passage through the region and proximity to Beijing that led to the next repair, in 1901. Like the late-Ming repair, this one during the Guangxu reign was more decorative than structural. The impetus for repair was the happy return of the royal family to their residence in the Forbidden City in Beijing after "exile" in the northeast. Since they also passed through Jixian en route to the Eastern Qing tombs in Zunhua, it was decided to redecorate what all records point to as Ji county's most eminent monastery for the last 900 years. Much of the painting of exterior wooden pieces today survives from the Guangxu period.

FIGURE 27. Shanmen, Dulesi, 984. [Steinhardt photograph]

During the Qing dynasty, the local population had been allowed to gather in front of the monastery, but not to enter it. Associations between the monastery and the Han family patrons seem long ago to have vanished. By the last dynasty, Dulesi seems to have been considered an imperial monastery. Yet upon the fall of the Qing, in 1911, the halls that had once protected the locals were flooded by thieves and plunderers. Worse was military occupation during the 1920s, the marks of which are still apparent in bullet holes lodged in timber building frames during target practice. In the late 1920s the Nationalist government ignored local opposition and sold the monastery. It is probably because of this transaction that anything is preserved today. In 1930, Dulesi became Ji County Village Normal School, and although its various courtyards were used for basketball and volleyball, the principal realized the value of the two Liao buildings and their imagery. They were preserved without alteration.

Dulesi is no longer an institution of secondary education, but its two Liao buildings (figs. 23 and 27) probably look much as they did in the 1930s.

MONASTERY PLAN

The size of the Liao religious complex is nowhere recorded and can no longer be determined, but Guanyin Pavilion has probably always been the focal point of Dule Monastery (fig. 23 and fig. 26, no. 1). Wall pieces that surround the enclosure today remain from the Qianlong restoration or later. Southernmost, beyond any wall that may have existed, is the Qianlong emperor's *zhaobi* (fig. 26, no. 2). To the north is a main axis with symmetrically positioned east and west courtyards that emphasize the centrality of the pavilion.

Continuing northward from the *zhaobi*, today one crosses Great West Avenue (Xidajie) and comes to a railing (*zhalan*; fig. 26, no. 3) on either side of which are flagpoles that formed a line with the ends of freestanding wall (fig. 26, nos. 4 and 5). Their marked distinction from comparable flagpole bases in the vicinity of Beijing led Liang to suggest that they might survive from the Liao period.[22] The wall at either end of this railing was set up in 1755 to restrict public entry; in the first part of this century it isolated the schoolchildren from outside traffic.

Less than 20 meters from the railing was one of the Liao monuments, the Shanmen, or front gate (fig. 27). It houses two guardian kings (renwang; dvarapalas), one on either side of the north-south passageway through it. Fondly known by the locals as Hem and Haw,[23] they are surrounded by wall paintings. Some of the paint may have been touched up during the Guangxu restoration.

A paved walkway (fig. 26, no. 7) led directly to Guanyin Pavilion and branched off to small side halls just before the stairs that led up to it. These stairs and sets of stairs at the east and west rose to a yuetai (literally, "moon platform") on which stood two flower beds, the western one containing a cypress tree (fig. 26, no. 8). The platform was the basketball court of the county normal school.

Rising more than 22 meters, in the 1930s the pavilion could be seen from the city wall more than 5 kilometers away,[24] just the way it had been drawn a century before in the Jizhou record (see fig. 25). Several meters behind is a Qing-period octagonal kiosk (fig. 26, no. 9). The school volleyball games were held in the courtyard behind it. Beyond the courtyard is one of two four-sided building complexes joined by cross paths. Music rooms and dormitories of the 1930s, the building group probably dates from the Ming period and is otherwise nondescript (fig. 26, no. 10). In the central west part of the courtyard between the kiosk and back building group is a bronze bell inscribed with names of casters and donors and dated 1489 (fig. 26, no. 11). The buildings of the east and west courtyards (fig. 26, nos. 12 and 13) are self-contained groups added in

Ming or Qing times. They were used by the school as cafeterias and lecture halls, perhaps similar to their purposes when constructed in monastic times.

SHANMEN

The Shanmen is the front gate of a Buddhist monastery.[25] Its distinction is simply that it is the only surviving Liao gate—for in comparison to the other extant examples of Liao timber-frame construction, it offers little in the way of structural uniqueness. It shares certain structural features as well as an early-Liao date with the pavilion behind it. Here we shall examine its architectural components, many of which will be treated again, sometimes with more detail.

The Dulesi Shanmen is a single-story structure.[26] At its foundation is a rectangular stone platform (taiji) 0.5 meter in height, which projects about 2.2 meters beyond the column line across the front and 1.3 meters at the sides. The extension of the platform beyond the gate is so narrow that there is no room for a worshiper to stand. Clearly the purpose of the Shanmen is to introduce the visitor to what lies within the monastery to its north. Positioned into the platform are three rows of four pillars each that support the rest of the timber frame (fig. 28). The intervals between the pillars, jian (bays), vary according to their positions. The widest bay in the structure is the central bay along the front facade. Known as dangxin jian or ming jian, it measures 6.17 meters. Two doors are joined into this bay. When they are open, a clear passageway even wider than the stone-paved walkway in front of it (fig. 26, no. 6) and behind it directs all space toward Guanyin Pavilion. The two outer bays across the front and back of the Shanmen measure 4.38 meters each, or 5.23 meters from the center line of one pillar to the next. Each of the side bays is 4.3 meters wide. Chinese terminology describes this as a three-by-two-bay structure. The designation of a building according to the number of bays across the front by the number of bays deep will be used throughout this book. One must keep in mind, however, that the reference is only to spatial intervals and not to distances—it is possible and even probable that in one Chinese structure, especially during the Liao dynasty, each bay from the central bay outward along either half of the front facade of a structure will have a different measurement (symmetrically positioned bays should have equal lengths), that side bays will have yet other dimensions, and that interior columns will not be placed along axes suggested by exterior pillars, giving way to yet different interior bay distances.

Granite plinths, or pillar bases (*chu*), whose style is more Qing than Liao,[27] are used for the pillars along the central Shanmen passageway. All are roughly square and measure 0.85 meter on each side. The wooden columns placed into them all rise 4.33 meters. This uniformity of height distinguishes the Shanmen from most other Liao buildings. It is probably not coincidence that this measurement is so close to the length of a side bay. It will be evident after discussion of more buildings that a modular system was used to generate timber lengths through a Liao structure. Pillar diameters are 0.51 meter at the base and taper to 0.47 meter at the top, giving way to an average height/diameter ratio of 8.65:1. The pillars bend inward very slightly, about 2 percent.

An architrave, or lintel (*lan'e*), passes through the pillar tops along both building axes (figs. 29 and 30). Into it are lodged *dougong,* known in Song China as *puzuo,* or corbel brackets. These bracket sets are found at five different places in the Shanmen, and their elements differ in size and number according to position in the individual set and location of the set on the gate. The five bracket-set locations can be seen in Figures 29 and 30. Scores of bracket-set varieties are present in Liao architec-

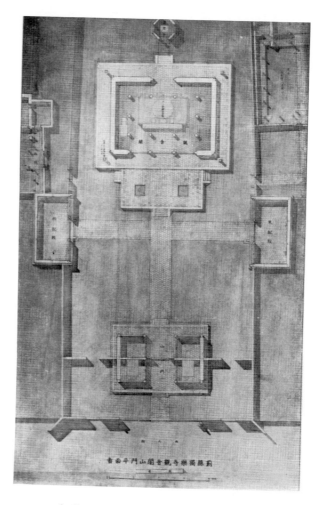

FIGURE 28. Reconstruction drawing of plan of Shanmen, Guanyin Pavilion, and two side halls. [After Liang, "Jixian Dulesi," frontplate 1]

ture. Since bracket sets are discussed in each of the early chapters and much of Chapter 8, only two distinctive features of the Shanmen bracket sets are mentioned here. Both of them are typical of other Liao construction. First, a *shu zhu* (dwarf pillar or post) was employed under the cap block *(ludou)*, keystone of the bracket set. Second, the transversal bracket arm known as *nidao gong* is noticeably long, 117 centimeters, or 71 *fen*—9 *fen* in excess of the length prescribed in the *Yingzao fashi* for a structure with these proportions.[28]

Besides the column and the bracket set, the other main timber component of the Shanmen is the beam. In Chinese construction, beams are distinguished by their position and by the number of rafters they span. Beams that run along the side axis of a building will be referred to here as crossbeams *(liang* or *ping liang)*. At the Shanmen, the principal crossbeams *(zhu liang)* span four rafter lengths *(chuan;* see fig. 30) and the gate is referred to as a structure with four-rafter beams *(sichuan liang* or *si-chuan fu)*. Like a building description of "three-bays-by-two," the beam designation is one of wooden members in relation to space rather than an actual measurement. In other words, *sichuan* tells us only that the beams cross four rafters; it says nothing about a beam's length or the intervals between any two rafters. Another beam, which can be referred to as a subsidiary crossbeam, *ci liang*, spans only the lengths of two rafters and is placed higher in the structure. Above the beams, running perpendicular to the crossbeams, are purlins *(lin* or *tuan)* also circular in section. The Dulesi Shanmen has five of these purlins. In contrast to what we find in later Chinese architecture, slight entasis is present in the beams. The bulge may explain some of the structure's strength. Ji county has suffered its share of earthquakes, the most recent in 1976,[29] yet the two Dulesi Liao buildings survive. The depth/thickness ratio of beams is approximately 2:1 (54:30 cm

for *da liang*, "great beams," and 50:26 cm for four-rafter beams), the proportions suggested in the *Yingzao fashi*. The Shanmen has a simple hipped roof *(si'a wuding)*. Its average rise *(juzhe)* is 50 percent.

Alternative names can be found for almost every wooden piece of a Chinese building, including those used in the preceding paragraph. In general, every component in Chinese construction has at least two names—one employed in the twelfth-century architectural manual *Yingzao fashi* and a second found in the Qianlong-period *Gongbu gongcheng zuofa zeli* (Engineering manual for the Board of Works). Other terms are the vocabulary of modern architecture. Occasionally one of the pre-modern manuals will have more than one name for the same thing, and sometimes the names for building parts have originated in literary works or have been found in premodern dictionaries. I have tried to name each building part by its most common Chinese name in the eighth through thirteenth centuries. Depending on the context, post-Song designations will be used if they are relevant. If my labeling of building parts seems inconsistent, the reason can be traced to the total lack of consistency in Chinese sources.

GUANYINGE

Guanyinge is the jewel of Dulesi and, one might argue, the gem of tenth-century Chinese architecture.[30] It rises more than 22 meters above the ground and is composed of more than a thousand individual pieces (see fig. 23).[31] Chen Mingda once wrote that the Shanmen reached the structural limitations of its time.[32] Guanyinge challenges them.

Guanyinge is the earlier of two multilevel wooden buildings that remain from the Liao dynasty. Except for pagodas—a foreign import whose presence in China was justified by its fundamental role in Buddhism but whose height nevertheless

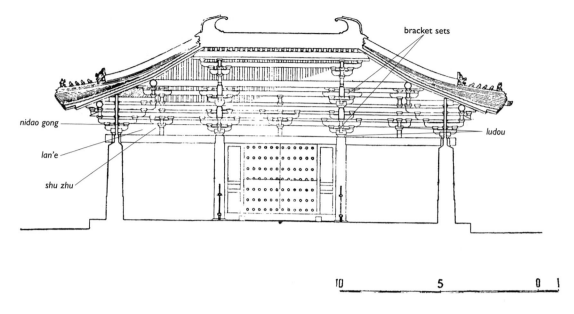

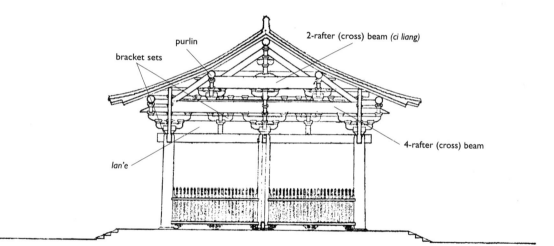

FIGURE 29 (top). Front elevation drawing of Shanmen, Dulesi. [After *Liang Sicheng wenji*, vol. 1, frontplate 7c]
FIGURE 30 (above). Side sectional drawing of Shanmen, Dulesi. [After *Liang Sicheng wenji*, vol. 1, frontplate 7a]

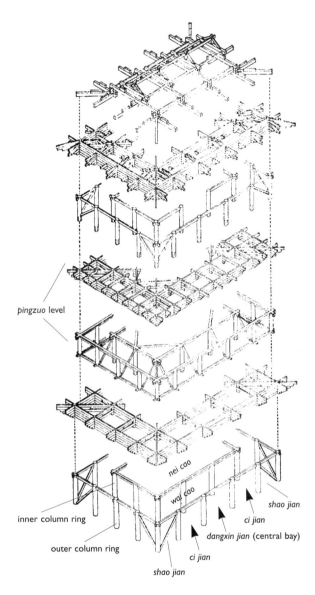

nei cao

wai cao

shao jian

ci jian

dangxin jian (central bay)

inner column ring

outer column ring

ci jian

shao jian

FIGURE 31. Line drawing of timber-frame layers of Guanyin Pavilion, Dulesi. [After Chen Mingda, *Jianzhu lishi yanjiu* 2, p. 52]

bespoke its foreign origins—Chinese hall construction is almost universally single level. Indeed, in a Chinese building complex, even when tall buildings are present, spatial magnitude was traditionally expressed along the horizontal axis. Upward construction, after all, could be interpreted as a sign that a builder had limited funds and was trying to get the most out of his square footage. Thus, ideally, buildings followed one another along north-south or east-west lines and were interrelated by covered arcades and walls that enclosed courtyards. The most dramatic example of the Chinese concept of horizontal space is the Forbidden City in Beijing, whose primary axis extended several kilometers through an otherwise crowded city; but much lesser building groups, even those with a single focal religious hall or residence, were composed of one-story structures. Liao architecture, as we shall see, was exceptional in its abundance of multistory construction.[33]

Native Chinese architecture confronted vertical space initially with watchtowers, sometimes freestanding and otherwise attached to city walls, and later with structures known as *ge*, translated here as "pavilions."[34] The ultimate origins of *ge* have never been worked out. Guanyinge of Dulesi is the earliest wooden pavilion in China now, but painted evidence at the Mogao Caves near Dunhuang pushes the date back to the Tang dynasty. So far, all early associations with *ge* are Buddhist and their specific function was to enshrine a deity.[35] (In modern Chinese parlance, the term "*lou*," a reference to a high building that need not be associated with Buddhism, merged with "*ge*" into "*louge*," a generic name for a multistory building that is not a pagoda.) *Ge* are common in surviving Liao construction, perhaps because they were, in fact, common or perhaps because of chance survivals. For the Liao monastery plan, *ge* and pagodas will be shown to have unique importance.

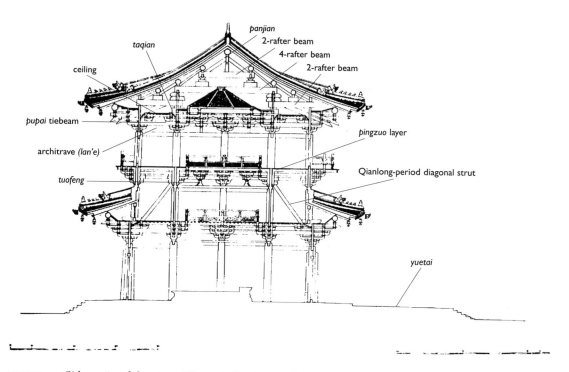

panjian
2-rafter beam
4-rafter beam
2-rafter beam
taqian
ceiling
pupai tiebeam
architrave *(lan'e)*
tuofeng
pingzuo layer
Qianlong-period diagonal strut
yuetai

FIGURE 32. Side sectional drawing of Guanyin Pavilion, Dulesi. [After *Liang Sicheng wenji*, vol. 1, frontplate 4]

The widespread use of *ge* in Liao architecture may seem surprising since Liao builders had not figured out the key to making high wooden buildings. As we see at Guanyin Pavilion, this Liao *ge* is essentially a set of independent one-story halls piled on top of each other (fig. 31). Bracket sets provide the only structural attempt at integration between stories. The layering of single halls with no pillar longer than the height of a story was a weak feature of construction at Guanyinge for which the Qianlong-period restoration compensated by the addition of diagonal struts on the interior between interior and exterior rows of columns (fig. 32). The straight posts that bolster the undersides of both sets of exterior eaves were added at the same time (see fig. 23).

The structural limitations of the time make the construction of the Guanyinge stories even more impressive. Outward indications suggest that this is a two-story building, but a third level, known in Chinese as *pingzuo* and sometimes translated "mezzanine," exists between them on the interior (see figs. 31 and 32). Stairs provide access to both upper stories (see figs. 33, 34, and 35). More striking still is the positioning of two rings of interior columns and the horizontal and vertical members they support. Even so, each ingenious feature is subordinated to the resident for whom the pavilion was constructed—the 16-meter Guanyin, tallest wooden Buddhist sculpture in China, that may predate the reconstruction of the monastery in 984 (see fig. 6).[36]

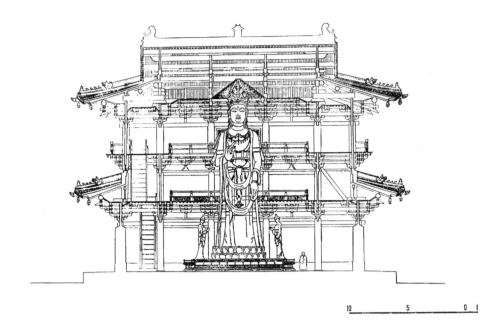

FIGURE 33. Front sectional drawing of Guanyin Pavilion, Dulesi. [After *Liang Sicheng wenji*, vol. 1, frontplate 5]

Guanyinge is a five-by-four-bay building (see fig. 28). The rigid superimposition of independent halls is nowhere better seen than in the measurements of these bays. The central bay across the front facade of all three levels measures 4.75 meters (fig. 33). The bays that flank it *(ci jian)* are 4.35 meters, again, for all three stories. Only the outside (east and west) bays of the front and back *(shao jian)* are of nonuniform lengths story to story, but in each case the measurement is smaller than the intermediate bay lengths. Similarly, the two interior bays on the east and west sides of the pavilion are 3.74 meters on all three levels, and the flanking side end bays, of different lengths story by story, are in each case smaller than the central bays (see fig. 32). The fact that the central bays above or below one another are of identical lengths makes it all the more surprising that no one came up with the idea of single, strong pillars running from the base to the top of the pavilion. Indeed, the three interior bays form a *(nei) cao*, inelo-quently translated "trough," distinct from the *wai* (outer) *cao*. The wooden structural frame follows the boundary of the *nei cao* on the mezzanine level (fig. 34), but for the third story the *nei cao* pillars are joined by timber pieces that lead to the hexagonal base of the ceiling frame over the bodhisattva's head (fig. 35).

An important feature of Chinese hall construction is indicated by the bay measurements. There is an obvious decrease in length outward from the central and longest bay (or bays, if an even number occurs) toward the end bays of any given side in timber-frame architecture. The principle of bay-length reduction across the front and back facades is found in the earliest surviving examples of Chinese wooden construction discussed in the next chapter. A construction principle related to the measurement of bays across the facade is known as "pillar rise" (*zhu shengqi*). The heights of pillars rise very slightly from those that flank the central bays to those under eave corners. There are other features of columns as well: the bottoms are slightly greater in diameter than the tops, and they incline slightly inward from the base, a principle known as *cejiao* and often translated "batter." In addition, it is believed that the original columns were all thick—approximately one-fifth their lengths—and discrepancies in the basically thick pillar widths were the result of weathering or aging.[37] (The fact that the ground-story pillar diameters are now only about one-tenth their heights, a proportion common in Qing construction, may suggest they have been replaced.) All of these features had been present in Tang architecture, and all enhanced a structure's stability.

Guanyin Pavilion is raised on a polished stone base about 1.06 meters in height whose bottom dimensions are 26.72 by 20.62 meters (see fig. 28). Takeshima Takuichi noted that the foundation was low in comparison to other Liao hall platforms.[38] In front projects a *yuetai* (literally "moon platform"), 16.21 by 7.68 meters, which rises just 5 centimeters short of the hall foundation. The *yuetai* is another standard feature of Chinese construction at least since the Tang dynasty. It was there that Liang saw students playing basketball in 1932. Three sets of stairs, one at the front center and one at each side, provide access to the "moon platform." Stairs led down from the hall platform at the north. In this century, small trees in flower beds stood on the east and west sides of the *yuetai* (see fig. 26, no. 8), but Takeshima believed he saw traces of earlier bell and drum towers in these spots.[39] The three central bays across the front facade of Guanyinge have doors, each with four panels and lattice windows at the top to let light into the hall (see fig. 23). The only other

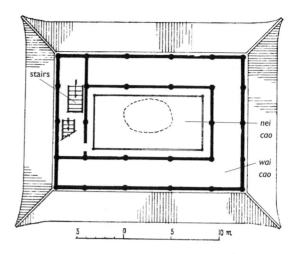

FIGURE 34. Plan of *pingzuo* level of Guanyin Pavilion, Dulesi. [After *Liang Sicheng wenji*, vol. 1, p. 72]

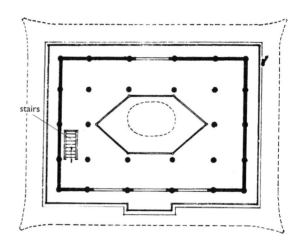

FIGURE 35. Plan of second story (third level) of Guanyin Pavilion, Dulesi. [After *Liang Sicheng wenji*, vol. 1, p. 72]

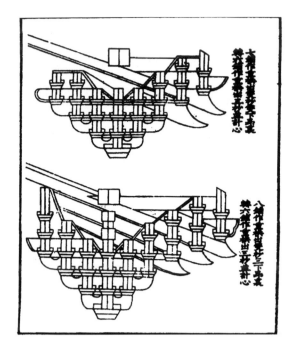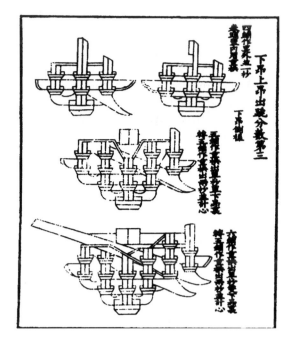

FIGURE 36. Three- through eight- *puzuo* bracketing. [Li Jie, *Yingzao fashi, juan* 30; after 1974 ed., *juan* 30, vol. 6, pp. 42–43]

entry to the hall is in the central back bay. Since the other bay walls do not even have windows, the interior is fairly dark.

By far the most fascinating use of timber is found in the Guanyinge bracketing. Twenty-four types of brackets are used in the hall. They differ according to their placement—a reflection of the load they must bear. Four bracket-set varieties are used under exterior eaves: at all but corner-pillar tops; above the corner pillars; intercolumnarly across the front; and intercolumnarly across the sides. Three kinds are found in the first story interior: above interior pillars; above corner pillars; and on architraves between pillars. The second story has five bracket-set types on its exterior: above-pillar sets are distinct from corner pillar-top sets as one expects, but there are three different compositions of intercolumnar bracketing—those used in the three central bays

across the front facade, those on the two front end bays, and the intercolumnar bays on the other three sides. Similarly, there are five types of mezzanine-story interior bracket sets. The top story has only three exterior bracket-set formats (for pillar tops, corners, and intercolumnar), and four variations are present on the third-level interior. Detailed descriptions of each type are provided in Liang Sicheng's initial study of Guanyinge.[40] Here we discuss only the unique bracket sets at Guanyinge or, on the other extreme, typical features of Liao bracketing.

One bracket-set type sets Guanyin Pavilion's importance apart from other Liao architecture. It is a formation known as 7-*puzuo. Puzuo,* the term for bracket sets used in the Song-dynasty architectural manual *Yingzao fashi,* is the structural unit that characterizes Chinese architecture as perhaps no other feature except the tile roof. The Qing term for *puzuo*—*dougong* (literally "cap [and] block")—is still in use today and refers to the two main bracket-set components. In the *Yingzao fashi*, six different bracket-set formations are illustrated and described (fig. 36). Study of Chinese structures suggests that from the Tang through Yuan dynasties, the period for which the Song manual is most relevant, a direct relationship existed between the *puzuo* number (eight being highest) and the importance, or rank, of a building.[41] The majority of surviving ninth-through-thirteenth-century buildings have 5- or 6-*puzuo* bracketing. In Tang architecture, the 7-*puzuo* formation is present at the East (Main) Hall of Foguang Monastery (see fig. 68).

In rudimentary terms, the *puzuo* number can be thought of as the number of transversal plus perpendicular bracket arms plus the number of cantilevers (when they exist). A key feature that sometimes characterizes 7-*puzuo* bracketing, for instance, is the presence of four *gong* (bracket arms) that project perpendicular to the building plane (figs. 37 and 38). In this case, the number 7 is derived by the two transversal bracket arms and the *shuatou* ("mocking head") above the perpendicular arms in addition to the four perpendicular *gong*. The perpendicular projection of bracket arms with respect to the front of a building gives them the label *hua gong*, distinguished from arms that project either transversally or between the 90-degree angle formed by transversal and perpendicular arms. There is a variation of corbel bracketing found under pillars of the top-level exterior of Guanyin Pavilion that can also be labeled 7-*puzuo*: this variation still has four perpendicular projections, but they occur as two bracket arms and two cantilevers (fig. 39). In Chinese, the bracketing is described as *si tiao* (four jumps or steps) or as *liang* (or *shuang*) *tiao*, *liang* (*shuang*) *xia ang* (two jumps, two down-pointing cantilevers). The transversal (or longitudi-

FIGURE 37. Front facade of Guanyin Pavilion showing 7-*puzuo* bracketing. [Steinhardt photograph]

nal) bracket-set projections do not have a general name such as *hua gong*. They are labeled according to their position in the bracket set. One of these names, *nidao gong*, was discussed earlier in reference to the Shanmen (see fig. 29). As at the Shanmen, *nidao* bracket arms are unusually long in comparison to other longitudinal *gong* in Guanyinge. These and other elements of bracket sets at the Dulesi buildings—including the *tailun*, a wooden piece between the top of the pillar and the cap block that occurs in some but not all Liao architecture—are labeled in Figures 38 and 43. Some are discussed again in Chapter 8.

The bracket set is the place in a Chinese hall where one begins the search for a relationship between proportional standards articulated in the *Yingzao fashi* and actual structures. For both the Shanmen and Guanyin Pavilion, many instances of this direct relationship were confirmed even during initial investigations at Dulesi by Liang Sicheng, Sekino Tadashi, and Takeshima Takuichi, and these cases are cited in their writings. The element

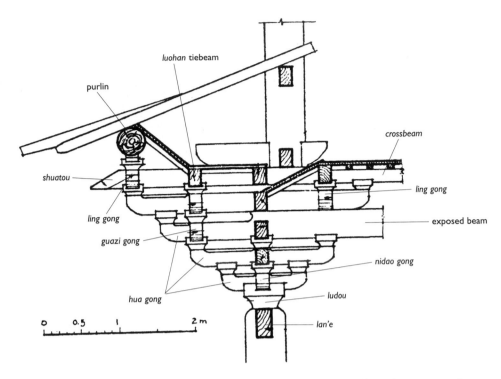

FIGURE 38. Sectional drawing of 7-*puzuo* bracketing, Guanyin Pavilion, first story exterior.
[After *Liang Sicheng wenji*, vol. 1, p. 77]

of the bracket set where the modular proportion is expressed is the *gong*, the bracket arm. It is described in Chinese in terms of a standard unit of timber, *dancai*, which is the length times the height of the cross-section of the bracket arm. At Guanyinge, three standard timber units occur: 27 by 18 centimeters for the *gong* of the first-story exterior bracket, 25.5 by 18 centimeters for interior bracket sets' *gong*, and 23.5 by 16 centimeters for bracketing on the mezzanine level. Proportionately, each of these is close to 3:2, the ideal standard timber proportion for high-ranking halls (*diantang*) expressed in the *Yingzao fashi* (*juan* 4).[42] When the measurement of a timber member does not equal a standard measurement (*cai* or *fen*), it is expressed in terms of

cai plus *zhi*. *Zhi*, simply, is a subsidiary unit. Adding the *zhi* to the length of the standard timber determines a length known as *zucai*. For Guanyin Pavilion, the respective *zucai* are 38.5 by 18 centimeters, again 38.5 by 18 centimeters, and 34.5 by 16 centimeters. The rank of the timber unit, however, a key feature in determining the overall rank of a building, is expressed by the *dancai*. Furthermore, one finds in *juan* 4 of the *Yingzao fashi* eight ranks, or grades, of timber units expressed according to the Song unit of measure, *cun*. When converted to centimeters, the three Guanyin Pavilion *dancai* correspond to the highest, second, and third timber grades. Since 7-*puzuo* bracket sets are employed in the same structure, one is not surprised to find that the building's high rank is also expressed in the measurements of its timbers. Further measurement of longitudinal bracketing components confirms the use of the three high *dancai* throughout entire bracket sets. Other wooden parts of Guanyinge have been measured and they too confirm the use of a proportional relationship either with the *dancai* or the *zucai*: these parts are the architrave; the flat additional tie-beam (rectangular in section) known as *pupai fang* that runs above the architrave (both labeled in fig. 32); and specific beams and rafters. Generally, then, measurement of wooden parts confirms the implementation of Song building standards in this Liao monument of 984.

The timber pieces that run through or above pillars in a Chinese structure and perpendicular or parallel to one another are beams and rafters. The beams and rafters of Guanyin Pavilion can be classified in various ways. One broad distinction separates those that are exposed ([*ming*] *rufu*) from those that are concealed. The concealed beams are generally unfinished (*cao* ["rough"] *rufu*). The feature that conceals them is the ceiling (*pingqi*, among other Chinese names). At Guanyinge the position and formation of every beam or rafter is a response to the ceiling or lack of ceiling at a given level; the use of certain struts and braces, none of which is unique to Guanyinge, is the result of the necessity of ceiling support. Due to the ceiling, for instance, the lengths of beams at Guanyin Pavilion are either two-rafter or four-rafter beams. The four-rafter beams are concealed. All beams are straight.

Three types of struts are used at Guanyin Pavilion. Camel's-hump-shaped struts (*tuofeng*) are placed on rafters and support bracket sets; short braces known as *taqian* join columns or kingposts to interior columns; and slanting posts (*panjian*) are found on kingposts under eave purlins (see fig. 32).

The drama of Guanyin Pavilion is achieved in ceiling construction combined with the main im-

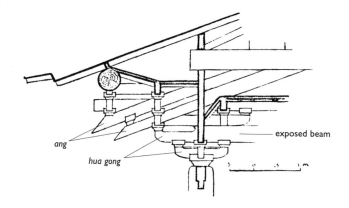

FIGURE 39. Sectional drawing of alternate configuration of 7-*puzuo* bracketing, Guanyin Pavilion, upper story exterior. [After *Liang Sicheng wenji*, vol. 1, p. 88]

age (see fig. 6). The pavilion contains the earliest known wooden example of a sunken ceiling form called *zaojing*, a word whose second character recognizes the resemblance between the frame leading up to it and a well. Based on painted examples of ceilings at the Mogao Caves in Gansu province to the west and painted brick tombs in Korea to the northeast, all dated fourth to eighth centuries, one might assume the wooden *zaojing* has a pre-Liao history.[43] The form is widespread in surviving Liao, Jin, and Yuan architecture.

The construction of the hip-gable roof that tops Guanyinge is, according to the Song system, known as *juzhe* (literally "raise-depress"). The words are taken from the key words in the *Yingzao fashi*, which explains that in building a roof one begins at the top, or main, roof purlin (*ji tuan*) and measures downward. "Raise" refers to the "raising" of a roof purlin ([*ping*] *tuan*) and "depress" to the depression, or slope, from one purlin to the next. We have already noted that purlins are named according to their top, central, or bottom positions under the roof eaves.

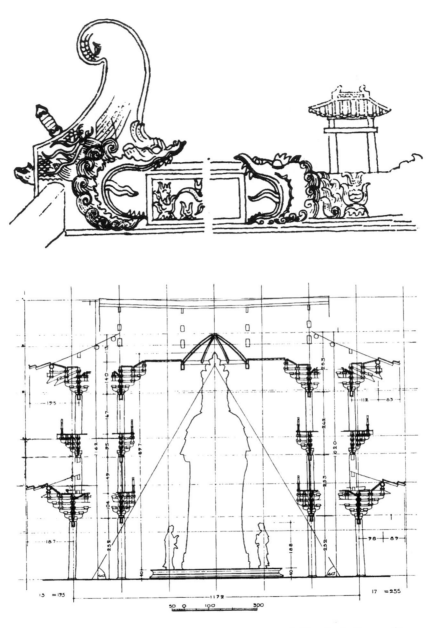

FIGURE 40 (top). Line drawing of decoration on main roof ridge, including pavilion, as seen by Liang Sicheng in 1932. [After *Liang Sicheng wenji*, vol. 1, p. 100]
FIGURE 41 (above). Line drawing of frontal section of Dulesi Guanyin Pavilion superimposed on grid. [After Chen Mingda, "Dulesi," 1987, p. 351]

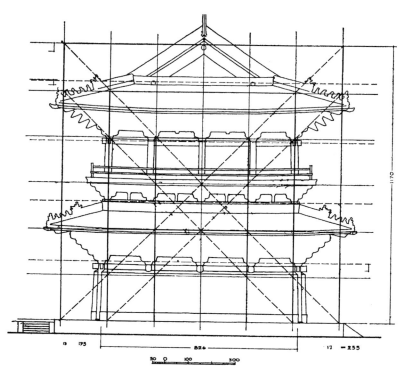

FIGURE 42. Line drawing of side elevation of Dulesi Guanyin Pavilion superimposed on grid. [After Chen Mingda, "Dulesi," 1987, p. 352]

Some, but not all, of the ceramic tile roof and its decoration along the main roof spine survive from the Liao period. A charming detail is a pavilion on top of the roof spine that Liang was told at one time contained an engraved stele (fig. 40).[44]

GUANYIN PAVILION AND THE WHITE PAGODA

Chen Mingda, a young member of the Society for Research in Chinese Architecture in the 1930s who accompanied Liang Sicheng on some of his searches for old buildings, returned to Dulesi in his later writing. In 1987 he published seven measured drawings of the two Liao buildings. Three are presented here as Figures 41–43.[45] The illustrations

indicate that the measuring and proportional relations within individual Liao structures could extend far beyond the *cai-fen* system articulated in the *Yingzao fashi* whereby the sizes of timber pieces are governed by the height and width of the lowest transversal bracket arm. The figures show that the cross section of either Dulesi building can be placed on a grid that proclaims its structural symmetry even though neither bay lengths nor roof rafter positions end up on grid lines. It seems unlikely that documents will be found to prove that Liao builders began construction drawings on grid paper.[46] Yet one has to conclude from these drawings that symmetry, and perhaps measured perfection, are implicit in the two Liao structures.

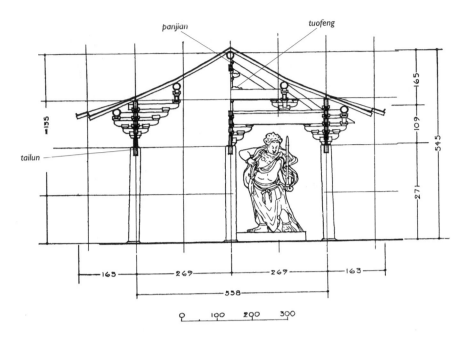

panjian   tuofeng

tailun

—155

165

109

545

271

165   269   269   163

558

0   100   200   300

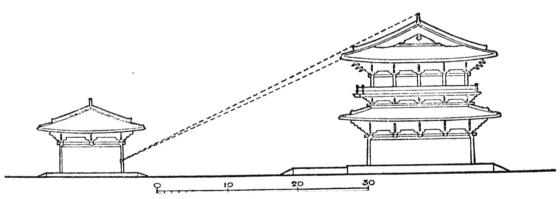

0   10   20   30

FIGURE 43 (top). Line drawing of side section of Dulesi Shanmen superimposed on grid. [After Chen Mingda, "Dulesi," 1987, p. 346]
FIGURE 44 (above). Line drawing of angle of vision from Shanmen to Guanyin Pavilion, Dulesi. [After Chen, *Yingxian Muta*, p. 50]

Chen Mingda made another drawing of the Liao architecture at Dulesi that only hints at the importance of planned space and spatial relationship in these buildings. Figure 44 suggests that if one stands at the back of the Shanmen, one's eyes are immediately drawn to the roof spine of Guanyin Pavilion—a focal point that lacks both meaning and intent. It seems clear that a different, but precise, meaning-laden line through architectural space was intended.

One begins at the central window of the upper story of the pavilion. When it is open, the eyes of the Guanyin image are visible (fig. 45). Standing at the statue's eye level, one is immediately drawn to the White Pagoda of Guanyin Monastery, 380 meters to the south (fig. 46). Although possibly not constructed until 1058,[47] the White Pagoda must be interpreted as an extension of Dule Monastery beyond its walls. It is an extension in accordance with Chinese ideas about the city. If the walled Dulesi is a city in microcosm, then the pagoda, whose funerary purpose will be in evidence shortly, is the necropolis, located extramurally, according to Chinese practice, at least since the Han dynasty when tombs were constructed outside the city walls of Chang'an. This creative interpretation of Chinese architectural space is just the first example of how Liao builders borrow from the Chinese architectural system and reinterpret its principles in new contexts. Moreover, as the prefectural and other records confirm, for the city of Jixian, through the Qing dynasty, Guanyin continued to look out beyond the monastery as a guardian deity in troubled times. It is thus understandable that such prominence is given to the Guanyin Pavilion and Guanyin Monastery directly south of it in *Jizhou zhi* (see figs. 24 and 25).[48]

Liang Sicheng became aware of the pagoda when he was conducting his investigation of Dulesi. Following his long study of Dulesi in 1932,

FIGURE 45. Eyes of Guanyin, Guanyin Pavilion, Dulesi. [Courtesy of Marilyn and Roy Gridley]

FIGURE 46. View from window of upper story of Guanyin Pavilion, Dulesi. [Courtesy of Marilyn and Roy Gridley]

FIGURE 47. White Pagoda, Guanyin Monastery, Jixian.
[Courtesy of Marilyn and Roy Gridley]

he published a short article on it telling the reader in the first paragraph that he had been told to look about half-a-kilometer toward the south, as the bodhisattva does, when he climbed up Guanyinge.[49] Although Liang had the right instinct—that the White Pagoda possessed great significance—neither he nor subsequent architectural historians knew what that significance was.

Liang also read stelae inscriptions. One of them, also recorded in *Jizhou zhi*, reads: "White Pagoda Monastery is in the southwest corner of the *zhou*. Its building date is unknown. Inside the monastery is a white pagoda, thus its name. In 1751 an official named Liang repaired the White Pagoda by imperial decree. When the work was completed, he erected a stone under the pagoda that was inscribed 'Repair of Guanyin *Bao* (Precious/Esoteric) Pagoda by imperial decree.'"[50]

Liang Sicheng found another stele dated 1594. Although this Wanli-period inscription makes a few important points about the date of this monastery and its relation to Dulesi, the two monasteries were clearly considered distinct entities. Summarizing his thoughts on the matter, Liang wrote: "Although one cannot say when this monastery [Baitasi] was established, it cannot have been earlier than Dulesi, and its plan must be related to Dulesi's—there is no doubt about it. When it comes to a discussion of scale, Dulesi is large and White Pagoda Monastery is small. Therefore, Dulesi must have been first and Baitasi came afterward, placed on its [Dulesi's] central axis."[51]

It was the aftermath of an earthquake in 1976 that brought about renewed interest in the White Pagoda and, ultimately, the interpretation of its purpose and relation to Guanyin Pavilion suggested here. Although the tremor caused no damage to the pavilion, the surface of the pagoda was cracked. In the spring of 1983, the Tianjin History Museum Archaeology Team and Jixian Cultural Relics Preservation Office began a structural and archaeological investigation of the pagoda.[52] One aspect of the work was peeling off the cracked exterior. Revealed beneath was a Liao pagoda (fig. 47) covered after the Ming period by the surface that Liang saw.

The Liao date for the inner pagoda was confirmed only by digging further into it (fig. 48). Among the findings was a two-layer sutra case—the exterior sandstone and the interior wood—engraved on its front, right, and left sides (fig. 49). In addition to the date, 1058, the date now assumed for the Liao pagoda, the inscriptions tell that the object was a reliquary containing the cremated remains of Han Zhibai, an official of the title *liushou* of the Zhongjing circuit (fourteen pieces), two pieces of another high-ranking official, Qin Jian, and six pieces of the monk Sixiao. Thus is confirmed the funerary purpose of the pagoda protected by the bodhisattva Guanyin's gaze beyond the walls of Dulesi.

Su Bai believes that Han Zhibai was not related to the Han family of Yuyang who are so closely linked to Dulesi.[53] Nevertheless, the family of Han Kuangsi is relevant to this structure. According to Su Bai, in 1058, Daozong, allowing for the fact that he had no son, ordered the son of the Prince of Wei, a member of the imperial family, to be Prince of Wenzhong for a year. The prefecture ruled by the Prince of Wenzhong was connected to Kuangsi's son, Kuangmei, whose burial ground was within it. Su Bai believes that the Buddhist pagoda was built by Han Zhibai in recognition of the fact that members of the powerful family of Han Kuangsi were buried in his district.

In their report of 1989, the archaeological investigative team proposed that the Liao pagoda was restored in the aftermath of an earthquake of 1057 recorded in the official Song history *Songshi*.[54] That earthquake is reported to have killed tens of thousands of people. The restoration team also suggested

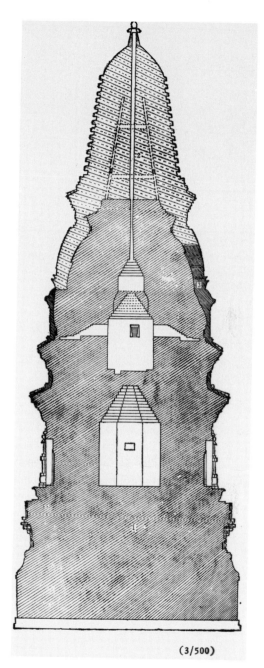

(3/500)

FIGURE 48. Sectional drawing of White Pagoda, Guanyin Monastery, showing interior reliquary compartments. [After "Tianjin Jixian Dulesi ta," p. 86]

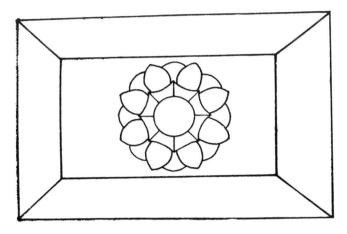

FIGURE 49. Line drawing of top of lid of two-layer box with lotus pattern on each lid, found inside White Pagoda, Guanyin Monastery, Jixian. [After "Tianjin Jixian Dulesi ta," p. 109]

that an earthquake southeast of Beijing during the Tang period, recorded in *Yuan yitong zhi* and corresponding, according to them, to at least 9 on the Richter scale, may have led to the destruction of Dulesi and ultimately to its restoration in 984.[55] Even though twice, it seems, building or rebuilding occurred in Jixian in response to destruction by natural forces, the second date, 1058, had added significance. The decade of the 1050s will be shown in this study to have been a time of Liao patronage and construction with additional meaning for the empire—meaning as potent as the decision to build a funerary pagoda to receive Guanyin's gaze.

By the completion of Dulesi in 984, major as-
pects of Liao architecture had been forged. Less than forty years after the formal establishment of their empire the Liao had emerged as master builders—not only builders capable of 7-*puzuo* corbel bracketing, multistory construction that included a hidden story, and a 20-meter empty space beneath a *zaojing* that housed a 16-meter image, but builders of architecture that would survive numerous earthquakes for over a thousand years. The Liao had demonstrated their penchant for extracting from the Chinese courtyard-space system to articulate symbolic space: they had introduced a monastery plan with unambiguous focus on a high, central building dedicated to a guardian deity whose power, symbolized by its gaze, extended beyond normal monastery confines. Moreover, it is clear through the study of just the first timber-frame pavilion that the Liao and those who came later to their monasteries left a historical record through which one can trace the integral part of a monument in the life of local populations and environment, from protectorate to military barracks to school. Finally, documentation of Liao architecture opens the discussion of patronage of medieval Chinese architecture —in this case initially through a powerful family of local origin and later through donation of the imperial family, the clergy, passersby, and the local population. Already by 984 the Qidan empire had produced a monument of unparalleled structural design, symbolism, and, ultimately, historical documentation.

3

Chinese Architecture before Dulesi

THE LIAO BROUGHT with them to China no building tradition that employed permanent materials. Yet neither Dulesi nor any earlier tenth-century interrelated building complex of wood, brick, tile, and stone elsewhere in Liao territory was a totally original conception of seminomadic Qidan lords and their followers. Moreover, it is unlikely that the Liao saw any of the earlier extant buildings that are the subject of this chapter. One has to assume that it was Chinese or Chinese-derivative architecture (built by Koreans, Bohai, or other peoples living within the Chinese sphere who became part of the Liao empire) that gave way to Dulesi and the other monuments of Liao patronage. Certainly the visual impact of Chinese architecture offered images of rulership and associated power that would have been compatible with the aspirations of Qidan emperors.

With regard to an association between kingship and power, architecture is the most potent of the arts. Although the Qidan may not have been aware of it, architecture had been employed by Asian empire builders time and again as symbols of power, sometimes by nonnative rulers trying to assume leadership over conquered peoples.[1] Yet among the art forms ripe for imperial patronage, architecture requires the greatest commitment from a ruler. Whereas an emperor or his official can say to a painter, sculptor, or ceramicist, "Make me this or that," and if the results are not pleasing discard it with ease, architecture requires a coordinated building program of time, planning, human resources, organization, and money.

Never would non-Chinese occupation of China be accomplished without Chinese buildings.[2] More nomadic than some non-Chinese groups who had ruled North China before them and others who would rule later, the Qidan never became fully sedentary. They continued to hunt and to maintain "traveling palace" locations for hunting and other native ceremonial and pleasure pursuits better kept away from Chinese cities.[3] The walled cities whose wooden buildings do not survive, and the urban and regional monasteries where they do, provided the locus for displays of Chinese-style architecture.

Although the potential sources of monastery and palatial architecture that must have been available to the Liao are vast, to document that they saw even one building from this theoretical list is next to impossible. Of the nine monasteries where Liao buildings survived into the twentieth century (Table 2), only two were newly built in Qidan times. The first potential sources of Liao timber architecture, therefore, are pre-Liao buildings, or at least ruins of them, the Liao found in their own territory. A search through local records of the sixteen prefectures acquired by the Liao in the 930s adds to a list of places where Tang monastery buildings might have stood after the Liao conquest. Still, not one pre-Liao wooden building stands today within the entire territory that was the Liao empire. The only place one can be sure the Qidan could have seen pre-tenth-century construction is in Buddhist worship caves, where, in some cases, the Liao made their own addi-tions to rock-carved facsimiles of architecture, perhaps with wooden facades.[4]

Yet it is only through an exploration of pre-Liao architecture that one can begin to understand how the transmission of Chinese or Chinese-derivative forms worked into the Qidan imperial program — and, therefore, how outstanding or unique Liao architecture is or is not. Information about Chinese wooden architecture in its earliest phases is far from definitive, but despite the small number of actual buildings, more is known about the architecture of this period than is sometimes realized. Modern literature on Chinese architecture focuses on two Tang halls from monasteries in Wutai and Taihuai counties of Shanxi built in the eighth and ninth centuries, respectively. After these, chronological lists of buildings in China generally offer the main hall of Zhengguo Monastery in Pingyao, Shanxi, just south of Liao territory, as China's third-oldest building with a date of 963.[5] In fact, several other less-well-known ninth-and-tenth-century buildings survive. (See Table 3.)

In an article published in 1986 entitled "General Discussion of Ancient Architecture in Shanxi" (in Chinese), Chai Zejun made several important statements about the survival of early Chinese architecture. He wrote that 106 of the 140 pre-thirteenth-century buildings, more than 70 percent of China's total, remain in Shanxi province.[6] Of the Shanxi buildings, more than seventy of them were in the southeastern part of the province beyond Liao territory.[7] Seven buildings studied by Chai—four from the Tang period and three from the period of the Five Dynasties and Ten Kingdoms (906–960)—can be considered pre-Liao. (See Map 2.)

We turn now to a summary of the early timber-frame tradition in China in order to understand the architectural sources of the Dulesi Shanmen and Guanyin Pavilion. (Timber architecture from the

TABLE 2. Liao Wooden Buildings

Monastery and Monument	Location	Date
Geyuansi	Laiyuan, Hebei	
Main (Mañjuśrī) Hall		966
Dulesi	Jixian, Hebei	
Shanmen		984
Guanyin Pavilion		984
Fengguosi	Yixian, Liaoning	
Daxiongbao Hall		1019
Guangjisi	Baodi, Hebei	
Sandashi Hall (destroyed)		1025
Kaishansi	Xincheng, Hebei	
Main Hall		1033
Huayansi	Datong, Shanxi	
Sutra Repository		1038
Haihui Hall (destroyed)		1038 (?)
Daxiongbao Hall		Liao-Jin (rebuilt ca. 1140)
Fogongsi	Yingxian, Shanxi	
Timber Pagoda		1056
Shanhuasi	Datong, Shanxi	
Main Hall		11th century
Puxian Pavilion (rebuilt 1953)		rebuilt 1154
[Shanmen, Jin]		1128–1143
[Sansheng Hall, Jin]		1128–1143
Kaiyuansi	Yixian, Hebei	
Pilu Hall (destroyed)		early 12th century
Guanyin Hall (destroyed)		early 12th century
Yaoshi Hall (destroyed)		early 12th century

TABLE 3. Pre-Liao Halls in North China

Monument	Location	Date
Hanyuan Hall, Daminggong (destroyed)	Chang'an, Shaanxi	662–881
Linde Hall, Daminggong (destroyed)	Chang'an, Shaanxi	662–881
Mizong Hall, Qinglongsi (destroyed)	Chang'an, Shaanxi	ca. 662–ca. 845
Main Hall, Nanchansi	Wutai, Shanxi	782
Five Dragons Temple	Ruicheng, Shanxi	831
Main Hall, Tiantai'an	Pingshun, Shanxi	Tang
Mizong Hall, Qinglongsi (destroyed)	Chang'an, Shaanxi	after 845
East Hall, Foguangsi	Taihuai, Shanxi	847
West Side Hall, Longmensi	Pingshun, Shanxi	925
Great Buddha Hall, Dayunyuan	Pingshun, Shanxi	940
Ten Thousand Buddhas Hall, Zhenguosi	Pingyao, Shanxi	963

early decades of the Song dynasty, 960–1279, is discussed in Chapter 8.) This discussion will encompass both religious and palatial architecture—for, as has long been known, halls that enshrined deities were derived from halls where emperors held court, and structural features of both types were shared.[8] (See Map 2.)

WOODEN BUILDINGS IN CHINA BEFORE THE MID-NINTH CENTURY

Physical evidence of interlocking timber building pieces can be traced back some 7,000 years in China to the Neolithic site at Hemudu in Yuyao county, Zhejiang province.[9] Architectural reconstructions of building complexes since then, from China's Bronze Age and early imperial period, suggest nothing other than timber-frame structures elevated on platforms.[10] Corroborative evidence from the period through the Han dynasty (ca. 206 B.C.–

A.D. 220) comes from incised designs of architecture on bronze vessels, relief sculpture, wall paintings and miniature models of buildings preserved in tombs, and freestanding pillars and towers (figs. 50 and 51).[11] The examples show that by the Han dynasty architectural components like the bracket set and tile roof were standard and had spread to the farthest reaches of the Han empire, including the present Inner Mongolian Autonomous Region and Liaoning, both in the heartland of Liao rule. Evidence of the timber-frame tradition in China between the Han and Tang (618–906) dynasties is preserved largely as relief sculpture and wall painting in Buddhist worship caves and tombs (fig. 52) and in at least one instance in column-top sculpture (fig. 53). The Yun'gang Caves, source of Figure 52, were less than 20 kilometers west of the Buddhist monasteries of the Liao western capital (present Datong). Since Liao additions were made at the Yun'gang

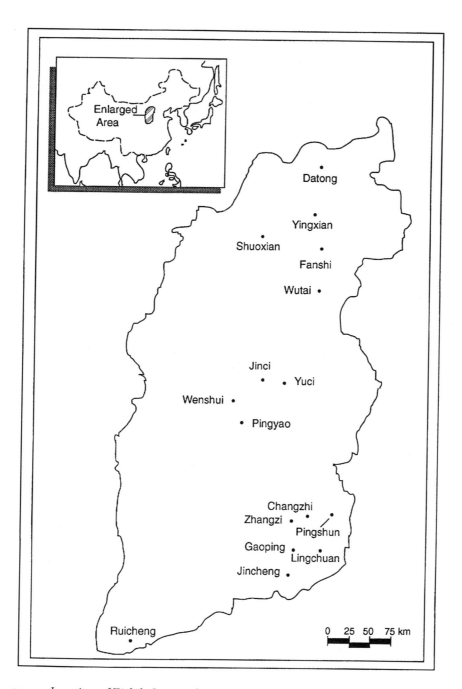

MAP 2. Locations of Eighth-Century through Thirteenth-Century Timber-Frame Halls in Shanxi

FIGURE 50 (top). Detail of wall painting from tomb excavated in Helinge'er, Inner Mongolia, Eastern Han period. [After Gai, *Helinge'er Hanmu bihua*, fig. 13]

FIGURE 51 (above). Pavilion: detail of wall painting from tomb in Beiyuan, Liaoning, Eastern Han. [Liaoning Provincial Museum; Steinhardt photograph]

FIGURE 52. Relief sculpture of "The Great Departure" (of Gautama Siddhartha) showing building in lower left, Cave 6, Yun'gang, Northern Wei. [After *Yun'gang shiku*, pl. 19]

Caves, there is little doubt that their interiors were known to the Qidan. The Yicihui column stands in Dingxing county, Hebei, just south of the Liao border with Song.

Tang Architecture in the Vicinity of Chang'an

For actual wooden buildings, one can probe only two centuries prior to Dulesi. For well-documented reconstructions of timber architecture, the earliest date takes one several decades into the Tang dynasty, to about the mid-seventh century. This was the decade in which construction of Tang palaces, adjacent to the capital Chang'an but beyond its outer wall to the northeast, commenced. The two palace complexes whose ruins have been recon-structed were begun in the 660s and burned in the 880s.[12] Also begun in the seventh century in Chang'an was Qinglong Monastery, one of whose halls has been theoretically reconstructed. All of these buildings had been destroyed before the Liao began construction in wood. The theoretically rendered buildings are discussed here as representatives of the metropolitan style of Tang China that would have spread to the provinces and eventually to the Bohai kingdom where Qidan conquerors saw Chinese-derivative architecture.

Daminggong

Daminggong is the name of the complex of palaces and related halls established by the second Tang

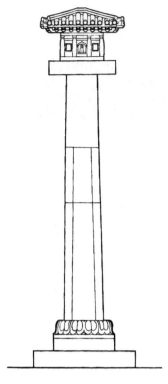

FIGURE 53. Line drawing of Yicihui Pillar, Dingxingxian, Hebei, A.D. 569. [After Liu Dunzhen, *Zhongguo gudai jianzhu shi*, 2nd ed., p. 106]

emperor, Taizong (r. 627–649), on a site that had been parkland during the preceding Sui dynasty (589–618). Its plan broke out of the strict north-south axis of buildings that characterized the original Tang palace-city, which included the residences of the Tang emperor and crown prince. Besides gates, two building complexes at Daminggong have been repeatedly excavated and have gone through several levels of reconstruction. Reconstructions of the audience-hall complex Hanyuan and the banquet-hall complex Linde are shown in Figures 54 and 55, respectively. Comparing these halls and their plans (figs. 56 and 57) to the Shanmen or Guanyin Pavilion, one finds several of the differences that characterize the evolution of architectural components from early Tang to Liao.[13]

One should begin first, however, with the Tang halls themselves. Hanyuan Hall complex was a main hall with three pavilions joining each side. The primary chamber is composed of two rings of pillars that distinguish an arcade from an enclosing corridor on the outside and from the large open interior space that has not even one pillar (see fig. 56). Although eleven-bays-by-four, this is the same *cao* formation implemented at Guanyin Pavilion where the interior of the five-by-four-bay structure was emptied for the bodhisattva image. The Linde Hall complex, by contrast, is a trihall structure, each hall of which is hypostyle in plan. That is, every exterior pillar initiates a complete row of columns that extends to the opposite end of the hall (see fig. 57). At present, it is the only example of this kind of construction known from the Tang period, but one has no reason to assume that it was unique. Section and elevation drawings of the Hanyuan and Linde Hall complexes also illustrate several features that are associated with early Tang construction but are not present at Dulesi (fig. 58). These include crescent-shaped beams (*yue liang*) and simple, single-step brackets or inverted **V**-shaped struts between the

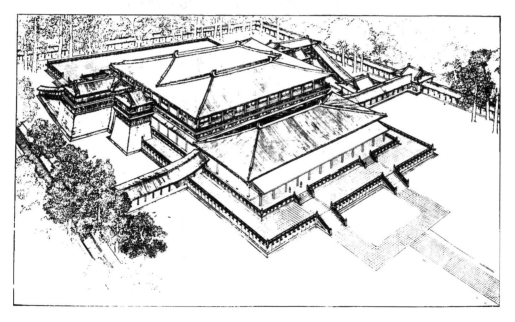

FIGURE 54 (top). Reconstruction of Hanyuandian, Daminggong, Chang'an, 660s–880. [After Steinhardt, *Chinese Traditional Architecture*, p. 93; published with permission of China Institute in America]
FIGURE 55 (above). Reconstruction drawing of Lindedian, Daminggong, Chang'an, 660s–880. [After Yang Hongxun, "Tang Daminggong Lindedian fuyuan . . . ," fig. 7]

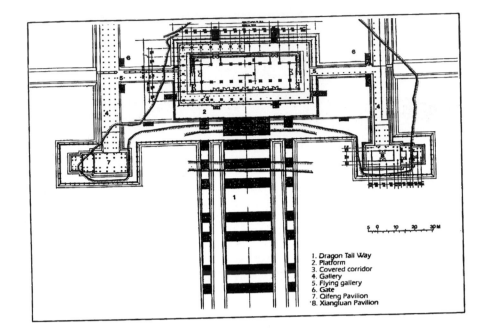

1. Dragon Tail Way
2. Platform
3. Covered corridor
4. Gallery
5. Flying gallery
6. Gate
7. Qifeng Pavilion
8. Xiangluan Pavilion

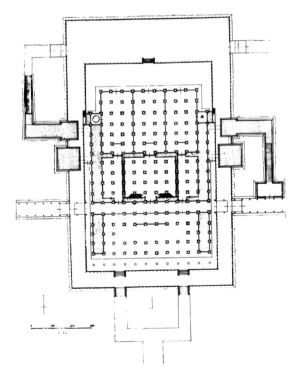

FIGURE 56 (above). Plan of Hanyuandian.
[After Steinhardt, *Chinese Traditional Architecture*, p. 95;
published with permission of China Institute in America]
FIGURE 57 (right). Plan of Lindedian. [After Yang
Hongxun, "Tang Daminggong Lindedian fuyuan . . . ,"
p. 240]

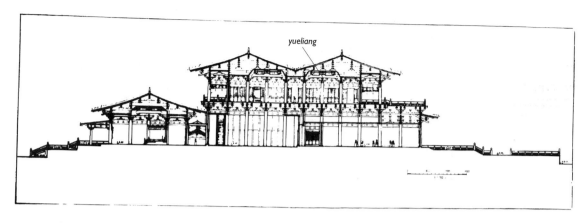

yueliang

FIGURE 58. Reconstruction drawing of side section of Lindedian. [After Yang Hongxun, "Tang Daminggong Lindedian fuyuan . . . ," fig. 4]

column-top bracket sets. Also present in the reconstruction drawings are architectural features typical of high-ranking Chinese architecture that are found at Guanyinge, including four-step bracket sets and the use of the *pupai fang,* the additional plate above the architrave.

Qinglongsi

Mizong Hall from the Tang capital has been the subject of almost as much theoretical reconstruction as the palace halls. It stood on foundation number 4 of what was once Qinglong Monastery, some 6 kilometers south of the Daminggong palaces (fig. 59). The Buddhist hall was built twice: before and after the 840s. The ground plans of both versions have been shown to reflect specific Buddhist rituals performed in the hall.[14] Thus only details of the timber frames will be discussed here in comparison to Liao architecture at Dulesi.

According to the Chinese reconstruction, bracketing in the earlier Qinglongsi hall was of the 6-*puzuo* type, a sign of significant status. Crescent-shaped beams and inverted-V-shaped struts, used in the reconstructions of both Daminggong halls (see

figs. 54 and 56), are believed to have been employed here as well, but they are not present in either Liao-period Dulesi structure. Several elements are present in all known seventh- and eighth-century Chinese architecture: a differentiation in size of bays across the front facade (with the central bay the widest); *juansha,* sometimes translated "entasis," or pillars that widened at the center and tapered at either end; *shengqi,* a "rise" in pillar heights toward the ends of an exterior facade; exposed beams (usually crescent-shaped); and the combination of *chashou* (inverted-V-shaped braces) and kingpost in the roof truss. All persisted into the 980s and are found at both the Dulesi Shanmen and Guanyin Pavilion.

Tang Religious Architecture in Shanxi

The main hall from Nanchan Monastery at the foot of Mount Wutai mentioned earlier (fig. 60) is one of three buildings in Shanxi province whose structural components suggest low status. The most published of the three, it is the one with which we begin. The first notice of Nanchansi's hall was published in one of the initial issues of *Wenwu* (Cultural Relics), soon to become a main source of in-

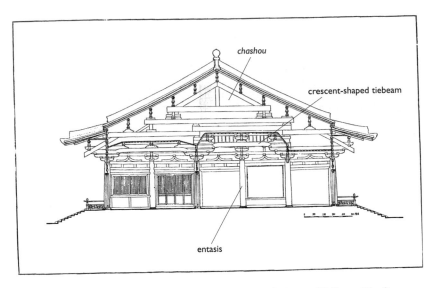

FIGURE 59. Reconstruction drawing of side section of Mizong Hall, ca. 662–845, Qinglong Monastery, Chang'an. [After Yang Hongxun, "Tang Chang'an Qinglongsi . . . ," p. 225]

formation on the excavation and study of old buildings in the People's Republic of China.[15] The obscure location that had eluded members of the Society for Research in Chinese Architecture may also have been the reason why persecutors of Buddhism had missed the small hall in 845. By 1961, however, the importance of the structure as the earliest dated wooden building in China was recognized when, in spite of certain restoration during the Song dynasty, the hall was designated an important cultural property. Although it fell during an earthquake five years later, piece-by-piece study and reconstruction in the 1970s led to the reassembly shown in Figure 60, as well as to restoration drawings that continue to aid our understanding of the structure of a lower-ranking Tang Buddhist hall.[16]

Two telltale signs of the Nanchansi hall's status are its simple frame and corresponding bracketing.

Twelve columns directly implanted into a brick foundation ring its exterior, but no pillars are employed inside to support the roof frame. The longest beam spans four rafters. It was used at either side across an approximately 10-meter span. What the reader now recognizes as standard features of Tang and Liao construction—a longer central bay across the front facade, pillar rise and batter, entasis, the *yuetai*, and camel's-hump-shaped braces—are all present (fig. 61). But, sign of the hall's modest status, not even a simple strut supports the hip-gable roof between the columns. The bracketing above exterior columns was 5-*puzuo*—not the lowest possible, but so far the lowest in surviving Tang or Liao buildings. Clearly this building type was not the inspiration for Guanyin Pavilion at Dulesi.

Less information is available about the other two Tang buildings in Shanxi, but the conclusion about their potential as architectural models for Dulesi is

FIGURE 60 (top). Main Hall, Nanchan Monastery, Wutai county, Shanxi, 782.
[Steinhardt photograph]
FIGURE 61 (above). Side sectional drawing of Main Hall, Nanchan Monastery, 782.
[Qi and Chai, "Nanchansi," p. 65]

FIGURE 62. Main Hall, Five Dragons Temple (Prince Guangren Temple), Longquanzhen, Ruichengxian, Shanxi, 831. [After Chai Zejun, "Shanxi gujianzhu gaishu," p. 255]

FIGURE 63. Main Hall, Tiantai'an, Pingshun county, Shanxi, Tang period. [After Li Yuming et al., *Shanxi gujianzhu . . .*, p. 194]

the same. The second pre-845 building in Shanxi is Five Dragons Temple (Wulongmiao), alternately known as the Temple to Prince Guangren, in Longquan village, Ruicheng county, at the southern tip of the province. Five Dragons Temple's date has been published as 833 but little other information has been made available about it.[17] It was a main hall, five bays across the front, with no *yuetai* (fig. 62). Since *yuetai* were used at earlier Tang and all but the simplest Liao buildings, its omission must be due to low status. The front end bays were noticeably narrower than the central one, and the hall had a hip-gable roof.

The last small main hall in Shanxi remains at Tiantai'an in Pingshunxian.[18] Also five bays across the front, hip-gable-roofed, and without *yuetai*, the hall has been described as "close to Nanchansi's."[19] It is nearly square, 7.15 by 7.12 meters at the bottom, with four-rafter beams, doors in the central bay and windows in the front side bays, entasis and rise evident in the pillars, camel's-hump-shaped braces, and no *pupai* tiebeam (fig. 63)—all features of Nanchansi Main Hall. The roof truss consists of a king-post and *chashou*. Its *dancai* was 17.5 by 12 centimeters and its *zhi* was 11 centimeters, the former consistent with the 3:2 proportion stipulated in the *Yingzao fashi* that has been confirmed at Guanyin Pavilion. In 1958 the hall was dated late Tang, but a more recent mention of the hall refers to it only as "Tang,"[20] perhaps due to structural similarities between it and the Nanchansi hall.

TANG ARCHITECTURE OF THE MID-NINTH CENTURY

The mid-ninth century is a clear point of division in the history of Chinese construction. The year 845 was marked by a widespread persecution of Buddhism sponsored by Emperor Wuzong known as the Huichang persecution because of the reign pe-

FIGURE 64. Reconstruction drawing of Mizong Hall, Qinglong Monastery, ca. 846. [After Yang Hongxun, "Tang Chang'an Qinglongsi . . . ," p. 216]

riod (841–846) in which it occurred. The dearth of extant architecture or sculpture from before the mid-ninth century in China, especially grandiose construction, attests to the program's success and seems to confirm that only out-of-the-way, insignificant buildings like the three just discussed are likely to have been spared.

One of the monasteries in the capital Chang'an that suffered certain destruction was Qinglong Monastery.[21] The second version of the monastery hall at Site 4 was rebuilt shortly after the persecution, about 846 (fig. 64). This date is just eleven years earlier than the year written on a beam of the East (Main) Hall of Foguang Monastery in Wutai county (fig. 65). The Foguang Monastery hall was used in the reconstruction of the later Qinglong Monastery hall at Site 4, and corroborative evidence of the ground plan and excavated material at Qinglongsi strongly suggest that the two Tang halls,

one in the capital, the other in the provinces, were structurally as close as any two buildings from the early period of Chinese construction.

Both ninth-century halls are, first of all, examples of *cao* construction (fig. 66), the only ground plan employed in Liao religious architecture. *Cao* (literally but ineloquently "trough") is, according to the *Yingzao fashi*, "the space enclosed by exterior, or eave, pillars (*yan zhu*), interior pillars (*wunei zhu*), and bracket sets above them. The distance between the central lines of *yan zhu* and *wunei zhu* is the depth of the [outer] *cao* (fig. 67)."[22] In modern parlance, the *cao* described in the passage from the *Yingzao fashi* are called "outer *(wai) cao*" and the interior space they enclose is "inner *(nei) cao*." Noticeable in Figures 66 and 67 is the elimination of pillars from the interior, as at Hanyuan Hall complex of the Tang imperial palaces at Daminggong (see fig. 56), but here in a Buddhist context to make

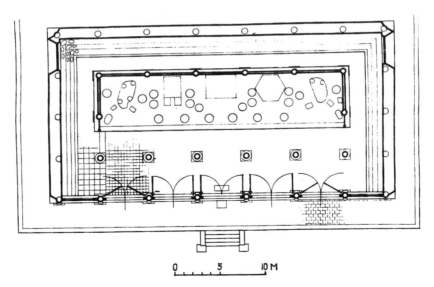

FIGURE 65 (top). Main Hall, Foguang Monastery, Taihuai county, Shanxi, 857.
[After *Ancient Chinese Architecture*, p. 68]
FIGURE 66 (above). Plan of Main Hall, Foguang Monastery, 857. [After Liu Dunzhen,
Zhongguo gudai jianzhu shi, 2nd ed., p. 137]

room for the altar. The framework itself is an example of a framework the *Yingzao fashi* calls *jinxiang dou dicao*, which can be translated something like "golden case *dou* (a liquid measure) lower trough." The formation is illustrated in Figure 67, which shows the inner and outer *cao* and the extension beams that connect parallel interior and exterior columns.

Like Qinglong Monastery, Foguangsi had a history that predated its destruction during the reign of Emperor Wuzong. Its present main hall, also known as the East Hall because of its position with respect to the monastery's east-west orientation, had a predecessor that may or may not have been located in the same place. The earlier hall had been built before the year 828 when the chief abbot of the monastery, Faxing, who had been in charge of its construction, died.[23] Nothing is known about the earlier hall's plan or details. The beam inscription in the main hall that provides the date 857 also informs us that it was built under the supervision of a monk named Yuancheng with funds provided by a woman named Ning Gongyu. Corroborative evidence for the date is found on a Buddhist pillar (*dhāraṇī* column) in front of the hall.

The main hall of Foguang Monastery is a seven-by-four-bay structure elevated on a platform of uneven height because of its position at the foot of a hill. Perhaps because of the uneven ground beneath it, not even a small *yuetai* such as was used at the post-845 Qinglongsi hall exists here. In addition to the twenty-two pillars that define the exterior of the 34-by-17.66-meter hall, fourteen are used in the interior; others have been eliminated to make room for the Buddhist altar. Pillar placement conforms to the principles of *cejiao* (slight lean forward), *juansha* (slight entasis and curve inward at the top), and diminishing length between each set from those that define the center front or back bays outward. Unlike Guanyin Pavilion of Dulesi, however, the

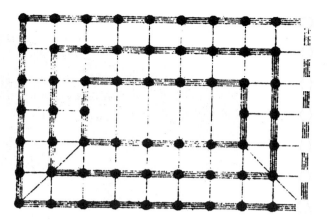

FIGURE 67. Plan of *cao* construction. [After Li Jie, *Yingzao fashi, juan* 31; 1974 reprint, vol. 7, p. 3]

pillars of Foguangsi Main Hall are all the same height, approximately 5 meters. The length is just 4 centimeters short of the width of the central front facade bay in accordance with the *Yingzao fashi* stipulation that a column's height must not exceed the length of any bay in a structure.[24]

The elements that comprise Foguangsi Main Hall's timber frame are labeled in Figure 68. Above the pillars are the architrave (no. 4) and then a board onto which the bracket sets are connected (*gongyan bi*) (no. 38). As at Guanyin Pavilion, bracket-set formations differ according to their positions inside and outside the hall, above or between columns, and at the hall corners. Not only does Foguangsi Main Hall boast some of the largest bracket sets known with respect to the lengths of columns below them (the length of bracket clusters measure fully half the pillar heights), but it is one of the few extant examples of 7-*puzuo* bracketing. As at Guanyinge, in 7-*puzuo* bracketing of the Tang period one finds two tiers of *hua gong*, each resting on a *dou*, two cantilevers, and a *shuatou* (decorative nose at the end of the uppermost bracket arm) (see fig. 38).

Other similarities in structural details of the

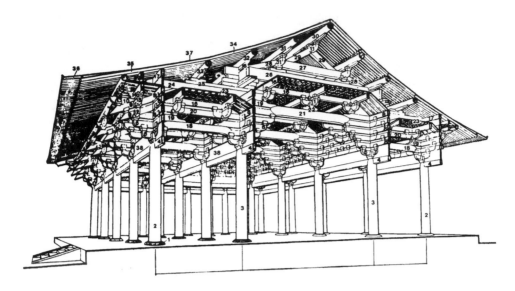

1. zhu chu: plinth
2. yan zhu: eave column
3. nei yan zhu: interior or hypostyle column
4. lan e: architrave or connecting-beam, lintel, girder
5. lu dou: capital-block
6. hua gong: transversal bracket-arm
7. ni dao gong: longitudinal bracket-arm
8. zhu tou fang: tie-beam or axial tie-beam
9. xia ang: down-pointing cantilever
10. shua tou: wooden member parallel to and on topmost transversal bracket-arm, intersecting eave purlin, with front end exposed
11. ling gong: longitudinal bracket-arm of intermediate length
12. gua zi gong: longitudinal bracket-arm of shortest length
13. man gong: longitudinal bracket-arm of longest length
14. luo han fang: luohan tie-beam
15. ti mu: wooden support between longitudinal bracket-arm and eave purlin
16. ping qi fang: paneled ceiling tie-beam
17. ya cao fang: wooden member on which the main-beam rests
18. ming ru fu: exposed tie-beam
19. ban tuo feng: semi-camel's-hump-shaped support
20. su fang: plain tie-beam
21. si chuan ming fu (yueliang): four-rafter exposed tie-beam
22. tuo feng: camel's-hump-shaped support
23. ping an: lattice ceiling
24. cao ru fu: rough tie-beam
25. jiao bei: wood support above rough tie-beam
26. si chuan cao fu: four-rafter rough tie-beam placed above ceiling
27. ping liang: cross-beam
28. tuo jiao: side brace connecting cross-beam with purlin
29. cha shou: inverted V-shaped brace
30. ji tuan: ridge purlin
31. shang ping tuan: upper purlin
32. zhong ping tuan: intermediate purlin
33. xia ping tuan: lower purlin
34. chuan: rafter
35. yan chuan: eave rafter
36. fei zi: flying rafter or cantilever eave rafter
37. wang ban: roof board
38. gong yan bi: board onto which bracket sets adhere
39. niu ji fang: ox-spine tie-beam

FIGURE 68. Infrastructural section of Main Hall, Foguang Monastery. [After Steinhardt, *Chinese Traditional Architecture*, ref. pl. 1; published with permission of China Institute in America]

Foguangsi East Hall and Guanyin Pavilion are apparent in comparisons of Figures 32 and 68. (Numbers in this paragraph refer to fig. 68.) In the roof frame, for example, one finds both two-rafter and four-rafter beams (no. 26). Unlike Guanyin Pavilion, however, both straight beams (nos. 24 and 26) and crescent-shaped beams (*yue liang*; nos. 18 and 21), the latter more prevalent in Tang architecture, are used in the mid-ninth-century hall. At the Foguangsi Main Hall the curved beams are exposed (*rufu*) to the public eye and, like all other architectural members that can be observed from below, show no rough or unfinished surfaces. Concealed beams are unfinished (*caofu*; no. 24) at both the ninth-century hall and Guanyinge. The ceiling, of course, is the means by which pieces of a roof frame can be hidden. The roof truss employs camel's-hump-shaped braces (no. 22) into which are locked bracket sets (no. 11) to help support tiebeams (no. 16)—here tiebeams that support the ceiling (*pingqifang*). The upper portion of the truss is supported by *tuojiao* (diagonal braces that connect crossbeams with purlins; no. 28) and inverted V-shaped braces (*chashou*; no. 29). *Timu*, braces on top of longitudinal bracket arms that bear the weight of eave purlins (no. 15), are also used. The rise (*juzhe*) of the roof—that is, the ratio of the distance between roof purlins to the height of the roof ridge—at the Tang main hall is 1:4.77. The *cai* is approximately 3:2, which is the ratio prescribed in the *Yingzao fashi* for a high-ranking hall such as this one and the ratio employed at Guanyin Pavilion.

Thus although the late Tang main hall and the Liao pavilion constructed 127 years later may appear quite different from the exterior (see figs. 23 and 65), every single timber component used at Guanyinge is found—many in almost exact likeness—at Foguangsi East Hall. It is not surprising that the Liao builders borrowed heavily from a style representing nearly the highest rank offered by the Chinese dynasty that had been defeated in the same century. What requires explanation is how the Northeast Asian patrons whose grandfathers had been tent dwellers and tribesmen came to combine these wooden pieces as they did. Although one can look to the wall paintings several thousand miles away near China's border with Central Asia and assume that fantastic pavilions like those painted on cave walls (fig. 69) were constructed in the Tang period, no wooden or archaeological evidence has yet come forth to confirm this. Moreover, as we study the other dozen Liao wooden buildings we will discover how common the *ge* was in the Liao monastery. Equally important, the case will be made that every extant Liao wooden building, imperial Qidan tombs, and certain brick pagodas (although they are so numerous and so often restored that it is harder to isolate the gems among them) all exemplify an ingenuity of construction for which few

FIGURE 69. Line drawing of wall painting from Mogao Cave 172, near Dunhuang, Gansu, showing *ge* behind Shanmen. [After Xiao Mo, *Dunhuang jianzhu yanjiu*, p. 72]

new components were constructed, but the likes of which are not known in Tang or Song or later Chinese construction. First, however, we need to investigate architecture of the decades between Tang and Liao.

CHINESE ARCHITECTURE IN THE TENTH CENTURY

Most of the eight decades between the fall of the Tang empire in 906 and the construction date of Dulesi recorded in the Liu Cheng Stele are part of a period of Chinese history known as the Five Dynasties and Ten Kingdoms. The first part of the label is a reference to ruling powers known as Later Liang, Later Tang, Later Jin, Later (or Northern) Han, and Later Zhou who rose and fell among themselves and in response to the Qidan threat between the middle of the first decade of the tenth century and the year 960 when the Song dynasty was officially established. The theater of war and power for these five dynasties was largely North and Central China including the portions of northern Shanxi and northern Hebei that were to become part of the Liao empire. With one exception, the handful of extant tenth-century buildings from this time period are either in what became Liao territory or close enough to it to be eligible sources of influence for the Liao timber tradition. The exception is the Main Hall of Hualin Monastery in modern Fuzhou, dated 964, which is discussed with architecture of the 970s at Longxing Monastery in Chapter 9.

It was in such a period of internal chaos and constant threat from non-Chinese people to the north that the art and architecture of Buddhism had made its most profound impact on Chinese culture half a millennium earlier.[25] In the turmoil of the tenth century, it was observed forty years ago, what might be termed a revolution occurred in every major type of Chinese painting and new schools were

born.[26] Chan Buddhism gave way to monochrome ink painting; figure painting achieved new levels in directness of observation and realistic, even disturbing, portrayal of intimacy; bird and flower painting was born; so too was romantic landscape painting and its associated philosophical literature. In a recent study of a fifth category of Chinese painting, jiehua, or "ruled-line painting," a type that has more direct relevance to architecture than most other forms of painting since buildings constitute such a large percentage of its subject matter,[27] James Cahill has observed dramatic changes in "A Noble Scholar," attributed to Wei Xian of the court of the Southern Tang kingdom (one of the ten) in the mid-tenth century.[28]

The development of architecture in this period is similar to that of figure painting. Detail by detail (technique by technique for painting), one may find a one-to-one correspondence between ninth-century styles (represented by Foguangsi East Hall in architecture and Zhang Xuan or Zhou Fang in painting) and those of the tenth century, but in both media the finished products in the tenth century exhibit a level of intensity theretofore unobserved in China. For the Liao, Dulesi was the initial attempt at spatial planning focused on a tall building, a structure of symbolic purpose for a local family and for the prefectural town. In the next century and a half, taller buildings of equally symbolic space were to remain the focal points of the Liao monastery. The expressive power of Liao architecture will be clearer after we look at other tenth-century buildings in North China and, later, Song architecture.

Hall of Ten Thousand Buddhas of Zhenguo Monastery

The only mid-tenth-century building that has achieved any recognition in the general literature on Chinese architecture is the main hall of Zhen-

FIGURE 70. Ten Thousand Buddhas Hall, Zhenguo Monastery, Pingyao county, Shanxi, 963. [After Li Yuming, *Shanxi gujianzhu . . .*, p. 158]

guo Monastery, some 10 kilometers north of Pingyao in north-central Shanxi province (fig. 70).[29] Its relative fame can be attributed to the location of the monastery—walking distance from Haodong station on what is today a major train route through northern Shanxi—and to the survival of its eleven Northern Han sculptures, the only statues of the period outside the Mogao Caves.[30] In fact, the Zhenguosi hall is the latest of three buildings from the period of the Five Dynasties in Shanxi. A fourth building, in Hebei, may date from the same time period, and at least one more was built in Shanxi before Dulesi but after the official start of Song rule.[31]

Of the two main halls, gate, and supporting structures arranged around two courtyards at Zhenguo Monastery today, only Ten Thousand Buddhas Hall (Wanfodian) survives from the tenth century. Little is known about the monastery's history. The date 963, in the third moon of the seventh year of the Northern Han reign *tianhui,* is recorded in the region's only local record, *Pingyaoxian zhi,* written in the Guangxu period (1875–1907) of the Qing dynasty.[32] The same date and the names of several craftsmen are written on a crossbeam of the hall.[33] More than twenty Ming or Qing stelae also survived at Zhenguosi in 1954. One that has some bearing on the date was carved in 1816 in conjunction with repair work. It tells us that

Zhenguosi of the village Haodong is in a wasteland with many difficulties. Its buildings are in a desolate state. Among them is the central hall, which is in a great state of disrepair. Yet its appearance is strangely ancient; it is decidedly not a structure of recent generations. There are those who say that the monastery was

FIGURE 71. "Zhenguo Monastery." [After Qi, Du, and Chen, "Liangnianlai Shanxisheng . . . ," p. 50]

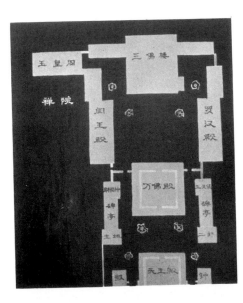

FIGURE 72. Plan of Zhenguo Monastery. [Courtesy of Carol Herselle Krinsky]

established in 963 of the Northern Han, and that this hall is an original from that time. Others say it was repaired under the Yuan or Ming. Unfortunately no stele can confirm [the date]. Surely it is several hundred years old.[34]

The stele inscription continues with the claim that repair work, which began in 1792, was in accordance with the spirit of the original old building. The plan of the monastery after these repairs, but not the structural details of the buildings, may be captured in a late-nineteenth-century drawing from *Pingyaoxian zhi* (fig. 71). It is not much different from the present configuration of buildings (fig. 72).

Ten Thousand Buddhas Hall is a three-bay-square structure, nearly square, raised on a low platform 11.57 by 10.77 meters at the base. The hall is supported by twelve perimeter pillars. The similarity between its plan and that of Nanchansi Main Hall discussed earlier (see figs. 60 and 72) immediately suggests that the tenth-century building was also of relatively low rank. In fact, it is architecturally more complex than the late-eighth-century hall. Wanfodian has, first of all, doors in the central bays of both the front and back facades, as well as windows in the other two front bays. Eight of the pillars are of uniform height, 3.42 meters, and 46 centimeters in diameter. Their lengths do not, in other words, exceed ten times their diameters. The four corner eave pillars exhibit rise: they are 3.47 meters in length. Pillar height may mark a transitional phase between the uniformity in length found at Foguangsi Main Hall and column rise observed at Guanyin Pavilion and, as we shall find, in other Liao wooden halls. Columns are cut off at the top and incline slightly toward the interior of the building. Characteristic of more humble buildings, they are implanted directly into the hall platform.

Only three varieties of bracket set are used in Ten Thousand Buddhas Hall, differentiated by placement above columns, between columns, and at the under-eave corners. The bracketing raises questions about the otherwise apparently humble status of Zhenguosi's hall: 7-*puzuo* bracketing is used above the columns and at the corners (fig. 73). At the corners, in addition, bracket arms project at 45-degree angles to the two building planes. The first- and third-step members of the 7-*puzuo* sets are described as *touxin*—literally "stolen heart," a reference to the lack of a lateral bracket arm (*gong*) that in some cases crosses through the bracket set. (The latter case is described as *jixin*, "added heart.") These bracket sets are even more dramatic than those at Foguangsi East Hall: they measure top to bottom 2.45 meters, a full 70 percent of the length of columns from the floor to the point where they begin. This feature seems contradictory for a building whose directly implanted pillars are characteristic of the fourth grade according to the *Yingzao fashi*.[35] The intercolumnar bracket sets that occur once between every two pillars are 5-*puzuo* (fig. 74). Exterior-facade bracketing is lodged into an architrave, but there is no *pupai* tiebeam.

As Ten Thousand Buddhas Hall has no ceiling, its entire frame is exposed (fig. 75). Long, six-rafter beams cross the full depth of the interior. Above are four rafter beams. *Tuojiao* and camel's-hump-shaped braces are used and a kingpost adds support between the inverted-V-shaped roof truss. The "rise" of the roof is 1:3.65, a full meter less than the rise at Foguangsi East Hall.

Alexander Soper characterized Ten Thousand Buddhas Hall as unassuming, but with the monumental bracketing scheme of the late Tang.[36] Chai Zejun has noted architectural similarities between it and Foguangsi East Hall.[37] Given its location, the Zhenguosi hall might best be interpreted as a structurally uncomfortable building whose bracket sets, most obvious indicators of the silent, symbolic language of Chinese building components, signaled the high status sought by Northern Han rulers, but

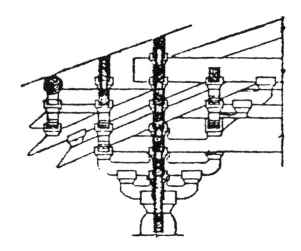

FIGURE 73. Line drawing of section of 7-*puzuo*, column-top bracketing, Ten Thousand Buddhas Hall, Zhenguo Monastery. [After Qi, Du, and Chen, "Liangnianlai Shanxisheng . . . ," p. 51]

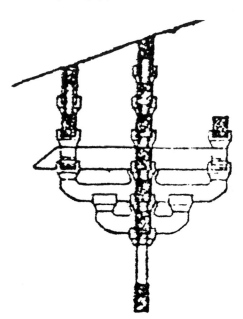

FIGURE 74. Line drawing of section of 5-*puzuo*, intercolumnar bracketing, Ten Thousand Buddhas Hall, Zhenguo Monastery. [After Qi, Du, and Chen, "Liangnianlai Shanxisheng . . . ," p. 51]

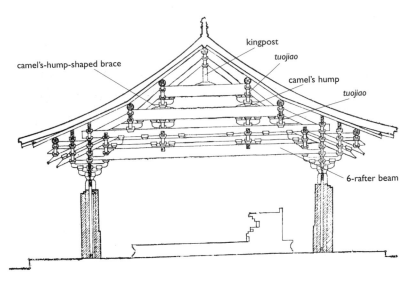

FIGURE 75. Side sectional drawing, Ten Thousand Buddhas Hall, Zhenguo Monastery. [After Chai Zejun, "Shanxi gujianzhu gaishu," p. 258]

which otherwise, in plan and size, was in fact a reflection of what those rulers could afford in troubled times. Huge bracket sets alone could not replicate the aesthetic grandeur of the Foguangsi hall of 857. Such architectural cacophony is never found in Liao monastery architecture. Liao builders followed Chinese dictates from base to roof and went on from there to create symbolic buildings with associations of power. In the tenth century, south of Liao territory, at Pingshun as well as Pingyao, religious architecture would continue to reflect the troubled times of tenth-century Chinese dynasties and kingdoms.

Dayunyuan Main Hall

Pingshun, near Shanxi's border with southern Hebei and northern Henan, was more distant from Liao territory than Pingyao. Its monastery, Dayunyuan, nestled in the mountains, was new precisely when the Liao empire was new. This second of the three Shanxi buildings from the decades of turmoil is the only example of Later Jin patronage.

The main hall, located in the center of a south-oriented building complex, is the only building of this monastery that retains a tenth-century date. A stele of the year 994 records that the monastery was established in 938 and this and other halls were built two years later. Repairs occurred in the 1470s and subsequently during the Ming and Qing periods.[38] The main hall is a three-bay-square building whose base dimensions are 11.8 by 10.1 meters (fig. 76). Like Ten Thousand Buddhas Hall, it has doors at the center front and back bays and windows in the other two bays of the front facade (fig. 77). The plan is somewhat more complex than that of the Zhenguosi hall, however, because there are two interior pillars that frame a wall between them. The two interior pillars are not adequate indication that space was conceived according to the *cao* system. It has been suggested that the *yuetai* in front of the hall is an addition of the Kangxi period,[39] yet combined with the interior pillars the construction appears to be of somewhat higher status than other three-bay-square halls discussed previously. The *cai* is 20 by 13.5 centimeters, consistent with the nearly 3:2 ratio observed in other early Chinese wooden buildings. That and the 10:11.5 proportion of *zhi* place the hall between the *Yingzao fashi* fifth and sixth ranks.[40]

Moreover, also different from buildings observed thus far, the pillars of Dayunyuan Main Hall are straight and narrow. There is both rise and a slight inward bend *(cejiao)*, but the pillars are probably the major cause for structural weakness for which later generations compensated by a wall whose thickness was over 2 meters.[41] Four different formations of bracket set are found at the Dayunyuan hall, the most impressive of which are 5-*puzuo*. In addition to the expected differences in bracketing according to the three main locations for corbel supports in a Chinese structure, more than one type is found in the same position under the eaves' purlins. Restoration may be an explanation, but another possibility is artistic license, for neither one nor the other appears to be structurally superior. Noteworthy details of the bracket sets are the earliest evidence of *pizhu* ("split bamboo") truncation on the end of the *shuatou* (fig. 78) and of half-wing-shaped *shuatou* in intercolumnar bracket sets (fig. 79). The former feature is prevalent in later Liao architecture; the latter feature is evident in the Liao timber pagoda of 1056. As has been observed in ninth- and tenth-century buildings, exposed beams are finished and are sometimes crescent-shaped, and camel's-hump-shaped braces and *tuojiao* are used. Yet like the structurally inexplicable variety in under-eaves' bracket-set formations, eight different camel's-hump-shaped braces, and *tuojiao* that extend the distance of two purlins are used in the one small hall. Whether it is the product of experimentation, artistic license, or another phenomenon,

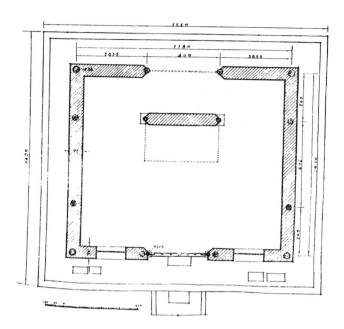

FIGURE 76. Plan of Great Buddha Hall, Dayunyuan, Shihuizhen, Pingshun county, Shanxi, tenth century. [After Yang Lie, "Shanxi Pingshunxian gujianzhu," p. 41]

FIGURE 77. Great Buddha Hall, Dayunyuan, tenth century. [After Chai Zejun, "Shanxi gujianzhu gaishu, p. 257]

FIGURE 78. Bracket set from front facade of Great Buddha Hall, Dayunyuan, showing *pizhu*. [After Yang Lie, "Shanxi Pingshunxian gujianzhu," pl. 4]

FIGURE 79. Half-wing-shaped *shuatou*, intercolumnar bracket set, Great Buddha Hall, Dayunyuan. [After Yang Lie, "Shanxi Pingshunxian gujianzhu," pl. 2]

this second Five Dynasties–period hall in Shanxi, like Ten Thousand Buddhas Hall, exemplifies the transitional point in the history of Chinese architecture coincident with the emergence of Liao.

The last of the Five Dynasties buildings in Shanxi, West Side Hall of Longmen Monastery, has the earliest date, but little else is known about it (fig. 80).[42] Found on a people's collective some 40 kilometers north of the Pingshunxian capital in 1973, the hall was built in 925 of the Later Tang. It is three-bays-square and retains the earliest example of a *xuanshan* (overhanging gable) roof. Its front facade has doors in the central bay and windows in the other two, pillars are placed onto an architrave with no *pupai* tiebeam, no intercolumnar bracket sets are employed, four rafters is the longest span of beams (some of which are crescent-shaped), and pillars are cut inward at the top.

Based on available information about the three Five Dynasties–period Shanxi halls, one can conclude that no major structural innovations are apparent in the middle third of the tenth century. Much of the Tang tradition, especially bracketing, was maintained, but because of economic or time constraints these brackets may have served as the only signatures of the grand possibilities represented by Foguangsi East Hall.[43] Given the political circumstances, it is also likely that if the Liao saw architecture of any of the Five Dynasties–period courts in North China, those buildings probably resembled these.

TANG-STYLE ARCHITECTURE OUTSIDE OF CHINA

The Liao no doubt saw Chinese-style buildings in the lands of Northeast Asia that became part of their empire. Specifically, they saw construction in northern Shanxi and Hebei, in Henan during the brief period of conquest under Liao Taizong, in what was once the Koguryŏ kingdom (presently

North Korea to Jilin province of China), and in the northern part of Jilin and Heilongjiang that had formerly been ruled by the Bohai. What they saw was exemplary of the widespread phenomenon known as the "international Tang style." Its expressions in all aspects of culture and statecraft became models for eighth- and ninth-century Asian states whose rulers aspired to emperorship. In art, the best-documented evidence of "international Tang" survives in Japan where in many specific cases buildings or sculpture can be used as primary evidence of what was lost from the Chinese tradition, in particular during the years of Buddhist persecution.[44] The Liao, however, saw none of the Japanese Tang-style buildings. Similarities between Liao and Japanese architecture, several of which are discussed in the next chapter, are examples of the phenomenon whereby cultural models as profound as those produced by Tang China could spread in two directions and give way to similar end-products at the farther reaches of the Tang cultural sphere.

As one might expect, there is a problem with this sort of comparative evidence: even when there is abundant documentation for Chinese craftsmen or foreign craftsmen trained in China or by Chinese, one is still faced with the dangerous game of building a scenario to explain structural or stylistic similarities. Due to record keeping and survivals, the evidence for Tang-style architecture in Japan is better than that for Northeast Asia. Only in the realm of city planning is it possible to observe aboveground the international Tang style in the Korean peninsula.[45] Underground the evidence is similarly strong. Korean-peninsula predecessors to the Liao funerary tradition are discussed in Part Two.

GEYUANSI

Finally, we turn to a relative newcomer in the investigation of Liao architecture: the one pre-Dulesi wooden building. The hall to the bodhisattva Wen-

FIGURE 80. West Side Hall, Longmen Monastery, Pingshun county, Shanxi, 925. [After Chai Zejun, "Shanxi gujianzhu gaishu," p. 256]

shu (Mañjuśrī) at Geyuansi (Monastery of the Ge Courtyard [Precinct]) was found in Laiyuan county, Hebei, near the Shanxi-Hebei border in about 1960. The two men who discovered it published it as Liao.[46] It was not until 1979, however, that the date of the hall, 966, was published based on an inscription on an octagonal stone pillar.[47] The Wenshu Hall is thus nearly twenty years earlier than Guanyin Pavilion and the Shanmen at Dulesi and just three years later than Ten Thousand Buddhas Hall at Zhenguo Monastery in nearby Shanxi.

Wenshu Hall is one of three main buildings and many auxiliary structures that remain at a monastery in the northwest corner of the out-of-the-way town of Laiyuan, nestled in mountains that are east of Mount Wutai at approximately the same latitude. The primary source for the monastery's history is *Laiyuanxian zhi*, written in 1875, which gives the following information: the monastery Dasi (Great Monastery) was founded in the late Han, burned and repaired in the Tang, and repaired again in the Song. A repair stele dated to the year 1568 says that

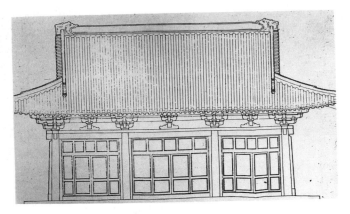

FIGURE 81. Front elevation drawing of Mañjuśrī Hall, Geyuan Monastery, Laiyuan, Hebei, 966. [After Mo Zongjiang, "Laiyuan, Geyuansi, Wenshudian," fig. 4]

the monastery was "first built in Liao times."[48] A four-rafter beam gives the repair date of the *taiding* period (1324–1327), a three-rafter beam records repair in 1507, and a tiebeam records repair during the Jiajing reign period (1522–1567).[49]

The Liao-period hall is three-bays-square and nearly square: 15 by 15.67 meters (fig. 81). Four door panels are placed in each front facade bay, a large *yuetai* projects in front of the hall, and two pillars are employed in the hall. Although there is no ceiling, and thus beams are exposed, beams that span six roof rafters are used (fig. 82). The same combination of long beams but no ceiling is employed at the main halls of Hualinsi, Zhenguosi, and Dayunyuan, but thus far not earlier than these. Another feature associated with the tenth century is the use of exclusively straight beams. Struts observed in earlier architecture and also used here include camel's-hump-shaped braces, diagonal *taqian*, and half-bracket arms to help support the six-rafter beam just below where it joins a side pillar.

Bracket sets are lodged into the architrave with an additional *pupai* tiebeam underneath it, a feature absent in the three Five Dynasties halls in

Shanxi province. But due to its presence in Tang architecture, the elimination is probably more a result of humble status than any other reason. Bracketing of 5- and 7-*puzuo* is employed.

One of the enigmas of this monastery is its name: Monastery of the Ge Courtyard. As mentioned earlier, the monastery is known in the local record of Laiyuan only as Dasi or, according to the 1979 study of the Wenshu Hall, as West (Xi) Great Monastery. Both are names typical of the nineteenth century — when the local record was written — for the oldest religious complex in a town. One of the three main buildings along the monastery axis is a *ge*, the Cangjingge (presumably for storing sutras), located north of Wenshu Hall (fig. 83). It is one of the buildings rebuilt in Ming or Qing times. It seems logical that the courtyard in front of this *ge* gave the monastery its name. Indeed, among the nine Liao monasteries, five had a *ge* or other multistory building along their main axes. Among the five are the two earliest Liao monasteries.

A more unusual feature of Geyuansi is the orientation of its three extant halls. From north to south, the Sutra Library, Wenshu Hall, and a Hall to the Divine Kings (*tianwang*) stand side by side facing west (see fig. 83). Two standard features of Chinese spatial planning are contradicted here. First, Chinese halls are oriented along the same axis, one in front of the other, so that passage can occur from the back door of one to the front door of the hall behind it. Second, in most instances, the fronts of buildings along this main axis face south. As we shall see, Geyuansi's orientation is not unique among the nine extant Liao monasteries. The temple complex whose buildings have the latest dates has a similar arrangement. Moreover, Liao is an exceptional dynasty in which one can find east-west orientation (with main buildings along an east-west line). My discussion of orientation in Liao monastery space in Chapter 6 will take issue

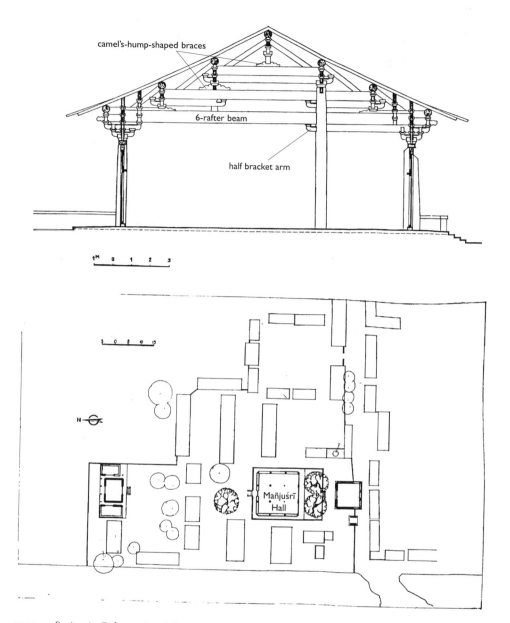

camel's-hump-shaped braces

6-rafter beam

half bracket arm

FIGURE 82 (top). Side sectional drawing of Mañjuśrī Hall, Geyuan Monastery. [After Mo Zongjiang, "Laiyuan, Geyuansi, Wenshudian," fig. 7]
FIGURE 83 (above). Plan of Geyuan Monastery, Laiyuan, Shanxi. [After Mo Zongjiang, "Laiyuan, Geyuansi, Wenshudian," fig. 1]

with published interpretations of the purposes of east-west orientation for the Qidan. That this new arrangement of space first occurs in the tenth century, however, again distinguishes that age of political confusion as the one in which new forms appear.

Finally, this earliest Liao wooden building offers evidence of another purpose, also associated with Guanyinge, that will be shown to be common in Liao monastery architecture. Among the scant literary documentation about Geyuansi is information about patronage. At Dulesi-Guanyinsi, an association between architecture and patron was preserved on a sutra case inside a pagoda. At Geyuansi a patron's name is found on the same *dhāraṇī* pillar where the date 966 is recorded. The name is Li Yanchao.[50] Li had been the right-hand man of one of the founders of the Later Tang kingdom. The his-tory of the Han family, so intimately associated with Dulesi and the adjacent Guanyinsi, can be traced over a longer period of time than that of the group of Li, but Dulesi was also a more prominent monument in a more important town, both in Liao and Qing times. Geyuansi's location, lesser patronage over time, and buildings as they are known to survive, seem fitting when the two early Liao monasteries are compared. It is clear, however, that patronage by powerful Chinese families was responsible for architecture in the second half of the tenth century in North China and that this sort of association between powerful patron and building is hard to prove prior to this time.[51] Examples of imperial and official patronage by the Qidan in subsequent chapters will do more to explain the prevalence of tall buildings along the main monastery axis, their purpose, and their symbolism.

4

Fengguosi

THE MONASTERY FENGGUOSI stands in the northeast corner of Yixian in Liaoning province. Located in the Zhongjing circuit and thus more out of the way than Dulesi or the Liao western capital Datong, Fengguosi was visited by the Japanese archaeologist and researcher of Chinese architecture, Sekino Tadashi, almost as an afterthought late one afternoon in October 1931 during a trip whose purpose was to see Buddhist caves of the Northern Wei period and brick pagodas.[1] Thus Takeshima Takuichi should have known what he might find when he visited Yixian more than ten years later, yet he wrote that he "came upon the monastery by chance" when he entered the western wall gate of the town.[2] For anyone who has seen it, the presence of Daxiongbao Hall is so overpowering that it is hard to believe its location has kept it unvisited and unstudied (fig. 84). Yet the documentation is indeed scant, consisting almost solely of twenty-plus stelae.[3]

HISTORY

The oldest stele at Fengguosi is a repair stele written in 1140 and cut in stone in the first moon of 1192. "The monasteries in the town," it says, "are as plentiful as the stars, and Fengguosi is of the divine class

FIGURE 84. Daxiongbao Hall, Fengguosi, Yi prefecture, Liaoning, 1019.
[Steinhardt photograph]

[number one]."[4] Through this and later stelae inscriptions, several of which contain the same or nearly the same passages, one can reconstruct the history of the monastery.

Relevant passages of the stele of 1303, much information from which is contained in the late-twelfth-century inscription, relate:

The Buddha dharma (*fa*) entered China in the generation of Wei, Jin, and Liang [Northern and Southern Dynasties]. Generation by generation, higher-ups and emperors made it their religion. When it came to Liao, they attacked the Northeast and made Linhuang their capital [Shangjing, their first capital]. Theirs was very much a Buddhist state.

West of the Liao River was a mountain called Yiwulu that spanned several hundred *li*. With slopes, trees, and grasses pure it [the monastery] could not but be established there. . . . One *jun* [military commandery district] was called Yizhou, formerly Dongying, today Yi- [a different character] zhou. Northeast was a monastery called Xianxi that later became Fengguo. That was its beginning. In 1020 the *chushi* [retired scholar] Jiao Xiyun founded it. The monk Qinghui later followed his work and completed it. In 1140 the

Buddhist monk Yizhuo successfully brought it to completion. Its main hall contained seven Buddhas. The Dharma Hall was extensive enough to hold one thousand monks. . . . [There were] more than two hundred bays of enclosing covered corridors with 120 sculpted images in them. . . . It was again repaired in 1303 by a Mongolian lord, Prince of Ningchangjun.[5]

Thus the stele inscription provides the date assigned to the hall, 1020, the year in which the monastery was founded by Jiao Xiyun. A monk named Qinghui supervised construction. An original monastery, presumably on the same site, was named Xianxisi. No specific date is ever given for its founding. The next names and dates associated with the monastery Fengguosi are from the first half of the twelfth century. Beginning in 1107,[6] the Buddhist monk named Yizhuo took on work at the monastery. His job was completed in 1140 at a cost of 10 million cash. During that time, forty-two images were either repaired or completed.

In his publication of 1944, Takeshima raised the possibility that the monastery had been used by the Liao prior to the official founding date of 1020. He found a reference to a Fengguosi in the biography of Li Huan, a tenth-century official of Jin who had come over to Liao upon the fall of his state, had served the third Liao emperor, and had even become a Hanlin scholar at Shangjing during his reign, but eventually had been imprisoned at Fengguosi.[7] Since Li Huan received his scholarly title in the 950s or 960s, it seems highly unlikely that he was still alive for incarceration after 1020.

In 1290 an earthquake shook Yizhou. A son-in-law of one of the Mongolian khans provided money for earthquake repairs that were completed in several years, sometime before the stele of 1303 that records them. The next dated stele, of 1355, is the first record that the seven Buddhas were greater than lifesize. It is also the first record that the Seven-Buddhas Hall had nine bays.[8] Other structures were present at the mid-fourteenth-century monastery: at least three *ge*, one in front of the Seven Buddhas Hall and one at either side of it; a Dharma Hall (*fadian*); a hall for vegetarian feasts or fasting (or an "abstinence hall"; *zhaitang*); three different kitchen areas; monks' quarters; a bathing chamber; a Ten Thousand Buddhas Hall; and many other courtyards of buildings. Although Daxiongbao Hall was huge, its size is proportionate to this number of buildings.

According to stelae records, Daxiongbao Hall was repaired at least sixteen other times between 1487 and 1888. The most recent damage to Fengguosi occurred as the result of bombing in 1948. Daxiongbao Hall was repaired again in the late 1980s.

DAXIONGBAO HALL

By the standards of any Chinese dynasty, Daxiongbao Hall is huge.[9] The nine-by-five-bay hall faces south on a 3-meter-high platform with base dimensions of 55.8 by 25.91 meters.[10] In front of its three central bays extends a *yuetai*, 37 meters east to west by 15 meters north to south. Two kiosks from the Qing dynasty—one hexagonal, the other square—and a stone incense burner stand on the *yuetai* today (fig. 85). A small *yuetai* remains at the back of the hall. It may at one time have provided direction to the Dharma Hall mentioned in stele inscriptions.

The base dimensions of the hall are 48.2 by 25.13 meters, fairly close to a 2:1 ratio. Access to the hall is through doors in the central front and back bays and in bays second from the end in the front facade. Each of the seven inner hall bays across the front highlights one of the Seven Historical Buddhas, or Buddhas of the Past.[11] They are raised on a single 87-centimeter-high platform (fig. 86). The ceiling above the platform offers a dramatic but subsidiary backdrop for the images. It is not a *zaojing*, but it functions in much the same manner as the Guanyin Pavilion ceiling at Dulesi. Moreover, just as two

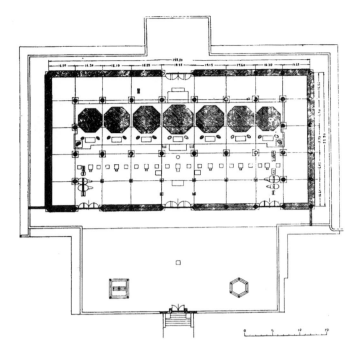

FIGURE 85. Plan of Daxiongbao Hall, Fengguosi. [After Takeshima, *Ryō-Kin jidai* . . . , p. 60]

bodhisattvas flank the image of Guanyin in the Dulesi pavilion, here each Buddha image is flanked by a pair of bodhisattvas, and a guardian king faces the south entry at either side of the altar. Behind the Seven Buddhas, facing the back door, is the bodhisattva Guanyin in *mahārāja-līlāsana* (fig. 87), the same deity in the same pose as the one at the back of Guanyin Pavilion at Dulesi. In other words, certain iconographic elements of the arrangement of the Liao pavilion of 984 have persisted thirty-six years and are found inside the next dated building of the dynasty.

Despite the hall's size, only twenty columns are used in the interior (see fig. 85). Except for the ends, an entire row that would otherwise block the view of images on the altar is eliminated. So too are the inner six pillars from the first east-west row north of

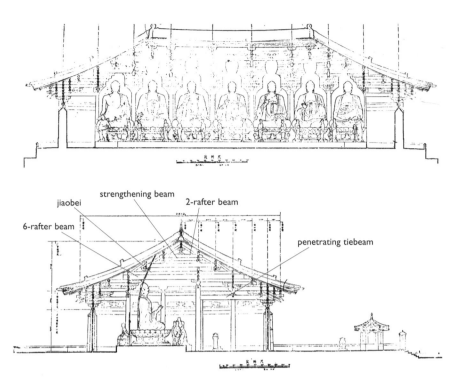

FIGURE 86 (top). Front sectional drawing of Daxiongbao Hall, Fengguosi. [After Du Xianzhou, "Yixian Fengguosi Daxiongdian . . ." (*Wenwu*, no. 2), p. 15]

FIGURE 87 (above). Side sectional drawing of Daxiongbao Hall, Fengguosi. [After Du Xianzhou, "Yixian Fengguosi Daxiongdian . . ." (*Wenwu*, no. 2), p. 15]

the hall front. The placement of pillars along the transversal building axis is in line with two-, four-, and six-rafter beams (see fig. 87). Tiebeams known as *toukuan* penetrate the pillars. Pillars taper at the top and exhibit a "rise" of 36 centimeters, which translates into 11.5 *cun*. The *Yingzao fashi* specifies a rise of 8 *cun* for a hall of these proportions and this stature.[12] Pillars also slant inward *(cejiao)* about 13 centimeters, or 2 percent. Eave pillars are 67 centimeters in base diameter and extend 5.95 meters in height. The height/base diameter ratio is thus 8.9:1. The ratio of plinths to pillars is 1.7:1. According to the *Yingzao fashi,* this ratio should have been 2:1.[13]

The *cai* at Daxiongbao Hall is 29 centimeters in

height by 20 centimeters wide. This ratio is very close to 3:2, or 9:6. The ratio, as noted in Chapter 2, is prescribed in the *Yingzao fashi* for halls from nine to eleven bays across the front. The Fengguosi Main Hall is thus far the only Liao example of a building that employs this grade of timber construction.[14]

Fittingly, bracket sets both above and between columns of the exterior facade are 7-*puzuo*. Figure 88 shows the section of one of these bracket sets; Figure 89 shows the same corbel cluster from the front. One of the special features in these sets is the *tailun,* an additional cap between the top of the column and the cap block *(ludou).* More striking is the fact that, despite a few differences that will be noted

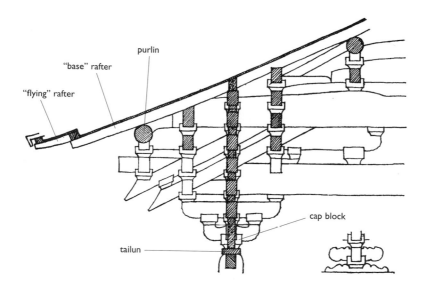

purlin

"base" rafter

"flying" rafter

cap block

tailun

FIGURE 88 (top). Side sectional drawing of 7-*puzuo* bracket set, Daxiongbao Hall, Fengguosi. [After Takeshima, *Ryo-Kin jidai* . . . , p. 62]

FIGURE 89 (above). Seven-*puzuo* bracketing from front facade of Daxiongbao Hall, Fengguosi. [Steinhardt photograph]

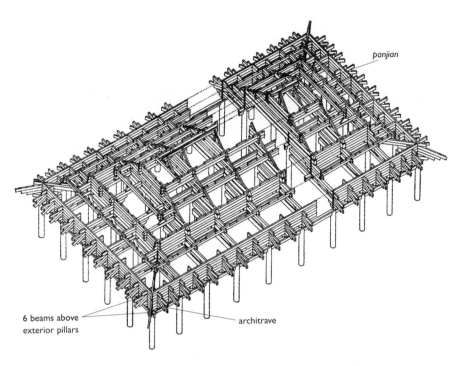

panjian

6 beams above
exterior pillars

architrave

FIGURE 90. Infrastructural drawing of timber frame of Daxiongbao Hall, Fengguosi.
[After Chen Mingda, *Jianzhu lishi yanjiu* 2, p. 54]

below, the column-top and intermediate bracket sets are more similar to each other than the corresponding sets at tenth-century halls such as the Northern Han Ten Thousand Buddhas Hall and Guanyin Pavilion or at Foguangsi East Hall. In general, only about half of the elements present in the column-top sets are used intercolumnarly. The large, heavy eaves may have required this kind of additional support, but it is also possible that Fengguosi's hall marks the beginning of a general change in intercolumnar bracketing. Foguangsi's East Hall is the earliest surviving building in which bracket sets, rather than simple struts, were used between columns. The simplified bracket sets of

the hall in Taihuai county are standard in tenth-century Shanxi halls with intermediate bracketing. Dulesi's Liao architecture in Hebei followed the same principle. After Fengguosi, however, architecture from monasteries in Datong will provide evidence of more complicated intercolumnar bracket sets and new features of bracketing both above and between columns of the exterior facade. It is impossible to know whether the impetus for such architectural change was structural, aesthetic, or the decorative whim of a designer or craftsman.

The *cao* system of space has already been used to describe the Foguang Monastery Main Hall and to distinguish it, not only from earlier hall types whose plans signaled specific ritual functions, but from very simple constructions like the three-bay-square tenth-century halls with few or no interior columns. Daxiongbao Hall of Fengguosi exhibits the most complex support system on top of these two rings of columns known between the ninth and twelfth centuries. Six beams that span the space between those columns are placed on top of the exterior (under-eave) pillars (fig. 90). The lowest of these beams were actually architraves *(lan'e)* with *pupai fang* under each one. The five beams above can go by the alternate names *yancao fang* (eave-*cao* ties). In the front outer *cao*, a four-rafter beam was placed under the special lintel. *Panjian,* the loop-type braces beneath purlins and above bracket sets, were found in the roof frame.

A beam called *jiaobei* was placed on the six-rafter beam. A strengthening beam *(shunfu chuan)* was placed under the upper flat beam to help the king-post and inverted V-shaped truss *(chashou)* support the main roof pole. All are labeled in either Figure 87 or Figure 90.

More than twenty-three different types of cross-beams *(liang)* and tiebeams *(fang)* have been identified based on their positions at Daxiongbao Hall. Combined with the seven bracket-set varieties, the hall framework offers more than thirty types of timber pieces between the column tops and the roof.[15] Yet only seven different cross sections are used for these wooden elements, and most of them are either 2:1 or 3:2 in section. The lintel, *pupai fang,* and transversal bracket arm were all close to 3:2 in section, while the four- and six-rafter crossbeams and extension beams were essentially 2:1. This standardization, as much as any other factor, is believed to have contributed to the hall's outstanding stability.[16] Still, as at Guanyinge, special wooden pieces were required to make the central space possible, in this case to fit around the huge altar and its images. Interior columns, for instance, were taller than pe-

ripheral columns. To enhance the ability of these pillars to support the 15-meter-long, six-rafter beams above them, auxiliary beams and additional bracket arms were piled one on top of the other. Four tiers of bracket arms, also employed here, had been used before in Chinese architecture, notably at the Main Hall of Foguangsi (see figs. 65 and 68). Yet their use here, coupled with another feature of this extraordinary hall, suggests far-reaching comparisons for this building in Liaoning.

FENGGUOSI MAIN HALL AND JAPANESE ARCHITECTURE

The architecture that immediately comes to mind when one looks at the four transversal tiers of bracket sets at Daxiongbao Hall is a group of buildings from the late twelfth century in Japan that are associated with a building style brought to the islands from China by a Buddhist monk named Chō-gen.[17] The building most often cited as an example of Chōgen's sponsorhip is the Great South Gate (Nandaimon) at the monastery Tōdai-ji in Nara. Its most distinctive feature is the seven-tier bracketing under its front eaves (fig. 91).

Shunjōbō Chōgen had begun his career as a student monk of Esoteric Buddhism at Daigō-ji, south of Kyōto. Sometime before 1167–1168, when he traveled to China, Chōgen had become a disciple of the monk Hōnen, founder of Japanese Pure Land (Jōdō) Buddhism. In 1181, in the aftermath of the destruction or damage to many of Nara's Buddhist buildings by the Taira clan, Chōgen was appointed by the ruling Minamoto family to direct the rebuilding at Tōdai-ji. By this time he was fully committed to the Pure Land sect. Even though there is neither sign nor emblem in the structure of the Tōdai-ji gate to which one can point as evidence of the Pure Land affiliation of its building supervisor, the gate and other architectural projects supervised by Chō-gen—notably a hall at a monastery named Jōdō-ji

FIGURE 91. Bracket sets on front facade of Great South Gate, Tōdai-ji, Nara, 1195. [Steinhardt photograph]

("Pure Land Monastery") in Hyōgo prefecture—share a few architectural features. Visually prominent are enormous bracket sets that project perpendicular to the building plane. They are an innovation of Chōgen's style in Japan believed to have been crafted by builders named Chen from South China.

The architecture associated with Chōgen has been labeled Tenjiku-yō in Japanese, literally "Indian style." Even at its inception, however, the forms of Tenjiku-yō were understood to be Chinese (not Indian) in origin—but distinct from a competing southern Chinese architectural style of the twelfth century described in the *Yingzao fashi*, a style known in Japanese as Kara-yō, literally "Tang style" or "Chinese style." The source of Tenjiku-yō is believed to be Fujian province on China's southeastern coast, a place Chōgen had visited. It is surely no coincidence that among extant buildings with bracket sets whose arms project purely in the transversal direction, one is located in Fujian. That building is Sanqing Hall of the Daoist monastery Xuanmiaoguan, constructed in Putian in 1016, just four years before Daxiongbao Hall of Fengguosi (see figs. 205 and 208).[18] Three years earlier, in 1013, a Buddhist hall in which four tiers of bracket arms were employed was constructed at Baoguo Monastery in Yuyao county, just outside of Ningbo, Zhejiang province, about the same distance from the Eastern Sea coast as Putian, but more than 500 kilometers to the north (see fig. 197).

Baoguosi has a history as old as Fengguosi's, dating to the Eastern Han dynasty. It suffered destruction in 845, southern China being no safer than north central China from the Huichang persecutions that ravaged Mount Wutai and Chang'an.

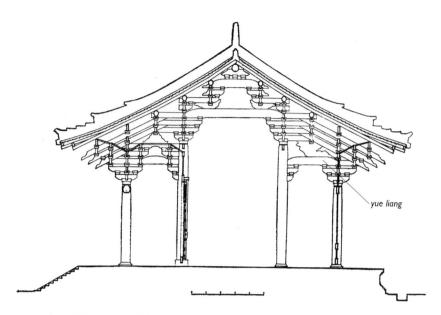

yue liang

FIGURE 92. Side sectional drawing of Daxiongbao Hall, Hualin Monastery, Fuzhou, Fujian province. [After Yang Binlun et al., *Jianzhushi lunwen ji* 9, p. 31]

When the monastery in Zhejiang was rebuilt in 880, its name was changed to Baoguosi. The Baoguosi hall, known also as Daxiongbaodian, has another feature in common with Daxiongbao Hall of Fengguosi: both have significantly lengthened columns around the inner *cao*.

The architectural style of the Fujian and Zhejiang halls can be traced back fifty years to the Main Hall of Hualin Monastery in Fuzhou, Fujian, dated to 964 (see fig. 172). A comparison between the main halls from Xuanmiaoguan, Baoguosi, and Hualinsi shows that the eleventh-century structures followed earlier architecture of China's far southeast, especially in the use of curved beams and roof construction (fig. 92; see also figs. 202 and 207).

Ultimately the similarities in the eleventh-century buildings—the one a product of Liao and the other of Song—must be traceable to a Tang source, perhaps one lost to the mid-ninth-century persecutions, perhaps one in part exemplified by bracketing at Foguangsi's Main Hall, but one surely present in architectural details of Hualinsi Main Hall. In our attempt to understand the construction of Daxiongbao Hall at Fengguosi, we are drawn to Japan for a second reason. Fengguosi's Main Hall, we have seen, is the only Chinese example of a seven-Buddha hall. In fact, it is the only Asian example. In Japan, one nine-Buddha hall is preserved. It is the eleventh–twelfth-century Main Hall (Hondō, literally "primary hall") of the monastery Jōruri-ji, north of the city of Nara. Like Fengguosi's main hall, at Jōruri-ji one bay is designated for each Buddha image and two additional bays give the hall a total of eleven (fig. 93).[19] At Jōruri-ji, all the Buddhas are Amitābha—Buddha of the Western Paradise—in nine different bodily manifestations. Again one

FIGURE 93. Main Hall, Jōruri-ji, Nara prefecture, eleventh–twelfth century. [After Amanuma, *Nihon kenchikushi zuroku*, vol. 1, p. 268]

probably is observing the results of what has been called "international Tang"—in this case giving way, on the one hand, to the Seven Historical Buddhas in their own bays in Liaoning and, on the other, to a monument of Pure Land Buddhism on the Kansai plain. Like curved tiebeams and four layers of bracket arms, the source of the Buddhist-image-in-its-own-bay must be Tang China. Beyond that general knowledge, one can only speculate on a specific locale and time in Tang China or on the role of Fujian as a point of embarkation to Japan.[20]

FENGGUOSI AND LIAO MONASTERY PLANS

Finally, like Dulesi—and, one assumes from its name, Geyuansi—Fengguosi was a monastery in which a *ge* figured prominently in its plan. Based on

stelae inscriptions cited earlier, two reconstruction drawings for Fengguosi have been proposed (figs. 94 and 95).[21] The distinction between them is the presence or absence of a gate and connecting covered corridor behind the *ge*; but in either case, the pavilion follows a Shanmen and precedes Daxiongbao Hall and the Dharma Hall on the main axis of the building complex.

The actual remains and reconstruction drawings of Fengguosi have been used, with texts, as evidence for a theoretical reconstruction of a nearby monastery, (Da) Guangjisi (fig. 96), of which only a brick pagoda survives today in Jinzhou (fig. 97).[22] Figure 96 shows a Shanmen, a hall to Guanyin, an extremely prominent octagonal pagoda in its own courtyard, and three additional halls along the main monastery axis from south to north. From the

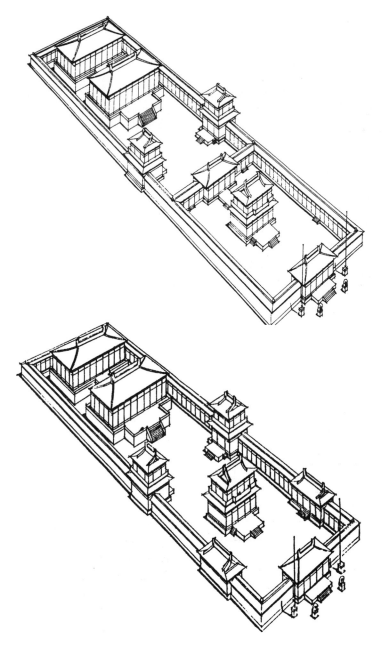

FIGURE 94 (top). Theoretical reconstruction 1 of Fengguo Monastery.
[After Cao Xun, "Dulesi renzong xunqin," p. 34]
FIGURE 95 (above). Theoretical reconstruction 2 of Fengguo Monastery.
[After Cao Xun, "Dulesi renzong xunqin," p. 35]

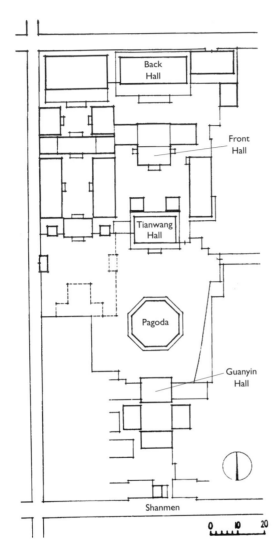

FIGURE 96. Theoretical reconstruction of (Da) Guangji Monastery, Jinzhou, Liaoning, Liao period. [After Cao Xun, "Dulesi renzong xunqin," p. 37]

three Liao monasteries discussed thus far, Geyuansi, Dulesi, and Fengguosi, one is inclined to justify a Liao date for the undated temple complex due to the isolation of Guanyin as the devotional deity in its own hall and to a central, prominent high building. New, however, are the substitution of pagoda for pavilion and the octagonal plan of that structure. The importance of the octagonal plan in Liao architecture will be explored in the next chapter. Here one can suggest an additional purpose of the multistory structure on the main axis at Guangjisi in Jinzhou in the light of evidence from Dulesi in Jizhou.

Recall from the discussion of Dulesi in Chapter 2 that the construction of Guanyinsi in the eleventh century has been interpreted as an extramural extension of Dulesi that symbolized the expansion of the bodhisattva Guanyin's protection farther into the prefectural town (see fig. 46). The approximately 20-meter base dimension of the Guangjisi pagoda suggests its height to have been adequate for comparably far-reaching vision from its highest window. In Fengguosi's prefecture of Yi, however, at least one Liao octagonal pagoda also was constructed. Dated to 1020, it survives today as the only old building at Jiafusi (fig. 98).[23] The interior of neither the pagoda at Jiafusi nor the one at Guangjisi has been accessible for decades, perhaps centuries. (My study of architecture in Yixian allowed no possibility for determining if a direct line from one Yixian monastery to the other, or from Guangjisi to an Yixian monastery, was feasible.) The prominence of a tall building, always visible long before one reaches the gates of its monastery, on the central axis at all five Liao monasteries considered thus far, suggests the crucial role of a multistory structure not just in its own building complex but in its town. If, in fact, the principle of extension of a monastery's protection beyond its walls was part of the

FIGURE 97. Brick pagoda, Guangji Monastery, Liao.
[After Sekino and Takeshima, *Ryō-Kin jidai no kenchiku* . . . , pl. 71]

thinking of Liao patrons, in Yizhou this idea may explain the construction of two monasteries, Fengguosi with a prominent *ge* and Guangjisi with a prominent pagoda, in the same year. Furthermore, it may be evidence that forty years after Dulesi was built, its plan had become standard, the role of Guanyin as a guardian deity had intensified, and from a high vantage point the bodhisattva's gaze could symbolically extend Liao power from one locale to another (fig. 99).[24]

Fengguosi's Daxiongbao Hall has not received the attention it deserves in the literature on Chinese architecture. Chinese writers' assessments of it simply point to the economical use of wood, in-cluding perfected standardization of timber, and the logical use of space.[25] In fact, Daxiongbao Hall may be the best structural example of the transfer of forms from Tang beyond its borders to North Asia, forms that were also transferred eastward across the sea to Japan. Furthermore, Daxiongbao Hall provides additional evidence of the importance of *ge* on the Liao monastery axis. Daxiongbao Hall is the second example of a monastery close to a monastery, this time in Yizhou and in Jinzhou, prompting one to speculate about the Liao vision of their extension of power, symbolized by the monuments and potency of Buddhism, beyond the physical boundaries of walls.

FIGURE 98 (right). Brick pagoda from Jiafu Monastery, Yi county, Liaoning, 1020. [After Sekino and Takeshima, *Ryō-Kin jidai no kenchiku . . .* , pl. 75]

FIGURE 99 (below). Upper levels of Guanyin Pavilion showing window for bodhisattva's eyes, Guanghua Monastery, Fuzhou, Fujian province, twentieth century. [Steinhardt photograph]

One aspect of documentation has been richer for the other two Liao wooden buildings but is lacking at Fengguosi: this aspect is patronage, specifically patronage by a prominent family of the town. Perhaps no family name has been carved into Fengguosi's stelae because a different patron was involved. At Dulesi and Guanyinsi, we have seen a direct link between the bodhisattva Guanyin and the families Han (and at Geyuansi with the Li family). At Fengguosi, perhaps the clue to patronage is the Seven Buddhas enshrined on the Daxiongbao-dian altar. The year 1020 occurred during the reign of the sixth Liao emperor, Shengzong. If one includes the father of the dynastic founder, the number of imperial Qidan lords that reigned by the time of the hall's dedication was seven, the same as the number of Buddhas inside Daxiongbao Hall.

Stronger evidence of the likening of a Qidan emperor to a deity will be presented in the next chapter. That evidence is found in the most magnificent wooden monument of Liao patronage, a structure known in China, simply, as Timber Pagoda.

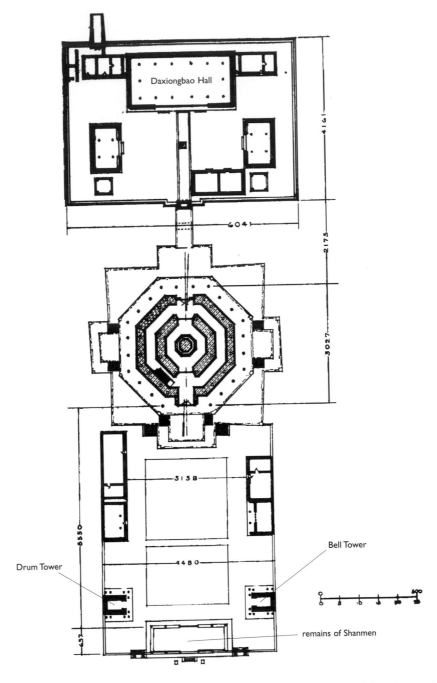

Daxiongbao Hall

Drum Tower

Bell Tower

remains of Shanmen

FIGURE 100. Reconstructed plan of Fogongsi. [After Chen Mingda, *Yingxian Muta*, drawing 1]

5

Yingxian Timber Pagoda

SUPERLATIVES ARE APPLIED to Chinese architecture with varying degrees of accuracy. For Yingxian's Timber Pagoda, two are correct. It is the tallest wooden building in China, and it is the oldest surviving wooden pagoda. The structure is unique and so famous, and has such a truly monumental presence, that Chinese people call it, simply, Muta (Timber Pagoda).

Even today the Timber Pagoda soars above the low *xian* town in which construction rarely exceeds 10 meters in height. One can imagine the dominance of the building in Yingzhou of Liao times. On a clear day the Muta is visible from a distance of 30 kilometers (see fig. 20).[1] The pagoda rises 67.31 meters and its entire 51.35-meter shaft is made of wood.

DESCRIPTION

The Timber Pagoda originally towered above its monastery, today Fogongsi, on the main north-south line behind the Shanmen and in front of Daxiongbao Hall (fig. 100), similar to the arrangements already observed in Liao monastery plans. In Liao times, the monastery is believed to have occupied a central postition in Yingzhou, just northwest of the intersection between the major north-south

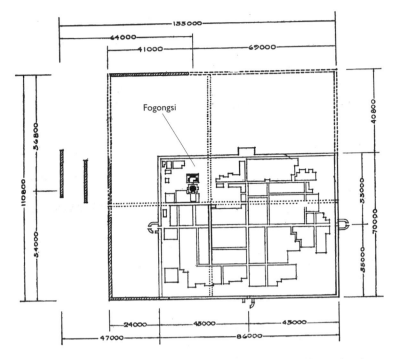

FIGURE 101. Theoretical reconstruction of Yingzhou in Liao times showing location of Fogongsi (Baogongsi). [After Chen Mingda, *Yingxian Muta*, p. 32]

and east-west city thoroughfares (fig. 101). The central position of the pagoda in its monastery, and the monastery in the town, are the first signs of the premier importance of the Muta.

From 1863 until its destruction by the Japanese in 1933, the entry to the pagoda precinct was a wooden monumental gateway *(paifang)* on which its craftsmen had recorded their names. About 107 meters beyond and 2 meters west, one came to an east-west street at one time faced by the Shanmen shown in Figure 100. Today only the foundation of the structure that, like its counterpart at Dulesi, once housed divine kings *(tianwang)* remains with a pair of bronze lions cast in 1594. Beyond to the east and west are two-story bell and drum towers, each three-bays-square, that faced east or west into the monas-

tery courtyard. Made in the Ming or Qing dynasty, the drum is gone, but the bronze bell in the belfry has an inscription dated 1622. The distance between the towers and the eastern and western monastery walls is about 44.8 meters. Behind them, but still inside the walls, were another pair of east-west oriented halls of different dimensions that were also probably constructed after the Liao dynasty. The 55.5 meters from the back exit of the Shanmen to the front of the pagoda is pure, open space. It is the large area necessary as foreground for what by Liao and later Chinese standards was a skyscraper. Originally the area behind the pagoda was equally vacant with a clear pathway to Fogongsi's Daxiongbao Hall. In later times the space was filled in by the auxiliary buildings shown in Figure 100.

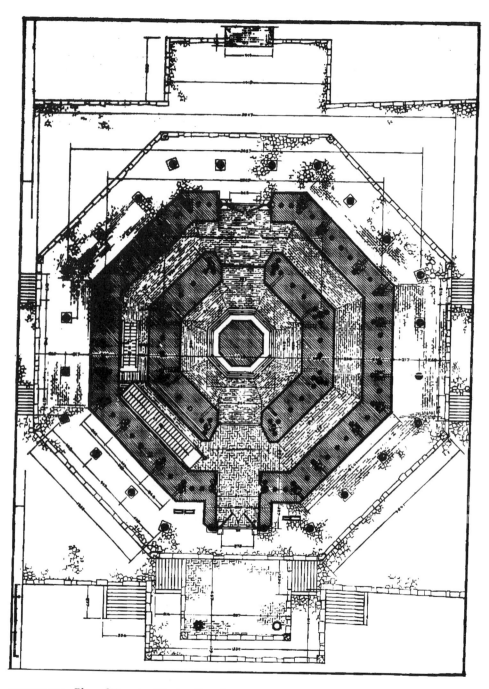

FIGURE 102. Plan of Yingxian Timber Pagoda. [After Chen Mingda, *Yingxian Muta*, drawing 5]

FIGURE 103. Front sectional drawing of Yingxian Timber Pagoda. [After Liu Dunzhen, *Zhongguo gudai jianzhu shi*, 2nd ed., p. 218]

The foundation of the pagoda was built in two levels. The lower is a quadrilateral of between 39.5 and 41.87 meters on each side. It rises 1.66 meters. *Yuetai* of different heights project at each side, the tallest just over 2 meters. Side stairs (*tadao*) provide access to the south *yuetai*. The north *yuetai* was originally accessed by ramps (*mandao*) that have been lost. The upper foundation is octagonal with a diameter of 35.47 meters and a height of 2.1 meters. *Yuetai* with side stairs project from all but its north side. Both foundations were made of stones of inconsistent size (fig. 102).

The timber frame of the base story consists of three independent rings of pillars, the outermost on the upper platform and supporting the eave ends, the middle and innermost joined to walls. The two interior rings define inner and outer *cao* of the hall. The *cao* function much as their counterparts at Guanyinge or any other hall: the outer *cao* is an arcade, and the inner *cao* contains the main images and sanctum. One sees in the plan that a staircase on the south provides access to the next story.

Like Guanyin Pavilion, each story of the Muta is an independent, self-contained structure and the plan of each story reveals every component of the one below it (except for the top story, which has no stairs). The only real variation in plan from story to story at the Muta (besides location of stairs) is at ground level. There the inner *cao* is encompassed by four pillars per face, forming three-bay sides. On higher levels, only eight pillars ring the inner *cao*. Twenty-four pillars still define the exterior of the outer *cao* in stories two through five, thus differentiating three bays on every exterior face, of which the central bay is the longest. Variation occurs in door or window placement and arrangement outside, and the shapes of altars of the inner *cao* vary. The altars of stories one and three are octagonal and the others are four-sided. Sculptures on the altars are nonuniform in position.

Observing from the exterior, one might think that the Muta is a six-story structure, each story defined by an exterior set of roof eaves. In fact, the base story supports two eave sets. But there is a more impressive interplay of structure and visual effect: between each of the five stories is a *pingzuo* (mezzanine level) hinted at from the exterior only by a porch. In actuality, then, Yingxian Timber Pagoda is a nine-level building (fig. 103). Chen Mingda (who drew figs. 41–43) has made drawings of the measured perfection, which extends through multiple planes of the Muta (figs. 104 and 105). As at Guanyinge, bracketing is the chief means of integration from level to level. The difference between exterior implication and interior construction, also a feature of both buildings, will be observed in another Liao wooden hall and, in fact, will be suggested as a feature of Liao architecture.

The placement of pillars of the five stories and four *pingzuo* is further evidence of the measured structural perfection in Yingxian Muta. The exterior columns of stories two through five are exactly above columns of the *pingzuo* beneath them. Their diameters are proportionately related not only to those of the columns closer to the interior of the pagoda on the same level but also to those of the story beneath them. Typical of medieval Chinese construction, the columns lean slightly inward and rise slightly toward the exterior of a given side. The ring of columns that differentiates the *cao* of a level is joined by floor tiebeams and architraves and *pupai* tiebeams at the tops. Tiebeams also join the column rings of a story (figs. 106 and 107). Additional square-sectioned pillars were placed beneath some bracket sets to help support their weight. These are the pillars, mentioned later, from which chemical analysis has yielded a date for the pagoda.

Another feature of the Timber Pagoda that puts it in the superlative category is the use of fifty-four different bracket-set types. The greatest variety occurs

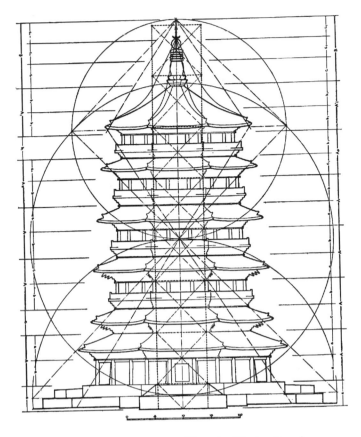

FIGURE 104. Elevation drawing of Yingxian Timber Pagoda showing measured perfection of dimensions. [After Chen Mingda, *Yingxian Muta*, p. 38]

in pillar-top bracketing under the exterior eaves. Figure 106 shows the exterior varieties across three sides of the first three stories and mezzanine levels.[2] The most intricate bracketing of the exterior is found at the eight corners where, in the first story, 7-*puzuo* bracketing is employed and in higher stories one finds 6- and 5-*puzuo* sets. The Muta is a prime example of the variation that can exist even within a defined type. Although certain features like three *ang* or two *ang* and one false *ang* define 7-*puzuo* bracketing, the number, size, and placement of caps and transversal or longitudinal arms may vary. In general, one finds bracketing that denotes highest status at corners, then pillar top, then intercolumnar; status is higher in lower stories as opposed to higher; status is higher on the exterior than in the interior. The logic is consistent with the fundamental Chinese concept of status, here defined by importance of position in holding up the structure.

Found at the Muta in greater number than any other structure are braces, struts, and posts that help support what might otherwise have been a precarious structure. One hundred and two props (*zhuzi*) were added on either side of main columns and under the lintels of every bay.[3] The other supports were of the general types mentioned earlier for Liao buildings like Guanyinge, but again greater variety and ingenuity in location can be found. The intricacy of construction is evident in a schematic drawing of a timber layer (fig. 107).

Despite the variety in timber pieces, a standard-size timber certainly was used for the transversal bracket arm and other pieces of the structure. The proportions of the *cai* are 25.5 by 17 centimeters, roughly the 3:2 ratio. The *zhi* is approximately 11 centimeters and thus the *zucai* is 36.5 centimeters. Chen Mingda's measurement of the pagoda has yielded a correspondence between the use of standard timber as specified in the *Yingzao fashi* and proportions of the architraves, *pupai* tiebeams, pillar diameters, lintels, certain beams, and, of course, bracket-set pieces, but the relationships are in some instances less than those measured for other Liao wooden buildings.[4] The structure's superb stability surely is a tribute to craftsmen who could override exact stipulations when necessity called for changes.

Of the numerous structural feats accomplished in this mid-eleventh-century building, ceiling construction, including its wooden support system, probably remains without parallel in China. Not only does each story function as an independent hall, but every hall story has inner and outer *cao*, a ceiling over the outer *cao* (see fig. 105), an altar with a complete sculptural program in the inner *cao*, and a ceiling over that altar and its sculpture. The first- and fifth-story ceilings have *zaojing* that, in the case of the first story, cut into the mezzanine layer and under the floor of the story above it; on the fifth level, the *zaojing* cuts into the roof timbers (fig. 108 and see fig. 105). The most impressive ceiling features are the *zaojing*. The core of the first-story *zaojing* consists of multidirectional beams of various lengths that join columns or struts and intersect other beams (fig. 109). The *zaojing* itself is a composite of four different lattice patterns that alternate between two for the eight triangles and two for the eight trapezoids (fig. 110). A different lattice pattern is employed for the *zaojing* of the fifth story (fig. 111). Figure 111 also shows some of the frame above the ceiling through the now lost lattices on the sides of the *zaojing*.

The imagery on each story is self-contained such that each story is its own three-dimensional Buddhist universe, or mandala (fig. 112), including not just sculpture but wall paintings, some of which survive from the Liao.[5] One wonders if the pagoda was not also conceived as one structural entity whose nine levels in composite form might have been a mandala.

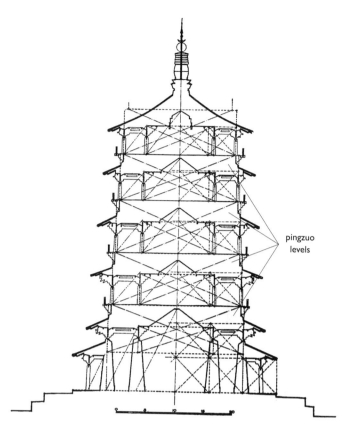

pingzuo
levels

FIGURE 105. Side sectional drawing of Yingxian Timber Pagoda showing measured perfection of dimensions. [After Chen Mingda, *Yingxian Muta*, p. 42]

FIGURE 106. Line drawing of exterior of first three stories of Yingxian Timber Pagoda. [After Chen Mingda, *Yingxian Muta*, drawing 18]

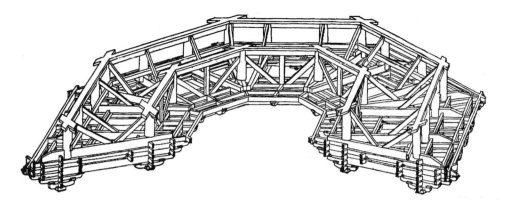

FIGURE 107. Schematic drawing of timber frame of one layer of Yingxian Timber Pagoda. [After Chen Mingda, *Yingxian Muta*, p. 49]

HISTORY AND DOCUMENTATION

The present Muta is widely believed to be a building of 1056 with repairs from the last decade of the twelfth century. Yet a different date is put forth in at least three sources: *Gujin tushu jicheng* (Illustrated encyclopedia of old and new; 1725), *Shanxi tongzhi* (Record of Shanxi province; 1892), and *Yingzhou xuzhi* (Record of Yingzhou continued; 1769) give its building date during the *tianfu* reign period (936–943) of the Jin dynasty (one of the Five Dynasties).[6] From a purely historical point of view, the mid-tenth-century date is unlikely. In 936, first year of the *tianfu* reign, the Northern Han attacked the sixteen prefectures of Shanxi and Hebei in Liao possession, an area that included Yingzhou. At that time, Yingzhou was not much more than a Liao military outpost. Judging from Ten Thousand Buddhas Hall at Zhenguosi, built by the Northern Han (see fig. 70), and the other tenth-century buildings that remain in Shanxi south of the territory of Liao control, it is unlikely the planning and money that brought the Muta into being could have been available. Moreover, war broke out again in 986 and

whatever did stand in Yingzhou would probably have been destroyed in the devastation. Anything that survived the war may well have been destroyed in the earthquake of 1021 that rocked Ying and a neighboring *zhou*.[7]

The 1056 date for the Timber Pagoda has one literary source: *Yingzhou zhi* (Record of Yingzhou), compiled from 1725 to 1735. Included in this local record, however, is a very important source written in 1599 by a man named Tian Hui.[8] Referred to in Chinese as "Tian's Record," the document is based on numerous stelae inscriptions preserved in the pagoda or at the monastery. Tian's record is one of the best sources of information on the Muta. It is therefore surprising that he seems never to have come across the *tianfu*-period date. (The earliest of the three records that gives the mid-tenth-century date, *Gujin tushu jicheng*, is contemporary to *Yingzhou zhi*.) Evidence of style and patronage that verify the date of 1056 will be presented shortly. What should be irrefutable evidence for a date is chemical analysis conducted by the Cultural Relics Bureau in 1977. Their findings dated square pillars in the pagoda to between 930 and 980 years old,

FIGURE 108. Śākyamuni and *zaojing* above its head, first story, Yingxian Timber Pagoda. [After Chen Mingda, *Yingxian Muta*, pl. 58]

giving those timber members a date of ca. 1000–1050.[9]

Other documentary evidence is found at the monastery itself.[10] The earliest inscription is on a stone *dhāraṇī* pillar dated 1194. It is brief and largely effaced; it seems to have revealed the names of monks associated with the monastery. The next three records about the monastery, chronologically, are much more important. One is a long inscription, dated 1353, on an octagonal stone column inside the pagoda's south portal. The other two were written in 1490: one, the "Śākyamuni Inscription," was written together with four placards on the fifth story of the pagoda by a man named Xie Jing; the second was engraved on the inner side of stairs to the pagoda. Tian's six-*juan* record is the only other Ming document. From the Qing period, in addition to the books mentioned earlier, scores of inscriptions survive in and around the pagoda.

Based on all the foregoing evidence, the following construction history is known. Whenever the monastery was founded, its original name was Baogongsi. The earliest date for Baogongsi in any record is 1056 (discounting the *tianfu* period date), when an imperial order was given to a monk with the surname Tian to build it. In Tian Hui's late-Ming record of this occurrence, the pagoda is referred to as Śākyamuni Pagoda, named after the main Buddha enshrined in it. Repairs were undertaken at the monastery in 1165 and to the pagoda in the 1190s. In 1305, an earthquake that destroyed 5,800 residences and killed more than 1,400 people was reported in the Datong circuit, possibly affecting the Timber Pagoda.[11] It was one of seven earthquakes between the time of construction and the end of the sixteenth century. During one quake that took place in the reign of Shundi (1333–1368), the ground shook for seven days yet the pagoda seems to have survived intact. The name change to Fogongsi, by which the monastery is still known, came

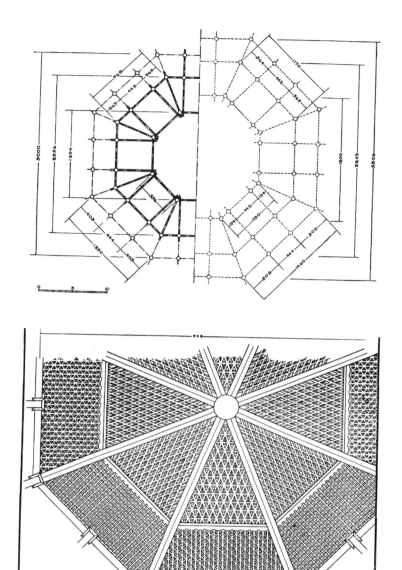

FIGURE 109 (top). Positions and measurements of beams of ceiling of first story of Yingxian Timber Pagoda. [After Chen Mingda, *Yingxian Muta*, p. 36]
FIGURE 110 (above). Line drawing of underside of *zaojing* of Yingxian Timber Pagoda. [After Chen Mingda, *Yingxian Muta*, drawing 7]

FIGURE 111. Ceiling and *zaojing* of fifth story of Yingxian Timber Pagoda. [After Chen Mingda, *Yingxian Muta*, pl. 129]

earlier, in 1315, when the character *"bao"* became taboo because it was used in an imperial name. The name Baogongsi was nevertheless used in the octagonal pillar inscription of 1353, but other than that, all fourteenth-century-and-later references are to Fogongsi. Some repairs were undertaken following imperial orders in 1320 by a man called Alibo and again in 1335. It is never specified whether this last Yuan-period repair provided the strength to withstand the mid-fourteenth-century quake or was a result of it: nothing specific about these renovations is known. Only in Jin inscriptions is the monastery described as "huge." The end of the Yuan dynasty marked an abrupt halt to imperial patronage in this part of China.

Natural disasters, repairs, and at least one imperial visit are recorded in Fogongsi's Ming and Qing history. In 1406, the Yongle emperor visited the monastery and inscribed one of its four-character placards. In 1464, a bronze tripod was cast for the platform south of the pagoda. In 1486, a kiosk was raised for a bell that remained from the Jin period. A tornado rocked Yingzhou in 1501, but like most of the other disasters recorded in *Yingzhou xuzhi,* one cannot confirm its destruction of the monastery. Repairs of 1508 were the result of the visit of a high-

FIGURE 112. Sculpture on second story of Yingxian Timber Pagoda.
[After Chen Mingda, *Yingxian Muta*, pl. 74]

ranking official named Wu Miaoyou in that year. Buddhist images were repaired in 1517. In 1579, a monk named Mingci, a townsman named Chen Lin, and others presented funds for repairs and for a bronze *dhāraṇī* pillar to be placed on the *yuetai* south of the pagoda. A pair of bronze lions was cast for the front gate fifteen years later. The last construction event known from the Ming dynasty was the casting of a bronze bell for the bell tower.

A century passed until the next recorded repairs were undertaken at the end of the Kangxi reign period. During these five months of 1720—in addition to repairs to the Timber Pagoda—east and west halls to local gods, bell and drum towers on old sites, a new enclosing wall more than 80 *zhang* in length, and other rooms and buildings were constructed. Moreover, numerous placards were written during this time. It was the first major repair since 1508, and it was to be the last until the 1990s. In 1726, a man named Xiao Gang, who was responsible for some repair work in nearby Zhizhou, built a brick gate behind the pagoda that became known as the "first [scenic] view." Xiao Gang was also the compiler of *Yingzhou zhi*. Minor repairs took place in 1786, 1787, 1844, and 1863, there was painting in 1863, minor work in 1887, and repair to images in 1894 and 1908. Serious damage resulted from shots fired on the Timber Pagoda by the Japanese in 1926, demonstrating once again that firearms present more of a threat to Chinese timber architecture than earthquakes, which shook the region again in 1953, 1966, 1968, and 1969 without structural damage to the Muta. In 1989, however, an earthquake resulted in structural damage that necessitated major repairs in the early 1990s. During repairs of the mid-1970s, artifacts were discovered inside images and at the base of the pagoda.[12]

Up to 1990, therefore, the noteworthy years for repair of the pagoda were 1191–1195, 1320, 1508, 1722, 1866, and 1928–1929. Structural change occurred only at the end of the twelfth century, however, about 150 years after initial construction. Chen Mingda points out that repair took place on average every 150 years,[13] a remarkable statistic in light of the pagoda's location in an active earthquake zone. The structural stability of this monument is admittedly magnificent. Still, it seems unusual that such a large and complex wooden structure would have been neglected for over a century at a time. Except for one intervention by the imperial Mongolian family in the fourteenth century, Yingxian Muta was largely neglected after the end of the twelfth century. A comparison between the amount and sort of information available for the Muta with that for Guanyin Pavilion of Dulesi—anecdotes, associations with heroes, a visit by the Qianlong emperor and several high-ranking officials for the pavilion versus a dry list of unspecific notices of repairs and earthquake records—underscores this point. Indeed, if not for Tian Hui, one would know almost nothing of Fogongsi's history. In the following section we shall see why this outstanding monument was erected in such an out-of-the-way place—a location no doubt a factor in the lack of attention paid to it after the Liao period.

GUANYINGE AND YINGXIAN MUTA

One begins to understand the importance of the Muta through comparisons with the other extant multistory Liao wooden building that stands at the focal point of its monastery: the much better documented, superbly by Liao standards, Guanyin Pavilion of Dulesi. To begin with, each is the focal point of enclosed religious space and each projects above its monastery's walls. Moreover, much of the structure of the Timber Pagoda is anticipated by Guanyin Pavilion. As has already been pointed out, both Liao buildings conceal mezzanine layers, indicated by *pingzuo* on the exteriors, between each of the apparent outer stories. Furthermore, both consist of complete interior and exterior rings of columns that define *cao*. In neither building does the height of a column exceed one story. Yingxian Timber Pagoda has fifty-four different types of bracket sets, the greatest number for a Liao building. Guanyinge has twenty-four, the second largest number. Foguangsi East Hall, by contrast, has only seven varieties of corbel clusters. The inner *cao* of the Timber Pagoda is dominated by Buddhist images beneath *zaojing*. Premier among these is the image of Śākyamuni on the first floor (see fig. 108). The presence of the bodhisattva Guanyin equally dominates the pavilion at Dulesi (see fig. 6).

More than the passage of time accounts for achievements surpassing the already impressive ones at Guanyin Pavilion. The splendid structure in Yingxian owes more to imperial patronage and construction date than any other Liao building.

Yingxian Timber Pagoda is intimately tied to the seventh and eighth Liao emperors, Xingzong (r. 1031–1055) and Daozong (r. 1055–1101). The man who became the seventh Liao emperor Xingzong (Zongzhen) was the son of an imperial consort named Noujin. Since the legitimate empress, Qitian, had failed to produce a son (two had died in infancy) by the time of Zongzhen's birth, the consort's child was adopted by Qitian. The foster mother was a native of Yingzhou. Thus, in accordance with Qidan custom whereby Yelü sons were raised by the families of their Xiao-lineage mothers, the future ruler was raised in Yingzhou.

In 1031, on his deathbed, Emperor Shengzong designated his fifteen-year-old son Zongzhen to succeed him. He also ordered that no harm come to the Empress Qitian. Nevertheless, Xingzong's birth mother, Noujin, managed to have Qitian implicated in a crime for which she was banished and eventually committed suicide. Noujin next made herself empress dowager (the posthumous name by which she is most often known is Qin'ai) and began plotting the replacement of the young emperor by his younger brother whom she herself had raised. The younger brother revealed the plot to Xingzong, however, who banished Noujin to the imperial necropolis at Qingzhou. Due at least in part to his debt to his younger brother and other members of Noujin's family, and perhaps to some fondness from his childhood, Xingzong visited Noujin in 1037. In 1039 he allowed her to return to the capital.

When Xingzong died at the age of thirty-nine in 1055, both his natural mother, Noujin (Qin'ai), and his wife, Empress Renyi, were alive. Renyi was the mother of his eldest son, Hongji, who became the eighth Liao ruler, Daozong.[14] Emperor Daozong was a devout Buddhist. Although it is not clear how close the new emperor's ties were to his grandmother (now Great Empress Dowager Qin'ai), Daozong nevertheless chose to erect the Timber Pagoda in Yingzhou, the place where his father had been raised by the legitimate empress, Qitian. Finally, it is suggested here that the year 1056 is related to Daozong's motivations as patron—to his interpretation of Buddhist doctrine of the past and to theological concerns of his own time.

Indeed, it is not only structural features that cause the Muta to stand apart from the other Liao wooden buildings. When the historical Buddha Śākyamuni died, a stupa was built over his remains. The first function of the building that in its East Asian forms has come to be referred to as a pagoda was that of relic mound. It is logical that a Liao ruler who was also a devout Buddhist would have followed the ancient practice and ordered the construction of the architectural symbol of the death of the historical Buddha as a shrine to his father's death. Implicit in this interpretation is the further

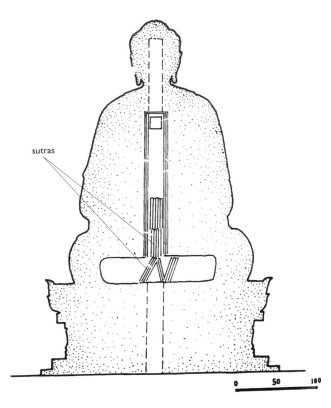

sutras

FIGURE 113. Section of Śākyamuni from fourth story of Yingxian
Timber Pagoda. [After *Yingxian Muta Liaodai mizang*, p. 10]

association between the enshrined deity and the
ruler to whom the monument was dedicated.

   The first evidence of the pagoda's funerary purpose comes from objects buried inside it and its images. The main image, Śākyamuni, on the fourth
story, for example, concealed a central pillar and sutras (fig. 113).[15] One may draw a further association
between the wooden pagoda and a form of rock-
carved worship cave common during the period of
Northern and Southern Dynasties (386–589).
Known as the "central pagoda-pillar style" (*zhongxin tazhu shi*) cave-temple, this common configuration of the Northern Wei (386–534) period in
northwestern China traced its origins to early Indian Buddhist worship spaces in which, as in the
later Chinese versions, the pillar, sometimes with
Buddhist imagery carved on it, symbolized the
Buddha and served as the focal point of circumam-
bulation (fig. 114).[16]

   Associations between the Muta's first-story central image, Śākyamuni, and the ruler Xingzong also
may be likened to Northern Wei precedent. In a
transformation of the timber monument into a symbol of the ruler's demise, the Qidan converts to the
Buddhist faith and to the forms of Chinese architectural space, it is suggested, conceived of the

monumental deity as a symbol of the deceased ruler. Sixty kilometers to the north at Yun'gang, Northern Wei emperors, it has been suggested, made a similar association between deity and ruler in the excavation of five Buddhist worship caves under the direction of the monk Tanyao in the 460s.[17] Associations between rulers and monumental deities are widespread in Asia.[18] However, although similar motives are likely, there is no indication that the Muta was built with a Northern Wei or other Asian precedent in mind. Rather, one observes in Daozong's construction of a pagoda with a monumental Buddhist image inside—the year after his father's death in the town where the father had grown up—the more direct kind of borrowing, adaptation, and interpretation in which Qidan patrons have been shown to have partaken. In cases of nonnative, seminomadic adaptations and reinterpretations, rulers do not seek subtley. They simply take from existing tradition (in this case, a monumental image of the Buddha) and reinterpret it as it suits their purposes.

It is in this context that the Seven Buddhas on the altar of Daxiongbao Hall of Fengguosi can be seen as symbols of Liao rulers through Shengzong plus the father of Abaoji. Similarly one can return to Guanyinge, the pavilion associated with the tenth-century Han family of Jizhou. The monumental bodhisattva Guanyin inside a pavilion might be interpreted as the appropriate memorial to a high-ranking official whereas the Buddha Śākyamuni inside the Muta could symbolize only the emperor himself. Yet another layer of symbolism might be associated with the employment of Guanyin. Since this bodhisattva has been shown to have been a clan deity of the Yelü, it is possible that in building a pavilion to Guanyin the Han sought to aggrandize their own importance or to make a statement about their political aspirations with respect to their overlords.[19] Such were the ways, it is believed, in which

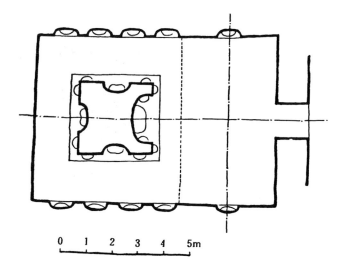

FIGURE 114. Plan of Mogao Cave 254, Dunhuang, Gansu, Northern Wei period. [After Xiao Mo, *Dunhuang jianzhu yanju*, p. 37]

forms and symbols of sedentary cultures and imported and absorbed faiths were adopted, adapted, and transformed through architecture in the first century of Qidan rule. Architecture was central to Qidan self-identification as Liao rulers of an Asian empire and to their definition of the hierarchy of power with respect to their subjects in this empire.

Concerning the date of the Timber Pagoda, the 1050s had another significance besides the death of Emperor Xingzong. Buddhologists in East Asia had calculated the year 1056 to be the one in which *mofa*—termination of dharma (the Buddhist law)— would occur and the universe as it was known would end. Upon its regeneration, Maitreya, Buddha of the future, would take on the role of Śākyamuni in the regenerated universe.[20] It was in the *mappō* (Japanese for *mofa*) climate that in the year 1052 Fujiwara no Yorimichi converted the Phoenix Hall of the Byōdō-in (his father Michinaga's residence in Uji) into a temple to Amitābha, whom the Pure Land sect taught would guide souls of the departed

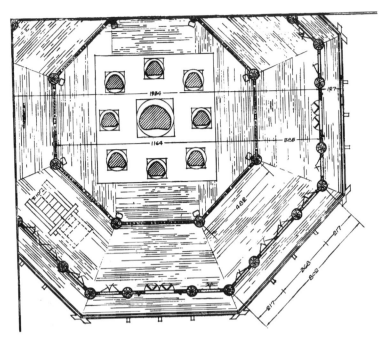

FIGURE 115. Plan of fifth story, Yingxian Timber Pagoda. [After Chen Mingda, *Yingxian Muta*, drawing 15]

to the Western Paradise. The same "end of the Buddhist Law" mentality, it has been suggested, gave way to the mass production of sutras carved in stone at the Liao Buddhist monastery Yunjusi in Fangshan, Hebei (see fig. 22).[21] Thus one can propose that, through borrowing and personalized interpretation, the Muta represented not only a death shrine to Emperor Xingzong but also an ultimate death shrine to Śākyamuni, Buddha of the age.

The funerary context of Liao architecture is a theme that bridges its wooden construction and its more explicitly funerary monuments, its tombs. The afterlife was also the motivation for the several examples of Liao metalwork discussed in the Introduction and an overriding concern of emperors, empresses, concubines, and relatives during the life

and especially upon the death of a ruler. Imperial death, after all, involved not only personal preparations for the afterlife but decisions about the continuation of the empire. Yet the genius of Liao imperial patronage is far from restricted to monuments motivated by impending demise.

For wooden architecture, the Buddhist context was equally powerful. It was a Buddhist context that engendered the octagonal plan of the Muta. It has already been suggested here that the combination of deities floor to floor of the Timber Pagoda comprises a mandala. The timber frame suggests the same possibilities. The plan of each level of Yingxian Muta is an eight-sided perimeter with a central core. The configuration is pronounced in the first story, in which Śākyamuni sits at that core (see fig.

108), in the fourth story where a wooden pillar rises through Śākyamuni's center (see fig. 113), and in the fifth and highest story whose deities consist of eight figures surrounding a main image (fig. 115). The scheme links it to one found at the center of the Tantric Womb World Mandala, whose earliest Chinese versions are believed to have been painted in the Tang dynasty and which was transmitted to Japan by the monk Kūkai in the first decade of the ninth century (fig. 116).[22] The comparison is strengthened by the presence of thunderbolts separating the eight deities that encircle the main image, Vairocana, and the eight pillars that join the walls of every exterior Muta story and those of many other Liao pagodas (see figs. 360–364). The double eight-petaled lotus on the lids of the reliquary buried inside Guanyin Pagoda in Jixian is similar in line drawing to the black outline that encloses the deities on the Womb World Mandala (see fig. 49). In Part Two I propose additional associations for this originally Tantric Buddhist form.

The Muta was built just over halfway through the Liao empire. Structurally it is the pinnacle of Liao architecture in wood. It is probably no coincidence that the tomb of the Muta's builder Daozong, together with the tombs of his father and grandfather in the same necropolis, will be shown in Part Two to be the acme of Liao subterranean construction. Liao wooden buildings later than the Muta are discussed below. Few compare with it, none surpasses it.

FIGURE 116. Center of Womb World Mandala, Tō-ji, Kyōto, Heian period. [After Sekiguchi *Nihon no Bukkyō*, vol. 2, *Mikkyō*, p. 253; courtesy of Shinchosa]

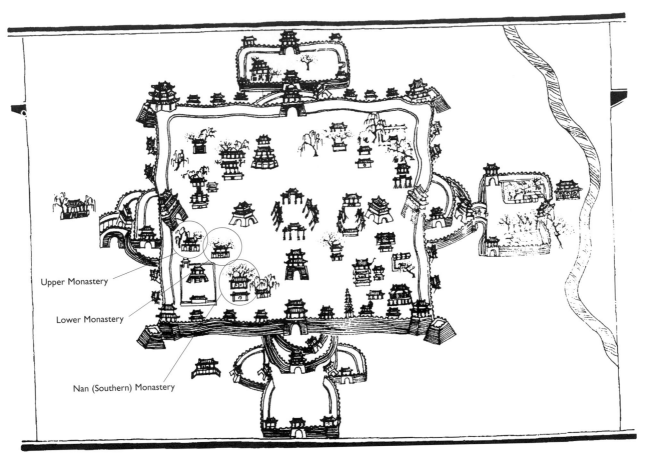

Upper Monastery

Lower Monastery

Nan (Southern) Monastery

FIGURE 117. "City of Datong" showing Huayansi and Shanhuasi. [Yang and Li, *Datongxian zhi, juan* 1 (illustration section)]

6

Liao Monasteries in the Western Capital

IF, BEFORE READING THIS BOOK, the words "Liao architecture" called to mind anything, it was probably an image from Datong, northernmost city in Shanxi province and western capital of the Liao from 1044 until the end of the dynasty. Except for Beijing, Datong is the one city in China proper that bears witness to China's conquest dynasties. Datong's predecessor, Pingcheng, had become the first Northern Wei capital south of the Great Wall in 398 and would remain so through the fifth century until the non-Chinese dynasty moved its capital farther south to Luoyang in Henan province in 493. Buddhist worship caves and

tombs survive from the fifth century.[1] The boundaries of the Northern Wei city have never been discovered.[2] And although only about 22 kilometers west of the present city, the Buddhist caves at Yun'gang do not appear on the only known map of Pingcheng or on plans of Datong bounded by Ming walls (fig. 117).[3] Nevertheless, the caves provided the Qidan with visual images of monumental Buddhist worship space.

The two major Liao monasteries were integral to Datong of the Ming and later. Both Huayansi, in its "upper" and "lower" building groups, and Shanhuasi (also known as Nansi, "Southern Monastery")

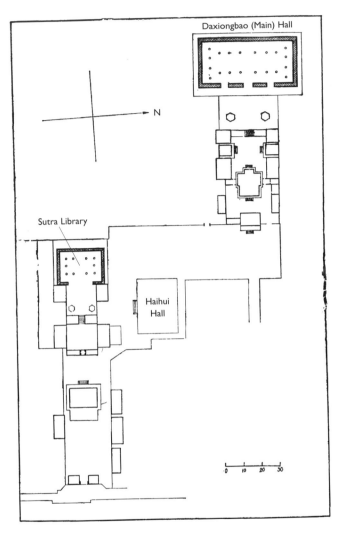

Daxiongbao (Main) Hall

N

Sutra Library

Haihui
Hall

0   10   20   30

FIGURE 118. Plan of Huayansi. [After Ding Mingyi, *Huayansi*, n.p.]

appear on maps published in local records (fig. 117). Although the buildings in Figure 117 may all look alike at first glance, only those three (Huayansi is pictured as "Upper Monastery" and "Lower Monastery") are monasteries. Most of the structures with pointed roofs are *miao*, temples to local gods or other deities. Many more than are plotted on the map were in the city in the 1940s when its religious structures were investigated by Willem Grootaers.[4] His study suggests the continuous history of Datong as a city of religious institutions.

HUAYANSI

The Buddhist monastery Huayan (Avataṁsaka) si is located south of Datong's main east-west street, near the western gate of a wall built around the city by the first Ming emperor Hongwu in 1372, just four years after the founding of the new Chinese dynasty. It was about this time that the monastery of Liao-Jin times was divided into two parts designated Upper Monastery and Lower Monastery.[5]

Like the city that enclosed it, the boundaries of the Liao monastery have never been exactly determined. Local records state merely that the Great Huayan Monastery stood south and a little east in the walled city, facing west.[6] The spread of "old" buildings—structures that date from the Liao or were rebuilt within a century after the fall of the Qidan to the Jin, who also designated Datong their western capital—is such that both upper and lower sections were certainly part of the Liao-Jin religious complex. Liao-Jin buildings at Huayansi numbered three when the monastery was most seriously investigated, during the two decades before the establishment of the People's Republic of China.[7] One of them, the Sutra Library, has a fixed date of 1038. The monastery's Main Hall was rebuilt in the twelfth century, but it retains much Liao flavor. Although the third Liao-Jin structure was lost during the Sino-Japanese conflict in the 1940s, it was stud-

FIGURE 119. Interior of Sutra Library, Huayansi, Datong. ["Clay Figures in the Huayan Temple, Liao Dynasty, Beijing Slide Studio, slide 1]

ied and photographed sufficiently before then to be discussed here.

The two extant early buildings are the main structures of the monastery today (see fig. 118). Stelae inscriptions record other buildings but give no information about how they were arranged. Because of the topography, Huayansi is more spread out than some of the other Liao monasteries, but it may not have contained more buildings than a monastery such as Dulesi which, like Huayansi, remained active into the twentieth century.

History

The earliest date associated with Huayansi is 1038. That year is written on the underside of a beam in the Bojiajiao (Bhaghavat) Sutra Repository, commonly known as the Sutra Library. The same date is recorded in *Shanxi tongzhi* and *Datongfu zhi*.[8] Construction was part of a program of religious building sponsored by Emperor Xingzong (r. 1031–1055), the Liao ruler memorialized at Yingxian Timber Pagoda. He presented twenty priests to Huayansi and had sutras copied for it.[9] During one year of the reign of Emperor Daozong (Xingzong's successor), 260,000 people, up to 3,000 a day, worshiped at Huayansi.[10] A construction date of 1062, also during the Daozong reign, is recorded for Huayansi in the *Liaoshi*.[11] The second reference also mentions the presentation of imperial images in stone and bronze. The *Liaoshi* does not say in which hall these images were placed. Since the twenty-nine images in the Sutra Library comprise the largest single repository of Liao sculpture in the world (fig. 119), it seems likely that this was the hall to which the Daozong presentation was made. Some of the images are said to have been imperial portraits.[12] It is certain that the images survived into the thirteenth century. The *Jinshi* (History of the Jin dynasty) records that in the fifth moon of 1166, Emperor Shizong saw old bronze images of a Liao emperor during his visit to the western capital.[13] In the biography of Shi Tianlin in the *Yuanshi* (History of the Yuan dynasty), it is reported that Khubilai Khan (d. 1294) was told by Shi of imperial bronze images in the old western capital.[14] Presumably these were the Liao emperors at Huayansi. The last construction date at Huayansi associated with Emperor Daozong is 1076, when the *dhāraṇī* pillar in front of the main hall (Daxiongbaodian) was made. Clearly Huayansi was a great recipient of imperial Qidan patronage.

The oldest historical record at the monastery is a stele carved in the year 1162. It is an extremely important document for the early history of Huayansi. According to the stele inscription, the monastery contained a sutra collection, no doubt the one housed in the Sutra Library.[15] During the *baoda* reign period (1111–1118) at the end of the Liao, the monastery suffered great damage. Only five buildings survived: a *zhaitang* (hall for "vegetarian feasts" or fasting; or an "abstinence hall"), a *chuku* (kitchen [storage]), a *baota* (a pagoda, perhaps one in Lamaist style), a Shou Situ Dashi *yingtang* (a countenance hall for the monk Shou Sita), and a *jingcang* (the sutra repository). The private hall for a monk is in all likelihood the small sideways-oriented Haihui Hall (see fig. 118) that survived until the 1940s. That and the Sutra Library are the only two of these five Liao buildings that stood in the twentieth century. According to the stele of 1162, one major building that suffered greatly during the Liao-Jin strife in about the year 1122 was rebuilt in 1140. It was Daxiongbao Hall, the third important early building at Huayansi. Also constructed in 1140

were several *ge*, a bell tower, gates, and *duodian*, literally "ear halls" (side halls connected to a main hall). Construction was supervised by six monks, one of whom was named Tongwu. Five of them died before the work of the surrounding covered corridor and "*dong*" (grottoes) was completed. The stele offers no explanation of these *dong*. They may be *luohan dong*, perhaps side halls containing statues of *luohan* such as are said to have been part of the Liao-Jin plan of Shanhuasi (discussed later in the chapter). A monk named Shengxue picked up where the others had left off and the repair work was finally completed by 1162 under the direction of the monk Cihui. Shengxue composed the stele inscription. Four years after this work was completed, the Jin emperor Shizong visited Huayansi.

The next stele at Huayansi, dated 1273, mentions repair work in 1250 during the reign of Güyüg Khan (third Mongolian ruler beginning with Chinggis), when the territory was already in Mongolian hands. A stele in the Sutra Library records repairs under the direction of monk Huiming in 1350, still during Mongolian rule. These repairs seem to have been fairly extensive, involving more than one hundred bays of buildings.[16] The Sutra Library was repaired in 1391. A repair stele of 1465 is the first source that records the Tang dynasty as the period the monastery was established. The same stele says that a Chan Buddhist master brought three golden images made in the capital (Beijing) to Huayansi in the late 1420s. This stele is the first one in which the terms "upper" and "lower" monastery were used, leading Takeshima to suggest that the dual concept began between 1427 and 1429 when Daxiongbao Hall was repaired.[17] During the quarter of a century between the two-year repair period and the death of the Chan priest, images were made and repaired, there was exterior repainting, and ceiling construction was undertaken. A stele of 1581 describes what Liang Sicheng and Liu Dunzhen refer to as an "ar-

FIGURE 120. Sutra Library, Huayansi, 1038. [After *Ancient Chinese Architecture*, p. 89]

chitectural overhaul."[18] There were three different repair periods in the seventeenth century, two in the eighteenth century, and at least one in the nineteenth century. Huayansi underwent more repairs and received more continuous imperial interest than Yingxian Muta. Today its space is somewhat disorganized and portions appear cramped. Fogongsi, by contrast, has retained its original spatial organization. Yet the changes at Huayansi are a sign of the kind of continued growth and activity that have not affected Yingxian.

Bhagavat Sutra Repository

The Sutra Library is a simple, even unimpressive, building from the outside (fig. 120). It is a five-by-four-bay hall with a hip-gable roof. The structure faces east on a high (approximately 3 m) foundation (31.52 by 24.09 m at the base) with a huge *yuetai*

(18.94 by 14.18 m) in front (fig. 121). The approach to the *yuetai* is fifteen stone steps with an entry gateway at the top. The entry and the hexagonal bell and drum pavilions on the *yuetai* are recognizable as standard additions of the Ming or Qing period like those at the other Liao monasteries discussed earlier. The incense burner, also standard in later imperial times, stands near the center of the *yuetai*. Less usual are two three-bay halls attached to the sides of the *yuetai*'s western end where it joins the hall.

The plan of the Sutra Library shows twenty-eight pillars forming two complete rings that define an inner and an outer *cao* (see fig. 121). Pillars are eliminated only from the central interior north-south line. (The hall is oriented east to west.) The altar juts out slightly at the eastern ends, but it is basically simple, as is the timber frame. Unlike Guanyinge or Fengguosi's Daxiongbaodian, the elimination

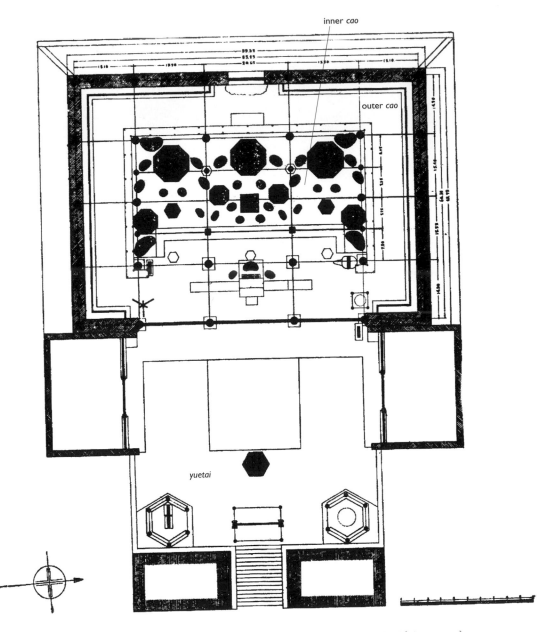

inner *cao*

outer *cao*

yuetai

FIGURE 121. Plan of Sutra Library, Huayansi, showing *yuetai*. [After Takeshima, *Ryō-Kin jidai* ..., p. 79]

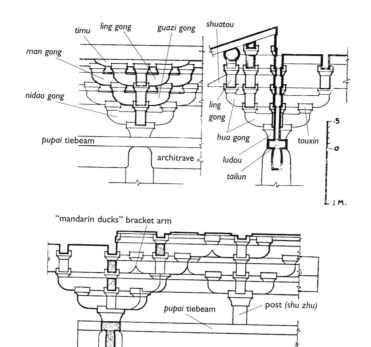

FIGURE 122 (top). Line drawing of frontal and side sections of pillar-top bracket set, Sutra Libray, Huayansi. [After Liang and Liu, "Datong," p. 20]
FIGURE 123 (above). Line drawing of sections of interior bracket sets showing male and female mandarin-duck bracket arms, Sutra Library, Huayansi. [After Liang and Liu, "Datong," p. 25]

of pillars did not correspond to unusual ceiling requirements. Six panel doors permitted entry via the three central front facade bays (see fig. 120). *Lian*, wooden panels that open and close, with lattice patterns different from that of the door windows, were placed above the doors for additional interior light and ventilation. The only other windows were in the central back bay. The hall is dark inside.

The pillars of the hall are of different shapes and dimensions, suggesting more than one period of repair. Their diameters range from 51 to 60 centimeters; they are cut off at the tops, but the rise is very slight across the front. Liang and Liu found the av-

erage pillar diameter to be 58.5 centimeters, corresponding to a *tingtang* rather than *diantang* in the *Yingzao fashi*.[19]

Bracketing at the Sutra Library is generally of the 5-*puzuo* type—the appropriate type for a *tingtang*. Among the bracket sets, one finds eight varieties that differ according to building position. Several types of bracketing at the Sutra Library are shown in Figures 122 and 123. Some of these bracket features, also found at other Liao structures such as Guanyin Pavilion, include the much-lengthened *nidao gong* in comparison to the *man gong* and the use of fan-shaped, or cluster, brackets above corner pillars un-

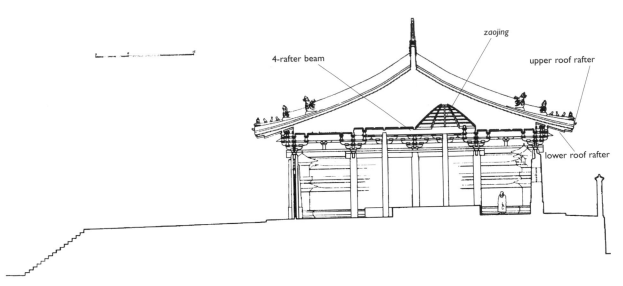

FIGURE 124. Side sectional drawing of Sutra Library, Huayansi. [After Liang and Liu, "Datong," pl. 4]

der the roof eaves. Another noteworthy feature observable in earlier Liao structures is the raising of the bracket set above the cap block by the addition of a post (*shu zhu*) between the cap block (*ludou*) and the *pupai* tiebeam into which the pillar is joined. The timber piece may be called *tailun*. The *cai*, or module, in the Sutra Library, based on the proportions of the bracket arm, is 24 by 17 centimeters, an appropriate ratio of approximately 3:2.

Sectional drawings of the Sutra Library show the relative simplicity of the structure, especially in comparison to Guanyin Pavilion, the Muta, or even Daxiong Hall of Fengguosi. The columns support three four-rafter beams and three *zaojing*, one above the head of each of the main images (figs. 124 and 125). The combination hip-gable roof, standard for *tingtang*, is eight purlins deep. There are two sets of roof rafters: the lower is square in section; the upper is circular (see fig. 124). The roof slope, with a grade of 24 degrees, is the most gradual among surviving Liao-Jin buildings.[20]

Certainly nothing in the description of the timber frame of the Sutra Library of Huayan Monastery suggests the extraordinary. Yet like Guanyin Pavilion and the Muta, exterior appearance is deceiving. The inside of the Huayansi library reveals another unique and unparalleled achievement in wooden construction of the kind achieved at Dule and Fogong monasteries.

No photograph can capture what one encounters upon entering the building of scriptures (fig. 126). In addition to the sutra collection that under Emperor Xingzong numbered 5,079 sutras,[21] the building is the largest in situ repository of Liao sculpture (see fig. 119). Recessed into every interior wall space except those occupied by doors or windows—nearly three walls in all—are wooden sutra cabinets. The cabinets are constructed in two or three

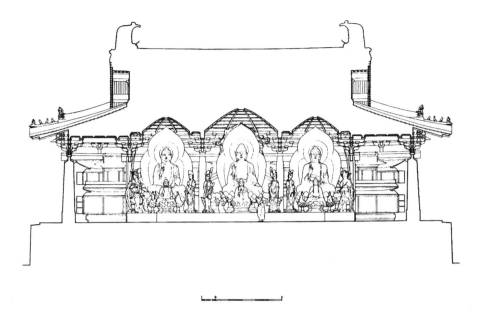

FIGURE 125. Front sectional drawing of Sutra Library, Huayansi. [After Liang and Liu, "Datong," pl. 5]

levels and in many respects may be likened to a multistory building.

On the north and south walls, one finds the equivalent of a Buddhist hall whose foundation is a patterned, Sumeru altar (fig. 127). Above is the "first story," an eleven-bay building with double doors in each bay. Behind these doors were stored sutras. The bracketing of this first story is composed of one pillar-top set and two intercolumnar sets of 7-*puzuo* type. Further above is a layer of roof eaves, another layer of the same number of brackets, and then a balustrade. Based on other Liao wooden architecture like Guanyinge and the Muta, one might expect to find a mezzanine story hidden behind the balustrade. The central three bays of the upper story are marked by a triple-entry gateway whose roof spines are capped at the ends by *chiwen*. These *chiwen* have turned-up fishtail ends that are characteristic, according to Liang and Liu, of Tang style.[22]

Under the exterior eaves of the upper story one finds again 7-*puzuo* bracketing, but of slightly different configuration than the corresponding brackets of the first story. In all, seventeen varieties of bracket set are used in the sutra cabinets, several of which are unique even among Liao architecture.[23] The ends of the upper story on the north and south hall sides are capped by gate towers.

Due to doors and windows, the configurations of the east-wall and west-wall sutra cases are slightly different from that of the north wall. Their space is divided into six bays on either side of the door or windows (fig. 128). Most impressive are the upper stories where elaborate pavilions, known in Chinese as *tiangong louge* (heavenly palace tower pavilions), cap the doors or windows to the exterior of the Sutra Hall, and four other roofed structures are raised two on either side of the center. On either side of the "tower pavilions" are balustraded,

FIGURE 126. Sutra Library, Huayansi, interior. [After *Ancient Chinese Architecture*, p. 90]

curved bridges of the kind that appear in Tang-period wall paintings from the Mogao Caves (see fig. 69). These were, it seems, reflections of actual Tang palatial architecture (see figs. 54 and 55).

The source of *tiangong louge* for the Sutra Library cabinetmakers was probably not wall painting in Gansu province. *Tiangong louge* are one of two types of sutra cabinets illustrated in *juan* 32 of the *Yingzao fashi* (fig. 129). The correspondence between these cabinets and Figures 127 and 128 is never identical, but it is close enough to strongly suggest the use of a printed guidebook, a precursor to the twelfth-century *Yingzao fashi*.

Haihui Hall

Haihui Hall, destroyed during military activity in the 1940s, was not architecturally outstanding.[24] It was a single-story, side-facing hall of five-bays-by-three, with a hip-gable roof, raised on a 1.21-meter foundation to the east of the Sutra Library (fig. 130). Although its timber frame is comparable to that of the Sutra Library, its orientation to the auxiliary building axis is a sign that its function was less significant.

Only one piece of evidence informs us of the function of this building, for its exterior structure tells anyone familiar with Chinese architectural language that it could not have been a main hall. One recalls that according to the stele of 1162, five buildings survived the chaos of the *baoda* period (when Liao fell and Jin took power). One of the five was, of course, the Sutra Library, dated 1038. Of the other four, this hall surely was not a pagoda. Nor would it have been a kitchen, because the precedent of other medieval monasteries confirms that the smells of kitchens necessitated that they be distant from the central monastery core. Perhaps Haihui Hall was the *zhaitang* (abstinence hall). The countenance hall, *yingtang*, a memorial chapel where the portrait or sculpture of a founder or other

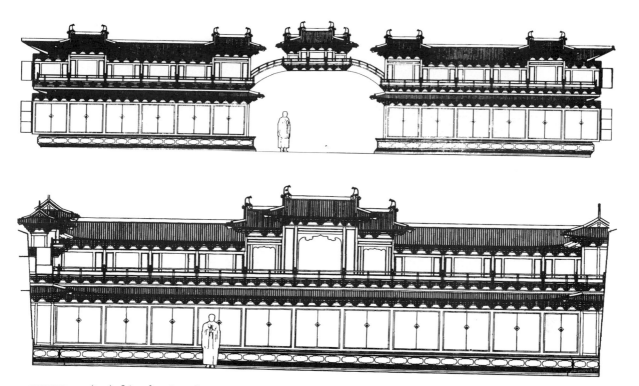

FIGURE 127 (top). Line drawing of sutra cabinets, Sutra Library interior, north wall. [After Liang and Liu, "Datong," pl. 6]
FIGURE 128 (above). Line drawing of sutra cabinets, Sutra Library interior, west wall. [After Liang and Liu, "Datong," pl. 8]

influential monk was housed, is a stronger possibility. If so, its proximity to the Sutra Library would have provided easy access for study. The reason for the name Haihui is uncertain.[25]

Haihui Hall measured 29.19 meters across the front and 20.15 meters in depth. Its central, front-facade bay was over 6 meters wide, and those that joined to its left and right declined in size toward the eave ends to just over 5 meters. Each side had only three bays, the middle one almost twice the size of the end two, which were not quite the same size. Inside were complete rows of columns across lines indicated by all four side pillars and additional small posts emerging from the altar to help support the roof frame (fig. 131). Access was provided by

doors in the central-front bay. The only other ventilation came through windows in the two adjacent bays. The dark interior would be typical of a countenance hall, yet the lack of exterior articulation and the *xuanshan* ("overhanging" gables) roof—the only roof of this type that survives from the Liao period and so far as one can tell the only unique feature of Haihui Hall among Liao buildings—made for a somewhat unattractive exterior (fig. 132). (A *xuanshan* roof is also found at West Side Hall of Longmen Monastery, discussed in Chapter 3.)

The simplicity of construction is shown in a sectional drawing of the hall (fig. 133). Standard features of Liao construction are the rise and batter of pillars, the use of the *tailun* (above pillars and be-

FIGURE 129. *Tiangong louge* ("Heavenly palace tower pavilions"). [*Yingzao fashi*, juan 32, 1974 ed., vol. 7, p. 95]

neath bracket sets) and the *timu* (above or below bracket sets; see figs. 122 and 123), and the appropriate ratios for *cai* and *zhi*—namely 23–24 by 15–18 centimeters (15:10.5) and 11 centimeters (thus 15:7), respectively. Only three varieties of *dougong* were employed, each between 5- and 4-*puzuo*.[26] Most of the beams are exposed; *taqian* (braces) are above exposed beams and parallel to them; purlins are right on them. All beams are straight. The roof slope is fairly gradual, one feature that distinguished Haihui Hall from the otherwise similar details of the Sutra Library. When Liang and Takeshima saw the hall, it had a ceiling across the central three bays, covering the heads of the three main images, but both concluded that much of the interior decoration was Ming period or later.

Daxiongbao Hall

The Sutra Library and Haihui Hall formed a self-contained unit together with the newer buildings in what is today the Lower Monastery of Huayansi.

The focal point of the monastery, however, is elsewhere. The compound of buildings discussed to this point was intended as an auxiliary to the main hall and its images.

Daxiongbao Hall of Huayan Monastery is the largest main hall that remains from the early period of Chinese construction, even larger than Daxiongbao Hall of Fengguosi. The nine-by-five-bay structure stands on an exceptionally high platform, even by Liao standards. Its elevation of 4 meters or more is approximately one-half the height of the hall pillars.[27] This foundation is certainly a sign of the hall's importance. Projecting in front of Daxiongbao Hall's five central bays is a *yuetai* of 32.42 by 18.48 meters with an archway at the top of the twelve stairs and hexagonal bell and drum kiosks, all three probably Ming or Qing additions like those at the Sutra Library. In the center of the *yuetai* are a bronze lantern with the date of 1594 and behind it a stone *dhāraṇī* pillar that, although its top has been lost, still has the date 1075 inscribed into it (fig. 134).

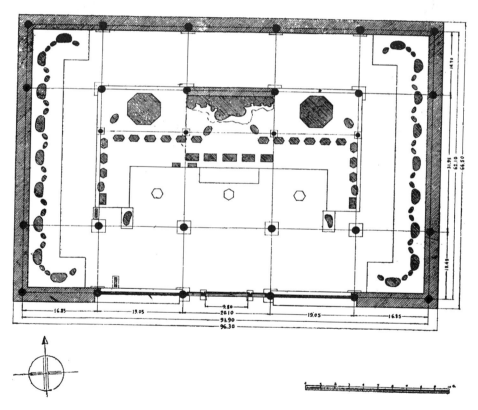

FIGURE 130 (top). Frontal rendering of Haihui Hall, now destroyed. [After Liang and Liu, "Datong," pl. 10]

FIGURE 131 (above). Plan of Haihui Hall. [After Takeshima, *Ryō-Kin jidai* . . . , p. 97]

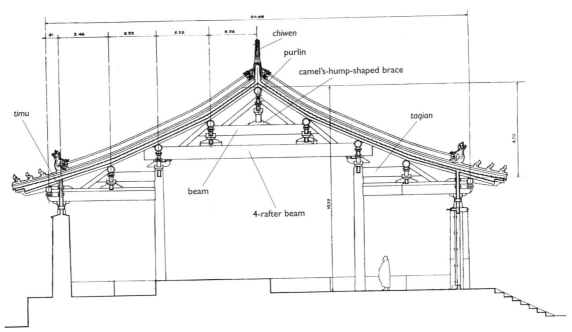

FIGURE 132 (top). Haihui Hall from side. [After Liang and Liu, "Datong," fig. 58]
FIGURE 133 (above). Side sectional drawing of Haihui Hall. [After Liang and Liu, "Datong," pl. 12]

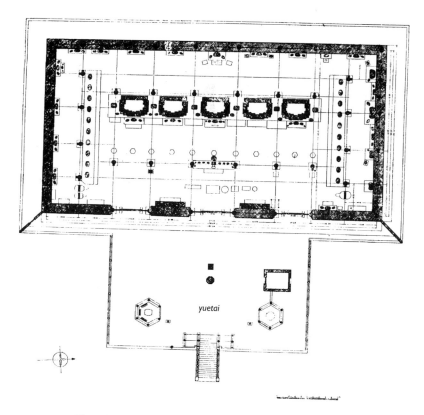

FIGURE 134. Plan of Daxiongbao Hall, Huayansi, 1140. [After Takeshima, *Ryō-Kin jidai . . .* , p. 116]

The *yuetai* is enclosed by a stone balustrade. This unique building approach is separated from the hall by several stone stairs, probably a sign of the hall's rank.

The date of the Main Hall is somewhat more controversial than that of the other Liao main halls or the other Liao-period buildings at Huayansi. Daxiongbao Hall is not mentioned in the stele of 1162 as one of the five Liao buildings that survived destruction in about 1120. The hall is believed to have been rebuilt in the twelfth century. The inscription on the stele of 1162 does name monks who came to reconstruct a nine-by-seven-bay hall in 1140,[28] but

Daxiongbao Hall is nine-bays-by-five. The year 1140 is nevertheless the date most often associated with Huayansi Main Hall and a mistaken character (7 rather than 5) is assumed in the stele inscription. Although Daxiongbao Hall is discussed here as a building of 1140, one should keep in mind that we do not have sufficient evidence at this time to differentiate a hall built in the mid-eleventh century from one built a century later in the same city.[29]

The bays across the front of Daxiongbao Hall decrease in length from 6.98 meters at the center to 5.15 meters at the ends. Like Daxiongbao Hall of Fengguosi, it can be entered only via three front

FIGURE 135. Daxiongbao Hall, Huayansi. [After "The Huayan Temple," Beijing Slide Studio, slide 2]

doors: in the center and in the third bays out from the center (fig. 135). The multipanel doors all have screens that open or shut above them, but there is no other light source. The shape of the door tops is unusual in comparison to doors of the Liao buildings discussed thus far. Known as *humen yazi* (vase-shaped entries with serrated edges), they are typical of Liao-Jin architecture in Datong and can be seen in the Main Hall of Shanhuasi also (see fig. 140). The doors were repaired during the Ming period. The exterior wall of the hall is described as *xiongqiang*, literally "breast wall," a reference to the differentiation between wall material below and above mid-level.

As in other Liao halls, pillars have been eliminated from the interior. Whereas sixty pillars would be necessary to complete a column grid suggested by the peripheral columns, forty-eight are used (see fig. 134). All forty-eight are aligned with one of the front facade pillars, but the interior pillars parallel to the six inner facade bay pillars are placed in two rows midway between lines suggested by the columns that define the northern and southern build-

ing faces. (Like that of the Lower Monastery, orientation of the Upper Monastery is east-west.) The back row of six interior pillars stands behind the altar on either side of each of five Buddhas and their attendants. The north-south interior rows of pillars one bay into the building are backing for two other long altars on each of which ten *luohan* sculptures are elevated. The east-west row of columns across the front of the hall is primarily for support of the timber superstructure; its central two pillars stand on either side of a small altar. This arrangement of columns, known as *jinxiang doudi cao*, corresponds to one of the four specified in the *Yingzao fashi*. The configuration is typical for buildings with inner and outer *cao* discussed in Chapter 2 (see figs. 66 and 67). The height of columns on either side of the *dangxin jian* (central front facade bay) is 6.98 meters, same as the length of the central front bay. Although the pillars rise to 7.3 meters at the ends, the central column lengths (equal to the measure of the bay they define) conform to the *Yingzao fashi* stipulation that the height of pillars should not exceed the width of any hall bay.[30] The pillars are cut only slightly inward at the tops. Their lengths are more than ten times their diameters, which are 65 centimeters. This measurement is about half the length of pillar bases (between 120 and 134 cm). The proportions of the *cai* are 29–31 by 20 centimeters, or 3:2, and the *cai/zhi* is approximately 30:14 centimeters. The hall corresponds in some but not all respects to the *Yingzao fashi* description of a high-ranking hall (*diantang*) built with first-grade timbers.[31]

Despite the huge proportions of Daxiongbao Hall, its bracketing is of the 5-*puzuo* type in ten variations. The most distinctive feature of the bracket sets is the use of fan-shaped bracketing of the kind also employed in the Huayansi Sutra Library and elsewhere in Datong's Liao-Jin monasteries (fig. 136). In these clusters, projection is along five directions—two parallel to, one perpendicular to, and two at 60-degree angles from the building facade. Other features of bracketing at the Huayansi Main Hall are typical of Liao construction as well, including the use of the *tailun*, the *timu*, and the *pizhu* ("sliced bamboo") end of the *shuatou* in pillar-top brackets (fig. 137). This end cut is a striking contrast to the wing-shaped molding of the bracket arm, sometimes called *yuanyang (jiaoshou) gong*; male and female mandarin ducks [joining] bracket arm, at the end of the second *hua gong* (transversal bracket arm) of intercolumnar sets (see fig. 123). All beams in the hall are straight, as we shall see at Shanhuasi's Main Hall. Beams penetrate bracket sets, thereby joining those on one building line with another. In all, there are four complete rings of beams. The *shunfu chuan* ("agreeable tiebeam connector"), employed as a brace at the Fengguosi Main Hall, is found at this main hall, as well, and so too are the *taqian* and *jiaobei* braces (see fig. 87). The latter join the main roof purlin to six-rafter beams. At present the only exposed beams are those of the outer *cao*, but the Liao-Jin hall had no ceiling. The lattice ceiling above the seven inner hall bays was installed during the Ming period, just like, according to Liang and Liu, the ceiling of Haihuidian.

The rise of the roof is 1:3.95. This number is consistent with three other Liao roofs: Fengguosi Main Hall's, which is 1:4, Guangjisi Main Hall's (1:3.95), and Shanhuasi Main Hall's (1:3.76). (The latter two will be discussed shortly.) The construction was according to the *juzhe* system described in the *Yingzao fashi*. Ceramic decoration on the roof, however, in particular the *chiwen*, or "owls' tails," at the ends of the principal roof rafter, is thought to be from the Jin period at the earliest.[32]

The fact that Daxiongbao Hall, and indeed the entire monastery of Huayansi, are oriented toward the east has escaped the notice of no one who has

FIGURE 136. *Fan-shaped bracketing, Sansheng Hall, Shanhuasi, Datong, Jin dynasty.* [Steinhardt photograph]

written about them. Chinese monastery and palace architecture is almost always oriented toward the south, the cardinal direction, whose associations with the Chinese ruler seated on his throne facing south are as old as the imperial tradition. Thus the first inclination of scholars, including Liang, Takeshima, and Soper, has been to seek meaning in the fact that Huayansi is oriented eastward. Justification for an eastward orientation has been found in references in the *Liaoshi* to Qidan worship of the sun (which rises in the east) and to the fact that the Qidan worshiped the sun during the winter solstice, in preparation for the hunt, for war, and in the ceremony of "recognition of the ruler." At the time of recognition, the emperors bowed to the sun four times. Then they turned toward the Muye Mountains, birthplace of the Qidan and site of their ancestral temple, and bowed toward them, to the god of metal, to his mother, to the tribal ancestress, and to other blood relatives.[33] Chai Zejun cites references from the *Liaoshi*, which says that the emperor entered from the east and faced east during a banquet with Song officials, and from dynastic histories of the Five Dynasties which relate that the

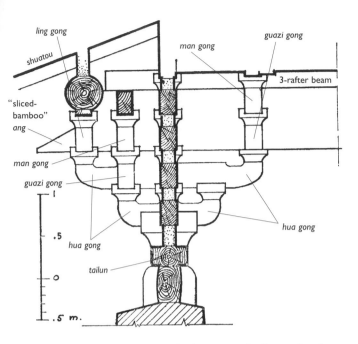

ling gong
shuatou
"sliced-bamboo"
ang
man gong
guazi gong
man gong
guazi gong
3-rafter beam
hua gong
hua gong
tailun

1
.5
0
.5 m.

FIGURE 137. Line drawing of side section of pillar-top bracket set, Daxiongbao Hall, Huayansi. [After Liang and Liu, "Datong," p. 67]

royal Qidan faced east monthly to worship the sun.[34]

Why, then, are Dulesi, Fengguosi, and Fogongsi oriented toward the south? Why is only Geyuansi oriented westward? And why was Kaiyuansi (discussed in the next chapter) composed of three buildings side by side, rather than one behind another, facing south? Perhaps the attempt to isolate Liao building complexes from the mainstream of Chinese traditional architecture has drawn undue significance to the issue of orientation. If eastward orientation deserves association with non-Chinese, North Asian custom, then, it is argued here, evidence points to the orientation as an occurrence of early Jin-period restoration of Liao monasteries. This aspect of Jin ideology may provide the best reason yet for a date of 1140 for Daxiongbao Hall.

In the discussion of Foguang Monastery we noted that its Main Hall is referred to as the East Hall because of its eastern position in the monastery. The East Hall is the only wooden building at Foguangsi that survives from before imperial Jurchen rebuilding there. The extent of Jin rebuilding is unknown, as is the configuration of Foguangsi in Tang times. When Jin rebuilding took place, from which time only Mañjuśrī Hall survives today, the monastery was oriented westward so that the East Hall was its focus and Mañjuśrī Hall was one of a pair of side halls that faced inward —and also southward (fig. 138). The date of Mañjuśrī Hall, and presumably that of Jin restorations, is 1137, just three years before the date associated with Daxiongbaodian.

What lies beneath Daxiongbao Hall of Huayansi has not been uncovered. Nor has the building been dismantled, so one cannot describe the extent of the 1140s restoration. It is certainly possible the hall was realigned or even moved at the time of Jin rebuilding. The orientation of Huayansi legitimately raises these questions when one also considers the relation between the Jin-period Mañjuśrī Hall to its monastery on Mount Wutai. With an undated Shanmen, it is conceivable that the south-facing Mañjuśrī Hall stands on what was once a north-south oriented Foguangsi. One cannot prove, therefore, that the east-west orientation of Huayan Monastery dates from the Liao period. Rather, a south-oriented Liao monastery may have been reoriented, perhaps during restoration by the Jin, in the same years that dynasty enacted reconstruction at Foguangsi about 225 kilometers to the south. The second Liao monastery in Datong, Shanhuasi, remained south-facing despite Jin repairs.

SHANHUASI

Shanhua Monastery faces south in the southern part of the Ming walled city Datong, west of the south city gate.[35] It is so far south that the temple complex has also been known as the Southern Monastery, as it is labeled in Figure 117. Its origins were during the *kaiyuan* period (713–741) of the Tang dynasty when, like so many monasteries throughout China, it was constructed through patronage of the Emperor Xuanzong (r. 713–755). At that time it was called Kaiyuansi, a name retained by only one of the Liao monasteries (with extant architecture).

History

Details about the early history of the monastery are taken primarily from stelae that survive there, the most important one dated 1176, but information is sketchy. At the time of Shi Jin, mentioned in reference to Geyuansi (in Chapter 2), the monastery became Da Pu'ensi. The only inscribed object from this period is a bronze bell dated 936. Destruction occurred here as at Huayansi during the chaos of the *baode* years, and of some ten original buildings only three or four survived. This is a crucial fact, for the plan of the monastery today shows nine buildings if one counts the side halls, or "ear halls" (*duodian*), adjacent to the main hall at the north as separate buildings (fig. 139). Otherwise, the count is seven plus whatever stood in front of the street that runs south of the monastery today. Writing after a visit in 1902, Itō Chuta said he thought he saw a drama pavilion and traces of other architecture in front of the road that runs south of the monastery, but neither he nor anyone else who has come to Shanhuasi since has been able to determine with certainty what was there.[36] Since the number 10 in a twelfth-century Chinese stele can easily mean "about ten," the important information from the inscription is that the monastery of that time probably had a plan much like the present one and, of that group of buildings, three or four were from the Liao period. Two Liao buildings stood at the monas-

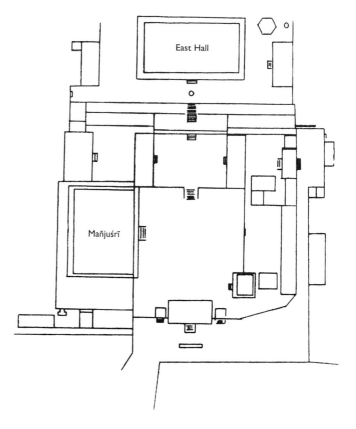

FIGURE 138. Plan of Foguang Monastery, Taihuai county (foot of Mount Wutai), Shanxi province. [After Yang Yutan et al., *Wutaishan simiao daguan*, p. 19]

East Hall

Mañjuśrī

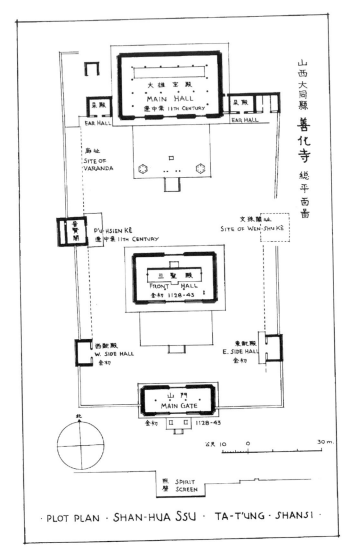

大雄宝殿
MAIN HALL
遼中葉 11TH CENTURY

呆殿
EAR HALL

呆殿
EAR HALL

廊址
SITE OF
VARANDA

普賢閣
P'U HSIEN KÊ
遼中葉 11TH CENTURY

文殊閣址
SITE OF WEN-SHU KÊ

三聖殿
FRONT HALL
金初 1128-43

西配殿
W. SIDE HALL
金初

東配殿
E. SIDE HALL
金初

山門
MAIN GATE
金初 1128-43

北

比例尺 10   0   30 m.

熙壁
SPIRIT
SCREEN

· PLOT PLAN · SHAN-HUA SSU · TA-T'UNG · SHANSI ·

山西大同縣善化寺總平面圖

FIGURE 139. Plan of Shanhuasi in 1930s. [After Liang Ssu-ch'eng, *A Pictorial History of Chinese Architecture*, p. 63; printed with permission of Wilma Fairbank]

tery now called Shanhuasi in the early 1940s. Today only the main hall should be considered a Liao structure.

The stele inscription of 1176 also records that in 1128, not long after the fall of Liao, a monk named Yuanman was ordered to undertake repair work. It was carried out without cessation for fifteen years, and when it ended in 1143 some eighty bays of buildings and some 500 images were repaired down to the utmost detail. Among the buildings, the inscription reports, were the main hall, east and west "ear" halls, a *luohan* hall, pavilions to the bodhisattvas Wenshu (Mañjuśrī) and Puxian (Samantabhadra), a front hall, main gate, and east and west connecting corridors. The Chinese labels on Liang Sicheng's plan of Shanhuasi (see fig. 139) show his assumption that the "front hall" referred to in the stele is the building known as Sanshengdian, named for the three main images enshrined there. Otherwise the Liao-Jin core described in the inscription was the same as one finds at the monastery today. The east and west side halls in Figure 139 are not referred to in the stele and are gone now, but Liang believed them to be part of the early-Jin-period restoration.

The author of the stele inscription was a Song official whose rank and presumed education account, in Liang and Liu's opinion, for the flowery prose.[37] Born far to the south in Huizhou, Anhui province, Zhu Bian was one of a group of Song emissaries who spent thirteen years as a prisoner in the Jin western capital during the first two Jin reigns.[38] Zhu's time of residence, in other words, covered thirteen of the fifteen years of repair work at Shanhuasi. And as Shanhuasi was one of the major monasteries in an otherwise sleepy town by Song standards, it is possible that even under incarceration he knew what was going on there. Whatever records existed prior to Zhu Bian's inscription are unknown. Why there is a thirty-three-year hiatus between its writing and the date carved in the stele is also unclear. (Perhaps a paper document became a stone one.) The Zhu Bian Stele of 1176 is nevertheless an important source about the early history and plan of the monastery that is corroborated by details of the destruction of Datong monasteries by Jin troops in about 1120 recorded in stelae at Huayansi and, of course, by the building plan.

Regarding the Main Hall of Shanhua Monastery, two points in Zhu Bian's text are most significant. First, he uses the word "*chongxiu*" (repair) with reference to it, not "*chongjian*" (rebuild). Second, he uses the term "*duodian*" (ear halls) to refer to the small buildings attached to the Main Hall. Shanhuasi's Main Hall is one of the earliest surviving examples of them, but the inscription is evidence that their current name is a twelfth-century term. Another unusual term in the stele inscription is "*xielang*," which might be translated "slanting covered corridor." The covered arcade that originally joined the Shanmen, side halls, bodhisattva pavilions, and ear halls is gone, but as Liang Sicheng's reconstruction of the plan of Shanhuasi in the 1930s indicates, the northern and eastern sides did not meet perpendicular to each other; rather, the eastern line slants inward from north to south to enclose a hall auxiliary to the ear hall. Although there is no indication whether the angled arcade had an intent, the passage in the stele inscription may well refer to this construction feature.

A puzzling and more tantalizing structure mentioned in the stele inscription is *luohandong*. *Luohan* images, one recalls, were placed in the Daxiongbao Hall of Huayansi, as well, and undefined "*dong*" were located somewhere in the monastery. At Fengguosi, according to the stele inscription of 1162, repairs included 120 "holy images" *(shengxian)* displayed in "enclosing covered corridors" *(wu)* on either side in front of the Buddha Hall.[39]

Based on this reference, it seems possible that at Shanhuasi the "caves" may refer to the enclosing corridors of that monastery, if not of one of its halls, probably also the location of *luohan* statuary at Huayansi. Perhaps the delineation of bays was likened to grotto entries outlined by rock. Finally, the inscription refers to interior wall paintings, none of which seems to have survived.

A second stele dated in the *mingchang* reign period (1190–1195) at the end of the twelfth century mentions the repair of Buddhist images but not of buildings. Only six more dates in Shanhuasi's history can be found in stelae or local records. In 1421 a monk named Dayong oversaw repairs. In 1445 the same monk received an imperial presentation of sutras, which he recited; in that year the monastery is first referred to as Shanhuasi. Stelae of 1576 and 1583 repeat some of the history recorded in other stelae and mention repairs to the foundation pavement and the placement of the bell and drum pavilions on the *yuetai*. More repairs took place in 1616 and again in 1633.

The most important tidbits from the later stelae are the record of the presentation of sutras by a Ming emperor and information about the performance of imperial ceremonies at Shanhuasi. Datong's monasteries, in other words, continued to receive imperial attention after the Liao-Jin period. Yet this information must be contrasted to another detail mentioned in the stele of 1740, which records the repairs of 1616 and 1633. Although the local record, *Datongxian zhi*, mentions repairs in 1740 and 1770,[40] by that time the monastery had fallen into a state of disrepair—apparently the parking of camels in one of the monastery halls had caused a wall to collapse. Even the most centrally located and urbanly situated monasteries, by Liao standards, were in remote areas of China exposed constantly to the impact of nomadic peoples and their lifestyle.

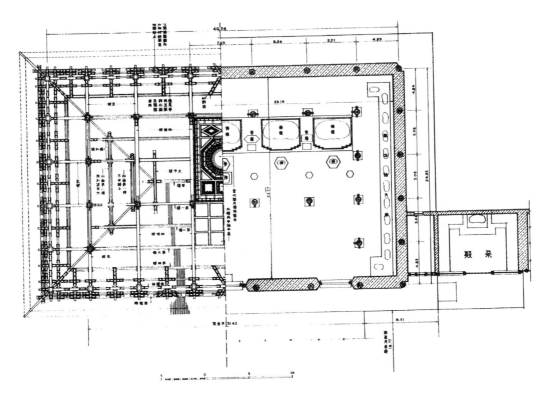

FIGURE 140 (top). Daxiongbao Hall, Shanhuasi, Liao dynasty. [After "Shanhua Temple, a Historic Site in Shanxi," Beijing Slide Studio, slide 6]
FIGURE 141 (above). Plan of Daxiongbao Hall and plan of its ceiling, Shanhuasi. [After Liang and Liu, "Datong," pl. 16]

Camels painted on the walls of tombs of the Liao consort clan (Xiao) were part of the backdrop of Liao architecture throughout its history. (For a discussion of the tombs at Kulunqi see Chapter 12.)

Daxiongbao Hall

Daxiongbaodian, the main hall of Shanhuasi, faces south in the northernmost position of the monastery (see fig. 139). The seven-by-five-bay (40.54 by 24.95 m), ten-rafter hall has a single-eaved hipped roof (fig. 140). Just as at Huayansi's Daxiongbao Hall, doors provide access to the hall in the front central and third bays. Like the Ming-renovated doors at Daxiongbao Hall of Huayansi, these have the "serrated tooth" edges above the door leaves and the screens that open and close above them. The hall has no other openings to the outside. Daxiongbao Hall is elevated on a platform of more than 3 meters in front of which projects a *yuetai* of 31.58 by 18.58 meters (fig. 141). Twenty stone stairs lead up to the *yuetai*, fronted by a balustrade that was probably added in 1581.[41] Bell and drum towers that once stood on the *yuetai* are gone, but the bronze incense burner remains. The length of bays across the front facade of Daxiongbao Hall decreases from 7.1 meters in the center to 4.92 meters on the ends. The pillars rise and have entasis; eight have been eliminated from the interior second and fourth east-west rows beginning on the south. The *cai* at Shanhuasi Main Hall is 26 by 17 centimeters (roughly 3:2) and the *zhi* is 15:6.6 — dimensions close to the *Yingzao fashi* suggestion for high-ranking halls and similar, too, to other surviving Liao buildings.

Eight varieties of bracket sets are found at Daxiongbao Hall of Shanhuasi, all formations of the 5-*puzuo* type. At Huayansi's Main Hall, bracket sets were also 5-*puzuo*. The rather low *puzuo* rank of bracketing may reflect the status of the western capital, for its two main halls are otherwise grand. Again, one of the outstanding features is the use of

cluster bracket sets (brackets whose arms project along more building planes than the longitudinal and perpendicular) (see fig. 136). Unlike the Main Hall at Huayansi, which may be a building from the early Jin period, this essentially Liao structure never has more than one intercolumnar set. At exterior eave-corner bracket sets, one sees the lengthened bracket arm that projects through several *huagong* and is curved off at the bottom to imitate male and female mandarin ducks (*yuanyang jiaoshou gong*) — the same composition of caps and arms pointed out at Huayansi's Daxiongbao Hall and Sutra Library (see fig. 123). Together with the cluster brackets, these are characteristics of bracketing of the Liao western capital that may or may not have been more general Liao-Jin architectural traits. At present, fan-shaped bracketing survives only in Datong and at Mañjuśrī Hall of Foguangsi dated 1137.

Other structural details present at the Huayansi Main Hall are also found here, including additional, smaller support pillars on the sides of main pillars and the use of exclusively straight beams (fig. 142). Beams span two, four, and six rafters. The timber frame supported by pillars is complex: as the labels in Figures 142 and 143 show, it required numerous specialized struts and joiners such as *jiaobei*, *taqian*, and *shunfu chuan*, in addition to the more common camel's-hump-shaped and inverted-V-shaped struts. All of them are present at the Daxiongbao halls of Huayansi and Fengguosi.

Finally, one finds similarities in the ceiling (or lack of ceiling) at the two Daxiongbao halls in Datong. Of five Buddhist images in the inner *cao*, the central one is covered by an octagonal *zaojing* (see fig. 143). Bracketing between the octagonal frame and central circular area where dragons are painted is as complex as 7- and 8-*puzuo* (fig. 144). Here one finds the only Shanhuasi example of such complex bracketing. It is in the details of wooden structure — the small-scale elements such as sutra-cabinet

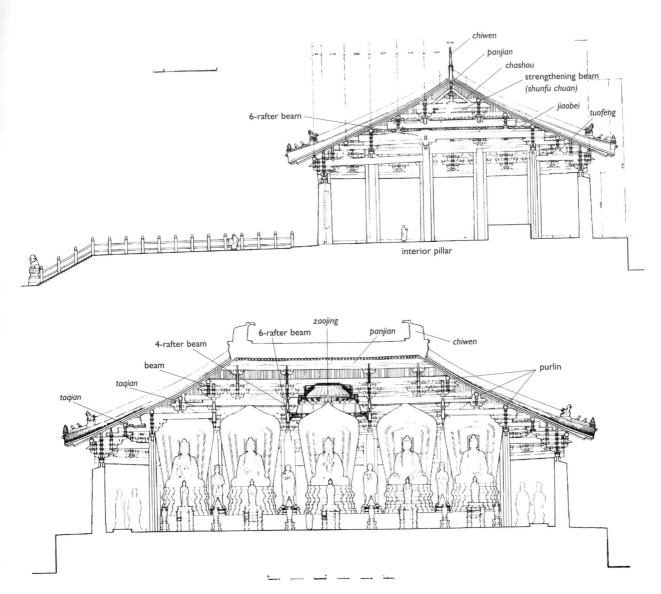

FIGURE 142 (top). Side sectional drawing of Daxiongbao Hall, Shanhuasi, showing additional pillar supports. [After Liang and Liu, "Datong," pl. 19]

FIGURE 143 (above). Frontal section of Daxiongbao Hall, Shanhuasi. [After Liang and Liu, "Datong," pl. 20]

woodwork or ceiling design—that the full potential of the timber craftsman shines forth. These are the details classified as "lesser carpentry" (xiaomuzuo), in contrast to "greater carpentry" (damuzuo), defined in the *Yingzao fashi* as structural members such as pillars and building frames.[42] Perhaps it was such workmanship that led Chai Zejun to write of the Main Hall of Huayan Monastery that "the creative spirit seemed beyond the limits of architectural creations of monks."[43] Besides the central *zaojing*, additional portions of ceiling at Daxiongbao Hall of Shanhuasi, like the entire Huayansi ceiling, are believed to be the result of Ming-period restoration.

Puxian Pavilion

The other Liao building at Shanhua Monastery was lost during the war and rebuilt in the 1950s as it now stands (fig. 145). The pavilion was heavily damaged even when Liang, Liu, and Takeshima saw it, but their investigations and Liang's drawings, in particular, make it possible to discuss it as a Liao structure.[44]

The uniqueness in structure and frequency of use of the pavilion (ge) in Liao monastery plans has already been pointed out. Any pavilion prominently positioned on the main axis of its monastery represents the highest achievement of the structural type in Liao architecture. Puxian (Samantabhadra) Pavilion is an example of one of a pair that faced inward on a secondary axis of a monastery. The twin pavilions dedicated to bodhisattvas that, according to monastery records, also stood at Fengguosi, Geyuansi, and Huayansi, were probably structurally similar to Puxiange and its counterpart at Shanhuasi. A comparison of this pavilion and the one dedicated to Guanyin as the focal point of Dulesi elucidates the correspondence between rank and structural detail in Chinese monastery architecture.

FIGURE 144. *Zaojing*, Daxiongbao Hall ceiling, Shanhuasi. [After Liang and Liu, "Datong," fig. 114]

FIGURE 145. Puxian Pavilion, Shanhuasi, rebuilt in 1953.
[Steinhardt photograph]

Attached to the monastery corridor and facing eastward into the monastery, Puxiange was a multilevel building raised on a platform with a lower *yuetai* approached by a narrow set of steps in front of it. Three-bays-by-two at the base, its plan was nevertheless an almost perfect square that measured 10.4 meters on each side. A door that faced the monastery courtyard with lattice windows above it was the only point of entry.

The key structural feature of Guanyinge and Yingxian Muta—the additional interior story between every two exterior stories—also is present at the Shanhuasi pavilion. Figure 146 shows the concealed interior level indicated only by a *pingzuo* on the exterior. As at Guanyin Pavilion, each of the levels was accessible by stairs; but as at the Muta, these stairs were not on top of each other from level to level.

The size of the pavilion allowed for a less complex structure than that of Guanyinge or the Muta. Each level was supported solely by a perimeter row of columns (fig. 147). The lack of division into inner and outer *cao* may be compared to the simple Tang and tenth-century buildings discussed in Chapter 3, in contrast to the Foguangsi and Liao main halls. Yet Puxiange could never be described as a simple structure. Although only perimeter columns support each level, the number is different for each. The top story, for instance, has three bays in either dimension, with the central bays about twice the width of the two end bays on any side. One recalls that Guanyin Pavilion's columns, too, were not positioned above or below one another from level to level. None of the bracketing at the pavilion is more than 5-*puzuo* in rank, but the wraparound clusters identify it as a hall from the western capital. Other features such as the rise in pillars across a front facade or the 3:2 ratio of the *cai* are generally standard for Liao architecture.

One feature of the first story of the *ge* is unique

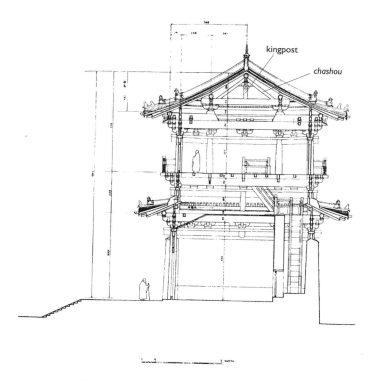

kingpost

chashou

FIGURE 146. Side sectional drawing of Puxian Pavilion, Shanhuasi.
[After Liang and Liu, "Datong," pl. 24]

among surviving Liao architecture: a self-contained miniature building, roof and all, in ruins even when Liang visited, was built inside the front bay of the first story. Its location is sketched in Liang's side-elevation drawing of the pavilion (fig. 148). An image or images might well have been contained within, but in addition a niche with two images and attendants stood against the back wall. Furthermore, the bodhisattva Puxian was enshrined with attendants in the central bay of the upper story. Thus although the name of the hall tells us the deity of focus, there were additional possibilities for worship, perhaps of alternate gods, in other places of the fairly small interior area. The unambiguous fo-

cus of worship on a single, gargantuan image seems restricted to structures on the main axis of a monastery. The side pavilions and their imagery should be viewed as branches to the main halls and their interior focuses of worship, perhaps in the manner of the deities peripheral to the center of a painted mandala.

The two other "early" buildings at Shanhuasi—the Hall of the Three Deities (Sansheng) and the Shanmen—were rebuilt in the Jin period and therefore are not discussed here. Still, until the war in the 1940s, Datong contained four Liao structures in addition to Daxiongbao Hall of Huayansi. Together they form the largest group of eleventh-

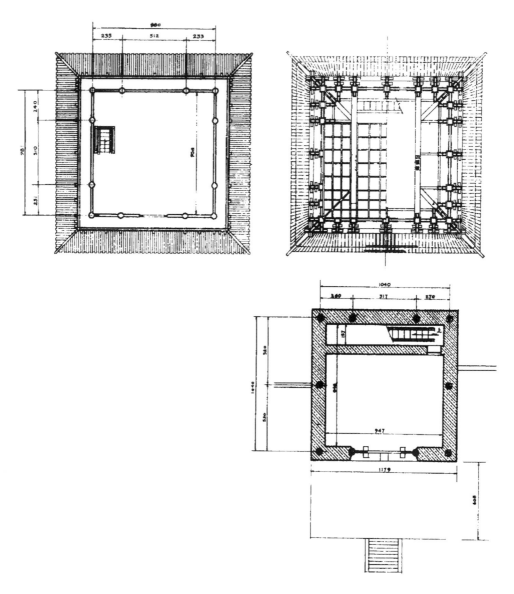

FIGURE 147. Plans of floors and timber frames of Puxian Pavilion, Shanhuasi. [After Liang and Liu, "Datong," pl. 21]

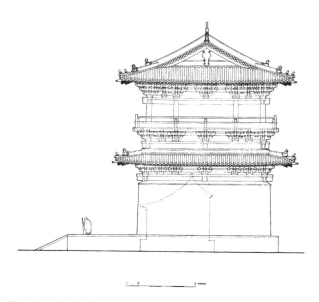

FIGURE 148. Line drawing of side elevation showing interior building, Puxian Pavilion, Shanhuasi. [After Liang and Liu, "Datong," pl. 23]

century buildings at one city in North China. Together with the Jin buildings, they form a group that in some ways is distinctively "Liao-Jin of Datong." Of this group of five halls, one pavilion, and one gate the outstanding exterior stylistic traits are the cluster brackets and specialized bracket arms (*yuanyang jiaoshou gong* and elongated *nidao gong*) used to support them. In addition, several braces, including the *jiaobei, shunfu chuan, taqian,* and *timu,* are used in greater abundance and with more flourish than at other extant examples of Liao construction.

Beyond certain features that may exemplify the level of workmanship in wood among local craftsmen, Datong's two Liao-Jin monasteries present a powerful, if somber, picture of the presence of Qidan seminomads who became Northern Chinese Buddhist rulers against the backdrop of the North Asian desert. Indeed it is remarkable that—with so much wooden monastery building and the techni-

cal ability to create sutra cabinets at Huayansi and *zaojing* at both monastery halls—neither foundations nor other archaeological evidence of palatial or other Qidan residential architecture has been uncovered here. Perhaps it is because native-style, tent dwellings were prevalent. Today the major monasteries stand with the Yun'gang Caves outside town as statements about the willingness of North Asian nomads or seminomads to use religious architecture as the symbols of their imperial presence. This architecture can surely be deemed architecture of imperial power—but of a different thrust than a pagoda to honor a ruler's birthplace, pay homage to his maternal ancestors, and signify his eternal presence as a Buddhist ruler. At Datong it was through ultimately Chinese-inspired buildings of religion that the Qidan made known their presence in a former Chinese outpost that had become one of the five focal points of their empire.

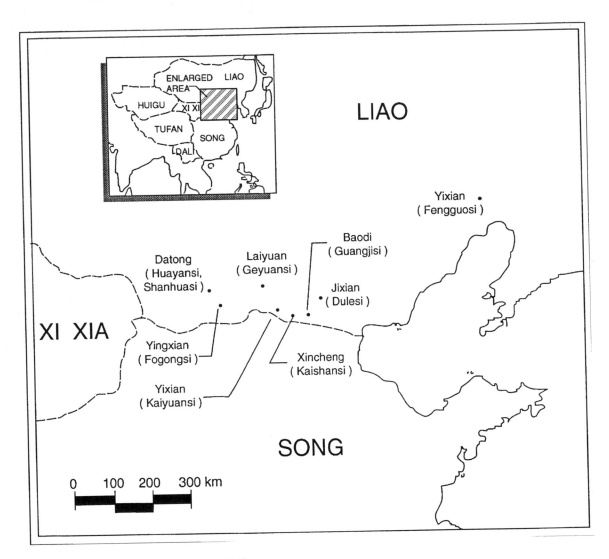

MAP 3. Locations of Liao Timber-Frame Halls

7

Other Liao Buddhist Halls

ONLY ONE OTHER Liao wooden building stands today. Sixty years ago there were five distributed among three monasteries in Hebei province. None of these buildings, however, unlike Guanyin Pavilion, the Daxiongbao halls, or Ying-xian Muta, is outstanding or unique. Nor were they constructed so early in the Liao period that they are best associated with Chinese architecture of the tenth century. Rather, it is through these buildings that one sees the broader picture of Liao architecture spread through the empire to *xian* less touched by imperial gifts (Table 3 and Map 3).

GUANGJI MONASTERY

Guangjisi in Baodixian, Hebei, is the monastery that was brought to Liang Sicheng's attention by the principal of the school into which Dulesi had been converted. Liang's first attempt to see old buildings at Guangjisi, known in the 1930s as Great West Monastery (Xidasi), was unsuccessful. He fared better the second time, but the journey through Baodi began with his inauspicious descent from a public bus into a market of thousands of pigs. Although only about 35 kilometers from Jixian and 90 from

FIGURE 149. Sandashi Hall, Guangji Monastery, Baodixian, Hebei, 1025 (destroyed). [After Liang Sicheng, "Baodixian Guangjisi . . . ," pl. 10]

Beijing, Guangjisi was so remotely situated that Liang decided to include a sketch map of the road from Dulesi to Guangjisi in his publication.[1]

In her biography of Liang Sicheng and his wife, Lin Huiyin, Wilma Fairbank describes the arrival of the research institute in Baodi:

> There, after an arduous journey from Peking, Sicheng and his party found the Kuang-chi Ssu [Guangjisi] to be another Liao temple, as the teacher [the principal of Dulesi] had guessed. The big brackets and deep eaves immediately identified it as having features of the Liao period. They came upon its main Hall . . . only to find that the Hall had been filled with hay to supply the horses of a cavalry unit stationed in the town. A group of workers were stacking hay, and the expedition could barely see the building through the dust-filled air. . . . In the haystacks were a number of stelae, the most important of which was dated 1025.[2]

The words Liang used to describe what he saw as he approached Sandashi Hall were typical charac-

terizations of Liao structure: somber architecture with heavy, dark, overhanging eaves (fig. 149). It was the one old building in a ruined temple complex, but it was only the second such structure Liang had seen. Moreover, it was clearly a Liao hall, with a date and historical sources to prove it.

History

Baodixian zhi (Record of Baodixian) is the only local record in which information about Guangjisi is available. From the six lines in this text we learn that the monastery stands on Xi (West) Avenue, that it has a hall to the three great ones, that the three images in this hall were repaired by Liu Yuan (a famous sculptor of the Yuan dynasty), and that there were twenty-one stelae at the monastery, nine of them from the Liao period.[3] Guangjisi is one of two monasteries shown in the illustration of the walled town in the Qianlong-period *Baodixian zhi* (fig. 150). It faces south toward what could plausibly have been called West Avenue, with the temples to the city god (Huangchengdi) and the war god (Guandi) on its east and west. The position of the monastery is not unlike the position of Dulesi in Jizhou (see fig. 25). Besides passages in this gazetteer, the history of Guangji Monastery is known primarily from the stelae Liang Sicheng found in 1932.

Unlike the sites of most other Liao monasteries, Baodi was not even a town during the Tang dynasty. It gained stature between 923 and 926 when it was realized that the site was a repository of salt. Its name at the time, Xincang (New Storage), is a reference to its role in the salt industry. The character "Bao" in the *xian* name means "precious" and is also a reference to the content of the local soil. This territory was part of the prefectures of North China held by the Qidan since the 930s. It became a *xian* only in 1171, at which time the territory was in Jin hands. By the twentieth century, Baodi's importance as a salt center had declined and today it is a

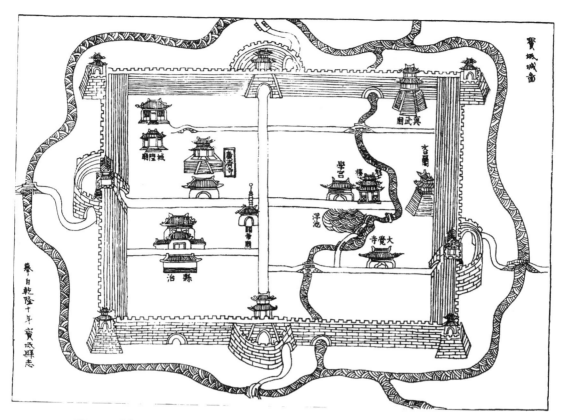

FIGURE 150. Picture of the Walled Town of Baodi. [Cai and Hong, *Baodixian zhi*, *juan* 1/2b–3a; after Taipei reprint, pp. 118–119]

dusty small town within the jurisdiction of Tianjin-shi (the city limits of Tianjin).

Like so many East Asian monasteries, the initial construction of Guangjisi was tied to the life of one monk. His name was Hongyan and he probably came from a town in the vicinity of Beijing.[4] Under his supervision and with the aid of locals, construction of this monastery commenced in 1005, but Hongyan was an old man before even the Main Hall was completed. Hongyan passed on the task of monastery building, including what seems to have been some repair, to a disciple named Daoguang. The monastery came to be established under the leader-ship of Daoguang and a second monk named Yi-hong through the generosity of one Wang Wenxi and others. Dozens of craftsmen were engaged in the actual labor. Some of these craftsmen were cited on stelae, but their names have become illegible.

According to the inscription on the oldest stele, from the Liao period, during the first year of construction all the labor involved "greater carpentry" (*damuzuo*). The second year, work was devoted to ceramic decoration, walls and windows, painting, Buddhist imagery, and wall painting. The order is logical: it is the same sequence in which construction is discussed in the *Yingzao fashi*. Yet this is the

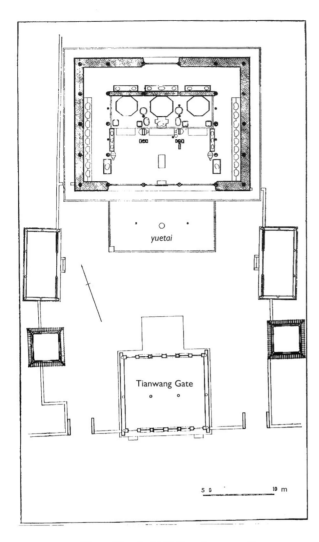

FIGURE 151. Plan of Sandashi Hall and surrounding buildings, Guangji Monastery, in 1932. [After *Liang Sicheng wenji*, vol. 1, pl. 2]

only Liao stele that explicitly provides this kind of detail. In the third year, sculpture in the Shanmen was completed. That year—1025, fifth year of the *taiping* period of the reign of Emperor Sheng-zong—is considered the date of the Sandashi Hall.[5] Three other dates, 1031, 1035, and 1059, are carved on the same stele. The last date, fifty-four years after initial construction, is believed to be the year in which the monastery was officially established by Emperor Daozong. The long construction period may be the reason the inscription uses the word *xiu* (repair) more than once in reference to construction—a hiatus in building could have necessitated repair before a structure was ever completed.

The next oldest stele (found by Liang at Guang-jisi) was dated 1534. Its inscription described the state of decay that had overtaken Sandashi Hall. In addition to repair of the Main Hall, 500 *luohan* were painted on the walls and five Buddhist images and two guardian kings were repaired over a five-year period. One of the monks involved in this repair work, Yuancheng, was from Panshan in Jizhou prefecture near Dulesi. A master carpenter, master mason, beam replacers, and modelers are all mentioned by name in the inscription.

The history of Guangjisi is also recorded on a stele of 1581. It relates that a tremendous amount of fighting took place in Baodi during the Liao-Jin transition. It is also the source of information about a timber pagoda that rose 180 *chi* (about half the height of Yingxian Muta) behind Sandashi Hall. This pagoda had been built and had suffered destruction under the Liao, had been repaired by the Jin, but had later burned. By the end of the six-teenth century, Baoxiang Pavilion stood in its place. The *ge* is mentioned again in a stele of 1745 which says that the structure rose several tens of *chi*. Liang could find traces of neither a pagoda nor a replacement *ge* behind the main hall, but the stele con-

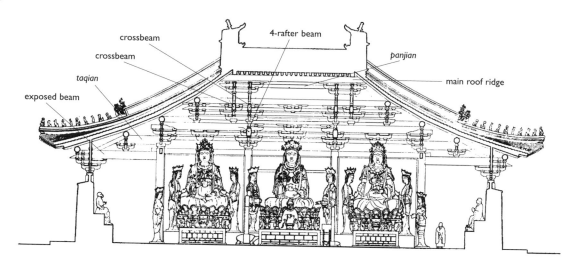

FIGURE 152. Drawing of frontal section of Sandashi Hall, Guangji Monastery. [After *Liang Sicheng wenji*, vol. 1, pl. 7]

firms that like most of the other Liao monasteries at Guangjisi, a multilevel structure had stood along the main building axis.

Repairs were continued at the end of the Ming dynasty in 1640 by a monk named Xuancheng through a donation from a man identified as Zhang Zhiyi in a stele inscription of 1829. That inscription further records a patron named Zhang Shanshi who contributed 2,000 *liang* of silver to the project.[6] This gift provided sufficient funds to repair wood, straighten columns, gild images, and add eighteen *luohan*. The last recorded repair was in 1872. When Liang Sicheng visited, he felt the monastery was in great need of repair.[7]

Sandashi Hall

From all indications, Sandashi Hall was the only Liao building at Guangji Monastery that survived into the twentieth century, probably that survived to the Qing or even the Ming period. It was a five-by-

four-bay hall whose base measured 24.5 by 18 meters (fig. 151). Support was by eighteen perimeter pillars and ten interior pillars, the latter group arranged with respect to an altar rather than along lines determined by the exterior columns, standard in Liao construction. The hall had three six-panel bays of doors across the front and a central bay of doors at the rear. A somewhat unusual feature was three bays of wall in the interior behind the three images that gave the hall its name. A *yuetai* projected 7.67 meters southward from the central three bays.

The Sandashi—Three Great Ones—were bodhisattvas. Each was seated on an octagonal platform that also supported a pair of bodhisattvas facing inward at the east and west ends (fig. 152). The row of bodhisattvas, each flanked by two bodhisattvas facing him, was the same arrangement (though with different iconography) found in the Seven Buddhas Hall at Fengguosi, built about fifteen years earlier. It may have been a preferred Liao arrangement that was compatible with different iconographic schemes. The three bodhisattvas on octagonal lotus platforms, six attendant bodhisattvas, and a small seated deity in the center front were raised together on a rectangular platform that spanned the three central interior bays between the second and third pillar rows from back to front of the hall (see fig. 151).[8] Additional bodhisattvas flanked and faced this group. Nine *luohan* were placed along each of the side walls and guardian kings protected the four corners—again, common imagery in Liao main halls. In all, forty-five images were in the hall in the 1930s. According to Liang Sicheng they were not so uniformly Tang in character as the sculpture in Guanyin Pavilion. Rather, he believed he was looking at important evidence of a specific workshop of the Yuan period.

Indeed, *Baodixian zhi* informs its reader that Liu Yuan, perhaps the most famous Chinese sculptor in the service of Khubilai Khan, was responsible for repair of sculpture in Sandashi Hall.[9] The same information is related in biographies of the Yuan sculptor who was a native of Baodi. The records say, further, that Liu Yuan "sculpted" a set of the three great ones and attendants.[10] None of the stelae found by Liang nor the historical record notes repairs.[11] What the fate of Guangjisi might have been in the Yuan period had the court sculptor not been a native of Baodi cannot be known. Still, the involvement of the famous craftsman who worked for the Mongolian rulers of China is also proof of imperial sanction, if not patronage, of the monastery during the Yuan dynasty. Unfortunately, when these images were found they were the only ones by Liu Yuan known. So far as can be determined, therefore, nothing by him survives today.

The hall columns exhibited features by now identified as typical of Liao construction and in accordance with *Yingzao fashi*'s dictates. Pillar diame-

ters ranged from 51 centimeters along the exterior to 54 centimeters in the interior, and their heights were between 8.6 and up to 11 times the diameter dimensions. All exterior columns inclined inward slightly and were cut inward at the tops. A few additional posts 0.25 meters in diameter helped support the ceiling between other interior columns.

Like so many of the Liao timber buildings, Sandashi Hall has been the subject of only one serious study; it is also one of the five buildings mentioned at the beginning of this chapter that were available for investigation sixty years ago but are now gone. (Puxiange of Shanhuasi, since it has been rebuilt, is not included among the five.) Thus Liang Sicheng's assertion that among the varieties of bracketing at Sandashi Hall—inside and out, above and between columns, and at the corners—not one can be found that does not exist at either the Dulesi Shanmen or Guanyin Pavilion is a statement of extreme importance.[12] It is the kind of statement about architecture associated with a certain time period and a certain people that one wants to believe; and even though Liang had seen only two Liao buildings when he wrote it, one has little reason to doubt him.

The rationale of Liang's observation is that a building with a date fifty years after the Dulesi halls and only 35 kilometers south (as the crow flies) must share many architectural features. Yet rarely does one find adequate proof for tenth- or eleventh-century Chinese buildings. One noteworthy feature of Sandashi Hall observed by Liang was the *yuanyang jiaoshou* bracket arm. He did not know at the time that it was a common detail he would observe in Liao architecture at Datong several years later (see fig. 123).

The ceiling frame of Sandashi Hall was completely exposed. Six types of beams or rafters and side supports like *taqian* and extension beams were

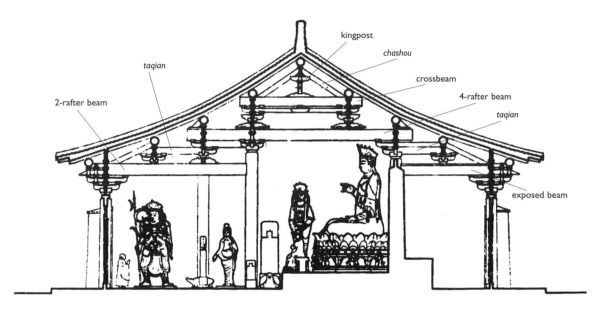

FIGURE 153. Side sectional drawing of Sandashi Hall, Guangji Monastery. [After Liang Sicheng, "Baodixian Guangjisi . . . ," pl. 5]

used. The beams and rafters, named by position and span, are labeled in Figures 152 and 153. When Liang Sicheng measured timbers at Dulcsi's two Liao-period buildings and here, he came up with another remarkable observation: although no two timbers were found to be exactly the same size, the variation in dimensions was amazingly minimal. Furthermore, the heights (between 0.25 and 0.205 m) and the widths (between 0.165 and 0.155 m) of all timbers corresponded closely to the second of the eight *Yingzao fashi* grades. Liang suggested that the discrepancies, although slight, may have been motivated by the craftsmen's desire not to waste wood.[13]

Further description of Guangjisi would only repeat information presented earlier in the discussion of other Liao wooden buildings. In fact, having examined eleven buildings at six other monasteries, we have seen enough evidence to conclude that certain buildings can be described as typically Liao or typically eleventh century, and Sandashi Hall of Guangjisi is one of them.

KAIYUAN MONASTERY

Another site where timber architecture built during the Liao dynasty still stood in the 1930s is the northeast corner of Yixian in Hebei province, a location better known for the western group of tombs of Qing emperors and, more recently, for the ruins of the capital of the Eastern Zhou state of Yan. Three Liao halls that remained at the Kaiyuan Monastery in the 1930s when Liu Dunzhen, Chen Mingda,

FIGURE 154. Pilu Hall, Kaiyuan Monastery, Yixian, Hebei, early twelfth century (?) (destroyed). [After Liu Dunzhen, "Hebeisheng xibu . . . ," pl. 2, *ding*]

Pilu Hall

Although structurally it could never be characterized as grand (Liu Dunzhen in fact describes it as severe),[16] Pilu Hall (fig. 154) had the most complicated plan of Kaiyuansi's three Liao buildings (fig. 155). The hall itself was strikingly simple. Pilu Hall was three-bays-square and perfectly square at the base. The only other example of a square hall that survives from the medieval period in China is the earlier version of Mizong Hall from the Tang monastery Qinglongsi, discussed in Chapter 3 (see fig. 59). Like the Tang hall, although the base dimensions were identical in either direction, the central bay was nevertheless longer than the ones that flanked it. Pilu Hall of Kaiyuan Monastery is also the first of the Liao buildings investigated thus far that was supported exclusively by perimeter columns, a structural feature shared by the other two halls from the monastery. The precedent for this extremely simple structure is found also in the eighth century, at the Main Hall of Nanchan Monastery, and was shown in Chapter 3 to have persisted to the tenth century. The importance of Pilu Hall, in contrast to two buildings that once flanked it, was expressed by the prominent *yuetai* and approach ramp. The *yuetai* is only a few meters shorter than the hall in any dimension.

Pilu Hall had several unusual, possibly unique, features. One was the use of octagonal columns. Octagonal columns are found in early Chinese architecture: the interior columns of the late Han tomb at Yi'nan are one of the most famous examples.[17] A more likely source of the Pilu Hall columns is found closer to home in the "Thunder Cave" of Yunju Monastery at Fangshan, another recipient of Liao patronage (only brick pagodas survive today) in the same region of Hebei province (fig. 156).[18] It has always been assumed that timber

and Mo Zongjiang visited the region during two different trips have since been destroyed.

As its name tells us, this monastery was one of the many established or renamed during the *kaiyuan* era (713–742) of the Tang dynasty. The three halls seen by members of the Society for Research in Chinese Architecture had been repaired in the decades before the collapse of the Liao empire. Despite repairs during each subsequent dynasty, the structures retained enough early-twelfth-century features to be studied as Liao buildings.[14] The layout of the three buildings is unique among monastery architecture known from Liao or Song. They stood almost side-by-side facing south.[15] Let us begin with the middle, and most complex, structure. It is the one likely to have been on a main north-south building axis.

architecture was replicated in underground tombs of more permanent construction materials. Replication in a Buddhist worship cave is equally plausible. After examining the significance of the octagon in Liao construction in Parts Two and Three, one may decide that the octagonal columns were symbolic. The octagonal columns joined a magnificent octagonal *zaojing* in the small Pilu Hall to create an interior beauty of which there was no hint from outside (fig. 157). This discrepancy between a lackluster exterior and what awaits the devotee inside has also been shown to be a feature of Liao timber construction.

Guanyin Hall

East of Pilu Hall was a building dedicated to Guanyin. Guanyin Hall too was square with a single-eaved, hip-gable roof. Again the central bay on each side of the approximately 9-meter-square hall was the longest, and in that bay was an intercolumnar bracket set (fig. 158). The bracket sets are difficult to see in what, to my knowledge, is the only photograph of the hall's exterior, but they were distinct: projection was only perpendicular to the building plane, and the brace known as *timu* was placed between the cap block and bracket arm, a scheme described at other Liao buildings discussed earlier. The corner brackets had both *timu* and *hua gong*. Such bracketing was used at Haihui Hall of Huayansi, as well, and can be found on Liao brick pagodas in several places in Liaoning and the Inner Mongolian Autonomous Region.[19] The bracket sets have three transversal arms that support either braces or tiebeams depending on their location on the exterior. Another unusual structural feature of Guanyin Hall is a *mojiao liang*, a rafter that spans the interior hall corner (fig. 159). This detail is present in at least three Yuan-period buildings—Ciyun Pavilion in nearby Dingxingxian, Hebei, and, ac-

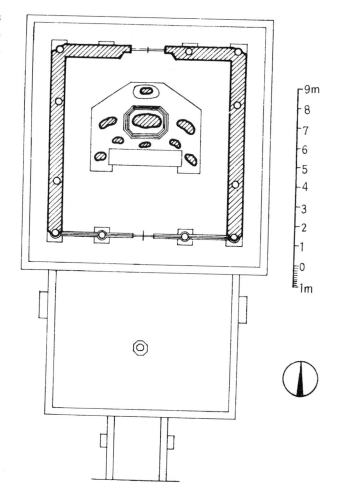

FIGURE 155. Plan of Pilu Hall, Kaiyuan Monastery. [After *Liu Dunzhen wenji*, vol. 2, p. 183]

FIGURE 156. Interior of "Thunder Cave," Yunju Monastery, Fangshan, Hebei province, Sui dynasty. [After "Yunju Temple," Beijing Slide Studio, slide 2]

cording to Liu Dunzhen, Shenggu Temple and Guandi Temple—but in no post-Yuan construction and in no earlier examples except Guanyin Hall of Kaiyuan Monastery.[20] Again, a fantastic *zaojing* was sunk into the ceiling directly above the head of the deity in the otherwise modest Guanyin Hall.

Yaoshi Hall

The hall to the Buddha Yaoshi was west of Pilu Hall. Its simple, hipped roof and front position among the three surviving monastery halls may be reason to suggest it was the main one. Liu Dunzhen, however, believed the differences might mean that Yaoshi Hall was not built at the same time as the other two halls.[21] Although it certainly was not a grand hall by Liao or any other medieval

Chinese standard (fig. 160), some of the wooden details of Yaoshi Hall were more complex than those of the buildings dedicated to Pilu and Guanyin. The exterior bracket sets were of the 5-*puzuo* variety and braces were placed directly on the cap block, but unlike Pilu Hall there was an intercolumnar set for each bay. The central bay of Yaoshi Hall contains the only Liao example of upper and lower *panjian* (braces). Yet as has been the case for other apparently unique details of Liao construction, this formation is described in the *Yingzao fashi*.[22] *Tuanfeng panjian*, as the formation is called, is thus another example of the Liao use of features of Chinese construction that either do not survive or were never actually constructed in Chinese territory.

FIGURE 157 (top). *Zaojing* of Pilu Hall, Kaiyuan Monastery. [After Liu Dunzhen, "Hebeisheng xibu . . . ," pl. 4, *jia*]

FIGURE 158 (above). Guanyin Hall, Kaiyuan Monastery, Yixian, Hebei, early twelfth century (?) (destroyed). [After Liu Dunzhen, "Hebeisheng xibu . . . ," pl. 4, *bing*]

FIGURE 159. *Mojiao* rafter, Guanyin Hall, Kaiyuan Monastery. [After Liu Dunzhen, "Hebeisheng xibu . . . ," pl. 5, *bing*]

KAISHANSI MAIN HALL

The only standing Liao hall (as opposed to gate) for which the term "extraordinary" cannot be argued is the Main Hall of Kaishan Monastery in Xincheng, Hebei. Xincheng is just under 200 kilometers from Laiyuan, site of Geyuan Monastery, and would have been no more than 25 kilometers from Kaiyuansi. Based on extant wooden architecture, monasteries along the strip of Hebei that surrounds the southern and southwestern boundaries of Beijingshi (city) today seem to have been less innovative or creative, and perhaps less well funded, than the buildings of Datong or the Muta or Guanyin Pavilion. Much timber architecture is, of course, missing, including buildings that would have stood

alongside the Liao brick pagodas at monasteries like Yunjusi (mentioned earlier). Here the Main Hall of Kaishansi is discussed as an example of the main worship space of a Liao monastery in a small town that seems not to have gained the attention of the imperial government (figs. 161 and 162).

The main source for Kaishansi's history is *Xinchengxian zhi*.[23] Only one stele is mentioned in the single modern report on the building, and it provides little information.[24] From the two sources one learns that Kaishansi was built in the Tang dynasty before the *xian* town. By the middle of the sixteenth century, the monastery had become very large. As for the town itself, it had been part of the state of Yan during the Warring States period (403–221 B.C.)—the remains of whose capital were men-

FIGURE 160. Yaoshi Hall, Kaiyuan Monastery, Yixian, Hebei (destroyed). [After Liu Dunzhen, "Hebeisheng xibu . . . ," pl. 5, *ding*]

tioned earlier as part of Yi prefecture—and part of Zhuojun (commandery) in the Han dynasty. The official beginning of what was to become Xinchengxian was the year 832. A new city, literally "*xincheng*," was built (under Later Tang rule [923–936] during the period of the Five Dynasties) in the southern part of this territory in 929, the recorded date when the city was walled. Xincheng was part of Zhuozhou, one of the sixteen prefectures ceded to Liao in the 930s. In the transport of tribute between Song and Liao, emissaries passed through Xincheng. Although it was a place of potential conflict, war did not break out in the region until it was attacked by the Jin between 1123 and 1125. Initially Qi Yingtao suggested the date 1004–1123 for the main hall—the parameters of the beginning of peace and

prosperity in the region and its fall to Jin—but eventually the year 1033 was discovered written on a wooden member.[25]

Kaishansi stood in the northeast corner of the walled town. The fact that it was known by locals as "Dasi" is the only clue to its possible location on the map of Xinchengxian published in the late Qing local record (fig. 163). At the intersection of Dajie (Main Street) and Great East Avenue is Dasi Alley, the most likely location of the monastery. A second possibility is that it is the monastery indicated just south of Great East Avenue.

The main hall, Daxiongbaodian, of Kaishan Monastery is a five-by-three-bay building raised on a 1.11-meter-high platform of base dimensions 30.39 by 18.49 meters. Like the majority of Liao main

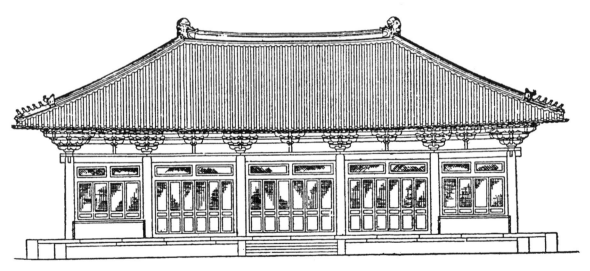

FIGURE 161 (top). Main Hall, Kaishan Monastery, Xincheng, Hebei, 1033. [Steinhardt photograph]
FIGURE 162 (above). Line drawing of Main Hall, Kaishan Monastery. [After Qi Yingtao, ". . . Kaishansi," p. 25]

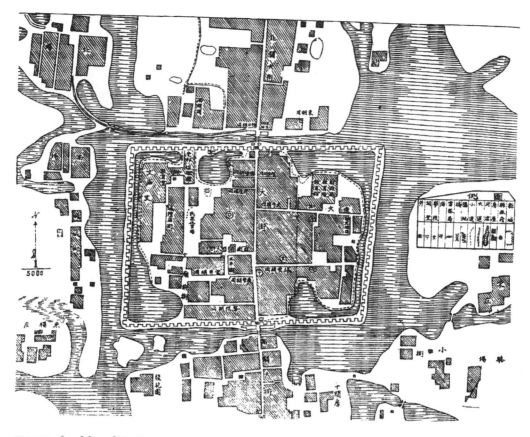

FIGURE 163. Map of Xinchengxian and its vicinity. [*Xinchengxian zhi*, first plan, between pp. 100 and 101]

halls, it faces south; and like all the Liao main halls, it is fronted by a *yuetai*, in this case 27.61 by 11.37 meters. The eave pillars across the front facade are 1.1 meters thick at the base (the same measurement as the height of the platform), rise toward the east and west sides of the building, and have entasis. Pillars are implanted into nearly square stone bases. The distance between pillars across the front and back building facades is widest between the central two columns. The exterior pillars *(jin zhu)* across the back incline inward about 10 centimeters (just under 2 percent of their 12.08-m heights) and the exterior side pillars incline 6.5 centimeters, or about 1.3

percent of their heights. At the Kaishansi Main Hall, exterior side pillars and those across the front and back, except for those on either side of the central bays, incline in a second direction: toward the center of the building plane. This double inclination has been noted by Qi Yingtao as a common feature in pre-Yuan timber architecture. He has observed it at Daxiongbao Hall of Fengguosi (see fig. 90), at the mid-eleventh-century Holy Mother Hall (see fig. 211) built by the Northern Song at the Jin Shrines, and at the Mituo Hall of Chongfusi (see fig. 221) from the Jin period. In other words, the feature was not universal but can be found in architecture of Chinese and non-Chinese patronage in North and South China. The two-directional inclination of pillars is not described in the *Yingzao fashi*.[26]

Four varieties of bracketing are employed on the exterior of Kaishansi Main Hall. The length of bracketing in comparison to the height of the hall columns has been measured as 33.6 percent of the column height, or 41.8 percent if one includes in the bracket-set length the span up to the tiebeams. The ratio is less than that of Tang halls like the East Hall of Foguangsi, but extremely large nevertheless. The rise of the roof is 1:3.9, close to the specifications for a *tingtang* in the *Yingzao fashi*. The sides of Kaishansi Main Hall's roof exhibit Liao examples of the feature known as *tuishan*, a pushing outward toward the side. Not found at the Shanmen of Dulesi or at Sandashi Hall, *tuishan* is employed in the Daxiongbao Hall of Fengguosi and at Shanhuasi Main Hall. It has a limited life in Jin architecture but becomes increasingly common in the Ming dynasty and later.[27]

The original arrangement of images inside the main hall cannot be proved because whatever remained in 1928 when the building became a Sun Yatsen educational hall was destroyed at that time. It appears, however, that the main devotional image was Guanyin; on either side of the bodhisattva were four esoteric bodhisattvas; *luohan* stood at the sides of the hall. Today the Main Hall of the former Kaishansi is a granary. Locals say that its walls bear old paintings which were covered by cement during the Cultural Revolution.[28]

THE LIAO TIMBER BUILDING:
AN OVERVIEW

Less has been said about Kaishan Monastery's Main Hall than about any of the other thirteen Liao wooden buildings (fourteen counting Huayansi Main Hall). We have considered enough details of Liao timber architecture that discussion of this hall would be largely repetitive. Yet to the extent that a building among the illustrious group that are Liao can be called standard, Kaishansi's hall is more standard than most. Thus it will serve here as a focal point to characterize the architectural structure of a Liao timber-frame hall and set it apart from other Chinese buildings. Words like "grand," "powerful," "awe-inspiring," and "somber" have been used freely in the preceding pages to refer to many of the fourteen wooden buildings discussed thus far. Justification for such praise is found in the way the building parts are joined and in the relationship between a Liao building and its architectural space and environment.

Foundation and Stairs

Every Liao timber building is elevated on an earthen foundation, above which is placed a stone platform approached by stairs. Writing of Guanyin Pavilion in 1932, Liang pointed out that the stone foundation could be thought of as the transition between the ground and the structure.[29] The stone foundation might also be interpreted as the manmade material that separates earth and wood, two of the five fundamental elements of the traditional Chinese universal order.[30] Although, in general, the foundation platform is higher for more important structures, no formula for the height of the platform compared to the height of the building is apparent. There are two general points to be made about Liao-Jin foundation platforms: in important buildings they rise approximately half the height of pillars; in middle and lower-ranking halls, they rise one-third to one-fifth the height. In every Liao case the heights exceed the prescriptions for foundations in the *Yingzao fashi*. Unlike Song buildings, foundations of front, middle, and back halls in Liao were of similar heights. Finally, both the Liao and Song systems were markedly different from the Qing, for which, according to the architectural manual *Gongbu gongcheng zuofa zeli* of 1736, the platform was to be one-fifteenth the height of the building.[31]

The approach to a Liao building is often a *yuetai* (literally "moon platform") that joins steps of an approach ramp to the platform in front of the hall. Occasionally *yuetai* also are found behind it. Often stairs lead to the hall from the two sides of the *yuetai*. Even when no *yuetai* is constructed in front of a timber hall, stairs or a ramp are still necessary to access it. The magnificent Yingxian Timber Pagoda—built, it has been suggested, in conjunction with the demise of a Liao emperor—was raised on a double-layer platform. Four *yuetai*, each with a pair of side stairs, gave access to the first story of the hall and an additional *yuetai* with side stairs led to the main entrance (see figs. 100 and 102).

Although *yuetai* were used in each of the Liao buildings except the Dulesi Shanmen and Haihui Hall and the Sutra Library of Huayansi, they are not so prevalent in medieval Chinese architecture in general. In a survey of forty-two buildings, Chai Zejun found *yuetai* at one out of four Tang buildings, none at three Five Dynasties halls, none at sixteen Song halls, but at sixteen of nineteen from the Liao-Jin period. From the Yuan period on, the *yuetai* was common.[32]

Ground Plans and Pillar Arrangement

Figure 164 shows the ground plans of fifteen Liao (-Jin) halls. No two of them are exactly alike. They range from the nine-by-five-bay Daxiongbao Hall of Fengguosi to several three-by-three-bay halls and a three-by-two-bay pavilion. Several of the small structures have plans that are closer to square, but the base dimensions have no relation to the number of bays across the front or in depth. (That is, a three-bay-square hall is not necessarily a perfect square at the base, nor is a square base an indication that the number of bays will be the same in width and in

depth.) Somewhat unusual are the Main Hall of Geyuansi and Pilu and Guanyin halls of Kaiyuansi, all longer in depth than across the front.

One of the most notable features of the plans is the elimination of pillars from the hall interiors. This aspect of construction was already present at the Main Hall of Foguangsi (see fig. 66). At every Liao one-story hall, anywhere from several interior columns to entire rows of them are missing from what would normally complete a grid defined by the exterior side pillars of the hall. One purpose of the elimination of interior columns observed at Guanyinge, at the Daxiongbao halls, and at less spectacular structures, is to make unobstructed room for statuary. But there was a result of the elimination that was not anticipated by Tang construction: structural detail would need to compensate for pillars so that an intricate ceiling could be supported above an empty space. (Sometimes, as we have seen at Geyuansi Main Hall, pillars had to be added or reinforced in order for the building to remain standing.) The elimination of interior columns would continue through the Yuan period, by which time buildings like the three halls that survive from the original central axis of the Daoist monastery Yonglegong at the southern tip of Shanxi are impressively devoid of interior columns.[33] The *Yingzao fashi* specifies four floor plans for *diantang*, or high-ranking halls. Known as *fenxin doudi cao*, *jinxiang doudi cao*, *dan cao*, and *shuang cao*, interior columns are eliminated in every one (fig. 165 and see fig. 67).

Absence of interior columns is also a feature of the plans of Moni Hall of Longxing Monastery (see fig. 187) and Holy Mother Hall of the Jin Shrines (see fig. 209), both eleventh-century Song buildings that are discussed in the next chapter. In the Ming and Qing periods, however, interior construction would change: complete column grids would occur with more frequency, especially in imperial

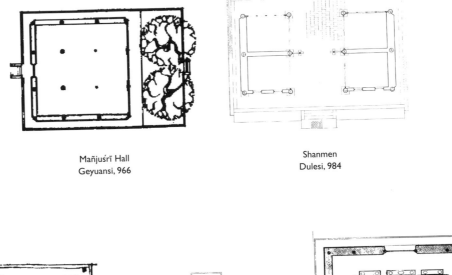

Mañjuśrī Hall
Geyuansi, 966

Shanmen
Dulesi, 984

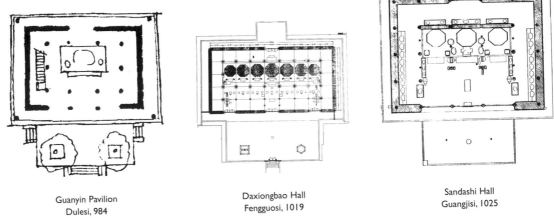

Guanyin Pavilion
Dulesi, 984

Daxiongbao Hall
Fengguosi, 1019

Sandashi Hall
Guangjisi, 1025

FIGURE 164. Plans of the fourteen Liao halls and Daxiongbao Hall of Huayan Monastery. [Taken from same sources as indicated in separate publication of each plan plus Zhang Yuhuan, *Zhongguo . . . jianzhu . . .* , pp. 74–75 (Shanmen, Dulesi; Main Hall, Kaishansi); *Liu Dunzhen wenji*, vol. 2, pp. 184–185 (Guanyin Hall and Yaoshi Hall, Kaiyuansi)]

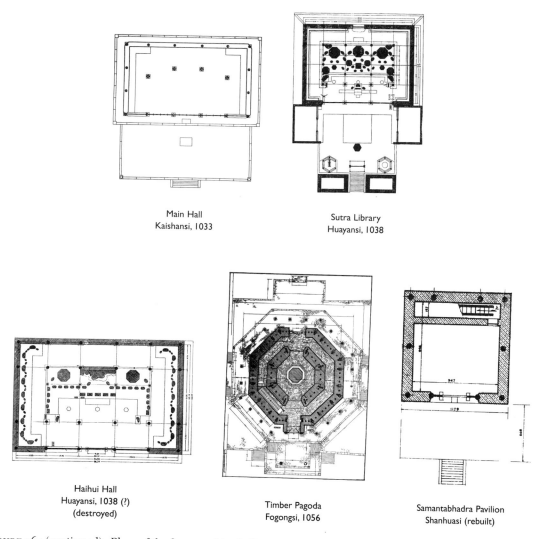

Main Hall
Kaishansi, 1033

Sutra Library
Huayansi, 1038

Haihui Hall
Huayansi, 1038 (?)
(destroyed)

Timber Pagoda
Fogongsi, 1056

Samantabhadra Pavilion
Shanhuasi (rebuilt)

FIGURE 164 (continued). Plans of the fourteen Liao halls and Daxiongbao Hall of Huayan Monastery.

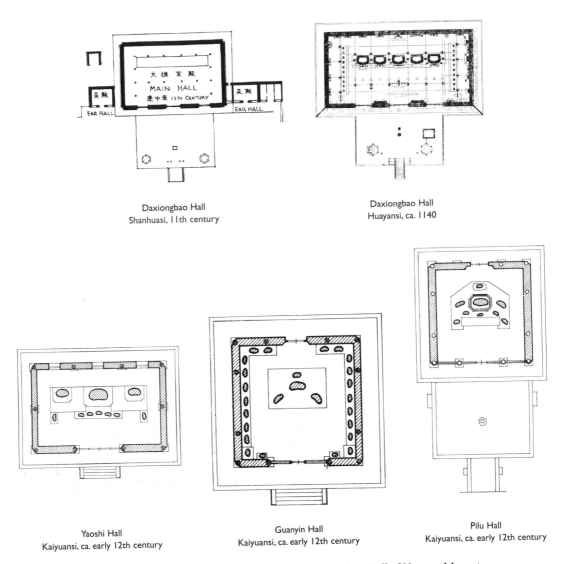

Daxiongbao Hall
Shanhuasi, 11th century

大雄宝殿
MAIN HALL
遼中葉 11TH CENTURY

EAR HALL

EAR HALL

朵殿

朵殿

Daxiongbao Hall
Huayansi, ca. 1140

Yaoshi Hall
Kaiyuansi, ca. early 12th century

Guanyin Hall
Kaiyuansi, ca. early 12th century

Pilu Hall
Kaiyuansi, ca. early 12th century

FIGURE 164 (continued). Plans of the fourteen Liao halls and Daxiongbao Hall of Huayan Monastery.

buildings, including the main halls of the Forbidden City and sacrificial halls at royal tombs.

An unusual feature of the plans of surviving Liao halls, as noted earlier, is the number that are longer in depth than width. This configuration breaks with the standard Chinese convention that the front of a hall is longer than it is deep. The three Liao examples of longer-depth halls are Pilu and Guanyin halls of Kaiyuansi and the Main Hall at Geyuansi. These buildings do, however, conform to other standard features: at every hall the central bay or bays across the front—and in most cases the central side bays (or bay when the number of bays is odd)—are the widest; the measurements of the bays on either side of the central bay decrease in length toward the outer ends of the hall; and symmetrically positioned bays are the same length. Earlier we referred to the central bay of a Chinese building as *dangxin jian* or *ming jian*. Those that flank it are *ci jian*. Next to *ci jian* are *shao jian*. Then come *ci-shao jian*, and finally, in an eleven-bay hall, the widest described in the *Yingzao fashi*, the outermost bays across the front would be called *jin jian*.

Certain features of the pillars of Liao halls are standard in Chinese construction from the Tang through Yuan periods: widening at the center and tapering off at the ends of pillars (*juansha*, sometimes translated as "entasis"); a slight increase in height of pillars across the front facade of a building from those that enclose *dangxin jian* to the outermost ones (*shengqi*, or "rise"); and a slight inclination of exterior pillars toward the center of the building (sometimes called "batter").[34] In pre-Yuan architecture, the outermost exterior pillars, in addition, incline toward the inner facade bays. (The same feature has been noted at Kaishansi Main Hall.)[35] The heights of exterior columns compared to interior columns can vary.

Columns of a wooden hall are named according to their positions, as well. The pillars on the interior

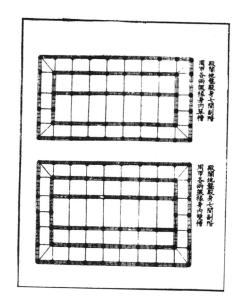

FIGURE 165. *Dan cao* and *shuang cao*. [*Yingzao fashi, juan* 31, 1972 ed., p. 4]

of a building are called *nei zhu*. On the exterior of a building, the two pillars that enclose the central bay (*dangxin jian*) are called *zhong zhu*. Other pillars across the front and back facades of a building, except those at the four corners, are called *yan zhu*, a reference to their important function of supporting the eaves (*yan*). *Jin zhu* also refers to pillars that line the front and back facades of a hall (except at the corners). Side exterior pillars, except those under the corners, are called *shan zhu*. The four corner exterior pillars are called *jiao zhu*.

Bracket Sets

Bracket sets of the Liao period were more complex than any that had preceded them and more diverse than any that would follow. Whereas the most complicated extant ninth-century building had seven types of bracket sets and Zhenguosi's tenth-century Hall of Ten Thousand Buddhas had only three variations, Yingxian Muta had fifty-four and Guan-

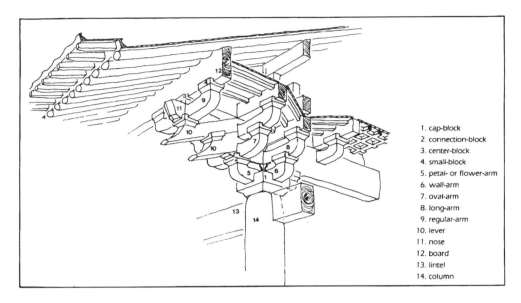

1. cap-block
2. connection-block
3. center-block
4. small-block
5. petal- or flower-arm
6. wall-arm
7. oval-arm
8. long-arm
9. regular-arm
10. lever
11. nose
12. board
13. lintel
14. column

FIGURE 166. Line drawing of bracket set at time of *Yingzao fashi*. [Drawn by Else Glahn; after Steinhardt, *Chinese Traditional Architecture*, p. 124; published with permission of China Institute in America]

yinge had twenty-four. Sometimes the differences between one type and another in a building with so many varieties are minute, but not always.[36] Here we discuss only the names for bracket-set pieces, exceptional types of bracket clusters, and what seem to be standard Liao bracket sets.

Like all Chinese bracket sets, the Liao set is composed of *dou* (blocks) and *gong* (arms). These two terms combine to make the modern word for bracket set, *dougong*. The term used in the *Yingzao fashi* is *puzuo*, which was also employed in combination with a number to designate the rank and associated complexity of a corbel-bracket cluster. In Qing architectural treatises, the term is *doukou*.

Dougong are found above pillars, between pillars, and above corner pillars on the exterior of a building and in the same places on the interior. Each member of this group is named differently. *Zhutou puzuo*, for instance, are pillar-top bracket sets, *bujian puzuo* are intercolumnar bracket sets,

and *zhuanjiao puzuo* are bracket sets above corner pillars. If there is no pillar into which a bracket set can be joined, it must be positioned in a bracket-arm cushion board (*gong dianban*). In discussing different bracketing types, the standard practice is to examine them according to position.

Figure 166 shows the standard elements of a Liao or Song bracket set.[37] By the Liao period, all column-top bracket sets were tenoned (joined without the use of nails) to columns by *ludou* (cap blocks), the largest cap (*dou*) in a bracket cluster. In Liao buildings, sometimes an additional piece called *tailun* is joined between the cap block and the rest of the bracket set (see fig. 122). Bracket arms are fit into the cap block along two planes, perpendicular to the building facade (*hua gong*), literally "flower arms," and parallel to it. The bracket arms that project parallel to the building facade are named according to their position from lowest tier to highest. The lowest is called *nidao gong* (wall arm). Next is *guazi gong* (melon arm), followed by *man gong* (kidney arm) and *ling gong* (order arm). Sometimes these last three arms are referred to as oval arm, long arm, and regular arm, respectively. Adjoined to the uppermost *gong* is a *shuatou* (mocking head), sometimes called the "nose" and in Chinese referred to alternately as the sparrow-, monkey-, or insect-head. By the Liao period, it was common for two cantilevers, or lever arms *(ang)*, to cut through the bracket set. This feature first appeared in bracketing in the Tang dynasty when it was a crucial piece in the support of the structure. By the Ming and Qing periods, cantilevers were often small and purely decorative. Another notable change in bracketing from the Tang period to the Qing is the reduced size of the bracket in proportion to the column on which it sits. Whereas at Foguangsi East Hall the height of the bracket set is half the height of the column—or one-third the base-to-roof height of the structure—in architecture of the Forbidden City the bracket-set to column proportion may be as small as 1:8. Liao-period bracket sets are still functional in all their parts and, although not half the height of the column, much closer to that proportion than 1:8. Perhaps their great variety confirms Liu Zhiping's comment that in the Tang dynasty bracketing was a status symbol.[38]

Like Chinese architectural history in general, the study of bracket sets has been predominantly the work of Chinese and Japanese architectural historians. Occasionally Japanese publications on Chinese architecture apply Japanese terminology for bracket-set components used in Japanese buildings. Figure 167 shows all the bracket-set parts labeled in Figure 166 and more, together with their Chinese, Japanese, and English names.

To understand just how the various pieces are put together, let us examine representative bracketing of high rank (7-*puzuo*) at Dulesi and bracketing of lower status (5-*puzuo*) from Liao buildings in Da-

tong. The justification for using these examples is twofold. First, the investigation of bracket formation during the Liao period began with Liang Sicheng's long article about Dulesi, followed three years later by the longer study of extant architecture in Datong.[39] Bracket sets at the five Liao and several Jin buildings that remain at these sites, therefore, are described, drawn, and photographed in more detail than most sets from buildings studied after them. Second, through a study of the two types, followed by a focus on unique aspects of other bracketing in Liao buildings, one can understand the justification for labeling the bracket clusters at Kaishansi Main Hall "standard."

Where are the twenty-four different bracket-set types at Guanyinge? On the base story exterior, there are four types: pillar top, corner-pillar top, intercolumnar across the front facade, and intercolumnar along the sides. Three kinds of bracket sets are found on the interior base story: atop pillars, above corner pillars, and intercolumnarly. Five more types are found on the exterior of the *pingzuo* level: pillar top, at the corners, intercolumnarly along the center and second bays of the front and back, intercolumnarly at the end bays of the front and back of the *pingzuo* level, and intercolumnarly along its sides. On the interior of the *pingzuo* level there are another five types: atop the pillars of the central bays, atop other pillars except those at the corners, atop corner pillars, intercolumnarly, and intercolumnarly at the end bays atop corner tie-beams. For the upper story exterior, bracket sets are different atop pillars, above corner pillars, and intercolumnarly; on the interior, four different types are found atop the pillars that define the central bay on the north side, atop other pillars, between the columns that define the central bay on the north side, and at the corners. From these twenty-four positions on three building levels, it is not difficult to see how a nine-level structure like the Muta could have

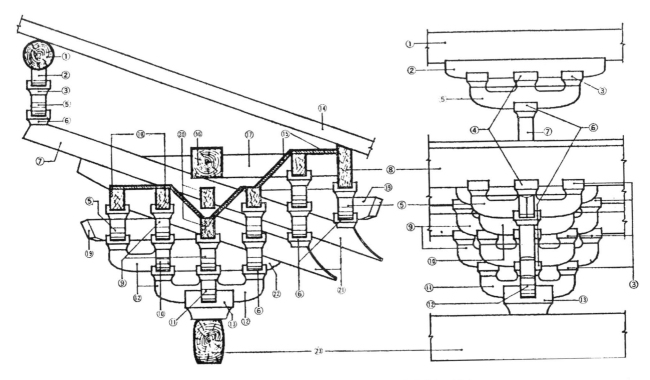

1. under-eaves purlin (*xia ping tuan; irimoya keta*)
2. strut beneath purlin and above bracket set (*timu; jitsu hijiki*)
3. cap (*[san]dou; to*)
4. additional cap on transversal bracket arm (*jixin dou; to*)
5. order arm (*ling gong; hakari hijiki*)
6. alternate cap (*jiaohu dou; to*)
7. tail rafter (*tiaohan; odaruki-shiri*)
8. pulling-the-eaves tiebeam (*liaoyan fang; hisashi no marugeta*)
9. kidney (second-level) bracket arm (*man gong; nichō no hijiki*)
10. melon arm (*guazi gong; ichichō no hakari hijiki*)
11. *nidao* bracket arm (*nidao gong; kabetsu hijiki*)
12. transversal bracket arm (*hua gong; tesaki hōkō no hijiki*)
13. cap block (*ludou; daito*)
14. rafter (*chuan; daruki*)
15. rafter-covering board (*zheyan ban; nokikō tenjō*)
16. pressing tiebeam (*yacao fang; kumimono ō[shi]*)
17. underneath tiebeam head (*chenfang tou; shinhō kashira*)
18. *luohan* tiebeam (*luohan fang; tōshi hijiki*)
19. mocking head (*shuatou; moku[ki] hana*)
20. pillar-top tiebeam (*zhutou fang; keta/toshi hijiki*)
21. lower cantilever (*xia ang; odaruki*)
22. flower-headed strut (*huatouzi; uyū*)
23. penetrating tiebeam (*lan'e [also architrave]; kashira nuki*)

FIGURE 167. Line drawing of sections of bracket set at time of *Yingzao fashi* with English, Chinese, and Japanese names of components. [After Tanaka, *Chūgoku kenchiku no rekishi*, p. 176; published with permission of Tanaka Tan]

fifty-four variations. The subtleties of most of the changes—fewer or more bracket arms, for example—do not alter structure. Such differentiation is probably more a credit to the ingenuity of craftsmen of these Liao buildings than to the structural necessity of one bracket arm more or less.

The exterior bracket sets across the front facade of the lower story of Guanyinge can be described as follows (see figs. 37 and 38). A cap block (*ludou*) is lodged directly above the top of the pillar. Four tiers of *hua gong* (literally "flower arms," perpendicular bracket arms) come out above the cap block. Above them is the *shuatou* (nose, mocking head) for a total of five levels. Interlocking with the *hua gong* and *shuatou* are a *nidao gong* on the first level and pillar-top tiebeams at four levels above it, again a total of five levels. The lower three (of these four) pillar-top tiebeams are carved so that their ends imitate the shape of a bracket arm. (One finds the same style at the Shanmen.) On every other tier, at the top of an individual bracket arm, an additional parallel bracket arm is placed. This formation is called *jixin*. Thus of the four tiers of *hua gong*, only the second and fourth tiers have the extra parallel bracket arms.[40]

Before we continue, however, one term merits explanation. Liao bracket sets may be differentiated as either "*jixin*" or "*touxin*," terms without obvious English equivalents. The "added" or "stolen" heart refers to the different systems of adding or not adding a bracket arm to enhance the stability of the bracket set. Whereas "*jixin*" involves the addition of a parallel bracket arm above a *hua gong*, "*touxin*" refers to a *hua gong* that does not support a parallel bracket arm.

The type of bracket set that is used on the exterior front facade of Guanyin Pavilion is described together with the *touxin* and *jixin* systems and the *puzuo* types in *juan* 4 of the *Yingzao fashi*.[41] The same section of the *Yingzao fashi* also names three differ-

ently positioned tiebeams, each of which is labeled in Figure 38. An unfinished tiebeam (*su fang*) lodged above the *nidao gong* is called a pillar-top tiebeam (*zhutou fang*). A tiebeam the next tier up is called *luohan fang*. Above the *luohan* tiebeam, joining it to an eaves' tiebeam, is a *xie'an zheyanban* (concealed [slanting] rafter board).

Guazi gong (melon arms) and *man gong* (kidney arms), especially long in this bracket-set formation, are placed above the second tier. It is above these that the *luohan* tiebeam is employed. Above the fourth tier only one bracket arm is used. Known as the *ling gong* (order arm), it interlocks with the *shuatou*. This system was also in use during the Qing dynasty.

Another component that was not labeled in Liang's original drawing of Figure 38 is *timu*—literally, a substitute piece of wood. Whereas in the Song dynasty *liaoyan fang* (eaves' tiebeams) were used alone, in Liao times an additional support (*timu*) was placed as a cushion between the eaves' tiebeam and the eaves' purlin (*liaoyan tuan*). (See fig. 122 for an illustration of *timu*.)

Because of the *jixin* system, the second and fourth tiers are heavier than the first and third and thus the outward projection of the second and fourth steps is less than that of the first and third. Above the unfinished tiebeams of every tier are *zheyan ban* (concealed [slanting] rafter boards). A small *lengmu* (joist) is used beneath the board to support it. Joists were not used in the Qing dynasty, but they are found in Tang and in Japanese architecture. Bracketing across the front facade of Guanyin Pavilion corresponds to the 7-*puzuo* system described in *juan* 4 of the *Yingzao fashi*. This feature, one recalls, distinguished the pavilion as one of the highest-ranking Liao structures that survives.

The second building whose bracketing we shall examine is the Sutra Library of Huayansi where, in contrast to Guanyin Pavilion, only eight different

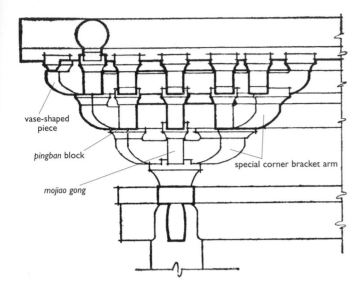

vase-shaped
piece

pingban block

mojiao gong

special corner bracket arm

FIGURE 168. Line drawing of exterior corner (column-top) bracket set, Sutra Library, Huayan Monastery, Datong, 1038. [After Liang and Liu, "Datong," p. 22]

types of bracket-set formations are used. At the Sutra Library, the most complicated bracket clusters are found on the exterior of the building; the corner sets are the most complex, followed by those above pillars and the intercolumnar ones (see figs. 120 and 122).

The exterior pillar-top bracket sets, the most intricate and highest-ranking system in the hall, are 5-*puzuo* (see figs. 36 and 120)—meaning the projection consists of two tiers of *gong* (plus the *dou* that support them) and a double bracket arm (*chong gong*) and the *jixin* system. The projection from the cap block outward is a *hua gong* with *jixin* (parallel bracket arm supported by that *hua gong*); *nidao gong, guazi gong,* and *man gong* are perpendicular to the *hua gong.* On both sides of the cap block are joined *nidao gong* on the lowest tier and three rows of tiebeams above. On the lowest of these tiebeams is a *man gong.* Because the interior of the *man gong*

appears to be cut out, there appear to be two bracket arms, but in fact there is only one.[42] Two layers of *luohan* tiebeams are employed, one on the melon arm and a second on the kidney arm, but the end of the *hua gong* is behind the block or cap block to allow for *jixin* in that part of the bracket set (see fig. 122). *Ling gong* are perpendicular to the second-tier *hua gong* and the sliced-bamboo-shaped (*pizhu*) end of the *shuatou.* Above all this is the *timu* that supports circular-ended purlins. At the ends of the *hua gong,* beneath the exposed tiebeams (*rufu*), blocks are placed every so often (but not in a precise sequence) and *ling gong* join either side of the caps—all to help support the ceiling inside the hall.

At Huayansi Sutra Library, the intercolumnar bracket sets on both the exterior and interior of the building are the same. Furthermore, they are different from pillar-top bracketing in only one respect: atop the *hua gong* of the second tier are projected only a *ling gong* (perpendicular to it) and *shuatou.* The resulting height differential led to the addition of a post (*shu zhu*) under the cap block (see fig. 123). In order to make the corner bracket sets on the exterior of the Sutra Library, special bracket arms with pointed ends were joined to the cap block (fig. 168). For interior corner bracketing, however, the piece was employed on only one side (fig. 169).

The intermediate projection of arms (on the interior and exterior) is at 45-degree angles to the building plane. (See fig. 168—exterior corner brackets contain members not included in interior ones.) On the lowest *hua gong* of these is a *pingban* block that supports the corner bracket arm of the second tier. It is at the same level in the bracket set as the *guazi gong* plane of projection. The 45-degree-angled bracket arm of the second tier supports the bracket arm directly above it and is at the same height in the set as the *ling gong* plane. On the third bracket arm is a *baoping* (vase-shaped) wooden piece that supports the large and smaller corner rafters. The bracket arms that project at 90-degree angles from the base are called *mojiao gong* ("rubbing the corner" bracket arms; see fig. 168). They extend two tiers of the bracket set. Pillar-top, fan-shaped bracketing on the exterior facade of the Datong monastery halls is more complex still (see fig. 136).

Yet all the features described here can be reduced to essentially four components—namely block, arm, cantilever, and joiners (including tiebeams)—that hold the other three together, and each is shaped so that it interlocks perfectly with any piece it touches. In fact, only two features can be found that appear to be associated specifically with Liao timber construction. One is an elongated *nidao* bracket arm. The other is the *yuanyang jiaoshou gong* ("mandarin-duck joining" bracket arm), the bracket arm that spans a position normally taken up by multiple *gong*, which also is found in non-Liao structures. (The fan-shaped bracketing so abundant in Datong architecture is better described as Liao-Jin.) Finally, it should be noted that for the Liao period one intercolumnar bracket set, such as the one seen at Kaishansi Main Hall, is standard.

Other Aspects of the Timber Frame

The number and position of beams and the various elements that compose the timber frame of most of the Liao buildings have now been described in some detail. In a study of extant Chinese wooden halls from Nanchansi Main Hall through Liao/Northern Song, Chen Mingda has suggested that the group can be divided into three basic types.[43]

According to Chen, the highest-ranking building is the Main Hall of Foguang Monastery. As mentioned in the description of the hall in Chapter 3, buildings of the Foguangsi Hall type can be seen in three separate timber layers (pillar, bracket set, and roof frame), each of which joins the other two (see fig. 68). All three layers are empty at the center. Yet

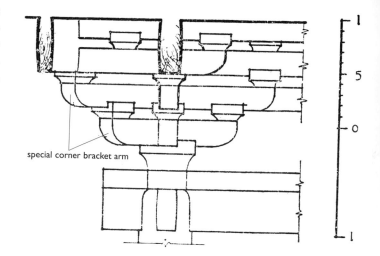

special corner bracket arm

FIGURE 169. Line drawing of interior corner (column-top) bracket set, Sutra Library, Huayan Monastery, Datong, 1038. [After Liang and Liu, "Datong," p. 25]

in order to achieve the vacant interior, the lowest beams must extend the depth of the structure. Every bracket set in halls of this type is 5-*puzuo* or higher. The Song-period Holy Mother Hall from the Jin Shrines (see figs. 210 and 211) also has these features.

Chen calls the next most structurally complex the Fengguosi Daxiongbao Hall Type. Membership in this group requires that every bracket set be 5-*puzuo* or higher, that there be two complete rows of rafters with bracket sets joined to each row, and that the boards onto which bracket sets attach join the two separate frames. Interior bracket sets are placed higher in the structure, and interior pillars are correspondingly taller, than their exterior counterparts. Exterior-eave and interior bracket sets become one entity to the extent that the exterior sets reach over to join the interior pillars (see figs. 90 and 170). Furthermore, the column grid of this type of hall need not be strictly symmetrical in front and back. Although in principal there are still complete

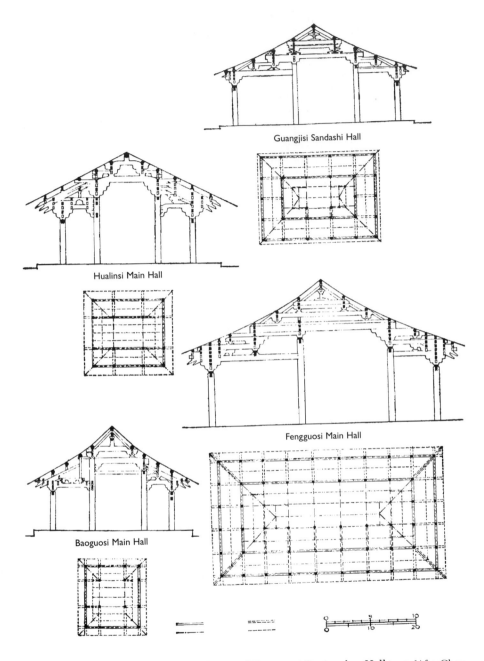

Guangjisi Sandashi Hall

Hualinsi Main Hall

Fengguosi Main Hall

Baoguosi Main Hall

FIGURE 170. Plans and sections of four buildings of Fengguosi Daxiongbao Hall type. [After Chen Mingda, *Jianzhu lishi yanjiu*, n.d., p. 55]

interior and exterior column frames (cao), interior pillars may be omitted from the inner bays or may be moved forward or backward, resulting in both two-rafter and four-rafter spans from the eave pillars. Inside the hall, camel's-hump-shaped braces (toufeng) may be placed on an interior architrave to cushion bracket sets that are not exactly above the columns. Three Liao halls exemplify this style. In addition to Daxiongbao Hall of Fengguosi, the Shanhuasi Main Hall and Sandashi Hall of Guangjisi were so constructed. Interestingly, other examples of this formation are found in South China: at the same two halls, the main halls of Hualinsi and Baoguosi, whose bracket sets were compared with those at Fengguosi in Chapter 4. The building style is also observed at Liangshan Gate at Tiger Hill, Suzhou.

The majority of wooden buildings that survive from medieval times are of the third type. Chen Mingda calls it the Haihui Hall Style. Both Type Two and Type Three in Chen's division are *tingtang* (halls) in contrast to the grander halls of Type One, the Foguangsi Main Hall style, labeled *diantang* (high-ranking halls). The Main Hall of Kaishansi and Puxian Pavilion from Shanhua Monastery share features that define this style of Haihui Hall, as do the Main Hall of Nanchan Monastery and the Ten Thousand Buddhas Hall from Zhenguosi. Three of these buildings, it has been pointed out, have no interior pillars. Beams are of four-rafter or six-rafter spans. Bracket sets are not used inside the *tingtang*. Rather, beam ends join interior and exterior pillars. It is thus possible for interior pillars to be positioned to support purlins, allowing these interior pillars to be more flexible in function. Interior pillars are also taller than exterior ones. *Tingtang* can appear upright to the point of rigidity (see fig. 130). Along the cross section (depth) of the hall, tiebeams join bracket-arms atop pillars to interconnect the transversal bracket-arm tiebeams underneath purlins (fig. 171).

In Liao architecture, several brace types are common joiners between rafters and rafters, or rafters and purlins, or rafters and bracket sets. At the Daxiongbao halls of Fengguosi and Huayansi (the latter a Liao-Jin structure), *jiaobei* join beams to the main roof purlin (see fig. 87). An "agreeable tiebeam connector" (*shunfu chuan*) is also found at Fengguosi's Main Hall (fig. 87). A diagonal brace known as *taqian* is found at Haihui Hall, at Sandashi Hall, at both Daxiongbao halls, and in a number of pre-Liao and Song buildings.

The Cai-Fen *Proportional System*

Chinese studies of medieval wooden halls are sprinkled with statements like "the height of a pillar should not exceed the width of any bay of the hall." The source of this statement—indeed, the source of virtually every specified proportional relationship of timber piece to timber piece in a Chinese hall frame—is the *Yingzao fashi*. The two most important chapters of the Song architectural manual for finding proportional specifications are *juan* 4 and 5, entitled *Damuzuo* 1 and *Damuzuo* 2. "*Damuzuo*," a term that can be translated "greater carpentry," should be understood in contrast to "*xiaomuzuo*" ("lesser carpentry"), details of the placement and function of smaller pieces of wood that are found in *juan* 7 through 11.

In the same decade when members of the Society for Research in Chinese Architecture discovered the crucial role of the *Yingzao fashi* in unlocking the system of Chinese wood joinery, they first explored old Chinese buildings. Thus Liang Sicheng and his colleagues' studies of Dulesi, Sandashi Hall, Liao-Jin architecture from Datong, and Foguangsi East Hall contained explanations of terminology from the *Yingzao fashi* interspersed with

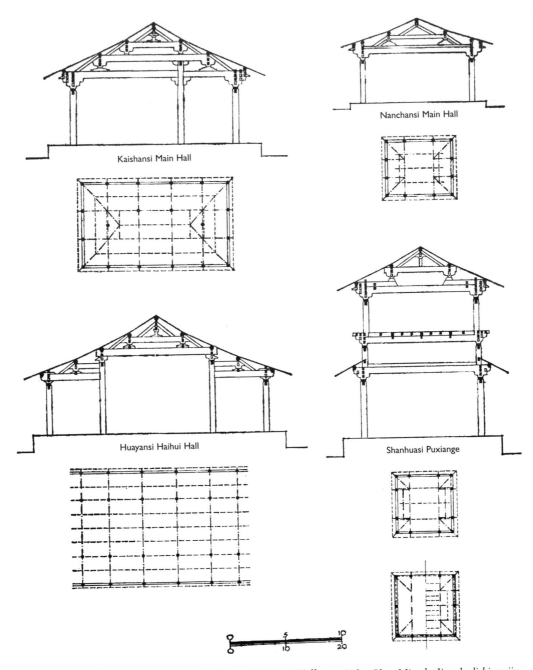

Kaishansi Main Hall

Nanchansi Main Hall

Huayansi Haihui Hall

Shanhuasi Puxiange

FIGURE 171. Plans and sections of four buildings of Haihui Hall type. [After Chen Mingda, *Jianzhu lishi yanjiu*, n.d., p. 47]

descriptions of timber pieces. Yet often these studies quote from the *Yingzao fashi* without explaining what the carpenters' jargon actually meant—for indeed it was carpenters' jargon. A study in 1992 concluded that Li Jie, compiler of the *Yingzao fashi*, had experience in building construction and had risen through the ranks to become an official rather than receiving his appointment by inheritance. Thus despite its two scholarly introductory chapters, which quote relevant passages about key architectural terms from the classical Chinese literature, the terminology of the manual produced at the Northern Song court is truly craftsmen's jargon written by one who understood it.[44] Unraveling this jargon has occupied scholars for much of this century. In the West, investigation of Chinese building standards begins with an early article by Paul Demiéville.[45] Much more expansive are the writings of Else Glahn.[46] Most thorough is the work of Chen Mingda and his students.[47]

An aspect of "greater carpentry" that merits more explanation is the *cai-fen* system—the proportional basis by which Chinese wooden architecture was cut and joined. It is because of this system's perfection that the fifteen buildings discussed here could stand. The two terms "*cai*" and "*fen*" have already been used in discussing Liao wooden buildings. *Fen* is best thought of as the module of a Chinese timber-frame building. While the measure of a wooden piece may vary from building to building, the proportions governing that component's own dimensions—as well as the proportional relationship between that member's dimensions and other architectural members of the same building—are consistent.

In scholarly writing, however, the proportional measurement of a building is more often expressed in terms of *cai* than of *fen*. *Cai* is an expression of the length/height ratio of the bracket arm (*gong*). *Cai* are divided into 15 *fen*. The cross section of a bracket arm should be proportionately 3:2 (or 15:10 *fen*). The actual dimensions of the timber pieces are given in terms of *cun*. *Cun* is sometimes thought of in English as an "inch," but *cun* in the *Yingzao fashi* does not have a specific length associated with it. Rather, *cun* is one-tenth of a *chi*, whose actual length changed through history, even during the Song dynasty. The maximum length of *chi* in the Song was 32 centimeters.[48] Sometimes a second measurement of *cai* is given in a discussion of a Chinese wooden building. Known as *zucai*, or "full *cai*," it is the sum of the measurement of *cai* (sometimes called *dan* [single] *cai*) plus *zhi* (or *qi*), a subsidiary standard timber of proportions 6 by 4 *fen*.[49]

Another system, one for ranking a building's timber, existed within the *cai-fen* system of the *Yingzao fashi*. Usually known as the eight grades of timber, it was through this system that the actual measurement of a timber piece was expressed. Grade 1 timbers were longest in both dimensions and Grade 8 were shortest; but the proportional relationship was at or close to 3:2. The highest-grade timber pieces were based on the module of 9 by 6 *cun*, for instance, and the second-highest were 8.75 by 5.5 *cun*. Many Liao buildings follow the proportions specified in the *Yingzao fashi* in large part, but the two Dulesi buildings follow them most closely. The module at Foguangsi East Hall of a century earlier is 3:2, as well, leaving one to feel confident that the *Yingzao fashi* was successor to similar manuals that have not survived but, on the other hand, wondering at the irony that Song buildings from the early twelfth century do not follow the contemporary architectural guide to the same extent as so many Liao and Tang buildings.

DEFINING LIAO ARCHITECTURE

What generalizations can one make about Liao wooden architecture? Structurally the fifteen buildings do not follow a detectable evolutionary scheme. One cannot begin with the Wenshu Hall from Geyuan Monastery of 966 and see how the Dulesi buildings borrowed from its structure and augmented it or how the building of 1019 inherited a structural style of 984. Nor can one observe regional styles in Liao wooden buildings. Except for the fan-shaped bracket set, eleventh- and twelfth-century Liao architecture of Datong is not notably distinct from northern Hebei's or from what survives in Liaoning.

What really defines Liao architecture as Liao is the aesthetic impact of the individual structures and the way the buildings were arranged in monasteries. In these two ways, evolution from Dulesi to Fogongsi and the distinct features of their layout and other Liao plans are evident.

In discussing several of the independent halls, I have quoted Liang Sicheng or Liu Dunzhen's initial feelings of somberness or the aura of power as he came upon a Liao building. In fact, as I noted in the Preface, my own pursuit of Liao architecture began because these structures "felt" intrinsically more interesting and more powerful than other Chinese buildings I had seen. One treads dangerous water in attempting to describe the aesthetic impact of a nationality's architecture—especially for a people with seminomadic origins—yet by the end of the next two chapters, in which we examine Liao buildings next to Song and Jin buildings whose structures were also guided, one assumes, by the *Yingzao fashi*, the somber power of Liao architecture should be more convincing.

For more tangible evidence of what makes Liao architecture Liao, we can turn to the monastery plan. Both Guanyin Pavilion and the Timber Pagoda suggest associations between the tall wooden structure and a deceased individual—the lower building for a powerful official, the higher one for the emperor. It is no coincidence that both Guanyinge and Yingxian Muta are not only on the main

building axes of their respective monasteries, but even after Liao times remained the architectural focal points.

Both theoretical reconstructions of Fengguosi (see figs. 94 and 95) show a prominent *ge* along the central axis. It is the only structure that might deflect the visual impact of Daxiongbao Hall. In his search through records of Baodi, it has been noted, Liang Sicheng determined that a multilevel *ge* or pagoda had also stood along its main axis. Thus one is certain that at four Liao monasteries, at least, Dulesi, Fogongsi, Fengguosi, and Guangjisi, the plan was different from what we most often think of as the typical Chinese monastery plan: several main halls along a central line, with pairs of pagodas or *ge* attached to or inside a covered corridor at either side. Although neither archaeological nor textual records can prove it, implicit in the name Geyuan Monastery is the notion that the monastery was named for its most prominent courtyard, one with a *ge*. If so, five of the nine Liao monasteries, at least one in every province where they survive, had a multilevel structure at a focal point along its main axis. The four *ge* and Muta, of course, are only a small percentage of extant Liao architecture whose multiple layers would have been visible from a great distance above monastery walls and even town walls (see figs. 97 and 98). Like Buddhist pillars built throughout his empire (in India) by King Aśoka in the third century B.C., these beacons signaled the spread of the Liao imperial Buddhist world. We shall return to the Liao pagoda and its symbolism in Part Three.

It is reasonable to conclude, too, that Liao wooden buildings were ingenious. Neither Tang nor Song architecture offers fifty-four or even twenty-four different bracket-set types in one building. More ingenious still is the *zaojing*. Magnificent *zaojing* would be sunk into ceilings after the fall of the Qidan empire, but the earliest that survive in wood are Liao. Guanyinge's is the very earliest. Even several of the simplest Liao halls, at Kaiyuansi in Yixian, conceal elaborate *zaojing*. This legacy of Liao construction further serves as an interior device of focus for the hall, multilevel or single-level, in which one or more *zaojing* shade the main images; in the case of the Muta, they are constructed one on top of another.

The *zaojing* is also an example of a third aspect of Liao ingenuity: the ability to conceal fantastic construction behind a simple exterior. Such differentiation between exterior and interior architecture and carpentry is evident in the placement of *pingzuo* levels in multistory architecture, by cabinetry in the Sutra Library of Huayansi, and in the *zaojing*, particularly those at Kaiyuansi. Should the earliest wooden *zaojing* actually be Dulesi's, the form itself might be a contribution of Liao architecture to the Chinese system.

The most profound legacy of Liao architecture is its expression of imperial power. By the end of the book it will be clear that the position of the *ge* or other high building in the center of a Liao monastery was just one of the ways the Qidan rulers conceived of architecture as a symbolic manifestation of their role as rulers of an Asian empire and, too, as a projection of their personal and imperial aspirations after life.

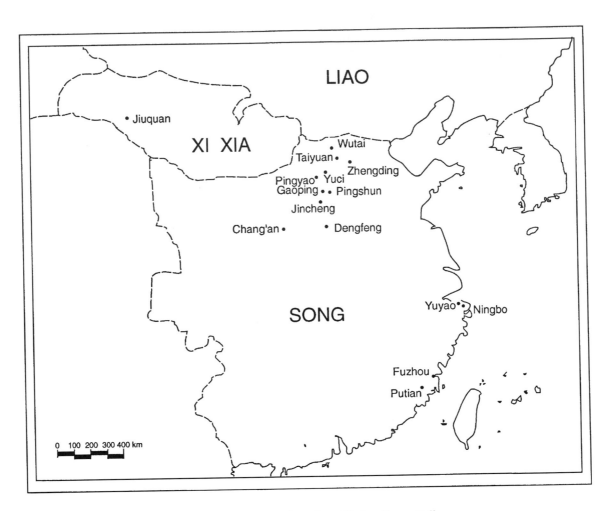

MAP 4. Locations of Selected Tenth-Century and Northern Song Timber-Frame Halls

8

Song Wooden Halls
at the Time of Liao

IN 1986, CHAI ZEJUN wrote that ninety-nine buildings from Liao, Song, or Jin survived in Shanxi province (see Map 2).[1] Chai did not provide a list or even clarify that he meant only wooden buildings—although for the post-Sui period, timber architecture is the exclusive subject of his study—but even if one counts structures that have been destroyed during the twentieth century, the maximum number from the Liao period in Shanxi province is six: the Sutra Library, Haihui Hall, and Daxiongbao Hall from Huayansi; the Muta in Yingxian; and the Main Hall and Puxian Pavilion at Shanhuasi. Some ninety more, in other words, are

known from the tenth through mid-thirteenth centuries in central and southern Shanxi or from the post-1125 period in the north. This is not the first time the remarkable survival rate for wooden architecture in Shanxi has been noted. Although no such reckoning of mid-tenth-through-mid-thirteenth-century buildings in other parts of China seems to have been undertaken, still it is safe to say that in addition to Shanxi architecture, scores more buildings, outside Shanxi and primarily from the Song dynasty, are extant in China (see Map 4).

Little scholarly attention—much less, in fact, than that for Liao—has been directed toward Song

FIGURE 172. Daxiongbao Hall, Hualin Monastery, Fuzhou, Fujian, 964 (restored). [Steinhardt photograph]

buildings.[2] Certainly most of the Song buildings were beyond the reach of Japanese architectural historians during the years of occupation. Most of these buildings were farther from Beijing, as well, the hub of Chinese interest in architectural history in the 1920s, 1930s, and 1940s. In other words, when scholarly attention returned to architecture after the founding of the People's Republic, the wooden buildings of North China were known through research and scholars could immediately turn (or return) to them. Moreover, the great interest in the Song architectural treatise, *Yingzao fashi*, both before and after the war, has deflected attention from the Song buildings themselves. The limited scholarship on Song architecture has been directed to Kaifeng and the potential recovery of the Song imperial tradition at the remains of the Northern Song capital at Bianliang and its monasteries like Xiangguosi.[3]

Here the discussion of Song architecture is limited to buildings contemporary to the Liao dynasty (in other words Northern Song) that are dated, accessible (if extant), or were published before de-

struction. (Thus the architecture of Xiangguosi is omitted.) Table 4 lists the Northern Song wooden buildings discussed in this chapter.

DAXIONGBAO HALL OF HUALINSI

The Daxiongbao (Main) Hall of Hualin Monastery faces south onto Pingshan Street inside the city of Fuzhou, capital of Fujian province (fig. 172). It is the only building that survives from the huge monastery that stood there in Tang and Song times. Restored and altered in the Ming and Qing dynasties, the Main Hall came to the attention of architectural historians in China in the 1950s, after which it was rebuilt according to its presumed tenth-century form.[4]

The date 964, fifth year of the first Song emperor, has been assigned to the Main Hall because it is found in a poem and local records.[5] Technically this date designates the hall as a building not of Song China. From the fall of Tang until 944, Fuzhou and its province, Fujian, were part of the kingdom of Min. Subsequently they fell to the Wuyue kingdom, which endured until 978. Primary sources about Daxiongbao Hall and Hualinsi are generally gathered in records of Min (an alternate name for Fujian), but the hall may be considered the sole example of Wuyue architecture. From the documents one learns that in the Song dynasty the Main Hall stood in front of a Tianwang (Divine Kings) Hall and behind a Dharma Hall (Fadian), the latter also dated to 964. By the Ming period, according to local records, a sutra library with a revolving cabinet inside, a founder's hall, and covered arcades were there. The plan, it seems, was in no way extraordinary.

Daxiongbao Hall of Hualinsi is elevated on a platform of uneven height. The grade below is reported to have been uneven due to the location against a hill, a situation found also at Foguangsi East Hall. Standing on a major street today,

TABLE 4. Northern Song Wooden Halls

Hall	Monastery	Location	Date
Daxiongbao Hall	Hualinsi	Fuzhou, Fujian	964
Middle Hall	Chongmingsi	Gaoping county, Shanxi	971
Foxiang Pavilion	Longxingsi	Zhengding, Hebei	971
Cishi Pavilion	Longxingsi	Zhengding, Hebei	971
Front Hall	Youxiansi	Gaoping county, Shanxi	990–994
Yuhuagong (destroyed)	Yongshousi	Yuci county, Shanxi	1008
Daxiongbao Hall	Baoguosi	Yuyao county, Zhejiang	1013
Sanqing Hall	Xuanmiaoguan	Putian, Fuzhou	1016
Holy Mother Hall	Jinci	Taiyuan, Shanxi	1023–1032
Moni Hall	Longxingsi	Zhengding, Hebei	1052
Daxiongbao Hall	Kaihuasi	Gaoping county, Shanxi	1073
Middle Hall	Yuhuangmiao	Jincheng county, Shanxi	1076
Jade Emperor Hall	Yuhuangmiao	Jincheng county, Shanxi	1076
Main Hall	Erxianguan	Jincheng county, Shanxi	ca. 1100
Main Hall	Qingliansi	Jincheng county, Shanxi	1102
Yuanjue Hall	Faxingsi	Changzhi, Shanxi	1111
Main Hall	Chuzu'an	Dengfeng county, Henan	1125
Hall of the Revolving Sutra Cabinet	Longxingsi	Zhengding, Hebei	N. Song

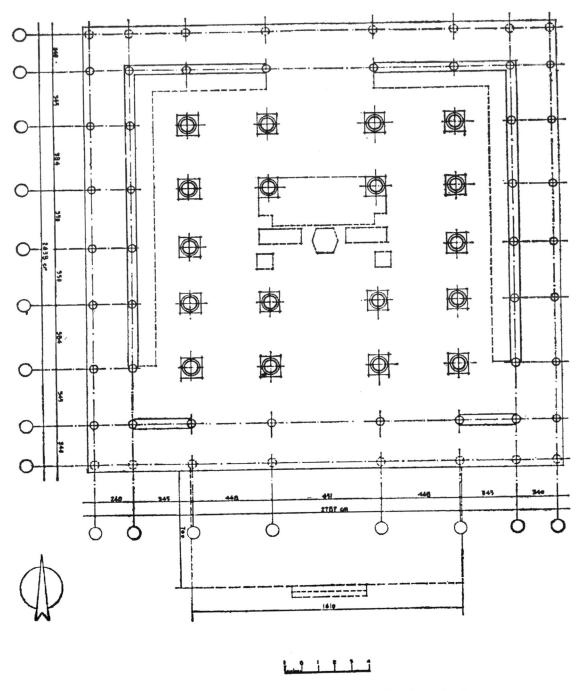

FIGURE 173. Plan of Daxiongbao Hall. [After Yang Binglun et al., "Fuzhou Hualinsi Dadian," p. 9]

however, none of the irregularity is noticeable. At one time the roof consisted of two layers of eaves, but now the timber frame supports a single, hip-gable-combination roof. Daxiongbao Hall is nearly square in plan (fig. 173). This is true both of the present hall and the foundations of earlier halls on which it was built. Figure 173 shows a three-by-four-bay hall whose dimensions are 15.87 by 14.68 meters with additional bays added to the sides and front. Today the outermost base dimensions are 27.3 by 26.4 meters, a ratio of 1.08:1—as close to a perfect square as one finds in Chinese halls. The squarish shape initially suggests comparison with the Main Hall of Nanchan Monastery of 782 and the Ten Thousand Buddhas Hall of Zhenguo Monastery of 963, both in Shanxi. The northern halls, however, are three-bays-square with no interior pillars.

Hualinsi's main hall was more complex. Approached by a *yuetai* with a *tadao* leading up to it, the hall was supported by four pillars east to west by five pillars north to south in complete rows except for two that were eliminated in front of the central altar. The elimination of interior pillars to make way for religious images, of course, has been shown to be a common feature of Liao Buddhist hall construction that can be traced to Tang architecture. Also consistent with Liao architecture and its Tang origins, the central front and back bays were wider than the two that flanked them. Arrayed in front of the 5.28-by-2.79-meter altar, on top of it, and along the side walls were more than sixty statues, most of them deities of Esoteric Buddhism. Today not even one remains. The caretaker told me in 1993 that their whereabouts were unknown.

The timber members of Hualinsi Main Hall were measured and recorded in the 1950s. Pillars beneath the exterior eaves were shuttle-shaped (*suo zhu*) but did not have entasis. They measured 64.6 centimeters in diameter at the base, 63 centimeters near the middle, and 53 centimeters at the top. The

FIGURE 174. Bracket set showing triple *ang*, Daxiongbao Hall, Hualin Monastery, after reconstruction. [Steinhardt photograph]

gradual thinning of wooden columns prescribed in the *Yingzao fashi* is confirmed, but it must be recognized that the shuttle-shaped column is known to survive in only one earlier Chinese structure—the Northern Qi-period Yicihui Pillar in Dingxing, Hebei (see fig. 53)—and in Japan at the Kondō and Chūmon of Horyū-ji, at the Yakushi-ji East Pagoda, and at the Tōshōdai-ji Kondō, all from the Nara period.[6] Interior pillars were also 64.6 centimeters at the bottom, but their uppermost portions could not be accessed for measurement. Pillars along the exterior facade rose gradually in height toward the corners with an 8-centimeter difference between lowest and highest. (Corner pillars measured 4.62 m and the average pillar height was 4.55 m.) This rise of 8 centimeters converts to about 2.26 *cun* in the Song system, the measurement specified in the *Yingzao fashi*, but less than that of the Liao-Jin buildings at Datong.[7] All pillars were lodged in bases that were 10.8 centimeters high and measured 1.69 times the base diameters of the pillars. This proportion was less than the one suggested in the

FIGURE 175. Longxing Monastery, Zhengding, Hebei, in 1987. [Steinhardt photograph]

Yingzao fashi but comparable to that of known Tang and Liao buildings.[8]

Interior pillars were higher than the exterior pillars under the eaves. Although the formation was the reverse of the specifications in the *Yingzao fashi* for a *tingtang* such as Hualinsi's Main Hall, we shall find it in later architecture of South China. The proportion of the pillar diameters to their height was about 1:7 on the exterior, where diameters were about 10 centimeters thicker than those inside the hall. They were much thinner than pillars at Foguangsi East Hall or Zhenguosi Ten Thousand Buddhas Hall, but fairly standard for a Liao-Song structure that, according to Zhang Buqian, averaged 1:9.5 or 1:9.6.[9]

Nine varieties of bracket sets were employed at Hualinsi Main Hall, eight on the exterior and only one inside. The number is just two more than at the East Hall of Foguangsi from the previous century, but fifteen fewer than at Guanyin Pavilion of Dulesi, built twenty years later. Two features of the bracket sets are noteworthy. Most important, Hualinsi's tenth-century hall exhibits a rare Chinese example of three *ang* (cantilevers) (fig. 174 and see fig. 92). The earliest surviving example of the double *ang* is the East Hall of Foguangsi. In later architecture, it is common for only one lever arm to function as a brace for bracket-set parts and the second to be decorative. Now and then one also finds a *shuatou* so elongated that it appears to be a cantilever. At Daxiongbao Hall of Hualinsi, however, all three lever arms are functional. The formation is 7-*puzuo*, but a version of it with three rather than two cantilevers (such as were employed at Foguangsi East Hall and Guanyin Pavilion). Furthermore, it has also been suggested that the earliest known example of *jixin* survives at this Daxiongbao Hall.[10]

The second outstanding timber feature of the Main Hall can also be seen in Figure 92: the crescent-shaped tiebeam (*yueliang*). This feature is also present in the East Hall of Foguangsi (see fig. 68, no. 21). It is not found at any extant Liao hall. The *pupai* tiebeam, by contrast, common in Tang and Liao architecture, is missing at Hualinsi Daxiongbao Hall. Braces observed at Liao halls and used here include *panjian* and *shunfu chuan*.

LONGXING MONASTERY

More Song buildings survive at Longxing Monastery in Zhengding, Hebei, than at any other temple complex in China (fig. 175). A stele found by Liang Sicheng at the monastery traces its origins to the year 586, but the earliest extant buildings are from the tenth century.[11] Zhengding had been attacked by Qidan forces before the present Song buildings were constructed. This battle confirms that Chinese architecture in this part of Hebei was seen by the Liao. In response to the attacks, an 84-meter pagoda was built some 60 kilometers farther north in Dingxing. Known as Liaodita, or "anticipating the enemy pagoda" (see fig. 358), it is the tallest extant brick structure in China. Indeed, from the tenth century onward, the central Hebei towns were crucial Song strongholds. During an attack on Zhengding, the Qidan destroyed the great bronze image of Guanyin in Dabei Monastery, located west of the city.[12] In the aftermath of this attack, the first Song emperor, Taizu (r. 960–975), commissioned the construction of a 23-*chi* image of the bodhisattva to be housed in a pavilion named Dabeige. This *ge*, dated to 971, goes by the alternate name of Foxiang Pavilion.

Foxiang Pavilion was the tallest structure at the imperial Song monastery, for which buildings were constructed in the tenth and eleventh centuries and in the Yuan, Ming, and Qing dynasties. In Song times, five main buildings and at least four, possibly six, subsidiary structures are believed to have stood along the main north-south axis: a Shanmen, Hall to the Sixth Patriarch, Moni Hall, Ordination Plat-

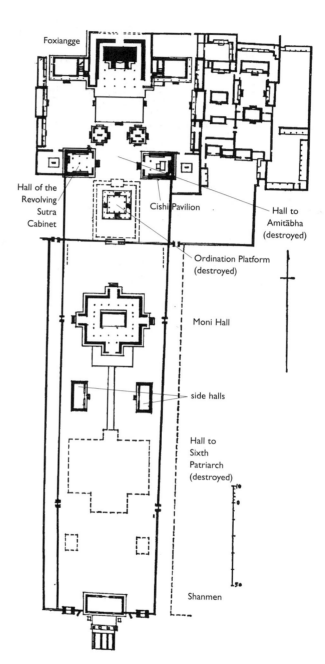

FIGURE 176. Plan of Longxing Monastery. [After *Liang Sicheng wenji*, vol. 1, p. 174]

FIGURE 177. Foxiang Pavilion, Longxing Monastery, Zhengding, Hebei, 971 with later restoration. [Photo courtesy of Gregory Walsh]

form, Foxiang Pavilion with a Sutra Library and Cishi Pavilion flanking the courtyard in front of it, and a hall to the Buddha Amitābha, besides side halls in front of Moni Hall and perhaps bell and drum towers on either side of the first courtyard. All are shown in Figure 176.

Foxiang Pavilion

The Guanyin inside Longxingsi's tallest structure is said to have risen 73 *chi* (approximately 24 m).[13] It has been suggested that knowledge of the bronze image of the bodhisattva in the Longxingsi pavilion was an impetus for the construction (or reconstruction in 984) of the Guanyin Pavilion at Dulesi.[14] The relationship is logical. Assuming the Dulesi builders were aware of Longxingsi, even though the

image in Guanyinge was not quite as tall as the Northern Song statue, the later construction of the Liao pavilion around its image signified a competitive relationship between Liao and Song, one in which religious sculpture and architecture were symbolic expressions of the power struggle. The Liao, however, would continue to erect structurally more and more challenging buildings whereas the Song pavilion at Longxingsi, as we shall see, was a much simpler wooden structure than Guanyinge. Even Song's later architecture would not exploit the potential of the Chinese timber frame the way Liao architecture had done in its initial decades. When Liang Sicheng visited Longxingsi in 1933, the upper hall portions were missing and the bronze image was exposed. The pavilion has since been reconstructed (fig. 177), however, so its Song features cannot be studied with the same enthusiasm as their counterparts at Cishi Pavilion.

Cishi Pavilion

Cishi Pavilion stands in the courtyard in front of Foxiangge, east of the main axis of the monastery (fig. 178). The pavilion to the bodhisattva Cishi (an alternate name for Mile, or Maitreya) is a three-bay-square structure whose sides are just under 14 meters each. Besides Maitreya, eighteen *louhan* statues, common in Liao and Song hall interiors, were arranged on either side of the interior (fig. 179). Inside one finds further evidence (in addition to the monumental Guanyin inside Foxiang Pavilion) to suggest that pavilion construction from this Song monastery may have served as a catalyst for Guanyin Pavilion of Dulesi: Cishi Pavilion appears to be a two-story hall from the exterior but in fact conceals an internal *pingzuo* level (fig. 180). When Liang Sicheng studied the building, an exterior layer of eaves marked the position of the *pingzuo* (fig. 181). The opinion of a Qing date for this eave layer was so strong, however, that it was removed during the 1958 restoration.[15] In spite of known restoration, the date 971, the year of its original construction for Song emperor Taizu, is generally assigned to the hall.

Except for the hidden story, the structural contrasts between the interiors of the imperial Song and Liao halls can be called startling—and in the comparison the genius of Liao construction is apparent. The side sectional drawing of Cishi Pavilion shows the structure to have been one of total rigidity and remarkable simplicity (see fig. 180). Every timber member is perfectly straight. The curved beams of Tang-Liao construction, preserved also in South China at Daxiongbao Hall of Hualinsi from 964 (see figs. 92 and 174), have vanished. Furthermore,

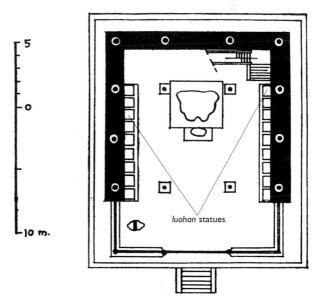

luohan statues

FIGURE 178 (top). Cishi Pavilion, Longxing Monastery, Zhengding, Hebei, 971. [Photo courtesy of Gregory Walsh]
FIGURE 179 (above). Plan of Cishi Pavilion. [After *Liang Sicheng wenji*, vol. 1, p. 198]

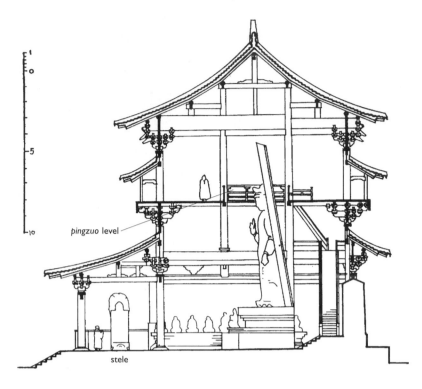

FIGURE 180 (top). Side sectional drawing of Cishi Pavilion. [After *Liang Sicheng wenji*, vol. 1, p. 198]
FIGURE 181 (above). Cishi Pavilion ca. 1933. [Liang Sicheng, "Zhengding diaocha jilüe," p. 197]

the complexity of wood joinery required to bridge the two layers of Dulesi's Guanyin Pavilion with the *pingzuo* is lacking. Instead, a huge, straight pillar rises from behind the altar to a roof purlin. Four straight interior pillars rise on the two sides of the altar and in front of it (see fig. 179). In addition, the hall lacks interesting or graceful bracket clusters, and their general simplicity—all are only 4- or 5-*puzuo*—as well as the massive vertical thrust of the multistory and other pillars, combine with the most blatant omission: a *zaojing*. In the Song hall, construction is of the most fundamental column-beam-and-strut formation and the covering over the head of the monumental bodhisattva is a simple, rigid frame. One feature that has not attracted much attention is the extended eaves that cover a front porch. (In fig. 181 one sees the stele that stood on that porch when Liang Sicheng's drawing was made ca. 1933.) At Foxiangge, believed to have been constructed in the same mode, the comparable exterior feature is an enormous rainshade so wide that rooms were added on two sides of the first story beneath it (fig. 182). The exaggerated eaves create a sharp horizontal contrast to the verticality of this tallest building in the monastery, one not so different from the rigid, perpendicular joining of wood inside Cishige. In the second half of the tenth century, it was the Liao, not the native Chinese, whose gods were housed in creative, dramatic, and architecturally challenging halls.

Hall of the Revolving Sutra Cabinet

The Hall of the Revolving Sutra Cabinet (Zhuan-lunzangdian) forms a pair with Cishi Pavilion in front of Foxiangge (fig. 183 and see fig. 176). Outside and in, the timber frame of the sutra hall is a *ge* of similar structure to Cishi Pavilion. Three-bays-square, it too concealed an interior *pingzuo*. (The exterior porch was removed during renovation in the late 1950s.) The pavilion also supported elon-

FIGURE 182. Detail of porch and eaves covering Foxiang Pavilion. [Steinhardt photograph]]

FIGURE 183. Hall of the Revolving Sutra Cabinet, Longxing Monastery, Zhengding, Hebei, Song period. [Steinhardt photograph]

gated eaves across the front.[16] Yet beginning with the plan, it is apparent that the library was structurally more complex than Cishi Pavilion.

First, the upper story distinguished itself from the Cishi Pavilion counterpart by the elevation of Śākyamuni and two bodhisattvas on an altar (fig. 184). The ground story had six interior pillars as opposed to four at Cishi Pavilion and images along either side wall, but most impressive was the revolving sutra container on an octagonal base. Pillars were positioned to accommodate it (fig. 185).

Seven meters across the base, the sutra cabinet is a superb example of wood joinery. A man named Fu Xi is credited with the invention of a turnable sutra cabinet in 544. Although a handful of such cabinets survive in China, the mechanism was never commonplace.[17] In addition to its mobility, the sutra cabinet has 8-*puzuo* bracketing. Thus it can be considered an example of technically superior *xiaomuzuo* such as the Liao achieved inside the Sutra Repository at Huayansi in 1038 (see figs. 126–128). Although there is no record that suggests the unique Liao building of the same purpose was inspired by the sutra hall at the imperial Song monastery, the connection between the Liao and Song pavilions dedicated to Guanyin leads one to suspect it. Among extant Liao construction, however, the *tingtang* structure with 5-*puzuo* bracketing is simple. Indeed, the exterior/interior contrast has been suggested as exemplary of the tendency in Liao architecture to create an interior unanticipated from the outside. At the imperial Song monastery in Hebei, the Pavilion of the Revolving Sutra Cabinet has the most intricate timber frame, but it does not achieve the structural complexity of Yingxian Timber Pagoda, Guanyin Pavilion, or Fengguosi's Daxiongbao Hall.

Zhuanlunzang Hall, for instance, has no *zaojing*. However, it was not composed of exclusively straight, perpendicularly configured timbers. Start-

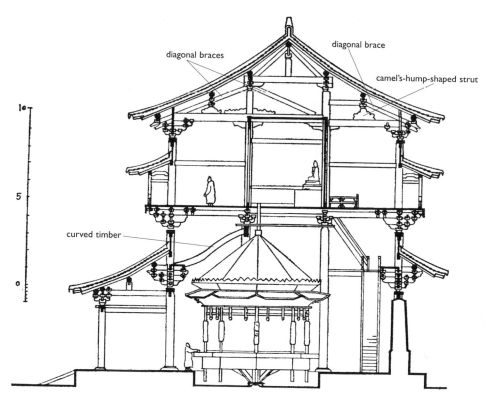

FIGURE 184. Side sectional drawing of the Hall of the Revolving Sutra Cabinet. [After *Liang Sicheng wenji*, vol. 1, p. 186]

ing at the top, one finds that immediately beneath the roof truss (beginning after the second purlin from the top), the column-beam-and-strut structure has been enhanced by three diagonal braces and camel's-hump-shaped braces (see fig. 184). The verticality of the image of Cishi and the long column behind it at Cishi Pavilion (see fig. 180) has been substituted by columns that span no more than the height of one story. A graceful, curved timber piece covers the front of the turning sutra cabinet. The placement of the curved member is doubly significant. First, it draws attention to the importance of the front of the hall; in back, only a piece of wood

lines the stairs to the second story. Second, both small posts reinforce the short, curved beams at the front and back of the hall, which, although present at Cishi Pavilion, easily go unnoticed (see fig. 180). Still, the structure of Zhuanlunzang Hall is not nearly so complex as that of Guanyin Pavilion. Despite its exquisite interior carpentry, it was just a side hall in its monastery.

Moni Hall

Moni Hall of Longxing Monastery is not only the most elegant Song building today but truly a unique one (fig. 186). In Song times, it was positioned third

FIGURE 185. Revolving Sutra Cabinet, Hall of the Revolving Sutra Cabinet. [Photo courtesy of Gregory Walsh]

FIGURE 186. Moni Hall, Longxing Monastery, Zhengding, Hebei, 1052. [Steinhardt photograph]

along the monastery axis, behind the Shanmen and a Hall to the Sixth Patriarch, but now it is showcased in front of Foxiang Pavilion.

Moni Hall is seven-bays-square with a slightly wider width than depth. A portico with hip-gable roof projects on each side (fig. 187). Clearly it was the intent of the builders to emphasize the porticoes (baosha), for not one window that might have diminished their prominence was included. Conforming to Chinese tradition, the front facade is the most pronounced, with a *yuetai* under this widest of the projections. The two sets of roof eaves and a perfectly symmetrical presentation are probably what

led Liang Sicheng to comment that Moni Hall's architecture was the sort that one might find in "ancient painting," but rarely in actual buildings.[18]

Beyond the beauty of its facade, the timber frame of Moni Hall (dedicated to Śākyamuni Buddha) may be as close to an ideal structure as any from the Song or Liao dynasties. Every strut, brace, and bracket set is reported to be consistent with the proportions in the *Yingzao fashi*.[19] For instance, the measure of four-rafter-length tiebeams (fig. 188) is equal to the length of the three central bays across the front.[20]

The plan of Moni Hall is close to that of the *cao*

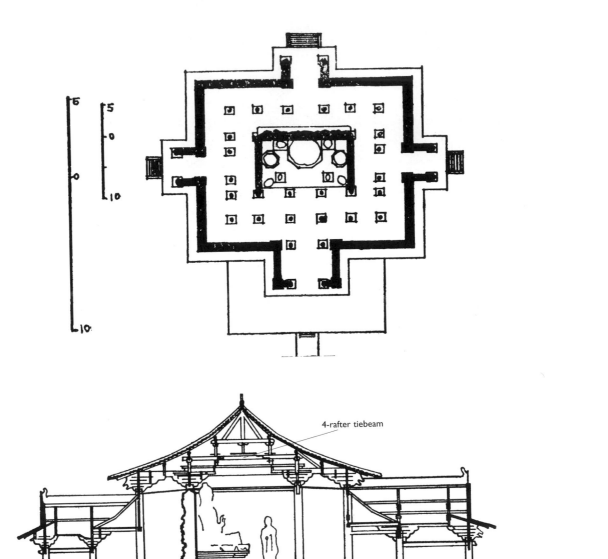

FIGURE 187 (top). Plan of Moni Hall. [After *Liang Sicheng wenji*, vol. 1, p. 177]

FIGURE 188 (above). Side sectional drawing of Moni Hall. [After *Liang Sicheng wenji*, vol. 1, p. 177]

system except that several columns from the northern side of the inner *cao* have been eliminated and replaced by altar pillars (see figs. 188, 66, and 67). The interior set as well as altar columns rise slightly higher than those of the outer *cao*, as we have observed at Hualinsi's Daxiongbao Hall, in order to support the upper roof eaves and their corresponding frame (see fig. 188).

When Moni Hall was first published in 1933, it was reported as a building from the reign of the first Song emperor with recognition of later (Ming-Qing) repairs. During restoration in 1978, the date 1052 was found inside the hall, both on the architrave and a bracket set.[21] The year is extremely significant in dating a detail of bracketing formerly associated simply with Song and later Chinese architecture. Liang Sicheng had noted this detail — a scooped-out end of the *ang* (cantilever) of the bracket sets — at Shengmu Hall of the Jin Shrines and recognized it as the *qinmian* (lute-face) *ang* described in the *Yingzao fashi* (fig. 189).[22] He did not know at that time that Shengmu Hall was built within decades of Moni Hall (during the *tiansheng* reign period, 1023–1032). The use of *qinmian ang* at Moni Hall may be a signature either of a short period of Song construction or of a regional style, for the alternate *ang* formation, *pizhu* (split bamboo), occurs at all the Liao halls, at Hualinsi's Main Hall, and at the related halls from South China to be discussed. Two other features of bracketing are noteworthy. First, corner bracket sets have triple *ang*; but unlike Hualinsi's Main Hall, one *ang* is actually a *shuatou* (fig. 190). Second, intercolumnar bracket sets, *bujian puzuo*, have arms that join at 45-degree angles (see fig. 189). The single, additional projection beyond the longitudinal and perpendicular planes does not constitute the "fan-shaped" bracketing observed in Liao-Jin architecture of Datong (see fig. 136). It is a feature found in Liao and Song

brick pagodas (see fig. 359) and in Qing architecture, at which time it is called *ruyi* (scepter) *dougong*. We shall return to Moni Hall in the discussion of Shengmu Hall of 1052 as we seek to understand the heights of main hall construction in Song as compared to Liao.

SONG ARCHITECTURE IN GAOPING

In the same year Foxiang and Cishi pavilions were constructed at Longxing Monastery in Hebei, building was undertaken at Chongming Monastery in Gaoping county, Shanxi. Today only the Middle Hall (Zhongdian) remains from the year 971 at the mountainous site 15 kilometers from the town limits (fig. 191).[23] A three-bay-square hall with hip-gable roof, it is exemplary of a type that seems to have been common in the tenth century, especially in Shanxi. That is, signatures of the "great tradition" of Chinese construction — 7-*puzuo* bracket sets atop columns and at the corners, for example, and 5-*puzuo* intercolumnar bracketing — are integrated into an otherwise structurally simple building. Indeed, often these are the only indications that the three-bay-square structure is a main hall. We observed the same phenomenon at Zhenguosi's Ten Thousand Buddhas Hall (see fig. 70). One explanation for the apparent dichotomy in architectural detail is that during this century of political reconfiguration in China, the time, money, and manpower available for construction in the more stable times of Tang were lacking. Instead, contenders for power such as the Northern Han builders of Zhenguosi and patrons of the Main Hall from Tiantai'an and Great Buddha Hall from Dayunyuan (see fig. 77) had to be satisfied with smaller buildings onto which they could append details of high status and power such as 7-*puzuo* bracket sets.[24] One unusual feature of construction at the Middle Hall is the piecing together of wooden beams (fig. 192). This,

FIGURE 189 (top). Bracket set showing "lute-faced" *ang* and *ruyi* (scepter) bracket arm, Moni Hall. [Steinhardt photograph]

FIGURE 190 (above). Bracket set with three lute-faced *ang* (*shuatou* and *ang*), Moni Hall. [Steinhardt photograph]

FIGURE 191. Middle Hall, Chongming Monastery, Gaoping county, Shanxi, 971. [After Li Yuming, *Shanxi gujianzhu . . .* , p. 199]

too, may indicate a desire to create a more grandiose structure than money would otherwise allow.

Two more Song buildings survive in this county, further adding to the number of old buildings that survive in Shanxi. The next earliest is the Front Hall of Youxian Monastery, also located in mountains, but about 10 kilometers due south of the Gaopingxian town. The Front Hall was built in the *chunhua* reign period (990–994) and was three-bays-square and nearly square in plan (fig. 193). It had unusually heavy roof eaves, 5-*puzuo* bracketing, and two *ang* in pillar-top sets as opposed to a single cantilever intercolumnarly. All bracketing here and at Chongmingsi's Main Hall was of the *touxin* formation observed at Guanyin Pavilion of Dulesi. (See the discussion of this term in Chapter 7.) Characteristic

of Song style, the *ang* was lute-faced. This feature, observed at Moni Hall of Longxing Monastery, would persist in Jin construction in North China (for example, at Maitreya Hall of Chongfu Monastery and Mañjuśrī Hall of Foguang Monastery, both discussed in the next chapter); but the Front Hall of Youxian Monastery is the earliest evidence of it.

The most important old building in Gaoping county, Shanxi, is Daxiongbao Hall of Kaihua Monastery, dated 1073 by an inscription carved into an eave's pillar (fig. 194). The same inscription provides the name of a female donor.[25] (One recalls that Foguang Monastery was also the recipient of female patronage.) Located in mountains 17 kilometers northeast of the town, Kaihuasi was founded between 923 and 926 and rebuilt from the 1070s to

FIGURE 192. Tiebeam composed of pieced-together wood, Middle Hall, Chongming Monastery. [After Li Yuming, *Shanxi gujianzhu* . . . , p. 199.]

1090s. Daxiongbao Hall occupies the central position in a monastery that seems to be divided into front and back sections. Still, this main hall is three-bays-square with a hip-gable roof. It is accessible via front and back central-bay doors, a feature that distinguishes it from more humble halls with only one point of entry, but both pillar-top and intercolumnar bracketing are 5-*puzuo*. Inside, architectural members are painted according to stipulations for interior painting in the *Yingzao fashi*.[26] More impressive, the walls are covered with Buddhist murals dated 1096.[27]

YUHUAGONG OF YONGSHOUSI

A handwritten report and accompanying illustrations in the final issue of the *Bulletin of the Society for Research in Chinese Architecture* is the only record of Yuhuagong, once the main hall of a monastery less than 50 kilometers southeast of Taiyuan in north central Shanxi province (fig. 195).[28] It is fortunate that Mo Zongjiang's study of the buildings investigated in June 1937 has been preserved, for the structure did not survive the war.

In 1937, the hall and a Shanmen, both oriented 11 degrees west of due south, remained. At one time, according to *Yucixian zhi* (Record of Yuci prefecture) of 1864, the monastery's high *ge* could be seen from a distance.[29] The same record relates that a monastery had been established at the site in A.D. 168 of the Han dynasty and that in the period of Sui-Tang it had been named Kongwangsi.

When Liang Sicheng and Mo Zongjiang studied Yuhuagong in the 1930s, it was the third oldest Chinese hall after the East Hall of Foguangsi and the Guanyin Pavilion of Dulesi. These were the only buildings confirmed to predate the *Yingzao fashi*.[30]

FIGURE 193 (top). Youxian Monastery, Gaoping county, Shanxi, showing Front Hall of 990–994.
[After Li Yuming, *Shanxi gujianzhu . . .* , p. 200]
FIGURE 194 (above). Daxiongbao Hall, Kaihua Monastery, Gaoping county, Shanxi, 1073.
[After Li Yuming, *Shanxi gujianzhu . . .* , p. 203]

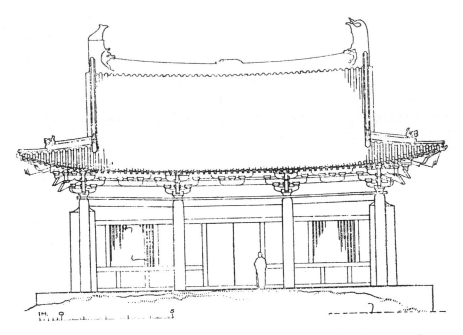

FIGURE 195. Line drawing of Yuhuagong, Yongshou Monastery, Yuci, Shanxi, 1008 (destroyed). [After Mo Zongjiang, "Yuhuagong," p. 22]

The three-bay-square structure was, therefore, somewhat remarkable. Now it must be viewed as one of a sizable number of three-bay halls built in the tenth century (in this case the date is 1008), many of which remain in Shanxi.[31]

Of added significance is the record of the monastery's pavilion, a feature that has been associated with Liao monastery planning. Yet at Longxingsi and extant Liao temple complexes with *ge*, the other buildings along the main axis were more grandiose than three-bay structures. The scarce records of the other Song monasteries in Shanxi discussed earlier do not indicate the existence of *ge*. Nor do they indicate, as is the case for Longxingsi, imperial patronage. Furthermore, the small scale of their main halls and frequency of the less-eminent roof form (the hip-gable combination) should indicate a Buddhist setting of somewhat modest importance.

Why, then, the tall pavilion—and why in combination with a three-bay-square main hall?

One of the features that most impressed Mo Zongjiang was the large scale of the bracket sets combined with their relative simplicity (fig. 196). Neither Mo Zongjiang nor Liang Sicheng seems to have been aware of the Ten Thousand Buddhas Hall of Zhenguo Monastery only 70 kilometers or so to the southwest. Although the bracket sets of Yuhuagong's Main Hall were only 5-*puzuo*—with a single *hua gong, touxin* and only one *ang* (plus a *shuatou*), and flat-shaped struts placed beneath the roof eaves intercolumnarly—as opposed to 7-*puzuo* bracket clusters at the hall of 963, the visual effect of the Northern Han hall and the early-eleventh-century hall would have been similar. The contrast between bracket size and hall size (150-cm-high clusters compared to 4-m-tall columns below

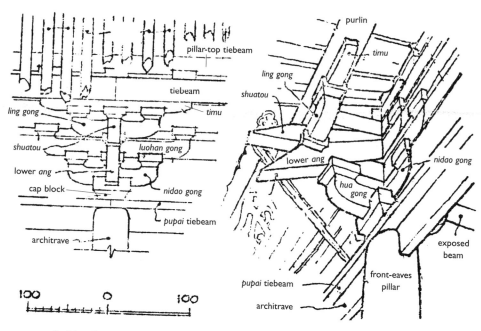

Labels in left drawing: pillar-top tiebeam, tiebeam, ling gong, timu, shuatou, luohan gong, lower *ang*, cap block, nidao gong, pupai tiebeam, architrave

Labels in right drawing: purlin, timu, ling gong, shuatou, lower ang, hua gong, nidao gong, pupai tiebeam, architrave, exposed beam, front-eaves pillar

Scale: 100   0   100

FIGURE 196. Line drawings of pillar-top bracket set, Yuhuagong, Yongshou Monastery. [After Mo Zongjiang, "Yuhuagong," p. 3]

them), in fact, was probably more startling at Yu-huagong's hall because its base dimensions, 13.33 by 13.2 meters, were almost 2 to 2.5 meters smaller than their counterparts at Ten Thousand Buddhas Hall.

A logical explanation is that in tenth-century and slightly later Shanxi province, divided like its neighbor Hebei into Liao and Song prefectures, the immense bracket sets remained the symbol of power they had been for wealthy Buddhist monasteries such as Foguangsi in the ninth century and for contenders for rulership like the Northern Han a hundred years later. If this is true, the date of Yuhuagong is significant. Constructed just four years after the signing of the Shanyuan Treaty that finalized the loss of Tang Chinese land to the Liao government, its purpose may well have been to mark the region as still inside the Song sphere. Large wooden clusters were its most powerful sign: they had been

an architectural symbol of Chinese power since the Tang dynasty. The *ge*, it is suggested, may have been another such sign.

The same two buildings, main hall and *ge*, had been used by Liao since their initial Buddhist constructions in wood. The Liao, I have suggested, not only adopted the Chinese *ge* but transformed it into a most powerful symbol of their own imperialism on Chinese soil. Could the erection of a *ge* at Yuhuagong in 1008 have been Song's reply to Liao? In 971, we have seen, the first Song emperor built a monastery whose tallest pavilion and bronze statue of Guanyin challenged Liao builders to construct the Guanyin Pavilion at Dulesi. The architecture of that pavilion, I have just argued, surpassed its Song counterpart technically and in the creative manipulation of wood. Perhaps in 1008 the situation, but not the role of architecture as a symbol of powerful

FIGURE 197. Daxiongbao Hall, Baoguo Monastery, Yuyao county, Zhejiang, 1013.
[Steinhardt photograph]

government, had reversed. Perhaps the construction of a monastery with a *ge* in Yuci was an attempt by local Song authorities to declare their continued presence in central Shanxi. As for the three-bay halls, perhaps they had become the norm in Shanxi, but it is just as likely that money was as tight in 1008 as it had been in the second half of the tenth century. In either case, these unassuming halls are *tingtang*, and thus their closest counterpart among architecture of the sixteen *zhou* is the Main Hall of Kaishansi (see fig. 161). Even it was five-bays-by-three.

DAXIONGBAO HALL OF BAOGUOSI

Keeping the cost down seems not to have been of concern to Song builders in southeastern China in the first part of the eleventh century. Daxiongbao Hall of Baoguosi, even in its restored state, provides

evidence of the heights of the Song timber-frame tradition unhampered by political concerns of the north (fig. 197).

Baoguosi is located in a spectacular mountain setting in Yuyao county about 15 kilometers west of Ningbo in Zhejiang province. Records say it was founded in the Han dynasty, was known as Lingshansi, and was destroyed in 845 during the *hui-chang* reign-period persecutions.[32] When rebuilt in 880 the monastery received its name Baoguosi ("Preserving the Nation" Monastery), typical of the nationalism represented by religious reconstruction efforts under Emperor Wuzong's (r. 840–846) successors.[33] Rebuilding took place between 1008 and 1016. In 1065, the monastery's name was changed again when it was subdivided into upper and lower precincts. Today it is known as Baoguosi.

Through local records and stelae one knows that

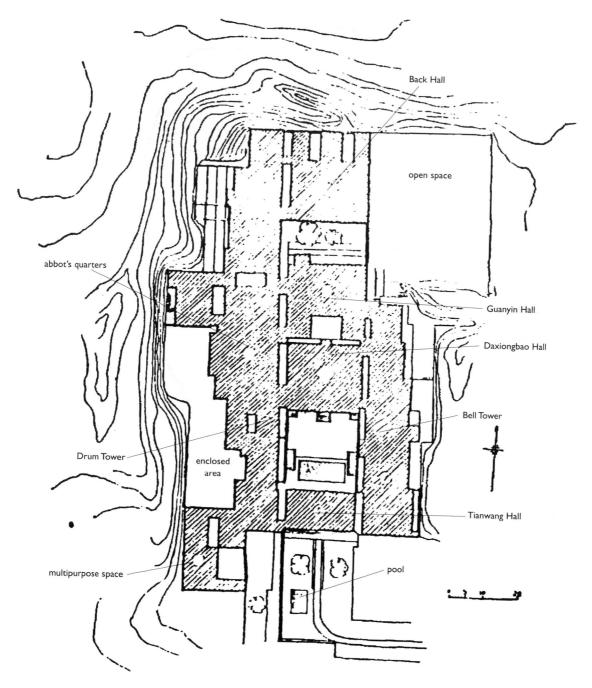

Back Hall

open space

abbot's quarters

Guanyin Hall

Daxiongbao Hall

Drum Tower

Bell Tower

enclosed
area

Tianwang Hall

multipurpose space

pool

FIGURE 198. Plan of Baoguo Monastery today. [After Dou Xuezhi et al., "Baoguosi," p. 54]

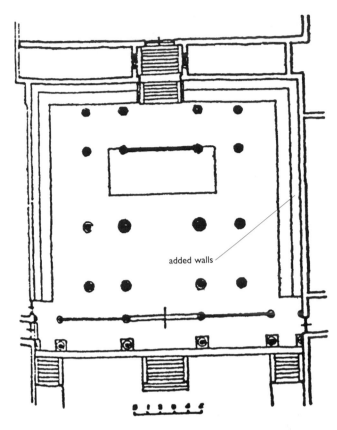

added walls

FIGURE 199. Plan of Daxiongbao Hall, Baoguo Monastery, ca. 1013. [After Dou Xuezhi et al., "Baoguosi," p. 55]

the monastery contained as many as twelve building groups, including a Shanmen that housed divine kings, a Dharma Hall, abbot's and monks' quarters, pavilion, bell and drum towers, guest houses, a sutra hall, a Pure Land Pond, and enclosing corridors (fig. 198). The only Song building is the main hall, Daxiongbaodian, built in 1013 and repaired, according to an inscription on a bracket set, in 1078. The remaining Baoguosi architecture is from the Kangxi period or later. Today Baoguosi is oriented southward, but in the Song dynasty its Shanmen (dismantled in 1954) faced east.[34] A location so far southeast, in the part of China subject to nonnative domination only in the Mongolian period, raises further questions about associations between eastward orientation and Liao monastery planning.

Daxiongbaodian faces just slightly east of due south along the main line of the monastery. Now a five-bay-square hall, in its Tang–early Song version Daxiongbao Hall was a three-bay-square hall (11.91 by 13.35 m). The two-bay-deep porch and side and back walls were added during the Kangxi period (fig. 199).[35] Unlike the many three-bay-square halls examined in this chapter and earlier, however, Daxiongbao Hall of Baoguosi was the only one whose front was shorter than its sides. The Qing increase in width has been attributed to the incorporation of images of the eighteen *luohan*,[36] but the initial cause for the base shape has never been explained. Perhaps it was the result of topography. Other unusual features of the Kangxi-period addition were three separate stairway approaches to the front.

The unusual construction continued inside. Most striking are the *zaojing*, positioned in each of the front three original interior bays (fig. 200), whose presence so sharply contrasts with the ceilingless and exposed roof construction of the two back hall bays. Although rare among what survives, the construction is logical for *tingtang* structures.

In *tingtang,* it was standard for interior columns to be significantly taller than peripheral ones, rising at one- to two-purlin-depth intervals.[37] At Daxiongbao Hall of Baoguosi, the rise was two purlin depths for the front columns of the second bay and one purlin depth for the front columns of the back bay.[38] The columns themselves were "melon-wheel-shaped" (*gualunzhuang*) and came in two varieties: eight-petaled columns were used across the front of the hall and for the horizontal row behind them; the rest of the columns were of the alternate *gualunzhuang* variety. Like the standard "shuttle-shaped columns" (*suo zhu*) observed at other buildings discussed earlier, the *gualunzhuang* columns tapered toward the top of the hall. The melon-wheel-shaped columns also survive in Song-period buildings in Fuzhou, Suzhou, and Changhuaxian, Zhejiang, but in these cases the structures are stone. Baoguosi's Main Hall is the only place *gualunzhuang* columns can be seen in wood.[39] The height/width ratio of column measurements was 7.6:1, relatively thick by Song standards.[40] Pillars were implanted into three different kinds of plinths.

Several features of Daxiongbao Hall of Baoguosi are found also at Hualinsi's Daxiongbao Hall of 964: Figure 201 shows rainbow-shaped beams (*yueliang*); Figure 202 shows the 7-*puzuo* bracketing, here with only two *ang.* These same bracket sets exhibit layer upon layer of *hua gong,* giving the wooden clusters a decidedly lateral thrust (figs. 203 and 204). This is the feature also noted at Daxiongbao Hall of Fengguosi in Liaoning, built just six years after Baoguosi's hall (see figs. 88 and 89) but more than a thousand kilometers to the north.

The significance of Daxiongbao Hall of Baoguosi in the history of Chinese architecture is two-fold. First, it provides evidence, together with the main hall from Hualinsi built half a century earlier, suggesting the separation between Tang architectural styles as they were transmitted to South China

FIGURE 200. *Zaojing* in front bay of Daxiongbao Hall, Baoguo Monastery. [Steinhardt photograph]

FIGURE 201. Rainbow-shaped tiebeam, Daxiongbao Hall, Baoguo Monastery. [Steinhardt photograph]

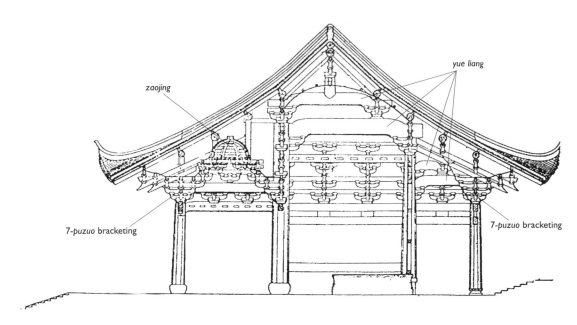

FIGURE 202. Side sectional drawing of Daxiongbao Hall, Baoguo Monastery, showing curved tiebeams, 7-*puzuo* bracketing, and layers of *hua gong*. [After Dou Xuezhi et al., "Baoguosi," p. 57]

compared to northern buildings, notably Liao ones. Important details of this southern Northern Song style are the curved beams, the squarish plan (longer in actual measurement or number of bays of its depth), and the frequent employment of 7-*puzuo* bracketing. Second, the two southern buildings plus another one in Fujian are the source material for a study of the transmission to Japan of what came to be known as Tenjikuyō.

SANQING HALL OF XUANMIAO DAOIST MONASTERY

The third building where the southern Northern Song architectural style is preserved is Sanqing Hall of Xuanmiaoguan, a Daoist monastery located 107 kilometers southeast of Hualinsi. A stele informs us that Xuanmiaoguan was constructed in 1016.[41] Little else is known about its history. *Putianxian zhi* (Record of Putian prefecture) calls it the "old *guan*

on the eastern side of the city."[42] Today only the Hall to the Three Pure Ones (Sanqing), a Tiandi (Emperor of Heaven) Hall, and Eastern Peak and Western Peak (Dong-, Xiyue) halls survive from what was once a much larger temple complex. That anything at all has been preserved is due at least in part to the multifunctionality of Chinese architecture. Today the former Daoist monastery is used for government offices and school buildings. Sanqing-dian is a middle-school lecture hall (fig. 205).

Sanqing Hall is five-bays-by-four. It follows Chinese precedent in the reduction of bay length from the center outward and in a longer front than side dimension (fig. 206). Little studied and rarely published, more of its original form is preserved than those of Hualinsi's or Baoguosi's main halls, with which it is most often compared. The most noteworthy architectural features of Sanqing Hall—its exposed roof construction, curved beams and

FIGURE 203 (left). Bracket sets at Daxiongbao Hall, Baoguo Monastery. [Steinhardt photograph]
FIGURE 204 (below). Bracket sets at Daxiongbao Hall, Baoguo Monastery. [Steinhardt photograph]

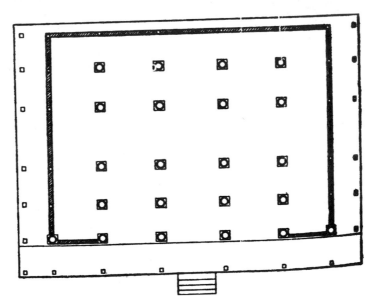

FIGURE 205 (top). Sanqing Hall, Xuanmiao Daoist Monastery, Putian, Fujian, 1016. [Steinhardt photograph]
FIGURE 206 (above). Plan of Sanqing Hall, Xuanmiao Daoist Monastery. [After Lin Zhao, "Xuanmiaoguan," p. 52]

FIGURE 207. Curved beams of Sanqing Hall, Xuanmiao Daoist Monastery. [Steinhardt photograph]

braces, and decidedly vertical presentation of the multiple *hua gong* that comprise its bracket sets (figs. 207 and 208), are shared by the two southeastern Daxiongbao halls. It is the bracketing that so clearly suggests the tenth- and eleventh-century halls of China's southeastern coastal provinces to be precedents for Tenjikuyō architecture (see fig. 91).

SHENGMU HALL OF THE JIN SHRINES

Shengmu, literally Holy Mother, is the second non-Buddhist Northern Song hall. Built during the first reign-period of Emperor Renzong (r. 1023–1032), the hall is one of several focal points in a building complex known as the Jin Shrines (Jinci) (fig. 209).[43] The hall dedicated to the mother of Prince Shuyu of the Zhou dynasty is the only extant Song building at the Taiyuan site (fig. 210). It is best known today for the more than forty clay statues of females, many surviving from the Song period.[44] Shengmu Hall was rebuilt in 1102.

The approach to Shengmu Hall is unique. Between a Jin-period offering hall (dated to 1168) and the Hall of the Holy Mother is a cruciform-shaped white marble bridge (see fig. 209). The impressive approach and imperial patronage suggest that the hall will be structurally spectacular—which, in fact, it is. It is the only Northern Song hall besides Moni Hall of Longxingsi that fits the specifications for the highest-ranking hall, *diantang*, prescribed in *juan* 31 and 32 of the *Yingzao fashi*.[45] The eminent hall structure is distinguished, however, by the use of an eight-rafter beam and interior and exterior columns of equal length (fig. 211).[46] Bracketing at Shengmu Hall is 7-*puzuo* with one false *ang*. All *ang* are of the *qinmian* variety noted in eleventh-

FIGURE 208. Bracket sets from interior of Sanqing Hall, Xuanmiao Daoist Monastery. [Steinhardt photograph]

century halls at Longxingsi in Hebei, as are the ends of *shuatou*, which in all respects appear as *ang* (see figs. 189 and 190). A final feature of its imperial associations are the gilt dragons that wind around the front pillars (fig. 212). This detail is recorded as having been built at the main hall of the Yuan palace-city in Dadu.[47] It persists in architecture of imperial patronage including Dacheng Hall from the Confucian Shrine in Qufu and the Temple to Guandi in Yuncheng, Shanxi, both of which have stone columns.

NORTHERN SONG ARCHITECTURE IN JINCHENG, SHANXI

Four dated Northern Song buildings from three temple complexes stand in Jincheng county of Shanxi province, some 50 kilometers from the unexplored architecture of Gaoping. Two of the building groups are Daoist and the third is Buddhist. All are even less well published than Gaoping's architecture.[48]

Two of them, the Middle Hall and Jade Emperor Hall, are found at Yuhuangmiao. Both are dated to 1076. Next is the Main Hall of Two Immortals Daoist Monastery, built ca. 1100.[49] The Buddhist structure, dated 1102, is the Main Hall, dedicated to Śākyamuni Buddha, of Qinglian Monastery, located on a mountain southeast of the Jincheng town center.[50]

MAIN HALL OF CHUZU'AN

The Main Hall of Chuzu'an stands just 2 *li* from the larger and famous monastery Shaolinsi (still a training site for highly disciplined Shaolin martial artists). This latest dated Northern Song building, the only one extant in Henan, is a humble, three-bay-square hall (fig. 213). The entire building complex occupies a plot only 75 by 35 meters.[51] The mountainous site about 10 kilometers northwest of Dengfeng traces its history at least to the year 537 when

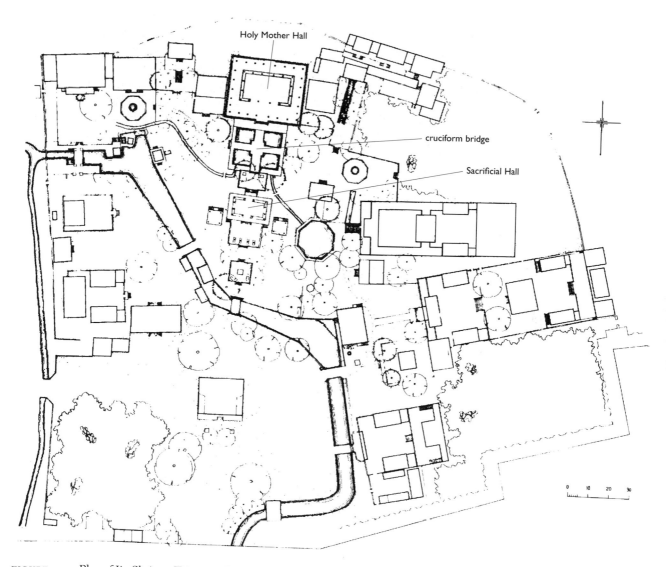

Holy Mother Hall

cruciform bridge

Sacrificial Hall

FIGURE 209. Plan of Jin Shrines, Taiyuan, Shanxi, Song dynasty and later. [After Liu Dunzhen, *Zhongguo gudai jianzhu shi*, 2nd ed., p. 196]

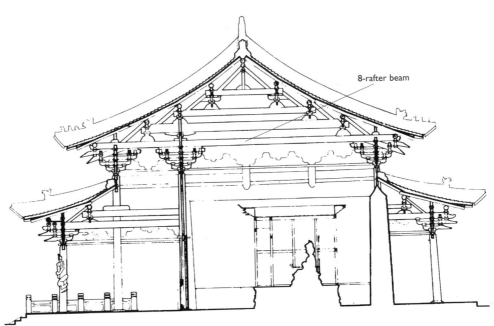

8-rafter beam

FIGURE 210 (top). Holy Mother Hall, Jin Shrines, Taiyuan, Shanxi, 1023–1032. [After *Ancient Chinese Architecture*, p. 87]

FIGURE 211 (above). Side sectional drawing of Holy Mother Hall, Jin shrines. [After *Ancient Chinese Architecture*, p. 88]

Bodhidharma, legendary founder of the Chan sect in China, visited Shaolinsi. Originally said to have housed a Shanmen, a Thousand Buddhas Pavilion, and auxiliary halls and to have been oriented north-west, today only the Main Hall of 1125 and two Qing-period pavilions survive. One of these pavilions is dedicated to Chuzu'an's founder.[52]

The three-bay-square *tingtang* has a single-eaved, hip-gable roof with green tiles. Its nearly square plan (11.14 by 10.7 m) consists of twelve exterior *(yan zhu)* and four interior *(jin zhu)* pillars; the two back interior pillars have been dislodged from their positions along the back interior bay to make room for an altar (fig. 214). It was on one of the front interior pillars that the date 1125 was discovered. Side exterior pillars measured 3.53 meters, including 12-centimeter-high bases. The pillars were thick by Song standards, with a height/diameter ratio of 7:1.[53] The pillars rose 7 centimeters toward the corners. Access to the hall was from the center front or back bays. The front bay was approached by a three-part *tadao*, the divisions suggestive of impe-rial construction. The only windows were in the side bays of the front facade.

The main question raised in the two studies of Chuzu'an's Main Hall is the degree to which con-struction is consistent with the text of the *Yingzao fashi*. Although this issue was of great concern to scholars of Chinese architecture in the 1930s and 1940s, sometimes eclipsing other questions of po-tential interest, it is of special pertinence here. The construction manual was first issued less than twenty-five years before Chuzu'an Main Hall was built, and in the same province. (The Song capital, Bianliang, was at today's Kaifeng.) The closest cor-respondences between text and construction are found in bracketing. The three types of bracket sets—found atop exterior pillars, between them, and atop columns on the inside—differ from those described in the text only in a slightly elongated

FIGURE 212. Front pillars with gilt dragons entwined on them, Holy Mother Hall, Jin Shrines. [Steinhardt photograph]

FIGURE 213. Main Hall, Chuzu'an, Dengfeng county, Henan, 1125.
[After Liang Ssu-ch'eng, *A Pictorial History of Chinese Architecture*, p. 89;
published with permission of Wilma Fairbank]

shuatou and a slightly lower than 3:2 *cai* ratio.[54]
One detail of intercolumnar bracketing found here
and at Liao buildings in Datong is the "male-and-
female mandarin ducks" bracket arm (see fig. 123).
The other feature associated with Liao construction
and found here is the brace known as *taqian*. (See,
for example, fig. 153.) Befitting a humble hall, there
is no ceiling. Nor is the *pupai* tiebeam employed.[55]
The longest beam at the Chuzu'an Main Hall extends six rafters. Chuzu'an Main Hall has been repaired numerous times, most recently in the twentieth century.

LIAO HALLS AND SONG HALLS

To compare them with Liao timber-frame halls, it
helps to divide Song halls into three groups. First
are the designs of imperial patronage: Moni Hall of
Longxing Monastery and Shengmu Hall of the Jin

Shrines.[56] Second are the three halls of southeastern China at Hualinsi, Baoguosi, and Xuanmiaoguan, interpreted in studies cited earlier as components of a lineage of southern-style construction
that would influence Japanese architecture of the
early Kamakura period. Last, and most numerous,
are three-bay-square halls, structural equivalents of
which also survive as wood-earthen facades to the
Mogao Caves (fig. 215).[57] Each of these types is represented by tenth-century timber construction.

Among the thirteen tenth-century timber-frame
buildings considered in this study, six constructed
between 963 and 984 are most instructive in helping us to determine the impact of that century's architecture on what was to follow. The six buildings
are the Main Hall of Zhenguosi in Pingyao dated
963 (see fig. 70), the Main Hall of Hualinsi of 964 in
Fuzhou (see fig. 172), the Main Hall of Geyuansi in
Laiyuan dated 966 (see fig. 81), Foxiang (or Cishi)
Pavilion of Longxingsi in Zhengding, both originally constructed in 971 (see figs. 177 and 178),
Guanyin Pavilion of Dulesi from 984 (see fig. 23),
and the Great Buddha Hall of Dayunyuan from
the Later Jin period (936–946; see fig. 77). Four of
these, the main halls of Zhenguosi, Hualinsi, Geyuansi, and Dayunyuan, are of the three-bay-square
variety noted earlier as the most prevalent among
surviving architecture of the Northern Song.

Much of the contrast between Liao and Song aspirations, symbolically expressed through architecture, is observed in pavilion structure. The contrast
between the pavilion in eastern central Hebei and
those in central Hebei, about 250 kilometers (as the
crow flies) to the southwest, can be observed in
building sections (see figs. 32, 33, and 180). Both
Cishi Pavilion and Guanyinge are two-story structures with *pingzuo* concealed inside—a feature
whose possible Tang origins still cannot be confirmed—but the Song pavilion is structurally far
simpler than the Liao hall. In fact, each of the fea-

tures used to emphasize the structural ingenuity of the Liao pavilion is simplified in the Song hall. One recalls from Figure 31 that Guanyinge was described as a set of individual one-story halls piled on top of one another. The lack of a pillar that spanned stories, in fact, was a potential structural weakness. Yet the Liao compensated for that possibility by intricate braces and joiners between the three levels. In all three Song pavilions, a massive column extends from the interior floor to the roof purlins. Although the building is structurally sound, the vertical thrust detracts from the drama of an empty interior. Its omission made possible a kind of interior drama and focus on the bodhisattva that remain unique in the Chinese universe of forms (see fig. 6). The Song, by contrast, indeed the imperial Song patrons, furthered the rigid interior atmosphere by the use of exclusively straight beams. The side section is essentially a checkerboard of different-sized rectangles in which the image awkwardly cuts through the grid lines. Rather than contesting the role of the bodhisattva in the hall, at Dulesi not only did the beams and columns respond to the focal image through elimination, size, or curved shape, but the pinnacle of the drama was intensified by the *zaojing*. Although *zaojing* construction may have been known to the builders of Cishi Pavilion, the structure nevertheless has a flat ceiling. On the exterior, too, the visual power of the Liao pavilion replaced the rigidity of Foxiangge. The excessive and massive eaves that cover the Song front porch (see fig. 182) combined with the straight walls and great height to produce as rigid an effect as the perpendicular pillars and beams inside. The genius of interior design around the Liao Guanyin was unmatched by any Song structure.

Equally important in understanding the tenth-century contribution to the divergent paths of Liao and Song architecture is a comparison of the monastery plans. Comparing Longxingsi, the most in-

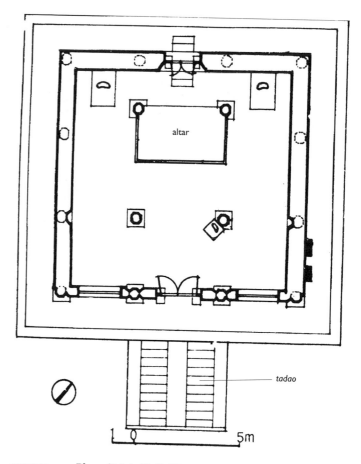

FIGURE 214. Plan of Main Hall, Chuzu'an. [After *Liu Dunzhen wenji*, vol. 2, p. 410]

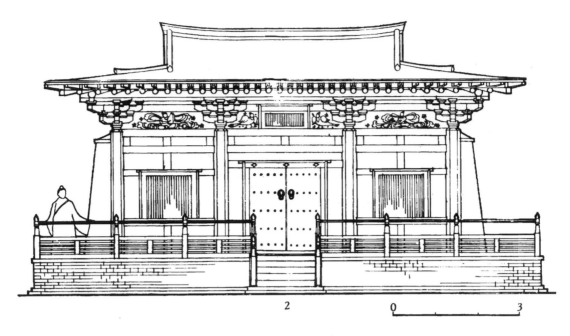

FIGURE 215. Line drawing of front facade of Mogao Cave 53, Dunhuang. [After Pan and Ma, *Mogaoku kuqian diantang yizhi*, p. 131]

tact Song monastery and one that received imperial patronage, with any of several that survive from Liao rulership, one can observe the results of tenth-century planning in the next century. Throughout the eleventh century, Liao builders continued to direct monastery space to a single symbol through which Qidan supremacy could be manifest. The ultimate surviving example of this desire to express imperial power in the form of a tall pagoda or pavilion that housed Buddhist deities and stood in front of one main hall is Fogongsi, constructed in Yingxian at the midpoint of the eleventh century (see fig. 100). The same purposeful, planned space is observed in Fengguosi, Guangjisi in Hebei, and Guangjisi in Liaoning (see figs. 94–97). (The Hebei Guangjisi pavilion had been destroyed.) At the Song monastery, by contrast, despite the tremendous height of Foxiangge, it was only one of four

prominent structures and two less impressive ones along the main building line (see fig. 176). Although one cannot miss the prominence of Foxiangge from any viewpoint (see fig. 175), an unambiguous focus is replaced not only by several architecturally fascinating buildings but by construction along subsidiary axes (see fig. 176).

In single-story Song halls such as Moni Hall or Holy Mother Hall at the Jin Shrines, one observes a fascination with delicate features and structural beauty like the *qinmian ang* and the four porticoes. At eleventh-century main Buddha halls of Liao patronage one finds, instead, an aesthetic of somber power. Bracket sets project against a stark exterior at the main halls of Fengguosi, Guangjisi, and Huayansi and at the Muta—in the last case one is not even aware of the scores of different bracketing details among them. In Liao construction, decorative ingenuity is reserved for the interior; the exterior's purpose is to inspire awe. (Compare figs. 86 and 149 with 186 and 190.)

The other four tenth-century halls reflect the varying but symbolic architectural aesthetics that would emerge in the eleventh century. Hualinsi's Daxiongbaodian has been shown to have preserved vestiges of Tang style that would flourish in the eleventh century in southeastern China and come to be symbols of Chinese Buddhism in Japan in the twelfth century. Ten Thousand Buddhas Hall of Zhenguosi also employed elements of Tang architecture—there for the purpose of expressing aspirations of imperialism according to Tang norms. Yet in 963, at the same building, the straight beams that gave Longxingsi's architecture its rigidity were present. The limited persistence of Tang-size bracketing in a small hall in the eleventh century—at, for example, the Main Hall of Yuhuagong (see figs. 195 and 196)—was due to the reality that in eleventh-century Northern Song territory in the north, Chinese power was not at full strength. Rather, architecture of the Northern Song in the north was easier to construct, and more rigid and less dramatic inside, than its Liao counterparts. Wenshu Hall of Geyuansi, the earliest Liao hall, has been shown to follow Tang precedents but not

to exhibit the symbolic power expressed by later Liao wooden halls. Simply, it was built too early and in too remote a region to be typical of Liao architecture. It should be viewed as a mid-tenth-century religious building not much different from those in nearby Shanxi, but in Liao territory. Its features, by contrast to those of Guanyinge of Dulesi built less than twenty years later, make the architectural achievement of the earliest extant Liao pavilion all the more impressive. Similarly the Main Hall from Dayunyuan, like Zhenguosi's Main Hall, the only wooden monument from a short-lived kingdom, offers little original or noteworthy. Like the other tenth-century buildings in Shanxi and the first Liao wooden building, it symbolizes the standard religious hall from which those of Liao and Song were to emerge.

Thus as tenth-century dynasties and kingdoms fell, and as painters in Bianliang, Chengdu, and Nanjing worked out the new styles that were to alter the history of Chinese painting, builders of Liao and Song sprang forth from Tang to erect what would become the model monuments of the next centuries. It was to be a legacy of Qidan patrons that their Liao halls, pavilions, and monasteries would take so seriously the potential of architecture to represent imperial goals and achievement.

FIGURE 216. Sanqing Hall, Xuanmiao Daoist Monastery, Suzhou, 1176, detail. [Steinhardt photograph]

9

Jin Architecture: A Liao Legacy?

IT HAS BEEN standard practice to write about Liao and Jin wooden buildings together.[1] The reasons for this interpretation of the history of Chinese architecture—in particular the rebuilding of Liao halls and refacement of Liao pagodas by Jin patrons—are understandable but, perhaps, not justifiable.

As we have seen, the distinctions between Liao and Song that were forged in the tenth century become even more polarized in the eleventh. In the twelfth and thirteenth centuries, buildings of southeastern China would exhibit the high ceilings, broadly overhanging and sloping eaves, and decorative quality that already characterized Song construction in the south in the eleventh century (fig. 216).[2] Jin architecture, we shall see, is lacking in these details. Our purpose here is to look at Jin wooden architecture independent of Liao and then try to determine whether construction in North China between 1126 and 1234 was merely an appendage to Liao architecture (and, if so, the implications of that statement) or whether Jin builders made a unique contribution to Chinese architectural history (and the implications of that contribution). Another important question is this: if not for Jin, which elements of Liao would have survived?

TABLE 5. Jin Wooden Buildings in Shanxi

Hall	Monastery	Location	Date
Main Hall	Upper Huayansi	Datong	ca. 1060, rebuilt Jin
Main Hall	Jingtusi	Yingxian	1124*
Sansheng Hall	Shanhuasi	Datong	1128
Shanmen	Shanhuasi	Datong	1128–1143
Mañjuśrī Hall	Foguangsi	Taihuaixian (Wutai)	1137
Amitābha Hall	Chongfusi	Shuoxian	1143
Guanyin Hall	Chongfusi	Shuoxian	Jin
Main Hall	Zetian Shengmumiao	Wenshuixian	1145
Mañjuśrī Hall	Yanshansi	Fanshixian	1153
Dongyue Dadi Hall	Dongyuemiao	Jinchengxian	1161–1189
Dacheng Hall	Wenmiao	Pingyao	1163
Xiandian	Jinci	Taiyuan	1168
Shanmen	Xianyingwangmiao (Fujunmiao)	Lingchuanxian	1184
Main Hall	Yanqingsi	Wutaixian	Jin
Ten Thousand Buddhas Hall	Chongqingsi	Zhangzi	Jin

*Even though the last Liao emperor, Tianzuo, officially reigned until 1125, the Jin were in control of Yingxian by 1124. Thus the Main Hall of Jingtusi is considered a Jin structure.

To answer these questions, one might write a book on Jin timber-frame architecture. That, of course, is not our purpose here. (If it were, one would have to start from scratch—for far less literature survives on that subject than has been available for this study.) Here we are going to survey the most noteworthy features of Jin's most noteworthy wooden halls.

At least fourteen wooden buildings survive from the Jin empire (see Table 5). Remarkably, even though the Jin empire was as expansive as Liao's, including four former Liao capitals among its five,[3] each of the fourteen is in Shanxi, the province already shown to be the most important for the study of extant Tang and Five Dynasties–Ten Kingdoms architecture and an important one, too, for Liao and Song (see Map 2).[4]

Four of the Jin buildings are at temple complexes that flourished in the eleventh century—three in Datong and one at the Jinci in Taiyuan. Two Jin buildings remain at monasteries of Mount Wutai (one at Foguangsi and one at Yanqingsi); a Jin building stands in Yingxian only a few kilometers from the Timber Pagoda; and Jin architecture survives in Jincheng and in Pingyao. Among Jin buildings discussed here, only one, at Yanshan Monastery, is at a site with no Liao-period history.

FIGURE 217. Mituo Hall, Chongfu Monastery, Shuo county, Shanxi, 1153. [After Li Yuming, *Shanxi gujianzhu . . .*, p. 78]

The most grandiose Jin hall is the one that has the strongest ties to the Liao tradition: Daxiongbao Hall of Huayansi. As noted in the discussion of that monastery (Chapter 6), the nine-bay building was constructed in 1060 and rebuilt in 1140 and provides evidence of what a Liao-Jin label may exemplify. After Daxiongbao Hall, the Amitābha Hall of Chongfusi in Shuoxian and Mañjuśrī Hall at Foguangsi are the most eminent Jin buildings.

Chongfu Monastery was established in 655, but in Liao times the site was an official residence.[5] By decree of Hailingwang (r. 1149–1160), the buildings were transformed into a Pure Land monastery named Chongfusi. At least ten structures are known to have stood there: Daxiongdian (also known as Sanbaodian), built in the same year, 1153, as the two extant Jin buildings to its north, the Mituo (Ami-

tābha)[6] and Guanyin halls (figs. 217 and 218), a Shanmen, Tianwang Hall, bell and drum towers, Thousand Buddhas Pavilion (for scripture storage), and west and east side halls to Wenshu and Puxian, respectively. Figure 219 is a reconstruction of this plan. The presence of the *ge* and the number of buildings along the main axis suggest that the plan followed the Liao or Northern Song arrangement in North China.

Mituo Hall is elevated on a 2.53-meter platform that extends a full bay beyond the hall on every side. Its five central-front bays and two of the back bays, the second ones from the ends, have doors; the hall has no windows, probably to avoid breaking the narrative continuity of the wall paintings that cover its interior walls.[7] Despite the proportion of bays across the front to sides (7:4) and the use of 7-*puzuo*

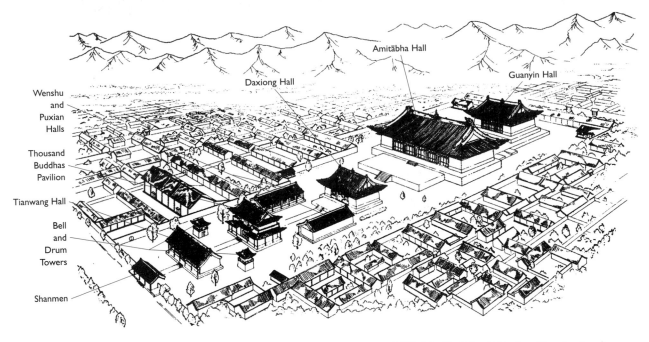

FIGURE 218 (top). Chongfu Monastery showing Mituo Hall and Guanyin Hall behind it. [After Li Yuming, *Shanxi gujianzhu . . .*, p. 78]

FIGURE 219 (above). Bird's-eye rendering of Chongfu Monastery. [After Chai and Li, *Chongfusi*, p. 2]

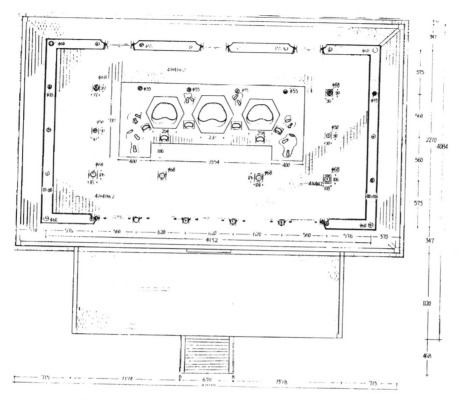

FIGURE 220. Plan of Mituo Hall, Chongfu Monastery. [After Chai and Li, *Chongfusi*, line drawing 4]

bracket sets above the columns of the front facade, the hall has a hip-gable-combination roof. As we have seen in other Liao wooden halls, columns were both eliminated and moved off axis inside the hall (fig. 220).

The timber frame of Mituo Hall exhibits several features unknown in earlier architecture. Added beneath exceptionally long lintels (*nei'e* or *youheng fang*)—12.45 meters for the central bay and 8.7 meters for the intermediate bays—was a new feature: a sublintel (*you'e* or *xiaheng fang*) to share the support of four-rafter beams that, in structures with more columns, might have been borne by lintels alone. Camel's-hump-shaped and numerous diagonal braces served as cushions between the lintels

(see fig. 221). Extremely simple (by medieval standards) bracket sets, composed of a single set of *hua gong*, are used above column-top bracket sets to support upper beams (see fig. 221). *Panjian* are positioned beneath the purlins of every bay, although in varying numbers. A Liao-Jin feature at Datong monasteries and employed here is fan-shaped, column-top bracketing in which arms project at 45- and 60-degree angles as well as perpendicular to the building plane.

The other seven-by-four-bay Jin hall is Wenshu (Mañjuśrī) Hall of Foguangsi, built in 1137 as one of a pair. (A hall to Puxian has been lost.) All discussions of the structure point out that, like Mituo Hall of Chongfusi, Wenshudian is an example of what

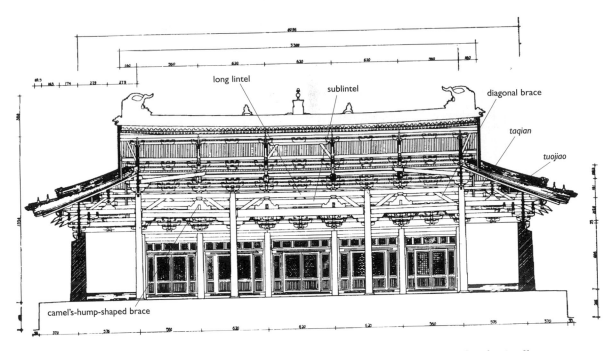

FIGURE 221. Frontal section of Mituo Hall, Chongfu Monastery. [After Chai and Li, *Chongfusi*, line drawing 6]

the *Yingzao fashi* calls *bajiachuan wu*, an eight-rafter structure in which four columns are used in the cross section, the center two of which are joined by a beam and the others to them by extension beams.[8] Raised on a less dramatic platform (only 83 cm) than Mituo Hall, but of the same number of bays, the building is approached by five steps. It has three front doors and two windows, a central back door, fan-shaped column-top bracket clusters, and a single-eave hip-gable roof (fig. 222). The hall is one of the most excessive examples of interior column elimination, retaining only four interior pillars, again necessitating the elongated lintels and camel's-hump-shaped and diagonal braces inside. Liang Sicheng described this combination as a "queen-post truss"; Zhang Yuhuan calls it the first Chinese employment of a true truss (fig. 223).[9] Neither Jin-period seven-by-four-bay hall has a ceiling.

The most spectacular Jin ceiling survives in one of the smaller halls, the Main Hall of Jingtusi, like Chongfusi a Pure Land monastery, built in 1124 (fig. 224).[10] Yet lack of ceilings and exposure of the roof frame seems to be a trait of Jin timber construction—the only other ceiling from the period covers the interior of the nine-bay Daxiongbao of Huayansi, originally a Liao structure.

The majority of extant Jin religious architecture in wood is structurally fairly simple. The ceilingless five-by-two-bay Shanmen and five-by-four-bay Sansheng Hall from Shanhuasi exhibit fan-shaped bracket sets (fig. 225) and interior column elimination characteristic of Datong and other architecture of the period. The five-by-three-bay Guanyin Hall from Chongfusi and the five-by-three-bay Mañjuśrī Hall from Yanshan Monastery in Fanshi, the latter of which only came to public attention in 1973 (fig.

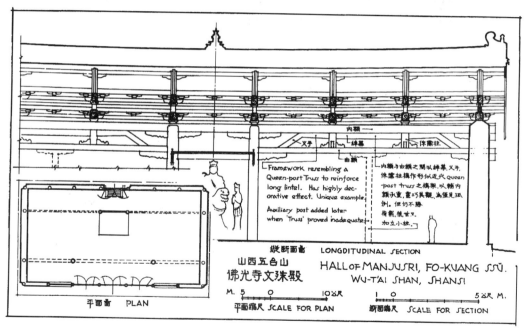

内額 ←
×子 绰幕 侏儒柱
由額
Framework resembling a
Queen-post Truss to reinforce
long lintel. Has highly decorative effect. Unique example.

内額与由額之間以绰幕,×子,
侏儒柱構作形似近代 queen
-post truss 之構架,以輔内
額永重,畫巧其觀,為僅見孤
例。但仍不勝
指载,後世又。
加立小柱。

Auxiliary post added later
when 'Truss' proved inadequate.

縱斷面畫　LONGDITUDINAL SECTION
山西五台山　HALL OF MANJUSRI, FO-KUANG SSŬ.
佛光寺文殊殿　WU-T'AI SHAN, SHANSI
M. 5　0　10公尺
平面縮尺 SCALE FOR PLAN
1　0　5公尺 M.
斷面縮尺 SCALE FOR SECTION

平面畫　PLAN

FIGURE 222 (top). Mañjuśrī Hall, Foguang Monastery, Taihuai county, Shanxi, detail of front, 1137.
[Steinhardt photograph]
FIGURE 223 (above). Plan and frontal section of Mañjuśrī Hall, Foguang Monastery. [After Liang Ssu-ch'eng,
A *Pictorial History of Chinese Architecture*, p. 87; published with permission of Wilma Fairbank]

FIGURE 224. Ceiling, Main Hall, Jingtu Monastery, Ying county, Shanxi, 1124. [After *Ancient Chinese Architecture*, p. 103]

226), are more important for their wall paintings than their structural details. If one were certain the paintings were replicas of architecture of the time, rather than idealizations, one would conclude that little of the splendor of Jin has survived (fig. 227).[11] The remaining Jin wooden architecture—the Main Hall of Yanqingsi (fig. 228), Xian Hall of the Jin Shrines, the Xianyingwangmiao Shanmen, the Song-Jin Main Hall of Qingliansi, and Ten Thousand Buddhas Hall of Chongqingsi—are all three-bay, hip-gable-roofed structures.

What, then, can one say of the Liao legacy or a distinctive Jin tradition? Frequent elimination of interior columns, intensified use of lintels and development of a roof truss, fan-shaped bracketing—these are the details associated with Jin architecture at this time. Yet even if none of them would have appeared in China without Liao construction, these few features are hardly worthy of the distinctions "legacy" or "tradition." Rather, one understands by contrast to Jin—or, perhaps more accurately stated, by examination of architecture in Shanxi province in the century after Liao—the truly unsurpassed construction systems offered by Qidan patronage. Can it only be coincidence of survival that *zaojing* were constructed in so many Liao halls, even otherwise humble buildings at Kaiyuan Monastery, but only one example of *zaojing*, at the Main Hall of Jingtusi, is known from the century after Liao rule? Is it just the luck of survival that Guanyinge, the Muta, and the Sutra Library of Huayansi startle the worshiper once inside, whereas a similar experience occurs only through wall paintings or in the one hall with a *zaojing* in Jin buildings?

Among Liao-controlled provinces, the one in which Jin architecture survives is the one with the

FIGURE 225 (above). Shanmen, Shanhua Monastery, Datong, 1128–1143. [Steinhardt photograph]

FIGURE 226 (left). Mañjuśrī Hall, Yanshan Monastery, Fanshi county, Shanxi, 1153. [After Li Yuming, *Shanxi gujianzhu . . .*, p. 136]

FIGURE 227. Line drawing of wall paintings from Mañjuśrī Hall, Yanshan Monastery, detail.
[After Fu Xinian, "Yanshansi," p. 123]

longest and most intensive construction history in China. Excellent Chinese craftsmen must have been available for Jin building projects in Shanxi. Certainly Han Chinese wall-painting workshops were laboring at a tremendous pace in twelfth-, thirteenth-, and fourteenth-century Shanxi.[12] How is it, then, that with the possible exception of Mituodian of Chongfu Monastery, what survives as the Jin tradition is so architecturally undistinguished? Perhaps the label "Liao-Jin" is misconstrued. The nomenclature, I would suggest, is largely the result of the accessibility of Datong and the resulting presentation beginning in the 1930s of its architecture as indistinguishably Liao or Jin. One role that may be Jin's, as noted in Chapter 6, is the tendency to reori-

ent monasteries east-west—a tendency that, due to this Liao-Jin label, has been greatly exaggerated for Liao building complexes.

The major role played by Jin in the Liao legacy was the preservation or restoration of what Liao had built. Most of the Liao monasteries, as we have seen, had Jin histories. Many also had Manchu histories, and that late restoration, as shown, for example, at Dulesi, is more detectable than Jin's. Yet the issue of Liao or Jin is not a matter of which architectural detail predates or postdates 1125. The issue is why, in their own construction, the Jin were satisfied to use, preserve, and restore but seem not to have attempted to duplicate architectural masterpieces like Guanyinge, the Muta, or Fengguosi's

FIGURE 228. Main Hall, Yanqing Monastery, Wutai county, Shanxi, Jin period. [After *Wutaishan*, fig. 34]

Daxiongbao Hall or to have progressed to even more grandeur or complexity. It is through contrast with Jin construction in Shanxi that one understands again, as was the case with Song construction of the tenth and eleventh centuries, what master builders the Liao were. They, more than any of their predecessors on China's soil, exploited the potential of the Chinese-invented timber frame. Those who had none before created a monumental, imperial building tradition. In so doing, they created an imperial identity and cultural legacy out of pavilions, pagodas, worship halls, and their posi-

tions in planned space. In the process they preserved some of what would otherwise have been lost to China by the Song, whose architectural tradition was exemplified in the north by Moni and Shengmu halls and in the south by the monasteries Hualinsi, Baoguosi, and their Southern Song successors. The imperial Qidan understood and interpreted as no one else the power of a Chinese building tradition and, as a result, provided a legacy for future China. In the process, Chinese posts and lintels soared to unprecedented heights.

The Funerary Tradition

II

10

The Imperial Qidan Funerary Tradition

AMONG THE MOST fascinating observations of the peoples referred to in Chinese texts as Donghu (literally "Eastern Barbarians," of which the predynastic Qidan are one group) are descriptions of their burial practices.[1] Sections entitled *Qidan zhuan*, *Suishu* (Standard history of the Sui), devoted to the years 581–617, and *Beishi* (Standard history of the Northern Dynasties), devoted to the years 368–618, both compiled in the early years of the Tang empire, relate that when the parent of a Donghu died, the mourner "placed the corpse on a tree." Not until three years had passed would the bones be gathered and burned. Following would

be wine libations. During this "ceremony," the mourner would make the supplication that "when he went hunting he might shoot many pigs and deer."[2]

PREDYNASTIC BURIAL PRACTICES

The practice of placing a corpse on tree limbs for a three-year period of disintegration continued into the Tang dynasty among the northern peoples who are believed to be ancestors of the Qidan. In reference to them, *Jiu Tangshu* (Old standard history of the Tang), compiled in the first half of the tenth century, records: "When a person dies, it is customary not to bury him in the ground. Rather, the corpse is sent by horse-drawn conveyance to the great mountains where it is placed on a tree without [mourning] garments or identification." The text continues by noting that when a male descendant dies, the parents and grandparents mourn from dawn until dusk, but in the case of a parent or grandparent's death, sons and grandsons do not mourn.[3]

The use of the term "custom" (*su*) in the Chinese text may not have been written with the same attention to word choice employed in the twentieth century, but these three descriptions, and those quoted in the Introduction for the reigns of Abaoji and Deguang, do confirm the existence of indigenous funerary practices among the predynastic predecessors of Liao. Nowhere is a tomb or underground structure described. Yet beginning with Abaoji, every Qidan ruler was buried in a *ling*, a Chinese term best translated as "royal tomb," for its occupant must have royal blood or a connection to the royal family. Excavated Qidan *ling*, as we shall see, as well as nonimperial tombs discussed in Chapter 12, show the Liao to have been tomb builders of exceptional creativity and ambition. The transformation from a corpse rotting on a tree to interment in a seven-chamber subterranean palace, which may have occurred within half a century of the onset of Liao rule, is truly startling. In his search for an explanation for such a dramatic change in practice, Jing Ai has emphasized the existence of sixth-century cremation burials (interment of ashes) in what became Liao territory.[4]

The purpose of linking the observations of Chinese writers about burial practices north of China with actual burial — including the story of the amputation and burial of Empress Yingtian's hand upon the demise of the first Liao ruler — is to try to explain Qidan ideology. One seeks an understanding of who the Qidan were, how they lived, and how they viewed their lives in the centuries before

Abaoji. How did they come to borrow, accommodate, adopt, adapt, use, or discard Chinese practices they encountered and to retain, discard, or amend native customs on their path toward North Asian imperialism? In the absence of Qidan descriptions of themselves, Chinese writers of standard histories and other texts have become de facto anthropologists. Most famous among these is probably the Southern Song author Wen Weijian (quoted in the Introduction), whose description of the culmination of the postmortem preparation of the second Qidan emperor Deguang as "imperial dried meat" is hard to forget. Even though a contemporary Chinese scholar may derive some comfort in a "logical" explanation for the process, implying that since Deguang died in the "heat of summer" preparation such as that described may have been the only way to preserve a corpse for the journey from central Hebei to his final resting place in present Inner Mongolia,[5] the same writer recognizes that other Yelü corpses were treated in the same manner. In the aftermath of sudden death in Song territory, Yelü Jian's corpse was hung upside down so that bodily fluids could drip out of the mouth and nose. A writing brush was used to prick his skin to allow additional internal fluids to drain out. His body was treated with alum to "guard against disease" and was then "returned," presumably to his place of birth, presumably for burial.[6] As late as 1092, when Yelü Di died in Huazhou, Henan province, his body too was hung upside down to allow internal fluids to drip out, after which the skin was pricked with a sharp brush so that more liquid could flow forth. Only then was alum spread over the body.[7] Together with the masks and netting of precious metals excavated at such Liao tombs as that of the Princess of Chenguo and her husband, Liao art and artifacts, perhaps more than those of any other dynasty, offer the most ideal sort of mutual confirmation of text and material culture.[8] Furthermore, the artifacts and associated burial practices suggest ties between the Qidan and other North Asian peoples—ties as far-reaching, perhaps, as to seventh-century-B.C. peoples of Siberia.

The descriptions of Song and earlier Chinese writers of Qidan practices regarding the corpse lead one to general studies of death ritual, the anthropology of death, and funerary architecture in search of a context those writers do not provide. Few would dispute, for example, the relevance to Liao material (or to Chinese tombs) of the lines from the first paragraph of Howard Colvin's *Architecture and the After-Life*:

> Faced with the supreme crisis of death, man has in the past devised elaborate social and religious rituals and has spent enormous sums on sculptured tombs and on buildings to house them. The rituals may now seem bizarre or at best picturesque, the tombs speak a dead language or symbolism, and few of the buildings still fulfil the religious purposes for which they were originally built. Some of them are, nevertheless, among the most celebrated of historic monuments, the most popular of tourist attractions.[9]

Beneficiaries of a century of cultural anthropology, today we in the West attempt to understand the Qidan, or, more generally, Donghu, through the fieldwork of Hertz, Van Gennep, and more recently Geertz and Huntington and Metcalf and through descriptions of preindustrial societies in other parts of the world.[10] For example, perhaps the Qidan indulged in a three-year period of corporeal rotting as a means of paying homage to a liminal phase of existence. Royal Qidan may have believed that the construction of a tomb by the heir apparent was a passage of centralized authority or an expression of the ever-present power of the current ruler's ancestors. It is a universal truth that in the face of death people are more introspective and more willing, on the one hand, to explore possibilities of other ideologies, even competing ideologies, and, on the other hand, to return to roots never evidenced in life, than in any other rite of passage such as birth, marriage, or initiation. It is reasonable, therefore, that in the architecture of death one might find some insights into the Qidan that remain veiled or indeed never even played a part in the construction of Chinese-style walled cities or timber halls.

Beyond remarkable descriptions such as those already quoted, the evidence through which one attempts to understand the role of tomb construction—and, more generally, architecture in Qidan and Liao society—remains the structures themselves. As for tombs, their number is staggering. If one is impressed that fourteen or fifteen wooden halls of Liao patronage stand, one is at a loss where to begin when confronted with the several hundred Liao tombs excavated and published by the early 1990s. No attempt will be made here (nor is one required) to discuss or even list every known Liao tomb. Certain tombs that aid our understanding of a Liao funerary, architectural tradition are discussed.[11] The tradition begins with royalty.

ZUZHOU

From the last chapter of Abaoji's biography in *Liao-shi*, one learns that the ruler died in the seventh moon of 926 and that in the ninth moon of that year his body was placed in a temple *(miao)* and buried at "Zuling" in the prefecture of "Zuzhou."[12] The site identified as Zuzhou can be found on current detailed maps of the Inner Mongolian Autonomous Region and on more specialized maps that show Liao sites together with modern ones (see Map 5). Located about 30 kilometers southwest of Balinzuoqi (also known as Lindong), a small town in the vast Chifeng county to which the ruins of Liao Shangjing are adjacent, access to Zuzhou is extremely limited.[13]

The first discussion of Zuzhou in modern times

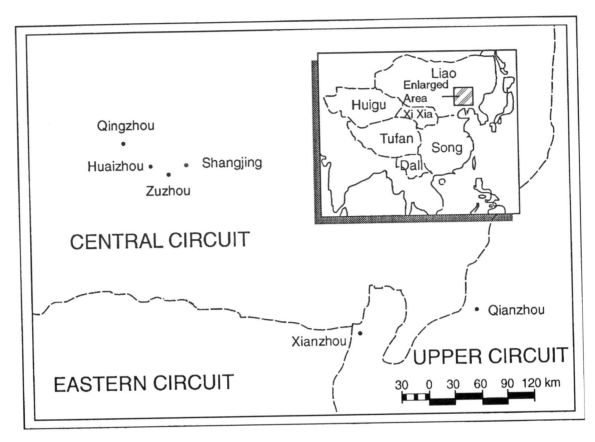

MAP 5. Locations of Mausoleums of Liao Emperors

was that of French missionary Joseph Mullie, who wrote of it in his seminal early work on Liao geography, "Les anciennes villes de l'empire des grands Leao au royaume mongol de Bārin." Traveling on horseback through brushwood an hour beyond a town residents called "Yellow City," he came upon broken pieces of wall that, based on his reading of *Liaoshi, juan* 37, he supposed to be Zuzhou.[14]

Mullie's reconstruction plan of Zuzhou (fig. 229) was based on *Liaoshi* and his findings at the site. "The city," he wrote, "is found in a narrow valley through which pluvial rain waters flow to the Bayan-gol River."[15] He noted its irregular outer shape, the lengths of wall pieces, and the position of gates. Although the entire city was on a slope, the grounds under the enclosed, northwestern area, referred to by him as the "inner city," and beneath southwestern portions were most elevated. The elevation of the western end suggests that from the vantage point of the inner city one could look down on the surrounding Shira-müren region (ancestral pasturelands of the Qidan). That the northwestern portion of Zuzhou was an "imperial city" was confirmed, Mullie believed, by ruins found there. They included yellow and green glazed roof tiles and plinths. None of these was recovered or published by Mullie, however, so one cannot be certain that they were from the Liao period.

The entry for Zuzhou is found in the first chapter of the geography section (*dili zhi*) of *Liaoshi*, following the entry for Shangjing. Located on the Shira-müren, against the backdrop of Muye-shan, the site called Zuzhou (literally "ancestral prefecture") was the birthplace of Abaoji's father, grandfather, great-grandfather, and great-great-grandfather.[16] According to *Liaoshi*, Abaoji came to his ancestral home often for the autumn hunt and had early on built "west tower" there.[17] Later a 2-*zhang*-high wall (about 7 m), 9 *li* in circumference and without battlements, was built. *Liaoshi* tells us the names of the four gates, one in each wall, and says that in the northwest corner of the 9-*li* Zuzhou was an "inner city" (*neicheng*) that contained four palatial-style halls (*dian*).[18] One hall, Liangming, housed an image of Abaoji's grandfather. Another, Eryi, housed a gilded image of Abaoji himself. The other two contained Abaoji's weapons and other military gear, his clothing, horse trappings, furs, and felts, all for the edification of his future heirs lest they forget their roots.[19] Officials and functionaries were quartered in the eastern part of the inner city of Zuzhou, as were 300 servants of Chinese, Qidan, or Bohai descent to see to the needs of the "palace." The "south wall" of *neicheng* had a triple-entry gate with gate towers above each portal. A major thoroughfare ran through the south(east)ern portion of the city. Multistoried towers (*lou*) were placed symmetrically at its four corners, and markets were located beyond the "southern" boundary. The city was divided by this road into eastern and western halves, each *xian* administered by its own governmental offices.

Having read these passages, several Japanese and Chinese archaeologists have investigated the ruins of "the city for offering respect to the tomb of Liao Taizu" since the expedition of Joseph Mullie.[20] In

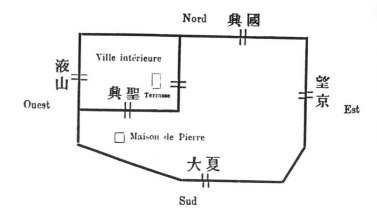

FIGURE 229. Plan of Liao Zuzhou, Chifeng county, Inner Mongolia, ca. 926. [After Mullie, "Les anciennes villes de l'empire . . . ," p. 146]

1966, Zhou Jie noted that the ruins of Zuzhou were accessible via two roads from the city of Lindong, both by way of "Stone House Village."[21] He speculated on the existence of such roads in Liao times.

In the 1980s, based on Chinese reconnaissances, Liao Zuzhou was mapped (fig. 230). Although the city was indeed five-sided as Mullie had discovered, its interior was overwhelmingly that of a Chinese imperial city—much more so than one might have expected for the "ancestral prefecture" of the first Qidan ruler. The major flaw was its orientation, southeast rather than due south. Turning the plan 45 degrees, one finds a city of fortified walls (including defensive projections in front of gates called *wengcheng* in Chinese) with a major north-south thoroughfare and markets to the south. On either side of this road were Changbaxian and Xianningxian, the administrative offices of the two *xian* noted earlier. The "north-south" thoroughfare terminated in an open area in front of Xingsheng Gate, southern entrance to *neicheng* and on line with Daxiamen, main "southern" entrance of the outer city. The open area combined with the approach to

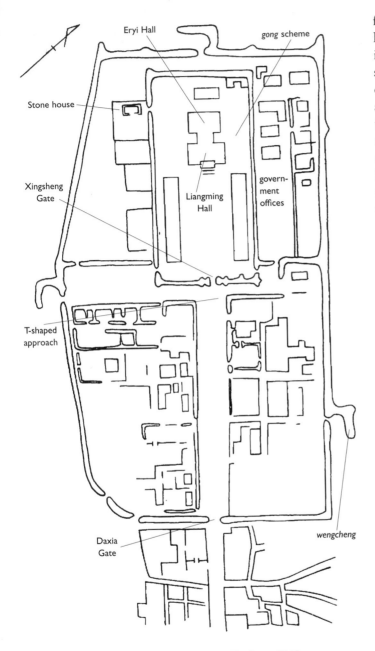

Eryi Hall

gong scheme

Stone house

Xingsheng
Gate

Liangming
Hall

govern-
ment
offices

T-shaped
approach

Daxia
Gate

wengcheng

FIGURE 230. Reconstruction plan of Liao Zuzhou, Chifeng county, Inner Mongolia, ca. 926. [After Zhang and Feng, "Zuzhou Shishi tansuo," p. 129]

form a **T**-shape. Halls for the storage of Abaoji's regalia lined the eastern and western boundaries of this inner city, but in the north center, toward which all space in Zuzhou was directed, were the halls that contained the portrait sculptures of Abaoji and his ancestors. They were arranged according to what is today nicknamed the *gong* scheme after the shape of the character: a configuration of two south-oriented halls joined by a covered arcade or smaller hall. This formation and the **T**-shaped approach to the imperial residential sectors were maintained in Chinese imperial planning until the fall of imperial China and can be found in the plans of the Three Great Halls and Three Back Halls of the Forbidden City in Beijing.[22] Employment of the *gong* scheme in a larger city or religious complex demarcated the most eminent space, reserved usually for the Chinese emperor. Space for officials was beyond Zuzhou's *neicheng* wall to its "east"; the "Stone House," discussed later, was in its own precinct to the "west."

Despite the city's small size by Chinese urban standards, a closer replica of the Tang primary capital at Chang'an would be hard to find. (Zuzhou was a city of approximately 600 by 300 m, and Tang Chang'an's outer wall measured 36.7 km in perimeter.) The main thoroughfare emanating from the southernmost outer wall and directed to the central entrance of the "palace-city" (original site of the ruler's residence), the **T**-shaped approach allowing for space between outer and inner cities, the *gong* plan, even the commercial district south of the south wall (whose roots can be traced to the pre-Tang, Northern Wei capital at Luoyang that flourished from 493 to 534)—all are pedigree elements of Chinese imperial planning.[23] Finally, Zuzhou more closely followed norms for Chinese capital building than Abaoji's first capital, Shangjing, the double-walled city whose perimeter had been enclosed eight years before his death (see fig. 4). That city, one recalls, had served to sequester the Qidan population from the nonnatives.

The resemblance of Zuzhou to a Chinese capital not only emphasizes the purpose of this Qidan "ancestral" architecture but also, perhaps, challenges the vision of the past, suggested by the Stone House or its images concealed inside Zuzhou's walls, in relation to the new dynasty's imperial future. Abaoji had gone far enough south and east in his conquests to have seen walled cities in North China and in Bohai territory. Thus the differences between the plans of Abaoji's two cities, Shangjing and Zuzhou, should be considered conscientious choices. For Shangjing, Abaoji had opted for a heavily fortified governmental center whose plan would serve his purposes at other Liao capitals too (and would be employed by the Jin in the subsequent centuries). For the scheme of his ancestral city, however, the burial ground and sacrificial site for himself and his ancestors, the architectural facade was much more closely allied with China's imperial past than with anything identifiably Qidan.

Anyone familiar with the Mongolian appropriation of Chinese architecture for the purposes of their dynastic legitimation would not be surprised by Zuzhou's plan. Yet Abaoji's architectural achievements were more impressive than those of Mongolian rulers with whom he might be compared. Abaoji was a dynastic founder who less than twenty years after the initial attempts at tribal confederation was engaged in constructing a city; for the Mongols it had not been Chinggis but his descendants who were to understand the potential of Chinese imperial planning and its symbolism in Asia.[24]

Still, the enigma of Zuzhou as an ancestral prefecture remains. The city has been discussed here, rather than in the Introduction, because it was not one of the five Liao capitals. Except for the space for "officials," who probably were appointed to guard the tomb, and funerary temples, there is little indication of government life. Had Abaoji desired to retain anything of his nativity, this would have been the likely place to do so. Yet the model for Zuzhou's architecture was Tang city planning. Perhaps the statues of himself or his ancestors, his clothing, and his weapons were reminders of his heritage, but they were concealed inside Zuzhou's temples; and these ancestral temples were enclosed by Chinese space after Chinese space. For Abaoji, architecture in his cities of life, and even more so in his city of death, was profoundly purposeful—he must have been aware of its message. Having so clearly cast his lot with Chinese architecture, it is no wonder his descendants built structures like Guanyin Pavilion and the Muta.

The Stone House

One place in Zuzhou that may have been reserved for rites of predynastic Qidan days is the "Stone House" (fig. 231). Mullie wrote of it as "la Maison de Pierre," taking this name from that of the local Mongolian population. Modern Chinese scholars refer to it similarly, as *Shishi*. Mullie recorded the dimensions of its walls as about 5.25 meters on the northern and southern sides by about 6 meters and 0.3 meter high.[25] When he saw it, the house was empty. Locals told him that at one time a white marble statue had stood in one of the corners, but it had been broken when knives were sharpened against it. Again Mullie found green-glazed tiles in the vicinity, this time reportedly large ones. He had no idea of the function of the building and published no photographs of it.

Mullie did, however, explore the theory that the Stone House was the West Tower referred to in *Liaoshi* and elsewhere, one of four "towers" said to have been erected in each direction from the capital Shangjing. He argued that the location relative to Shangjing was correct, that it was near what he

FIGURE 231. Stone House from front, 1988. [Courtesy of Marilyn and Roy Gridley]

was convinced were vestiges of Zuzhou's *neicheng* (including ruins of its wall), that the wall of Zuzhou itself (the outer wall) showed evidence of the four gates referred to in *Liaoshi*, and that the site was in the mountain range known as Zushan ("ancestral mountains"). His one reservation was that the perimeter of what he defined as the Zuzhou wall was barely 3 *li*, only one-third of the measurement recorded for it in *Liaoshi*.

It was the Japanese archaeologist Torii Ryūzō who first published pictures of the Stone House. Through a series of five photographs in his monumental *Ryō no bunka* (Liao culture) of 1936, Torii preserved a rare panoramic view of the Shira-müren that captures the "house," the ruins of Zuzhou's wall, close-up shots of the structure from different views, and a look into its interior.[26] Alongside the illustrations, Torii provided the reader not only

with captions, but with an important aspect of the material that can be gleaned from them.

Torii chooses the word "dolmen" (in Japanese, French, and English) to identify the structure. Indeed, the resemblance between the Stone House and prehistoric upright stones with flat megaliths across their tops is more than superficial. The concept of a dolmen, however, raises more probing questions: Is this structure Liao? Were the statues in it Liao? And if the answer is yes in both cases, can the Stone House be related to the widespread existence of such structures in non-Qidan, even non-Donghu, or perhaps non-Asian cultures? Does the structural similarity between the Stone House and prehistoric stone structures or tombs suggest that the early tenth-century Qidan were part of a society similar in organization or ideology to prehistoric Western Europe?

FIGURE 232. Stone House, Korban-toroghai, Inner Mongolia. [After Torii, *Ryō no bunka: Zufu*, vol. 2, pl. 93]

One dare not go farther than speculating about these potential cross-cultural similarities. Even though Torii conceded in his captions that the Stone House may have been Abaoji's, he published in the pages that follow a similar cube-shaped stone house with front opening photographed on the sand dunes of a place he calls Korban-toroghai (fig. 232). The second stone house is undated and unassociated. It may be evidence that the Stone House of Zuzhou belongs to a regional type; but it might also belong to a people of different times, lifestyle, and worship practices than the Qidan.

In 1991 two short papers containing significant data and some speculation about the Stone House were published.[27] According to Zhang Songbo and Feng Lei, authors of one article, the Stone House stands in the southwestern corner of the remains of Liao Zuzhou, in Balinzuoqi district of Chifeng county, the same location determined by Father Mullie.[28] The two authors raise the most pertinent questions about the structure: who amassed the labor and wealth to build it; what was its purpose; was there any precedent for it; and what might it tell us about Qidan worship practice or ritual? Although they do not answer these questions, they do present important information. Here we too are concerned with answering these questions, but we are also interested in the role of the Stone House in what has been referred to repeatedly as the Liao architectural tradition.

The Stone House is a structure of seven huge stones, each of which measures a minimum of 30 square meters.[29] Each stone weighs several tens of tons. It is believed they were quarried from a place about 15 kilometers to the south. How they were transported is unknown. The "house" faces southeast. On the southwest-northeast side it measures 7 meters, on the southeast-northwestern side 5.7 meters, and its height is 3.6 meters—all somewhat lengthier than Mullie's measurements. In plan, it forms a U-shape: an entry of 1.4 meters in width and 1.95 meters high creates an opening at the front. Above it, and joining the door to make a T-shaped opening, is what Chen Yongzhi describes as a window, 2.3 by 0.9 meters in dimension. On the interior, he says, is a stone platform, 4.3 by 2.5 meters, and rising from 40 to 70 centimeters.[30]

Although neither *Liaoshi* nor other texts in which the early history of the Qidan is related mentions stone houses (or other buildings in stone), *Weishu* and *Beishi* do. The standard history of the Northern Wei (386–550), *Weishu*, talks of "chiseling [into] stone to make a temple to the ancestors,"[31] and *Beishi* records that Emperor Xiaowendi (r. 471–499) built a Stone House and Lingquan Hall on Fangshan (in Hebei) the summer of 478 whose purpose was ancestral worship.[32] This evidence is not enough, however, to link the Qidan or proto-Qidan to the Xianbei. Moreover, it is nearly impossible to determine a date for massive pieces of stone in dolmen arrangement.

The key to the associations between the Stone House and Abaoji seems to be not texts but archaeology. The Stone House must be interpreted in the light of Zhang and Feng's reconstruction drawing of Zuzhou (see fig. 230). We have already noted that Figure 230 provides archaeological confirmation of the five-sided wall sketched by Mullie as the enclosure of Zuzhou. In addition, the reconstruction drawing shows the Stone House outside of *neicheng* but inside the Zuzhou outer wall. Since *Liaoshi*, among other sources, tells us Zuzhou was walled by Abaoji, we have to assume that whether the Stone House preexisted Abaoji or was built by him, he wanted it inside his ancestral city.

Interpretations of the purpose of the Stone House inside Zuzhou range from a place for incarceration of imperial prisoners to the western of the four towers of the Qidan empire.[33] More will be said about the second of these hypotheses later. Here I wish to argue that the Stone House was Abaoji's ancestral temple. Leaving aside possible associations between pre-Liao Chinese ancestral temples *(taimiao)* and this structure, I believe Abaoji's ancestral temple was the locus of his worship of his direct ancestors and the primogenitors of the Qidan. According to Qidan legend, a male (Qishou Khan) on a white horse and a female riding in a cart drawn by a gray ox met at the confluence of waters in the Muye Mountains. They produced eight sons, each of whom went on to marry and found a tribe.[34] Abaoji and his father are also said to have been born on Muyeshan. Zhang and Feng make a strong case that the Stone House contained images of Abaoji's direct ancestors, as well as, perhaps, Qishou, his wife, and their eight sons. The Qidan rulers are said also to have sacrificed to tablets of Heaven and Earth set up on Mount Muye facing eastward. (The Stone House's southeastern orientation would have allowed for this.) It is a fact that the erection of ancestral tablets, temples of unspecified material or form to house them, and statues and portraits of ancestors were used in ceremonies throughout the duration of Liao rule.[35] Finally, if this permanent megalithic structure was indeed a monument to Abaoji's ancestors, one might view the wooden Muta—Emperor Daozong's monument to his father—as the adaptation by a more sinified, Buddhist Liao ruler of a native funerary tradition represented by a stone monument at the time of the dynastic founder.

West Tower

If the Stone House and West Tower were not the same structure (Mullie believed they were), then West Tower was a separate entity in Zuzhou. Discussion of Xilou far predates the early-twentieth-century Jesuit's writings.

West Tower is mentioned twice in tenth-century records. In 926, Yao Kun, the man who reported to Abaoji about the demise of the Later Tang emperor at Luoyang, is said to have arrived at Xilou for his audience with Abaoji.[36] Hu Jiao, a Chinese official who spent six years in the Shangjing circuit in the mid-tenth century, left a record of what he saw entitled *Xianbei (lu) ji* (Record of [captivity among] the Xianbei). Hu's account identifies West Tower as a monument demarcating the upper capital, Shangjing.[37] *Liaoshi*, however, places West Tower in Zuzhou: in the geography section *(dili zhi)* it says that Taizu frequently hunted in this place (Zuzhou), first building West Tower and later walling the city that he called Zuzhou.[38] Mullie, as has been pointed out, followed the text of the *Liaoshi*, as did Chavannes and Pelliot, all therefore believing Hu Jiao to have confused the place where he saw West Tower (actually Zuzhou) with Shangjing.[39]

Wittfogel and Feng nevertheless supported Hu Jiao's statement. They found it difficult to believe that a man who lived in the vicinity for so long could have confused the location of what seems to have been a dominant monument, and, further, they based their assumptions on passages in *Qidanguo zhi*. In *Qidanguo zhi*, it is explained that four *lou* lie in the Qidan domain: the southern one on Muyeshan; the eastern at Longhuazhou near the confluence of the Shira-müren and Laoha rivers; the northern at Tangzhou, 300 *li* north of Shira-müren; and *xilou* at Shangjing.[40] The four identifications, according to Wittfogel and Feng, are corroborated by passages in *Liaoshi* that name specific monasteries such as Tianxiongsi, a monastery of Shangjing, "at" *xilou*.[41] According to this interpretation, a directional tower is an alternate name for each of the four *zhou*. Wittfogel and Feng waffle in their interpretation by the last line of their note, however,

holding out the possibility that West Tower was initially Shangjing but after the establishment of Zuzhou the reference (or structure) could have changed to Zuzhou.[42]

Chen Yongzhi in a sense follows Wittfogel and Feng. He interprets West Tower as a reference to Abaoji's governmental center, first at Shangjing and later at Zuzhou.[43] Yet he also wants to see West Tower and the Stone House as one and the same structure. By his reckoning, therefore, West Tower was at Shangjing from 901 until 912, the year in which he finds the first reference to Stone House. Thereafter, he agrees with what Mullie somewhat timidly tried to suggest—that the Stone House, despite its lack of height or any other characteristic generally associated with a *lou*, and West Tower were the same building.

What is certain is this: beginning in the first years of the tenth century, the Qidan built a walled, Chinese-style city and monumental structures near the birthplace of their dynastic founder. If later records are not anachronistic, the tenth-century Qidan, or at least Chinese who observed them, referred to some structure or place in that enclosure by the Chinese word for a multilevel building. Abaoji's ancestral city emerges as a Tang-style city with incorrect orientation whose Stone House, perhaps, was one accommodation to native Qidan construction. In large part, however, the design of this ancestral city is evidence that in the early decades of confederation, the Qidan already had cast their lot with Chinese architectural models and, one supposes, their associated symbolism of empire.

Zuling

The location and appearance of Abaoji's tomb, however, remain elusive. We are told that Zuling should be about 5 *li* (2.5 km) northwest of Zuzhou at a site replete with mountains and springs called "great springs" by the local population.[44] The site is

FIGURE 233. Zuling (?), Chifeng county, Inner Mongolia. [Courtesy of Marilyn and Roy Gridley]

said to have been defined by two huge mountains with a valley between—a natural *shanmen* (mountain gate) formed by those peaks. The Liao called this natural entrance Black Dragon (*heilong*) Gate. The peaks are about 100 meters apart. They can be entered and exited only from one direction, and an earthen wall with gate on either side is said to join them (fig. 233).[45] The Liao are said to have given names to the scenery such as "Hidden Ladder," "White Horse," and "Solitary Stone."

Several *li* north of Black Dragon Gate, numerous ceramic tiles and pillar bases have been excavated (fig. 234). All are believed to have been part of buildings of the funerary complex. Tortoise-back bases for stelae, as well as other stelae, one estimated to have had about 5,000 characters of which 21 are legible, have been excavated together with the torso of a monumental image.[46]

Yet to this day Abaoji's tomb has not been discovered and no one has been able to confirm its location in this valley. Unsuccessful Chinese archaeologists have concluded that the destruction of Zuling by Jin troops in 1120 may indeed have been as comprehensive as their records describe.[47] There is logic to this thought, for construction at Zuzhou suggests that Abaoji would have desired an architectural display for his mausoleum. Yet one has to allow for the possibility that in this one most final and personal aspect of his life, Abaoji sought to follow the ways of his ancestors. Perhaps, to avoid the personal desecration that later conquerors might inflict, he did not wish his corpse to be found. It remains a puzzle, too, where his empress Yingtian and concubines lie. It has been suggested that their graves are marked by two mounds deeper into the northwest and northeast of the valley.[48] Once has no evidence of what lies under those mounds, however, and thus the resting place of Empress Yingtian's hand is another mystery.

HUAIZHOU

Huaizhou was the chosen burial prefecture for the second Liao emperor, Taizong, and his son Muzong, fourth ruler of Liao (whose tomb area was known as Fengling). No more than 30 kilometers northwest of Zuzhou, portions of the *zhou* had been captured by Abaoji. The rest had been taken by Deguang. Subsequently it became his *ordo* (the center of his military operations).[49] Its male population has been estimated at 25,000 of all nationalities.[50] Taizong himself had ordered the walled enclosure of Huaizhou, and in 946 his nephew and successor, Shizong, paid his respects there.[51]

Liaoshi tells the story of how Taizong's final resting place was chosen. On the day of Deguang's death in Hebei (on his way home from the attack on the Song capital at Bianliang and still in Song territory), a number of his horsemen had a vision while hunting in Zuzhou. They saw Taizong mounted on a white horse in pursuit of a white fox. He killed it with just one shot of the arrow, but when the horsemen arrived at the spot, they found only the fox and arrow. Taizong had disappeared. At this place a temple *(miao)* was erected, and on Feng-huang (Phoenix) Gate in Huaizhou an image of Taizong on horseback shooting the fox was painted.[52]

Until recently, the burial site of Liao Taizong remained a mystery.[53] In 1976 and again in 1983 expeditions went out from the cultural relics agencies in Zhaomeng and Balinyouqi to search for it. Huai-

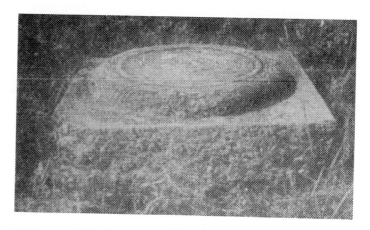

FIGURE 234. Pillar base excavated at proposed remains of Zuling. [After Zhou Jie, "Nei Menggu . . . Liao Taizuling," 1966, pl. 9, no. 9]

zhou was discovered about 20 kilometers northeast of a people's collective in Balinyouqi county. From the site, excavators report, one could see Shangjing to the southeast.[54] Archaeologists found a walled enclosure of strict north-south orientation (fig. 235). Three walls had gates. Water flowed where the western edge of the wall would have been. The outer wall had four corner towers. Inside the wall were two "palatial" remains and smaller *hangtu* foundations suggesting residential architecture. In the mountains north of the city wall, one large monastery and smaller temple remains were uncovered.

The Huaizhou wall measured 524 meters north to south by 496 meters east to west. It was between 8 and 12 meters thick at the base and only a meter or two at the top. Gates seem to have measured from 12 to 18 meters and corner towers 15 by 11 meters or 14 meters square. The main palatial foundation was also walled. It had been elevated on a *hangtu* foundation 100 by 174 meters that was 7 meters high and had consisted of a Shanmen, a front hall of 40 by 24 meters, and a smaller building behind it. The sec-

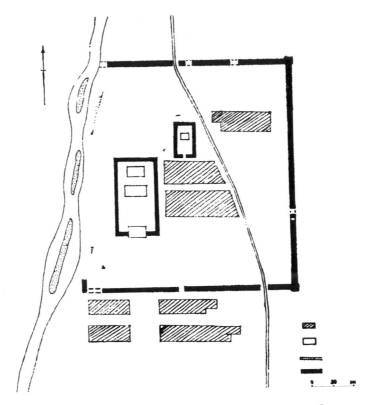

FIGURE 235. Reconstruction plan of Huaizhou, Chifeng county, Inner Mongolia, tenth century. [After Zhang Songbo, "Liao Huaizhou . . . , p. 67]

ond enclosure was 50 by 81 meters. In the Qing period, Ganggangmiao village had been founded on the ruins of the first enclosure. The village persisted into the 1980s and perhaps was the reason that anything from Huaizhou has survived. That is, perhaps the Qing villagers had revived religious buildings with Liao origins, a common practice throughout the northern lands of the Qing empire as far west as Russian Mongolia.[55] Animal-headed ceramic tiles, circular roof tiles, drainpipes, *chiwen* (roof-end decorations), copper coins, and tricolor-glazed ceramics were found among the remains of temple complexes north of the walled region.

The *Liaoshi* records that Huailing was located 20

li (about 10 km) west of Huaizhou. But it was 3 kilometers north of Huaizhou that excavators uncovered what they believe to be the ruins of Huailing, final resting place of Deguang. Like the site believed to be the tomb of Abaoji, it was situated in a river valley between two mountains (fig. 236). The entry to the tomb, in fact, is at the mouth of a canal. Enough pieces of stone wall remained for excavators to determine that the wall had enclosed inner and outer tomb areas. Pieces of the wall and numerous *hangtu* foundations are shown in the site plan (see fig. 236). Excavators reported they found remains of Deguang's grave and a sacrificial hall for it in the "inner enclosure" and two major palatial-

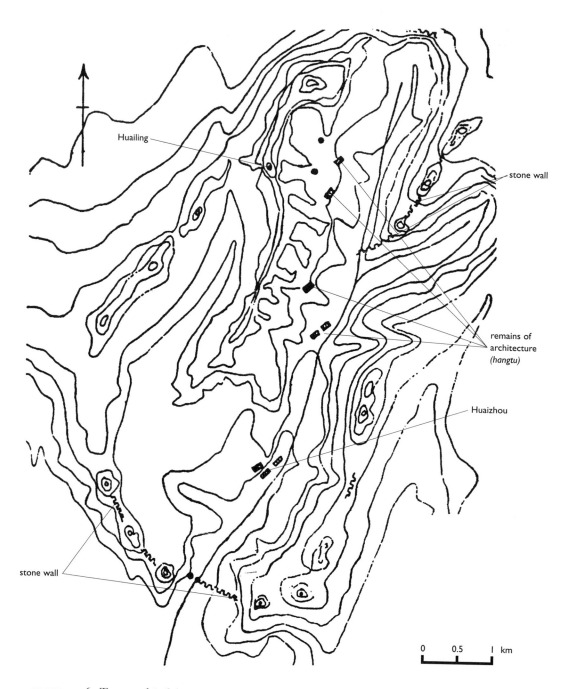

Huailing

stone wall

remains of
architecture
(hangtu)

Huaizhou

stone wall

0   0.5   1 km

FIGURE 236. Topographical drawing of Liao Huaizhou. [After Zhang Songbo, "Liao Huaizhou . . . , p. 69]

style halls in the "outer enclosure," but they are not labeled, making it difficult to determine which foundations might refer to specific structures. Various pieces of Liao ceramics and stone were found throughout the city and at its entry.

Deeper into the valley, two more tombs were uncovered. Both were oriented 20 degrees west of north. Westward and northward, following their associations with autumn and winter, as we shall see in the next chapter, were the most frequent alignments for Chinese tombs. Similarly, Chinese imperial tombs were situated northwest with respect to Western Han and Tang Chang'an and to Ming Beijing. At Huailing, too, it seems that early Qidan royalty relied on Chinese precedent for siting.

The *Liaoshi* tells us that Liao Taizong's successor, Emperor Shizong, established Taizong's funerary *zhou* in 946.[56] Shizong, however, was not Deguang's son and was not buried at Huaizhou. The fourth Liao ruler Muzong, who was Deguang's son, was buried "beside" his father's mausoleum at a place designated Fengling. Although one would like to assume that one of the two building complexes walled in stone was Muzong's tomb, confirmation of both burial sites has proved as difficult as for the tomb of Abaoji.

XIANZHOU

Xianzhou, near the modern city of Beizhen in Liaoning, in the Liao eastern circuit, was the *ordo* of the third Liao emperor Shizong. He had inherited it from his father, Abaoji's murdered eldest son, Yelü Bei, who had the title Prince of Dongdan. (Dongdan referred to the territory in the heart of the former Bohai kingdom.) Xiaowen, son of the fifth Liao emperor and younger brother of the sixth, was also buried at Xianzhou. The area was known for sericulture, but not even one building is mentioned in the brief description of Xianzhou in the *Liaoshi*.[57]

QIANZHOU

We are only slightly better informed about Qianzhou, location of the mausoleum of the fifth Liao emperor, Jingzong, and his wife, Empress Chengtian. Qianzhou too is in former Bohai territory, about 5 kilometers due south of modern Beizhen. In addition to Jingzong's tomb (Qianling), Ningshen Hall and Chongdegong (palace complex) stood there.[58] Qianling was also the place where the last Liao emperor, Tianzuo, who died in Jin captivity, was laid to rest in 1145.[59]

QINGZHOU AND QINGLING

"Qingzhou," the *Liaoshi* tells us, "is a place of majestic valleys and dangerous precipices."[60] It was one of the seasonal wild-animal hunting grounds for the royal Qidan. Emperor Muzong had walled it, calling it Black Waters (Heihe) prefecture. Emperor Shengzong loved to hunt there as well: he named the prefecture Qing and designated it for the site of his future mausoleum. His eldest son and successor, Xingzong, honored his father's wishes and had Yongqingling built in the *zhou*.[61] Qingzhou was to be the resting place of Xingzong and his son Daozong as well. Referred to in the general literature as "Qingling," the three tombs represent Liao imperial funerary architecture for a period of more than one hundred years. More important, they are the epitome of subterranean tomb construction in the tenth and eleventh centuries.

Qingling today is almost as remote as it was a thousand years ago (fig. 237).[62] The tombs seem to have slipped into near obscurity between Daozong's interment in 1101 and the 1920s when Father Mullie discovered the site and Father Kervyn found a stele from one of the tombs. At the same time, a local warlord named Tang Zuorong managed to remove a number of relics prior to excavation by the Japanese in 1931.[63] A millennium ago, however, the

FIGURE 237. Qingzhou, Chifeng county, Inner Mongolia. [After Tamura and Kobayashi, *Keiryō*, vol. 2, pl. 2]

site 50 kilometers northwest beyond Huaizhou and about 75 kilometers northwest of Shangjing was the hub of the most complicated of Liao ceremonies. Wittfogel and Feng provide a long description of an imperial Liao funeral in their section on Liao customs and traditions. The following account is based on their description in combination with their notes and the textual sources for both.[64]

Sixteen days after Shengzong died in a traveling camp, his body was placed in Taiping Hall, which one assumes to be in Qingzhou. The next month the emperor's widow led a procession of imperial relatives to Taiping Hall, to which families had already been designated as guards of the future mausoleum town. That same month, the new emperor mourned before a portrait of his late father. Ten days later he burned Shengzong's bows and arrows in Taiping Hall. The next month (the third since his death), the coffin was taken into the funeral hall. The following month Xingzong burned offerings there. Xingzong returned again in the fifth month to examine the progress that had been made. The next month, the sixth since Shengzong's death, the equivalent of a burial finally occurred:

On the night preceding the transfer of the coffin [to the mausoleum], when the fourth drum had been struck, the emperor led the courtiers in and offered libations thrice before the coffin. The coffin was taken out through the northwestern gate of the hall and was placed on a hearse. It was covered with a plain mat. The shamans purified it [from evil spirits]. At dawn the next morning the funeral cortege went to the sacrificial place. Libations were offered five times. The head shaman offered up prayers. The imperial clan, the relatives of the empress, high officials, and all the officials of the capitals made offerings according to their rank. Then clothes, bows, arrows, saddles, bridles, pictures, horses, camels, imperial equipment, and other objects were all burned.

The coffin went to the mausoleum and was entombed. Then an epitaph was offered up. The emperor presided in a tent. Ordering a fire to be made, he faced the fire, made a libation, and bowed thrice. Then he faced east and bowed twice to Heaven and Earth. He mounted a horse and led the funeral company through the logs of the divine gate. Then he dismounted and bowed twice toward the east.

The next day, early in the morning, the emperor led the courtiers and titled ladies to the mausoleum to perform the first libation ceremony. Ascending the hall of the deceased emperor's image, he received the objects bequeathed [by the emperor].

On the third day the second libation ceremony was performed as before.

Xingzong's burial place was selected by his successor, Daozong. By the time Daozong died, his successor, who had no idea in 1101 he would be the last Liao emperor, wore Chinese mourning clothes for the first time under Liao rule. After various libations by relatives and officers of various ranks,

> the coffin was placed on a cart which the imperial princes pushed to the place where a ram was offered. It was an old custom of the Liao empire to slaughter a ram here as a sacrifice. The imperial clan, the relatives of the empress, and the officials of the capitals and prefectures offered sacrifices according to their rank. After they arrived at the burial place, the coffin was taken down from the cart and placed on a sedan chair. The emperor took off the mourning dress and went ahead of the coffin on foot to Changfu Hill.

During this night the emperor entered the mausoleum and granted the objects bequeathed by the deceased emperor to the imperial clan, the relatives of the empress, and high officials. Then they came out. It was ordered that the former emperor's sleeping tent be passed through the logs of the divine gate which was in front of the mausoleum. The emperor did not go personally but sent a close attendant dressed in regular court clothes.

In the first libation the emperor and the empress led the imperial clan, the consort clan, the military and civil ministers, the commanding prefects, and the titled ladies from the rank of *furen* up in making obeisance and offering sacrifice. They went twice around the mausoleum and then descended. Libations were made again as before. They took their departure from the mausoleum and returned.

There is one final passage of relevance to imperial funerary architecture:

> After the death of an emperor, households [of retainers] were assigned, and a treasury for money as well as a depot for grain [were] set up. Within the domed tent a small felt hall was built; gold images of the deceased emperor, empress, and concubines were cast and placed in it. On all festivals, anniversaries of imperial deaths, and the first and fifteenth days of each month, sacrifices were offered up in front of the domed tent.[65]

Few specific buildings are mentioned in these descriptions. In the record of Shengzong's funeral, one reads about only three structures: Taiping Hall, a divine gate made of wood (logs), and a hall for the deceased emperor's image. Taiping Hall seems to have been the equivalent of a funerary hall—a multifunctional building that at certain times housed the corpse in a coffin and was also the location for parts of the ceremony. If Chinese precedent was followed, the divine gate probably was in front of Taiping Hall. Xingzong's interment involved a hall that could subsequently function as his and his descendants' ancestral hall in which an image—perhaps a statue of Shengzong or an earlier ancestor (or ancestors)—was kept. Based on the textual description, other aspects of the ceremony, such as offerings or the presentation of the deceased emperor's hunting gear, could have been enacted outdoors or in tents like the ones mentioned. The precious stele discovered by Father Kervyn that ultimately led to the ripple of European scholarly interest in things Liao in the 1920s may also have been erected outdoors. The subterranean tomb remains, as we shall see, stand in sharp contrast to the lack of monumental evidence above ground.

Published reconstruction drawings of the site by Tamura and Kobayashi show a gate followed by a long approach—a tremendously long and winding approach to what is believed to be the earliest of the three tombs (on the east)—and a single building fronted by an enclosed courtyard for each tomb (fig. 238). If significant buildings have not been lost, the arrangement is not much different from what archaeologists believe stood at the graves of the first, second, and fourth Liao emperors (Zuling, Huailing, and Fengling). Pre-Ming Chinese imperial tombs did not contain much more aboveground architecture, but noticeably lacking in Qingzhou is evidence of monumental sculpture lining the long pathway to the tomb and remains of walls that en-

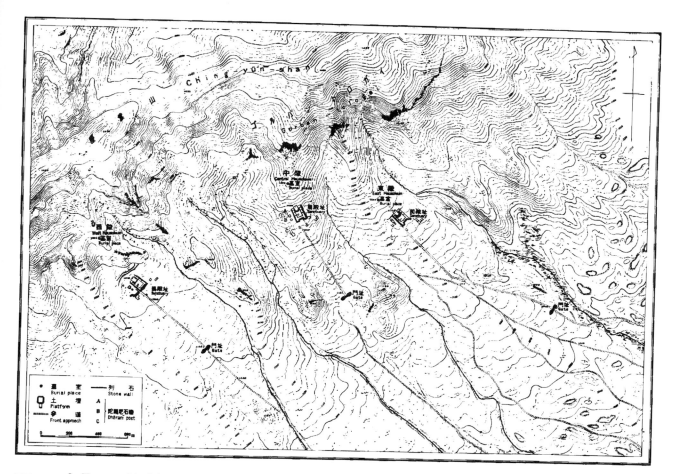

FIGURE 238. Topographical drawing of Liao Qingzhou. [After Tamura and Kobayashi, *Keiryō*, vol. 1, fig. 7]

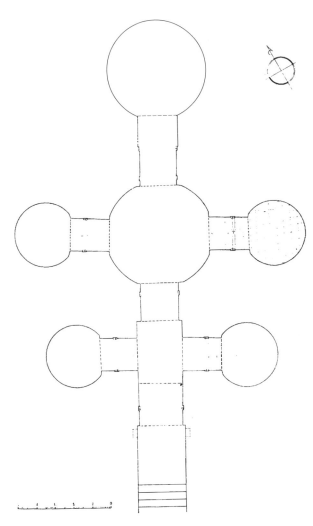

FIGURE 239. Plan of Eastern Mausoleum, Qingzhou.
[After Tamura and Kobayashi, *Keiryō*, vol. 1, p. 19]

closed the mausoleums. Stone wall pieces and a statue, one recalls, were found at the site identified as Zuling. Examples of Chinese tombs with "spirit paths" are discussed in the next chapter. In Chapter 12 we shall see proof that at least one member of the Yelü clan had sculpture along the approach to his tomb. It is unfortunate that not even one statue has been found at the Qingzhou tombs, because the layout and, as we shall see, Chinese precedent are suggestive of spirit paths.

Yongqingling

Yongqingling, mausoleum of sixth Liao emperor Shengzong, is nestled against Mount Mian. The excavators wrote that when they found it, it was completely hidden below the ground.[66] The plan of the tomb underground can be described as three main chambers and four side rooms, each of which is joined by a corridor to one or two others, oriented along a northwest-southeast axis (fig. 239). The back chamber and each of the side rooms is circular—or as close to circular as possible given the constraints of adjoining space—and the central chamber has four curved sides. The connective corridors, approach rooms, and front chamber were rectangular in plan. Each of the seven rooms had its own vaulted ceiling (fig. 240). From entry to back chamber the main axis spanned 21.4 meters. The greatest length from side to side was 15.5 meters. The interior construction was bricks held together by mortar. Bricks were 36 by 18 by 6 centimeters. Originally, wooden doors had provided access to nine entryways, but all were removed by the warlord Tang Zuorong. Above entryways, evidence remains of brick imitation of timber architecture in the form of lintels and brackets.

Since its discovery, the most fascinating aspect of the Eastern Mausoleum has been its wall paintings.[67] In all there are over seventy male figures (described by the excavators as portraits), landscapes of

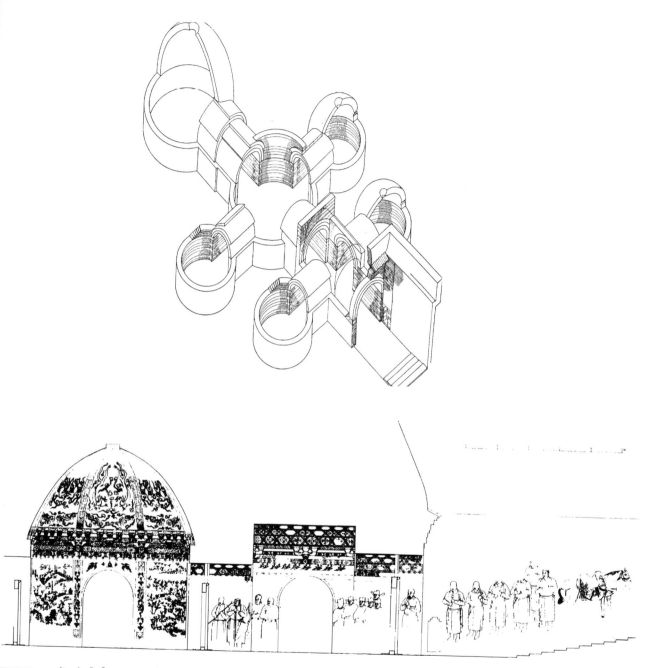

FIGURE 240 (top). Infrastructural section of Eastern Mausoleum, Qingzhou. [After Tamura and Kobayashi, *Keiryō*, vol. 1, p. 31]

FIGURE 241 (above). Sectional drawing of paintings on either side of entry to Eastern Mausoleum, Qingzhou. [After Tamura and Kobayashi, *Keiryō*, vol. 1, fig. 39b]

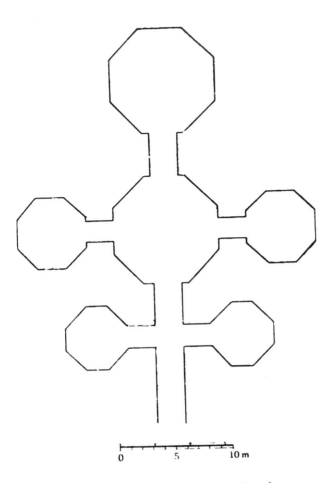

FIGURE 242. Plan of Central Mausoleum, Qingzhou.
[After Tamura and Kobayashi, *Keiryō*, vol. 1, p. 159]

the four seasons, and decoration on or imitation of architectural detail (fig. 241). A few aspects of the paintings will be discussed later, but only as they pertain to architecture.

Yongxingling

Yongxingling, tomb of Shengzong's successor Xingzong, was backed by the Yong'an Mountains, 640 meters west of Yongqingling. It is called the Central Mausoleum because of its position relative to the other two (see fig. 238). The underground tomb is larger than Yongqingling, 30 by 26 meters, but this is only one of the differences. The interior space of Yongxingling consisted of six rather than seven units: two main chambers and four side rooms (fig. 242). A continuous passageway, rather than an antechamber that divided the space, led into the central room. More significant, however, the shape of every room was octagonal. The tomb was terribly damaged by the time Tamura and Kobayashi got there. If paintings had once covered its walls, none is mentioned.

Yongfuling

Yongfuling, the Western Mausoleum, was 1,400 meters west of Yongxingling. Located right on Qingyunshan, as opposed to a slope in front of it, its plan is nearly the same as that of Yongxingling (fig. 243). When Torii entered he found traces of wall paintings, but in too poor a state of preservation to describe.

The identification of the three tombs from east to west according to the chronological sequence of Liao emperors has not been agreed on unanimously, but the opinion of Sekino and Takeshima is echoed and supported by Tamura and Kobayashi.[68] There are several reasons for this identification: tomb size (the largest for the first of the three rulers); *fengshui* (Chinese geomancy); location of cenotaphs; the remains of a complete program of wall paintings only in the tomb of Shengzong (best-known artist and patron, as well as earliest, of the three); evidence of reopening and repainting in Yongqingling (presumably coincident with the death and burial of Shengzong's empress Renyi) as opposed to no evidence of reopening at Yongfuling (logical since Daozong's predeceased wife was moved there for reburial when he was laid to rest); and an association between a Tianzuo-reign-period date on a tile found at the western tomb in 1934, which, if identified properly, would be the one that emperor built for his father.

Architecturally, the Eastern Mausoleum can be shown to be unique—both in the shape of its interior chambers and in the complete covering of walls and ceilings with paintings. Although Tamura and Kobayashi see the Central Mausoleum as "transitional," sharing features with both its eastern and western neighbors,[69] the Central and Western mausoleums share the most fundamental similarity: use of the octagonal plan as opposed to circular for its rooms. This shape may be another indication of an association with seventh Liao ruler Xingzong (its occupant). Built by Xingzong's successor, Daozong, the other monument most clearly associated with his direct patronage is the Timber Pagoda, also octagonal in plan. The pagoda was constructed the year after Yongxingling, also to commemorate Xingzong's death and, it has been suggested, to recognize the potential implications of that year according to the Buddhist reckoning of time. As we examine more Liao architecture with octagonal plans in Chapters 12 and 13, the profound importance of the octagon and its frequency and significance at the midpoint of the eleventh century in North Asian construction will become apparent.

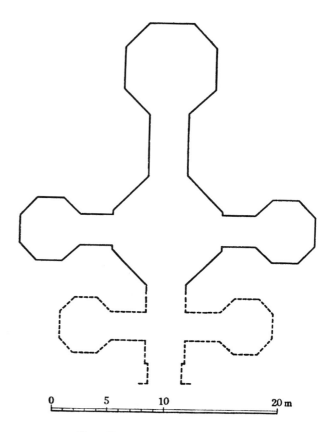

FIGURE 243. Plan of Western Mausoleum, Qingzhou. [After Tamura and Kobayashi, *Keiryō*, vol. 1, p. 174]

FIGURE 244. Tomb of legendary emperor Shao Hao, Qufu, Shandong province, stone added in Song dynasty. [Steinhardt photograph]

11

Chinese Funerary Architecture before Qingling

JUST AS THE GUANYIN PAVILION of Dulesi has been, from the point of view of Chinese architectural historians, the representative monument of Liao timber construction, Qingling has been considered the high point of the imperial funerary tradition. Before continuing with the Liao contribution to funerary architecture, therefore, it is necessary to investigate the extent to which Qingling is part of a longstanding Chinese tradition of tomb architecture.

EARLIER CHINESE TOMBS

The history of subterranean tomb construction in China may not be as long as that of interlocking timber-frame architecture, now traceable to the fifth millennium B.C. in Zhejiang province, but it is much easier to document.[1] Chinese tomb construction can easily be traced to the third millennium B.C., and some would begin the history of regal tomb architecture at that time. Grave sites of China's earliest recorded rulers, the "legendary emperors," are now Chinese tourist spots (fig. 244).[2] The royal Shang cemetery and countless graves of

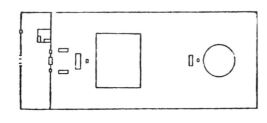

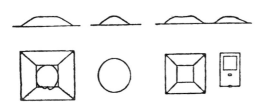

FIGURE 245. Plans and sectional drawings of tombs of Zhou kings Wen and Wu, and other Zhou tombs, late second to early first millennium B.C. [After Xie, *Zhongguo lidai diwang lingqin kaolue*, p. 37]

all ranks of society from the Shang period in the second millennium B.C. have been identified. In the Shang period, royal tombs with long approach ramps and thousands of grave goods were located northwest of the city of Anyang (Yinxu), and even some commoners and slaves were buried in simple pit tombs.[3] There is no evidence so far that Shang tombs were marked above ground.

By the first millennium B.C., aboveground mounds for underground burials can be confirmed.[4] Excavation suggests that the shapes of mounds above rulers' graves were circular, square, or a combination of the two shapes (fig. 245). Underground, first-millennium-B.C. tombs ranged from simple pits to multiple four-sided chambers, often containing wooden coffins. Sometimes tombs of this period provide evidence that the various rooms had different functions.[5] The mound that stands above the grave of China's First Emperor,

Qin Shi Huangdi, as well as the contents of neighboring burial pits, are famous.[6]

We have skimmed over the achievements of the first 2,000 years of Chinese funerary construction in two paragraphs because it is impossible to prove they had any direct bearing on the Liao architecture of death. It is highly unlikely that the Qidan had any awareness of Shang, Zhou, or Qin tombs. Even if in their conquest or seasonal hunts the Liao happened upon a Zhou grave, it probably would not have captivated Qidan imagination for its "Zhouness." In any case, there is no literary record of such an encounter. Nor is there reason to believe that the first Qidan builders of tombs were cognizant of the classical Chinese texts that had led to first-millennium-B.C. Chinese tomb construction. Nevertheless, it is worth pointing out three features of Chinese tomb construction of the last two millennia B.C.: tombs were constructed for all levels of society; before the end of this period, burial was underground and mounds covered these tombs; and subterranean chambers were four-sided. These points are relevant because the number of tombs from the end of the first millennium B.C.—the Han dynasty (206 B.C.–A.D. 220)—remaining in Liaoning and Inner Mongolia even today (see figs. 50 and 51) suggest that the Liao might well have come into contact with them. And by that time, Chinese tomb construction had a history far longer than 2,000 years—it was already an established tradition.

CHINESE TOMBS FROM HAN TO TANG

Han tomb architecture below ground was as complex in plan and design as that of any time period before Liao. Excavation of Han imperial tombs has begun only recently, but the sites of most are known. Many, including mounds that cover the burial sites, can still be seen near the former Western and Eastern Han capitals, respectively, in Xi'an and Luoyang suburbs (figs. 246 and 247).[7] Figure

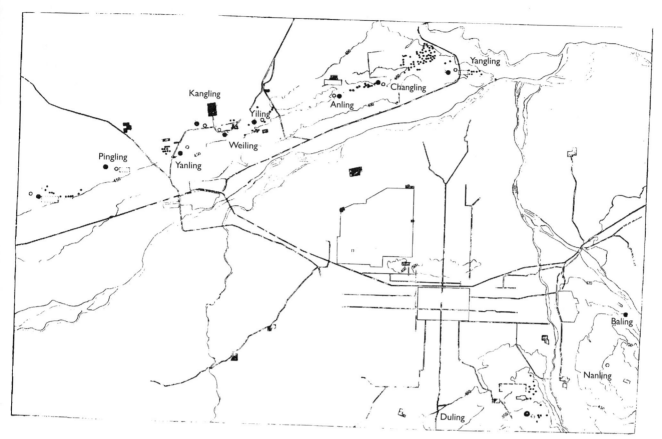

FIGURE 246. Plan of Western Han (206 B.C.–A.D. 23) capital, Chang'an, showing locations of imperial tombs. [After *Han Duling lingyuan yizhi*, pp. 3–4]

FIGURE 247. Maoling (tomb of Emperor Han Wudi [r. 140–87 B.C.]).
[Courtesy of Elizabeth Owen]

246 shows eleven imperial Han tombs in the vicinity of the former Western Han capital, Chang'an, and makes clear that under a strong empire such as the Han, the Chinese system was to bury all rulers in the same general vicinity, roughly northwest of the capital city. Scores of princely and aristocratic graves from the Han have been excavated and reconstructed.[8]

Wang Zhongshu discusses Han tombs according to five main types.[9] According to Wang, the simplest and oldest Han tombs were vertical pit burials. Even these rudimentary structures have included some of the most sophisticated Han art and artifacts, such as painting on silk, military maps, and star charts.[10] Horizontal pits were another element of Han funerary construction. This type is best represented by the graves of Prince Liu Sheng and Princess Dou Wan, carved into cliffs in Mancheng, Hebei, also in the second century B.C.[11] More complex Han tomb construction involved the use of brick. In general, large hollow bricks were employed in earlier Han tombs and small solid ones

were standard later. Han brick tombs have been studied throughout the twentieth century.[12] Their plans range from two connected chambers, each with its own vaulted ceiling, to three main chambers, sometimes with side rooms, to three interconnected chambers with seven other rooms, all constructed along a main axis (figs. 248 and 249).[13] There is no question that Han tombs were inside Liao territory, even in capital cities. The mounds of three Han tombs can be seen in Liaoyang still.[14] Some of their wall paintings have been moved to the Liaoning Provincial Museum (see fig. 51).

The Liaoyang tombs are of the last type identified by Wang Zhongshu. Subterranean tomb chambers are constructed of stone slabs, and passage is from room to room without intermediary corridors (fig. 250). Comparable construction in Shandong is the late-Han (possibly later in the third century) tomb at Yi'nan.[15] A different Han tomb form, not discussed by Wang, is represented by the late-Han Mahao Cave Tomb in Leshan, Sichuan.[16] Carved horizontally into natural rock like the tomb of Prince Liu Sheng, the stone walls offer an impression more similar to the Liaoyang or Yinan tombs than to brick tombs where vaulted-ceiling chambers are joined by corridors.

The Han is also the period credited with the introduction of monumental stone sculpture that lines the approach to a tomb. This formation of human and animal sculpture and freestanding gate towers—and, after the Han period, also stelae—is called *shendao* (spirit path.)[17] Above ground, the spirit path is probably the most identifiable feature of all subsequent imperial Chinese tomb construction. Spirit paths can also be found along the approaches to tombs of imperial relatives and high-ranking aristocracy. No description of a ceremony at Qingzhou refers to a spirit path, and sculptural evidence of one is lacking, but as we have noted, the long approach to each tomb suggests a spirit path.

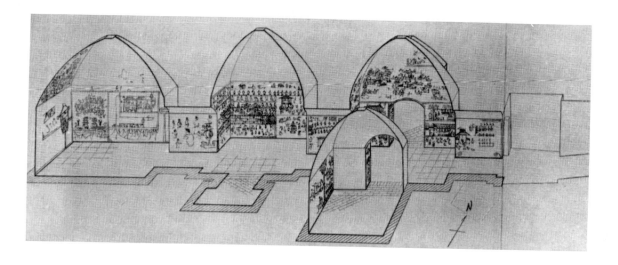

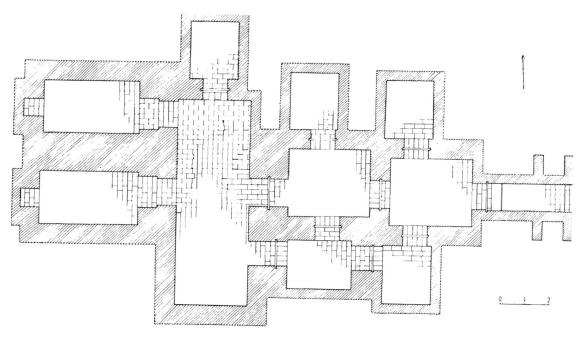

FIGURE 248 (top). Infrastructural drawing of tomb at Helinge'er, Inner Mongolia, second century A.D. [*Helinge'er Hanmu bihua*, p. 21]

FIGURE 249 (above). Plan of tomb in Anping, Hebei province, A.D. 176. [After *Anping Dong Han bihuamu*, p. 4]

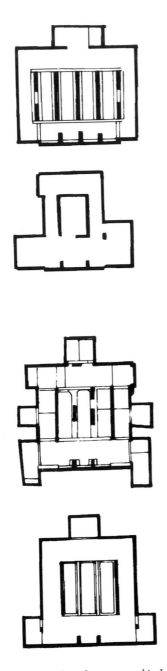

FIGURE 250. Plans of tombs excavated in Liaoyang, Eastern Han. [After Fairbank, *Adventures in Retrieval*, p. 170; published courtesy of Wilma Fairbank]

Even though the majority of Chinese emperors' and empresses' tombs remain unexcavated, thus far the evidence has yielded nothing, imperial or non-imperial, between Han and Liao that approaches the complexity of design in subterranean construction of Han or Qingling. For the 360 years after Han—the periods of the Three Kingdoms (220–280) and the Northern and Southern Dynasties (ca. 265–ca. 581)—funerary architecture is studied according to its location and the nationality of its patron. For the Six Dynasties of southeastern China whose capitals were in the vicinity of modern Nanjing, imperial burials had spirit paths lined by fanciful animals, freestanding pillars with animal capitals, and stelae. Burial was marked by mounds.[18]

Tombs of the Northern Dynasties—in particular the Northern Wei (386–534) and one group of their predecessors, the Xianbei (whose tombs have been identified through the sixth century)—are inside Liao territory and thus their potential impact on Qidan burial is greater than that of the distant Southern Dynasties.[19] A tomb excavated at Guyuan, Ningxia Hui Autonomous Region, for example, has become very well known because of the lacquer coffin decorated with scenes of Chinese filial piety. Its structure, however, is extremely simple: a single, four-sided, domed chamber approached by a diagonal path from the ground.[20] The tomb of Li Xian, also excavated in Guyuan, was only slightly more complex: it had three vertical shafts from ground level to the tomb path, perhaps for lowering grave goods.[21] This burial has become known in the West because a gilt silver ewer was excavated inside.[22] Similarly, the tomb of Sima Jinlong, some of whose contents have been on exhibition at the Huayansi, is known for its lacquer screen on which scenes from "Admonitions of the Court Instructress" are illustrated, but the underground structure is one domed chamber approached by a ramp.[23] All three tombs were identified by aboveground mounds.

FIGURE 251. Detail of paintings from west wall of tomb of Lou Rui, Taiyuan, Shanxi province, Northern Qi period. [After *Wenwu* (1983, no. 10), lower color plate]

The Li Xian tomb and two others from sixth-century North China are especially interesting because of the wall paintings that decorate them. A tomb dated to A.D. 550 in Cixian, Hebei, has been identified as belonging to a Ruru princess married to a Xianbei.[24] One feature of the princess' burial has fascinated scholars: the apparently unique painting of a carpet pattern on the floor of the passageway into the tomb. (Unfortunately, it has never been published.) Standard bearers on the eastern wall of the ramp into the tomb chamber and women holding fans or perhaps parasols, however, call to mind the murals in the tomb of Tang Princess Yongtai, who was buried outside the capital in 706. We cannot prove these murals were directly responsible for wall paintings in a princess' tomb in Chang'an 150 years later, but the two are similar not only in subject matter but in line quality.[25] The comparison is raised here because it spans two centuries and several provinces. In Chapter 13, similar far-reaching comparisons in space, and more distant in time, will be shown relevant to Liao tombs and their decoration.

The last noteworthy "Xianbei" tomb belongs to Lou Rui, an official under Northern Qi rule who was buried in Taiyuan. With a plan no more complex than those in Cixian, in Guyuan, or that of the Ruru princess, Lou Rui's tomb is covered with wall paintings of horsemen with hunting dogs (fig. 251). In style they are affiliated with Chinese painting, but their subject matter anticipates later non-Chinese tomb decoration.[26] The format—horizontal registers of narrative—has a source in Han tombs such as the ones at Wangdu or Anping.

The tombs identified as Xianbei and discussed here were all located in or just south of the southwestern and south central regions of Liao territory—that is, in the Liao western and central circuits or just to their south. During the third through sixth centuries, tomb building flourished in the eastern Liao circuit, and, as well, in the vicinity of Beiyuan and Liaoyang and farther northeast under Korean and Bohai patrons. These tombs are discussed in Chapter 13.

TANG FUNERARY ARCHITECTURE

Tang was a nearly 300-year dynasty whose influence on all aspects of East Asian life and art has been common knowledge since initial investigation of this dynasty.[27] The timber-frame structures of Tang, moreover, were shown in Part One to have served as the foundation for Liao wooden architecture. Thus one would expect the impact of the Tang funerary tradition on Liao imperial mausoleums to have been equally strong.

Tang imperial tombs are well known and well published. The turn-of-the-century scholarship of Edouard Chavannes and haunting photographs of Victor Segalen were enhanced for historians of Chinese art beginning in the 1960s when the first tombs of imperial princes and princesses in suburban Xi'an were opened.[28] Most recently, aboveground remains at the tombs of the Tang emperors have been studied by Ann Paludan.[29] The visible components of a Tang royal tomb complex have been part of the official record since the Song dynasty (fig. 252).[30] Indeed, with such excellent literary and archaeological documentation, few questions remain about the appearance of a Tang royal tomb above ground or about the subterranean space of princely burials.

Qianling, imperial tomb of third Tang emperor Gaozong (d. 683) and his wife (and usurper of the throne) Empress Wu, who reigned until her death in 705, occupied an area over 5,000 meters north to south by about 1,500 meters east to west (fig. 253 and see fig. 252).[31] One's introduction to the ceremonial space was a pair of *que* at the southern terminus; more than 2,500 meters beyond them one came to the beginning of the spirit path. Institutionalized in

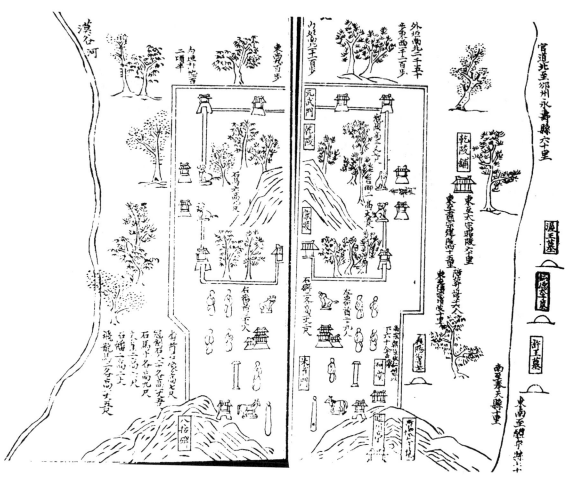

FIGURE 252. Plan of Qianling, mausoleum of Tang Emperor Gaozong (d. 683) and Empress Wu (d. 705) and satellite tombs of Tang royalty, Qian county (Xi'an suburbs), Shaanxi province. [After Li Haowen, *Chang'anzhi tu, juan zhong*/5a–b]

FIGURE 253. Spirit path leading to Qianling. [Steinhardt photograph]

imperial tomb architecture in the Han dynasty, each emperor's tomb, as well as the tombs of princes and princesses, had its own *shendao*. The animals, humans, and stelae carved for the spirit path ended at the outer enclosure of the mound (see fig. 253). At Qianling, this enclosure could be accessed by a gate at the center of each side.

Only a southern entry pierced the original enclosure at the tomb of Princess Yongtai (fig. 254), and the mound above her smaller tomb was a truncated pyramid. At both the princesses' tombs and at Qianling, the burial chambers were directly beneath the mound. The burial rooms of the tombs of Princess Yongtai, her brother, and her uncle, all of whom were executed or forced to commit suicide at the hand of Empress Wu, were approached by diagonal ramps from the ground-level entry. Approximately six vertical shafts made it possible to lower goods into side niches of this ramp. A hall led into the first of two burial chambers, both four-sided and joined by a shorter corridor. Each of the two brick chambers had a domed ceiling.

Structurally, the tombs of Tang princes and princesses are simpler underground (they have fewer main chambers and no side niches) than those at Qingzhou, but one assumes that the burial spaces for emperor and empress were more complex. The tombs of Tang princely figures and those associated with the Xianbei also are structurally simpler than the tombs of Han officials at Wangdu, Helinge'er, or Anping. Despite the time differences, it is the Han tombs that offer the best comparisons with the three at Qingzhou.

CHINESE TOMBS OF THE TENTH THROUGH FOURTEENTH CENTURIES

Tombs of Chinese royalty from the first half of the tenth century in Nanjing and Sichuan are, more than anything else, built on the models of the imperial Tang system. In the Nanjing region, tombs of the first two rulers of the Southern Tang kingdom, Li Bian (d. 943) and his son Li Jing (d. 961), are located in the Zutang Mountains about 15 kilometers south of the modern city. Although no traces of a

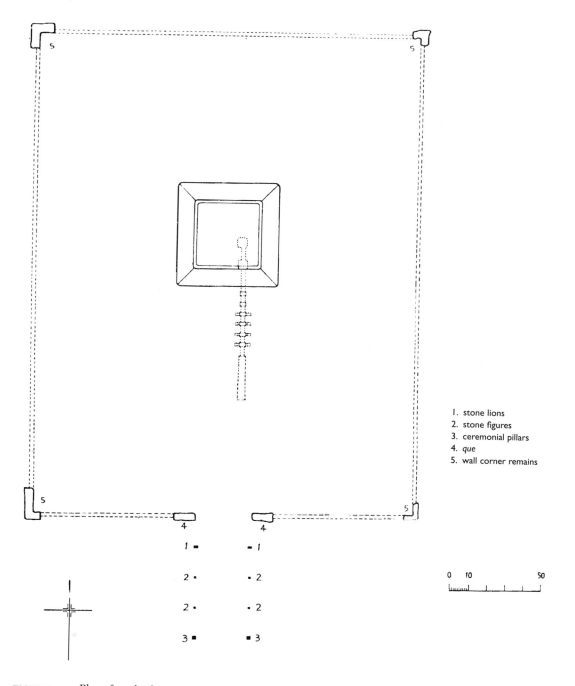

1. stone lions
2. stone figures
3. ceremonial pillars
4. *que*
5. wall corner remains

0 10   50

FIGURE 254. Plan of tomb of Princess Yongtai, Qian county, Shaanxi, 706. [After Liu Dunzhen, *Zhongguo gudai jianzhu shi,* 2nd ed., p. 159]

spirit path were found in the 1950s excavation of the burials, the nearly identical tombs were more complex in plan and more costly to build than those of the Tang princes and princesses (fig. 255). The Southern Tang tombs, for instance, had three main subterranean chambers, each with one to three side niches.[32] Each main chamber had a domed ceiling. The tombs had more relief sculpture than painting on the inside and had actual columns as well as painted columns on the walls. Still, each chamber was four-sided in plan.

The royal tomb Yongling built for Wang Jian, emperor of the Kingdom of Shu in modern Chengdu who died in 918, also exhibits no evidence of a spirit path, but 15 meters of its mound remained in the 1940s.[33] Underground the tomb consisted of three main chambers, the central one approximately twice the size of the front and back chambers, for a total length of nearly 25 meters (fig. 256). Construction was of red sandstone with thirteen arches separated by stone slabs to form the ceiling. As Cheng Te-k'un points out, Sichuan was a refuge for Tang officials following the demise of their empire, and one is thus inclined to view the tomb's architecture as following Tang customs.[34] Despite its elaborate interior, however, the tomb was a simple series of three chambers. More important, even if one could confirm that the Qidan knew about Tang tombs, it is highly unlikely that underground architecture of Sichuan was known to them. Since the thirteen arches are unknown elsewhere, one probably should conclude for the time being that even if the Yongling interior followed a specific Tang precedent, it seems to have had a very limited afterlife.

It is more likely that Song royal tombs caught the attention of the Liao emperors. Deguang had been in the Song capital Bianliang, and subsequent missions between Liao and Song brought Qidan into Henan province. The first seven (of nine) Song emperors and the father of the dynasty's founder are buried in Gongxian, Henan province. Besides the eight imperial males, twenty-one empresses plus consorts, relatives, and officials were laid to rest in the 56-square-kilometer area.[35] Each imperial tomb has at least one auxiliary burial.

Above ground, the complexity of the Northern Song royal tombs lies somewhere between a Tang emperor's tomb like Qianling and the tomb of a Tang prince. That is, each of the eight tombs was approached by a spirit path that consisted of an entry marked by *que*, another pair of *que* behind it, and a long row of stone sculptures on either side (fig. 257). The total distance from the first gate to the last pair of sculptures, however, was only about 150 meters. All Song royal tombs were approached by spirit paths and enclosed by walls with an opening on each side like those at Qianling (see figs. 252 and 253); at their centers were truncated, pyramidal mounds (fig. 258). We have no underground plans of Song imperial tombs. One wonders, in particular, if the shapes of chambers were four-sided—following the precedent of Tang and the first half of the tenth century—or if a change to the circular or octagonal chambers of the three Qingzhou tombs had occurred.

The possibility of such a transformation is real: three nonimperial Song tombs excavated in Henan province about 60 kilometers southeast of Gongxian at a site called Baisha offer evidence of an underground tomb chamber that is not four-sided. Tomb 1, the largest and most complex, had a hall leading to the four-sided antechamber and another hall joining it to the back chamber, which was hexagonal (fig. 259).[36] Tombs 2 and 3, by contrast, had small anterooms at the ends of the stepped ramps into the underground chambers that led directly to the hexagonal main chamber.[37] According to Xu Pingfang, from the middle of the Song period on-

FIGURE 255. Infrastructural section of tomb of Southern Tang Emperor Li Bian (d. 943), Jiangning county (Nanjing suburbs), Jiangsu. [After Liu Dunzhen, *Zhongguo gudai jianzhu shi,* 2nd ed., p. 161]

FIGURE 256. Infrastructural section of tomb of Emperor Wang Jian (d. 918) of Former Shu kingdom, Chengdu, Sichuan province. [After Wang Wenlin, *Nan Tang erling,* p. 8]

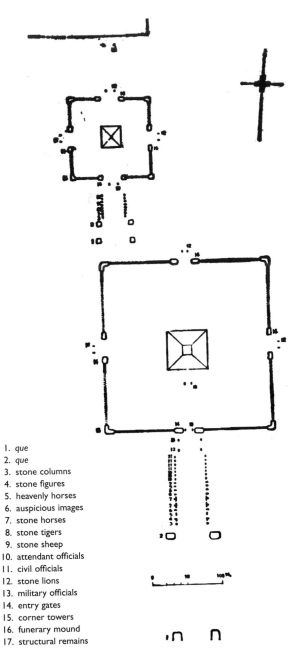

1. que
2. que
3. stone columns
4. stone figures
5. heavenly horses
6. auspicious images
7. stone horses
8. stone tigers
9. stone sheep
10. attendant officials
11. civil officials
12. stone lions
13. military officials
14. entry gates
15. corner towers
16. funerary mound
17. structural remains

FIGURE 257. Plan of Yongzhaoling, tomb of Northern Song Emperor Renzong (d. 1063), Gong county, Henan. [After Liu Dunzhen, *Zhongguo gudai jianzshu shi*, 2nd ed., p. 237]

FIGURE 258. Yongdingling, tomb of Northern Song Emperor Zhenzong (d. 1022), Gong county, Henan. [Steinhardt photograph]

ward (specifically from the reign of Shenzong [r. 1068–1087]), four-sided and circular chambers gave way to a variety of shapes, including hexagonal and octagonal.[38] This is precisely the period in which the earliest of the Qingzhou tombs, that of Shengzong, was constructed. Among excavated tombs in Henan, Shanxi, and Hebei (all Song provinces closest to Liao territory), as well as Hubei, Shaanxi, and Gansu, not to mention tombs farther south, hexagonal and octagonal underground chambers are known.[39] Like earlier tombs, most of the Northern Song tombs had imitations of timber-frame construction carved or painted on their walls (see fig. 259).

In China and to its north, such variety in underground chamber configuration dropped off sharply after the fall of Liao and Song. Jin tombs, for example, can be found with both four-sided and octagonal underground rooms, but rarely does one find a tomb with more than one chamber plus side

niches.[40] In China under Southern Song rule, one can view as representative the single-chamber stone tomb of Huang Sheng, who died in 1243 and was buried outside of Fuzhou, Fujian province, or the similar single stone-chamber tomb of Yu Gongzhu and his wife from Pengxian, Sichuan.[41] As for Southern Song imperial tombs, they were constructed without spirit paths in Shaoxing, Zhejiang province, not far from the capital in Lin'an (today Hangzhou). Little remains of these tombs whose construction, it had been hoped, would be part of a temporary stop while the dynasty regrouped before reclaiming its lands to the north.[42]

The approximately twenty Yuan-period tombs that have been uncovered in today's Inner Mongolian Autonomous Region, Liaoning, Shanxi, and Gansu are uniformly single-chambered. All but one are four-sided-chamber tombs.[43] Mongolian emperors were returned to their homeland in present Outer Mongolia for burial at unmarked and still

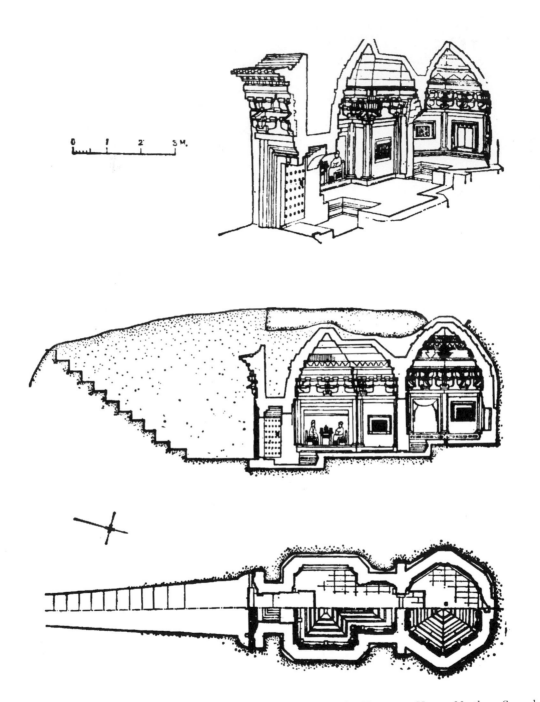

FIGURE 259. Infrastructural drawing, plan, and section of Tomb 1, Baisha, Yu county, Henan, Northern Song dynasty. [After Liu Dunzhen, *Zhongguo gudai jianzhu shi*, 2nd ed., p. 240]

undiscovered locations. Still, even among the non-imperial tombs, the return to four-sided underground burial chambers may be significant.

One cannot prove the origins of hexagonal and octagonal chambers to be Song or to be Liao. They appear in great numbers in both Song and Liao territory in the mid-eleventh century, about the time of the Shengzong reign. For the Liao, however, octagonal spaces have symbolism and meaning. Since in China the forms seem to have neither pre-Song nor post-Song histories in architectural planning, the style must have been learned from Liao. There is no evidence that associated meanings traveled with the forms to Song China.

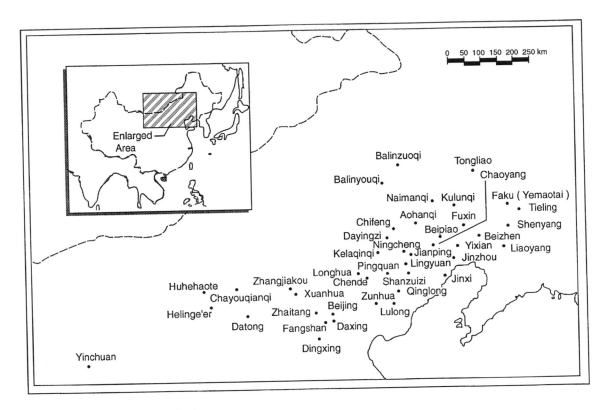

MAP 6. Sites of Selected Liao Tombs

12

Liao Tombs beyond Qingling

WELL OVER ONE HUNDRED Liao tombs have been excavated within the area of the "five circuits," and more than another hundred await opening.[1] No single study has adequately addressed the subject of Liao tomb architecture or decoration. Most research on Liao tombs begins and ends with excavation. The overwhelming majority of known Liao tombs have been discovered by an accidental confrontation between an agricultural or construction worker and a mound or underground remains. Only for tombs of emperors have excavators started out with a text and searched for the burial site. Information about nonimperial tomb occupants has come forth as randomly as the tombs themselves—occupants are known through chance uncovering of a funerary inscription or other obvious identification at the site. Research focused on tomb occupants has addressed two main questions: can one determine whether certain nationalities, Han Chinese or Qidan, preferred certain types of burials, and can one differentiate between burial styles of aristocrats and commoners?

Here, too, the database for our discussion is excavation reports, about forty of them. (See Map 6.) There are several criteria for selecting approximately thirty (some merely mentioned, others subject to more lengthy discussion) Qidan burials and about a dozen Han Chinese burials: dated tombs; tomb plans with extraordinary features; tombs that serve as excellent representatives of a widespread type. My purpose here is not to present a definitive study of Liao funerary architecture, but to relate the subterranean architecture to aboveground buildings discussed in Part One and to sharpen our understanding of the significance of architecture in the Liao empire.

DATED TOMBS OF YELÜ AND OTHER IMPERIAL RELATIVES OR QIDAN ARISTOCRACY

Two features of the three imperial Liao tomb complexes at Qingzhou are especially noteworthy. First is the lack of surviving monumental stone sculpture that is believed to have defined a spirit path to the tomb. Second are the varied room plans, above all the apparent substitution of octagonal for circular underground chambers in the mausoleum of Emperor Xingzong (see figs. 239 and 242). Concerning the first point, one of the most important Liao tomb finds was that of Yelü Cong, who died in 979. A complete set of sculptural pairs still lines the approach (fig. 260).[2]

Tomb of Yelü Cong

Yelü Cong's tomb is located in a mountainous region of Chifeng county. Oriented southeast, its spirit path consisted of five pairs of stone sculptures between a stele and the funerary mound. The stele is positioned on the back of a tortoise and serpents entwine around the top, both standard features of Chinese imperial construction. Standing 256 centimeters, the stele has a Chinese translation of the *Avalokiteśvara (Guanyin) Sutra* written in standard script *(kaishu)* on the front and back. The first and second pairs of sculptures are reclining sheep that extend 65 centimeters high. Behind them are the

third pair, tigers, the more complete of which stands 120 centimeters. Fourth are a pair of military officials in armor, wearing high boots, with hands positioned on swords. Then comes a pair of civil officials, taller than their military counterparts and judged to be Han Chinese.[3] Last was a rectangular platform about 20 meters in width. Pieces of it were strewn in the vicinity when archaeologists visited. Another stele that rose 236 centimeters was placed about 30 meters west of the tomb. It was carved on all four sides with up to eighty-nine characters in a line. What could be read of its inscription is appended to the publication by Li Yiyou about this tomb.

The occupant of the tomb has been identified as the man referred to in the *Liaoshi* as both Yelü Changzhu and Yelü Hezhu.[4] His paternal grandfather was the younger brother of Abaoji.[5] The family's ancestral home was in the vicinity of Lingyuan and Jianping prefectures of Liaoning, and their territory extended to present Kelaqinqi, Jingcheng, and Pingquan, the latter territories in the center of the central circuit. It seems also to have included today's Chengde. Still, in 979, the lands were a full hundred kilometers from the Song border and hundreds or even thousands of kilometers from Chinese spirit paths. We do not know specifically what inspired Yelü Cong or his descendants to erect a double row of monumental stone sculpture at the approach to his tomb. Perhaps he saw one, read about one, or had one described to him.

For the Tang, Song, Yuan, and later dynasties, texts not only specify the erection of a spirit path in front of an imperial or official tomb but prescribe which animals or humans (and in what numbers) should line that path.[6] Each of the stone pairs in the Liao tomb has a counterpart in imperial Song spirit paths. Specifically, kneeling sheep (symbolizing filial piety), tigers (symbolizing martial arts), and civil and military officials are part of the approach

FIGURE 260. Spirit path from tomb of Yelü Cong, Chifeng county, Inner Mongolia, 979. [Photo courtesy of Tian Guanglin]

to the tomb of the first Song emperor, Taizu, who was buried in 976 in Gong county, Henan.[7] The animals chosen by the Yelü official, however, sheep and tigers, were more common at official Han and Tang tombs than any imperial ones.[8] Certainly some Chinese source led to Yelü Cong's tomb display—perhaps one (or knowledge of one) in a Chinese outpost that by the tenth century would have been out of vogue in China but served its symbolic function on the Shira-müren plain.

One cannot but marvel at the complete takeover of something so purely Chinese as a spirit path for a Qidan grave in Chifeng county just twenty-two years after a Qidan ruler had his internal organs re-

placed with vegetal substances in preparation for burial. Although Yelü Cong's is the only Qidan spirit path known to survive, the approach to this official's tomb was probably not unique. It is the best evidence that the miscellaneous pieces of large human sculpture found at the site identified as Zuling and at the Qingzhou tombs were parts of imperial spirit paths.

Tomb of the Emperor's Son-in-Law, Prince of Wei

The only dated Qidan tomb earlier than Yelü Cong's is the tomb of a *fuma* (emperor's son-in-law): Zeng, Prince of Wei. Its date, 959, is provided

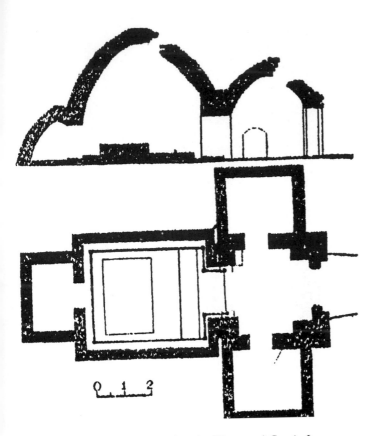

FIGURE 261. Plan and section of tomb of Emperor's Son-in-Law, Prince of Wei, Dayingzi, Chifeng county, 959. [After Zheng Shaozong, "Chifengxian Dayingzi Liaomu . . ." (*Kaogu xuebao* 1956, no. 3), p. 2]

by a Chinese funerary inscription.[9] The *fuma's* tomb is located in mountainous terrain northwest of the village of Dayingzi in Chifeng county, about 45 kilometers from the city of Chifeng. Discovered as the result of heavy rains, it was excavated during a period of twenty-seven days in the autumn of 1954. During the excavation, two other tombs were uncovered also. Underground the prince's tomb consisted of two main, domed chambers, two side rooms off the front chamber, and a back room, also domed, all in brick (fig. 261). The total length of the tomb was 10.6 meters, from entry to back room, and 8.7 meters between the ends of the two side rooms. Every chamber was four-sided and doors led from one to the next. The corpse was placed in the central chamber. A diagonal path followed a 20-degree angle from the ground into the tomb. Its dimensions were 5 by 1.25 meters. The entry from this path into the tomb was a double-panel door 1.22 meters in height, 0.66 meter across each panel, and 0.13 meter thick. It was arched at the top and there were traces of painted figures on it.

Although the tomb had been robbed, over 2,000 objects remained in it. The majority were imperial gifts. Thus it seems one can confirm, even in this early example of a Qidan burial, the line from the *Liaoshi* quoted in Chapter 10 relating that upon an emperor's death some of his possessions were distributed to relatives.

Tomb of Yelü Yanning

The third dated tomb with a royal Qidan occupant belongs to Yelü Yanning. Located in Chaoyang county of Liaoning province, this tomb's occupant was identified by a bilingual funerary inscription (Qidan and Chinese), but his name is not found in the *Liaoshi*.[10] The inscription tells us the occupant died in his thirty-ninth year, in 985, thus making this a rare, early example of a bilingual inscription. He was buried the next year. Based on the inscrip-

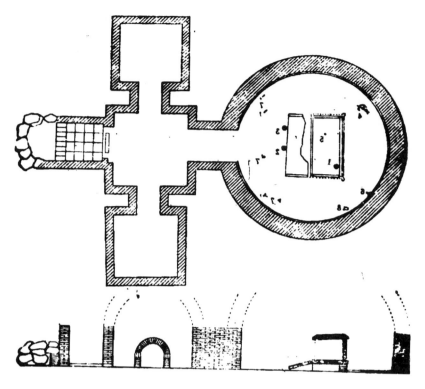

FIGURE 262 (above). Plan and section of tomb of Yelü Yanning, Chaoyang county, Liaoning, 986. [After "Liaodai Yelü Yanning mu . . . ," (*Wenwu* 1980, no. 7), p. 19]

FIGURE 263 (left). Stone man excavated at tomb of Yelü Yanning. [After "Liaodai Yelü Yanning mu . . . ," (*Wenwu* 1980, no. 7), pl. 5, fig. 1]

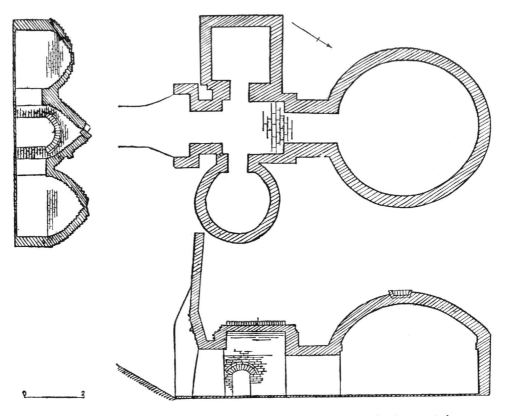

FIGURE 264. Plan and section of Tomb 1, Shazigou, Aohanqi, Inner Mongolia, Liao period.
[After Shao Guotian (*Kaogu* 1987, no. 10), p. 890]

tion, he has been identified as an imperial relative whose territory extended northeastward from Chaoyang into Heilongjiang.

Underground the tomb was brick and was oriented only 8 degrees west of due north-south. With no evidence of aboveground markings, the subterranean portion consisted of two main brick chambers, the front chamber nearly square (2.64 by 2.56 m), approached by an entryway and joined on either side by a nearly square room. The second main chamber, joined to the front chamber by a corridor, was circular. Both had vaulted ceilings (fig. 262). The tomb had been robbed, but remains made it clear that wooden pillars had been used in addition to the brick; in fact, iron nails were found.[11] It still contained a stone coffin on which were carved the four directional animals *(sishen)*. Among the remains was the upper portion of a stone man (fig. 263) which, we have seen, was not unique among Qidan burials. The plan of Yelü Yanning's tomb is similar to that of the Prince of Wei: both consisted of two main chambers and two side rooms off the antechamber. However, Yelü Yanning's tomb of 985 is the earliest Liao evidence so far of a circular burial chamber. (Emperor Shengzong's tomb [see fig. 239] was not built until 1031.)

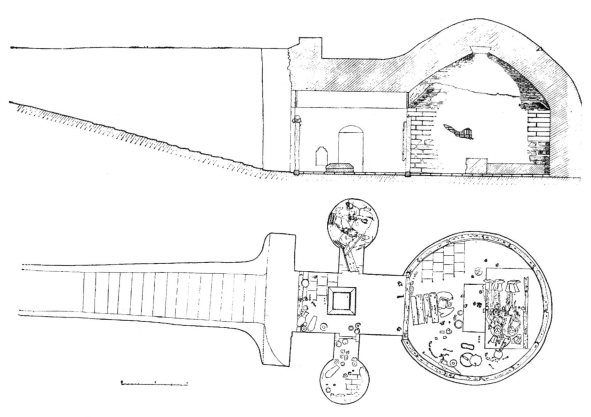

FIGURE 265. Plan and section of tomb of Princess of Chenguo and her husband, Qinglong, Naimanqi, Inner Mongolia, 1018. [After *Liao Chenguo gongzhu mu*, p. 7]

Excavations of 1982 and 1983 yielded another tomb in Shazigou, Aohanqi (Aohan Banner), Inner Mongolia, of very similar plan (fig. 264).[12] The only notable difference was that the side eastern chamber (of the roughly north-oriented tomb) was circular instead of squarish. Based on the dating of Yelü Yanning's tomb, it is likely that the Shazigou tomb is also pre-eleventh century.

Tomb of Yelü Jiayili's Concubine

The next dated Qidan tomb was identified only by funerary inscription. The concubine of Yelü Jiayili had died in 1008 and been buried the following

year in Pingquan county of Hebei, near modern Chengde. Her tomb is reported to have been brick with two chambers. It was washed away with several other tombs in floods of 1916.[13]

Tomb of the Princess of Chenguo and Her Husband, Xiao Shaoju, Son-in-Law of the Emperor

The joint burial of the Princess of the Chen state and her husband is one of the most important finds in the history of Liao excavation. The princess died at the age of eighteen in 1018 during the reign of her uncle, sixth Liao emperor Shengzong. (She was the

FIGURE 266. Princess of Chenguo and her husband as they were found during excavation. [After *Liao Chenguo gongzhu mu wenwuzhan*, n.p.]

daughter of former Emperor Jingzong—thus her husband's title.) Her husband was the brother of Shengzong's wife, Empress Qitian. In other words, tomb finds might foretell the manner and accoutrements of an emperor's or empress' burial.

The tomb was found with two others in the town of Qinglongshan, in Naimanqi, Inner Mongolia, just miles from the Liaoning border, in the summers of 1984 and 1985. By 1986 all three tombs had been excavated.[14] Tomb 3, belonging to the princess and her husband, was the only one intact. Oriented 136 degrees west of north, the positioning was close to that of the tomb from Shazigou (see fig. 264). Underground the tomb stretched 16 meters — 5.4 meters shorter than the length of the Eastern Mausoleum but extremely long for a Liao tomb nevertheless. (Yelü Yanning's tomb was less than half as long.) The tomb was composed of an entry area, a rectangular chamber that contained the stone epitaph, two circular side niches attached to it by corridors, and a large, circular, vaulted burial chamber (fig. 265). The entire tomb was brick. The princess and her husband were placed on a funerary bed along the back wall of the main circular chamber. Originally the bed had been covered with curtains. Among the more than 300 objects inside the tomb, the most spectacular were the metal burial suits (fig. 266).

Virtually every inch of the prince and princess' bodies was covered with metal or metal netting. The faces were covered with gold death masks that joined silver-wire netting for the bodies (figs. 267 and 268). Netting for the heads and feet was further protected by gold crowns and silver and gold boots. Although studies have not confirmed that the corpses were opened and refilled with vegetable matter, the bodily encasement is evidence of the practice described for the second Liao emperor, Deguang. Among the many paintings that remain inside the tomb were a "sky" painted dark blue, a

FIGURE 267. Gold death mask of Princess of Chenguo's husband. [After *Liao Chenguo gongzhu mu*, pl. 4, no. 1]

sun on the eastern wall, and a moon on the western wall.[15] The gold masks, as noted in the Introduction, link Liao burial practice with those of certain North Asian groups of the last millennium B.C.[16]

Tomb of Xiao Jin

The tomb of Xiao Jin in Fuxin county, Liaoning, is another tomb of Qidan female royalty. This aunt of sixth emperor Shengzong's wife Qitian was also the daughter of the Prince of Qin (Han Kuangsi), who has been associated with Dule Monastery. She was buried in a domed, octagonal chamber in 1029.[17] Xiao Jin's tomb has the earliest dated octagonal floor plan from the Liao period. Otherwise the tomb plan is similar to the plans of the tombs of the Chenguo princess, Yelü Yanning, and from Shazigou, with a large antechamber and two smaller side rooms (in this case four-sided) adjoining it, but here the orientation is 15 degrees east of north-south (fig. 269). At this time, 1028–1029 is considered a turning

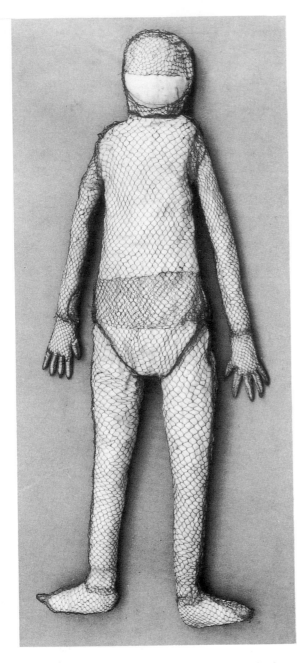

FIGURE 268. Silver-wire netting excavated at tomb of Princess of Chenguo and her husband. [After *Liao Chenguo gongzhu mu*, pl. 7]

point in Liao tomb construction. Another tomb with an octagonal burial chamber, dated 1028, is reported to have been uncovered at Youqiaozi, Ningcheng county, Inner Mongolia, in 1956.[18]

Tomb of the Princess of Qinjin

The tomb of the Princess of Qinjin, dated to 1046, was found in the same county of Hebei as the tomb of the Yelü Jiayili concubine. The princess had died the year before and was buried in a tomb of unusual shape.[19] The underground structure had at least two main rooms: a front chamber, long and narrow with two circular side niches, and an adjoining circular back burial chamber. Orientation was east-west (fig. 270). The princess, older sister of Emperor Shengzong and daughter of his mother Ruizhi who became Empress Dowager Chengtian, is believed to have been born about 970 and was married to a member of the Xiao family.

Several less precisely dated tombs are believed to be from about the same time. Four of the earliest excavated Liao tombs, from Yixian, Liaoning, are assigned to Yelü or Xiao royalty by funerary inscriptions.[20] Tomb 1, believed to contain the remains of Xiao Xianggong, has a main circular chamber and a rectangular antechamber that adjoins it (fig. 271). Its date is pre-1044. A tomb whose occupant is not identified but is dated by inscription to 1057, by contrast, has an octagonal main chamber and two four-sided rooms joining an approach to it (fig. 272). Again, the mid-tenth century appears to be the time when circular burial chambers become octagonal.

QIDAN TOMBS OF THE 1030S TO 1090S

The tombs discussed thus far have interiors faced with brick and occasionally wood. In 1982, two earthen tombs were excavated in Aohanqi, Inner Mongolia. Both had octagonal burial chambers and the better-preserved one (fig. 273) is dated 1032–1054 (the *zhongxi* reign period of Emperor Xing-

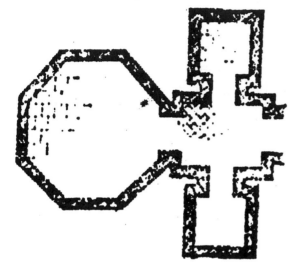

FIGURE 269 (left). Plan and section of tomb of Xiao Jin, Fuxin county, Liaoning, 1029. [After Li and Yuan *(Fuxin Liao-Jinshi yanjiu)*, p. 34]

FIGURE 270 (below). Plan of tomb of Princess of Qinjin, Pingquan county, Hebei, 1046. [After Zheng Shaogong *(Kaogu* 1962, no. 8), p. 429]

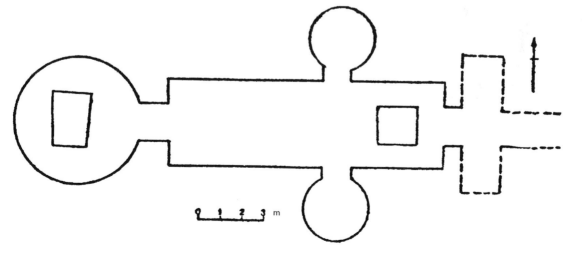

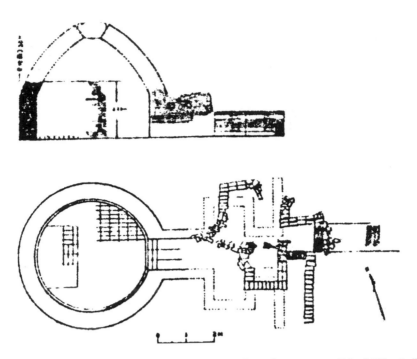

FIGURE 271. Plan and section of tomb of Xiao Xianggong, Yixian, Liaoning, pre-1044. [After Li Wenxin (*Kaogu xuebao* 1954, no. 8), p. 167]

zong),[21] presumably because of the shape of its burial chamber.

By the middle of the eleventh century not only were main chambers predominantly of hexagonal or octagonal shape but side chambers had the same configurations. Such a tomb was made for Yelü Yixian in Fuxin county, Liaoning, in 1052.[22] The same kind of tomb was made in Aohanqi (fig. 274), but it is undated.[23] In 1057, Xiao Zhenwei was laid to rest in Yixian, Liaoning. His tomb consisted of a main octagonal chamber and two four-sided side rooms off the approach to it; the orientation was northwest-southeast (fig. 275).[24]

The next dated Liao tomb whose plan is published also was excavated in Aohanqi.[25] An unknown occupant was buried in a simple brick tomb with a single, hexagonal burial chamber lined with wood (fig. 276).[26] It was approached by a path just over 1.5 meters in length that connected it to the ramp from the outside. Another aspect of this tomb's simplicity are the three bracket sets on the lintel of its entry: they are only of the 4-*puzuo* type. The tomb is believed to have contained a wooden coffin. The tomb also contained three sutras. The date 1079 was found on them and therefore has been assigned to the tomb.[27]

Xiao Cemetery at Kulunqi

Kulun Banner in Inner Mongolia, not far from the border with Jilin province, has been a hub of excavation of Liao tombs since the 1970s. The majority have been given the date ca. 1080. The main struc-

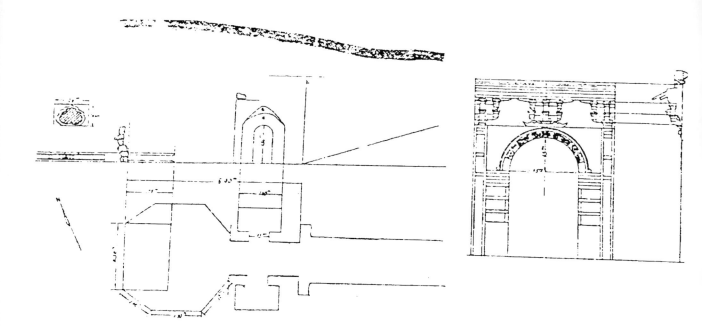

FIGURE 272. Plan and section of Liao tomb excavated at Yixian, Liaoning, 1057. [After Li Wenxin (*Kaogu xuebao* 1954, no. 8), p. 174]

tural criterion behind the dating is the consistent use of hexagonal and octagonal main and side chambers. Other crucial factors in assigning dates to the tombs have been excavated objects, but these too have been dated more by association with similar dated pieces than because of inscriptions or engravings.

The tomb known as Kulunqi Tomb 1 was the first published.[28] Most discussions about it and the seven subsequently excavated and published tombs from the same site have focused on the wall paintings and their iconography. Yet with only one dated coin (1079, found in Tomb 1) and no inscribed objects to identify the tomb occupants, tomb architecture offers better possibilities for determining whose tombs these are and when they were made.

The plans of all eight Kulunqi tombs are shown in Figure 277. Whether a simple, single chamber like Tomb 8 or a complex arrangement like Tombs 1 and 7, all room plans are hexagonal or octagonal (except for Tombs 3 and 4). Another noteworthy feature of the Kulunqi tombs with hexagonal or octagonal main chambers is an extremely long subterranean approach ramp to each one. Tomb 1's ramp is the longest: 42 meters. One purpose of the approach is to provide wall space for paintings. The complex approach-ramp programs of Tombs 1, 2, 7, and 8 have been interpreted as "departure" and "return" scenes. (The mounted male and female figures on either wall of the Princess of Chenguo's tomb may represent the same ideas.) Interpretations of these scenes range from general ideas, such

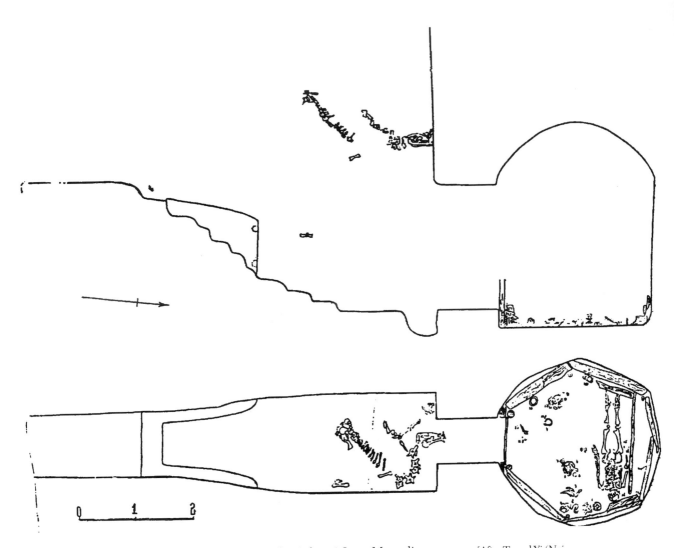

FIGURE 273. Plan and section of Liao tomb excavated in Aohanqi, Inner Mongolia, 1032–1054. [After Ta and Yi (*Nei Menggu wenwu kaogu* 1984, no. 3), p. 76]

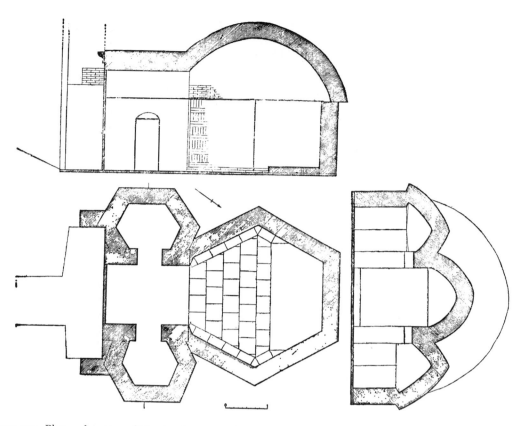

FIGURE 274. Plan and section of Liao tomb excavated in Aohanqi, Inner Mongolia. [After Shao Guotian (*Kaogu* 1984, no. 11), p. 1004]

as passage to and from life or passages during life, to specific events from the life of the interred, including, at Kulunqi Tomb 1, the wedding ceremony of a Qidan princess.[29]

Based on the dated coin and comparisons between the plans of Kulunqi tombs (other than Tombs 3 and 4) and dated Liao tombs with similar plans including some discussed earlier, Tombs 5 and 6 were dated ca. 1080, Tombs 1 and 8 to 1080 or later, and Tomb 7 to after 1080.[30] The most recent study of Kulunqi tombs has refined the dating of Tomb 3 to the last years of the Shengzong reign; Tomb 4 is later than Tomb 3, perhaps as late as the reign of Xingzong; Tomb 1 is from the Daozong reign; Tomb 2 is the latest of Tombs 1–4.[31] Furthermore, the same study has suggested that the Kulunqi burial ground was part of the private city of the Princess of Yue, daughter of Shengzong. She, like many Yelü females and males, is known to have married a member of the Xiao clan, in her case Xiao Xiaozhong. A descendant of his is believed to be buried in Tomb 1 and a less eminent descendant in Tomb 2. Tombs 3 and 4 are believed to be Xiao family plots, but from before the year of Xiao Xiaozhong's marriage to the emperor's daughter.[32]

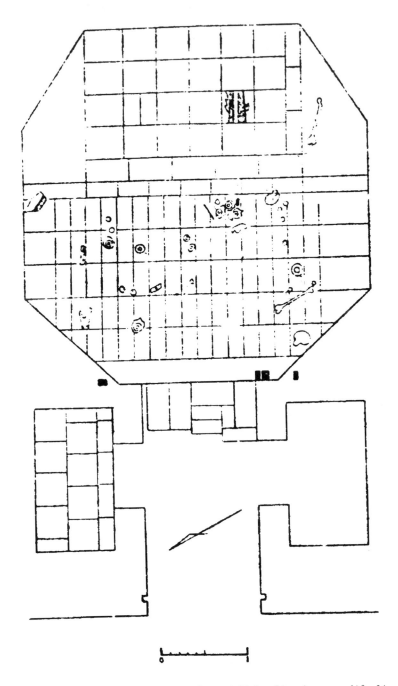

FIGURE 275. Plan of tomb of Xiao Zhenwei, Yixian, Liaoning, 1057. [After Li Wenxin (*Kaogu xuebao* 1954, no. 8), p. 175]

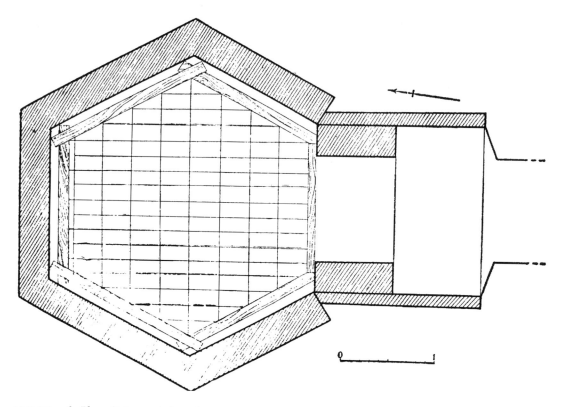

FIGURE 276. Plan of Liao-period tomb excavated at Baitazi, Aohanqi, Inner Mongolia. [After Shao Guotian (*Kaogu* 1978, no. 2), p. 119]

Inside the Tombs

An analysis of architectural decoration inside two of the tombs may shed light on the self-perceived status of the presumably Xiao or Xiao-related occupants and on the dates of the Kulunqi tombs. Figures 278 and 279 depict the lintels of the entries to Kulunqi Tombs 1 and 7, respectively. Among the eight tombs, Tombs 1 and 7 are most alike in plan, each having an octagonal main chamber and hexagonal side rooms; but Tomb 1 has the greater complexity of a partially carved out, roughly octagonal antechamber and a passageway joining it to the main chamber and off of which project the side rooms (see fig. 277a). (As mentioned earlier, both tombs have been dated to the 1080s or later.) Tomb 1, in addition, has paintings of birds and flowers framed around the arc-shaped lintel. Such decoration, as well as human-headed winged females, is also present in the same position at Tomb 8 (fig. 280), but not at Tomb 7. More remarkable is the formation of bracket sets and roof rafters carved in imitation of wooden architecture above the lintel. The three complete bracket sets at the Tomb 1 entry are significantly more complex than the three at Tomb 7. The Tomb 7 clusters are, simply, 5-*puzuo* formations, the kind preserved at Kaishansi Main Hall in Laishui, Hebei (see fig. 162). Those in Tomb 1 are

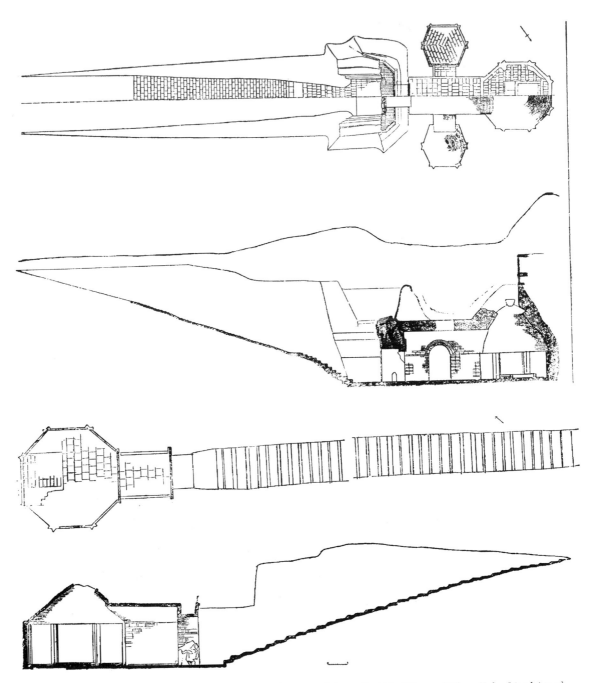

FIGURE 277a (top). Plan and section of Kulunqi Tomb 1, Inner Mongolia. [After Wang and Chen, *Kulun Liaodai*, p. 5]
FIGURE 277b (above). Plan and section of Kulunqi Tomb 2. [After Wang and Chen, *Kulun Liaodai*, p. 36]

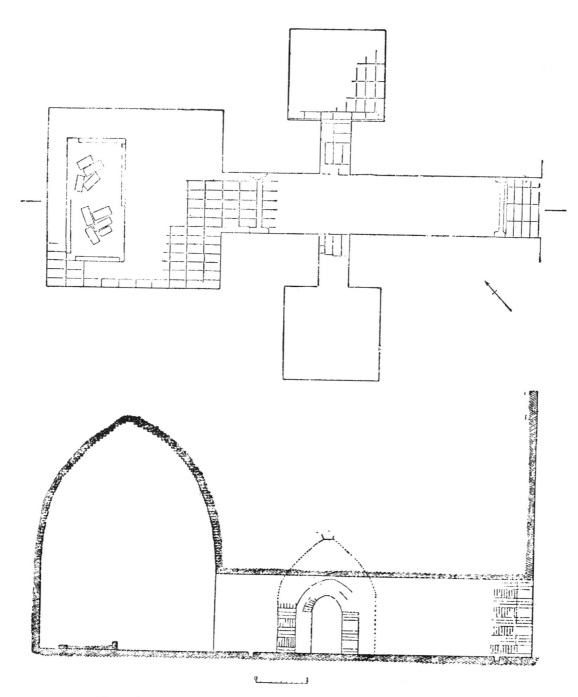

FIGURE 277c. Plan and section of Kulunqi Tomb 3. [After Wang and Chen, *Kulun Liaodai*, p. 48]

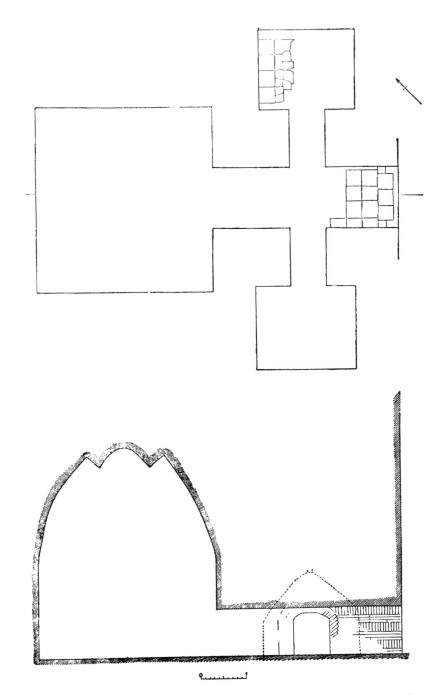

FIGURE 277d. Plan and section of Kulunqi Tomb 4. [After Wang and Chen, *Kulun Liaodai*, p. 57]

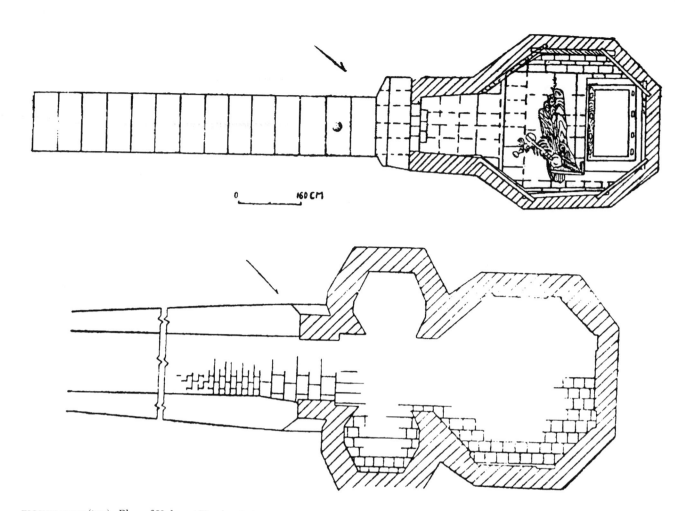

FIGURE 277e (top). Plan of Kulunqi Tomb 5. [After "Kulunqi diwu-, liuhao . . ." (*Nei Mengu wenwu kaogu* 2), p. 35]
FIGURE 277f (above). Plan of Kulunqi Tomb 6. [After "Kulunqi diwu-, liuhao . . ." (*Nei Menggu wenwu kaogu* 2), p. 38]

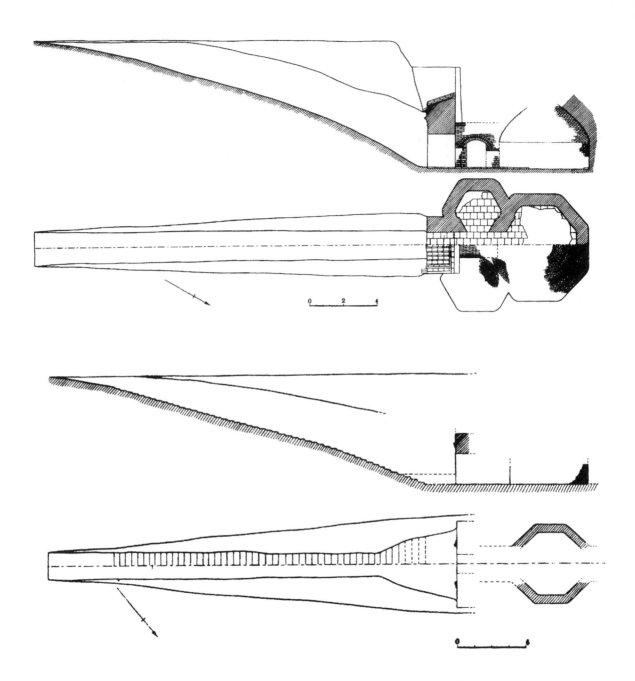

FIGURE 277g (top). Plan and section of Kulunqi Tomb 7. [After Qi Xiaoguang (*Wenwu* 1987, no. 7), p. 75]
FIGURE 277h (above). Plan and section of Kulunqi Tomb 8. [After Qi Xiaoguang (*Wenwu* 1987, no. 7), p. 81]

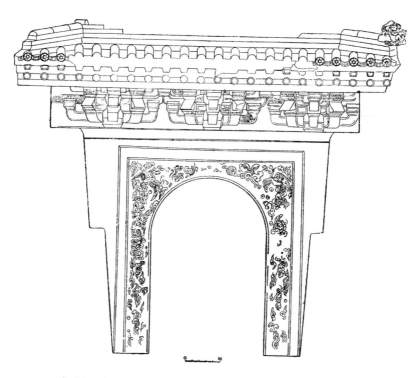

FIGURE 278. Line drawing of lintel at entry to Kulunqi Tomb 1. [After Wang and Chen, *Kulun Liaodai bihuamu*, p. 6]

6-*puzuo*, the higher rank indicated by the *ang* in each cluster. More interesting, they are fan-shaped.

These features are of interest for many reasons. First, at all three imperial tombs from the Qingling site, the bird and flower motifs surround the doorway but bracket sets are 5-*puzuo* (fig. 281). Indeed, the bracket sets above the doorway to Kulunqi Tomb 1 are more detailed than any other doorway sets from the Liao period. So too are the two layers of roof rafters—the upper square in section and the lower circular—combined with the *pupai* tiebeam (compare figs. 278 and 281). All of these features present a sharp contrast to the alternating rectangles at Kulunqi Tomb 7. Tomb 7's quickly rendered shapes might be artisans' "abbreviations"—a feature

that sometimes signifies work from a later time when it was no longer necessary to show every detail with care. ("Rectangles" might stand for bracket sets.) Second, from the discussion of wooden architecture in Part One we have seen that even though fan-shaped bracketing is a feature that has long been associated with Liao architecture, it survives in actual buildings only at Datong. (See, for example, fig. 136.) Its use in Tomb 1, underground in Inner Mongolia, seems to suggest that the feature was more widespread than can be confirmed by the fourteen wooden buildings.

The complexity of bracketing—certainly 6-*puzuo* as opposed to 5-*puzuo* and perhaps fan-shaped clusters—should be understood as a sign of

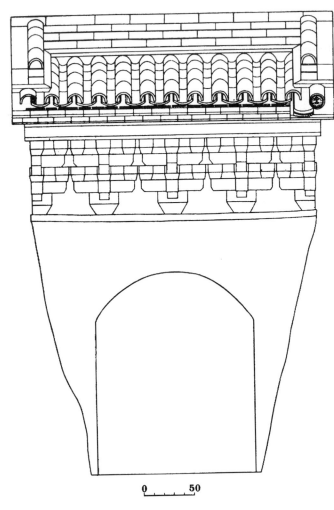

FIGURE 279. Line drawing of lintel at entry of Kulunqi Tomb 7. [After Qi Xiaoguang (*Wenwu* 1987, no. 7), p. 75]

rank. Thus the lack of such bracket sets and tie-beams at the three emperors' tombs in Qingzhou is problematical. Two explanations seem plausible. One is that Kulunqi Tomb 1 is quite late, decorated at a time close to the Jin period when fan-shaped bracket clusters were in fashion, perhaps as late as Tomb 7 and its "abbreviated" forms. Second, and more likely, the architectural motifs painted and carved underground in Kulunqi Tomb 1 are examples of the power of architecture and associated symbolism concealed in a funerary context. Perhaps the Xiao or their tomb builders were aware of the details of underground construction for the ruling Yelü clan at Qingzhou and, with that knowledge, chose the privacy of their burial sanctums for architectural details whose silent symbolism rendered them of higher status than that of the family into which their children so often married. Such a statement, of course, could never have been made in life.

LATE LIAO TOMBS

Four tombs with Qidan occupants are dated 1089 or later. The first of these, in Jinxixian, Liaoning, is Xiao Xiaozhong's. No plan has been published nor has one even been described.[33] The second is nearly 300 kilometers northeast in Fakuxian, the county in which the Yemaotai tombs (discussed later) were excavated. It belongs to Xiao Yi and an unidentified occupant. The third belongs to Xiao Paolu, buried in 1090. The last tomb is dated to 1116.

Tomb of Xiao Paolu

Xiao Paolu's tomb was stumbled upon by workers of Bojiagou People's Collective, Faku county, Liaoning, in 1965 and excavated within a few months after the find.[34] Although no traces of it remained aboveground, its subterranean interior consisted of a 10.3-meter-long approach ramp, a 3.08-by-1.65-

meter antechamber, 1.6-meter-square side chambers joined perpendicular to it, and a main octagonal chamber with one 2.4-meter-long wall and the others approximately 1.8 meters. The "diameters" of these chambers ranged from 4.8 to 5.2 meters. Above the entrance to the tomb were bracket sets of the 5-*puzuo* type, a *pupai* tiebeam, and a lintel with floral patterns, all carved in brick.[35] Yet this tomb is distinguished by an extraordinary feature. Along its interior floor run two main drainage canals from the entry ramp into the tomb. The canals divide to provide water for the anterior side niches and for four branch waterways in the main room (fig. 282).

Xiao Paolu does not have a biography in *Liaoshi*. He is, however, identified by a cenotaph. (A female co-occupant, believed to be his wife, appears to have been about forty at the time of death.)[36] More important information about Xiao Paolu is provided by a long funerary inscription preserved in the tomb. According to this inscription, he served under both Liao Xingzong and Daozong. During Xingzong's reign he twice led attacks on the Xi Xia, in 1044 and 1049, but the latter attack was unsuccessful. Xiao died at the age of seventy-two *sui* in 1090.

Even though his tomb had been plundered, complete skeletons of a dog and sheep remained in it. Also found were stone human figurines.

Tomb of Xiao Yi

The next dated Liao tomb, from 1112, was uncovered in Fakuxian as well. This tomb was large compared to most other known Liao graves: excavators spent almost five months uncovering it.[37] The tomb was approached by a 13.5-by-3.2-meter diagonal ramp whose side walls were covered with wall paintings. The subjects have been defined as the typical Liao "going out" and "returning home" of the occupant.[38] The tomb path widened at either side in

FIGURE 280. Line drawing of decorative detail from lintel at entry to Kulunqi Tomb 8. [After Qi Xiaoguang (*Wenwu* 1987, no. 7), p. 83]

FIGURE 281. Reconstruction drawing of lintel detail from Eastern Mausoleum, Qingzhou. [After Tamura and Kobayashi, *Keiryō*, vol. 1, fig. 101]

front of the entry to the tomb chambers, so that in plan it formed a T (fig. 283). A narrower path led to the antechamber, at either side of which projected octagonally planned rooms. Beyond the anteroom was the main chamber, also octagonal in plan.

The plans of Xiao Yi's and Xiao Paolu's tombs are similar in many ways. Perhaps not coincidentally, both are in the same county. Xiao Yi's tomb is larger—the "diameter" of its main chamber, for instance, is about 5.82 meters—but the key similarity is the presence of waterways on the floor, in this case one main canal leading to the side room and dividing into two to enclose Xiao Yi's stone coffin.

Although more than twenty Liao tombs have been excavated in the vicinity of Yemaotai, and many more in the rest of Faku county, thus far these are the only two with waterways. The feature is of prime symbolic importance. A waterway is the terrestrial complement to heavenly bodies such as those painted on the Princess of Chenguo's tomb ceiling—the ceiling design long known to be standard in underground microcosmic reconstructions of the world of life. Although the waterways do not have a continuous history in East Asia, one was constructed on the floor of the tenth-century tomb of Southern Tang Prince Li Bian (d. 943) in Nanjing (fig. 284 and see fig. 255 for a plan of his tomb).[39] A common Tang source, of course, is likely. Furthermore, we have another example of an architectural detail that survives, so far, only in Southeast China and in Liao territory. That the two Liao examples of tomb waterways would be constructed for the same aristocratic family in the same county seems logical. Yet why Yemaotai, Faku county, was the place remains a mystery.

The latest dated Qidan tomb is from 1116 in Shanzuizi, Inner Mongolia. Between 1969 and 1970 four Yelü family tombs were excavated there. Only the one shown in Figure 285, whose plan is similar to that of Xiao Yi's tomb, is dated.[40] Like other Liao

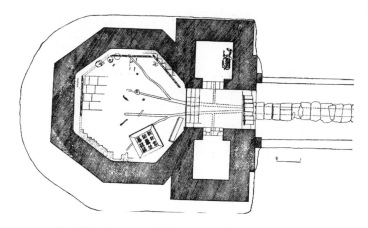

FIGURE 282. Plan of tomb of Xiao Paolu, Bojiagou People's Collective, Faku county, Liaoning, 1090. [After Feng Yongqian (*Kaogu* 1983, no. 7), p. 625]

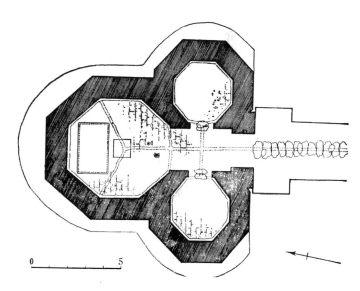

FIGURE 283. Plan of tomb of Xiao Yi, Faku county, Liaoning, 1112. [After Wen Lihe (*Kaogu* 1984, no. 4), p. 325]

FIGURE 284. Detail of floor of tomb of Prince Li Bian (d. 943), Nanjing, Southern Tang, showing drainage canal. [After Wang Wenlin *Nan Tang erling*, p. 34]

tombs from the 1080s and later, such as those at Kulunqi, a long 4.8-meter ramp led from ground level to the tomb. To either side of the narrower pathway to the main chamber were hexagonal side rooms. The main chamber was octagonal in plan with a vaulted ceiling. A Song coin of 1038 was the only dated object in the tomb, but a twenty-five-line inscription provided dates for the male occupant. Archaeologists read these years as 1082–1116 but lack of clarity and missing characters made it impossible for the name to be deciphered.

GENERAL FEATURES OF ARISTOCRATIC QIDAN TOMBS

Between 1981 and 1992 five scholars wrote general articles on Liao tombs. Each discussed at least some of the dated Qidan tombs covered here and for the undated tombs suggested ranges of dates based on plans and architectural features of dated tombs. Due to the unique imperial status of their occupants, the three tombs at Qingzhou were

noted but not considered sufficiently typical to shed light on Qidan or even aristocratic Qidan tomb architecture.

Standard in all six studies (two by the same author) was a division of tombs into early-, middle-, and late-Liao periods. Early is defined as before 983, the year in which Liao Shengzong acceded to the throne. This period can include the predynastic Qidan era; one author, Liao painting authority Xiang Chunsong, defines it as beginning in 893.[41] Middle Liao lasts more than seventy years, the reigns of Shengzong, Xingzong, and early Daozong. Late Liao spans more than sixty years from the remainder of the Daozong reign until 1125.

Xiang Chunsong's was the first study. Published in 1981, the material was confined to burials in the Zhaowudameng region of Inner Mongolia. Still, Xiang's research is extremely useful. His is the only article presenting plans of all the tombs he has surveyed (figs. 286 and 287). In the early period, according to Xiang, Zhaowudameng tombs have only one main chamber, which is usually circular or four-sided in plan but in at least one instance was hexagonal and, in another, nearly triangular (fig. 286, nos. 1–9). Subterranean tomb material was both brick and stone. In some of the tombs, the corpse was placed on a coffin bed (*guan*). Three tombs, including one with a hexagonal chamber, have a pair of niches on the approach ramp side of the burial chamber.[42] Orientation is not noted in any of the plans, however, and since several have not been published elsewhere it is impossible to generalize about the direction of the ramps or niches.

Xiang believes that in the middle period of Liao tomb construction, a time he calls "flourishing Liao," one observes a gradual move toward unified format in plan and, at the same time, the emergence of multichamber plans and more elaborate decorations, both in the burial goods and in decoration in the form of imitation of wooden architectural motifs in brick. The database for Xiang's middle period is Figure 286 (nos. 10–13) and 287 (nos. 1 and 2). The idea of a unified plan is put forth despite the presence of circular, four-sided, hexagonal, and octagonal main chambers. According to Xiang, the octagon should be interpreted as a straight-edged version of the circle (for example, in fig. 287, nos. 9 and 10). I view the form differently. Indeed, later in the book I argue that the emergence and employment of the octagon in a burial chamber had temporal origins and meanings. Although Xiang's late-Liao group exhibits variety in room shape, every Zhaowudameng tomb he studied but one type (fig. 286, nos. 6) had four structural features: a diagonal approach ramp from ground level to the tomb (mudao), a flat connective path to the burial chamber (yongdao), a main burial chamber (zhushi), and symmetrically positioned smaller rooms (ershi) (fig. 287 [all tombs]; fig. 286, no. 2). The main chamber varies from circular to hexagonal to octagonal in plan—as do side chambers, which can also be four-sided and need not be the same shape in a given tomb (fig. 287, no. 8). One finds, according to Xiang, a mix of construction materials (brick, stone, wood) but always the forms of aboveground timber architecture.

In 1982, the year after Xiang Chunsong's study, Jing Ai published in Chinese an article entitled "Liao-Jin-Period Cremation Burials."[43] A cremation tomb is defined as one in which human remains have been burned prior to placement in a subterranean burial chamber. Jing reports evidence of preburial cremation among preliterate cultures of Gansu province and cites records of this practice in Tang-period texts of earlier "barbarian" peoples.[44] For the Liao period, the author had gathered more than fifty examples of cremation tombs at more than twenty Liao sites in Beijing, Hebei, Shanxi, Liaoning, Jilin, Heilongjiang, and Inner

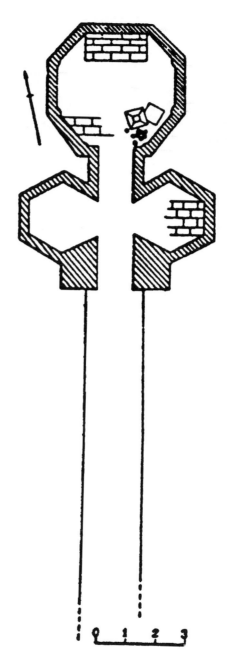

FIGURE 285. Plan of Yelü tomb uncovered at Shanzuizi, Inner Mongolia, 1116. [After "Nei Menggu Shanzuizi . . ." (Wenwu ziliao congkan, 1981, no. 5), p. 167]

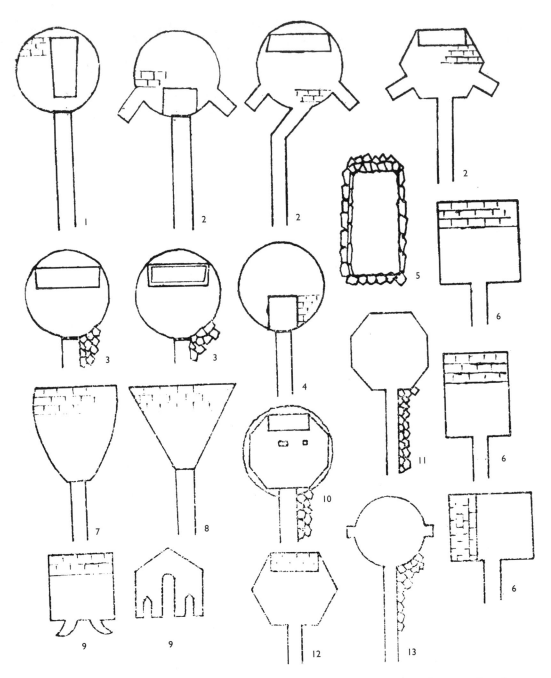

FIGURE 286. Thirteen types of Liao tomb plans. [After Xiang Chunsong, ". . . Liaodai muzang," p. 74]

Mongolia—in other words, in every portion of the Liao empire, although those in the northeastern provinces of China were more plentiful. (For the Jin, by contrast, he had found only slightly more than thirty among about twenty sites.) Evidence of cremation burial was found in both simple, earthen-pit tombs and more elaborate chambers made of stone and brick but was more numerous among the earthen pit types. Among brick tombs, cremation burials occurred in tombs whose main chambers were round, rectangular, hexagonal, and octagonal, with single and multiple chambers, with and without wall paintings, with and without vaulted ceilings, and with and without imitation of wooden forms in brick. Remains were sometimes placed on coffin beds (guanchuang) and sometimes in stone, wooden, or ceramic coffins. Most often, in more than one-third of the cases Jing studied, coffins were stone, but their tops ranged from flat to forms that imitated hip-gable roofs. Sometimes the wooden coffins were decorated, frequently with the four Chinese directional animals (sishen). Some stone coffins were wider at the head than the foot, following the style (sometimes in other materials) in vogue among North Asian peoples, including the Xianbei, since the post-Han centuries.[45] Among coffins, wooden ones were rarest; ceramic coffins, of which both glazed and unglazed examples are known, were also rare.

One of the noteworthy finds reported in Jing Ai's study was coburial of cremated and noncremated corpses in the same tomb. Although several examples of up to six or eight corpses in the same tomb were found in Liao and Jin-period burials, Jing believes that tombs were opened after initial interment for new corpses (presumably relatives) and that only in the Liao period were cremated remains buried at the same time as noncremated ones. Sometimes, but not always, the bodies were in different rooms. In his article Jing published a complete list of the tombs he studied. He notes that cremation tombs flourished between 1012 and 1021, but beyond this point few generalizations can be made. One of the most surprising results of Jing Ai's study is that not only was the practice spread through Liao territory, but for those whose nationalities could be determined (Han or Qidan) the division between the two was fairly equal.

The existence of so many cremation burials among the Han population of the Liao empire is truly significant. As Jing notes, with the exception of monks, pre-Liao cremation is almost nonexistent among the Chinese population. Yet Jing's data confirm that cremation burial was transmitted not only to the Han population under Liao rule (in, for example, Shanxi province) but also into Song territory in Shanxi, Gansu, and Henan and was adopted by the Jurchen. Jing identified at least twenty-five examples of Song cremation tombs.[46] Under the Song empire, too, remains were found in circular and hexagonal single-chamber tombs and in multichamber burials. Remains were placed on coffin beds and in brick and, occasionally, even earthen tombs. Here, too, cremation burial was alongside corpses in sarcophaguses.

Some distinctions can be made between Song cremation burials and Liao examples. Most important, when remains were placed in containers in Song tombs, those containers often took the form of pagodas (one recalls that the Han family of Jixian in Liao territory encased cremated remains in a box) and impoverished Song Chinese often buried cremated remains in jars in the vicinity of Buddhist monasteries.[47] In other words, even though cremation burial seems to have increased among the Han population of North China in the tenth through thirteenth centuries—an increase that may have been influenced by the spread and popularity of the custom in the empire to China's north—the incidence of cremation in Song China was undoubt-

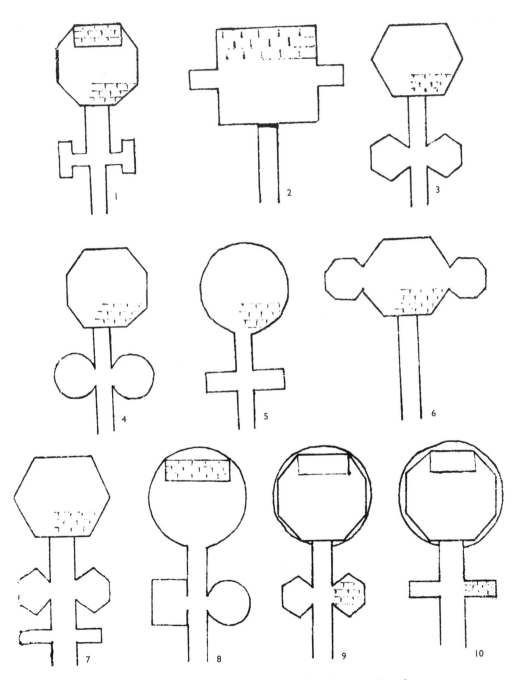

FIGURE 287. Ten Liao tomb plans. [After Xiang Chunsong, ". . . Liaodai muzang," p. 75]

edly due to Buddhist practices of the interred. A Liao practice may have encouraged that same method for the Chinese, but one cannot go further and conclude that Qidan who engaged in cremation burial had become Buddhist. In the Yuan period, cremation tombs of Han Chinese have been uncovered in Shanxi, Fujian, Guangdong, Yunnan, and Inner Mongolia,[48] a truly diverse spread of land. The Ming government prohibited the practice except among minorities or when a person had died of a serious illness.[49]

In 1987, Yang Jing published a study of Liao cremation burials in which he wrote that they accounted for one-third of all excavated Liao tombs.[50] Using dated excavations, Yang too divided Liao burials into three periods. But more than the others who have written on the subject, he stressed that cremation burial was employed in some of the most structurally complex tombs. Yang suggests, in fact, that cremation burial came to the Han population of the Qidan empire by way of its use among the non-Chinese. Yang does not believe, however, that Buddhist practice was necessarily the cause for the large number of cremation tombs among the Qidan population in Liao times. (He does attribute the rise in the practice among the Han population to Buddhism.) Rather, citing texts about the rotting of the corpse followed by burning and placement in the ground, Yang thinks it is a continuation or reinstatement of native custom.

The same year that Yang Jing published his study and again four years later, Li Yiyou—a member of the Research Institute of Inner Mongolian Cultural Relics and Archaeology, chief archaeologist, and the most prolific writer about Liao tombs and, more generally, Inner Mongolian archaeology—published two studies of Liao burial practice and tomb construction.[51] Their purpose was to propose criteria for dating and determining the nationality of occupants in Liao-period tombs based on dated tombs

with known occupants. Of special value are the tombs mentioned in Li's studies—many his own excavations, which remain unpublished. Li Yiyou contends that the postmortem customs of the Qidan and Han were diffcrent. Furthermore, he writes that burial practices described in the *Liaoshi* are pertinent only to the emperors and their wives. To assess the issues of his concern—periodization and ethnic affiliation—Li believes the only reliable evidence is excavated data.[52] His database, as mentioned earlier, numbers several hundred.[53]

Li Yiyou makes numerous points that are supported by the dated tombs with Qidan occupants we surveyed earlier. Like Xiang Chunsong, Li divides the Liao into early, middle, and late periods: his early period ends after the Jingzong reign; the middle commences mid-Shengzong; his late Liao begins with Daozong's reign. Li cites the use of hexagonal and octagonal chambers as characteristic of the late period but occurring in the middle period, whereas circular and four-sided burial chambers predominate in the early and middle periods.[54] The earliest dated tomb with octagonal and hexagonal chambers, according to Li, is the tomb of the Princess of Qinjin (see fig. 270).[55] Yet he writes that the majority of aristocratic Qidan burials occurred in tombs with a single chamber, and sometimes "ear chambers" or niches,[56] and that in his opinion the multiplicity of chambers and lavishness of decor were reflections of the occupant's status rather than an earlier or later date.[57]

Li's studies also address the subject of tomb orientation. He believes that, as sun worshipers, the early Liao oriented their aboveground architecture, and also their tombs, toward the east.[58] In Part One we noted that, regarding monastery orientation, extant wooden Buddhist halls were most often oriented southward. Such is not the case for tombs. Yet one still can take issue with Li Yiyou and argue that Qidan tomb orientation is more accurately described as southeastern. The significance of that 45-degree turn is that this new positioning can be traced to Liao Taizu's construction of Zuzhou and Shang-jing (see figs. 230 and 4). The importance of southeast is emphasized also by a comment credited to the Song emissary Shen Kuo, who wrote that "all Qidan tombs are on the southeastern slope of a mountain."[59] The most accurate way of describing Liao tomb orientation is that it is decidedly not north-south—virtually every other possibility can be found.[60] Indeed, as one traces the orientation of dated tombs in China from Shang through Qing, imperial and nonimperial, an overwhelming number are not oriented north-south, whereas aboveground architecture is.

Li Yiyou also makes more specific points than Xiang or Jing about the use of coffin beds and sarcophaguses. He believes, for instance, that when a corpse entered a grave it was most often placed on a coffin bed.[61] The stone or brick coffin bed was generally in the same half of the main chamber as its innermost wall. In larger rooms one might find space between the coffin bed and innermost wall, but just as often it was set against that wall. Most Qidan did not use coffins, according to Li, but when they did the coffins were usually placed on platforms or coffin beds. Occasionally Qidan were buried in multiple coffins: the inner was wooden and the outer made of stone. Yemaotai Tomb 7, whose wooden inner coffin will be discussed shortly, is one example of this arrangement.

The burial of wooden and stone human figurines (some are part stone and part wood) is a practice Li Yiyou associates with "middle Liao."[62] Li explains the number of statues as the result of the kind of transformation from sacrificial burial to sculptural surrogates that had occurred in China by the time of the First Emperor in the third century B.C. He believes the transformation took place among the Qidan during Liao rule as a result of Chinese influence. Abaoji's burial preparation, like those for members of the royal Shang household, had included the execution of several hundred persons (but not his widow). The remains of Shengzong's tomb also include sacrificial burials of males and females. Even Kulunqi Tomb 1, latest of the eight according to evidence presented earlier, had ten corpses that may have been sacrifically buried, but the evidence is not definitive because the grave had been robbed.[63] Until the last years of Liao rule, tombs of the Qidan had a host of grave goods including, even after the Xingzong emperor's prohibition of 1042–1043, gold and silver objects and sacrificial burial of sheep and horses.[64]

The most recent study of Qidan burial practices was published in 1992 by Tian Guanglin and Zhang Jianhua.[65] Devoted just to Qidan burial customs and tombs, it is divided into predynastic, imperial, aristocratic, and commoner graves. Tian and Zhang extensively cite texts, but most of the material in their article can be found in the five earlier studies.

Together the six studies provide a comprehensive, although selective, survey of what has been excavated in Liao territory, what this information might suggest about structural chronology and occupant nationality, and how certain aspects of burial can be confirmed by textual evidence. One of the most important observations one draws from these studies, and from the tombs themselves, is that Liao tomb construction and burial practices were not part of a unified system. Furthermore, although we find clear evolution in tomb style from the mid-tenth century to the early twelfth, burial practices conform to no evolutionary pattern during these two centuries. (Han Chinese material is discussed in some of the six studies, but the authors' views are saved for later in this chapter.) Disposal of the corpse among dated tombs with occupants of just Yelü or Xiao lineage, for instance, can range

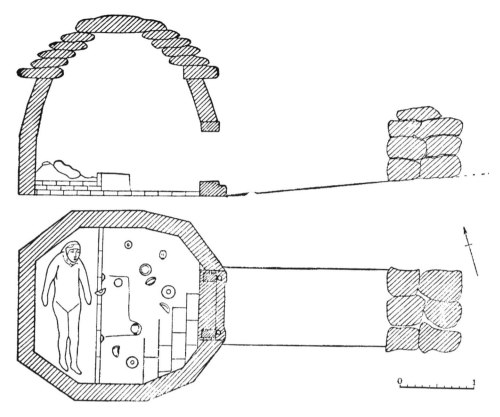

FIGURE 288. Plan and section of Haoqianying Tomb 6, Chayouqianqi, Inner Mongolia. [After Lu and Du (*Wenwu* 1983, no. 9), p. 2]

from cremation to deterioration (burning of the corpse and burial of ashes to, one assumes from texts, leaving the body outdoors for natural rotting and subsequent interment of bones perhaps after three years) to corporeal preservation. Except when sutras or stupa-shaped reliquaries have been excavated, it has been impossible to link burial customs to religious practices.

All three burial practices (cremation, natural deterioration, unnatural intervention for preservation), and combinations of them, are known throughout Liao rule, in all the Chinese provinces that once comprised the Liao empire, in tombs of brick or stone or combinations of them, in single-chamber and multichamber settings. Excavators have found all varieties of ceramic types and objects in Qidan tombs, gold and silver objects even from decades when sumptuary laws seem to have forbidden such lavish burials, and evidence of sacrificial burial not just of human beings but of dogs, horses, and sheep. Corpses and other remains have been placed on platforms and on coffin beds, in single-layer and multiple-layer coffins. When brick surfaces have been decorated, the forms imitated Chinese timber architecture including known bracket-set types, subsidiary tiebeams, and fan-

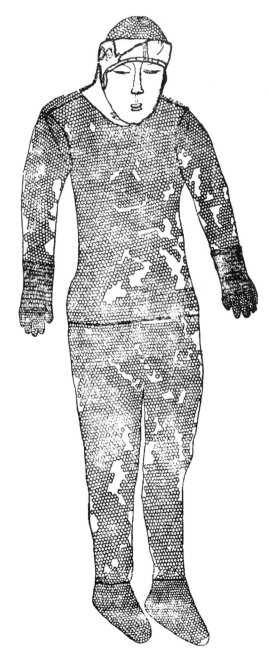

FIGURE 289. Line drawing of copper-wire netting and face mask found on female corpse from Haoqianying Tomb 6. [After Lu and Du (*Wenwu* 1983, no. 9), p. 4]

shaped bracket sets. Microcosmic reproductions of the world of life have included floor-level waterways, and scenes from the daily lives of the Qidan have decorated their tomb walls. Life-size animals and men have lined long, aboveground approaches to Qidan tombs. Finally, rarely does one find a Liao tomb in isolation. Famous among necropolises is Kulunqi, but burials also have been grouped together in Yixian (Liaoning), Faku, and Aohanqi.

UNIQUE FEATURES OF QIDAN BURIALS

Many of the features just listed have counterparts in earlier tombs on China's Central Plain or farther south. Three details of Qidan burial practice, however, set the Qidan apart from their Chinese neighbors. The first—encasement of the corpse in metal wire netting—affirms Wen Weijian's famous text cited in the Introduction and is corroborated by evidence from the dated tomb of the Princess of Chenguo and her husband. The second is removal of internal soft tissue. The third, multiple-layer coffins, has far-reaching architectural significance.

Tomb 6 at Haoqianying

In the early years of the People's Republic, ten tombs identified by mounds were encircled by mountains about 20 kilometers southwest of Jining at a site called Haoqianying in Chayouqianqi, Inner Mongolia. By 1972 all but three had been destroyed. Tomb 6, southernmost of the group, was excavated in 1981.[66] Haoqianying Tomb 6 is distinct from most Liao tombs in that its walls and ceiling were lined with stone (fig. 288). Oriented roughly eastward, its main chamber was octagonal but the sides were not of uniform length. The ramp down to the tomb was 7.4 by 1.1 meters; not enough survives to determine if originally there had been steps at the top. Four large stones sealed and covered the entry. Two of the stones formed a double-panel door, each panel about 78 by 34 by 5.5 centimeters that opened

FIGURE 290. Remains of female uncovered in Haoqianying Tomb 6 with copper-wire netting and gilt-bronze face mask. [After Lu and Du (*Wenwu* 1983, no. 9), pl. 1, no. 1]

outward. The main chamber's dimensions were roughly 2.12 meters north-south by 2.2 meters east-west. It was lined at the bottom by a rock layer about four rocks high (approximately 1.59 m). The floor was covered with cut rectangular stones.

Besides the abundance of stone, which is unusual but not unique, the most outstanding feature of Haoqianying Tomb 6 was the female body inside it. The corpse was found on her left side on a coffin bed that had been damaged by mud and water over the centuries. It is believed that resulting resettlement caused the body to turn sideways.[67] Although the tomb had been robbed, many pieces of the burial garments were preserved. Most impressive was the covering of copper-wire netting and a gilt-bronze face mask. The copper-wire netting con-

sisted of six parts: headgear, chestgear and backgear, arm covers, pants, shoes, and gloves (fig. 289). The gilt-bronze mask (fig. 290) and wire headgear were connected to a piece of cloth wound around her upper head. The body was placed in the tomb wearing a silk garment embroidered with flowers and lined with thin silk, a short, sleeveless tunic and pants (also silk), silk boots, a belt with a clasp, a hat, and a piece of cloth covering the pubic region (fig. 291). Beneath the copper-wire netting but on top of the silk garments was a layer of coarse brown silk gauze. Archaeologists believe the gauze was wrapped around her from top to bottom, with each limb also wrapped downwards.[68] The gauze was tapered to body size. Its thickness around her thighs was about 22 centimeters, for instance, but near the

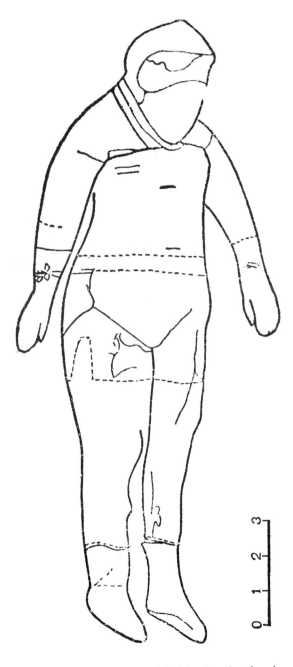

FIGURE 291. Line drawing of clothing found on female corpse from Haoqianying Tomb 6. [After Lu and Du (*Wenwu* 1983, no. 9), p. 3]

ankle it was 16 to 15 centimeters. Toes and fingers were individually wrapped and certain portions of hand covering were only 2 centimeters in thickness. Her body was completely preserved—the first time such a complete corpse had been found in the region. Hair remained, too, wrapped in a bun on top of the corpse's head. There was evidence that a 5.5-centimeter patch had been shaved from it. The other two Haoqianying tombs also had copper-wire-net suits and face masks, but in 1983 this initial excavation of a copper-wire suit in this western region of Inner Mongolia was the most complete one.[69]

The Haoqianying Tomb 6 discoveries have not received the attention they deserve. Chinese scholars and exhibition organizers have instead turned to the tomb of known occupants, the Princess of Chenguo and Xiao Shaoju, for evidence of corporeal encasement in metal netting—even though Haoqianying Tomb 6 is distinguished both by the complete copper-wire-net suit and by the remarkable state of preservation of the corpse.[70] Archaeologists found traces of blood on the right side of the corpse's chest and on top of her right shoulder at the Haoqianying tomb. Although they admit that the corpse was not well enough preserved to confirm whether the skin was damaged in life, they cautiously speculate that the body could have been pricked open for the kind of preburial drainage described in the passage from Wen Weijian quoted in the Introduction.[71] The same study postulates further that the female's chest could have been opened in order to fill it with vegetable matter and—in affirmation of yet other details of aristocratic Qidan life known from texts (in this case that the Qidan ate squirrel meat)—the author points out that the bones of four squirrels were found in Haoqianying Tomb 6.[72]

So far, we have no evidence that the Liao indulged in trepanation, the practice made famous by peoples of the North Asian steppe in the first millennium B.C.,[73] but noteworthy comparisons are suggested between branches of these North Asian seminomads and the Liao-period Qidan. In preparing corpses for burial at the Pazyryk *kurgan*, for instance, one female had had her scalp folded back, her skull chiseled open, her brain removed, and then the skull cavity filled with vegetable matter.[74] The portion of skull that had been opened was resewn. Similarly the abdomen had been opened, the organs replaced by vegetable substances, and then resewn. This particular female's thigh had also been opened, the muscle removed, and then resewn, leading to speculation of endocannibalism of the kind reported by Herodotus among a people of North or Central Asia.[75] One has no reason to speculate about endocannibalism among the Liao. Yet it is worth repeating that a patch had been shaved from the head of the female in the Haoqianying tomb, raising the possibility of preparation for trepanation. It is certainly possible that death practices of the kind exhibited at Haoqianying Tomb 6 are related to death rituals of earlier North Asian seminomads who moved in life and stopped to build for permanency only in death.

As we shall see by the end of Part Two of this study, a strong case can be presented for viewing the Liao as one in a succession of North Asian empires who mutually borrowed and followed similar practices on the eastern and western ends of North Asia, north of China's Central Plain. Yet the comparisons can be subtle and even inconclusive. The same practices—in this case, the use of metal death masks and encasement of the corpse for eternal preservation—that lend themselves to associations between the Liao and North Asian seminomads, who predated them by almost fifteen hundred years, can also be interpreted as evidence of the infiltration of Chinese views about death and the afterlife into Qidan territory. The Shang, for instance, a thousand years earlier than the builders of tombs

FIGURE 292. Bronze face mask uncovered at Anyang, Henan province, mid-second millennium B.C. [After Li Chi, *Anyang*, pl 20; published with permission of University of Washington Press]

at Pazyryk, covered the faces of corpses with death masks. Line-by-line comparison between the Liao-period mask in the Museum of Art and Archaeology at the University of Pennsylvania (see fig. 9) and one from the mid-second millennium B.C. excavated at Anyang offers more than superficial similarities (fig. 292). Yet if it is easy to recognize the pitfalls of comparing Liao practices with those of China's North Central Plain in the second millennium B.C. (even if the two civilizations could be shown to have indulged in common customs), it is less easy to discount the fact that by the Han dynasty (206 B.C.–A.D. 220), whose tombs have been shown to survive beneath Liao cities, the Chinese were the ultimate

FIGURE 293. Wooden model used for encasement of stone sarcophagus, excavated at Yemaotai, Faku county, Liaoning, Liao period. [Liaoning Provincial Museum; Steinhardt photograph]

practitioners of a funerary culture whose stated objective was to preserve physical remains. Symbols of this Han-dynasty objective were jade burial garments—a native Chinese precedent, if we follow this line of thinking, for Liao silk-gauze wrappings, copper-wire suits, and golden death masks.[76]

Clearly, it is extremely difficult to determine a cultural identity for a people like the predynastic or dynastic Qidan. One means of trying to assess the extent of "Chineseness" or "Qidanness" in pockets of the Liao empire between 947 and 1125 is through excavated tomb objects. The results of these excavations suggest that in burial and decisions about the afterlife, "native" (predynastic Qidan or other North Asian) ideas predominated. This allegiance to nativity was, however, concealed underground.

Part One of this study showed that the moment the Qidan decided to move into the Chinese arena they built walled cities with timber-frame buildings inside them. The aboveground building programs occurred at lightning speed—walled capitals were being built before a dynasty named Liao was conceived. Funerary architecture, too, favored imitation of a Chinese system. It appeared on the Mongolian plain as early as Liao residential cities. Examples range from Abaoji's funerary city Zuzhou and his tomb site, Zuling, to Yelü Cong's spirit path of 979.

Through the combined investigation of burial practice and funerary architecture one sees who the Liao were and the critical role of architecture in this self-identification process. Only by looking underground can we understand how architecture was linked to the imperial legitimation process of the

FIGURE 294. Wooden architectural model with stone sarcophagus in front of it, excavated at Yemaotai. [Liaoning Provincial Museum; Steinhardt photograph]

Qidan: aboveground, it was the symbolic medium of Chinese imperialism for external public display; but at the same time, behind or beneath those sacrificial halls, mounds, and stone statues, it offered a way in which to play out, in the secrecy of death, native Qidan practices. Nevertheless, funerary architecture is inextricably linked to wooden temple halls, and the Qidan expressed their admiration for the Chinese building tradition underground as well as above it. This homage is in evidence in the relief carving in brick in the Kulunqi tombs, where higher than imperial status was expressed through the visual display of China's silent, but established, architectural symbolism.

A similar phenomenon can be observed in the multiple sarcophaguses found in at least three Qidan tombs in Inner Mongolia and Liaoning. In these cases, the Liao sarcophaguses may be more "Chinese" than anything that survives from China at the same time.

"Lesser Carpentry" in Qidan Tombs

In August 1992, I saw an extraordinary wooden architectural model in the four-room museum in Balinyouqi, Inner Mongolia. The model was three-bays-square with a hip-gable roof and 5-*puzuo* bracketing. The accompanying label said only "Model of House from Qidan Tomb." The museum cashier (the only person willing to talk to me about it) told me it had been excavated at Bayan'erdeng-sumu People's Collective, also in Balinyouqi. No form of persuasion would convince this cashier to let me take a photograph, and to my knowledge the piece remains unpublished. Yet when I asked about

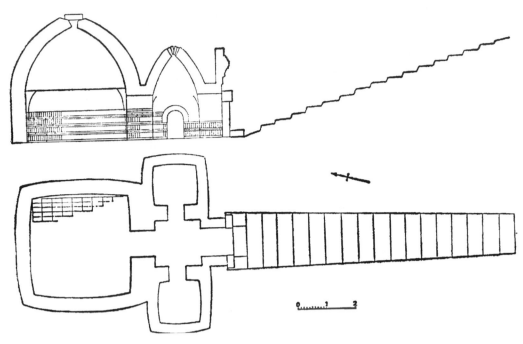

FIGURE 295. Plan and section of Yemaotai Tomb 7, Faku county, Liaoning, Liao period.
[After "Faku Yemaotai Liaomu jilue" (*Wenwu* 1975, no. 12), p. 27]

it in Beijing, colleagues at Qinghua University told me "everyone knew about it" but no one could get a photograph.[77] The next year I saw a similar, but not so spectacular, architectural model in the Liaoning Provincial Museum in Shenyang (fig. 293). It stood in one of the Liao-period rooms behind a stone sarcophagus (fig. 294). Although the condition of both the Liaoning and Inner Mongolian models was pristine, I sensed more work had gone into reassembly of the model in Shenyang.

Yemaotai Tomb 7

The stone and wooden sarcophaguses in the Liaoning Provincial Museum had been excavated at Yemaotai, Faku county, Liaoning, in the spring of 1974, from a tomb that had gained immediate inter-national attention for the silk scrolls uncovered there.[78] Yemaotai had been an important site for Liao tomb excavation for two decades. It was the county where both tombs with floor-level waterways had been uncovered (see figs. 282 and 283). Oriented 17 degrees east of south, the entire underground length of Yemaotai Tomb 7 was 16.7 meters of which 8.7 meters were occupied by a seventeen-step diagonal approach to the 7-meter-long burial chamber (fig. 295). The underground chambers numbered four: a main chamber fronted by an antechamber and adjoining side rooms, all nearly perfectly square in plan and all with vaulted ceilings. Vaulted archways marked the entries from room to room. Much of the tomb interior was mud-brick that imitated the forms of timber architecture. Ar-

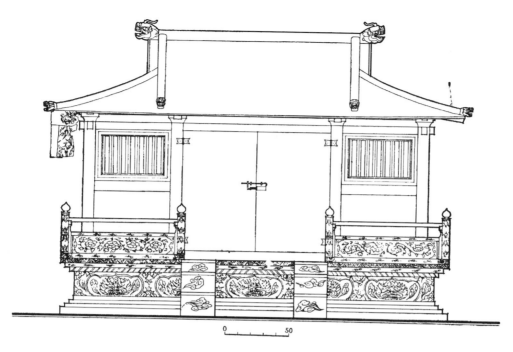

FIGURE 296. Line drawing of front elevation of wooden outer sarcophagus, Tomb 7, Yemaotai. [After Cao Xun (*Wenwu* 1975, no. 12), p. 61]

chitectural members were painted vermilion, and floral design enlivened the bracket sets and door lintels.[79]

The wooden model stood in back of the main chamber. The stone sarcophagus was inside it. The inner sarcophagus contained bones of an elderly woman, more than ten pieces of her silk burial garments, and a waistbelt from which were suspended a variety of precious objects. Finally, she was covered with silk embroidered with gold thread. A crystal ball was in her hand; a silver plug was in her nostrils. Outside the stone sarcophagus, on the east and west walls of the wooden "house," hung the paintings referred to earlier. A large lacquer box was placed on the stone coffin and a stone table with more than ten vessels, some still containing food,

was in front of it. Wooden tables were placed in the southeast and southwest corners of the wooden structure.

The cypress-bark "house" for the stone sarcophagus was a three-by-two-bay structure with plank walls and a combination hip-gable roof (fig. 296). Its central bay, 123.7 centimeters in length, was occupied by a double-panel door, and mullioned windows were located in the upper portions of the 67.2-centimeter and 68.2-centimeter side front bays. Ten pillars, four-sided in section (square-sectioned corner pillars and rectangular elsewhere), all of them perfectly straight like every other architectural member of the building, supported the roof. With base dimensions of 2.15 by 1.25 meters (and 88 cm high),[80] the stone sarcophagus occupied most of the

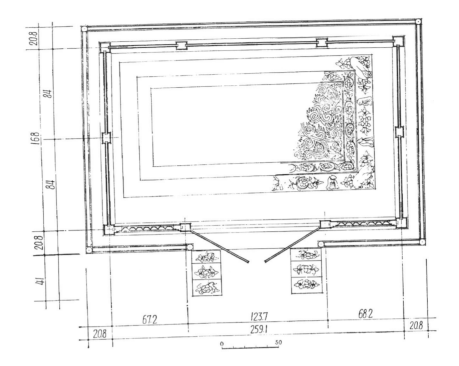

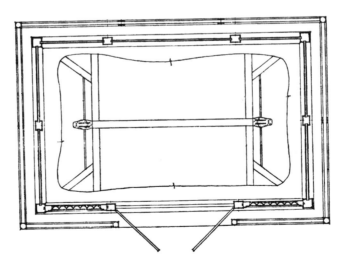

FIGURE 297 (top). Plan of interior of wooden sarcophagus showing position of inner stone sarcophagus from Tomb 7, Yemaotai. [After Cao Xun (*Wenwu* 1975, no. 12), p. 61]

FIGURE 298 (above). Line drawing of roof ridge superimposed on plan of wooden sarcophagus from Tomb 7, Yemaotai. [After Cao Xun (*Wenwu* 1975, no. 12), p. 54]

interior space (fig. 297). The "structure" was approached by a two-step *tadao* and surrounded by a wooden balustrade into which decoration was inlaid (see figs. 296 and 297). Like the main building, the balustrade around it had ten posts positioned directly in front of the pillars. The balustrade and structure were raised on an elaborately decorated seven-layer base. The balustrade posts, in contrast to those of the hall, were circular in section. Although untapered and of equal length, these pillars leaned 1 centimeter inward. The front doors were attached to the front inner pillars by butterfly-shaped iron joiners. Above the pillars were the simple *dou*. No bracket-arms were employed.

The roof is by far the most interesting feature of the wooden model. All four of its sides project at the same angle, nearly 45 degrees. Not only does the uniformity separate this small building from standard Chinese timber-frame architecture—so too does the sharpness of the angle. In large-scale Chinese architecture (*damuzuo*), the angle of eaves' projection is rarely more than 28 degrees.[81] Equally fascinating are animal heads attached to the ends of the main roof ridge (fig. 298). They are important evidence in the identification of a Liao date for painted wooden panels and other pieces in the Art Museum of Princeton University.[82] Finally, several bamboo nails were used in construction of the roof. They are evidence of an exchange with Song China, for bamboo is not native to any portion of Liao territory.[83]

The structural system employed in the wooden building is named *jiuji xiaozhang* in the *Yingzao fashi*. It is among forty-two items listed in *juan* 6 to 11 under the category *xiaomuzuo*,[84] "lesser carpentry" (literally "small things made of wood"), in contrast to building standards described for full-size wooden construction (*damuzuo*, or "greater carpentry") such as the buildings discussed in Part One. *Jiuji xiaozhang* is a "nine-spine (or [roof] ridge) small-

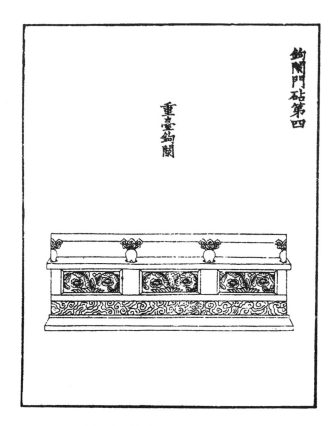

FIGURE 299. Multilevel balustrade. [After Li Jie, *Yingzao fashi, juan* 29, 1974 reprint, vol. 6, p. 21]

scale container." The last word, *"zhang,"* more literally is a curtain or cover, but in this context it must refer to the covering for the sarcophagus.[85] The Song architectural manual states that the proportions of *jiuji xiaozhang* should not exceed 1 *zhang*, 2 *chi* in height—not counting the length of *chiwen* (about 4.32 m), the projections on the ends of the roof ridges—and 8 *chi* in width (2.82 m).[86] *Xiaozhang* is not illustrated in the *Yingzao fashi*, but a multilevel balustrade with decoration that may have served as a model for the balustrade on this wooden sarcophagus is depicted (fig. 299).

The stone sarcophagus was carved or painted on

FIGURE 300. Incised decoration on inner side of stone sarcophagus, Tomb 7, Yemaotai. [After "Faku Yemaotai Liaomu jilue" (*Wenwu* 1975, no. 12), p. 35]

all interior and exterior surfaces. The combination of incised and painted decoration on one side of its interior included male guards at either side of a two-panel, partially open door, a figure looking out that door, female entertainers, and winged humans and animals including a frontal winged creature at the top center (fig. 300).[87]

Excavators have dated Yemaotai Tomb 7 to the seventh, eighth, or ninth decades of the tenth century.[88] This date is based largely on the fact that all four tomb chambers are four-sided in plan. The earliest dated Liao tomb, that of the emperor's son-in-law, Prince of Wei, has the most similar plan (see fig. 261) and a date of 959; beginning in the Sheng-zong reign (983–1031), we have observed an abundance of hexagonal and octagonal subterranean chambers; and even by the time Yelü Yanning was

buried in Chaoyang county, in 986, circular chambers were employed (see fig. 262). The same time frame, 959–986, has been the starting point for studies of the two silk paintings. (See note 78 for a bibliography.)

Seeking Comparisons

The Yemaotai sarcophagus can be compared to the small, three-bay-square halls that were fairly numerous in tenth-century and later Song China. Similar comparisons have been made between sarcophaguses of Tang princes and princesses and buildings like the Main Hall of Nanchan Monastery.[89] Conceptually the Liao were engaged in the same practice of fashioning an architectural replica for mortal remains. Yet among extant Song burials, mortuary houses are unknown. Perhaps the lacuna

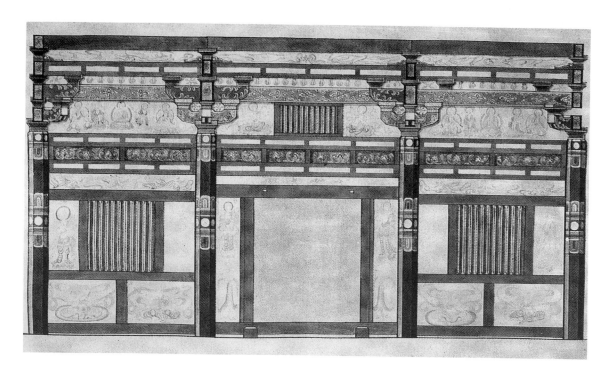

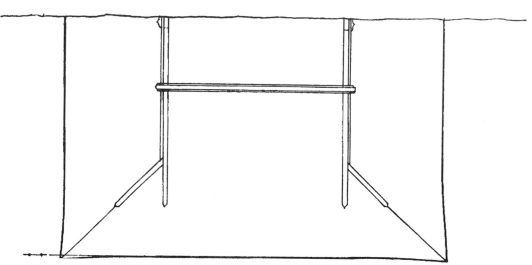

FIGURE 301 (top). Reconstruction drawing of front facade of Mogao Cave 427 showing pillar-top bracket sets, Dunhuang, Gansu province. [After Xiao Mo, *Dunhuang jianzhu yanjiu*, color pl. 7]
FIGURE 302 (above). Line drawing of roof ridges from front facade to Mogao Cave 53.
[After Pan and Ma, *Mogaoku kuqian . . .* , p. 129]

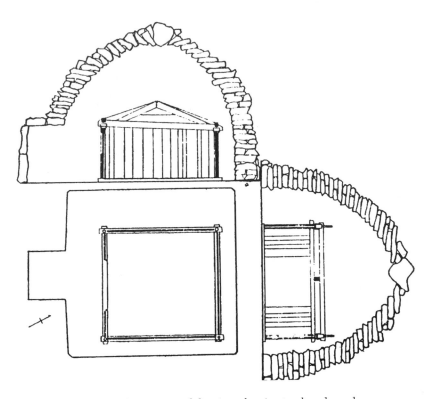

FIGURE 303. Plan and two sectional drawings showing tomb and wooden sarcophagus excavated at Beipiao, Liaoning, Liao period. [After Zhang and Li (*Liaohai wenwu xuekan* 1990, no. 2), p. 25]

is due to the percentage of the Song population that was Buddhist and, furthermore, did not place ashes in a house. Still, one observes another instance in which a Tang royal practice was preserved by Liao adaptation of the Chinese custom and transformation of it—in this case to accommodate Qidan custom. (A Chinese-style funerary "house" encases uncremated human remains.)

Given the lack of Song stone or timber sarcophaguses, a Song architectural expression that might be labeled *xiaomuzuo* becomes more intriguing. Facades to Mogao Caves 53, 427, 431, 437, and 444 near Dunhuang were mentioned in Chapter 8 as evidence of the Song building tradition in wood (fig.

301 and see fig. 215). The facade of Cave 53 is especially significant because its roof is the clearest extant Song example of *jiuji* structure (fig. 302). In other respects—the projection of its front facade beyond the pillars, the additional window at the top of the central bay, the *hua gong* of its bracket sets, and the intermediate balustrade posts between those parallel to hall bay pillars—the facade of Cave 53 is structurally more complex. The pillar-top bracket sets at the facade hall of Cave 427, however, have no transversal bracket arms (see fig. 301), making them more similar to the plain *dougong* of the Liao wooden sarcophagus.

It is unlikely that either the Liao wooden sarcophagus container or the Mogao Cave facades could have been made without factual knowledge of Song timber construction—specifically, a precursor to the *Yingzao fashi*. Due to the portability of the printed word, architectural prescriptions of the Song court would have made it possible for Qidan officials to adapt Song building standards to their burial practices and, moreover, for Song Buddhists to clarify the space of their worship caves thousands of kilometers to the west.

Although several other wooden or partially wooden architectural models that contained sarcophaguses have been uncovered in Liao tombs, none is as grand a structure as the Yemaotai or Balinyouqi Museum examples. In 1988, a wooden *xiaozhang* was excavated in a simple, stone-lined, single-chamber tomb in Beipiao, Liaoning (fig. 303).[90] The *xiaozhang* was a simple, four-sided plank container supported by pillars with a single entrance in the front center and no windows (fig. 304). An interesting feature of the house was the use of palm fiber in its floorboards—a material available only from South China but used by the Qidan in the preservation of corpses.[91] The tomb had been robbed before excavation, but it is believed to have contained a male and female and gold and silver objects. The latter would constitute evidence that, according to excavators, like theories about Yemaotai Tomb 7 and other Liao tombs, it predated the Shengzong-reign ban on gold and silver burial items.[92] Finally, a stone sarcophagus whose form imitated wooden architecture was uncovered in a Liao tomb in Zhangkangcun, Jinzhou, Liaoning, in 1960 (fig. 305).[93]

TOMBS OF HAN CHINESE IN LIAO TERRITORY

Han Chinese who lived in Liao territory usually were buried there. Thus far tombs of Chinese occupants have been identified through funerary

FIGURE 304. Reconstruction drawing of wooden sarcophagus excavated at Liao tomb in Beipiao. [After Zhang and Li (*Liaohai wenwu xuekan* 1990, no 2), p. 26]

inscriptions for, as we have observed, cremation tombs that might in pre-Liao days have been assumed to belong to Chinese Buddhists have been identified (also through inscriptions) as Qidan. Moreover, not every Han Chinese was Buddhist nor can it be assumed that every Buddhist was cremated, especially those who could afford a subterranean tomb of the kind described here. Furthermore, Han Chinese were buried all over the Liao empire, including places that before Liao times had not had large Chinese populations (not just Hebei and Shanxi but Liaoning and Inner Mongolia). The dated or exceptional tombs discussed here belong to officials in the service of the Liao.

Tomb of Zhao Dejun and His Wife

The earliest dated Liao tomb with a Chinese occupant is the joint burial of official Zhao Dejun and his wife, née Zhong. According to a funerary in-

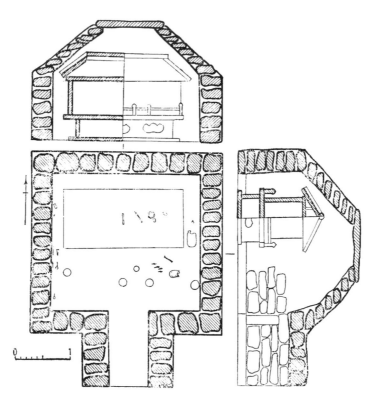

FIGURE 305. Plan and two sectional drawings of tomb with stone sarcophagus that imitates "house," excavated in Zhangkangcun, Jinzhou, Liaoning. [After Liu Qian (*Kaogu* 1984, no 11), p. 996]

scription found about 10 meters in front of the tomb, he died in 937 and she was buried in 958. Although the tomb was constructed sometime in the initial decades of Liao rule, it remains unique among Chinese, aristocratic Qidan, pre-Liao Qidan, and Song graves.[94]

Located in the southern suburbs of Beijing, the tomb was oriented eastward. It consisted of nine distinct chambers, each of them circular in plan (fig. 306). The central chamber, 4.12 meters in diameter, was largest. It was the coffin chamber. Nothing remained inside the coffin, but it is believed that the occupants had been cremated prior to interment.

The majority of the room's contents and decoration had been destroyed. Still, it was clear that originally its walls were punctuated by eight pillars and four doors, all imitating timber-frame architecture, and the walls had also been painted (fig. 307). In fact, all nine chambers had architectural decoration that included pillars, tiebeams, bracket sets, door and window frames, and lintels. All had originally been painted.

The suburban Beijing tomb is the only known tomb that might be suggested as a precedent for the construction of the earliest tomb at Qingzhou, the Eastern Mausoleum believed to belong to Liao

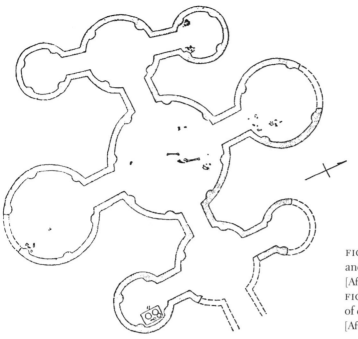

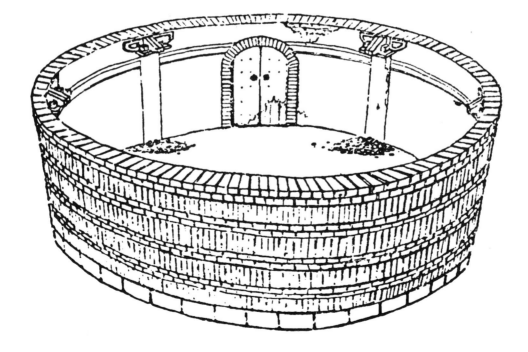

FIGURE 306 (left). Plan of tomb of Zhao Dejun and his wife, Beijing suburbs, mid-tenth century. [After Su Tianjun (*Kaogu* 1962, no. 5), p. 247]

FIGURE 307 (below). Reconstruction drawing of chamber from tomb of Zhao Dejun and his wife. [After Su Tianjun (*Kaogu* 1962, no. 5), p. 247]

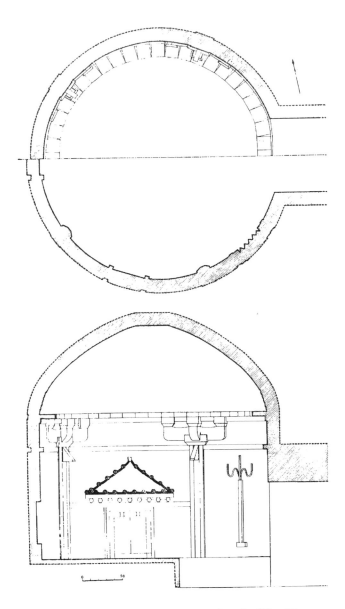

FIGURE 308. Plan and sectional drawing of tomb of Han Xiang, Qian'an, Hebei, 1017. [After Tang Yunming (*Kaogu* 1973, no. 5), p. 277]

Shengzong (see figs. 239 and 240). The connective paths in the Shengzong tomb are more elaborate, but the emperor's grave had fewer chambers—a total of seven of which the central antechamber was rectangular and no side rooms joined the back circular chamber. Zhao Dejun has a biography in *Jiu Wudaishi* (Old standard history of the Five Dynasties), and his grandson has a biography in *Songshi* (Standard history of Song).[95] There is no clear record of a connection between this branch of the Zhao family and the Liao royal household. Still, the existence of a tomb with this plan in what was to become the Liao southern circuit, eighty years before the death of Shengzong, provides the first formal evidence of an architectural model for an imperial Qidan tomb.

Tomb of Han Xiang

Several tombs with Han Chinese occupants who died at the end of the tenth century or beginning of the eleventh have been identified, but none has a published plan.[96] The next dated Han tomb with a published plan is the tomb of Han Xiang, who died in 1013 at about the age of forty and was buried in 1017.[97] Oriented 100 degrees east of north, Han's tomb consists of a circular brick chamber 2.94 meters in diameter (fig. 308). The interior decor imitated timber-frame architecture with four octagonal columns joined by tiebeams (but without the *pupai* tiebeam) such as was found inside Zhao Dejun and his wife's tomb (see fig. 307) and in an undated tomb with a Chinese occupant (figure 309).[98] Between the pillars on all sides but the eastern entry were false double-panel doors with notches at the top and roof decoration with imitation tiles. Han Xiang has no biography in *Liaoshi*. According to his funerary inscription, he was a descendant of Han Zhigu of the Han family of Jixian.

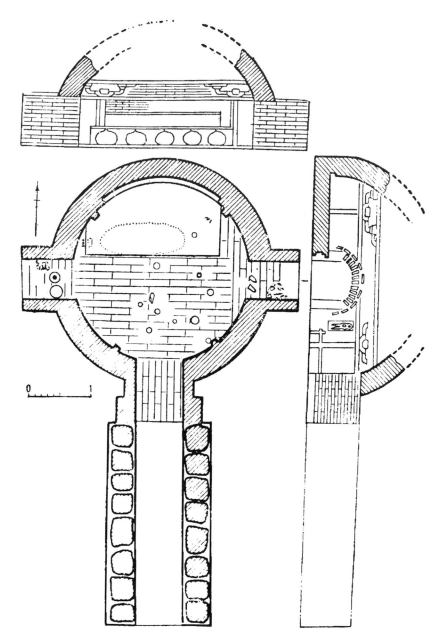

FIGURE 309. Plan and two sectional drawings of Tomb 1 from Zhangkangcun, Jinzhou, Liaoning, Liao period. [After Liu Qian (*Kaogu* 1984, no. 11), p. 990]

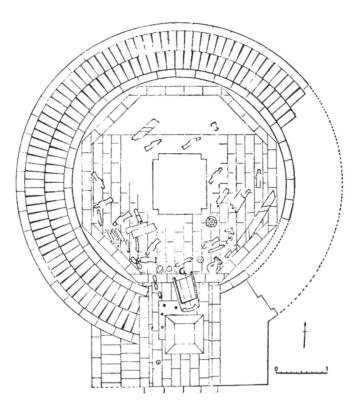

FIGURE 310. Plan of tomb of Ma Zhiwen and his wife, Daxingxian, Beijing, Liao period. [After Zhang Xiande (*Wenwu* 1980, no. 12), p. 31]

Undated Tombs of Han Officials in the Vicinity of Beijing

Five undated tombs or tomb groups of Han officials under Liao rule buried in the second decade of the twelfth century have been excavated. Three are in the vicinity of Beijing, one is in Datong, and a group of tombs remain in Chaoyang, Liaoning. Besides these, three undated tombs are within the city limits of Beijing or a nearby suburb.

Tomb of Ma Zhiwen and His Wife

Ma Zhiwen and his wife, Zhang Guan, were buried in a single-chamber, circular brick tomb with an oc-tagonal wooden frame in today's Daxingxian, a suburb of Beijing. In roughly the center of the tomb was a squarish platform on which were eleven wooden figures. Near the entry was Zhang Guan's funerary inscription (fig. 310).[99]

Despite the variety of Liao-period burials, Ma Zhiwen and Zhang Guan's tomb has been described as atypical. First, only one funerary inscription was contained in the tomb: the wife's. It recorded the ties between her ancestors on both sides and the Qidan royal family or to officialdom under Liao rule.[100] Ma had, instead, an inscribed stone *chuang* (funerary pillar), 39 centimeters high and 20 in its base diameter, with a lotus pattern on the base (fig. 311). Pieces of a second *chuang* of hexagonal base were also found in the tomb chamber. Zhang Xiande has cited one precedent for this combination of wife's funerary inscription and husband's funerary pillar: the tomb of Dong Xiang and his wife in another town on Beijing's outskirts, Xuanhua, where three other Han officials' graves, to be discussed, were later uncovered.[101] Dong Xiang's *miezui zhenyan* (true words of extinguishment of suffering) record his meritorious deeds and extraordinary career as an official in Liao service.

In the Dong Xiang joint burial, a wooden coffin with a wooden figurine was found. Ma and Zhang's tomb had no coffin. Instead, ashes remained inside a simple, barely carved wooden effigy that Zhang Xiande has suggested originally wore clothing and headgear (fig. 312).[102] The bendable knees of the figures from both tombs raise the possibility that in burial they were positioned kneeling.[103] This human form for containment of human remains is rare but not unique. In addition there were images of the twelve calendrical animals. Furthermore, in October 1965, human figurines with ashes were found in Mogao Caves—more evidence of similar practices that can be found on both northern sides of China.[104] Cremated remains and the stone funerary pagoda, of course, also suggest that Ma Zhiwen was a Buddhist. Although the tomb is undated, a change in 1012 of the name of a location mentioned in the funerary inscription suggests pre-1012 as a date of this tomb.[105]

Tomb of Han Yi

Han Yi's is one of three tenth-to-eleventh-century tombs in Babaoshan, currently a Beijing cemetery. Epitaphs of Han family members who died in 1069 and 1157 were found at Babaoshan more than seventy years ago and have since been moved to Beijing's Shoudu Museum. Han Yi's tomb is undated, but his funerary inscription records he was the

FIGURE 311. Funerary pillar, tomb of Ma Zhiwen and his wife, Daxingxian, Beijing. [After Zhang Xiande (*Wenwu* 1980, no. 12), p. 33]

FIGURE 312. Wooden figurine, with bendable knees, that contained human ashes, tomb of Ma Zhiwen and his wife, Daxingxian, Beijing. [After Zhang Xiande (*Wenwu* 1980, no. 12), p. 33]

grandson of Han Yanhui, a high-ranking official instrumental in Abaoji's accession to power.[106] Thus it is likely that Han Yi was buried before the end of the tenth century.

Han Yi's tomb was approached by a stepped ramp. Between the door at which the ramp terminated and the main, circular, brick tomb chamber was an entry passageway (*yongdao*) (fig. 313). The doorway was tightly sealed and pieces of brick found in the vicinity led to the suggestion that it had been repaired.[107] Bricks of the doorway were arranged (from bottom to top) diagonally, horizontally, and in line with the arched door lintel. Above were imitations of 5-*puzuo* bracket sets, tiebeams, and ceramic roof tiles.

The walls and ceiling of the tomb interior were virtually covered with paintings. Seven pillars that supported bracket sets and additional intercolumnar bracket sets lined the circular walls in the manner that molding of architecture had decorated the interiors of the Zhao Dejun and Zhangkangcun tombs (see figs. 307 and 309). Attendants, goods of daily life, and even a three-panel screen with birds and flowers were painted opposite the entryway.[108]

At the top center of the vaulted ceiling was a lotus, and emanating from it were floral motifs, clouds, and birds, separated at the bottom of the ceiling by twelve animal-headed humans. What these painted figures may represent will be discussed shortly. Unlike the tomb of Ma Zhiwen and his wife, both Han Yi and his wife (née Wang) had cenotaphs, although his had lost its cover, and there was a coffin.

Liao Tomb at Zhaitang

In our discussion of Chinese officials' tombs in Liao territory, thus far circular rooms with architectural decoration that imitated timber architecture, painted or molded to the walls, have predominated. A single-chamber, nearly square, brick tomb dated to the Liao period was excavated in the far Beijing suburb of Zhaitang in 1979 (fig. 314).[109] It is one of the simplest tombs associated with the Liao period. Its plan, in fact, is more typical of Jin or Yuan-period tombs: the former was often a single chamber with two small side niches; the latter was universally one room, in all but one case a four-sided room.[110] Yet the wall paintings in this tomb are among the most

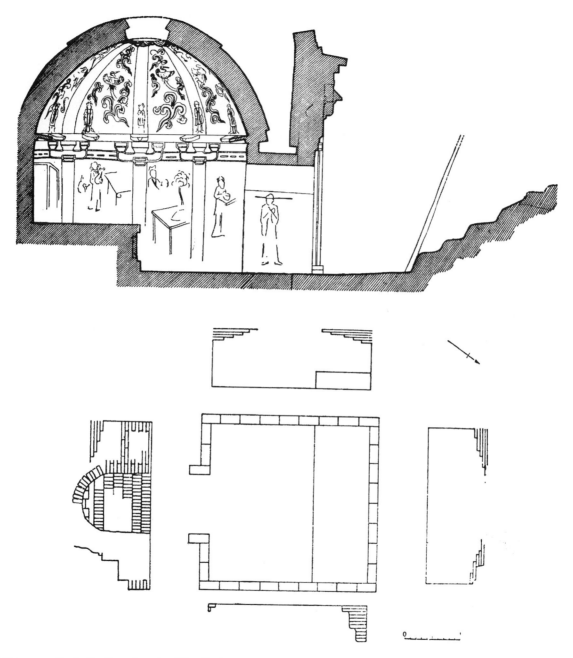

FIGURE 313 (top). Section of tomb of Han Yi, Beijing, Liao period. [After Huang and Fu (*Kaogu xuebao* 1984, no. 3), p. 363]
FIGURE 314 (above). Plan and sectional drawings of Liao tomb in Zhaitang, Beijing. [After Lu and Zhao (*Wenwu* 1980, no. 7), p. 23]

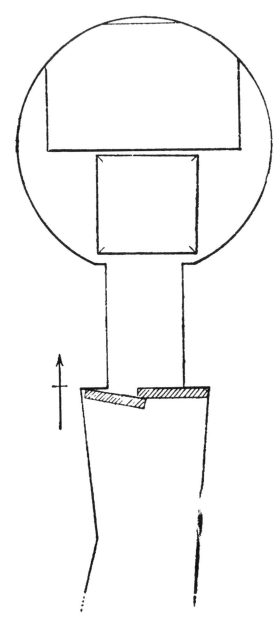

FIGURE 315. Plan of tomb of Zhao Kuangyu, Liaoning.
[After Deng, Sun, and Li (*Wenwu* 1983, no. 9), p. 32]

finely executed from the Liao dynasty and include the only example identified thus far of a filial piety story from the period, a theme that is more widely depicted in Jin-period tombs.[111] The key evidence for a Liao date has been a *dhāraṇī* column found in the vicinity of the tomb with the date 1111 and the suspension of a mirror from its ceiling, a feature of tombs from Xuanhua to be discussed shortly. Stylistically the tomb plan and wall paintings have more in common with Jin material than with Liao. As we have seen in our study of timber-frame architecture, stylistic features do not necessarily conform to the rise and fall of dynasties. Just as the east-west orientation of Kaiyuansi in Hebei was more similar to a Liao-Jin monastery plan in Datong or the Jin rebuilding at Foguangsi than to other Liao monastery arrangements, the representation of scenes of filial piety may have more to do with an early-twelfth-century date than an association with standard Liao-period imagery.

Tombs of the Zhao Family in Chaoyang

Like the Han, the Zhao were a powerful and influential Chinese family in Liao government and politics. One branch of the Zhao, the Lulong Zhao, had been important in China's history since the Tang dynasty. Zhao Siwen, descended from the Zhao of Lulong, was the ancestor of the branch of the family who lived in present Chaoyang county, Liaoning, in the eleventh century. Tombs of this branch of the Zhao were uncovered in Chaoyangxian through the 1970s. Three tombs published in 1983 contained funerary inscriptions that made it possible to reconstruct the family genealogy from Zhao Siwen's great-grandfather, Zhao Shaoyang, through the generations of his twelve sons and even great-great-grandchildren.[112]

Like most of the Han Chinese tombs in Liao territory surveyed thus far, all three Zhao tombs had a single circular chamber, a wooden coffin, and cremated corporeal remains inside (fig. 315).[113] The occupant of this tomb, Zhao Kuangyu, died in 1019 but was moved in 1060, presumably to the place where he lies today. The chief importance of this tomb group is in the documentary evidence provided by funerary inscriptions, much of which can be corroborated by Song and Yuan-period primary sources.[114] Moreover, the Zhao family tombs are the first of Han Chinese with circular plans outside of Beijingshi or one of the sixteen prefectures surrendered to Liao by Song China.

Tombs of Han Chinese: 1111–1119

Ding Family Tombs in Baiwanzhuang, Beijing

In 1958, two tombs whose occupants were identified by funerary inscriptions were excavated in the Baiwanzhuang district of Beijing.[115] Tomb 1 consisted of two southward-oriented, circular chambers joined by a corridor (fig. 316), and Tomb 2 had a single octagonal burial chamber, 1.8 meters on each side. The first tomb belonged to the Han official Ding Wenyou, who died in the fifth moon of 1112 and was buried two months later. The second belonged to his only son, Ding Hong, who predeceased his father by a year. Both tombs were seriously damaged and had been robbed, but it was clear that originally their interior walls had been covered with paintings. The method of the son's burial is not identified, but Ding Wenyou's ashes had been placed in a wooden box on top of a funerary bed. In addition to a funerary inscription, the father had an epitaph on which twelve figures were arranged on the four sides of its cover.

Tomb of Liu Chengsui at Datong, 1119

In the late 1950s five tombs of Han Chinese were also excavated at the Liao western capital, Datong. Each had a single circular chamber, some had traces of wall paintings, and one was dated by inscription. That tomb, Tomb 29, belonged to Liu Chengsui, who was buried in 1119.[116]

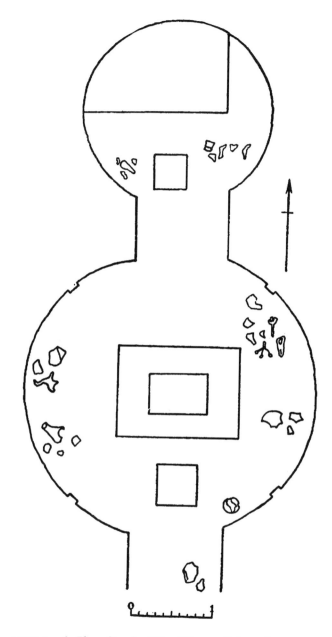

FIGURE 316. Plan of tomb of Ding Wenyou, Baiwanzhuang, Beijing, 1112. [After Su Tianjun (*Kaogu* 1963, no. 3), p. 145]

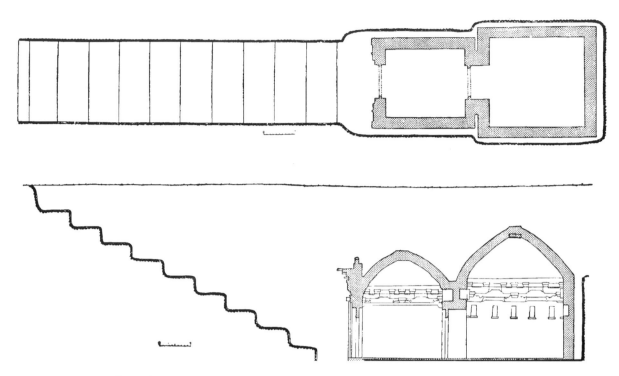

FIGURE 317. Plan and sectional drawing of tomb of Zhang Shiqing, Zhangjiakou, Xuanhua county, Hebei, 1116. [After Zheng Shaozong (*Wenwu* 1975a, no. 8), p. 32]

Zhang Family Tombs in Xuanhua, Hebei

The capital of Xuanhua county is 140 kilometers from Tian'anmen Square and about 60 kilometers from the city limits of Beijing. The Han official Zhang Shiqing was buried in Xiabali village, Zhangjiakou, Xuanhua county, in 1116 at the age of seventy-four. By that time a grandson of his had married a woman from the Yelü clan.

Zhang Shiqing's burial chambers were approached by an approximately eleven-step ramp that stretched 11.5 meters in length and was 2.7 meters wide.[117] The underground tomb consisted of two adjoining rectangularly planned brick rooms, the front one 2.55 by 2.2 meters with a vaulted ceiling 3.2 meters in height and the back one 3.10 me-

ters square (fig. 317). The tomb was brick and its walls were carved in imitation of timber-frame architecture. The tomb had been plundered, but many of its burial objects and extensive paintings on the walls and ceilings remained.

Zhang Shiqing was buried in a manner already observed in the grave of the Han official Ma Zhiwen (see fig. 310). After cremation, his ashes were put in a wooden figurine (see fig. 312). For Zhang, that encasement was then placed in a wooden coffin. Cremation, alone, in a Han Chinese burial is usually considered adequate indication that the occupant was Buddhist. Evidence of Zhang Shiqing's faith is stronger. His funerary inscription states that he read the *Lotus Sutra* more than a hundred thousand times.[118] A painting on the east wall of the

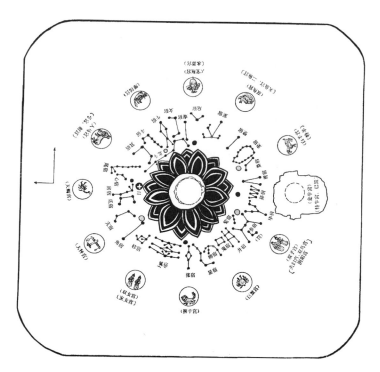

FIGURE 318. Line drawing of ceiling painting from tomb of Zhang
Shiqing. [After Zheng Shaozong (*Wenwu* 1975a, no. 8), p. 44]

back chamber of his tomb includes two Buddhist
sutras.[119]

The most important decoration on Zhang Shiqing's tomb was painted on the vaulted ceiling of
the back chamber (fig. 318). The painting can be
viewed as consisting of five concentric circles. Innermost is a circular bronze mirror facing toward
the outside. Second are two nine-petal lotus flowers. Third were the Big Dipper (*beidou*), the sun,
and eight smaller stars. Fourth were the *ershiba xiu*,
the twenty-eight lunar lodges. Last were the twelve
symbols of the Western Zodiac. In 1975 and 1976,
interpretive studies of this tomb ceiling were published. In both studies the ceiling design was referred to as a "*xingtu*," or star map.[120] In the second
study, the author Xia Nai wrote that the lunar

lodges and the zodiac signs were unique in Chinese
ceiling design.

Celestial bodies on tomb ceilings were not rare
even during the Han period,[121] but lunar lodges are
more infrequent. One example of a ceiling with
paintings of the twenty-eight lunar lodges was excavated in a tomb in Astana, Xinjiang province, dated
to the Tang period.[122] The lunar lodges also appear
on an epitaph from the Southern Tang kingdom
found in Jiangsu (fig. 319). In this stone example
they are coupled with twelve animals symbolically
associated with the Chinese calendar.[123] On the
sides of the epitaph are the *sishen*.

Twelve has been the number of standing figures
painted and inscribed on epitaphs of the tombs of
the Chinese officials Ding Wenyou and Han Yi dis-

FIGURE 319. Stone epitaph found at Jiangsu, Southern Tang. [After *Zhongguo gudai tianwen wenwu tuji*, pl. 72]

cussed earlier. Sometimes the calendrical animals appear with human bodies, and indeed it is they who are portrayed also in Liao-period tombs of Han officials before Zhang Shiqing's. Zhang Shiqing's ceiling stands apart from the norm in the Tang, Southern Tang, and perhaps other Liao depictions, however, because the twelve animals individually encircled in the outermost of its five rings are, as Xia Nai pointed out, symbols of the Western Zodiac. The Western Zodiac signs have a history in West Asia at least 500 years before the interment of the Liao official Zhang Shiqing. They were painted, for instance, on the ceiling of a bathing room at the Umayyad palace at Qusayr 'Amr in about 715.[124] Their route across Asia to northern Hebei in the

twelfth century is not clear, but Xuanhua was not the only North Asian location, and ceiling painting not the only context, in which the Western Zodiac signs appeared.

Fifteen years after the publication of Zhang Shiqing's tomb, Xuanhua Tombs 2 and 3 were published.[125] Tomb 2, located about 6.4 meters north, contained the remains of Zhang Gongyou, who died in 1117. (It is not certain the two Zhangs were related.) Tomb 2 was brick, as well, with wall decorations that imitated wooden architecture, and it too was oriented southward. It had a single hexagonal chamber of dimensions 2.9 by 2.4 meters with walls that reached 1.8 meters before the beginning of the vaulted ceiling (fig. 320). Near the north wall were remains of a coffin bed and coffin, both made of wood. Wall paintings and ceiling paintings were preserved in their entirety. Zhang Gongyou's ceiling painting, like Zhang Shiqing's, was formed of five concentric circles (fig. 321). Beginning at the top was a mirror followed by a lotus with two sets of petals. In this case each set numbered eight. Third were the signs of the Western Zodiac, then the twenty-eight lunar lodges plus the sun and moon (the latter two perhaps should be considered a separate ring), and last the calendrical animals in human guise. Unique is the juxtaposition of zodiac signs and calendrical animals.

Tomb 3 at Xuanhua belonged to Zhang Shiben and his wife, who were buried in 1144, twenty years after the fall of the Liao dynasty. Although no funerary inscription has linked the occupants of even two of the tombs, the common family name and location, combined with the painting programs on all three ceilings, suggest the occupants were related. Because of the similarity of the paintings, Tomb 3's ceiling is discussed here despite its post-Liao date.

The plan of Tomb 3 was more typical of Liao tombs of Han Chinese officials than the earlier two Xuanhua tombs. Located about 40 meters southeast of Tomb 1, it consisted of a single, circular, brick chamber, 2.64 meters in diameter, whose interior imitated motifs of wooden architecture (fig. 322). Orientation was to the south and the ceiling above the chamber was vaulted. The walls up to the ceiling were 1.52 meters high. Painted on them were pillars with bracket sets on top and windows. Tomb 3's ceiling was the simplest of the three. It had, first of all, no bronze mirror at its center. Rather, the center was the painted interior of a lotus flower with two layers of six petals each; in the second concentric circle (from the inside) were the twenty-eight lunar lodges; the last circles were two rings of flowers, eight pairs framed by lines in each ring (fig. 323).

I believe that the tomb ceiling designs at Xuanhua were intended to represent specific Buddhist affiliations and postmortem aspirations of their occupants and, moreover, that the ceiling programs connected the practice of Buddhism in the early twelfth century in Hebei to that of an international Buddhist community of North Asia. Further, the ceiling motifs show that at least by the final decades of Liao rule, Chinese subjects of the empire had become as creative as the dynasts in their implementation of architectural programs. It is believed, furthermore, that the ceiling designs at Xuanhua were more explicit than constellations or "star maps," the likes of which had been painted on Chinese tomb ceilings since the Han dynasty. Rather, the Xuanhua ceilings represent specific mandalas painted elsewhere in Asia at the same time.[126]

The Buddhist explication of the ceiling paintings of Zhang family tombs begins with the mirror. The mirror, alone, might be interpreted as a *zhaoshen jing*, a "mirror that lights the body," an object found in Chinese coffins since the Han dynasty.[127] Yet the placement directly above the remains of the deceased, in both tombs, is the first clue to the interpretation proposed here. It is the position prescribed in *Yuanjing mantuluo* (Circular mirror

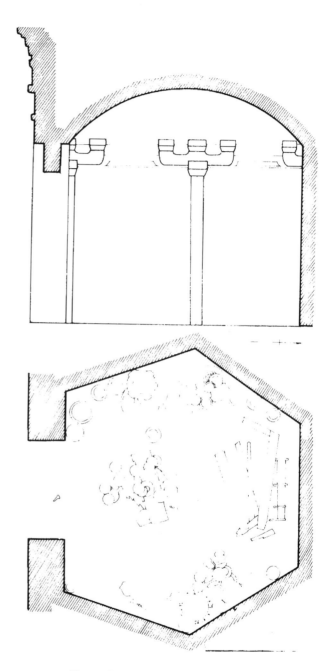

FIGURE 320. Plan and sectional drawing of tomb of Zhang Gongyou, Zhangjiakou, Xuanhua county, Hebei, 1117. [After Tao, Liu, and Zhao (*Wenwu* 1990, no. 10), p. 2]

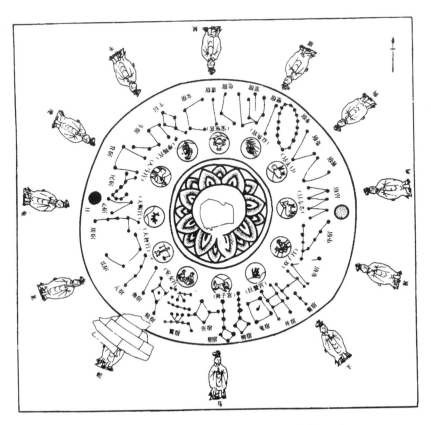

FIGURE 321. Line drawing of ceiling painting from tomb of Zhang Gongyou.
[After Tao, Liu, and Zhao (*Wenwu* 1990, no. 10), p. 9]

mandala), practiced by Tantric Buddhists, including the Qidan. In the practice of this mandala, the devotee is to imagine two mirrors, one at his heart and a second at the heart of the Buddha in front of him.[128] In the positioning of the heart (or its remains if the body has been cremated) under the mirror one observes the kind of three-dimensional interpretation of a Buddhist concept that I have suggested was employed by Liao Daozong in the erection of the Timber Pagoda at Yingxian.

Continuing outward, the lotus is almost a generic Buddhist symbol, depicted in art as a symbol of Śākyamuni even before the appearance of the anthro-

pomorphic Buddha. One of the primary meanings of the lotus in a Buddhist context is its symbolism of rebirth in a Buddhist paradise. The placement of the mirror, representing the body of the deceased, inside the lotus would suggest such a rebirth. The varied number of petals on the Xuanhua tomb ceilings gives cause for momentary consideration. One would be pleased to find rings of eight petals in each case: eight is the number of sides at the Timber Pagoda, the number of petals on the lids of the reliquary inside the White Pagoda at Jixian (see fig. 49), and, as we shall see in the final two chapters, a defining number for the Tantric world of Liao Buddhism. Since the numbers are different, one might argue that artists fit the petals into designs—drawing too wide or too close together resulted in six or nine petals as opposed to eight. Or perhaps the number was intentional in each case, and the petals represent iconography that at this time is not obvious.[129]

The symbols of the Western Zodiac are the most intriguing. They lead us to another mandala, the Star *(Xing)* Mandala, also known as the Big Dipper *(Beidou)* Mandala.[130] In a version that survives at the Hōryū-ji, the Buddha is at the center, enthroned on a lotus (fig. 324), replacing the mirror in the ceiling paintings. Planetary deities and zodiac signs encircle the Buddha in the same concentric ring position as planets, and in the outermost ring of the Hōryū-ji mandala the twenty-eight lunar lodges are shown as Buddhist divinities. The occupants of the fourth and fifth rings (lunar lodges and zodiac signs), in other words, are switched in the painting and ceiling designs. Also changed is the direction of progression of the signs of the zodiac: on the Hōryū-ji mandala, the twelve celestial symbols proceed clockwise; on the ceilings, they proceed counter-clockwise. This may be the explanation for the upward positioning of the mirror—the ceiling direction is the same as the mandala's if viewed from above, or outside, the tomb. Thus it would be intended for the terrestrial world or higher, perhaps as an interface between the occupant's ashes and his former or future existences.

The specific path of the Star Mandala to Japan is unknown, but one assumes the source to have been continental Asia. In addition to the Hebei ceilings and the silk painting now in Japan, a version of the Star Mandala was found among excavated ruins of the eleventh–twelfth-century Xi Xia. It is now in the Hermitage (fig. 325). The similarities between Liao and Xi Xia funerary architecture is a main subject in the next chapter.[131]

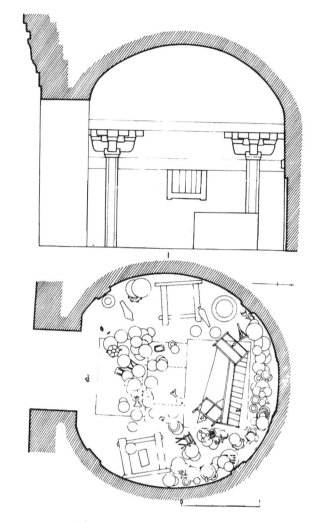

FIGURE 322. Plan and sectional drawing of Tomb 3 at Zhangjiakou, Xuanhua county, Hebei. [After Tao, Liu, and Zhao (*Wenwu* 1990, no. 10), p. 11]

FIGURE 323. Ceiling painting from Tomb 3, Zhangjiakou, Xuanhua county, Hebei. [After Tao, Liu, and Zhao (*Wenwu* 1990, no. 10), pl. 4]

LIAO TOMBS IN RETROSPECT

Before turning to tombs northwest of China during the Liao centuries, it might be helpful to summarize the major points of this long chapter. Among the several hundred tombs believed to be from the Liao period, we have focused on dated tombs with known Qidan or Han occupants. Of these, certain burial practices are in evidence only among tombs of aristocratic Qidan—most noteworthy, the use of metal death masks and encasement of the corpse in suits of metal netting. A variety of preburial procedures for the corpse have been observed in Qidan tombs. They range from cremation to deterioration before interment to removal and replacement of bodily organs in preparation for preservation after interment. Once inside the tomb, corpses have been placed without protection on funerary beds, inside single coffins, and inside stone sarcophaguses that were further enclosed by exquisite wooden replicas of Song-style architecture. The materials of tombs varied from earth to stone to brick to wood to combinations of all. In their plans, one finds circles, squares, rectangles, hexagons, octagons, and combinations, with chambers numbering from one (with perhaps adjoining spaces) to nine. A few generalizations about these plans can be made: in the earliest tombs, those from the mid-

FIGURE 324. Star (Big Dipper) Mandala, Hōryū-ji, Nara prefecture. [After Ishida Hisatoyo, *Mandara no mikata*, p. 67; published courtesy of Iwanami Shoten]

FIGURE 325. Planetary Deities (Star Mandala), showing planetary deities in foreground and signs of Western Zodiac in background, Xi Xia, eleventh–twelfth century. [Hermitage; courtesy of Electa]

tenth century up to the time of the Shengzong reign, four-sided and circular room plans are common; but by the eleventh century, perhaps inspired by their use at the Central Mausoleum at Qingzhou, octagonal room plans appear in lesser royal and aristocratic Qidan tombs and at Baisha in Song China. We have also observed the octagonal patterns in the plan of the Timber Pagoda, on a reliquary box in Jixian, and on ceilings of Zhang tombs in Xuanhua. Its supreme significance in Liao construction will be a theme in the final chapters.

Some features of Liao-period tomb construction are found among the Qidan and Han Chinese, and many of these have a history that can be documented for a millennium before Liao rule in many regions of China. Since the origins of the concept of subterranean burial—traceable in China at least from the second millennium B.C.—tombs have, in at least some ways, been replicas of residential architecture. They have contained actual objects from life or items superior in quality for the deceased's postmortem use. Walls have been decorated with paintings, carvings, and the two together.

Wall scenes have reflected actual events or generalized depictions of the life of occupants, as well as heroic deeds and Chinese superheroes. The number of chambers and complexity of construction—reflections of time and money expended for a tomb—have always been indicators of an occupant's wealth and status.

One can isolate certain features that are typical of Han burial during Liao rule: tombs are more consistently oriented north-south than in the variety of directions one finds among the non-Han population; coffins are more often wood than stone; more bodies have been cremated; fewer animal corpses (horses, dogs, squirrels) have been found; there is no evidence of sacrificial human burial; and the shapes of tomb chambers are more often circular or rectangular. In only a few cases do tombs have chambers with more than four sides. Those cases have been in territory closer to the Qidan homeland, Liaoning and Inner Mongolia. It is with the configurations of tomb plans contemporary to Liao but to their south and west that we begin the next chapter.

FIGURE 326. Da Xia royal cemetery in 1930s, Yinchuan, Ningxia Hui Autonomous Region, eleventh–thirteenth centuries. [After Castell, *Chinaflug*, pl. 114]

13

The Funerary Traditions of North and Northeast Asia

W̲E HAVE JUST CONCLUDED our study of Liao-period tomb architecture by pointing out that tombs of both the Qidan and the Han Chinese under Liao rule shared certain ideological and stylistic features with a Chinese tradition that had more than 2,000 years of history prior to the interment of Abaoji at Zuling. Yet we have observed also that a superlative creativity in the use of architecture—one not unlike the unparalleled creative employment of wooden architecture and its symbolism by Liao builders—is present in Qidan and Han tombs and their decoration. Through imitation, adoption, adaptation, or absorption, Qidan funerary creativity emerged from Chinese models in the manufacture of "funerary houses" that replicated the prescriptions of *xiaomuzuo* in a Song Chinese architectural text. And in Han Chinese tombs, "underground palaces" of death were further transformed into three-dimensional mandalas with two-dimensional mandalas painted on their ceilings.

If there is one form through which the the Liao manifest their creative and symbolic genius in architecture, it is the octagon. An investigation of octagonal forms, therefore, will conclude this study. To explicate these forms in floor and ceiling plans, in full-size and miniature replica, above and below

FIGURE 327. Great Xia Tombs 1 and 2 in 1970s. [After Shi Jinbo et al., *Xi Xia wenwu*, pl. 23]

ground, one is drawn to Liao's neighbor to the west, the Xi Xia (1038–1227), and to Liao's predecessors on Northeast Asian Qidan soil, the Korean kingdoms, in particular Koguryŏ, of the fifth through eighth centuries.

XI XIA ROYAL TOMBS NEAR YINCHUAN

Xi Xia, literally Western Xia, is one of the Chinese names by which the people also known as Tangut are referred. Their origins are generally traced to an Ordos tribe that dates from the Tang dynasty or earlier named Dangxiang in Chinese texts. The Tanguts survived the fall of the Uyghur and Tibetan empires in the 840s and shortly after the fall of Tang in 906 began to function as a semi-independent state. In 1038, under the ruler Li Yuanhao (r. 1032–1048), Xi Xia (or Da Xia, "Great Xia") proclaimed its independence. That same year, the ruler changed his family name from the one he shared with the Tang royal house to Weiming and began the construction of tombs for himself, his father, and his

grandfather. Through its 200-year history the Xi Xia empire was bounded by Asian empires on all sides—Song China to its south and east, Liao and then Jin to its northeast, Tibet to the southeast, and seminomadic empires across the north and westward.[1]

The site Weiming Yuanhao chose for the tombs of his ancestors and his future descendants lies about 40 kilometers west of Yinchuan, present capital of Ningxia Hui Autonomous Region and formerly known as Xingqing, capital of the Xi Xia dynasty. According to a sixteenth-century Chinese local record, *Jiajing Ningxia xinzhi* (New record of Ningxia of the Jiajing reign period; 1522–1567), the necropolis had 360 mounds.[2] As Yuanhao feared that the site of his tomb would become known and be plundered, he had a new mound erected daily to mislead robbers. As an additional precaution, all workers were forced to commit suicide after the initial three tombs were completed. In fact, the tomb site and nearby capital seem to have eluded the intrepid explorers of the region, including Marco Polo, Piotr Koslov, Sergeĭ Ol'denburg, and Sir Aurel Stein. Apparently the first description and photographs came from Wulf Diether Graf zu Castell, who published them in his air survey of China, *Chinaflug*, in 1938 (fig. 326). The site looks little different today (fig. 327).

The Tangut necropolis extends over 10 kilometers north to south by 5 kilometers east to west. Nine tombs are imperial: one group of six and another of three.[3] Chinese excavation began in the 1970s, at which point the tombs were arbitrarily numbered. It has since been determined that Xi Xia construction began in the south. Thus the two southernmost tombs would have belonged to Weiming Yuanhao's grandfather, Li Jiqian (963–1004), and his son who predeceased him, Li (or Zhao) Deming (984?–1032). They were subsequently renumbered Tombs 1 and 2. Only one other tomb has been identified, that of Weiming Zunxu, Emperor Shenzong (r. 1211–1223). This tomb still goes by its original number, Tomb 8.[4]

The nine royal Xi Xia tombs have standard architectural features both above and below ground. The aboveground structures commence with *que*, that is, gate towers (fig. 328, no. 1). At Xi Xia Tomb 8, they were raised on brick platforms made of pounded earth. The *que* were faced with lime, a material soft enough for carving replicas of timber-frame architecture on them. Fifty meters beyond, almost due north (the tomb was oriented 5 degrees east of north), were a pair of stele pavilions. Foundation remains show that one was approached by steps from the east and west and the other from the west (fig. 328, no. 2). Other Xi Xia royal tombs had a pair of stele pavilions on the east and a single pavilion west of the main approach to the tomb. Thirty-five meters beyond the stele pavilions, pairs of life-size stone sculptures of men and animals lined the approach to Tomb 8. It ended at the southern gateway

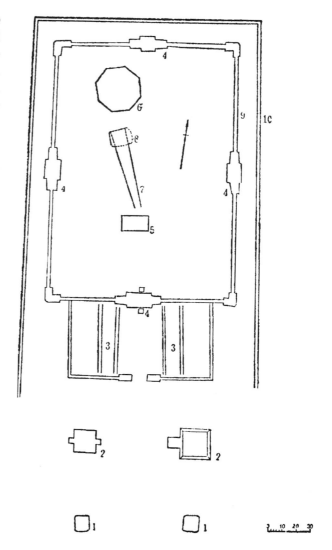

1. *que*
2. stelae pavilions
3. spirit-path sculpture
4. gates
5. offering hall
6. octagonal hall
7. path to underground burial area
8. subterranean tomb area
9. location of inner wall
10. location of outer wall

FIGURE 328. Plan of Great Xia Tomb 8, Yinchuan, Ningxia Hui, 1223. [After "Xi Xia bahaoling fajue jianbao" (*Wenwu* 1978, no. 8), p. 6]

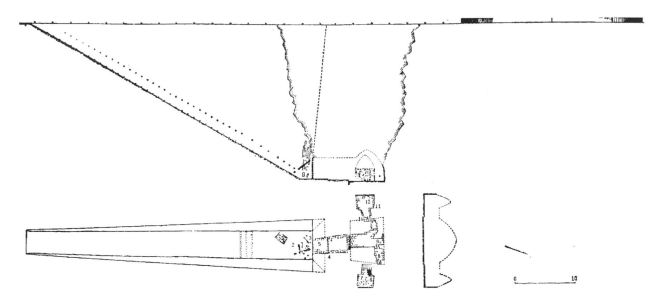

FIGURE 329. Underground plan and section of Great Xia Tomb 8. [After "Xi Xia bahaoling fajue jianbao" (*Wenwu* 1978, no. 8), p. 6]

(fig. 328, no. 4) of the inner walled enclosure to the tombs (fig. 328, no. 9),[5] one of four such gates located at the center of each side. The outer walled enclosure, about 15 meters from the inner wall, today extends on only three sides (fig. 328, no. 10) but one assumes it had a southern edge that joined or was south of the *que*. Corner towers were lodged into the inner wall, but there is no evidence that they existed at the outer enclosure. Two structures dominated the inner enclosure. Almost directly north of the southern gate was an offering hall. Only its foundation platform stands today (fig. 328, no. 5). Northwest was an octagonal, multilevel earthen structure that had, according to Castell, been faced with brick (fig. 328, no. 6).[6] Excavators believe that a timber frame supported the octagonal building.[7]

Other standard features of the nine Xi Xia royal tombs were underground (fig. 329). A subterranean path to Xi Xia Tomb 8 (see fig. 328, no. 7) began at the central axis of the tomb inside the inner walled enclosure several meters north of where the offering hall is thought to have stood. The 49-meter path was cut 30 degrees into the ground; it began at a width of 4 meters, but its terminus was 8.3 meters wide. Its direction was about 20 degrees west of due north. The walls on either side of the path appear to have been prepared for painting, but if any painting had been done it was peeled off by the time of excavation. Underground, Xi Xia Tomb 8 consisted of an antechamber, a main chamber, both rectangular in shape, and squarish side niches attached east and west of the main room. The main chamber and side rooms all had vaulted ceilings. The underground walls of Xi Xia Tomb 8 were earthen and the floor was made of earthen bricks.

In 1986 and 1987, excavation in the northern sectors of the 50-square-kilometer Xi Xia necropolis uncovered the remains of aboveground architectural groups.[8] Reconstructed plans show interconnected buildings arranged around courtyards and at least one example of an extrafacial fortification on the northern portion of the western wall (fig. 330). Although the plan does not suggest a specific Chinese funerary prototype, China is the logical source for the wall-enclosed, courtyard-style formation. The two most likely purposes of the buildings are sacrificial halls to the interred or their ancestors or, perhaps, guard stations for those who attended the graves. Another suggestion is that these buildings housed artisans.[9]

OTHER XI XIA REMAINS

Mounds from more than seventy nonimperial tombs fill in spaces not enclosed by inner or outer walls of the nine royal tombs. They tend to cluster in groups of two to ten around the major tombs. One of these, Tomb 108, has been excavated.

In plan, Tomb 108 is a highly simplified version of a Xi Xia tomb (fig. 331). Aboveground three structures survive. Most prominent is an octagonal, stepped mound (fig. 332) situated west of center about 10 meters from the northern enclosing wall (orientation is several degrees west of north). The wall itself measured 58 meters north to south by 55.6 meters east to west. Near the south center was a 3.25-meter opening. Some 40 meters south of the southeastern corner of the wall was a 10-meter-square stele pavilion with an engraved stone that identified a tomb occupant as a Tangut prince.[10] Underground a stepped approach oriented 20 degrees west of north led to a single earthen burial chamber. Directly under the octagonal mound were three corpses. It appeared that this tomb had not been robbed.

The position of the Xi Xia corpse with respect to the mound was surely not coincidental. In fact, evidence from Xi Xia Tomb 8 suggests that there, too, the burial chamber was directly beneath the more clearly octagonally shaped aboveground mound (fig. 333). Through the mounds one begins to understand the introduction of octagonal-shaped

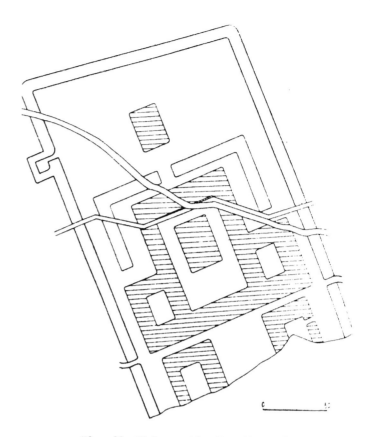

FIGURE 330. Plan of fortified area within Great Xia royal cemetery. [After "Xi Xia lingyuan beiduan . . ." (*Wenwu* 1988, no. 9), p. 58]

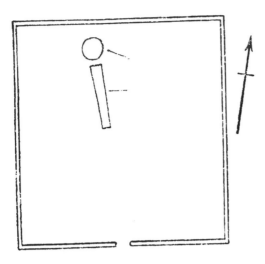

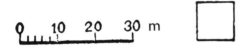

0 10 20 30 m

FIGURE 331. Plan of Tomb 108, Great Xia royal
cemetery. [After Wu and Li (*Wenwu* 1978, no. 8), p. 71]

chambers at the Central Mausoleum at Qingzhou
and thereby the greater significance of the octagon
above and below ground in tenth–twelfth-century
North Asian architecture.

One recalls that the plan of the Eastern Mausoleum at Qingzhou, believed to be earliest of the
three (see fig. 239), had five circular-shaped rooms
(the back and both sets of side chambers) and a central chamber whose shape might be interpreted as
circular or as octagonal or, perhaps, as a shape transforming from circle to octagon (with four circular
and four straight sides). Yet by the time of the construction of the mausoleum of Shengzong's successor, the Central Mausoleum of Xingzong, six out of
six funerary chambers were decidedly eight-sided
(see fig. 242). There is thus no question that Liao
Xingzong, to whose memory the octagonal Timber
Pagoda was dedicated, was buried inside an octagon. The royal Tanguts used the same shape in the
construction of their tombs, but they placed it directly above rather than around the corporeal remains, perhaps as a roof of their burial chamber.
Looking up to the octagon and seeing oneself in it
can, perhaps, be viewed as a concept similar to the
Zhang officials' looking up to mirrors enclosed by
lotuses, some of them eight-petaled, and seeing
themselves in them (as discussed in Chapter 12).

The importance of the octagon is underscored in
the case of Xi Xia by the fact that tomb construction
for them began seventy-five years after the Song dynasty was under way. Thus there is a greater likelihood their royal tomb builders had an awareness of
Song royal funerary configurations than did tenth-
century Qidan royalty. (Zuling was constructed for
Abaoji before the name of the Song dynasty was
known.) For the Liao, use of the octagonal burial
chamber required a transformation of a royal tradition; for the Xi Xia, it was an initiation into the
realm of royalty. Thus in comparing the Xi Xia
tombs with examples of Song or Five Dynasties or

FIGURE 332 (left). Remains of octagonal(?) stepped mound from Tomb 108, Great Xia royal cemetery. [After Shi Jinbo et al., *Xi Xia wenwu*, pl. 27]

FIGURE 333 (below). Entrance to Great Xia Tomb 8 showing octagonal mound above burial chamber, Yinchuan. [After Shi Jinbo et al., *Xi Xia wenwu*, pl. 26]

FIGURE 334. Octagonal miniature pagoda, wood, excavated at Tomb 2, Wuwei, Gansu province, Xi Xia period, ca. 1198. [After Shi Jinbo et al, *Xi Xia wenwu*, pl. 255]

Tang royalty, we find that, similar to those of earlier Chinese rulers, the Xi Xia tombs had princes' and lesser mortals' graves as satellites. But unlike the graves of Tang and Five Dynasties and Song emperors and their children, Xi Xia rulers were buried beneath eight walls. Above ground the graves of Chinese royalty had been marked by truncated pyramids, or less rigidly sided mounds, since the time of the First Emperor through the Song dynasty.[11] For Xi Xia rulers and some princes, the four sides were transformed into eight.

The three-dimensional octagon is found in remains of Xi Xia material culture underground (in miniature) and in caves. Evidence of it survives at two of the sites with significant Xi Xia remains besides greater Yinchuan in Ningxia Hui Autonomous Region.[12] In 1977, two Xi Xia tombs were excavated in Wuwei county, Gansu province.[13] One was oriented north-south with a southern entry. The second, to its south, had an eastern entry. Both had one brick underground chamber with brick-faced walls and brick floors. They had arched stone doorways, vaulted ceilings over their burial chambers, and a bilevel platform at the back wall of the burial chamber, opposite the entry. Neither tomb's plan has been published.

Many of the objects in the two tombs were wooden and some, therefore, had rotted. There were, for instance, twenty-nine painted wooden panels. The paintings that could be deciphered depicted predominantly male and female figures and animals. Most important, by far, was a wooden, miniature pagoda. Its shape was octagonal. The pagoda measured 76 centimeters in height and stood on a two-level base (fig. 334). Its body consisted of eight panels, each 34 by 12.5 by 2 centimeters. The sides were held together by two rows of bronze nails. Painted on the pagoda in red (and scarcely discernible in the photograph) were bracket sets.[14] The roof of the pagoda was formed of eight pieces of

FIGURE 335. Octagonal pagodas, Bai Monastery, 45 kilometers northwest of Yinchuan, Ningxia Hui, Xi Xia period. (Althouth known as twin pagodas, the profile of the structure in the distance is more similar to Figure 336 than it is to the one in the foreground. [After Shi Jinbo et al., *Xi Xia wenwu*, pl. 12]

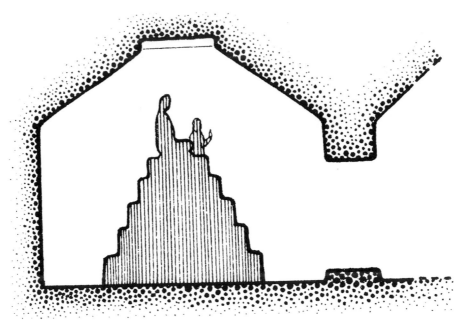

FIGURE 336. Sectional drawing of Cave 29, Yulin Caves, Anxi, Gansu province, Xi Xia period. [After *Tonkō Bakukō kutsu*, vol. 5, p. 166]

wood that curved at the top to give it a triangular profile. Eight small pieces of wood were superimposed on the roof, under the multilayer *harmikā* (the pagoda's crown). Written in the wood across the eight sides of the pagoda top was an inscription that identified the tomb occupant as the Han Chinese official Liu Deren, who died in 1198 and was buried two years later. The occupant of the second tomb was a member of the same family who was buried in 1201.[15]

The archaeological report on the Xi Xia tombs at Wuwei does not mention ashes inside the miniature pagoda. Moreover, the platforms at the back of the two tombs could have been funerary beds. Nevertheless, the small pagoda is reminiscent of the physical forms of both the Yingxian Timber Pagoda and—from its bilevel base to its curved octagonal roof, painted bracket sets, and *harmikā*—of brick pagodas that dotted the landscape of the Tangut empire (fig. 335). Could its function as a reliquary be proved, it would be comparable to the box inside the eleventh-century White Pagoda in Jixian.

The second Gansu site where evidence of Xi Xia patronage remains is Anxi, home of the Yulin Caves. Yulin, named for the river along which these caves were carved, is one of six cave sites excavated by the Xi Xia in the eleventh–thirteenth centuries.[16] A standard Xi Xia plan is a squarish cave with pyramidal, flat ceiling. In Cave 29 of the Yulin group one finds at the center the Buddha on a stepped mound (fig. 336). In profile the image is that of a Xi Xia octagonal pagoda (see fig. 335). Buddha and flanking bodhisattvas elevated at the core of this cave chamber are reminiscent of the image of Śākyamuni at the base of Yingxian Timber Pagoda.

On two sides of North Asia the Xi Xia and the Liao emerge as creative adapters of architectural space, capable of associating symbolism with that space in imperial, especially imperial funerary, contexts in the eleventh and twelfth centuries. The Xi Xia royal tombs were simpler than their Liao counterparts at Qingzhou. Underground they had a single, main domed chamber with two domed auxiliary rooms. Yet noticeable at each of the royal Tangut tombs and missing from contemporary Liao or Northern Song tombs is the octagonal, multistory, earthen mound. This mound calls to mind the stupas that spread across the Xi Xia empire from Khara-Khoto to Ningxia. The placement of corporeal remains of Tangut royalty beneath above-ground octagonal stupas (see fig. 333), it is suggested here, served the same purpose as the enshrinement of a Buddha atop a mound but inside a cave (see fig. 336), as a miniature octagonal pagoda in the tomb of a Han official in service of the Xi Xia in Gansu (see fig. 334), as a reliquary with octagonal lotus design in an eleventh-century funerary pagoda constructed by the official family Han in Liao service (see fig. 49), as the ultimate funerary monument to a deceased Qidan ruler (Yingxian Timber Pagoda of 1056; see fig. 20), as the enshrinement of a bodhisattva whose gaze located a pagoda for later Han-family officials (see fig. 46), and as the lotus-encircled mirror in the tomb ceiling of Zhang-family officials in Hebei (see figs. 318 and 321). One cannot prove that impending *mofa* (end of the Buddhist Law) was an impetus for the abundance of eleventh-century funerary architecture focused on the Buddha in the center of his world, but it can be strongly suggested for the mid-eleventh-century Timber Pagoda and for Jixian Guanyin Pagoda and its reliquary box.[17]

Thus through their architecture both above-ground and underground, in caves, and in miniature buildings of the tenth to thirteenth centuries,

North Asian empires emerge as masters in the adoption and adaptation for their own purposes of forms and symbols of more sedentary cultures. On the most fundamental level was the adoption of the stupa—house of relics of the historical (sixth century B.C.) Buddha Śākyamuni—and its adaptation into a house of immortality for Qidan, Tangut, and Han Chinese deceased. Yet the migration and transformation from Indian relic mound to octagonal pagoda above and below ground was neither direct nor without nuance. The only thing about which one can be certain is that in the tenth to thirteenth centuries, knowledge of the stupa and its significance was learned from sedentary Asia.

REGIONAL SOURCES OF LIAO ARCHITECTURE

The fact that similarities can be found in Liao and Xi Xia tombs, even if the builders shared ideological purposes or even if they practiced the same forms of Tantric Buddhism,[18] in no way suggests that two groups on different sides of North Asia learned from each other. The Liao and Xi Xia empires were contemporary; more likely there is a common, earlier source. One possibility, of course, is China. But to understand how the processes of transmission or borrowing occurred, one needs to be much more specific. Scholars seeking to interpret sedentary ways among seminomadic empire builders have tended to turn to huge empires for models for the nonnative manifestations in the centuries that directly precede the rise of the new powers. For the tenth and eleventh centuries, the Tang is not only a plausible model but an attractive one because of the number of easily observable cases of Tang culture consciously admired, borrowed, transmitted, or sought beyond its borders under the rubric "international Tang." Not just Korea and Japan, but empires from the Uyghurs in northwestern Asia to the Bohai in the northeast to

Vietnam in the south are known to have plucked from Tang culture certain aspects of their empires—from government institutions to capital city plans and, in less public affairs, from Buddhist sects to court painting beginning in the seventh and eighth centuries and continuing for the duration of these empires.[19]

But Tang Chinese models, especially in their pure and original forms, were not the impetus for Liao tomb construction. Indeed, "pure forms" is the key to this interpretation of Liao funerary architecture. The cultural centers of Tang China—sources of the imperial culture that emanated to governmental institutions, city-plan models, and Buddhist or secular painting—were her great cities: Chang'an, Luoyang, Yangzhou, Chengdu. If Qidan royalty or aristocracy knew of mausoleums in these cities, it was probably by description. From description, for instance, a spirit path even grander than Yelü Cong's could have been constructed for Liao emperors. Wooden worship halls could have been built from descriptions as well, although they and their statuary could as easily have been observed in countless Chinese towns and outposts.[20] *Xiaomuzuo* sarcophaguses could have been built from handbooks. Indeed, a stone sarcophagus with architectural decoration was excavated in a Xi Xia tomb at Longdeguanzhang People's Collective.[21] But Liao tombs, I would argue, were not based on verbal descriptions or handbooks. The imperial Qidan found architectural sources for their tombs close to home.

Although we have no record of a Qidan official stumbling upon a tomb in what are today Liaoning or Jilin province or Korea, having it opened, and ordering it copied for his own burial, there were at one time tens of thousands of pre-Liao burials in this region of the former Liao empire,[22] and scores survive. The majority of these tombs were constructed by Korean kingdoms in the centuries fol-

lowing the fall of the Han dynasty. Those of particular interest belong to the Koguryŏ kingdom (37 B.C.–A.D. 668).

Koguryŏ Tomb Architecture

Although the kingdom known as Koguryŏ was founded in 37 B.C., it is only from the time after the Chinese colony at Lelang fell to Koguryô, in A.D. 313, that dated tombs with identified occupants survive. It was at that time, the fourth century, that cairns, referred to in *Sanguo zhi* as "piled-up stones to cover the tomb,"[23] were replaced by earthen mounds over underground burial chambers. These chambers were carved out of stone, but their walls and ceilings were often faced with earth to provide a painting surface.

The oldest dated Koguryŏ tomb contains the remains of the Chinese general Dong Shou, who surrendered to Koguryŏ and subsequently died there in 357. Known as Anak Tomb 3, in the Korean province Hwanghae, the roughly north-south oriented tomb was approached by a subterranean, diagonal path. It consisted of a nearly square antechamber and a main burial area of more than 7 meters by more than 4.5 meters, divided into a back chamber with vestibule on three sides and a front area with two side niches (fig. 337).[24] Octagonal columns lined two sides of the burial chamber. The configuration of adjacent stone chambers and the use of octagonal columns calls to mind the interiors of late Han tombs both in Yi'nan, Shandong province, and much closer to Anak at Beiyuan, Liaoning (see fig. 51).[25] Yet in the ceiling form of Dong Shou's tomb one sees the first evidence of what was to become a trademark of Koguryŏ subterranean construction: the Anak Tomb 3 ceiling began at the tops of four adjoining walls and was stepped to smaller and smaller quadrilaterals until the top two levels, where two squares were positioned at 90-degree angles (fig. 338). In Korean, the ceiling form is

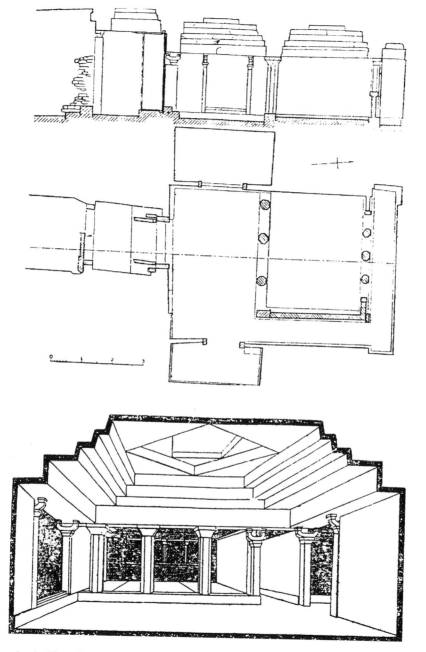

FIGURE 337 (top). Plan of tomb of Chinese general Dong Shou (Anak Tomb 3), Hwanghae province, (North) Korea. [After Hong Qingyu (*Kaogu* 1959, no. 1), p. 28]

FIGURE 338 (above). Drawing of interior of tomb of Dong Shou. [After Hong Qingyu (*Kaogu* 1959, no. 1), p. 29]

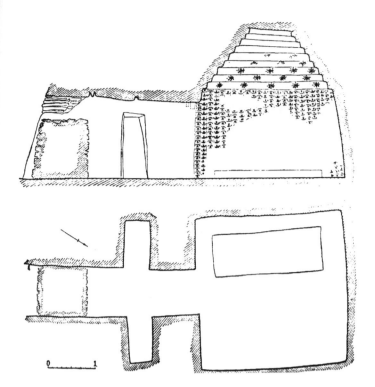

FIGURE 339. Plan and sectional drawing of Tomb 332, Tonggou, Ji'an county, Jilin province, Koguryŏ kingdom. [After Li Dianfu (*Kaogu* 1983, no. 4), p. 308]

called *malgak chochŏng* ("off-corner ceiling"), a reference to its formation by setting stone slabs diagonally across the four corners of the ceiling and four more corner slabs above them. The result is a central square resting on four cornices.[26] Eventually, out of this formation, octagonal forms would burst forth.

Sometime in the third century, before the construction of Dong Shou's tomb, the Koguryŏ kingdom moved its capital to Tonggou (now Ji'an) on the bank of the Yalu River that today separates Jilin province of China from North Korea. Although the dating of Koguryŏ tombs is still very imprecise, the several important tombs that stretch along this river

are dated to the fourth century. Beginning in 427 when the capital of Koguryŏ was moved south to P'yongyang and continuing through the fall of the kingdom 240 years later, most tomb construction was in the vicinity of the second capital. By the end of the fourth century and into the fifth, a common tomb configuration was a T-shaped plan with one main chamber and two side niches along the approach (fig. 339). Tomb 332 at Tonggou, Ji'an county, dated to about the late fourth century,[27] is an example both of this plan and the nine-level ceiling that characterizes main chambers in the Ji'an region at this time.

In wall and ceiling painting motifs, one finds more impressive links between Koguryŏ tomb interiors and Liao tombs. They include imitations of wooden architecture, heavenly bodies such as constellations (fig. 340), and lotus flowers at the center of ceilings (fig. 341). Paintings of celestial bodies and architecture on the walls of underground tomb chambers, like portraits of the deceased or the *si-shen*, have a pre-Koguryŏ history in Han tomb ceiling and wall painting.[28] The lotus may have a more subtle explanation.

Buddhism was officially introduced to Koguryŏ in 372 and had entered China about three centuries earlier. At the time of this initial introduction, according to Wu Hung, certain symbols may have been proto-Buddhist auspicious omens in the new Chinese context, rather than the standard and specific Buddhist symbols they were to become.[29] Borrowing from this model in our thinking about Koguryŏ tomb decoration, the lotus at the top center of the Ssangyŏng-ch'ong (Twin Pillars Tomb) ceiling may have carried a primary connotation of "Chineseness" or "auspiciousness" in fourth- and fifth-century Koguryŏ tombs as well as, or even instead of, a profoundly Buddhist meaning. By the time of the decoration of the Zhangjiakou tombs (see figs. 318, 321, and 323), however, the lotus had an undeni-

FIGURE 340. Ceiling of back chamber, Changchun Tomb 1, Ji'an county, Jilin, Koguryŏ kingdom. [After Chen and Fang (*Dongbei kaogu yu lishi 1*), 1982, p. 169]

able connection to the Buddhism practiced by the interred.

Archaeologists have dated Changchun Tomb 1 to the fourth century based on stylistic associations between this tomb and other Ji'an tombs including the famous Tomb of the Dancers (Muyong-ch'ong).[30] This date may also be significant in terms of the similarities in ceiling formation observed between a tomb like Changchun Tomb 1's ceiling (see fig. 340) and those of certain Japanese *kofun* of the pre-Buddhist centuries A.D. (fig. 342).[31]

Changchun Tomb 1 is a double-chamber tomb (fig. 343). Approached by a 1.4-meter-long ramp,

1.53 meters wide and 1.9 meters high, the tomb was made of stone with walls covered with white to provide a suitable painting surface. The door frame was wooden and painted. The antechamber of Changchun Tomb 1 was 2.37 by 2.9 meters at the base and rose 3.35 meters in height. Its ceiling was built up of six layers, three thicker and three thinner, with triangular stone cornices and a central square top. A *yongdao* measuring 1.12 by 1.34 by 1.63 meters joined the antechamber to the back room. Nearly a perfect square, the floor dimensions of the back room were 3.2 by 3.3 meters. It rose 3.05 meters in height. The back chamber housed two stone coffin

FIGURE 341. Lotus on top center of ceiling of antechamber, Ssangyŏng-ch'ong (Twin Pillars Tomb), Yongkang, P'yongyang, Korea, Koguryŏ kingdom. [After *Chōsen koseki zuroku*, vol. 2, pl. 173]

beds and a pine coffin. Orientation of this tomb is nearly east-west (255 degrees). Thus, technically, much of the structure and construction of Changchun Tomb 1 at Ji'an anticipates funerary construction under the Qidan.

Tombs with similar plans are plentiful in the vicinity of the second Koguryŏ capital. They include the Tomb of the Dancers and Tomb of the Wrestlers (Kakjo-ch'ong).[32] The Twin Pillars Tomb (Ssangyŏng-ch'ong) in P'yongyang, source of the ceiling shown in Figure 341, is also of this scheme but with a significant addition. The Twin Pillars Tomb is named for two stone octagonal columns that stand between the antechamber and main room (fig. 344). The only other known implementation of two columns in this position is the Buddhist worship cave Sŏkkuram, outside Kyongju, built after 668 by the United Silla kingdom (668–935) (see fig. 346). Another significant aspect of this Buddhist chapel will be explored shortly.

By the last phase of Koguryŏ tomb construction, after the fifth century but before the collapse of the kingdom to United Silla, the octagonal ceiling appears. Anticipated even in the ceiling of the tomb of Dong Shou (see fig. 338), the ceiling of the Tomb of Divine Kings and Earthly Spirits consists of two oc-

FIGURE 342. Chamber wall of Ōtsuka Tomb, Jumyo prefecture, Chikuzen. [After Umehara and Kobayashi, *Chikuzen-kuni*, pl. 12]

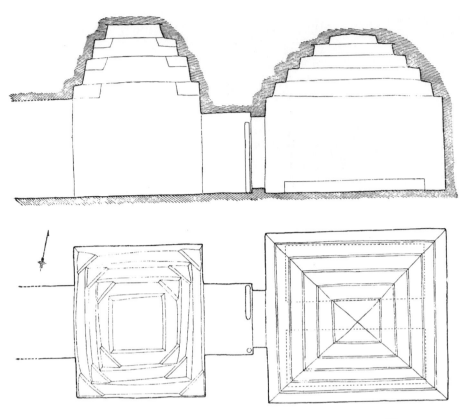

FIGURE 343. Plan and sectional drawing of Changchun Tomb 1, Ji'an county, Jilin.
[After Chen and Fang (*Dongbei kaogu yu lishi* 1), 1982, p. 155]

tagonal drums culminating in a dome (fig. 345). The inverted-V-shaped braces, in stone in the antechamber and painted in the main room, define the ceiling as in the tradition of post-Han and pre-Tang to early Tang Chinese architecture.[33] In all that we have seen in this book, and among what is known from Tang in wood, the exquisiteness and complexity of the ceiling of the Tomb of Divine Kings and Earthly Spirits are achieved only above the head of Guanyin in the deity's pavilion at Dule Monastery and in later Liao wooden architecture.

In the search for Qidan architectural prototypes, therefore, one has the best success close to their home. There one finds structural sources of Liao tombs and the feature that so characterizes the power and creativity of Liao wooden architecture: the *zaojing*.

Sŏkkuram

Another Korean structure located not far from the border of the Liao eastern circuit was Sŏkkuram. Cut from natural rock in the eighth century by, according to legend, Kim Tae-sŏng when he was minister to King Kyong-dok (r. 742–765), the two pillars alluded to in the discussion of the Twin Pillars Tomb are prominent in a plan of the structure (fig.

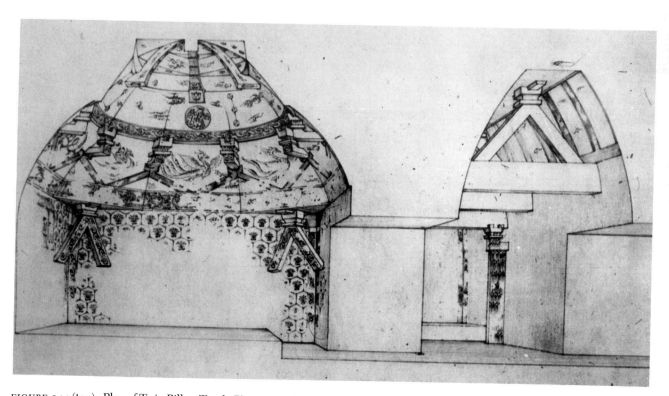

FIGURE 344 (top). Plan of Twin Pillars Tomb, P'yongyang, Korea, Koguryŏ kingdom. [After *Chōsen koseki zuroku*, vol. 2, pl. 162]
FIGURE 345 (above). Interior drawing of Tomb of Divine Kings and Earthly Spirits, Koguryŏ kingdom. [After Sekino et al., *Kokuri jidai no iseki*, vol. 1, pl. 174]

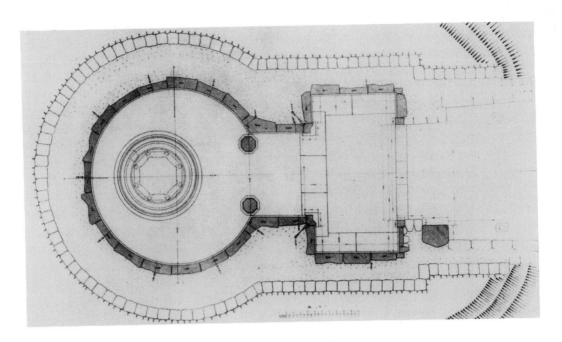

FIGURE 346 (top). Plan of Sŏkkuram, Northern Kyongsang, Korea, eighth century. [After McCune, *The Arts of Korea*, p. 138; published courtesy of Tuttle Press]

FIGURE 347 (above). Sectional drawing of Sŏkkuram, Northern Kyongsang, Korea, eighth century. [After McCune, *The Arts of Korea*, p. 138; published courtesy of Tuttle Press]

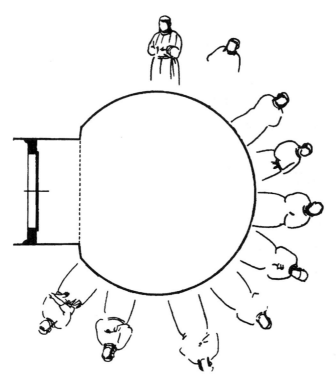

FIGURE 348. Line drawing of east front niche, Eastern Mausoleum, Qingzhou, ca. 1030. [After Tamura and Kobayashi, *Keiryō*, vol. 1, p. 48]

346). The plan of this cave-chapel has much in common with Liao tombs.

Sŏkkuram is composed of a rectangular antechamber, connective path, and circular main chamber. The focus of the main room is an enthroned Buddha, identified as both Śākyamuni and Amitābha.[34] The eyes of the deity look across the sea to Japan. These eyes are symbolic of the deity's role as guardian of Korea from threats from the east. It is the same sort of protectorate suggested for Guanyin in the pavilion in Jixian. Furthermore, as at Guanyinge and in the Daxiongbao Hall of Fengguosi, an image of the bodhisattva Guanyin is behind the main image. Yet the most impressive similarities between the configuration of Sŏkkuram and

Liao architecture are found in Liao's imperial funerary showcase.

As the side section of Sŏkkuram indicates (fig. 347), the stone walls of the cave are lined with figures. First are a pair of guardians at the entrance, followed by three pairs of guardians of the Buddhist faith. Next are four divine kings (in two pairs), then four bodhisattvas (also in two pairs), then ten disciples of the Buddha surrounding the main image. Eight seated figures, two of whom are Brahmā and Indra, form a higher ring around the main image. The arrangement of main image surrounded by celestial and secular guardians is recalled in wall paintings of the Eastern Mausoleum at Qingzhou. Not only do Chinese and Qidan officials line the

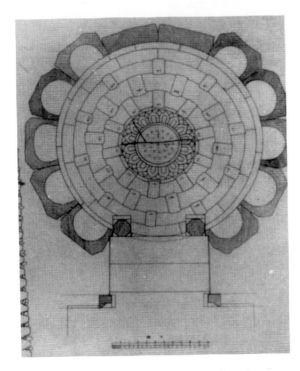

FIGURE 349. Line drawing of lotus on ceiling above head of Buddha, Sŏkkuram, Northern Kyongsang, Korea, eighth century. [After McCune, *The Arts of Korea*, p. 139; published courtesy of Tuttle Press]

borrowing to adoption to adaptation of forms and symbols of sedentary peoples by the Qidan. Sometimes, especially in the realm of religion, the context is known; but at other times, especially in the realm of rulers, it has been suggested that a secular image has been generated by a religious one. Based on interpretation of Śākyamuni inside the Muta, we can even propose that a Buddha in a cave-chapel encircled by bodhisattvas and guards was the symbolic model for transformation into a ruler's corpse and the officials that surrounded him at the Eastern Mausoleum in Qingzhou. The painting of officials who served a ruler or prince in life has a continuous history in Chinese funerary painting since the Han dynasty, but the arrangement in a circular chamber is new in tenth-century Inner Mongolia under Qidan patronage. Finally, the lotus pattern in the top center of the ceiling above the head of the Sŏkkuram Buddha must be noted (fig. 349). In this case, one's attention is drawn to the ceiling paintings at the Xuanhua tombs (see figs. 318, 321, and 323) and the earlier Ssangyŏng-ch'ong Tomb (see fig. 341).

LIAO AS A NORTH ASIAN EMPIRE

Other details of burial in the northeastern provinces of China and on the Korean peninsula in the Three Kingdoms centuries suggest additional connections between the Qidan and earlier empires and kingdoms on their own soil. We have already noted the common practice of burial with death masks.[35] In fact, precious-metal death masks and crowns (see fig. 8), now confirmed by excavation to be Liao, were in earlier times assigned provenances of Three Kingdoms' Korea or even Han.[36] Looking to recent catalogs of gold treasures from Korean and Liao tombs, one finds a host of similar burial goods including plates, combs, buckles, and jewelry.[37]

The label "Korean" used in the last sentence is intentionally nonspecific because the issue here is not one of dating. The point is to emphasize ideological

walls of the entry to the Liao tomb and stand on either side of the side-chamber entries, but individual males ring the walls of the east and west side niches of the front chamber (fig. 348 and see fig. 241). The extent of damage has been such that by the time the Eastern Mausoleum murals were copied in the 1930s or 1940s, it was uncertain how many figures had been painted originally—but twelve appears to have been the number. The fact that the Qingzhou images are purely secular does not rule out a Korean Buddhist cave-temple as a stylistic source.

In the course of this inquiry we have suggested evidence for a range of processes from copying to

links between Qidan and their Northeast Asian predecessors. Tomb remains confirm that not every Asian empire which arose in the aftermath of Tang looked to Tang China for its cultural and artistic models in the focused way that Japan had done since the Nara period. The Liao empire, it is suggested here, learned much from its territorial ancestors. Shortly we shall consider evidence to support the idea that just as one finds commonality in imperial tomb construction and material culture between the Qidan and their Northwest Asian contemporaries, the Tanguts, we observe similar commonality on the two northern sides of China in the fifth and sixth centuries. In contrast to the way Liao civilization has been viewed previously, the tenth-to-twelfth-century Liao empire is best understood as one that rose and fell in North Asia.[38] Drawing this cultural transmission line across North China, rather than as segments radiating from urban centers like Chang'an and Luoyang, one perceives the logic in finding similarities in burial practice among North Asian nomads, even in the first millennium B.C., and the Qidan. This is not to suggest that transmission was always direct. Rather, processes such as removal of corporeal organs and replacement with vegetable matter could have persisted in a variety of nomadic locales in North Asia but can be documented only when North Asian groups come into contact with sedentary record keepers.

Among the North Asian empires that logic dictates would have had a profound cultural impact on Liao is one about which far too little is known: the Bohai. The Bohai kingdom came about in the last years of the seventh century under the leadership of Da Zurong, who moved an amalgam of Tungusic tribes and members of Korean elite from Koguryŏ into the vicinity of the Mudan River in Jilin and Heilongjiang.[39] Enduring until its defeat at the hands of Liao in 926, for part of its history the Bohai

kingdom was tributary to Tang. (One recalls that upon this defeat Abaoji's eldest son, Bei, was sent to govern the Dongdan kingdom.)

In terms of Bohai construction, most is known about their cities and palaces.[40] For two of their five capitals, Shangjing and Dongjing, planning clearly derived from Tang models. Underground, if one can generalize from the few published tomb excavations, Bohai construction seems to have been primarily stone, the material we have associated with pre-Koguryŏ construction. Such arrangements are also found among Liao tombs. If none has been discussed thus far, it is because no occupant of this sort of tomb has been identified. But to date the locations of Liao tombs with mounds of piled stone are primarily in Jilin, with a few examples in Liaoning and Inner Mongolia.[41] The structural form persists in Jin tomb architecture.[42] The connection is surely no coincidence. Whereas the heart of the Liao empire was along the Liao River in Liaoning and Inner Mongolia, the Nüzhen (Jurchen) heartland was in Jilin and Heilongjiang, the center of Bohai rule. Thus again one observes nonnative North Asian empire builders looking close to home for funerary architectural models. (The Jin and Liao of Jilin and Heilongjiang were primarily influenced by Bohai tomb structures.)

FIFTH–SIXTH-CENTURY TOMBS IN GANSU AND NINGXIA

Several fifth-to-sixth-century tombs from northern Chinese provinces were discussed in Chapter 11 as part of the history of Chinese funerary construction prior to Liao. One was the tomb of Lou Rui in Shanxi province (just south of the sixteen *zhou*). As noted in that discussion, these tombs were included in the chapter on Chinese tombs because both in China and the West they have found their way into publications on the history of Chinese art and archaeology. Probably two main factors have justified

FIGURE 350 (top). East wall, front chamber, Tomb 6, showing inverted V-shaped braces and piled bricks, Jiayuguan, Gansu province, Wei-Jin period. [After Wang Tianyi, *Jiayuguan bihuamu . . .* , pl. 31, no. 1]

FIGURE 351 (above). Entrance and burial chamber of King Muryŏng, Songsan-ni, Kyŏngju, Paekche kingdom, 523. [After Kim Won-Yong, *Recent Archaeological Discoveries in the Republic of Korea* pl. 16; published courtesy of UNESCO Publishing]

FIGURE 352. Line drawing of south wall, front chamber, Dingjiazha Tomb 5, Jiuquan, Gansu province. [After *Jiuquan Shiliuguomu bihua*, p. 13]

the inclusion of Northern Wei–sponsored statues and structures in standard histories of Chinese art in contrast to fewer Liao and almost no Korean counterparts in the same books: first, more of China proper was in the hands of the Northern Wei and their immediate successors (Eastern and Western Wei, Northern Qi and Northern Zhou) than the sixteen *zhou* that belonged to the Liao empire; and second, a large percentage of that material is Buddhist and has been considered "mainstream" for understanding not just Chinese art of the fourth through sixth centuries but later Buddhist art.

Just before the Northern Wei moved into China and during the first years of their empire, tomb construction activity was intense at two sites in Gansu province. Both provide evidence that enhances our

understanding of the interconnections between North Asian empires and that part of China. In the third century, tomb walls at Jiayuguan were made by Wei-Jin builders with standard-sized, baked bricks arranged perpendicular to each other in rows of horizontal or rows of vertical pieces (fig. 350). In many of the Jiayuguan tombs, the purpose of this arrangement was to fit in bricks that had been painted in workshops outside the tomb.[43] Less than 50 kilometers southeast, at Dingjiazha Tomb 5 in Jiuquan, dated late fourth to early fifth century, a similar structure was employed, although painting was done right on this tomb's wall and ceiling surfaces.[44] Precisely the same configuration of bricks—with three horizontal rows for entry walls and four horizontal rows in side walls uninterrupted

FIGURE 353. Ceiling of Mogao Cave 285 viewed from east, Dunhuang, Gansu province, Western Wei period. [After *Tonkō Bakukō kutsu*, vol. 1, pl. 143]

by entries or niches—was employed at the tomb of King Muryŏng (501–523) in Songsan-ni, Kyongjŭ, in the Paekche kingdom (fig. 351).[45]

Similarly, one can compare the arrangement of painted images on the walls of Three Kingdoms Korean tombs with those of Dingjiazha Tomb 5. On both sides of China in the late fourth to early fifth centuries, for instance, enthroned deities reign closest to the ceiling; below them, in the world of humankind, figures engaged in daily pursuits are painted without serious concern for relative position (fig. 352). A large tree is the focal point on the walls of Changchun Tomb 1, Dingjiazha Tomb 5 (see fig. 352), and even farther west on a wall of Tomb 13 in the Astana cemetery, Turfan, Xinjiang province, dated to the Jin period (265–313).[46] The lotus flower in the center of the highest point in a domed or lantern ceiling—as we noted in Ssangyŏng-ch'ong (see fig. 341)—is found in the center of the ceiling of the antechamber in Dingjiazha Tomb 5. On these same tomb ceilings one finds, as well, celestial bodies; on the walls, one finds tomb occupants such as have been observed on the ceiling of tombs of the Northern Dynasties in northern Shanxi and Ningxia (see Chapter 11).

The themes and structures in all the contemporary Northeast and Northwest Asian locations—Ningxia, Gansu, Shanxi, Korea, and now the Hexi Corridor—may well have been learned from Han China. Their common existences, like the interconnections between Liao and Xi Xia funerary architecture, are examples of how North Asian patrons in some cases draw from common sources and how, perhaps unknowingly, they share painted, carved, or structural details on two sides of China. No suggestion is made here of an awareness of Hexi Corridor underground construction by Koreans or vice versa; nor is such a process between Liao and Xi Xia proposed. The fourth–sixth and tenth–thirteenth century groups are exemplary results of borrowing, importation, adoption, or adaptation of aspects of sedentary art and architecture by empire builders and aristocrats in newly formed empires. What I am proposing, rather, are common Han sources for provincial Han funerary architecture on both sides of China and for tombs built with an awareness of those provincial examples in the century after Han lost control of Liaoning and Gansu in these two provinces. Thereafter, Northeast and Northwest Asia generated some of their own art forms. In some instances in Northeast Asia, native seminomadic burial practices from much earlier times were preserved, only to reappear in Liao tombs.

Finally, we cannot conclude without noting the most famous post-Han Gansu site, for links with Korean kingdom funerary art can also be found there. This site is the Mogao Caves near Dunhuang. In ceiling center after ceiling center, one can find the square superimposed at the midpoints of sides of a larger square, sometimes with a lotus in the center of it (fig. 353).[47] Yet they are flat: plans of the cave ceilings show only quadrilaterals. Indeed, it is in tombs of the Koguryŏ kingdom of Northeast Asia that the true octagonal lantern ceiling proliferates. And it is also in Northeast Asia, above the head of the bodhisattva Guanyin in the Liao-period pavilion at Dulesi, that the earliest wooden version of this ceiling survives.

The Architectural
Legacy of Liao

FIGURE 354. Pagoda, Songyue Monastery, Songshan, Henan province, 523. [After *Ancient Chinese Architecture*, p. 53]

14

Conclusion

THE WORD "PAGODA" was first used in the sixteenth century by Portuguese to refer to temples dedicated to the worship of the *bhagavati* (divine female) seen on the Malabar coast of southern India.[1] Characteristic of these Indian temples were high towers. The Chinese word most often translated as "pagoda" is *"ta,"* which in Chinese is a reference to the Indian stupa, a mound constructed over Buddhist relics.[2] Here, as in Chinese and most Western-language literature on East Asian art and architecture, pagoda refers to the Chinese, Korean, or Japanese architectural form that traces its origins to the Indian stupa.

The earliest dated freestanding pagoda in China is the twelve-sided structure at Songyue Monastery on Songshan, Dengfeng county, Henan (fig. 354). In 523, the year it was built, the only competing Chinese pagoda form was four-sided in plan. Numerous examples of the four-sided pagoda survive in Buddhist worship caves of the Northern Dynasties (386–581) at Yun'gang, Shanxi province, in the Mogao Caves near Dunhuang, and at Maijishan, the latter two sites in Gansu province. Some are painted on the cave-temple walls. Others, such as those in Yun'gang Caves 2, 6, 7, and 21 or Mogao Caves 254 or 257 (fig. 355), are carved into the cave. At

FIGURE 355. Interior of Mogao Cave 257 showing four-sided pagoda. [After *Tonkō Bakukō kutsu*, vol. 1, pl. 38]

Yun'gang, Maijishan, and in the Mogao Caves, when the four-sided form has circumambulatory paths carved around it, the form is referred to as *zhongxin tazhu* (central-pagoda-pillar) style.[3] Studies of this and other fifth-and-sixth-century Buddhist cave interiors show the origins of the pagoda form and related ritual to derive from Indian worship and praxis.[4] The pagoda plan and profile are understood as deriving ultimately from the Indian stupa that became taller and narrower as it migrated eastward into Western China and combined with a native Chinese multistory structure: the Han-period watchtower or gate-tower.[5]

The limited archaeological evidence for the pre-Sui Chinese pagoda seems to corroborate the evidence from cave interiors and perhaps from the Songshan pagoda as well. The most reliable information comes from the ruins of Yong'ningsi in Luoyang, Henan province. Built in 514, Yong'ningsi was the largest monastery in the Northern Wei capital.[6] At its core, almost the exact center of its four-walled enclosure, was a pagoda (fig. 356). Elevated on a square foundation approximately 8 meters in height, the base form of the pagoda is not definite. If it was circular, or nearly so, the shape would link its form with the Indian stupa. A circular plan also might explain the dodecagonal shape of Songyuesi pagoda, unique both for its time and later in China. Perhaps the twelve sides were the attempt of early sixth-century builders experienced only in constructing flat walls to imitate a circular plan by small straight-wall segments. As figure 356 indicates, the pagoda was one of only two main buildings in this grandest monastery in the Northern Wei capital. Although we do not have enough evidence to suggest a direct link between the Liao monastery plan and one from Northern Wei times, both non-Chinese dynasties built architectural masterpieces (such as Yong'ningsi pagoda and Yingxian Muta) in simple, focused spaces.

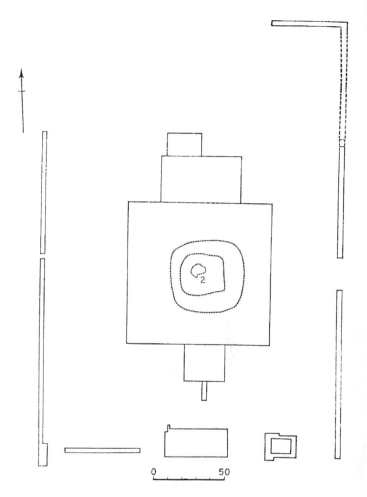

FIGURE 356. Plan of Yong'ning Monastery, Luoyang, Henan province, first half of sixth century, showing central location of pagoda. [After "Han-Wei Luoyangcheng . . ." (*Kaogu* 1973, no. 4), p. 205]

FIGURE 357. Great Wild Goose Pagoda, Ci'en Monastery, Xi'an
(Chang'an), ca. 706. [Steinhardt photograph]

Our knowledge of the position of pagodas in Tang monasteries is not much better than it is for the pre-Tang period. Nowhere do a wooden hall and pagoda survive at the same Tang monastery.[7] For isolated pagodas, the Sui-Tang evidence is better. Pagodas dated sixth through the ninth century remain in Zhejiang, Shandong, Yunnan, and the Tang capital Chang'an. All are four-sided at the base.[8] The most famous is the Great Wild Goose Pagoda (Dayanta) from Ci'en Monastery in Chang'an (fig. 357).

In the tenth century—the same century in which dramatic changes were forged in the timber frame—a new pagoda plan appears. It is octagonal.

Numerous examples remain in southeastern China: at Tiger Hill in Suzhou, at Qixiasi in Nanjing, at Lingyinsi in Hangzhou, at Longhuasi in Shanghai, and at Luohansi in Suzhou.[9] Although it is unlikely that Liao builders could have seen structures so far from their territory, the number of extant tenth-century examples suggests that the octagonal form could have been known in the north, and would have been built before the first half of the tenth century, close to or even within what was to become Liao territory. From the eleventh century survives "Liaodita" (fig. 358) at Kaiyuan Monastery in Dingxian, Hebei, a structure only kilometers from the sixteen *zhou* whose nickname, as mentioned in Chapter 8, reflects its purported function as a watchtower from which the Song could monitor Liao activity.

THE LIAO PAGODA

Yet it is the Liao who have received credit for introducing the octagonal pagoda plan to China. The reputation is deserved, too, for the Liao pagoda of octagonal plan is distinct from its Song counterparts and from pagoda construction that came before it. Alexander Soper's description of this form, written more than thirty years ago, sums up its characteristics precisely:

> Liao Buddhism created a distinct brick pagoda type, capable of great beauty and dignity. The distinguishing features are an octagonal plan, and an elevation in which three stages—base, shaft, and crown—are sharply differentiated. The base is fairly high, and is subdivided into courses enriched by sculpture. The shaft is relatively plain, serving as a background for Buddhist groups in relief; some sort of corner accent maintains verticality. The crown is a series of close-set roofs, usually thirteen. The bottom-most eaves are bracketed in a fashion based on Chinese carpentry; most often the rest will be corbelled out. The whole multiple crown diminishes as it rises, and is topped by some sort of spire.[10]

The few scholarly studies of Liao pagodas have focused on identification of stylistic features and classification into subgroups of distinguishable styles. The reason for so little work—apart from the limited research on Liao art and architecture discussed in the Preface—may be explained by the initial publication on the subject, which was overpoweringly extensive and even today might be hard to surpass. Indeed, one-half of Sekino Tadashi and Takeshima Takuichi's *Ryō-Kin jidai no kenchiku to sono Butsuzō*, published in 1925 and 1944, is devoted to the pagoda and its exterior decoration. The 110

FIGURE 358. "Liaodita," Kaiyuan Monastery, Ding county, Hebei province, eleventh century, showing interior of pagoda during course of repair. [Steinhardt photograph]

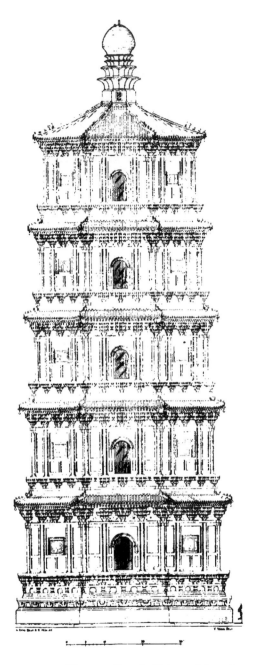

FIGURE 359. Zhenguo Pagoda, Kaiyuan Monastery, Quanzhou, Fujian, 1237. [Drawn by Gustav Ecke; after Ecke, "Structural features . . . ," pl. 2]

plates in some cases record monuments lost since the photographic work of the 1920s and in other cases remain the only published pictures of the twenty-four pagodas on which the study is focused. The text, published nineteen years after the photographs, ranges from discussion of general features of the Liao pagoda, to proposed typologies of the form, to inscriptions, to proposed identifications of relief sculpture. This work was the basis for Alexander Soper's carefully reasoned and succinct discussion in *The Art and Architecture of China*. It also provided data for an earlier study of Liao pagodas by Gustav Ecke published in 1948.[11] The third major investigator of the pagoda in the West, Ernst Boerschmann, published a book on the subject in 1931 and discussed the pagoda in his various other writings on Chinese architecture.[12] In China, the only pre-1949 scholarly publication was an article by Bao Ding on early (Tang-Song) pagodas published under the auspices of the Society for Research in Chinese Architecture.[13] Even in recent years only a few pagodas have received serious attention from Chinese scholars and very few book-length studies have appeared.[14]

Gustav Ecke's work on pagodas stands out for its superb measured drawings (fig. 359) and for the questions posed in his text. He uses "stone-built *ting* pagodas" of the Liao to query whether, as Wittfogel and Feng had done in their nearly contemporary study of Liao culture, "alien intruders, whether 'invading' or 'infiltrating,' ever add under the sway of their dominion to the commonwealth of Chinese design? Did [the Liao] enrich . . . Chinese [art] . . . with new vital impulses? Or, . . . adopt Chinese tradition as if it were their own?"[15] Viewing the Qidan as one in a line of non-Chinese rulers who had a potential impact on Chinese art and culture, Ecke frames his investigation of the Liao brick pagoda in terms of acculturation and cultural assimilation. Judging from phrases like "barbarous magnificence," "uncouth grandeur," and "stupendous display of skilful carpentry,"[16] it is clear that his awe of Liao pagodas was comparable to Liang Sicheng's feelings about the wooden building tradition.

The majority of Liao pagodas fall into two categories. (There are four types in all.) The first type is represented by perhaps the grandest of brick Liao pagodas: the Great Pagoda (Data) of Data Monastery, located within the ruined walls of the former central capital in present Ningcheng, Inner Mongolia, just kilometers from its border with Liaoning (fig. 360). Data rises 80 meters—13 meters higher than the total height of the Muta. Each of its eight base sides measures 13.96 meters. The base may be thought of as consisting of four parts: a smooth-sided edge atop a dirt platform; a band decorated on each side with three *wan* symbols framed by posts; a brick portion approximately ten layers thick; and a platform dividing base from shaft.

The eight faces of the shaft serve as backdrops for relief sculpture. At Data, the central bottom of each shaft face is occupied by a Buddhist deity seated on a lotus throne. Each of the eight main deities is framed by an arched lintel. On the southern shaft the deity and its frame are distinct from the other eight, thereby indicating south as the monument's cardinal direction (fig. 361). Here the deity is in the *vajramudrā* (pose) indicated by the encasement of the first finger of the left hand with the right hand. Furthermore, a Mongolian inscription has been added: "Dayičing ulus-un Tügernel Elbegtü-in dötöger on köke bars jil." The translation is: "Fourth year [blue tiger] of the Qing emperor Xianfeng," or 1854.[17] One assumes this to be the year of restoration.

On the southern shaft the main deity is flanked by two smaller, standing bodhisattvas, each beneath a canopy. Above each canopy floats an *apsara*. Higher still, and between them, a larger canopy with four streamers covers the head of the main de-

FIGURE 360. Data, Great Pagoda Monastery, Ningcheng (formerly Liao central capital, Zhongjing), Liao period with later restoration. [Steinhardt photograph]

FIGURE 361. Southern shaft face, Data, Datasi, Ningcheng.
[After Sekino and Takeshima, *Ryō-Kin jidai . . .* , vol. 2, pl. 25]

ity. A decorative band that extends across all eight faces of the shaft joins the top of the face with another band of decorative casing between the shaft and the third part of the pagoda, the crown. Other details distinguish the southern shaft face of Data from the others as well. Especially distinct is the main deity, Mahāvairocana, who wears an elaborate crown of exaggerated height and is backed by a pointed and highly decorative *mandorla*. A comparison with imagery of the other three cardinal shaft faces shows the depiction to be somewhat similar (see fig. 361); but on the intermediate faces (northeast, northwest, southeast, southwest), guardians rather than bodhisattvas flank the main deity (fig. 362). Two pairs of guardians, those on the southeast (see fig. 362) and southwest, are covered by sets of three seated deities rather than by canopies.

Connecting the shaft to the pagoda's crown, the third part of Data, is a layer of bracket sets whose form imitates wooden architecture. The crown itself consists of thirteen layers of roof eaves, the lowermost projecting more than twice as much as those above it. Thirteen is a standard number for roof eaves in Liao brick pagodas (see fig. 11). The number, moreover, appears to be exclusive to Liao pagoda construction. Other Chinese brick pagodas

FIGURE 362. Southeastern shaft face, Data, Datasi, Ningcheng.
[After Sekino and Takeshima, *Ryō-Kin jidai . . .* , vol. 2, pl. 26 no. 1]

have many eave stories: from fifteen at Songyuesi Pagoda (see fig. 354) to ten (or eleven if one counts the base-story eaves) at Liaodita (see fig. 358) to ten at Liuhe Pagoda of Kaihua Monastery in Hangzhou (dated to 1163), but so far thirteen is a number reserved for Liao construction.[18]

The second style of Liao brick pagoda has seven stories, each with its own roof eaves. The upper six stories are decorated with imitation bracket sets along their tops and bottoms (fig. 363). Originally this form of pagoda was accessible to the top story via interior stairways and arched doorways on one or more sides at every story or every other story (fig.

364). In contrast to the Data-style pagoda, however, the seven-story structures bear less complex iconography: on any of the eight faces of any level may be displayed a pair of bodhisattvas, guardians, or pagodas. Like so many of their structural predecessors back to the initial Indian stupa, all extant octagonal Liao pagodas of both varieties are (or were originally) topped by a *harmikā*.

The third type is represented by the North and South pagodas in Chaoyang, Liaoning, possibly the earliest pagoda that can be given a Liao date (fig. 365).[19] Chaoyang North Pagoda and its mate in the southern part of the town (Chaoyang South Pa-

FIGURE 363. Wanbu Huayanjing Pagoda (White Pagoda), Huhehaote (Hohhot), Inner Mongolia, probably late Liao with later repairs. [Steinhardt photograph]

FIGURE 364. White Pagoda, Qingzhou (Balinyouqi), detail of south side, Liao period. [After Sekino and Takeshima, *Ryō-Kin jidai . . .*, vol. 2, pl. 10]

goda, which bears more signs of restoration) are unique among extant Chinese and Liao construction. Although the four-sided plan places the North and South pagodas as standard forms of the Tang (see fig. 357), the imagery on their shaft faces appears to be a post-Tang contribution.[20]

In Chaoyang, it is likely that the iconography was carved onto earlier, probably Tang, pagoda bodies. Thus the Chaoyang pagodas can be viewed as "early Liao" and as examples of a "transitional" Tang-Liao stage. Even though pagodas with octagonal plans such as those in southeastern Chinese provinces mentioned earlier were built under Five Dynasties

and Song rulership, and sometimes even included imagery, it was Liao builders who transformed pagodas, including their faces, into backdrops for complex iconographic programs. Again the Liao emerge as borrowers of an earlier architectural form and adaptors of it for their own purposes. During the process, the tall buildings were transformed into uniquely Liao monuments.

Furthermore, Liao pagoda shaft imagery has been shown to be fairly specific in the choice of deities. Thus far, all enthroned deities on the Chaoyang or any of the octagonal pagodas with thirteen-story crowns are identified as members of the

FIGURE 365. South Pagoda, Chaoyang, Liaoning, Liao period with later repairs. [Steinhardt photograph]

Esoteric Buddhist pantheon. (The Liao, of course, practiced Esoteric Buddhism.) The main image on the southern face of Chaoyang North Pagoda (here the preeminence of south is defined by a *yuetai* that projects from the pagoda base) is Ratnasaṁbhava, the Dhyāni (Meditational) Buddha associated with south (fig. 366).[21] On the eastern face is Akṣobhya and on the west Amitāyus. The deity of the north was so effaced that Sekino and Takeshima did not attempt identification, but based on the other three and its northern position, it would have been Amoghasiddhi. In this instance, key to identifying the main images are the vehicles of the thrones on which they are elevated (horses, for example, for Ratnasaṁbhava). The four faces, however, represent only four of five Dhyāni Buddhas. The location of the ultimate one, positioned in the center of a two-dimensional mandala, will be addressed shortly.

Some of the imagery observed on the eight faces of the Data also appears at Chaoyang North Pagoda. The central Buddha on each face is crowned by a canopy from either side of which emanates an *apsara*. Beneath the *apsaras*, bodhisattvas make offerings to the main image. On the far ends of each face are four-sided pagodas of thirteen stories with Buddhas enthroned on the visible faces (at least), and above the pagodas are canopies from which, again, emanate *apsaras*. Alexander Soper has pointed out that with two stupas on each shaft, the total is eight, probably the Eight Great Stupas of the Mahāyana tradition.[22] The entire image is not only framed but bordered by pillars on each end. The pillars are also found at the seams of the Data faces and, in fact, at the points where shaft faces of all octagonal pagodas with thirteen stories join. Counterparts to actual wooden members of Yingxian Timber Pagoda (see fig. 20), the columns are examples of the way Liao builders borrowed and adapted from forms of Chinese architecture to create

FIGURE 366. Southern face of North Pagoda, Chaoyang, Liaoning. [After Sekino and Takeshima, *Ryō-Kin jidai . . .*, vol. 2, pl. 41]

unique structures through which they could manifest their own brand of Esoteric Buddhism.

The last type of Liao brick pagoda is represented by the White Pagoda at Guanyinsi in Jixian (see fig. 47). In this form, the octagon is as important as elsewhere in Liao brick architecture. Characteristic are two large octagonal shafts, octagonal sets of roof eaves, and a profile that narrows, sometimes dramatically, toward the top. The uppermost section is defined by thirteen levels capped by a rounded top. (The railing that often encloses a *harmikā* is missing.) This combination of octagon and circle, as well as the origins and meaning of the *harmikā*, have been analyzed by John Irwin.[23]

The eight shaft faces of Data (see figs. 361 and 362) are where we begin our explanation of how Liao adapted the octagonal form. We compare them to the central eight-petaled lotus court of the Womb World Mandala (see fig. 116). In the version of this mandala, dated to the second half of the ninth century, in the Tō-ji, Kyōto, believed to preserve details of a mandala transmitted from China to Japan in the first decade of the ninth century by the Japanese monk Kūkai,[24] the eight deities that encase Mahāvairocana are four *tathāgata* ("enlightened" Buddhas) and, between them, four bodhisattvas (Samantabhadra, Mañjuśrī, Avalokiteśvara, and Maitreya) with long histories in the

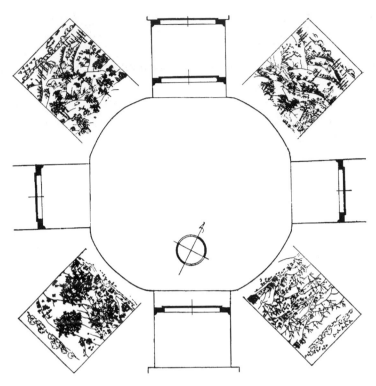

FIGURE 367. Schematic drawing of positions of paintings and adjacent rooms of central chamber, Eastern Mausoleum, Qingzhou. [After Tamura and Kobayashi, *Keiryō*, vol. 1, fig. 85]

Mahāyana tradition (although here in Esoteric emanations).

The iconography of Liao pagodas with eight shaft faces depicting Buddhist deities does not precisely follow the pattern of the Womb World Mandala. In the case of the brick pagoda at Yuantong Monastery in Tieling county, Liaoning, Buddhas and bodhisattvas are found on alternate shaft faces;[25] but in other instances, including Data, another iconography occurs. Here a most complex situation arises: one bodhisattva is named by inscription in a cartouche on each of the shaft faces (from the south and moving eastward they are Maitreya, Avalo-

kiteśvara, Kṣitigarbha, Sarvanivāranaviṣkambhī, Mañjuśrī, Vajrapani, Samantabhadra, and Ākāśagarbha); but the sculptures are of Buddhas.[26]

Although the writing in the cartouches may be newer, if the names were part of the Liao conception of the pagoda, then the total iconographic program might be interpreted as a complete scheme in which images of some and names of others combine. Thereby the Liao (or their designers) emerge as creative as well as accurate iconographers. Such creativity, of course, has been shown to characterize their adaptation of Chinese architecture. Whether the intent of the placement of deities on the Data shaft faces was to reproduce a known mandala or simply to represent eight deities around a center, the Great Pagoda of the Liao central capital exemplifies the transfer and transformation processes whereby Buddhist painting came to be transformed to three dimensions. In such transformations, a painted deity could become three-dimensional and the thunderbolts painted between deities could become pillars between shaft faces. Taking the process one step farther, mortals could become gods.

Architecture of the Qidan thus emerges as without equal in this art of transformation. One can now return underground to the Eastern Mausoleum central chamber—that ambiguous room whose shape has been charted as between circle and octagon (see fig. 239)—and find other associations (besides the one suggested in the discussion of Sokkurăm in the preceding chapter) between its wall paintings and Chinese views of the cosmos, on the one hand, and between wall paintings and religious sculpture on the other. Four sides of that central space led to other chambers: passages to the four directions (space). Between them were paintings of the four seasons (time) (fig. 367). According to the approximately 45-degree alignment of the tomb (similar orientation to Abaoji's funerary city; see fig. 230), the seasons are positioned in their proper places in the Chinese cosmos. (Spring is east, summer is south, and so on.) In Tamura and Kobayashi's line drawing, the configuration is as vivid as a true mandala.

What, then, of the center? To understand the Liao explication of octagonal imagery in three dimensions, we must return to our first example of it: the Timber Pagoda. Recall the plan of the fifth story of the Muta, where eight pillars encircle a central image, Vairocana (see fig. 115). Beyond them on the exterior are eight more wooden pillars—counterparts of the stupa-pillars or pillars

that line the edges of the brick pagodas discussed earlier and counterparts, too, of the thunderbolts on the Womb World Mandala. The configuration of the top story, the eight plus the center, caps the main image (Śākyamuni) and its *zaojing* (see fig. 108), creating from base to ninth level a three-dimensional diagram of Buddhist deities, often eight per level, that emanate around an ultimate Buddha. In a pure version of the Womb World Mandala, of course, the main image must be Mahāvairocana. At the Muta, it is Mahāvairocana on the fifth story and Śākyamuni at ground level. Whether or not this was a conscious substitution (perhaps the Muta imagery was intended to replicate a Śākyamuni mandala), the center of the Muta, suggested to represent a Liao emperor's demise, also represented an ultimate Buddhist divinity. The next step is to view the empty interiors of the Data and the Chaoyang North Pagoda as representing the ultimate Buddha, perhaps Vairocana, the ninth and fifth deity, respectively, for completion of three-dimensional mandalas. Basing our interpretation on these ideas of the Muta and Data, the center of the central chamber of the Eastern Mausoleum of Shengzong would represent the deceased ruler, aspiring to attain buddhahood, surrounded by space and time.

The significance of the octagonal plan is so apparent in Liao pagodas that one has added reason to reiterate one last time the choice of an octagonal pattern—for the reliquary box buried inside the White Pagoda one-half kilometer south of Dulesi (see fig. 49), for the octagonal reliquary uncovered in the tomb of an official in service of the Xi Xia in Gansu (see fig. 336), for the choice of decidedly octagonal chambers in the Central Mausoleum at Qingzhou (see fig. 242), and for the use of aboveground octagonal mounds in royal Xi Xia burials in Yinchuan (see figs. 327, 332, and 333).

THE LIAO LEGACY

The octagonal pagoda is the Liao legacy. It is the bequest of the Qidan to architecture in China and North Asia. The Liao octagonal pagoda is an example of the borrowing of artistic forms (the four-sided pagoda, or Indian stupa, and the mandala) by different branches of the faith and endowing them with new meanings. It is the medium through which the Liao implemented the iconography of their borrowed religion. Like the Buddhist hall and imperial tomb, the pagoda is a symbol of Qidan imperial power in Asia. Through the statuary in his hall, through an octagonal funerary space, and through relief carving and the body of the pagoda itself, the Qidan ruler could liken himself to Buddhist divinities. The focus on perpetual monuments by the Qidan is not surprising. The Timber Pagoda, the pavilion and White Pagoda in Jixian, and every tomb were intimately bound to death—the one "passage," we have seen, that inspired permanent architecture among the Qidan's North Asian forebears.

The legacy of Liao in architecture, however, would not have been possible without the continuation of octagonal construction and revitalization of pagodas and other Liao buildings. In the immediate post-Liao centuries, the octagonal pagoda came to be a fixture in Jin monasteries. Subsequently, sometimes the Mongols and often the Manchus returned to Liao monastery sites and revitalized them. We have seen the role of Qing settlement and restoration at Liao sites: in the town adjacent to Huaizhou; as the result of an imperial tour through Jixian en route to the imperial tomb site; and in the refacement and inscriptions at Data in Damingcheng (Ningcheng). Without Manchu restoration, despite changes from Liao or Jin originals that occurred in the process, it is likely that many fewer Liao buildings would have survived.

Yet the octagonal plan had its own power in Man-chu ideology, one that probably enhanced the appeal of Liao pagodas in seventeenth-century Northeast Asia. In that century, the octagonal plan was a motivating force as powerful for the Manchus as it had been in the same regions of Asia seven and six centuries earlier.

Planning Shenyang

Like most cities in China proper or its surrounding territories, the Shenyang of today has a history that dates from the Neolithic period, more than 7,000 years ago.[27] From the Warring States period, when it was part of the state of Yan, the urban history of the site is fairly continuous. Evidence of the Qin-Han city survives in the archaeological and textual records. In 684, the walled city Dinglifu, 2 *li*, 200 *bu* in perimeter, was a Bohai town. Abaoji resettled the area in 919 with people from Jizhou, Hebei province. The Liao walled city, known as Shenzhou, was reused by the Jin, but the city was destroyed at the end of that dynasty. Under Mongolian rule the walls were repaired and portions of the wall along the old Liao boundary were still in use in the Ming walled city. It was this site that the first Manchu ruler, Nu'erhachi (Nurhachi), finally settled on in 1625, after short-lived capitals at four nearby sites, for the capital of his dynasty. It is unclear why Nu'erhachi ultimately chose this city rather than the former Liao-Jin eastern capital, Liaoyang, 80 kilometers southeast, that he had selected as his capital just a year earlier.

Nu'erhachi died one year after the move to Shenyang and it was left to his successor, Hong Taiji, to complete the capital. The city whose construction the second Manchu ruler oversaw consisted of adjacent walled enclosures: the one to the east contained an administrative hall, ten pavilions, two storage halls, and a treasury; the western one enclosed the main halls of state and residential palaces. That western section is the middle one in

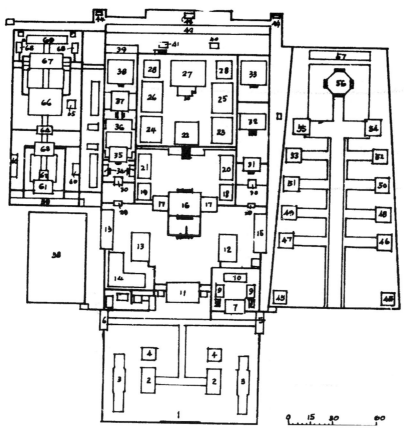

1. Screen Wall	16. Chongzheng Hall	33. Jingdian Hall	55. Pavilion of the Right Wing
2. Anterooms to the Throne	17. Side Gates	34. Side Halls	Commander
Rooms	18. Rihua Tower	35. Huiguang Hall	56. Dazheng Hall (of Administration)
3. Side Rooms	19. Xiaji Tower	36. Baojiu Palace	57. Storehouse for Imperial Chariots
4. Music Pavilions	20. Shishan Studio	37. Jiansi Studio	58. Imperial Storehouse
5. Civil Officials' Rooms	21. Xiezhong Studio	38. Chonghu Pavilion	59. Tuanfang Chamber
6. Military Officials' Rooms	22. Fenghuang Tower	39. Seven Bay Hall	60. Side Halls
7. Ancestral Temple Gate	23. Hengqing Palace	40. Zhan Chamber	61. Miao Tower
8. Shunshan Rooms	24. Fuyong Palace	41. Tang District	62. Platform
9. Offering Halls	25. Guansui Palace	42. Twenty-eight Bay Granary	63. Jiaying Hall
10. Ancestral Temple	26. Linzhi Palace	43. Palace Inspection Room	64. Gate
11. Da Qing Gate	27. Qingning Palace	44. Inspection Rooms	65. Stele Pavilion
12. Xiangfeng Tower	28. Side Halls	45. Pavilions	66. Wensu Pavilion
13. Feilong Pavilion (Storehouse for	29. Gate	46–53. Pavilions of the Eight	(Imperial Library)
Imperial Treasures)	30. Gate	Manchu Banners	67. Yangxi Studio
14. Southern Tower	31. Shunhe Hall	54. Pavilion of the Left Wing	68. Side Halls
15. Seven Bays of Rooms	32. Jiezhi Palace	Commander	69. Nine Bay Hall

FIGURE 368. Plan of Gugong, Shenyang, Liaoning province, eastern and central sectors, seventeenth century; western sector, eighteenth century. [After Steinhardt, *Chinese Imperial City Planning*, p. 170; courtesy of University of Hawai'i Press]

FIGURE 369. Dazheng Hall, Gugong, Shenyang, seventeenth century with later restoration. [Courtesy of Barry Till and Paula Swart]

Figure 368. Although Shenyang became a summer capital after the Qing move to Beijing in 1644, the western sector was not added until 1782, by the Qianlong emperor.

The dominant structure of the eastern sector is an octagonal hall (fig. 369). The standard interpretation of the Dazheng Hall plan is that its eight sides symbolized the eight banners under which Manchu administration was divided. This explanation is plausible since four pairs of the ten pavilions in this sector were also dedicated to each of the Manchu banners (and the other two were for commanders of the right wing and left wing of banners).

Evidence from the city plan of Shenyang in Hong Taiji's day, however, leads one to find additional meaning in the octagon. Figure 370 is a plan of Shenyang after 1680 (thirty-six years after the Qing capital was transferred southwest), the year in which a circular outer wall was added. It was drawn by Fang Dianchun and Zhang Keju, who based their scheme on information in *Peijing zashu* and *Shenyangxian zhi*.[28] According to the texts, the inner square wall and four dots beyond the circular wall were constructed under Hong Taiji. The dots refer to monasteries or pagodas, perhaps monasteries with pagodas, rebuilt in 1643. The remainder of the city at that time consisted of the two-part palace area located in the exact center of the square and eight squares radiating around it. Although one may be inclined to view the diagram as symbolic of the eight banners radiating around the emperor, Fang and Zhang also note that the configuration is that of the center of the Diamond World Mandala (fig. 371).[29] The Diamond World Mandala and the Womb World Mandala (see fig. 116) were transmitted to various points of Asia together and used in pairs in Esoteric ceremonies.[30] Based on the evidence presented earlier, by which we interpreted certain Liao pagodas as three-dimensional versions of mandalas such as the Womb World Mandala, it is equally plausible that a mandala inspired Shenyang's plan. In this case one would view the ruler in his palace at the north center—the position of the main deity in, for instance, the Diamond World Mandala—and religious architecture would demarcate the four world quadrants. Thus both a religious source and a purely Manchu administrative connotation exist for the eight-sided imagery.[31]

One can also propose several examples of native Chinese symbolism for the plan of Shenyang. The nine-quadrants scheme calls to mind the magic square, a part of Chinese architectural symbolism since the construction of the composite ritual hall, the Mingtang (fig. 372).[32] Furthermore, the number 9, symbol of the Chinese emperor, is also the number of north-south and east-west cross streets (three times three by three times three) prescribed for Wangcheng (the ideal Chinese ruler's city) in the *Kaogong ji* (Record of trades) section of *Zhou li* (Rituals of Zhou), believed to be a Han text based on Zhou precedent.[33] The most famous rendering of the textual description was published in *Sanli tu* (Illustrations of the three "ritual classics") in 1676 (fig. 373). But since earlier versions existed, the *Kaogong ji* scheme, the same plan resurrected at Khubilai's court for the design of his great capital Dadu

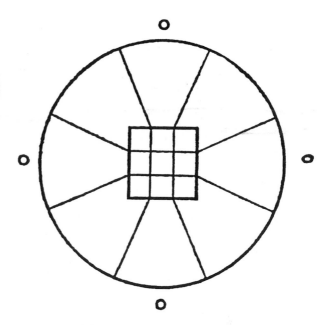

FIGURE 370. Schematic plan of Shenyang in the seventeenth century. [After Fang and Zhang, "Shenyang Gugong," p. 47]

beneath Ming-Qing Beijing,[34] could have inspired the Manchu capital plan at Shenyang. The fact that such a plan had Chinese and Manchu pedigree, the latter also traceable to a Liao penchant for octagonal planning, made Shenyang's design a suprasymbolic city design. In all cases, such clear implementation of symbolism in architectural planning, beginning with the first Manchu rulers, suggests that they were not only ready restorers of octagonal buildings constructed by their non-Chinese predecessors in Northeast Asia but also perpetuators of the Liao legacy.

Identity through Architecture

Still, it was the Liao who played the greatest part in the architectural heritage that was to be their own. Although Liao monasteries retained old Chinese elements with meaning such as the pagoda (a sym-

FIGURE 371. Diamond World Mandala, Tō-ji, Kyōto, second half of ninth century. [After Ishida, *Mandara no mikata*, 1984, p. 33; published with permission of Iwanami Shoten]

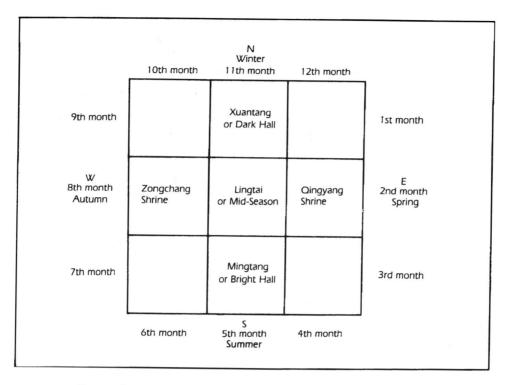

FIGURE 372. Rooms of Mingtang shown in positions of a magic square. [After Steinhardt, *Chinese Traditional Architecture*, p. 75; courtesy of China Institute in America]

bol of the Buddha) or icons of the Buddhist pantheon inside monastery halls, the central, prominent tall buildings and monumental main images beneath *zaojing* suggest the overlaying of what had to be retained with the explicit message of strong new imperialism focused on imagery of the ruler, his power, and his position in the Buddhist world. The simple spatial arrangement of one tall building and one main hall, interestingly, is found also in the Lamaist religious architecture at the Manchu summer resort Chengde.[35]

How the Liao came to create such masterful buildings and meaning-laden architectural spaces is explained by more than religion. Architectural components—bracket arms, beams, struts, braces

—hold no intrinsic meaning in Chinese culture. They are simple wooden parts. It is only when they are used out of context (as by the Liao or later by the Manchus) that those components acquire meaning. Even in Chinese-patronized construction such as a brick tomb, copies of wooden architectural elements can transform the palace of life into the house of death. The same building parts have a simpler but equally powerful meaning for Qidan patrons. In temple architecture, a building with corbel brackets such as Guanyinge or Yingxian Timber Pagoda, or one less explicitly symbolic, is a *Chinese* building as much as a *Buddhist* building. Below ground level, the wholesale adoption of subterranean burial in a tomb, like the making of a perma-

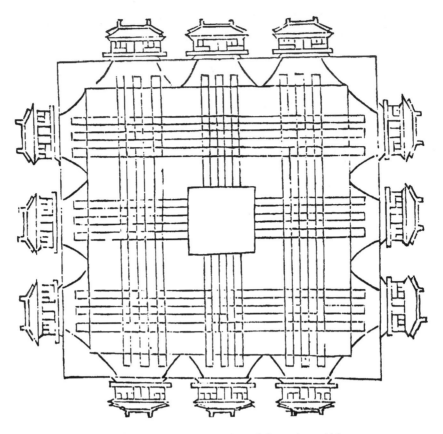

FIGURE 373. "Wangcheng." [After Nalan, *Sanli tu*, 1676, pt. 1, *juan* 4/2b]

nent capital or palace complex, even if neither palace nor its city were used year round, are examples in architecture of absorption of nonnative forms with their meanings and, moreover, vehicles for moving the absorbers into the new culture.

Liao architecture provides few examples of the borrowing of once symbolic forms for purely decorative purposes or evidence of the collaboration of Chinese and non-Chinese style with no meaning at all. Such instances are better found in painting or the minor arts. Liao architecture of life and death was grand in scale: it required the kind of human and economic commitment that demands mean-

ing. The purposes of the Guanyin Pavilion, the Muta, and the royal tombs at Qingzhou were powerful and explicit. And the Liao were true master builders. They made an imperial tradition, a monumental and a symbolic one, for people who had never had one before. In this endeavor they were more successful than many of their predecessors at China's borders.

Apart from its pivotal role as a bridge between earlier, seminomadic North Asia of the Korean peninsula and later Manchu construction, Liao architecture is an entity in Chinese architectural history because in the process of cultural identification through architecture the Liao became participants in and preservers of the Chinese concept of tradition, perhaps unknowingly, at China's borders during centuries when native Chinese architectural initiatives were not at their peak. Between 947 and 1125, the Liao created an imperial identity and left a cultural legacy with architecture as a key medium. The imperial Qidan emerge as geniuses in the making of their own architectural tradition, in providing a legacy of construction for future Northeast Asia, and in advancing Chinese architecture to its highest level in medieval times.

Notes

1. INTRODUCTION

1. Khitan and Kitan are the most common English names of this people. Throughout this book they are referred to as Qidan, the pinyin romanization of the two-character modern Chinese pronunciation of the name.

2. Scholars continue to debate many aspects of the history of Inner Asia in the first millennium. The information offered in this paragraph and the next two is intended to provide a general framework for events that led up to the formation of the Liao empire. Here I have relied mostly on Franke and Twitchett (1994, 44–53). I thank Professor Twitchett as well for two prepublication versions of his chapters on Liao from this work and for many

helpful discussions. In addition I have consulted Wittfogel and Feng (1949), Otagi (1959), Pulleyblank (1983), and Sinor (1990).

3. On the Xianbei see Eberhard (1949) and Pulleyblank (1983).

4. On the Bohai see Komai (1977, pt. 2).

5. The sixteen prefectures of North China were ceded to Liao in 937. Their reclamation continued to be a rallying point for Song mobilization against Liao for the rest of Liao-Song history.

6. This aspect of Qidan burial practice is discussed in Chapter 10. For a bibliography see the notes for that chapter.

7. Some have speculated that statues of Qidan ancestors were worshiped in the so-called Stone House. For a discussion see Chapter 10.

8. For general discussions of shamanism see Eliade (1964), Hoppal (1984), and Balzer (1990).

9. On Liao Shangjing see *Linhuang shiji* (1988, 21–29), Steinhardt (1990, 123–125), Murata (1981, 131–137), and Tamura (1964, vol. 1, 315–326).

10. For information on what may have been in these Bohai capitals see Komai (1992), Li Dianfu (1988), Zhao Hongguang (1988), Liu and Wei (1987), "Bohai Shangjing" (1987), Wei Zuncheng (1982), Chen Xianchang (1980), and Harada and Komai (1939). Virtually nothing is known about the Bohai city on whose ruins Liao Shangjing was built.

11. At other Bohai capitals evidence of Tang-inspired planning is clear. For one such city, plus Japanese and a Korean example, see Steinhardt (1990, 93–121).

12. This was a main theme in my dissertation (Steinhardt 1981a) and the subject of Steinhardt (1983).

13. Steinhardt (1989).

14. Franke and Twitchett (1994, 59). On Liao city building see also Yao Congwu (1959, vol. 1, esp. 193–216) and Jagchid (1981).

15. Torii identified the image as Guanyin in 1936. On this image see Gridley (1993b, 30, 151–153). Gridley has presented additional evidence for the association between the Guanyin at Shangjing and Liao Taizong in several unpublished papers and talks. In a seminar at Harvard during spring semester 1976, Wai-kam Ho suggested that this image might be a white-robed Guanyin.

16. This duality is characterized in a poem by Su Che (1039–1112) translated in Wittfogel and Feng (1949, 220).

17. The reference here is to nomads and seminomads of the Russian and Siberian steppes. Their burial customs are compared with those of the Qidan in Chapter 10.

18. On this painting in the Museum of Fine Arts, Boston, see Paine (n.d., painting 2). For a list of paintings attributed to or associated with Li Zanhua see Cahill (1980a, 44–45). A contemporary painter of Qidan subjects whose works are more likely to be authentic was Hu Gui (act. 923–935). For a list of his works see Cahill (1980a, 34).

19. Tuotuo et al. (*Liaoshi, juan* 72, p. 1211).

20. Tuotuo et al. (*Liaoshi, juan* 71, p. 1200).

21. The power and influence of imperial Liao wives, widows, and mothers cannot be underestimated. On their roles in politics see Holmgren (1986a).

22. All the Liao imperial tombs are discussed in Part Two.

23. On this piece, its history, and related objects see Fontein and Wu (1973, 185–187).

24. A number of crowns are on exhibition in the museums in Jianping and Chaoyang. The Jianping crown is published in Fontein and Wu (1973, 186).

25. For a discussion of Liao masks and a bibliography on related pieces see Fontein and Wu (1973, 192–194).

26. The source of this passage is Wen's "Luting shishi," preserved in *Shuofu, juan* 8 (p. 49a), edited by Tao Zongyi. It is quoted or translated in almost every writing on the subject of Liao burial practice, including Li Yiyou (1991, 90), Wittfogel and Feng (1949, 280), and Fontein and Wu (1973, 192). The use of "five-colored string" may be noteworthy. According to Victor Mair, it was first used by the Aryans (Āryas), Indo-Europeans who entered India from the northwest in the second millennium B.C. They called it *pañca-rūpa-sūtra*.

27. Figure 10 is an illustration of one of the so-called Yizhou *luohan*. This group of Buddhist images first came to the attention of the West in publications of Friedrich Perzyński (1913; 1920). The debate about the sculptures has continued in writings of Wolf (1969), Smithies (1984), and Gridley (1995–1996). In 1994, Paul Goldin found unpublished correspondence between Perzyński and Langdon Warner in the Rübel Library, Harvard University, suggesting that Perzyński himself had questions about the authenticity of the group of statues.

28. This date is published in *Zhongguo mingsheng cidian* (1986, 239). It is not based on an inscription. Nor was the pagoda dated in Takeshima (1944).

29. Little has been written about Liao Dongjing, and I am not aware that its remains have been surveyed. For information see Murata (1981, 137–139) and Chen Shu (1963, 92–93).

30. During the period of Deguang's conquest, these portions of North China, including Bianliang, were un-

der the control of a dynasty called Later Jin (ca. 936–ca. 947). I thank F. Mote for providing me with unpublished portions of his *Later Imperial China*, in which this murky period of North China's history is clarified.

31. This is a polite expression, of course, for an admission that Taizong realized he could not maintain a power base so far south. For the quotation see *Liaoshi, juan* 4, p. 60.

32. Franke and Twitchett (1994, 74).

33. On Liao Nanjing see *Beijingshi* (1985, 69–79); Xu Pingfang (1984b); Hou Renzhi (1984; 1982; 1962; 1959); and Zhu Qiqian (1936).

34. For more on these monasteries and their architecture see Zhao and Yang (1986a; 1986b).

35. Joseph Mullie (1922) was the first to identify and publish a plan of Zuzhou. It is discussed in Part Two with subsequent Liao imperial tomb sites.

36. On differences between government in the northern and southern parts of the empire see Wittfogel and Feng (1949, esp. 434–450) and Franke and Twitchett (1994, 77–80). I thank F. Mote for providing me with the population figure for Chinese residents in the southern portion.

37. For more on Chengtian see Holmgren (1986a).

38. On "rebirth" see Wittfogel and Feng (1949, 273–274).

39. Tamura (1964, vol. 1, p. 333). For more on Liao Zhongjing see Murata (1981, 140–145), Tamura (1964, vol. 1, pp. 330–341), Chen Shu (1963, 89–90), and *Liao Zhongjing jianjie*.

40. For an extensive discussion of this important reign see Franke and Twitchett (1994, 87–114).

41. Tuotuo et al. (*Liaoshi, juan* 41, p. 506). This point will come up again in Chapter 5.

42. On the Xi Xia kingdom see Dunnell (1984; 1988; 1996a) and Franke and Twitchett (1994, 154–214).

43. On the date of the pagoda see Zhang Hanjun (1994, 66). I thank Marilyn Gridley for this reference.

44. On the pagodas in Zhuoxian see Liu Dunzhen (1935, 33–34) and Ecke (1948). For pictures of the pagoda in Jinzhou, Liaoning, see Sekino and Takeshima (1925, vol. 2, pls. 71–74).

45. On the sutras carved in stone see Ledderöse (1990). They were the subject of papers presented by Lothar Ledderöse in March 1991 and April 1992, both in Washington, D.C.

46. On this man and his rise to power see Tao (1976, 14–21) and Franke and Twitchett (1994, 220–226).

47. In fact, most information about Liao monasteries in the *difang zhi* is found in the *siyuan* (["living"] monasteries) section rather than in *guji* (ancient relics).

48. All are cited in full in the Bibliography.

49. Torii (1931).

50. On this extraordinary couple see Fairbank (1994).

51. Although Zhu did not agree with all of Liang's ideas on how to go about identification of old buildings (the issue was texts vs. fieldwork), he knew Liang was the only man for the job. For more on this subject see Fairbank (1994, 49–54).

52. Luo Zhewen and Wu Liangyong were also among this early group of students. Both remain prolific scholars in the fields of Chinese architecture and city planning, respectively, but their research is not focused on the Liao period.

53. Liang (1984, xvii).

54. Boerschmann (1911; 1923; 1925; 1931). (Several of Boerschmann's books were published under similar titles by different publishers in different years, some in German and English editions. The works I consulted are listed in the Bibliography.)

55. Sirén (1924; 1926; 1930).

56. I thank Gustav Ecke's widow, Tseng Yuho (Betty Ecke), for correspondence of 20 November 1990 from which information in this paragraph is drawn.

57. Ecke (1935–1936; 1936–1937; 1942; 1948); and Ecke and Demiéville (1935).

58. Notes from a conversation in October 1988. I gratefully acknowledge the many discussions I had with Alexander Soper about this book and other matters between 1981 and his death in 1993.

59. Sekino's major works relevant to this book are 1932, 1933, and 1938; see also Sekino and Itō (1925), Sekino and Takeshima (1925), and Tokiwa and Sekino (1928–1929). Sekino also was responsible for major contributions to the study of Japanese architecture and Korean architecture and archaeology.

60. Tamura Jitsuzō (1977).

61. *Liang Sicheng wenji* (vols. 1–4) and *Liu Dunzhen wenji* (vols. 1–3).

2. DULESI

1. Liang Sicheng's work (1932a) remains a classic study of a Chinese wooden building. The Society for Research in Chinese Architecture existed for two years before Liang and his colleagues visited Dulesi. Up to that time the group's publications relied extensively on texts. The Dulesi article was the first study of a Chinese building based on fieldwork and measurement of the structure.

2. Liang's approach to the study of a building is discussed in Liang (1932a, 7–10). In this initial investigation he conscientiously used Western architectural terminology, including Latin names for building parts, in his discussion of the Chinese timber-frame structures.

3. Liang Sicheng (1932a, 7).

4. Chen Mingda (1987, 344).

5. On bell towers or drum towers "at the crossroads" of towns see Tanaka Tan (1983).

6. The primary sources consulted for the wooden Liao architecture of Dulesi are the Liu Cheng Stele ("Chongxiu Dulesi bei"), reprinted in Chen Shu (1982, 101); Qi Xiting (*Jixian zhi*, p. 532); Shen Rui, comp., *Jizhou zhi*, vol. 2, p. 344; Zhu Yizun with later additions, *Rixia jiuwen (kao)* (1982 reprint), *juan* 114, pp. 7a–9a; and Miao Quansun et al., *Shuntianfu zhi*, *juan* 25/19a–b (pp. 1607–1608). Twentieth-century sources are Chen Mingda (1987); "Dulesi" (1976); Han Jiagu (1986); Liang Sicheng (1932a); Luo Zhewen (1976); Qi Yingtao (1992i); Sekino (1932); Sekino and Takeshima (1925); Su Bai (1985); Takeshima (1944); Xie Guoxiang (1989); and unpublished papers from "Jinian Dulesi chongjian yiqian zhounian," which I thank Tanaka Tan for sending me.

7. Zhu Yizun (1968 reprint, vol. 16, *juan* 114/7b).

8. Liang Sicheng (1932a, 16).

9. Susan Naquin tells me she has found similar references to An Lushan in her research on temples in Beijing and its environs.

10. For the text of the inscription see Chen Shu (1982), cited in note 6.

11. Liang Sicheng (1932a, 16).

12. Han Kuangsi is identified as Qinwang in Tuotuo et al. (*Liaoshi*, *juan* 13, p. 141). Wittfogel and Feng (1949, 584), refer to Han Kuangsi as Qinwang.

13. Su Bai (1985).

14. Han Kuangsi's biography is also summarized in Franke and Twitchett (1994, 89).

15. Su Bai (1985).

16. The inscription is reprinted in Liang (1932a, 19) and discussed on pp. 18–19. Liang found the stele inscription about its author in *Kangxi Chaoyixian houzhi* (a source unavailable to me). It is the text referred to in this paragraph.

17. Longxing Monastery had a pavilion known as Dabeige (or Foxiangge) built in 971. It has been suggested that the image of Guanyin at Longxingsi may have challenged construction at Dulesi (for a similarly tall building and monumental image). If so, it would hardly be coincidence that the Liao and Song pavilions had the same names. For more on this subject see the discussion of Longxingsi in Chapter 8.

18. Liang (1932a, 19: discussion of "Xiu Dulesi ji" stele inscription).

19. Liang (1932a, 20). He does not specify which of the four structures was Ming.

20. For a translation of one version of the biography of Lu Ban and sources of others see Ruitenbeek (1993, 152–154).

21. For the full story see Liang (1932a, 20).

22. Ibid., p. 24.

23. Ibid.

24. Ibid.

25. Literally, "mountain gate." According to one interpretation the term is evidence that in China the entrance to a monastery may be likened to passage from cities and their vulgarity into the pure realm of the mountains. According to other interpretations, Shanmen should refer only to the entrance gate of a monastery located in mountains or to the entrance gate of a Chan Buddhist monastery. On the meaning of Shanmen see, for example, *Mochizuki Bukkyō daijiten*, vol. 1, pp. 1691b–1692a.

26. Information on the Dulesi Shanmen in this and succeeding paragraphs is taken from Liang (1932a), Sekino (1933), and Chen Mingda (1987).

27. Liang (1932a, 31) makes this comparison between Qing and Song. It is also true for Qing and Liao.

28. Zhang Yuhuan (1985, 75).

29. Chen Mingda (1987, 344) provides information on earthquakes that might have affected Dulesi. Although the numbers may not be exact because his source is local records, this region of Hebei has always been prone to earthquakes.

30. For a brief discussion of three other tenth-century wooden buildings see Steinhardt (1995; 1994, 29–32) and Chapter 3 of this book.

31. Zhang Yuhuan (1985, 80).

32. Chen Mingda (1987, 347).

33. The absence of multistory construction is more evident in Ming-Qing architecture than in earlier building complexes. Although the Song also constructed pavilions on the main monastery axis (discussed in Chapter 8), a notable difference between Liao and Song architectural complexes is the greater number of additional, single-story Song buildings on the main axis. As a result of fewer one-story buildings in Liao religious compounds, the space is more focused on the tall buildings.

34. On *ge* see Lü Jiang (1988).

35. All these examples are from wall paintings. In the pre-Buddhist period, especially during the Han dynasty, high buildings are usually called *lou* (towers) or *que* (gate towers). In contrast to *que*, the *lou* must be freestanding. At the approach to a tomb, however, *que* may also be freestanding. Such is the case for numerous Han and Three Kingdoms and Southern Dynasties (222–589) tombs in the vicinity of Nanjing. In the post-Tang period south of Liao, the pavilion becomes a secular image in poetry and painting. In the Song dynasty and after, pavilions such as that of Prince Deng or the Yellow Crane (Yueyangge) became famous images in painting. (See, for example, Xu Zhen and Zhang Rongqing 1990 or fourteenth-century paintings by Xia Yong in the Freer Gallery of Art and the Museum of Fine Arts, Boston.)

36. Liang Sicheng consistently suggests the statue is from the Tang period. As Marilyn Gridley points out (Gridley 1993b, 90), the Liu Cheng Stele mentions that the image was repaired in 984. Still, she concludes (pp. 84–93 and 110) that the image is closer to Tang style than

other clearly eleventh-century Liao sculptures. Construction around the image makes extensive repair after 984 unlikely.

37. Liang (1932a, 53).

38. Takeshima (1944, 23).

39. Ibid.

40. Liang (1932a, 55–71).

41. Steinhardt (1988, 68).

42. For explanations of the modular system in *Yingzao fashi, juan* 4, see Chen Mingda (1981, vol. 1, pp. 52–64) and Xu and Guo (1984, 40–41, 46).

43. The major study of the Asian ceiling in English is still Soper (1947). Illustrations of what Soper called "Lanternendecke" are found in the various publications on the Mogao Caves, Kizil Caves, and Korean tombs of the Three Kingdoms period. A few are illustrated here in Chapter 13. Although any of them might have given way to or been influenced by wooden construction, the Guanyinge ceiling of Dulesi remains the earliest example of a wooden *zaojing*. It may not be coincidental that the earliest *muqarnas*—the ceiling built up of squinches usually with at least one part of the plan octagonal—is also believed to date from the tenth century (contemporary with Dulesi). According to this theory, the source of this ceiling form associated with Islamic construction is the eastern part of the Islamic world, Iran or farther east in Islamic Central Asia. On this idea see Ettinghausen and Grabar (1987, 172, 222–224). Another theory about the origin of the *muqarnas* places it farther west, in Baghdad, but still during the Liao dynasty (eleventh century). (See Tabbaa 1985.) Either date allows for the possibility that the *zaojing* was an inspiration, from verbal descriptions or firsthand observation, for the *muqarnas* or, alternatively, that a very early form of this ceiling moved eastward into Chinese territory. In any case, the continuous construction of *zaojing* in China after the tenth century is excellent evidence that when called upon to construct a ceiling such as the one in the Ming-period mosque in Xi'an, Chinese technology was available.

44. Liang (1932a, 82).

45. Additional drawings are published in Chen Mingda (1987), the source of information for this paragraph and the following one.

46. There is evidence to suggest that Chinese cartographers did employ grids for mapmaking in the period of the Northern and Southern Dynasties. The first to explain the use of the grid is said to have been Pei Xiu, born in the Wei dynasty (220–265). None of his maps survives, but the text in which he postulated the grid system, the preface to his *Yugong diyu tu* (Maps of the regions of Yugong [Tribute of Yu]), is preserved in *juan* 35 of Fan Xuanling et al., *Jinshu* (Standard history of the Jin). For an alternative interpretation and further discussion of Pei Xiu see Harley and Woodward (1994, 110–113, 124–127). Mapping on grids was common by the Song dynasty. Examples of copies of Song and later maps on grids are found in any standard history of Chinese cartography. See, for example, Wang Yong (1958) and Cao Wanru et al. (1990).

47. Han Jiagu (1986, 52) and "Tianjin Jixian Dulesi ta" (1989, 114) believe the White Pagoda to have been built at the same time as Guanyinge. "Tianjin Jixian Dulesi ta" suggests it may have been rebuilt in 1058, following the earthquake of the previous year. I thank Marilyn Gridley for making me aware of the different dates.

48. The entries for them are found in vol. 2, p. 344 (*juan* 3/1b), and in vol. 2, p. 462 (*juan* 3/60b), respectively.

49. Liang Sicheng (1932b, 93).

50. For the inscription see Liang (1932b, 93).

51. Ibid., p. 94.

52. "Tianjin Jixian Dulesi ta" (1989).

53. Su Bai (1985, 45 and nn. 96 and 98).

54. "Tianjin Jixian Dulesi ta" (1989, 113). The investigative team believes the earthquake of 1057 to have measured 7.8 on the Richter scale.

55. Ibid., pp. 112–114.

3. CHINESE ARCHITECTURE BEFORE DULESI

1. The Northern Wei patronage of the "Tanyao Caves" (nos. 16–20) at Yungang, Shanxi province, in the 460s is a famous pre-Liao example of patronage of monumental art and architectural programs as a means of imperial legitimation.

2. The accession of emperorship by the Mongols, three centuries after the Qidan, is one of the best examples of the central role of architecture in dynastic legitimation. On this subject see Steinhardt (1981a; 1983). For the Liao, as we shall see, architecture was equally important and, furthermore, had unique religious-symbolic associations. Cases for the crucial role of architecture in empire building can also be made for each of the groups mentioned above, but most are beyond the scope of this study.

3. On Qidan customs see Wittfogel and Feng (1949, esp. 237–284).

4. Specifically, the Liao added sculpture at Yun'gang Caves 3 and 11. On their contributions see Mizuno and Nagahiro (1951–1956, vols. 1, 8, 9) and Mizuno (1950, 48).

5. See, for example, *Ancient Chinese Architecture* (1982, 247); Zhang Yuhuan (1985, 593), and Chen Mingda (n.d., 49 and 64). One finds references to the later Tang hall as located in both Wutai and in Taihuai counties. Even the Zhenguosi Main Hall is also sometimes omitted in standard survey literature such as Liu Dunzhen (1984a). It is because of these publications that I was surprised to hear from a member of the Shanxi Province Cultural Relics Bureau in 1986 that these three buildings were the oldest, second oldest, and fourth oldest wooden structures in China. In fact, we shall see that that chronology is now outdated. The locations of many of Shanxi's old buildings are in *xian* that until very recently were off-limits to foreigners.

6. Chai Zejun (1986, 245). Chai's article is, to my knowledge, the first publication about pre-Liao/Song buildings in Shanxi, but his list of Shanxi architecture is far from complete. Fewer than 106 pre-thirteenth-century buildings are on it, and one has no idea what or where the other 30 percent of early wooden buildings are. Chai (1990) also includes a list of Tang through Jin buildings (pp. 44–45), not restricted to Shanxi province.

7. Chai Zejun (1986, 245).

8. This principle of Chinese construction is explained in Soper (1942, 1–21).

9. Hemudu is now an open site with a museum in which Neolithic timber pieces can be seen. For a picture see also *Ancient Chinese Architecture* (1982, 19).

10. For examples of reconstructions see Yang Hong-xun (1976; 1981), Fu Xinian (1981a), and Qi Yingtao (1983).

11. Han precedents for timber-frame architecture are too numerous to list. Several examples are found in Liu Dunzhen (1984a, esp. 70–77) and in illustrations in Wu Hung (1989).

12. The bibliography on Daminggong is long. The most important references are Ma Dezhi (1959a; 1959b; 1961), Guo Yifu (1963), Liu Zhiping and Fu Xinian (1963), Fu Xinian (1973), Yang Hongxun (1987b), and Saehyang Chung (1990). Architectural evidence that gave way to these reconstructions is discussed in Steinhardt (1991, esp. 29–31). Additional bibliography for Tang architecture is found in Steinhardt (1991, ff. 16).

13. Naturally, certain architectural features are standard in eighth- through thirteenth-century construction. Most of them are explained in the discussion of Tang architecture in Steinhardt (1991).

14. On Qinglongsi see Lu Zhaoyin (1964), "Tang Qinglongsi" (1974), Chang Yao (1986), Ma Dezhi (1986; 1989), Yang Hongxun (1987g), and Steinhardt (1991).

15. Chen Mingda (1954, 89).

16. On Nanchansi Main Hall see Chen Mingda (1954), Chai and Liu (1980), Qi and Chai (1980; 1982), and Steinhardt (1984, 102–107).

17. Chai Zejun (1986, 254–255) publishes the hall as 831.

18. "An" can have several translations. One is a nunnery, or convent, as opposed to "si," a monastery. It can also refer to a very humble, possibly grass, dwelling, leading to the English translation, "hermitage."

19. "Jin dongnan Lu'an, Pingshun, Gaoping he Jincheng sixian de gujianzhu" (1958, 34) mentions the hall in three sentences and provides no illustrations. No buildings from Pingshun had been discussed four years earlier in Qi et al. (1954). The only other references to this hall of which I am aware are Yang Lie (1962, 49), in which the hall is simply mentioned by name; Chai Zejun (1986, 255–256); and Li Yuming (1986, 193–194).

20. "Jin dongnan" (1958, 34) and Chai (1990, 44).

21. Officially only four monasteries, Ci'ensi, Chong-fusi, Zhuangyansi, and Ximingsi, two on each side of Great Red Bird Road, which bisected the city, were preserved. The periodical literature about Qinglongsi raised doubts about its total destruction, however, until an inscription on a bronze bell, first mentioned in Ma Dezhi (1989), confirmed the totality.

22. Li Jie (1103; 1974 ed., *juan* 31, vol. 7, p. 3).

23. The best source on Foguangsi Main Hall remains Liang Sicheng (1953).

24. Li Jie (1103; 1974 ed., *juan* 5, vol. 2, p. 8).

25. Naitō (1922) theorized that China's greatest cultural watersheds have occurred in periods of the greatest internal turmoil. See also Miyakawa (1955).

26. Sirén (1956, vol. 1, pp. 150–153). During this century the brushes of Juran and Li Cheng, Huang Quan, Guanxiu, and Gu Hongzhong and Zhou Wenju dramatically altered the future histories of landscape, bird and flower, Chan Buddhist, and figure painting, respectively.

27. The use of ruled lines raises the possibility that *jiehua* employed a module, as, of course, did timber-frame architecture.

28. Cahill (1980b).

29. On Zhenguosi see Qi et al. (1954) and Chai (1986, esp. 256–260; 1989, 25–27).

30. On these images see Fu Tian-chou (1981).

31. The fourth building is the Main Hall (Dachengdian) of the Confucian Temple in Zhengding, Hebei. It is discussed in Qi et al. (1954, 54–55), but it is so heavily restored that I have not included it here. The Song building is discussed in Chapter 8.

32. *Pingyaoxian zhi* was not available to me. Information from it and Figure 71 are taken from Qi et al. (1954).

33. Ibid., p. 49.

34. The inscription is reprinted in Qi et al. (1954, 50–51).

35. Ibid., p. 51.

36. Sickman and Soper (1971, 420).

37. Chai (1986, 259).

38. On Dayunyuan Main Hall see "Jin dongnan Lu'an, Pingshun, Gaoping, he Jincheng" (1958, 43–44), Jiu Guanwu (1958), Yang Lie (1962, 40–49), and Chai (1986, 258).

39. Yang Lie (1962, 44).

40. Ibid.

41. Ibid., p. 45.

42. The only information I have found about West Side Hall is Chai (1986, 256). The building is listed in Chai (1990, 44), but no information is provided.

43. This idea is developed in Steinhardt (1995).

44. The best example of a Tang-style building in Nara is the Kondō of Tōshōdai-ji, built in 759 under the directorship of a Chinese Buddhist monk. In sculpture, pieces such as the Buddhist triad at Yakushi-ji appear so similar to Chinese Buddhist statuary of the metropolitan capitals that some believe the three images were made in China. Sometimes, moreover, Tang images or copies of Tang images, especially in sculpture and painting, have been carried to the farthest reaches of Chinese-influenced Asia, in some cases leading to intentional revivals of Tang styles and other times to uncomfortably Tang-esque works and hybrid works of unknown circumstances of production. Pictures of Tang-inspired buildings, sculpture, and painting of the Nara period (710–794) can be seen in Ooka (1973). For studies of the transmission of Tang painting motifs into Central Asia see Cahill (1958), Steinhardt (1981b; 1987), and Watson (1981). Still, it is important to remember that not every Nara-period Japanese building or statue or painting was inspired by a Chinese prototype.

45. A plan of one of the Tang-style cities in Korea is published in Steinhardt (1990), as are plans of many of the Japanese cities; see pp. 93–121.

46. Feng and Jia (1960).

47. Mo Zongjiang (1979).

48. *Laiyuanxian zhi* was not available to me. The inscription is published in Mo Zongjiang (1979, 57).

49. Feng and Jia (1960, 66).

50. Mo (1979) names specific relatives of Li Yanchao and provides information about them based on his reading of the Five Dynasties' history, *Wudaishi*. Unfortunately, the names Mo gives do not correspond to the numerous Li family members for whom information is given in the standard history of the Five Dynasties period. Mo does not provide sufficiently detailed references to check his sources.

51. A female patron's name, Ning Gongyu, was found on a *dhāraṇī* pillar at Foguangsi. Another ninth-century example of patronage of a Buddhist monument by a powerful military leader is the decoration of Mogao Cave 156 by General Zhang Yichao. In Zhang's case, he had been awarded the title of imperial commissioner after successfully liberating the Dunhuang region from the Tibetans. For more on Zhang Yichao see Yang Jidong (1995). Zhang's success is displayed in cave murals. For illustrations see Akiyama and Matsubara (1969, 87). It is premature to suggest that the breakdown of a strong, central Chinese government (or subsequent rule by a non-Chinese power) might have made it easier for powerful families to patronize monuments.

4. FENGGUOSI

1. The result of this visit was Sekino's (1933) publication about Fengguosi. There are indeed Northern Dynasties Buddhist caves in Yixian. When I attempted to see them in 1992, I was told the road to them was closed.

2. Takeshima (1944, 73).

3. The *Liaoshi* makes no reference to Fengguosi in its discussion of Yizhou. See Tuotuo et al. (*Liaoshi, juan* 39 [*dili zhi, juan* 3], p. 487).

4. As recorded in Takeshima (1944, 50). The term I translate as "divine class" is "*shen.*"

5. Ibid., p. 52.

6. Ibid.

7. Tuotuo et al. (*Liaoshi, juan* 103, pp. 1445–1451). For Takeshima's discussion see Takeshima (1944, 54).

8. Takeshima (1944, 56–57).

9. Standard Buddhist dictionaries such as *Foguang dacidian*, *Bukkyō jiten*, and *Mochizuki Bukkyō daijiten* do not list Daxiongbaodian or Daxiongdian. Instead, under the terms "*dadian*" or "*jindian*" one can find a passage that says Daxiongbaodian is an alternate name for *dadian* or the Japanese Kondō. Nevertheless, "Daxiongbaodian" is a name as common for the main hall of a monastery, especially in Song and Liao times, as the name "Dachengdian" is for the main hall of a Confucian temple complex throughout Chinese history. (The origins of Dachengdian can be traced to two Song sources, one an edict of Song Huizong [r. 1101–1125] and the other a reference in *Quan Songwen, juan* 196, from Chen Yaozuo's "Suzhou

xinxiu Dachengdian ji," vol. 5, p. 382. I thank Chang Che-chia for this information.) "Daxiongbaodian" probably should be understood as "Daxiong," a title for the Buddha, plus "*baodian*," a "Buddha hall," both of which are listed in standard Buddhist dictionaries. I thank F. Mote for this suggestion.

10. After Sekino (1933) and Takeshima (1944) more recent data on Daxiongbaodian are found in Du Xianzhou (1961) and Shao Fuyu (1980).

11. From left to right across the altar they are Śākyamuni, Kanakamuni, Viśvabhū, Vipaśyin, Śikhin, Krakucchanda, and Kāśyapa. For more on the Seven Buddhas at Fengguosi see Gridley (1993b, 148–150).

12. Du Xianzhou (1961, 8).

13. Ibid., p. 12.

14. Chen Mingda (n.d., esp. 53–56) designates the timber-frame hall style the Fengguosi Style. For more on this and Chen's other groupings for the Chinese timber-frame hall see the discussion of the timber frame in Chapter 7.

15. Zhang Yuhuan (1985, 76–77).

16. Ibid., p. 76.

17. My introduction to Chōgen and his work came by way of lectures by John Rosenfield when I was a graduate student and more recently at the University of Pennsylvania in May 1987. On Chōgen's architecture see also Tanaka Tan (1975; 1977a; 1977b). The only discussion in English is Soper (1942, esp. 211–224) and Paine and Soper (1981, 379–383).

18. For discussion of Sanqing Hall and the other Song buildings mentioned here see Chapter 8.

19. Soper (1942, 149–152 and ff. 262) offers a good summary of literature on Jōruri-ji until 1942. For a brief English discussion see Ōmori Kenji (1964).

20. Rhie (1977b) has shown similar parallel developments between the Buddhist sculpture at Fengguosi and Japanese sculpture contemporary to that housed in the Amida Hall of Jōruri-ji.

21. Cao Xun (1984). The model of Fengguosi in the Liao period on exhibition at the monastery follows Figure 94.

22. This reconstruction is also presented in Cao Xun (1984). The boundaries of Jin prefecture have changed in this century. In some of the Japanese publications from the first half of the twentieth century, Fengguosi is included in Jinzhou(xian) rather than Yizhou. On Guangjisi, see also Takeshima (1944, 240–244).

23. Jiafusi is only about 5 kilometers north of Jinzhou, but in Yizhou. See Takeshima (1944, 244–247).

24. The bodhisattva's gaze beyond the upper story of a Guanyin pavilion can be seen today. At a recently reconstructed (brick!) Guanyinge at Guanghuasi in Fuzhou, the upper-story open window functions as it does at Dulesi (fig. 99). In the Fuzhou monastery, the pavilion is not on the main axis. Still, perhaps it is no coincidence that again the same principle is found in former Liao territory of northeastern China and in the southeastern province of Fujian.

25. Du Xianzhou (1961, 13) and Zhang Yuhuan (1985, 76–80).

5. YINGXIAN TIMBER PAGODA

1. Chen Mingda (1980, 2). Chen (1980) is the main source of information on Yingxian Timber Pagoda. In addition, four primary sources are discussed later in this chapter: Chen Menglei et al. (1725, *juan* 108/48a); Wang Xuan et al. (1892, *juan* 169; Taipei reprint, vol. 6, p. 3250); Wu Bing, *Yingzhou xuzhi* (1769, *juan* 4); and *Yingzhou zhi* (Qing period). (The latter two works were not available to me.) Relevant passages from all of them are reprinted in Chen (1980).

2. For additional illustrations of bracket sets see Chen (1980, drawings 20–23).

3. Zhang Yuhuan (1985, 88).

4. Chen (1980, p. 6 and elsewhere).

5. For discussion of the iconography of sculptures on stories two through five see Gridley (1993b, 63–66).

6. Relevant passages from these sources are found in Chen (1980, 229–236).

7. *Yingzhou xuzhi* (1769, *juan* 1), quoted in Chen (1980, 225).

8. For the passage see Chen (1980, 23).

9. Zhang Yuhuan (1985, 88). The testing of pounded mud-brick wall yielded a date of 1000 plus or minus seventy years.

10. Information in this paragraph comes from stelae

inscriptions quoted in Chen (1980, 229–236). Some of the inscriptions are also quoted in local records.

11. Chen (1980, 225), whose source is Song Lian et al., *Yuanshi, juan* 55.

12. The initial report of the sutras found in the Timber Pagoda of Fogongsi was published by Yan et al. (1982). It was superseded by the major publication *Yingxian Muta Liaodai mizang* in 1991.

13. Chen (1980, 23).

14. For more on the Xingzong's childhood, mothers, their involvement in politics, and the accession of Daozong, see Franke and Twitchett (1994, 114–116 and 123–125). On the powerful influence of wives, mothers, and concubines at the Liao court see Holmgren (1986a).

15. The texts have been reconstructed and are reproduced in full in *Yingxian Muta Liaodai mizang* (1991).

16. For a brief discussion of such caves, including some Indian precedents, see Xiao Mo (1989, 35–42).

17. Not every scholar accepts this interpretation of the Tanyao Caves. John Huntington (1986) suggests that the five monumental Northern Wei images represent Śākyamuni, two manifestations of Maitreya, and two manifestations of Amitābha. Those with whom Huntington takes issue, including Alexander Soper, are cited in his article.

18. Famous examples are ninth- to twelfth-century Khmer monuments at various sites around Angkor, Cambodia.

19. Marilyn Gridley (1992; unpublished talks) has discussed the association between the Guanyin at Shangjing (see fig. 5) and Liao royalty. Chapter 12 presents evidence suggesting that in details of tomb construction the Xiao clan exhibited their desire to be viewed as more eminent in status than the ruling Yelü.

20. On the "end of the dharma" see Stone (1985) and Marra (1988).

21. Ledderöse (1990).

22. For a succinct description and discussion of this mandala see Ishida (1987, esp. 29–42). More detailed studies are listed in Ishida's bibliography. The role of Kūkai in the transmission of the mandala to Japan is discussed throughout Ishida's book, especially on pp. 12–21. Interestingly, the ground plan of the Great Buddha Hall at Tōdai-ji in Nara, dedicated to the Esoteric Buddha Vairocana, is similar: eight pillars enclose the central altar. (For an illustration see Mino Yutaka 1986, 35.) Also similar is the plan of the Yumedono (Hall of Dreams) in the east precinct of the Hōryū-ji, Nara, built in 739. (For an illustration see Kuno and Suzuki 1966, 172.) Posthumously, Prince Shōtoku came to be worshiped at the Yumedono. Yet another Nara-period octagonal hall survives at Eizan-ji, also in Nara prefecture. On this building see Fukuyama and Akiyama (1950). The purposes and symbolism of the octagonal hall in East Asia have not been worked out. (Nor have the associations of the octagonal ceiling, which may or may not be related.) At this point, it is important to note that in addition to the abundance of octagonal configurations in Esoteric mandala, several examples of buildings with octagonal plans that can be associated with royal death are known.

6. LIAO MONASTERIES IN THE WESTERN CAPITAL

1. The most famous Northern Wei tomb in Datong, belonging to Sima Jinlong, contained the lacquer screen with illustrations of "Admonitions to the Court Instructress" on it. Artifacts from this tomb are sometimes displayed in a hall of Huayansi today. On excavations of Northern Wei material from Pingcheng see Mizuno (1938); "Datong nanjiao" (1972); "Shanxi Datong nanjiao" (1983); "Shanxi Datong Shijiazhai" (1972); and Su Bai (1978). On Liao additions to the Yun'gang caves see Mizuno (1950, 48).

2. The only premodern map of Pingcheng is the highly idealized plan in Yang Shoujing's (1839–1915) *Shujingzhu tu*. (For an illustration see Steinhardt 1990, 79.) The limited excavation of Pingcheng is discussed in Su Bai (1978).

3. The source of the map of Pingcheng is cited in note 2. For a map of Datong see Yang and Li (1830), *juan* 1, illustration section (source of fig. 117).

4. Grootaers (1945). Neither Huayansi nor Shanhuasi is discussed by Grootaers. On Datong also see Wang Huguo (n.d.).

5. Wang and Wu (1776) and Wang Xuan et al. (1892) are the main primary sources for the history of Huayansi and Shanhuasi. Huayansi is not unique in its division.

Guangshengsi, for instance, in Hongdong, Shanxi province, is also divided into upper and lower monasteries. Location against a hill may have been geomantically desirable, but it led to a natural division of a temple complex into two parts.

6. Wang and Wu (1776, *juan* 15/22b).

7. The most important secondary studies are Liang and Liu (1934) and Takeshima (1944, 74–124), the latter based on fieldwork in the 1920s. Other studies are Ding Mingyi (1980) and Yuan and Tang (1982).

8. Wang Xuan et al. (*Shanxi tongzhi, juan* 169/27a; Taipei reprint, vol. 6, p. 3248); and Wang and Wu (1776, *juan* 15/22b).

9. Liang and Liu (1934, 8). Liang and Liu are not specific about their source. They write only that this information comes from one of three dynastic histories (Song, Liao, or Jin) or *Qidanguo zhi*.

10. Ibid.

11. Tuotuo et al. (*Liaoshi, juan* 22, p. 262) relate that Daozong was in the western capital in the twelfth moon of 1062. The same information is given in *juan* 41 (*dili zhi* 5), p. 506.

12. Tuotuo et al. (*Liaoshi, juan* 41, p. 506). The presentation of imperial portraits also occurred during the Tang period. See Schafer (1963).

13. Tuotuo et al. (*Jinshi, juan* 6, p. 137). Since all the Liao statues in Huayansi's Sutra Library are clay, the mention of bronze imagery is problematic.

14. Song Lian et al. (*Yuanshi, juan* 153, pp. 3619–3620).

15. The text of the stele is published in Takeshima (1944, 110–111).

16. Information from stelae is summarized in Liang and Liu (1934, 7–15) and Takeshima (1944, 107–114).

17. Takeshima (1944, 113).

18. Liang and Liu (1934, 14).

19. Liang and Liu (1934, 28). Takeshima (1944, 80) gives 55 centimeters as the average pillar diameter.

20. Liang and Liu (1934, 27).

21. Liang and Liu (1934, 51); their source is a Jin-period stele they found at the monastery.

22. Liang and Liu (1934, 47) cite Huang Chaoying (of the Song dynasty) as their source of information. In my opinion, the *chiwen* is one of the most unreliable features

by which to suggest a date for a building. They are easily breakable and it seems the tendency for late repair in an early style would be great.

23. Liang and Liu (1934, 36).

24. Of the three architectural styles into which he suggests Chinese timber frames can be divided, Chen Mingda has labeled the least eminent as "Haihui Hall style." See Chen (n.d., 50). (This study is discussed in Chapter 7). Of the architectural historians who studied Haihui Hall before its destruction (Liang, Liu, and Takeshima), none had any doubt that it was a Liao building. They are the only references for this building, which is discussed here only to highlight its characteristically Liao features.

25. In correspondence of April 1996, Marilyn Gridley pointed out that Haihui Hall housed a Ming-period image of Guanyin on Mount Potala, thus suggesting Haihui ("meeting on the sea") to be a reference to the meeting convened by that bodhisattva on Mount Potala where he expounded Buddhist scriptures.

26. The 5-*puzuo* bracket sets discussed thus far are not identical to the 5-*puzuo* bracketing here. The *Yingzao fashi* descriptions and illustrations (see fig. 36) are of one standard form of each type. Although every type has variations, the key to identification remains a count of the relevant components.

27. According to Chai Zejun (1990, 43), platforms tend to be high through the Yuan period, such that the typical middle-to-low-ranking hall stands on a platform one-fifth to one-third the height of its pillars. The Qing architecture manual *Gongbu gongcheng zuofa zeli*, published in 1734, says that platforms should rise 15 percent of the height of a hall's columns.

28. See Takeshima (1944, 110–111) for the text of the stele.

29. Liang and Liu, Takeshima, and Chai all accept 1140 as Daxiongbaodian's date.

30. Chai Zejun (1990, 46) has found these consistencies between the *Yingzao fashi* and Daxiongbao Hall.

31. For more on Daxiongbaodian's *cai* and *zhi* see Liang and Liu (1934, 65) and Chai (1990, 46).

32. In this case Chai (1990, 58) uses the *chiwen* as a means of dating a hall. See note 22.

33. On these ceremonies see Wittfogel and Feng (1949, 215, 274). Their source is Tuotuo et al. (*Liaoshi, juan* 7).

34. Chai (1990, 41–42). And, as we shall see, east-west orientation was clearly significant to the Jin.

35. Wang and Wu (*Datongfu zhi, juan* 15/22a) say it is located in the southeast; but since the plan of the Ming city is certain, there must be a misprint in the text. Information about Shanhuasi is found in Wang Xuan et al. (*Shanxi tongzhi, juan* 169/27b; Taipei reprint, vol. 6, p. 3248); and *Datongfu zhi, juan* 15/22a–b. The secondary sources for information about this monastery are Liang and Liu (1934, 77–161), Takeshima (1944, 125–155), and *Shanhuasi* (1987).

36. Itō's recollection is published in Takeshima (1944, 125).

37. Liang and Liu (1934, 78).

38. Tuotuo et al. (*Songshi, juan* 373 [*liezhuan* 132], pp. 11551–11553).

39. Takeshima (1944, 50).

40. Liang and Liu (1934, 82).

41. Takeshima (1944, 135), based on information from a stele dated 1583.

42. The large members of the Chinese timber frame (*damuzuo*) are described in *juan* 4 and 5 of the *Yingzao fashi. Juan* 6 through 11 are devoted to "lesser carpentry."

43. Chai (1990, 59).

44. On Puxiange see Liang and Liu (1934, 103–111) and Takeshima (1944, 141–143).

7. OTHER LIAO BUDDHIST HALLS

1. Liang Sicheng (1932c) is the only study of the hall; these comments are on p. 2; the sketch map of the site is his fig. 1.

2. Fairbank (1994, 57).

3. Cai and Hong (*Baodixian zhi, juan* 15/1a–b; Taipei reprint, vol. 2, pp. 733–734).

4. The town was called Wuqingjingyi. In addition to the one near Beijing, towns of the same name exist in Shaanxi and Gansu. The information about Hongyan comes from the stele found by Liang Sicheng. See Liang (1932b, 10–11).

5. Liang Sicheng (1932c, 12).

6. I thank F. Mote for pointing out to me that they may be one and the same man. Zhiyi may be the man's name, but it may also refer to him as of "righteous purpose" and Shanshi may be a reference to him as a "benefactor."

7. Liang Sicheng (1932c, 18).

8. Marilyn Gridley has suggested in correspondence of May 1996 that the small, seated deity in front may be a post-Liao addition.

9. Cai and Hong (*Baodixian zhi, juan* 15).

10. On Liu Yuan see Li Fang (1912, *juan* 3/1b–2b).

11. Liang Sicheng (1932c, 9–18).

12. Ibid., p. 28.

13. Ibid., p. 40.

14. Liu Dunzhen (1935, 9–15). Again, this is the only modern study of this monastery.

15. This is the monastery referred to in the discussion of orientation in Chapter 6. Historically, one finds side-by-side halls in the late-fourth-century B.C. bronze engraving of a funerary temple complex uncovered in Pingshan, Hebei. For three illustrations see *Wenwu*, no. 1 (1979):pl. 8, no. 3; p. 23; and p. 24. Could this arrangement be shown to be related to funerary purposes, Kaiyuansi would be another example of the association between Liao monastery construction and immortality.

16. Liu Dunzhen (1935, 10).

17. For discussion of this tomb and illustrations see Shih Hsio-yen (1959).

18. Octagonal columns were also used in various of the Mogao Caves near Dunhuang from the Northern and Southern Dynasties period.

19. Liu Dunzhen (1935, 13) notes that the bracket form is found at pagodas in Damingcheng (a post-Liao name for the Liao central capital, today Ningcheng [see fig. 360]), Chaoyang (see fig. 365), and Fenghuangshan.

20. Liu Dunzhen (1935, 13–14).

21. Ibid., p. 14. Liu Dunzhen did not say whether he believed the hall to be earlier or later.

22. Li Jie (*Yingzao fashi, juan* 30; 1974 ed., vol. 6, p. 64).

23. *Xinchengxian zhi, juan* 3/8b–9a (Taipei reprint, vol. 1, pp. 78–80).

24. Qi Yingtao (1957).

25. Qi Yingtao (1957, 28) gives the date as 1004–1123. Subsequent publications such as Chen Mingda (n.d., 49; 1980) date the hall to 1033.

26. Qi Yingtao (1957, 26).

27. Ibid., p. 27.

28. This statement was made during conversation with a local on 13 August 1992. I was told the man with the key was on holiday and there was no possibility of entering.

29. Liang Sicheng (1932a, 52).

30. The five elements are wood, fire, earth, metal, and water. For discussion of them and their associations in the writings of Dong Zhongshu (second century B.C.) see De Bary et al. (1964, esp. 201–206).

31. Chai Zejun (1990, 43).

32. Ibid., pp. 45–48.

33. Steinhardt (1988, esp. 65–66). For illustrations of plans of these halls see, for example, *Eiraku-kyū hekiga* (1981, 11).

34. These features are all discussed in Steinhardt (1991).

35. Qi Yingtao (1957, 26).

36. On Liao bracketing see Liang Sicheng (1932a, 31–39 and 55–65 for Dulesi's architecture) and Chen Mingda (1980, 45–48 and drawings 20–33). On bracket sets generally see Liang Sicheng and Liu Zhiping in Liang Sicheng et al. (n.d., 113–177), Han Baode (1973), Qi Yingtao (1981, esp. 32–37; 1992c, 56–58), Steinhardt (1984, 122–125), and Chen Mingda (1990, 40–44).

37. The labels are based on the work of Else Glahn (1981).

38. Liu Zhiping (1957a, 82).

39. Liang (1932a) and Liang and Liu (1934). Thus by the time Chen Mingda (1980) was published, the terminology of the bracket set was well known among Chinese architectural historians. Publications of the 1980s and later tend to assume knowledge of the parts of a bracket set according to publications of the Society for Research in Chinese Architecture in the 1930s.

40. This paragraph and those that follow are based on Liang (1932a, 55–57).

41. Li Jie (*Yingzao fashi, juan* 4; 1974 ed., vol. 1, pp. 88–92).

42. Liang and Liu (1934, 19). The same bracket formation is found at Guanyinge, Daxiongbao Hall of Fengguosi, and Sandashi Hall.

43. Chen Mingda (n.d., esp. 50–56). Chen's study was expanded and published as a monograph under the same title by Wenwu chubanshe in 1990. In the later version it is clear that fourteen of the twenty-four buildings he studied were from the Liao period. For his list and data see pp. 64–68.

44. Sui An-der (1992).

45. Demiéville (1925a). Other early studies are Yetts (1926–1928; 1930).

46. Glahn (1975; 1981).

47. Chen Mingda (1981), some of which is included in Liang Sicheng (1983a; 1983b), Xu and Guo (1981), and Guo and Xu (1984). See also Chen Zhongchi (1962), Takeshima Takuichi (1972), Guo and Xu (1979), Xu and Guo (1984), and Xu Bo'an (1985).

48. Chen Mingda (1981, vol. 1, p. 262).

49. I have followed Chen Mingda (1981, vol. 1, p. 49) for the pronunciation of this character. Chen's reading follows a special reading determined by Liang Sicheng. In modern Chinese the character is pronounced "*qi*."

8. SONG WOODEN HALLS AT THE TIME OF LIAO

1. Chai Zejun (1986, 259). The abundance of premodern architecture in Shanxi was also noted in Chapter 3; see note 6 of that chapter.

2. Besides articles on specific Song buildings mentioned in these notes, the following works are useful: *Liang Sicheng wenji* (1985, esp. 114–146); Zhang Yuhuan (1985, esp. 89–105); Qi Yingtao (1992j); and Chen Mingda (1990, after p. 38). No monograph on Song architecture or a Song building has been written. Monographs on Song tombs are mentioned in the endnotes for Chapter 11.

3. Two texts relevant to this reconstruction are Tao Zongyi's *Zhuogeng lu* (Record of rest from the plow), published in 1368, of which *juan* 18 is devoted to the Northern Song capital, and Meng Yuanlao's *Dongjing menghua lu* (Record of dreaming of *hua* in the eastern

capital [of the Song]) of 1148. The erroneous belief that the Forbidden City in Beijing replicated the architecture of the Northern Song capital, held by, among others, Zhu Qiqian, also fueled interest in reconstruction. On Xiangguosi see Soper (1948) and Xu Pingfang (1987).

4. The four main studies of Daxiongbao Hall of Hualinsi are Lin Zhao (1956), Zhang Buqian (1958), Fu Xinian (1981b), and Yang Binglun et al. (1988). They are the sources for the discussion of the structure of Daxiongbao Hall presented here.

5. Relevant records and literary sources are found in Zhang (1958, 1–2). His sources are *Minzhong ji* of 1043, available in several reprinted versions, and *Sanshanzhi* (see *Song-Yuan difangzhi congshu*, vol. 12, *juan* 33, pp. 7985–7986). The earliest extant stele is dated 1182.

6. Yang Binglun et al. (1988, 14).

7. Zhang Buqian (1958, 5).

8. Ibid., p. 13.

9. Ibid., p. 5.

10. Ibid.

11. On Longxingsi see Zheng Dajin et al. (*Zhengdingfu zhi*, *juan* 9/53b–55a; Taipei reprint, vol. 3, pp. 979–983). Liang Sicheng (1933a, 14–29) is the main secondary source on Longxingsi; the stele is mentioned on p. 14. In May 1935, after this report was published, members of the Society for Research in Chinese Architecture again studied Longxingsi and other architecture in Hebei. Their report is published in Liu Dunzhen (1987, 1–23).

12. Liang Sicheng (1933a, 26).

13. Ibid., p. 27.

14. Marilyn Gridley made this suggestion in a talk at the University of Pennsylvania in April 1992. One recalls that the stele inscription giving 984 as the date for Dulesi's Guanyinge is ambiguous about how much might have survived from a Tang building period.

15. Liang mentions other features of Cishi Pavilion he suspects to have been restored in Liang Sicheng (1933a, 26).

16. Restoration is the main concern of post-1930s publications about Longxingsi. On restoration of the Sutra Library see Luo Jiang (1956) and Yu Wuqian (1958).

17. On revolving sutra cabinets see Goodrich (1942).

The most famous surviving Qing-period revolving sutra cabinet is at Tayuan Monastery on Mount Wutai.

18. Liang Ssu-ch'eng (1984, 77).

19. Liang Sicheng (1933a, 18).

20. Ibid., p. 16.

21. *Liang Sicheng wenji* (1982, vol. 1, 183).

22. See, for example, Liang Ssu-ch'eng (1984, 81).

23. To my knowledge, Chongmingsi is published only in Chai (1986, 259–260) and Li Yuming (1986, 199).

24. This argument is presented in Steinhardt (1995).

25. On Kaihuasi see Wang Xuan et al. (*Shanxi tongzhi*, *juan* 170; Taipei reprint, vol. 6, p. 3259) and Chai (1986, 263). This fact is reported in Chai's article.

26. Ibid.

27. On the wall paintings see *Kaihuasi Songdai bihua* (1983).

28. Mo Zongjiang (1945, 1–24).

29. Wang Pingge (*Yucixian zhi*, *juan* 3/10a [see also 9b]; Taipei reprint, vol. 1, p. 221). Yongshousi is also mentioned in Wang Xuan et al. (*Shanxi tongzhi*, *juan* 168; 1892 Taipei reprint, vol. 6, p. 3216).

30. Mo Zongjiang (1945, 12). The article does not mention the Shanmen of Dulesi, perhaps because it is a gate, but scholars were aware of it. As for the architecture of Longxingsi, at the time of the Society for Research in Chinese Architecture's investigation, one recalls, the dates recorded on wooden members had not yet been discovered.

31. Before I was aware of the number of extant three-bay-square halls in China, I sought structurally comparable material among the sizable number of Japanese three-bay-square halls from the twelfth century. Those, however, are directly linked to worship of Amitābha Buddha. In China, the three-bay-square halls serve worshipers of many deities. Thus I do not see a connection between the tenth-to-eleventh-century Chinese buildings and those from the late-Heian period (twelfth century) in Japan. For illustrations and introduction to the Japanese halls see Suzuki (1980, 174–182).

32. Local records for Baoguosi include *Ningbofu zhi* and *Cixian zhi*. The other important sources are *Baoguosi zhi* and stelae, both of which are used (but not cited) in secondary sources listed in note 34. *Baoguosi zhi*

was not available to me. I did not have enough time at Baoguosi to read or copy the stelae.

33. Twitchett and Fairbank (1979, 669) make this general point about the change in monastery names.

34. On Daxiongbao Hall of Baoguosi see Dou Xuezhi et al. (1957), Lin Shimin (1980), and discussions in Chen Mingda (n.d.), Fu Xinian (1981b), and Huang Yongquan (1956).

35. Dou Xuezhi et al. (1957, 55).

36. Ibid.

37. Ibid.

38. Ibid.

39. Ibid.

40. Ibid.

41. The only study of Xuanmiaoguan of which I am aware is Lin Zhao (1957). The stele inscription is mentioned in his article. See also the discussion in Fu Xinian (1981b).

42. According to Lin Zhao (1957, 53), whose source for this capsule history of the temple complex is *Putianxian zhi* (a source not available to me).

43. My sources of information are sections of books that deal with Chinese architecture more generally and publications of the Society for Research in Chinese Architecture. A good discussion, for example, is found in Chai Zejun (1989, 27–30), a publication of the Institute for Preservation and Research of Ancient Architecture in Shanxi. The main older publication is Lin and Liang (1935, 56–61).

44. On these statues see McNair (1988–1989).

45. Zhang Yuhuan (1985, 91). The four types of *diantang* (listed previously) are explicated in Li Jie (*Yingzao fashi, juan* 31; 1974 ed., vol. 7, pp. 5–8).

46. According to the *Yingzao fashi*, in all four constructions the great beam is supposed to span ten rafters.

47. Xiao Xun (1398; 1963 reprint, p. 1).

48. My main source on these buildings is Li Yuming (1986, 207–213). The three buildings are listed by Chai Zejun (1990, 44) but not discussed.

49. Chai lists this building as *shaosheng* 4, which corresponds to the year 1097. Li Yuming (1986, 209) gives the date as *daguan* 1, or 1107. Since I have not been able to confirm either's sources, I give the date here as ca. 1100.

50. A cross section of this building is published in Zhang Yuhuan (1986, fig. 5–6–17). It is not included in the Chinese version of this book (1985).

51. On Chuzu'an's Main Hall see Liu Dunzhen (1937, esp. 112–114) and Qi Yingtao (1979).

52. Qi Yingtao (1979, 61).

53. All measurements are provided in Qi Yingtao's article.

54. Qi Yingtao (1979, 63).

55. Architectural historians in China tend to note the existence or omission of the *pupai* tiebeam—the beam placed underneath the *lan'e* (architrave) to reinforce it—as a key feature for dating a building. So far it has not proved a definitive means. Its earliest use is at this time thought to be at the Main Hall of Dayunyuan. At Guanyin Pavilion of Dulesi the additional tiebeam is found only on the *pingzuo* level.

56. Other studies of Song imperial architecture might use textual evidence in order to include buildings from the Northern Song capital as well. For reasons mentioned at the beginning of the chapter, they have been omitted from discussion here.

57. Recent studies have led to important research on facades of Mogao Caves 53, 431, and 444. Their architectural details confirm what has been discussed in this chapter concerning freestanding wooden buildings, but these structures do not shed new light on the subject of Liao architecture. Serious discussion of the facades is therefore omitted, although they will be relevant to a funerary object discussed in Chapter 11. For more information on the facades see Pan and Ma (1985, 123–133) and Xiao Mo (1989, 313–323).

9. JIN ARCHITECTURE

1. See, for example, Sekino and Takeshima (1925), Takeshima (1944), Liang and Liu (1934), Sickman and Soper (1971), Liu Dunzhen (1984a), and *Liang Sicheng wenji* (1985). In all these discussions, the focus is on Liao buildings or Liao-Jin architecture from Datong. Only Zhang Yuhuan (1985) separated Jin architecture from Liao.

There are, by contrast, an increasing number of studies of Jin civilization. See, for example, Chan Hok-lam (1970), Tao Jing-shen (1976), and Tillman and West (1995).

2. Even through the period of Mongolian rule, the southern tradition in architecture continues in the south. A good example of it is the Main Hall of Zhenrusi in Shanghai. For an illustration see *Ancient Chinese Architecture* (1982, 126).

3. The Jin ruled from five capitals, as had Liao, but in the course of their history used a total of six capital cities. The sixth, the initial capital, Shangjing, was moved to a second site farther south. On these cities see Steinhardt (1990, 128–136).

4. Shanxi is the main province for the study of Jin tombs, as well, but not the only one. It is also the location of Jin imperial tombs, in Changzhi, southern Shanxi. Shanxi is also the most important province for Jin drama and wall painting.

5. On Chongfusi see Wang Xuan et al. (*Shanxi tongzhi, juan* 170; Taipei reprint, vol. 6, p. 3255); Chai Zejun and Li Zhengyun (1993); Chai Zejun (1989, 39–42); Li Liangjiao (1959); and Luo Zhewen (1953). On its Guanyin Hall see Luo Zhewen (1953, 37–42).

6. Although Mituo Hall has been translated as Maitreya Hall in Zhang Yuhuan (1986) and Chai (1989), Mituo is a shortened version of Amituofo, or Amitābha. The Chinese rendering of Maitreya is Mile.

7. On these paintings see *Fogongsi Shijiata he Chongfusi Liao, Jin bihua* (1983) and Jin Weinuo (1988, pls. 48–51).

8. Li Jie (1974, *juan* 31; vol. 7, p. 16).

9. The term is used in Liang Ssu-ch'eng (1984, 40). See Zhang Yuhuan (1985, 104–105) on trusses in Jin architecture.

10. No study has been devoted to this extraordinary ceiling or its hall. Information is found in Chai (1986, 267).

11. On these paintings see Karetsky (1980), Fu Xinian (1982), and *Yanshansi Jindai bihua* (1983).

12. After Yanshansi, the wall painting tradition in Shanxi continued at Yonglegong, Guangshengsi, and Xinghuasi, to name a few sites. Examples of these paintings can be seen in Jin Weinuo (1988, pls. 80–127). In a

talk at the Metropolitan Museum, New York City, in May 1993, Richard Barnhart suggested that wall painting talent at the time of Mongolian rule may have emerged from the ranks of former court painters. Perhaps what appears to be a serious burst of wall painting in the Jin period may be attributed to unemployed figure painters from the former Northern Song court who went west to Shanxi rather than south to Lin'an (Hangzhou).

10. THE IMPERIAL QIDAN FUNERARY TRADITION

1. As mentioned in note 1 to the Introduction, this book makes no attempt to shed new light on, or debate, the ethnic origins of the Qidan. It follows opinions or summarizes discussions of those who have engaged in the questions such as Wittfogel and Feng (1949), Pulleyblank (1983), Sinor (1990), and Franke and Twitchett (1994).

2. Wei Zheng (*Suishu, juan* 49, p. 1881) and Li Yanshou (*Beishi, juan* 94 [*liezhuan* 82], p. 3128).

3. Li Xu (*Jiu Tangshu, Beidi zhuan, juan* 199 [*liezhuan* 149]; Taipei reprint of *Sibu beiyao* ed., pt. 2, *juan* 199/5b.

4. Jing Ai (1982, 108). Indeed, if one looks hard enough, one can even find other "Inner Asian" precedents that might be construed as explanations for Liao burial practices. As precedent for Empress Yingtian's burial of her hand, for instance, one might turn to the death of the Uyghur *khaghan* Moyancuho in 759. In that year his wife, the Princess of Ningguo, broke with established custom and slashed her face rather than accompany her husband into the grave. (This incident is related in Sinor 1990, 327). There is no reason to believe Yingtian sought a precedent for her actions. Even if she did, the decision nevertheless marks a radical change in attitude toward death and life—implying that she understood the potential of a Qidan empire and, further, that Yingtian determined her principal purpose was to influence events in that empire's future.

5. Li Yiyou (1987a, 189).

6. Li Yiyou (1991, 90).

7. Zhang Shunmin, "Huaman lu," preserved in *Shuofu, juan* 18, also accounted in Li Yiyou (1987a, 189).

8. For more on the tomb of the Princess of Chenguo

see the discussion in Chapter 12. Six studies have attempted to assess texts that describe Qidan burial practices in the light of excavations or to categorize the tombs themselves. They are Jing Ai (1982), Feng Yongqian (1987), Yang Jing (1987), Li Yiyou (1987a; 1991), and Tian and Zhang (1992).

9. Colvin (1991, ix).

10. Relevant sections of Robert Hertz and A. Van Gennep are summarized in the introduction to Huntington and Metcalf (1979). See also Hertz (1960). Of Clifford Geertz's numerous writings, those listed in the Bibliography are considered especially relevant.

11. The word "tradition" has been used numerous times here and in my conclusions to the study of Liao timber-frame architecture. My usage follows definitions on p. 1934 of the second edition of *Webster's Unabridged Dictionary* (1980)—namely, "a long-established custom or practice that has the effect of an unwritten law; specifically, any of the usages of a school of art or literature handed down through the generations and generally observed" and "the delivery of opinions, doctrines, practices, rites, and customs from generation to generation by oral communication."

12. Tuotuo et al. (*Liaoshi, juan* 2, pp. 23–24).

13. In the summer of 1992 I was told by residents of both Balinyouqi and Balinzuoqi that, due to water damage, no roads to Zuzhou were open. Foreigners did go to Zuzhou in 1987 and 1993.

14. Mullie (1922, 139).

15. Ibid., p. 141. It is a futile exercise to try to reconstruct Mongolian place-names from Mullie's French romanization of them. The few of them referred to here that are not obvious (such as Yellow River) are given as Mullie wrote them (such as Bayan-gol River).

16. Tuotuo et al. (*Liaoshi, juan* 37, pp. 442–443).

17. Tuotuo et al. (*Liaoshi*) say, simply, "*shi zhi xilou*": "Initially [they] established [or put up] West Tower." The reference is decidedly ambiguous. More will be said later on the possible interpretations of the passage.

18. The Chinese text uses the term "*neicheng*." Like most Chinese references to cities or the walls that encompass them, the word is interchangeable with similar terms. Here *neicheng* refers to the enclosed area in the north-western sector of the larger city (when the plan is shown oriented due north-south as in fig. 229). For more on the terminology of Chinese cities see Steinhardt (1990, 26–28).

19. Tuotuo et al. (*Liaoshi, juan* 37, pp. 442–443). The implication here is that Abaoji wanted to display—for those who had been part of his effort to establish this city, the Qidan, and for his progeny—obvious signs of their native Qidan lifestyle lest they become too enamored with China ways and abandon too much of their own past. I thank F. Mote for pointing out the true meaning of this passage. In light of the text, the role of Chinese imperial architecture on the Qidan road toward empirehood is again emphatic. The buildings and walls were clearly Chinese in style, but the style was so readily adopted because it was adaptable to concerns of an empire-builder like Abaoji. Behind the concealing Chinese facades of buildings and walls could be displayed the emblemata of the Qidan purposes: recognition of their nomadic ancestors, recognition of Abaoji as dynastic founder, examples of the kind of clothing he wore and weapons he used when he conquered a sedentary society. In the Chinese architectural setting, the halls functioned as a museum—they were showcases of items whose time had passed. Their placement in this context turned them into historical artifacts.

20. Published studies include Wang Yuping (1955), Shimada Masao (1955), Zhou Jie (1966), *Liao Shangjing yizhi jianjie* (1983, 5–7), and Wei Changyou (1989). The information offered here is taken primarily from Zhou, Wei, and the Shangjing guidebook. Wei makes no mention of Zhou Jie's work in his article.

21. Zhou Jie (1966, 23).

22. All of these features of Chinese imperial city planning are discussed at length in Steinhardt (1990). On the *gong* plan see Steinhardt (1984, 155); for illustrations of the T-shaped approach and *gong* plan see pp. 132–133, 158, 166, 174, and 180. A fourteenth-century illustration of the central capital of the Jin dynasty (Steinhardt 1990, fig. 133), shows, as discussed in note 19, that at the Jin capital, too, tents and other emblemata of native Nüzhen custom were concealed behind Chinese-style city walls.

23. For illustrations of these cities see Steinhardt (1990, 11, 82, 86, 89). It is conceivable that Abaoji had

some awareness of the appearance of Luoyang. In 926, an envoy from the Later Tang capital (at Luoyang) made a personal report to Abaoji about a coup in that city. I thank Marilyn Gridley for this suggestion. On the incident see Franke and Twitchett (1994, 66).

24. The classic case of the adaptation of Chinese urban patterns in the implementation of a new, non-Chinese dynasty's vision is that of Khubilai Khan and his city Dadu. See my dissertation (Steinhardt 1981a) and Steinhardt (1983).

25. Mullie (1922, 141).

26. Torii Ryūzō (1936, vol. 2, pls. 87–91).

27. Zhang and Feng (1991) and Chen Yongzhi (1991).

28. Zhang and Feng (1991, 127).

29. Chen Yongzhi (1991, 135). Chen's description of the Stone House is more detailed than that of Zhang and Feng. Most of the information in this paragraph is found on p. 135.

30. Chen Yongzhi (1991, 135). Mullie wrote that the house was "empty." Marilyn Gridley, who saw the platform in 1988, relates that it is so low that Mullie could easily have mistaken it for the floor.

31. Zhang and Feng (1991, 131) mention this reference but do not cite the specific passage.

32. Again, Zhang and Feng (1991, 131) mention a passage (in Li Yanshou, *Beishi*, seventh century), but they do not cite the specific section.

33. Chen Yongzhi (1991, 135–138).

34. Numerous studies recount this legend, including Zhang and Feng (1991, 136) and Wittfogel and Feng (1949, 272). Wittfogel and Feng say the tablets of Abaoji's ancestors were on Muyeshan, but not that they were inside the Stone House.

35. Wittfogel and Feng (1949) cite many cases. See, especially, pp. 272–283.

36. The account of the meeting between Yao Kun (the man referred to in note 23) and Abaoji is translated in F. Mote, "Later Imperial China" (unpublished manuscript); I thank Professor Mote for sending me this passage from his manuscript. The implied conversation between Yao Kan and the Qidan ruler again raises the possibility of a connection between architecture in Luoyang and Liao construction. The question was posed to me in Heidel-berg in 1996. Specifically, it was asked if the Qidan had knowledge of the octagonal *mingtang* constructed in Luoyang during the reign of Wu Zetian (684–705). Recent reconstructions of this structure and a taller pagoda behind it are published in *Luoyangshi zhi* (1995); see p. 52 for a picture of excavation at the *mingtang* site. On that *mingtang* see also Forte (1988). If the reconstruction is correct and that *mingtang* was indeed octagonal, then one might query structural relations between a Tang *mingtang* and octagonal architecture of the Liao in general.

37. Hu Jiao's account survives in Ye Longli (*Qidanguo zhi, juan* 25) and in Ouyang Xiu (*Wudaishi ji, juan* 73). The reference to West Tower can be found in *Qidanguo zhi, juan* 25 (Taipei 1968 reprint, p. 175).

38. Tuotuo et al. (*Liaoshi, juan* 37, p. 442).

39. For Chavannes' opinion see Chavannes (1897, 398). These main Western opinions about West Tower are summarized in Wittfogel and Feng (1949, 175, n. 5).

40. Ye Longli (*Qidanguo zhi, juan* 23; Taipei 1968 reprint, p. 168).

41. Wittfogel and Feng (1949, 175).

42. Ibid., p. 176.

43. Chen Yongzhi (1991, 137).

44. The bibliography for Zuling is about the same as for Zuzhou. See especially: Wang Yuping (1955); Zhou Jie (1966); *Liao Shangjing yizhi jianjie* (1983, 8–11); and Wei Changyou (1989).

45. Figure 233 shows the site identified by Jin Yongtian, director of the Balinzuoqi Museum, to Marilyn Gridley as Zuling in 1988. The same scene is published in Zhou Jie (1966) and Zhang and Feng (1991).

46. For discussion of the figure and other excavated objects see Zhou Jie (1966, 264–265).

47. Wei Changyou (1989, 144).

48. Ibid.

49. The etymology of the word "*ordo*" is beyond the scope of this book. For an explanation of the *ordo* system under Liao government and in pre-Liao times see Wittfogel and Feng (1949, esp. 508–517).

50. Ibid., p. 542.

51. Tuotuo et al. (*Liaoshi, juan* 37, p. 443). Shizong's father was Bei (Abaoji's eldest son), who had been executed in 937.

52. Ibid.

53. This is not to say that many people ever went in search of the burial place of the second Liao emperor. The only reconnaissance report known to me is Zhang Songbo (1984).

54. Ibid., p. 67.

55. Among the numerous monasteries in Inner Mongolia and Liaoning where Liao pagodas survive (some of which are discussed in Chapter 14), it is rare to find one without Jin and/or Qing renovation or restoration. The Manchus and the Qing-period Mongols were responsible for the preservation through renovation of monastery architecture from earlier times across the northern fringe of their empire, even into today's Russian Mongolia. During his excavation of the site of thirteenth-century (Mongolian period) Qara-qorum, for instance, Sergei Kiselev found the monastery Erdeni-ts'u. For discussion and illustrations see Kiselev (1965, esp. 123–127).

56. Tuotuo et al. (*Liaoshi, juan* 37, p. 443).

57. Ibid., *juan* 38, p. 463.

58. Ibid., *juan* 38, p. 465.

59. Ibid., *juan* 30, p. 352.

60. Ibid., *juan* 37, p. 444.

61. Essentially, this is all the information provided about Qingzhou in the *Liaoshi*. However, the funerary stele found by Father Kervyn referred to in the next paragraph adds details and, most important, the description of Emperor Shengzong's funeral that follows can be visualized through the architecture.

62. In 1992 I was told there was no possibility of getting there. The next summer, however, a group that included several foreigners was permitted to enter one of the tombs.

63. Four Japanese studies provide the majority of information about the three tombs. Beginning with the earliest they are Torii Ryūzō (1931; 1936, relevant sections of four vols.); Tamura and Kobayashi (1953); and Tamura Jitsuzō (1977).

64. Wittfogel and Feng (1949, 278–283).

65. Ibid., p. 283.

66. Tamura and Kobayashi (1953, vol. 1, English abstract, p. 5).

67. The wall paintings were first published in Torii (1931) and have attracted more attention than the tomb architecture. A dissertation by Tsao Hsingyuan (Stanford, 1996) addresses many issues of Liao wall painting.

68. Tamura and Kobayashi (1953, vol. 1, esp. 55–59).

69. Ibid., p. 58.

11. CHINESE FUNERARY ARCHITECTURE BEFORE QINGLING

1. Interlocking pieces of wooden architecture have been excavated at the Neolithic site Hemudu in Zhejiang province. For illustrations see *Ancient Chinese Architecture* (1982, pl. 2).

2. Standard references on the history of Chinese tombs are Xie Mincong (1976), Yang Kuan (1985), Sun Zhongjia et al. (1987), Yang Daoming (1991), and Luo Zhewen (1993). Sites identified as the tombs of the legendary emperors can be found in various Chinese provinces. A few emperors have mausoleum-shrines at more than one site. It is calculated that Shao Hao, son of Huangdi (the so-called Yellow Emperor), acceded to the throne in 2597 B.C., and he is said to have made Qufu his capital. The stone was added in 1111 during the reign of Northern Song emperor Huizong.

3. For an introduction to Shang funerary architecture one can begin with K. C. Chang (1986, esp. 317–339) and continue with Chang (1980). On the royal Shang tombs see Chang (1980, 110–124). For plans of the royal tombs see p. 114; for a structural model of Anyang showing the northwestern position of the royal tombs with respect to the rest of the city see p. 130.

4. Yang Kuan places the beginnings of aboveground mounds in the Spring and Autumn period. See Yang Kuan (1985, 2–3).

5. One of the best examples of the differing functions of underground chambers is the fifth-century B.C. tomb of Marquis Yi of Zeng in Suixian. On it and similar tombs see Thorp (1981–1982). For more on Eastern Zhou tombs see Li Xueqin (1985).

6. This tomb is discussed and illustrated in numerous publications. See, for example, Fong Wen (1980, 334–373) and Thorp (1983).

7. On the Western Han imperial tombs see Liu and Li (1987) and *Han Duling lingyuan yizhi* (1993). For a survey

of the textual documentation for Han tombs and other data see Yang Kuan (1985, 219–241).

8. One hardly knows where to begin with bibliography on Han tombs. Three sources are Wang Zhongshu (1982, 175–205), Pirazzoli-T'Serstevens (1982), and Lim (1987). Several important studies of more specific subjects are Xu Pingfang (1981), *Wangdu Hanmu bihua* (1955), *Changsha Mawangdui yihao Hanmu* (1973), Gai Shanlin (1978), and *Anping Dong Han bihuamu* (1990). This list of publications is selected because, for comparisons with the tombs at Qingzhou, royal or aristocratic Han tombs seem most relevant.

9. Wang Zhongshu (1982, 175–205).

10. These three items are examples of the numerous spectacular artifacts among the thousand-plus-object inventory from the Mawangdui tombs. In addition to *Changsha Mawangdui yihao Hanmu* (1973), see reports on the Mawangdui maps in *Wenwu*, no. 2 (1975): 35–42 and 43–48, *Wenwu*, no. 1 (1976): 18–23, and Zhan Libo (1976).

11. On these tombs see Capon and MacQuitty (1973) and Thorp (1991).

12. Much of this bibliography is found in Lim (1987, 205–209).

13. Good examples of multiple chambers with side rooms are the tombs at Helinge'er, Wangdu, and Anping; for a bibliography see note 8.

14. I saw the remains of these tombs from the roadside at a site labeled "Hanmu cun" in 1993. On the Beiyuan tombs and related tombs see Fairbank (1972, 141–180). Other Han tomb sites in the Liao eastern circuit are at Yingchengzi and Lelang. All three were studied and published by Japanese archaeologists. In addition to Fairbank (1972) see Harada (1930) and Mori and Naitō (1934).

15. For two tombs in Shandong that fit this description see Wang Zhongshu (1982, figs. 262–263). On the Yinan tomb see also Shih Hsio-yen (1959).

16. See Lim (1987, 194–199).

17. Ann Paludan places the origins of the spirit path in the Eastern Han dynasty. On this subject see Paludan (1988; 1989; 1990; 1991) and Weber (1978).

18. For general material on tombs of this period see Xu Pingfang (1981), Paludan (1991, 52–83); Zhu Xie (1936a;

1936b), Till and Swart (1982, 19–67), Yao and Gu (1981), and Lin (1984).

19. The group "Xianbei" brings us into waters as murky as those of the Donghu. Art historians such as James Caswell have tried to identify monuments of Xianbei patronage by clothing worn by their figures. (See Caswell 1988 and for an illustration of a group of worshipers often labeled Xianbei see *Yun'gang shiku* 1977, pl. 63.) Linguistically, the Xianbei are considered proto-Mongolian. The Modern Standard Mandarin word "Xianbei" may be reconstructed as Šärbi. The Tabgatch (Tuoba) were probably a ruling clan of the Šärbi. (I thank Victor Mair for this information.) Here I associate the Xianbei only with four tombs. Each of them has been identified as "Xianbei" by Chinese archaeologists through excavated objects, costume in wall paintings, or the occupant. For more on these tombs see Dien (1991), Su Bai (1977), and Friedley (1979). These four tombs are discussed here rather than in Chapter 13 for three reasons: because of the proposed association between the tomb of the Ruru princess and the tomb of Princess Yongtai; because stylistically the wall paintings in these tombs are closer to those in Tang tombs than to those in tombs from Gansu and Koguryŏ discussed in the later chapter; and because it was from Northern Zhou, during whose reign the Li Xian tomb was built, that the founding emperor of the Sui dynasty (the man who built the city that was to be the Tang capital and where the Tang imperial tombs lie) usurped power.

20. The most extensive publication on this tomb is *Guyuan Bei Weimu qiguanhua* (1988), but the long bibliography on it includes "Ningxia Guyuan Bei Weimu" (1984), Wang Long (1984), Han and Luo (1984), Sun Ji (1989), Soper (1990), Luo Feng (1990), Karetsky and Soper (1991), and Owen (1993).

21. See "Ningxia Guyuan Bei Zhou Li Xian fufu mu" (1985) and Luo Feng (1985).

22. On this ewer and similar finds in "Xianbei" tombs see Wu Zhuo (1987; 1989), Harper (1990), and Pirazzoli-T'Serstevens (1994).

23. On Sima Jinlong's tomb see "Shanxi Datong Shijiazhai Bei Wei Sima Jinlong mu" (1972) and *The Quest for Eternity* (1987, 124–125).

24. See "Hebei Cixian Dong Wei Ruru gongzhu mu" (1984). The Ruru are also known as Ruanruan and, according to Pulleyblank (1983), may be the Avars (Awars).

25. The standard bearers are published in "Hebei Cixian Dong Wei Ruru gongzhu mu" (1984, 15). Female figures in the mural paintings from the tomb of Tang Princess Yongtai are published in countless books and articles. See, for example, Sickman and Soper (1971, cover and fig. 120).

26. On Lou Rui's tomb see "Taiyuanshi Bei Qi Lou Rui mu" (1983) and Su Bai et al. (1983).

27. The theme of Tang as an international empire that cast its influence throughout Asia is accepted among sinologists and has been mentioned earlier. On this subject see, for example, Wright and Twitchett (1973) and Watson (1974).

28. Many of Segalen's photographs are republished in Segalen (1978). For Chavannes' illustrations see Chavannes (1893; 1909–1915). As for so many of the tombs referred to in this chapter, the bibliography on Tang tombs is long. Two good summary studies are He Zichang (1980) and Su Bai (1982); the latter focuses on wall painting but includes a list of the tombs. Xie Mincong's list of tombs and sites is found in Xie Mincong (1976, 89–90).

29. Paludan (1991, esp. 84–120).

30. See Song Minqiu (1075) and an illustrated version by Li Haowen (Yuan period).

31. For the initial excavation report see "Tang Qianling" (1960). See also Chen Guocan (1980).

32. On these tombs see Wang Wenlin et al. (1957).

33. On the royal Shu tomb see Cheng Te-k'un (1945; 1982b) and Feng Han-yi (1947).

34. Cheng Te-k'un (1982b, 92).

35. On Song royal tombs see Guo Husheng et al. (1964), Cheng Te-k'un (1982c, 103–105), and *Gongxian* (1985); for a general discussion of Song tombs see *Xin Zhongguo de kaogu* (1984, 567–601).

36. On the tombs at Baisha see Su Bai (1957). In 1986 I was told the tombs were submerged in water and there was nothing to see.

37. For illustrations see Su Bai (1957, pls. 31 and 43).

38. *Xin Zhongguo de kaogu* (1984, 598).

39. Lists of tombs and classification are found in *Xin Zhongguo de kaogu* (1984, 598–599); a bibliography for those tombs can be found in notes on pp. 648–649.

40. On Jin tombs see *Xin Zhongguo de kaogu* (1984, 607–609), Laing (1978), and Steinhardt (1990–1991, esp. 219, n. 21).

41. On the Fuzhou tomb see *Fuzhou Nan Song Huang Sheng mu* (1982); on the joint burial of Yu Gongzhu and his wife see *Nan Song Yu Gongzhu* (1985).

42. The only publication on these tombs of which I am aware is Demiéville (1925b).

43. Steinhardt (1990–1991).

12. LIAO TOMBS BEYOND QINGLING

1. These are either dated tombs or burials that can be identified as Liao based on inscriptions or excavated objects. The most wide-ranging research on Liao tombs has been undertaken by Li Yiyou of the Institute of Cultural Relics and Archaeology of Inner Mongolia. (See the Bibliography.) In 1992 Li told me that more than 200 Liao tombs were known. Li (1987a, 187) says that more than one hundred had been excavated in the last thirty years. Li (1991, 80) says that several hundred Liao tombs are known. Feng Yongqian studied seventy dated Liao tombs for his 1987 publication. Dieter Kuhn studied ninety-eight tombs from fifty sites for his 1990 publication. For general information in addition to Li, Feng, and Kuhn, see Tian and Zhang (1992). One difficulty with some of the Chinese publications, in particular those of Li Yiyou, is that excavated but unpublished tombs, as well as tombs that await excavation, are discussed.

2. The only publication on this tomb is Li Yiyou (1982). It was reprinted as Li Yiyou (1991). I thank Marilyn Gridley for obtaining the photograph published as Figure 260 from Tian Guanglin for me.

3. Li Yiyou (1982, 175).

4. Ibid.

5. Ibid., p. 176. Li's sources on Yelü Cong are *Liaoshi* and a stele inscription from the site.

6. Ibid., pp. 179–180, whose sources are *Fengshi jianwen lu*, *Shilin guangji*, and *Yongle dadian*.

7. For illustrations of a royal Song spirit path see Fig-

ure 258. For a discussion see Paludan (1991, 126, 129); for extensive photographs of Northern Song imperial tombs see Paludan (1991, 121–155).

8. Li Yiyou (1982, 181).

9. On the Prince of Wei tomb see Zheng Shaozong (1956).

10. On this tomb see "Liaodai Yelü Yanning mu" (1980) and Ji Xunjie (1987).

11. "Liaodai Yelü Yanning mu" (1980, 18). According to the report, iron nails were also used in undated Liao tombs excavated at Dayingzi (site of the Prince of Wei tomb) and at Jianping, Liaoning. Those tombs are published in *Kaogu*, no. 2 (1960).

12. On the Shazigou tomb see Shao Guotian (1987).

13. On the tomb of Jiayili's concubine see Zheng Shaozong (1981).

14. The initial articles on the tomb of the Chenguo princess were published in *Wenwu*, no. 11 (1987). These included the excavation report (pp. 4–24), Zhang Yu's study of burial garments (pp. 25–28), and Li Yiyou's study of belts found in the tomb (pp. 29–35). See also Zhang Yu (1987b), Shi Guiping (1987), and Zhang Bozhong (1992). An undated pamphlet, "Liao Chenguo gongzhumu wenwuzhan," was published in conjunction with exhibitions of tomb finds shown in Huhehaote and at the Shaanxi History Museum in Xi'an, both in 1992. The major publication is now *Liao Chenguo gongzhu mu* (1993). In it, one finds a few discrepancies concerning previously published dates of the three tombs.

15. One finds numerous examples of the painting of heavenly bodies on the ceilings of Chinese tombs. The practice was already in place in the Western Han dynasty in Tomb 61 and the Tomb of Bu Qianqiu, both in Luoyang. (On them see Chaves 1968 and Cahill 1979, both of which cite Chinese excavation reports.) When constellations were not painted, it was still common to depict the *sishen*—four directional animals—on the tomb walls associated with their directions for directional and seasonal (space and time) markers. Examples of this practice are too numerous to name. It continued after the Han dynasty and outside China. See, for instance, the Tang-contemporary Takamatsuzuka tomb near Asuka, Japan. (See Kidder 1972 and 1973, for example.)

16. Death masks are discussed later with reference to Tomb 6 at Haoqianying.

17. On Xiao Jin's tomb see Li Yufeng and Yuan Haibo (1988).

18. An article on this subject by Li Yiyou in the initial issue of *Nei Menggu wenwu kaogu* is cited by Li and Yuan (1988). The article does not appear in the run of the periodical that commenced in the 1970s, however, nor vol. 1 of the 1990s.

19. On this tomb see Zheng Shaozong (1962).

20. They are published in Li Wenxin (1954).

21. On these tombs see Ta La and Yi You (1984).

22. Even though the excavation report was published twice, the plan of Yelü Yixian's tomb has not been published. See *Wenwu ziliao congkan* 1 (1977) and *Beifang wenwu*, no. 2 (1988).

23. Shao Guotian (1984) dates the tomb "mid-Liao."

24. This is one of several Liao tombs discussed in one of the earliest publications on the subject. See Li Wenxin (1954) from which Figures 271 and 272 are taken.

25. Three Liao tombs with Qidan occupants probably have dates between the Aohanqi tomb of 1032–1054 and this one. The tomb of Yelü Yixian is the least securely dated of this group. The other two are the tomb of Yelü Renxian of 1071 and the tomb of Xiao Dewen of 1075. Neither plan is published. On Yelü Renxian's tomb see *Kaogu*, no. 7 (1988); on Xiao Dewen's tomb see Li Wenxin (1954).

26. On this tomb see Shao Guotian (1978).

27. Ibid., p. 121.

28. The Kulunqi tombs have been published in the order in which they were excavated. Tomb 1 was first published in Chen Xiangwei and Wang Jianqun (1973) with subsequent studies of its wall paintings by Johnson (1983) and Rorex (1984). Tomb 2 was published in Wang Jianqun (1978). Tombs 5 and 6 were published in "Kulunqi diwu-, liuhao Liaomu" (1982) and Tombs 7 and 8 in Qi Xiaoguang (1987). For further studies of wall paintings in the various tombs see Wang Zeqing (1973), Zheng Long (1982), and Jin Shen (1982). The most recent and definitive study is Wang and Chen (1989), the only reference, to my knowledge, for Tombs 3 and 4.

29. These are examples of the sorts of associations be-

tween Liao burial practice and tomb decoration suggested in Chapter 10 to correspond to general explanations of ceremonies celebrating life's liminal phases. Themes of passages through life have been associated with Han tombs at Helinge'er and Anping and with tombs from the Yuan period. On this last point see Steinhardt (1990–1991). On the wedding of a Liao princess see Johnson (1983).

30. In the initial reports cited in note 28.

31. Wang and Chen (1989, 76).

32. Ibid., p. 67.

33. The tomb is discussed in Yan Yu (1960b).

34. On the Xiao Paolu tomb see Feng Yongqian (1983).

35. See Feng Yongqian (1983, 626) for photographs. Their quality is too poor for reproduction here.

36. Ibid., p. 627.

37. See Wen Lihe (1989).

38. Ibid., pp. 327–329.

39. Wang Wenlin (1957, 34). According to Sima Tan and Sima Qian (*Shi ji, juan* 6, p. 265), on the floor of Qin Shi Huangdi's tomb was a stone map of the empire on which mercury flowed through the rivers. Another fascinating and at this time unique tomb floor is that of the Ruru princess (discussed in Chapter 11) on which a carpet motif was painted.

40. On this tomb and the others from the site see "Nei Menggu Shanzuizi 'Gu Yelüshi' mu" (1981).

41. Xiang Chunsong (1981).

42. On these tombs see Xiang Chunsong (1982).

43. Jing Ai (1982).

44. Ibid., p. 104.

45. A famous example is the lacquer sarcophagus excavated at Guyuan; for a bibliography see Chapter 11, note 20.

46. Jing Ai (1982, 109, 114). Ebrey (1990), too, notes the sharp rise in cremation burial among the Chinese population of Song China in the tenth century. The greater number of cremation burials in Qidan territory in close proximity to China is logical. For more on this subject see Ebrey (1990) and Ebner von Eschenbach (1994). Jing Ai's study was not used by Ebrey or by Ebner von Eschenbach.

47. Jing Ai (1982, 109).

48. Ibid., p. 109.

49. Ibid., p. 110.

50. Yang Jing (1987, 213).

51. Li Yiyou (1987a; 1991).

52. Li Yiyou (1991, 80).

53. For Li's various estimates see note 1.

54. Li Yiyou (1987a, 190).

55. Li Yiyou (1991, 84).

56. Li Yiyou (1987a, 190).

57. Li Yiyou (1991, 83).

58. Li Yiyou (1987a, 190).

59. Li Yiyou (1991, 84).

60. To my knowledge, no one has published statistics on tomb orientation for Chinese or Liao tombs. This observation is based on my own informal survey.

61. Li Yiyou (1991, 91).

62. Ibid., p. 94.

63. Wang and Chen (1989, 8–9 and 79–80).

64. Li Yiyou (1991, 94).

65. Tian and Zhang (1992).

66. The Haoqianying tomb find is reported in several articles in *Wenwu*, no. 9 (1983). See Lu Sixian and Du Chengwu (1983) and Ji Chengzhang (1983). An article by Li Yiyou on Qidan hairstyles also is published in this issue of *Wenwu*; see Li Yiyou (1983).

67. Lu and Du (1983, 2).

68. Ibid., p. 5.

69. The other two Haoqianying tombs are discussed in the same articles cited in note 66.

70. For a list of other Liao tombs where metal netting or face masks have been uncovered see Li Yiyou (1987a, 188). He does not include Haoqianying Tomb 6.

71. Ji Chengzhang (1983, 9).

72. Ibid.

73. For a description of trepanation by northern steppe nomads (sometimes known as Scythians) see Jettmar (1967, 117–118).

74. Ibid.

75. Ibid., p. 118.

76. The bibliography on Han burial practices and the Han "quest for eternity" is long. See, for example, Loewe (1979; 1982), Kuwayama (1991, 1–15), and Poo (1990). The jade burial garments worn by Prince Liu Sheng and Prin-

cess Dou Wan are published in most discussions of Han art or archaeology. See, for example, Capon and Mac-Quitty (1977, pls. between pp. 48 and 49), Pirazzoli T'Serstevens (1982, 107), or Wang Zhongshu (1982, fig. 280).

77. It was the ambiance—a museum of largely twentieth-century or natural history displays in this out-of-the-way town in Inner Mongolia—that enhanced my utter surprise at finding this funerary house and led me to personalize this paragraph. I assume that the Balinyouqi Museum or a local Cultural Relics team plans to publish this find.

78. The silk paintings hung on either side of the coffin. Articles on this tomb and its contents are in *Wenwu*, no. 12 (1975). For the initial report see "Faku Yemaotai Liaomu" (1975). On the paintings see Yang Renkai (1975; 1983; 1984), Vinograd (1981), and Cahill (1980b).

79. "Faku Yemaotai Liaomu" (1975, 26). Not enough painted architectural members remain in Qidan tombs to permit a general statement about the frequency of this practice. Excellent examples of painted architectural molding in a Song tomb interior are published in Su Bai (1957). Painting of architectural components did occur at the three Qingzhou tombs (see fig. 281).

80. The excavation report ("Faku Yemaotai Liaomu" 1975) says 2.25 by 1.24 meters. These dimensions are from the detailed discussion of the wooden sarcophagus, Cao Xun (1975).

81. Cao Xun (1975, 51).

82. The Princeton panels were acquired in 1995. Their accession numbers are 1995–76 through 1995–109. Several can be seen in an advertisement in *Orientations* (January 1994).

83. Cao Xun (1975, 54).

84. Li Jie (*Yingzao fashi*; 1974 ed., vol. 2, pp. 23–134; vol. 3, pp. 1–28).

85. The articles in *Wenwu*, no. 12 (1975) (see notes 79 and 80 above) also refer to the piece as *xiaoshi*, literally "small house." *Shi* is probably a reference to its function as a house for mortal remains. *Shi* is also the word used in the label in the Balinyouqi Museum to refer to their architectural model.

86. Li Jie (*Yingzao fashi*, *juan* 10; 1974 ed., vol. 2, p. 121).

87. These figures and their style have been important in the identification of the undated wooden pieces of unknown provenance in the Art Museum, Princeton University.

88. "Faku Yemaotai Liaomu" (1975, 32–33) and Cao Xun (1975, 58).

89. Numerous stone sarcophaguses from the Tang period can be seen in the Shaanxi Provincial Museum in Xi'an. For a comparison between one of these and the Main Hall from Nanchansi see Perlstein (1984).

90. On this tomb see Zhang Hongbo and Li Zhi (1990).

91. Zhang and Li (1990, 27).

92. Ibid., pp. 27–28.

93. The tomb was not published until 1984. See Liu Qian (1984). In addition, Zhang Bozhang (1985) published information that a wooden coffin similar to the one excavated at Yemaotai Tomb 7 was uncovered at Erlinchang, Tongliao, Inner Mongolia. Neither a detailed description nor a picture has been published.

94. On this tomb see Su Tianjun (1962).

95. For the biography of Zhao Dejun see Xue Juzheng (*Jiu Wudaishi*, *juan* 98 [*liezhuan* 13], pp. 1308–1310); for the biography of his grandson, Tuotuo et al. (*Songshi*, *juan* 254 [*liezhuan* 13], p. 8889).

96. These include the tomb of Jiang Chengyi in Xuanhua, Hebei, reported in *Kaogu*, no. 10 (1960) and the tomb of Wang Yue found at Kezuo, Liaoning, reported in *Kaogu*, no. 9 (1962).

97. On Han Xiang's tomb see Tang Yunming (1973).

98. This is the second tomb excavated at Zhangkangcun, Bozhou, Liaoning. See Liu Qian (1984, 990–994).

99. On the tomb of Ma Zhiwen and his wife see Zhang Xiande (1980).

100. The inscription is published in full in Zhang Xiande (1980, 36–37).

101. On the tomb of Dong Xiang and his wife see "Jin'-nian Beijing faxian de jizuo Liaomu" (1980).

102. Zhang Xiande (1980, 34–35).

103. Ibid., p. 35.

104. Ibid.

105. Ibid., p. 36.

106. For the report on Han Yi's tomb see Huang and Fu (1984).

107. Ibid., p. 362.

108. For an illustration see Huang and Fu (1984, pl. 21) or Laing (1992, 60).

109. The tomb in Zhaitang is published in Lü Qi and Zhao Fusheng (1980).

110. On standard forms for Yuan and Jin tombs see Steinhardt (1990–1991, 198–209).

111. It is a story of reverence for one's elder brother (*ge*). For illustrations see Su Bai (1989, 166–167). For illustrations of filial piety in Jin or Jin-Yuan tombs see Li Fengshan (1985) and Tao Fuhai and Jie Xigong (1986).

112. Information about this tomb, including the epitaph, is found in Deng et al. (1983). This article suggests that some tombs excavated in the first half of the twentieth century belong to this same family.

113. At least one tomb of a Han Chinese with an octagonal plan is known. It was uncovered in 1956 in Ningchengxian. The tomb of Li Zhishin, who died in 1008, is published in Li Yiyou (1981). The octagonal shape may be due to the Inner Mongolian location.

114. Deng et al. (1983, 37–38).

115. On these tombs see Su Tianjun (1963).

116. All five tombs are discussed in Bian Chengxiu (1960).

117. On Zhang Shiqing's tomb see Zheng Shaozong (1975a).

118. Ibid., p. 37.

119. For an illustration see Zheng Shaozong (1975a, pl. 3).

120. The studies are Zheng Shaozong (1975b) and Xia Nai (1976).

121. As has been pointed out before in reference to the joint burial of the Princess of Chenguo and her husband; see note 15 for references and examples of Han tomb ceilings with constellations.

122. It is published in Li Zhengchi (1973). For more on the lunar lodges see Schafer (1977).

123. On the calendrical animals see Ho (1991).

124. For illustrations see Creswell (1932, fig. 339).

125. On Tombs 2 and 3 from Xuanhua see Tao et al. (1990). As of August 1993, the burial site included ten tombs. Tomb 4, belonging to Han Shixun, a merchant, consisted of a square front chamber joined by a causeway to a hexagonal back chamber, both oriented due south, like Tombs 2 and 3. For discussion and illustrations see Liu Haiwen et al. (1992). For a brief announcement of the other six tombs, including interior photographs of Tombs 6, 7, and 10, see Zheng Shaozong (1993).

126. The ceiling paintings from the Xuanhua tombs have been discussed in graduate seminars of mine in 1991 and 1993. In particular I thank Tansen Sen and Chang Che-chia for research that led to the interpretation of the ceiling designs proposed here.

127. *Zhaoshen jing* are discussed in Kuhn (1994, p. 35 and n. 77).

128. This idea was put forth in a seminar paper by Chang Che-chia.

129. I thank Marilyn Gridley for this suggestion.

130. On related mandalas see Howard (1983).

131. They are also a subject of Steinhardt (1993).

13. THE FUNERARY TRADITIONS OF NORTH AND NORTHEAST ASIA

1. For background on the Xi Xia see Dunnell (1984; 1988; 1996a; 1996b) and Dunnell's chapter in Franke and Twitchett (1994). On Xi Xia tombs see Steinhardt (1993).

2. *Jiajing Ningxia xinzhi, juan* 7 (1982 reprint, 361–362).

3. On the Xi Xia necropolis and related material see "Ningxia Shijushanshi" (1981), "Xi Xia bahaoling" (1978), Chen Bingying (1985), Till (1986), Niu Dasheng (1986), Wu Fengyun (1986), Wu and Li (1978), Shi Jinbo et al. (1988), and "Xi Xia lingyuan beiduan" (1988).

4. On Tomb 8 see "Xi Xia bahaoling" (1978).

5. Examples of sculpture from the spirit paths can be seen in Shi Jinbo et al. (1988, pls. 223–227).

6. Castell (1938, 185).

7. "Xi Xia bahaoling" (1978, 62).

8. On these excavations see "Xi Xia lingyuan beiduan" (1988).

9. Ibid., p. 66.

10. The suggestion is that he was Prince Zheng Xian (ca. 1063–ca. 1129). See "Xi Xia bahaoling" (1978, 74–75).

11. For a review of Chinese imperial tombs, in addition to Chapter 11, see Yang Kuan (1985) and Luo Zhewen (1993).

12. A problem in dealing with Xi Xia civilization is that the territory of the former empire has been divided into Russian-dominated and Chinese-dominated Asia. The major fortified city known through Russian and Soviet excavations is Khara-Khoto, surveyed and published to greater and lesser extents by Koslov (1923) and Stein (1928, vol. 1, pp. 429–462); the city's material remains have been published by Kozloff (1909; 1910), Ol'denburg (1914), Pelliot (1914), Kazin (1961), Lubo-Lesnichenko (1968), and Lubo-Lesnichenko and Safronovskaia (1968). At present, the territory is part of China. Known as Heicheng (Chinese for Khara-Khoto, "Black City"), results of excavation there are published in Guo Zhizhong and Li Yiyou (1987). Still, the most recent publication on Khara-Khoto, Piotrovsky (1993), makes no reference to the Chinese excavations. Khara-Khoto, one recalls, is where the Star Mandala in the Hermitage, discussed in Chapter 12, was excavated.

13. These tombs are published in Ning Duxue and Zhong Zhangfa (1980), Chen Bingying (1980), and "Gansu Wuwei faxian" (1974).

14. Ning and Zhong (1980, 65).

15. For the inscription and more on the Liu family see Ning and Zhong (1980, 66).

16. On the Xi Xia caves in Gansu province see Liu Yuquan (1982, 164–177) and Wang Jingru (1980).

17. Also related to the octagonal imagery, the mid-eleventh-century date, and the funerary associations is an eight-sided stone *chuang* with the date 951, found on top of a coffin dated to the year 1051. The discovery was made at Beizheng, Fangshan county, Hebei. For more on it see Qi Xin and Liu Jingyi (1980); for discussion of its imagery see Gridley (1993). I thank Prof. Gridley for making me aware of this piece.

18. On Xi Xia Buddhism see Dunnell (1996a). There is still no serious study of Liao Buddhism.

19. As has been mentioned several times in this book, there are countless specific and general examples of the borrowing of Tang culture abroad. One readily thinks of Japanese and Korean versions of Chinese cities; Japanese, later Chinese, and other Asian paintings in the style of Tang court painters Zhang Xuan and Zhou Fang; and Japanese examples of Tang-style Buddhist sculpture that in some cases, such as the bronze triad in Yakushi-ji, Nara, have been argued to be Chinese originals.

20. Many cases can be presented for the influence of Tang Buddhist sculpture on Liao Buddhist sculpture. See, for example, Gridley (1993). For some monasteries, such as Dulesi, construction occurred on a former Tang monastery site.

21. For discussion and illustrations of this piece see Zhong Kan (1978, 57–58).

22. McCune (1962, 72).

23. Kim Won-yong et al. (1979, 150).

24. On Dong Shou's tomb see Su Bai (1952) and Hong Qingyu (1959).

25. On the Yi'nan tomb see Shih Hsio-yen (1959). On tombs from Beiyuan see Fairbank (1972, 141–180). Tombs from both sites are mentioned in Chapter 11.

26. Pak (1978, 185).

27. On Tomb 332 see Li Dianfu (1983). Sanchengxia Tomb 983 has the same plan; it is published in Li Dianfu (1983, 312). A third example is Moxiangou Tomb 1 in Ji'an county, Jilin, published in Fang Qidong (1964).

28. Chinese tombs that exhibit these features are discussed in Chapter 11. For illustrations of Koguryŏ tomb wall paintings see Kim Won-yong et al. (1979).

29. Wu Hung (1986).

30. On this tomb see Chen Xiangwei and Fang Qidong (1982). The Tomb of the Dancers is published in most discussions of Koguryŏ tombs. For illustrations see, for example, Jin Weinuo (1988, pls. 70–74) and Kim Won-yong et al. (1979, pls. 21–24).

31. This suggestion is based on visual evidence. On *kofun* with wall paintings see Saitō Tadashi (1976).

32. For illustrations of these tomb plans see Sekino et al. (1929).

33. Many examples of the inverted-V-shaped interco-

lumnar braces are found in relief sculpture and painting of the Northern and Southern Dynasties period. See, for example, Cave 6 and Cave 21 from the Yun'gang Caves in Shanxi and Cave 5 from Maijishan in Gansu.

34. On Sŏkkuram see Adams (1986, 115–133) and McCune (1962, 94–97). On the identity of the main image see Adams (1986, 119–121).

35. See the discussion of Tomb 6 at Haoqianying in Chapter 12.

36. The reidentification of gold and silver masks and crowns is discussed in Fontein and Wu (1973, 185–187, 192–194).

37. For examples of Liao gold see Deydier (1990; 1991). For Korean pieces see Goepper and Whitfield (1984).

38. I thank Pamela Crossley for an interesting discussion of this point in 1992.

39. On the Bohai see Komai Kazuchika (1977).

40. On Bohai cities, palaces, and excavations see Wang et al. (1957), Wei Zuncheng (1982), Liu Xiaodong and Wei Cuncheng (1987), "Bohai Shangjing" (1987), Zhao Hongguang (1988), Li Dianfu (1988), Jiang Huachang (1988), and Komai Kazuchika (1992).

41. For examples of Liao tombs with mounds of piled stone see Li Shaobing (1988), Hong Feng and Zhi Li (1988), and "Hebei Luanping Liaodai Bohai" (1989).

42. Hong and Zhi (1988) give a Liao-Jin date for the Jilin tomb that is the subject of their article.

43. On the Jiayuguan tombs see *Jiayuguan bihuamu* (1985) and Wang Tianyi (1989).

44. On this tomb see *Jiuquan Shiliuguomu* (1989); for an illustration of the arrangement of bricks see p. 3, fig. 7.

45. King Muryŏng's tomb is the only intact royal tomb from the Paekche kingdom. See Kim Won-yong (1983, 53–61).

46. For illustrations of similar trees painted on the walls of Dingjiazha Tomb 5, Changchuan Tomb 1, and Astana Tomb 13 see *Jiuquan Shiliuguomu* (1989, fig. 20), Chen Xiangwei and Fang Qidong (1982, 160), and *Xinjiang Weiwu'er Zizhiqu Bowuguan* (1996, 10–11), respectively.

47. The bibliography on paintings in the Mogao Caves is voluminous. See, for example, *Tonkō Bakukō*

kutsu, five volumes plus an index in the Sino-Japanese collaborative series *Chōgoku sekkutsu*. Other examples of these ceilings are found in Cave 249 (vol. 1, pls. 98 and 100), also Western Wei, and Cave 420 (vol. 2, pl. 78) from the Sui period.

14. CONCLUSION

1. Willetts (1958, 392).

2. On the stupa see Mitra (1971, 21–30), Seckel (1968, 113–135), Snodgrass (1985), Dallapiccola and Lallement (1980), and Kottkamp (1992).

3. For a discussion of the central-pagoda-pillar-style cave see Xiao Mo (1989, 35–42).

4. On the relation between central-pillar-style caves and ritual see Xiao Mo (1989, 35–42) and Abe (1989).

5. Every standard history of Chinese or Buddhist architecture explains the development and evolution of the pagoda in this way. See, for example, Seckel (1968, 113–135), Sickman and Soper (1971, esp. 374–390), or Seckel (1989, 64–74).

6. On Yong'ningsi see "Han-Wei Luoyangcheng" (1973, 204–206), Jenner (1981), and Wang Yi-t'ung (1984, p. 13 and elsewhere).

7. At Foguangsi, a *chuang* (funerary pillar) remains from the Tang period.

8. The pagodas are Guoqingsi Pagoda at Tiantaishan, Zhejiang, dated 597; Simenta of Shentong Monastery, Licheng county, Shandong, dated 611; Qianxun Pagoda from Chongsheng Monastery, Dali, Yunnan, from the eighth century; Shandao Pagoda from Xiangjisi in Chang'an dated 706; and Xiaoyanta from Xianfu Monastery in Chang'an, built in 707 with repairs as late as the Ming dynasty. For illustrations of three of these see *Ancient Chinese Architecture* (1982, 56, 65, and 73).

9. For illustrations see *Ancient Chinese Architecture* (1982, 74, 76, 78–79).

10. Sickman and Soper (1971, 442).

11. For Gustav Ecke's publications on the Chinese pagoda see Ecke (1935–1936; 1942; 1948) and Ecke and Demiéville (1935). A Chinese article by Liang Sicheng was based on Ecke's work; see Liang (1933b).

12. Boerschmann's writings on Chinese architecture

have been published in English and German. Sometimes the contents of books overlap. On the pagoda see, for example, Boerschmann (1911; 1923; 1925; 1931).

13. Bao Ding (1937).

14. Besides Chen Mingda (1980), three important recent books are Zhang Yuhuan and Luo Zhewen (1988), *Zhongguo mingta* (1993), and Ji Chengkai and Ji Jialong (1993). As for recent monographic studies of Liao pagodas, Ji Ping (1991) and Bao Enli (1987) are recommended.

15. Ecke (1948, 333).

16. Ibid., pp. 337, 339, 341, respectively.

17. I thank the late Francis Cleaves for translating this inscription for me. He suggested that Mongolian was used rather than Manchu, despite the Qing-period date, because the local population was Mongolian.

18. For illustrations of Liuhe (Six Harmonies) Pagoda see *Ancient Chinese Architecture* (1982, 110).

19. Chaoyang South Pagoda is shown as Figure 365 because the North Pagoda was under scaffolding when I was in Chaoyang in 1992. (The North Pagoda is believed to be more restored.) During the course of this repair, imagery from all four faces (the south face is shown in fig. 366) has been removed and restored. Major studies of the pagoda and its iconography are under way in China. See, for example, Dong Gao (1990; 1991) and Zhang Hongbo and Lin Xiangxian (1992).

20. Buddhist iconography does occur on the lintels at Dayanta, but not on the shaft walls.

21. For more on the Dhyāni Buddhas see Getty (1962, 28–43).

22. Sickman and Soper (1971, 443).

23. Irwin (1980).

24. For an introduction to Kūkai and his role in the transmission of the Mandala of the Two Worlds see, for example, Ishida (1987, 11–24 passim).

25. For illustrations of this building see Sekino and Takeshima (1925, vol. 2, pls. 93–95).

26. I thank Marilyn Gridley for explaining the correct identifications of these eight images and noting that a different group of deities is named in the inscriptions.

27. For a summary history of Shenyang see Fang Dianchun and Zhang Keju (1985).

28. Ibid., pp. 50–52.

29. Ibid., p. 51.

30. On the Diamond World Mandala see Ishida (1987, esp. 42–46).

31. And perhaps a native Qidan source. In the early history of the empire, "Qidan" were divided into eight tribes. For a list see Wittfogel and Feng (1949, 94).

32. For introductory information about the composite ritual hall and magic squares see Steinhardt (1984, 70–77); for more information see Soothill (1951); and on magic squares see Cammann (1960; 1962).

33. On early Chinese texts, including the passage from *Kaogong ji*, relevant to Chinese city planning, see Steinhardt (1990, 29–36).

34. Steinhardt (1983).

35. Anne Châyet made this point at an NEH Seminar on the city of Chengde in Ann Arbor in July 1994. As for the Manchu palace complex at Chengde, it was formed around nine courtyards, symbol of the nine heavens that gave way to the frequent use of nine and its multiples in Chinese imperial space.

Glossary

Abaoji　阿保機

Aguda　阿骨打

Alibo　阿里伯

Amituofo　阿彌陀佛

an　庵

An Dule　安獨樂

An Lushan　安祿山

Anak　安岳

ang　昂

Anping　安平

Anxi　安西

Anyang　安陽

Aohanqi　敖漢旗

Babaoshan　八寶山

Baisha　白沙

Baitasi　白塔寺

Baitazi　白塔子

Baiwanzhuang　百萬莊

bajiachuan wu　八架椽屋

Balinyouqi　巴林右旗

Balinzuoqi　巴林左旗

Bao　寶

baoda　保大

Baodixian　寶坻縣

Baogongsi　寶宮寺

Baoguosi　寶國寺

baoping　寶平

baosha　抱廈

baota　寶塔

Baoxiang　寶祥

Bayan'erdengsumu　巴彦爾燈蘇
　　木

Bei (see Yelü Bei)

beidou　北斗

Beijing　北京

Beipiao　北票

Beishi　北史

Beiyuan　北園

Beizhen　北鎮

Beizheng　北鄭

bencheng　本城

Bianliang　汴梁

Bingshan　屏山

Bohai　渤海

Bojiagou　柏家溝

Bojiajiao　薄伽教

bu　步

Bu Qianqiu　卜千秋

bujian puzuo　補間鋪作

Byōdō-in　平等院

cai　材

Cangjingge　藏經閣

cao　槽

cao (ru) fu　草 (乳) 栿

caofu　草栿

cejiao　側腳

Chai Zejun　柴澤俊

Chan　禪

Chang'an　長安

Changbaxian　長霸縣

Changchuan　長川

Changfu　長福

Changhuaxian　長化縣

Changzhi　長治

Chaoyang(xian)　朝陽 (縣)

chashou　叉手

Chayouqianqi　察右前旗

Chen　陳

Chen Lin　陳麟

Chen Mingda　陳明達

Chen Shu　陳述

Chengde　承德

Chengdu　成都

Chengtian　承天

Chenguo　陳國

chi　尺

Chifeng　赤峰

Chikuzen　筑前

chiwen　鴟吻

Chōgen (see Shunjōbō Chōgen)

chong gong　重栱

chong jian　重建

chong xiu　重修

Chongdegong　崇德宮

Chongfusi (Jin)　崇福寺

Chongfusi (Tang)　崇福寺

Chongmingsi　崇明寺

Chongqingsi　崇慶寺

Chongshengsi　崇聖寺

chu　礎

chuan　椽

chuang　幢

chuku　廚庫

Chūmon　中門

Chun Shan　春山

chunhua　淳化

chushi　處士

Chuzu'an　初祖庵

ci jian　次間

ci liang　次梁

Ci'ensi　慈恩寺

Cihui　慈慧

cishao jian　次稍間

Cishi(ge)　慈氏 (閣)

Cixian (*zhi*)　磁縣 (志)

Ciyunge　慈雲閣

(Da) guangjisi (see also Guangjisi)
　　大廣濟寺

da liang　大梁

Da Pu'ensi　大普恩寺

Da Xia　大夏

Da Zurong　大祚榮

Dabeige (si)　大悲閣 (寺)

Dachengdian　大成殿

Dadingfu　大定府

Dadu　大都

daguan　大觀

Daigō-ji　醍醐寺

Dajie　大街

Dali　大理

Damingcheng　大明城

Daminggong　大明宮

damuzuo　大木作

dan cao　單槽

dancai　單材

Dangxiang　黨項

dangxin jian　當心間

Daoguang　道廣

Dasi　大寺

Data (si)　大塔 (寺)

Datong (xian/fu)　大同 (縣/府)

Daxiamen　大夏門

Daxing(xian)　大興(縣)

Daxiongbaodian　大雄寶殿

Dayanta　大雁塔

Dayingzi　大營子

Dayong　大用

Dayunyuan　大雲院

Dazheng(dian)　大政 (殿)

Deguang　德光

Dengfeng　登封

di　弟

di ba　帝杷

dian　殿

diantang　殿堂

difang zhi　地方志

dili zhi　地理志

Ding Hong　丁洪

Ding Wenyou　丁文迿

Dingjiazha　丁家閘

Dinglifu　定理府

Dingxing(xian)　定興 (縣)

dong　洞

Dong Shou　冬壽

Dong Xiang　董庠

Dong Zhongshu　董仲舒

Dongbei　東北

Dongdan　東丹

Donghu　東胡

Dongjing　東京

Dongjing menghua lu　東京夢華
　　錄

Dongpingjun　東平郡

Dongying　東營

Dongyue Dadidian　東岳大帝殿

Dongyuemiao　東岳廟

dou　斗

Dou Wan　寶綰

dougong　斗栱

doukou　斗口

Dulesi　獨樂寺

Dulesi Dabeige ji　獨樂寺大悲
　　閣記

Dunhuang　敦煌

duodian　朵殿

duxiang　督餉

ershi　耳室

ershiba xiu　二十八宿

Eryi　二儀

fa　法

Fadian　法殿

Faku(xian)　法庫 (縣)

fang　枋

Fangshan　房山

Fanshixian　繁峙縣

Faxing　法興

fen　分

Fengguosi　奉國寺

Fenghuangshan/men　鳳凰山
　　(門)

Fengling　奉陵

Fengshi jianwen lu　封氏見聞
　　錄

fengshui　風水

fenxin doudi cao　分心斗底槽

Fogongsi　佛宮寺

Foguangsi　佛光寺

Foxiangge　佛香閣

fu　祓

Fu Xi　傅翕

Fujiwara no Yorimichi　藤原賴
　　道

Fujunmiao　府君廟

fuma　駙馬

Fuxin　阜新

Fuzhou　福州

Ganggangmiao　崗崗廟

Gaochang　高昌

Gaoping　高平

ge　閣

Geyuansi　閣院寺

gong　工

gong　栱

gong dianban　栱墊板

Gongbu gongcheng zuofa zeli　工
　部工程做法則例

gongcheng　宮城

Gongxian　鞏縣

gongyan bi　栱眼壁

Gu Hongzhong　顧閎中

gualunzhuang　瓜輪狀

guan　觀

guan　棺

guanchuang　棺床

Guandi　關帝

Guanghuasi　廣化寺

Guangjisi　廣濟寺

Guangren　廣仁

Guanxiu　貫休

Guanyinge　觀音閣

Guanyinsi　觀音寺

guazi gong　瓜子栱

guji　古蹟

Gujin tushu jicheng　古今圖書
　集成

Guoqingsi　國清寺

Guyuan　固原

Haihuidian　海會殿

Hailingwang　海陵王

Han　漢

Han Derang　韓德讓

Han Kuangmei　韓匡美

Han Kuangsi　韓匡嗣

Han Shixun　韓師訓

Han Xiang　韓相

Han Yanhui　韓延徽

Han Yi　韓儀

Han Zhibai　韓知白

Han Zhigu　韓知古

Hancheng　漢城

hangtu　夯土

Hangzhou　杭州

Hanlin　翰林

Hanyuan(dian)　含元 (殿)

Haodong　郝洞

Haoqianying　豪欠營

"Haw"　哈

Heihe　黑河

heilong　黑龍

Helinge'er　和林格爾

"Hem"　嗊

Hemudu　河姆渡

Hexi　河西

Hondō　本堂

Hōnen　法然

Hongji　洪基

Hongyan　弘演

Hōryū-ji　法隆寺

Hu Gui　胡瓌

Hu Jiao　胡嶠

hua gong　華栱

Huailing　懷陵

Huaizhou　懷州

Hualinsi　華林寺

"Huaman lu"　華墁錄

Huang Chaoying　黃朝英

Huang Huashan　黃花山

Huang Quan　黃筌

Huang Sheng　黃昇

Huangcheng　皇城

huangchengdi　隍城帝

Huayansi　華嚴寺

Huazhou　滑州

Huhehaote　呼和浩特

huichang　會昌

Huichang　會昌

Huiming　慧明

Huizhou　徽州

humen yazi　壺門牙子

Hwanghae　黃海

Hyōgo　兵庫

ji tuan 脊槫	*Jiu Tangshu* 舊唐書	Keisenmachi 桂川町
Jiafusi 嘉福寺	*Jiu Wudaishi* 舊五代史	Kelaqinqi 喀喇沁旗
Jiajing Ningxia xinzhi 嘉靖寧夏新志	*(jiuji) xiaozhang* (九脊) 小帳	Kim Tae-sŏng 金大城
jian 間	Jiuquan 酒泉	*kofun* 吉墳
Ji'an 集安	Jixian/zhou 薊縣/州	Kondō 金堂
Jianping 建平	*jixin* 計心	Kongwangsi 空王寺
Jiao Xiyun 焦希贇	*Jizhou zhi* 薊州志	Kuangmei (see Han Kuangmei)
jiao zhu 角柱	Jōdō 淨土	Kūkai 空海
jiaobei 繳背	Jōdō-ji 淨土寺	Kulunqi 庫倫旗
Jiayuguan 嘉峪關	Jōruri-ji 淨琉璃寺	Kyŏngju 慶州
jiehua 界畫	*juan* 卷	Laishui 淶水
Jietaisi 戒台寺	*juansha* 卷殺	Laiyuan (*xian zhi*) 淶源 (縣志)
jin 金	Jumyo 嘉穗	*lan'e* 闌額
jin jian 金門	*jun* 君	Laoha 老哈
jin zhu 金柱	*jun* 郡	Lelang 樂浪
Jincheng 晉城	Juran 巨然	*lengmu* 愣木
Jinci 晉祠	*juzhe* 舉折	Leshan 樂山
Jing 璟	Kaihuasi 開化寺	*li* 里
jing 鏡	Kaishansi 開善寺	Li Bian 李昪
Jing Ai 景愛	*kaishu* 開書	Li Cheng 李成
jingcang 經藏	*kaiyuan* 開元	Li Cunshen 李存審
Jingtusi 淨土寺	Kaiyuansi 開元寺	Li Deming 李德明
Jining 集寧	Kakjo-ch'ong 角抵塚	Li Huan 李瀚
jinshi 進士	*Kangxi Chaoyixian houzhi* 康熙朝邑縣後志	Li Jing 李璟
Jinshi 金史	Kansai 關西	Li Jiqian 李繼遷
jinxiang doudi cao 金箱斗底槽	*Kaogong ji* 考工記	Li Keyong 李克用
Jinxixian 錦西縣	Kara-yō 唐樣	Li Xian 李賢
Jinzhou/xian 錦州/縣	Ke Gong 柯公	Li Yanchao 李彥超
		Li Yiyou 李逸友

Li Yuanhao　李元昊

Li Zanhua　李贊華

lian　簾

liang　樑

liang　兩

Liang Sicheng　梁思成

liang tiao　兩跳

liang xia ang　兩下昂

Liangmingdian　兩明殿

Liangshan(men)　兩山 (門)

Liao　遼

Liaodita　料敵塔

Liaoshi　遼史

liaoyan tuan　料檐槫

Liaoyang　遼陽

Licheng (xian)　黎城 (縣)

lin　檁

Lin Huiyin　林徽因

Lin'an　臨安

Linde(dian)　麟德 (殿)

Lindong　林東

ling　陵

ling gong　令栱

Lingchuanfu/dian　陵川府/殿

Lingyingsi　靈隱寺

Lingyuan　凌源

Linhuang　臨潢

Liu Cheng　劉成

Liu Chengsui　劉承逐

Liu Deren　劉德仁

Liu Dunzhen　劉敦楨

Liu Sheng　劉勝

Liu Yuan　劉元

Liu Zhiping　劉致平

Liuhe(ta)　六和(塔)

liushou　留守

Longdeguanzhuang　隆德關莊

Longhua(si)　龍化(寺)

Longmeigong　龍眉宮

Longmensi　龍門寺

Longquan　龍泉

Longxingsi　隆興寺

Longxu　隆緒

lou　樓

Lou Rui　婁叡

louge　樓閣

Lu Ban　魯班

ludou　櫨科

Lulong　盧龍

Luohan/*luohan*　羅漢

luohan fang　羅漢枋

Luohansi　羅漢寺

Luoyang　洛陽

Lushansi　祿山寺

Ma Zhiwen　馬眞溫

Mahao　麻浩

Maijishan　麥積山

malgak chochong　抹角藻井

man gong　慢栱

Mancheng　滿城

mandao　慢道

mappō (see *mofa*)

Mian　緬

miao　廟

Michinaga (Fujiwara no)　道長
　　(藤原の)

miezui zhenyan　滅罪眞言

Mile　彌勒

Min　閩

Minamoto　源

ming jian　明間

ming rufu　明乳栿

mingchang　明昌

Mingci　明慈

Mingtang　明堂

Minzhong ji　閩中記

Mituo(dian)　彌陀殿

Mo Zongjiang　莫宗江

mofa　末法

Mogao　莫高

mojiao gong　抹角栱

mojiao liang　抹角梁

Monidian　摩尼殿

Mudan　牡丹

mudao　墓道

Muta　木塔

Muyeshan　木葉山

Muyong-ch'ong　舞踊塚

Naimanqi　奈曼旗

Nanchansi　南禪寺

Nandaimon　南大門

Nanjing　南京

nei cao　內槽

nei cheng　內城

nei zhu　內柱

nei'e fang　內額枋

nidao gong　泥道栱

Ning Gongyu　甯公遇

Ningbo (*fu zhi*)　寧波 (府志)

Ningchangjun　寧昌郡

Ningcheng　寧城

Ningshendian　凝神殿

Noujin　耨斤

Nu'erhachi　努爾哈赤

Nuzhen　女眞

Ōtsuka　王塚

Ouyang Xiu　歐陽修

Ouyang Xuan　歐陽玄

paifang　牌坊

panjian　襻間

Panshan (*zhi*)　盤山 (志)

Peijing zashu　陪京雜述

Pengxian　彭縣

Pilu　毗盧

ping liang　平梁

ping tuan　平槫

pingban　平版

Pingcheng　平城

pingqi(fang)　平棊(枋)

Pingquan　平泉

Pingshun(xian)　平順(縣)

Pingyao(*xian zhi*)　平遙(縣志)

pingzuo　平坐

pizhu　劈竹

Pu'ensi (see Da Pu'ensi)

pupai fang　普拍枋

Putian (*xian zhi*)　莆田 (縣志)

Puxian (ge)　普賢 (閣)

puzuo　鋪作

P'yongyang　平壤

qi　旗

Qi Yingtao　祁英濤

Qian'an　千安

Qianling (Tang)　乾陵

Qianling (Liao)　乾陵

Qianxun　千尋

Qianzhou　乾州

Qidan　契丹

Qidan guozhi　契丹國志

Qidan zhuan　契丹傳

Qin Jian　秦鑒

Qin'ai　欽哀

Qinghua　清華

Qinghui　清慧

Qingliansi　青蓮寺

Qingling　慶陵

Qinglongshan (zhen)　青龍山
　　(鎭)

Qinglongsi　青龍寺

Qingyunshan　慶雲山

Qingzhou　慶州

Qinjin　秦晉

qinmian ang　琴面昂

Qinwang　秦王

Qishou　奇首

Qitian　齊天

Qixiasi　栖霞寺

Quanzhou　泉州

que　闕

Qufu　曲阜

renwang　仁王

Renyi　仁懿

Rixia jiuwen kao　日下舊聞考

rufu　乳栿

Ruicheng　芮城

Ruizhi　睿智

Ruru　茹茹

ruyi dougong　如意斗栱

Sanbaodian　三寶殿

Sandashi　三大士

Sanguo zhi　三國志

Sanqing (dian)　三清 (殿)

Sanshan zhi　三山志

Sanshengdian　三聖殿

Sekino Tadashi　關野正

shan zhu　山柱

Shandaota　善導塔

shangfu　尚父

Shanghai　上海

Shangjing　上京

Shanhuasi　善化寺

Shanmen　山門

Shanxi tongzhi　山西通志

Shanyuan　澶淵

Shanzuizi　山嘴子

Shao Hao　少昊

shao jian　稍間

Shaolinsi　少林寺

shaosheng　紹聖

Shaoxing　紹興

Shazigou　沙子溝

Shen Kuo　沈括

shendao　神道

Shenggu(miao)　聖姑(廟)

Shengjing tongzhi　盛京通志

Shengmudian/miao　聖母殿/廟

shengqi　升起

shengxian　聖仙

Shengxue　省學

Shentongsi　神通寺

Shenyang (xian zhi)　瀋陽 (縣
　　志)

Shi Fang　室昉

Shi Jin　石晉

Shi Tianlin　石天麟

Shilin guangji　事林廣記

Shishi　石室

Shiwei　室韋

Shoudu (Bowuguan)　首都 (博
　　物館)

shu zhu　蜀柱

shuang　雙

shuang cao　雙槽

shuang xia ang　雙下昂

shuatou　耍頭

shunfu chuan　順袱串

Shunjōbō Chōgen　俊乘坊重源

Shuntianfu (*zhi*)　順天府 (志)

Shuoxian　朔縣

si　寺

si tiao　四跳

si'a wuding　四阿無頂

sichuan　四椽

sichuan fu　四椽袱

sichuan liang　四椽梁

Sima Jinlong　司馬金龍

Simenta　四門塔

sishen　四神

Sixiao　思孝

Sŏkkuram　石窟庵

Songsan-ni　宋山里

Songshi　宋史

Songyuesi　嵩岳寺

Ssangyŏng-ch'ong　雙楹塚

su　俗

Su Bai　宿白

Su Che　蘇轍

su fang　素枋

sui　歲

Suishu　隋書

suo zhu　梭柱

Suzhou　蘇州

ta　塔

tadao　踏道

taiding　泰定

Taihuai(xian)　台懷 (縣)

taiji　台基

tailun　台輪

Taimiao　太廟

taiping　太平

Taipingdian　太平殿

Taira　平

Taiyuan　太原

Takamatsuzuka　高松塚

Takeshima Takuichi　竹島卓一

Tamura Jitsuzō　田村實造

Tang Zuorong　湯佐榮

Tangzhou　湯州

Tanyao　曇曜

Tanzhen　談眞

Tanzhesi　潭柘寺

taqian 剳牽

Taxiasi 塔下寺

Tayuansi 塔院寺

Tenjiku-yō 天竺樣

Tian Hui 田惠

Tian'anmen 天安門

Tiandi 天帝

tianfu 天福

tiangong 天宮

Tianjin (shi) 天津 (市)

Tianningsi 天寧寺

tiansheng 天聖

Tiantai'an 天台庵

Tiantaishan 天台山

tianwang 天王

Tianwangdian 天王殿

Tianzu 天祖

Tieling (xian) 鐵嶺(縣)

timu 替木

ting 亭

tingtang 廳堂

Tōdai-ji 東大寺

Tonggou 通溝

Tonghua 通化

Tongliao 通遼

Tongwu 通悟

Torii Ryūzō 鳥居龍藏

Tōshōdai-ji 唐招提寺

toukuan 頭貫

touxin 偷心

tuan 槫

tuanfeng panjian 槫縫襻間

tuishan 推山

Tujue 突厥

Tuoba 拓拔

tuofeng 駝峰

tuojiao 托腳

Tuotuo 托托

Uji 宇治

wai cao 外槽

wan 卍

Wanbu Huayanjing 萬部華嚴
    經

Wanfodian 萬佛殿

Wang 王

Wang Jian 王建

Wang Wenxi 王文襲

Wang Yubi 王于陛

Wangcheng 王城

Wangdu 望都

Wei 魏

Wei 衛

Wei Xian 衛賢

Weiming 嵬名

Weiming Zunxu 嵬名遵頊

Wen Weijian 文惟簡

wengcheng 甕城

Wenmiao 文廟

Wenshu 文殊

Wenshuixian 文水縣

Wenwu 文物

Wenzhong 文忠

wu 廡

Wu Miaoyou 武廟游

Wudai shiji 五代史記

Wulongmiao 五龍廟

wunei zhu 屋內柱

Wuqingjingyi 武清井邑

Wutai 五台

Wuwei 武威

Wuyue 吳越

Xi 奚

Xi Xia 西夏

Xia Nai 夏鼐

Xiabali 下八里

xiaheng fang 下橫枋

Xiamen 廈門

xian 縣

Xi'an 西安

Xianbei ([lu] ji) 鮮卑 ([錄] 記)

Xian(dian) 獻 (殿)

Xiang Chunsong 項春松

Xiangguosi 相國寺

Xiangjisi 香積寺

Xianningxian 咸寧縣

Xianxisi 咸熙寺

Xianyingwangmiao 顯應王廟

Xianzhou　顯州

Xiao Dewen　蕭德溫

Xiao Gang　蕭綱

Xiao Jin　蕭僅

Xiao Paolu　蕭袍魯

Xiao Shaoju　蕭紹矩

Xiao Xianggong　蕭相公

Xiao Xiaozhong　蕭孝忠

Xiao Yi　蕭義

Xiao Zhenwei　蕭愼微

xiaomuzuo　小木作

Xiaowen　蕭文

Xiaoyanta　小雁塔

xiaozhang (see jiuji xiaozhang)

Xidajie　西大街

Xidasi　西大寺

xie'an zheyanban　斜安遮掩版

xielang　斜廊

Xilou　西樓

Ximingsi　西明寺

Xincang　新倉

Xincheng (xian zhi)　新城 (縣
　志)

xing　星

Xingsheng (men)　興聖(門)

xingtu　星圖

xiong　雄

xiongqiang　胸墻

xiu　修

"Xiu Dulesi ji"　修獨樂寺記

Xiyue　西岳

Xuancheng　軒成

Xuanhua (xian)　宣化 (縣)

Xuanmiaoguan　玄妙觀

xuanshan　懸山

Xue Jing　薛敬

Yakushi-ji　藥師寺

Yalu　牙魯/淥

Yan　燕

yan　簷

yan　鹽

yan zhu　簷柱

yancao fang　簷槽枋

Yanchao (see Li Yanchao)

Yangzhou　揚州

Yanjing　燕京

Yanqingsi　延慶寺

Yanshansi　巖山寺

Yantao　彥韜

Yanxiang　彥鄉

Yao Congwu　姚從吾

Yao Kun　姚坤

Yaoshi　藥師

Yelü　耶律

Yelü Bei　耶律倍

Yelü Changshu　耶律昌朮

Yelü Cong　耶律琮

Yelü Di　耶律迪

Yelü Hezhu　耶律合住

Yelü Jian　耶律建

Yelü Jiayili　耶律加乙里

Yelü Nugua　耶律奴瓜

Yelü Renxian　耶律仁先

Yelü Yanning　耶律延寧

Yelü Yixian　耶律義先

Yemaotai　嚜茂台

Yicihui　義慈惠

Yihong　義弘

Yila　移剌

Yi'nan　沂南

Yinchuan　銀川

Yingchengzi　營城子

yingtang　影堂

Yingzhou (xu) zhi　應州 (續) 志

Yingtian　應天

Yingxian/zhou　應縣/州

Yingzao fashi　營造法式

Yinxu　殷墟

Yiwulu　醫巫閭

Yixian　義縣

Yixian/zhou　易縣/州

Yizhuo　義擢

Yong'an　永安

yongdao　甬道

Yongdingling　永定陵

Yongfuling　永福陵

Yongkang　龍岡

Yongle dadian　永樂大典

Yonglegong　永樂宮

Yongling　永陵

Yong'ningsi　永寧寺

Yongqingling　永慶陵

Yongshousi　永壽寺

Yongtai　永泰

Yongxingling　永興陵

Yongzhaoling　永照陵

you'e　由額

youheng fang　由橫枋

Youqiaozi　右橋子

Youxiansi　遊仙寺

Yu Gongzhu　虞公著

Yuan yitong zhi　元一統志

Yuancheng　圓成

Yuanjing mantuluo　圖鏡曼荼羅

Yuanman　圓滿

Yuantongsi　圓通寺

yuanyang jiaoshou gong　鴛鴦交
　手栱

Yuci (xian) zhi　榆次 (縣) 志

Yue　越

yue liang　月梁

yuetai　月台

Yugong diyu tu　禹公地域圖

Yuhuagong　雨花宮

Yuhuangmiao　玉皇廟

Yulin　榆林

Yuncheng　運城

Yun'gang　雲崗

Yunjusi　雲居寺

Yutian　玉田

Yuyang (jun)　漁洋 (郡)

Yuyao　餘姚

zaisheng　再生

zaojing　藻井

Zeng　曾

Zetian　則天

zhaitang　齋堂

Zhaitang　齋堂

zhalan　柵欄

zhang　丈

Zhang Gongyou　張恭誘

Zhang Guan　張錧

Zhang Shanshi　張善士

Zhang Shiben　張世本

Zhang Shiqing　張世卿

Zhang Xuan　張萱

Zhang Yichao　張議潮

Zhang Zhiyi　張志義

Zhangjiakou　張家口

Zhangkangcun　張扛村

Zhangzi　長子

Zhao　趙

Zhao Dejun　趙德鈞

(Zhao) Deming　(趙) 德明

Zhao Kuangyu　趙匡禹

Zhao Shaoyang　趙少陽

Zhao Siwen　趙思溫

Zhao Zan　趙贊

zhaobi　照壁

Zhaomeng　昭盟

zhaoshen jing　照身鏡

Zhaowudameng　昭烏達盟

Zhengding　正定

Zhenguosi　鎮國寺

Zhenrusi　眞如寺

zheyan ban　遮眼板

zhi (qi)　契

Zhizhou　知州

Zhong　种

zhong zhu　中柱

Zhongdian　中殿

Zhongjing　中京

zhongxin tazhu (shi)　中心塔柱
　(式)

zhou　州

Zhou Fang　周昉

Zhou li　周禮

Zhu Bian　朱弁

Zhu Qiqian　朱啓鈐

zhu shengqi　柱升起

Zhu Yizun　朱彝尊

Zhuangyansi　莊嚴寺

zhuanjiao puzuo　轉角鋪作

zhuanlunzang　轉輪藏

Zhuogeng lu　輟耕錄

Zhuoxian/zhou/jun　涿縣/州/郡

zhushi　主室

zhutou fang　柱頭枋

zhutou puzuo　柱頭鋪作

zhuzi　柱子

Zongzhen　宗眞

Zubu　祖卜

zucai　足材

Zuling　祖陵

Zunhua　遵化

Zushan　祖山

Zutang　祖堂

Zuzhou　祖州

Bibliography

ASIAN LANGUAGES

"Aluke'erqinqi Dao'erqige faxian yizuo Liaomu" [A Liao tomb excavated in Dao'erqige, Aluke'erqinqi] 阿魯科爾沁旗道爾其格發現一座遼墓. 1992. *Nei Menggu wenwu kaogu*, nos. 1–2, pp. 149–152.

Amanuma Shunichi 天沼俊一. 1927. *Nihon kenchiku shiyō* [History of Japanese architecture] 日本建築史要. 2 vols. Nara: Hichōen.

——. 1933. *Nihon kenchikushi zuroku* [Illustrated history of Japanese architecture] 日本建築史図録. 5 vols. Kyōto: Hoshino shoten.

Anping Dong Han bihuamu [An Eastern Han tomb with wall paintings at Anping] 安平東漢壁畫墓. 1990. Beijing: Wenwu chubanshe.

Bai Bin 白濱, ed. 1984. *Xi Xia shi lunwen ji* [Collected essays on Xi Xia history] 西夏史論文集. Yinchuan: Ningxia renmin chubanshe.

"Balinyouqi Niaozhurishan faxian yizuo Liaomu" [A Liao tomb excavated at Niaozhurishan, Balinyouqi] 巴林右旗鳥珠日山發現一座遼墓. 1992. *Nei Menggu wenwu kaogu*, nos. 1–2, pp. 148 and 145.

Bao Ding 鮑鼎. 1937. "Tang, Song ta zhi chubu fenxi" [Preliminary analysis of Tang and Song pagodas] 唐宋塔之初步分析. *Zhongguo yingzao xueshe huikan* 6, no. 4, pp. 1–29.

Bao Enli 包恩梨. 1987. "Liaoning Liaodai zhuanta de zhuandiao yishu" [Brick art on the Liao-period brick pagoda in Liaoning] 遼寧遼代磚塔的磚雕

藝術. In *Zhongguo kaogu xuehui diliuci nianhui lunwen ji* 中國考古學會第六次年會論文集. Beijing: Wenwu chubanshe, pp. 209–218.

Beijing gucha mingsi [Ancient monasteries in Beijing] 北京古剎名寺. 1993. Beijing: Zhongguo shijieyu chubanshe.

Beijingshi [History of Beijing] 北京史. 1985. Beijing: Beijing chubanshe.

"Beipiao Koubuyingzi Liaomu fajue jianbao" [Excavation report on a Liao tomb at Koubuyingzi, Beipiao] 北票扣卜營子遼墓發掘簡報. 1978. *Wenwu ziliao congkan* 2, pp. 129–134.

Bian Chengxiu 邊成修. 1960. "Shanxi Datong jiaoqu wuzuo Liao bihuamu" [Five Liao wall-painted tombs from the suburbs of Datong, Shanxi] 山西大同郊區五座遼壁畫墓. *Kaogu*, no. 10, pp. 37–42.

"Bohai Shangjing gongchengnei fangzhi fajue jianbao" [Brief report on excavation of residential remains inside the walls of the palace-city of Bohai Shangjing] 渤海上京宮城內房址發掘簡報. 1987. *Beifang wenwu*, no. 1, pp. 38–41.

Cai Yindou 蔡寅斗 and Hong Zhaomao 洪肇楙. 1673. 1969 reprint. *Baodixian zhi* [Record of Baodi county] 寶坻縣志. Taipei: Chengwen shuju.

Cao Anji 曹安吉 and Zhao Da 趙達. 1992. *Yanbei gujianzhu* [Ancient architecture in North China] 燕北古建築. Beijing: Dongfang chubanshe.

Cao Guicen 曹桂岑 and Guo Youfan 郭友范. 1981. "Gongyusi ta ji" [Notes on the pagoda of Gongyu Monastery] 鞏峪寺塔記 *Kejishi wenji* 7, pp. 115–118.

Cao Wanru 曹婉如 et al., eds. 1990. *Zhongguo gudai ditu ji* [Atlas of ancient Chinese maps] 中國古代地圖集. Vol. 1: *Zhanguo – Yuan* [Warring States period to Yuan dynasty] 戰國至元. Beijing: Wenwu chubanshe.

Cao Xun 曹汛. 1975. "Yemaotai Liaomuzhong de guanchuang xiaozhang" [The small-scale "container" and coffin bed in a Liao tomb at Yemaotai] 葉茂臺遼墓中的棺床小帳 *Wenwu*, no. 12, pp. 49–62.

———. 1984. "Dulesi renzong xunqin" [Dulesi—recognizing ancestors and seeking relations] 獨樂寺認宗尋親. *Dulesi chongxiu yiqianzhounian jinian lunwen* 獨樂寺重修一千周年紀念論文. Unpublished.

———. 1988. "*Yingzao fashi* de yige ziwu" [An error in the *Yingzao fashi*] 營造法式的一個字誤. *Jianzhushi lunwen ji* 9, pp. 54–57.

Chai Zejun 柴澤俊. 1986. "Shanxi gujianzhu gaishu" [General discussion of ancient architecture in Shanxi] 山西古建築概述. In *Zhongguo gujianzhu xueshu jiangzuo wenji* 中國古建築學術講座文集. Beijing: Zhongguo zhanwang chubanshe, pp. 244–298.

———. 1989. *Shanxi gujianzhu mujiegou moxing* [Models of ancient architecture in Shanxi] 山西古建築木結構模型. Beijing: Beijing Yanshan chubanshe.

———. 1990. "Datong Huayansi Daxiongbaodian mujiegou xingzhi fenxi" [Structural analysis of Daxiongbao Hall of Huayan Monastery in Datong] 大同華嚴寺大雄寶殿木結構形制分析. In *Zhonghua gujianzhu* 中華古建築, eds. Zhang Yuhuan 張馭寰 and Guo Husheng 郭湖生. Beijing: Zhongguo kexue jishu chubanshe, pp. 41–61.

Chai Zejun 柴澤俊 and Li Zhengyun 李正雲. 1993. *Shuoxian Chongfusi Mituodian xiushan gongcheng baogao* [Report on the restoration of the Amitābha Hall at Chongfu Monastery in Shuoxian] 朔縣崇福寺彌陀殿修繕工程報告. Beijing: Wenwu chubanshe.

Chai Zejun 柴澤俊 and Liu Xianwu 劉憲武. 1980. "Nanchansi" [Nanchan Monastery] 南禪寺. *Wenwu*, no. 11, pp. 75–77.

Chang Yao 暢耀. 1986. *Qinglongsi* [Qinglong Monastery] 青龍寺. Shaanxi: Sanqin chubanshe.

Changsha Mawangdui yihao Hanmu [Han Tomb 1 at Mawangdui, Changsha] 長沙馬王堆一號漢墓. 1973. 2 vols. Beijing: Wenwu chubanshe.

Chen Bingying 陳炳應. 1980. "Gansu Wuwei xijiao Linchang Xi Xia mu tiji, zangsu lüeshuo" [Notes on burial customs and inscriptions based on the Xi Xia tomb at Linchang in the western suburbs of Wuwei, Gansu] 甘肅武威西郊林場西夏墓題記、葬俗略說. *Kaogu yu wenwu*, no. 3, pp. 67–69 and 62.

———. 1985. *Xi Xia wenwu yanjiu* [Research on cultural relics of the Xi Xia] 西夏文物研究. Yinchuan: Ningxia Renmin chubanshe.

Chen Gaohua 陳高華, ed. 1984. *Song, Liao, Jin hua-*

jia shiliao [Histories of Song, Liao, and Jin painters] 宋、遼、金畫家史料. Beijing: Wenwu chubanshe.

Chen Guocan 陳國燦. 1980. "Tang Qianling shiren xiang jiqi xianmingde yanjiu" [Research on the ranks and names of stone figures at Tang Qianling] 唐乾陵石人像及其銜名的研究. *Wenwu jikan*, no. 2, pp. 189–203.

Chen Lu 陳陸. 1941. "Liao Youzhou shirong ju lie" [The appearance of Liao Youzhou] 遼幽州市容舉例. *Zhonghe ribao* 2, no. 9, pp. 38–48.

Chen Menglei 陳夢雷 et al. 1725. 1965 edition. *(Qinding) Gujin tushu jicheng* [Synthesis of books and illustrations past and present] (欽定) 古今圖書集成. Taipei: Zhonghua shuju.

Chen Mingda 陳明達. 1954. "Nanchansi" [Nanchan Monastery] 南禪寺. *Wenwu cankao ziliao*, no. 11, p. 89.

———. 1980. *Yingxian Muta* [Yingxian timber pagoda] 應縣木塔. Beijing: Wenwu chubanshe.

———. 1981. *Yingzao fashi damuzuo yanjiu* [Research on "greater carpentry" in the Yingzao fashi] 營造法式大木作研究. 2 vols. Beijing: Wenwu chubanshe.

———. 1982. "Zhongguo fengjian shehui mujiegou jianzhu jishu de fazhan" [Development of Chinese timber-frame architecture of the feudal society] 中國封建社會木結構建築技術的發展. Pt. 1. *Jianzhu lishi yanjiu*, 1, pp. 56–95.

———. 1987. "Dulesi Guanyinge, Shanmen jianzhu goutu fenxi" [Structural drawings and analysis of Guanyin Pavilion and the Shanmen of Dule Monastery] 獨樂寺觀音閣山門建築構圖分析. In *Wenwu yu kaogu lun ji* 文物與考古論集. Beijing: Wenwu chubanshe, pp. 344–56.

———. 1990. *Zhongguo gudai mujiegou jianzhu jishu: Zhanguo-Bei Song* [Techniques of ancient Chinese timber-frame architecture] 中國古代木結構建築技術：戰國—北宋. Beijing: Wenwu chubanshe.

———. 1992. "Tang-Song mujiegou jianzhu shice ji, lu, biao" [Notes, records, and charts on the timber frame Tang through Song] 唐宋木結構建築實測記錄表. In *Jianzhu lishi yanjiu* 建築歷史研究,

ed. He Yeju 賀業鉅. Beijing: Zhongguo jianzhu gongye chubanshe, pp. 231–261.

———. n.d. "Zhongguo fengjian shehui mujiegou jianzhu jishu de fazhan (xu)" [Development of Chinese timber-frame architecture of the feudal society (continued)] 中國封建社會木結構建築技術的發展 (續). *Jianzhu lishi yanjiu* 2, pp. 42–93.

Chen Shu 陳述. 1963. *Qidan shehui jingji shi gao* [History of Qidan society and economics] 契丹社會經濟史稿. Beijing: Sanlian chubanshe.

———. 1981. *Liaodai shihua* [On Liao history] 遼代史話. Zhengzhou: Henan Renmin chubanshe.

———, ed. 1982. *Quan Liaowen* [Liao writings] 全遼文. Beijing: Zhonghua shuju.

———. 1984. "Qidan kaogu dui Zhongguo tongshi yanjiu de gongxian" [The contribution of Qidan archaeology to research on the history of China] 契丹考古對中國通史研究的貢獻. *Nei Menggu wenwu kaogu* 3, pp. 6–12.

———. 1986. *Qidan zhengzhi shigao* [History of Qidan government] 契丹政治史稿. Beijing: Renmin chubanshe.

———, ed. 1987a. *Liao-Jin shi lunji* [Collected essays on Liao-Jin history] 遼金史論集. Vol. 1. Shanghai: Shumu wenxian chubanshe.

———, ed., 1987b. *Liao-Jin shi lunji* [Collected essays on Liao-Jin history] 遼金史論集. Vol. 3. Shanghai: Shumu wenxian chubanshe.

Chen Tanglian 陳棠棟 and Li Xingsheng 李興盛. 1988. "Nei Meng Xinghcjianshan Liaomu fajue jianbao" [Excavation report on the Liao tomb at Xinghejianshan in Inner Mongolia] 內蒙興和尖山遼墓發掘簡報. *Beifang wenwu* no. 4, pp. 43–45.

Chen Xianchang 陳顯昌. 1980. "Tangdai Bohai Shangjing Longquanfu yizhi" [Remains of Longquanfu, the Bohai upper capital during the Tang period] 唐代渤海上京龍泉府遺址. *Wenwu*, no. 9, pp. 85–89.

Chen Xiangwei 陳相偉 and Fang Qidong 方起東. 1982. "Ji'an Changchuan yihao bihuamu" [A tomb with wall paintings, Changchuan 1, in Ji'an] 集安長川一號壁畫墓. *Dongbei kaogu yu lishi* 1, pp. 154–173.

Chen Xiangwei 陳相偉 and Wang Jianqun 王健群. 1973. "Jilin Zhelimumeng Kulunqi yihao Liaomu fajue jianbao" [Brief report on the excavation of Liao Tomb 1 at Kulunqi, Zhelimumeng, Jilin] 吉林哲里木盟庫倫旗一號遼墓發掘簡報. *Wenwu*, no. 8, pp. 1–18.

Chen Yongzhi 陳永志. 1991. "Zuzhou Shishi zaitan" [Another investigation of the Zuzhou Stone House] 祖州石室再探. In *Nei Menggu Dongbuqu kaoguxue wenhua yanjiu ji* 內蒙古東部區考古學文化研究集. Beijing: Haiyang chubanshe, pp. 135–139.

Chen Zhongchi 陳仲箎. 1962. "Yingzao fashi chutan" [Preliminary investigation of *Yingzao fashi*] 營造法式初探. *Wenwu*, no. 2, pp. 12–17.

"Chifeng Dawopu faxian yizuo Liaomu" [A Liao tomb excavated in Dawopu, Chifeng] 赤峰大臥鋪發現一座遼墓. 1959. *Kaogu*, no. 1, pp. 47–48.

Chifeng shi [History of Chifeng] 赤峰史. 1991. Beijing: Wenwu chubanshe.

Chōsen koseki zuroku [Illustrated history of ancient remains in Korea] 朝鮮古蹟圖錄. 1916. 2 vols. Tokyo: Kokka-sha.

Cui Dewen 崔德文. 1992. "Liaodai Tiezhou guzhi xintan" [New excavation at the remains of the ancient Liao site at Tiezhou] 遼代鐵州故址新探. *Beifang wenwu*, no. 2, pp. 46–48.

"Datong Huayansi Daxiongbaodian shice" [Investigation of Daxiongbao Hall of Huayan Monastery in Datong] 大同華嚴寺大雄寶殿實測. In *Zhonghua gujianzhu*, eds. Zhang Yuhuan and Guo Husheng. Beijing: Zhongguo kexue jishu chubanshe, pp. 213–248.

"Datong nanjiao Bei Wei yizhi" [Remains of the Northern Wei in the southern suburbs of Datong] 大同南郊北魏遺址. 1972. *Wenwu*, no. 1, pp. 83–84.

De Xin 德新, Zhang Hanjun 張漢君, and Han Renxin 韓仁信. 1994. "Nei Menggu Balinyouqi Qingzhou Baita faxian de Liaodai Fojiao wenwu" [Buddhist relics discovered in the White Pagoda of Qingzhou in Balinyouqi, Inner Mongolia] 內蒙古巴林右旗慶州白塔發現的遼代佛教文物. *Wenwu*, no. 12, pp. 4–33.

Deng Baoxue 鄧寶學, Sun Guoping 孫國平, and Li Yufeng 李宇峰. 1983. "Liaoning Chaoyang Zhao-shizu mu" [A Zhao family tomb in Chaoyang, Liaoning] 遼寧朝陽趙氏族墓. *Wenwu*, no. 9, pp. 30–38.

Deng Qisheng 鄧其生. 1980. "Woguo gudai jianzhu wumian fangshui cuoshi" [How Chinese roofs prevent water damage] 我國古代建築屋面防水措施. *Kejishi wenji* 5, pp. 135–141.

Ding Mingyi 丁明夷. 1980. *Huayansi* [Huayan Monastery] 華嚴寺. Beijing: Wenwu chubanshe.

Dong Gao 董高. 1990. "Chaoyang Beita 1986–1989 nian kaogu kancha jiyao" [Notes on excavation 1986–1989 at Chaoyang North Pagoda] 朝陽北塔1986–1989年考古勘察紀要. *Liaohai wenwu xuekan*, no. 2, pp. 15–23.

———. 1991. "Chaoyang Beita 'Siyanfotu' jizhi kao" [Research on the remains of four Buddhist images at Chaoyang North Pagoda] 朝陽北塔思燕佛圖跡址考. *Liaohai wenwu xuekan*, no. 2, pp. 97–109.

Dong Wenyi 董文義. 1984. "Balinyouqi Chaganba shiyihao Liaomu" [Liao Tomb 11 at Chaganba, Balinyouqi] 巴林右旗查干壩十一號遼墓. *Nei Menggu wenwu kaogu*, no. 3, pp. 91–93.

Dou Xuezhi 竇學智 et al. 1957. "Yuyao Baoguosi Daxiongbaodian" [Daxiongbao Hall of Baoguo Monastery in Yuyao] 餘姚保國寺大雄寶殿. *Wenwu cankao ziliao*, no. 8, pp. 54–59.

Du Chengwu 杜承武. 1987. "Liaodai muzang chutu de tongsi wangluo yu mianju" [Copper-wire netting and face masks excavated in Liao-period tombs] 遼代墓葬出土的銅絲網絡與面具. In *Liao-Jin shi lunwen ji* 遼金史論文集, vol. 1, ed. Chen Shu 陳述. Shanghai: Shumu wenxian chubanshe, pp. 271–294.

Du Xianzhou 杜仙洲. 1961. "Yixian Fengguosi Daxiongdian diaocha baogao" [Report on the investigation of Daxiongbao Hall of Fengguo Monastery in Yi county] 義縣奉國寺大雄殿調查報告. *Wenwu*, no. 2, pp. 5–13.

"Dulesi" [Dule Monastery] 獨樂寺. 1976. *Wenwu*, no. 10, pp. 74–76.

Eiraku-kyū hekiga [Yonglegong wall paintings] 永楽宮壁画. 1981. Beijing: Waiwen chubanshe.

"Faku Yemaotai Liaomu jilüe" [Notes on a Liao tomb at Yemaotai, Faku] 法庫葉茂臺遼墓記略. 1975. *Wenwu*, no. 12, pp. 26–36.

Fang Dianchun 方殿春. 1988. "Lun Beifang yuanxing muzang de qiyuan" [On the origins of circular tombs in North China] 論北方圓形墓葬的起源. *Beifang wenwu*, no. 3, pp. 38–42.

Fang Dianchun 方殿春 and Zhang Keju 張克舉. 1985. "Shenyang Gugong" [The Forbidden City in Shenyang] 瀋陽故宮. *Beifang wenwu*, no. 3, pp. 47–52.

Fang Qidong 方起東. 1964. "Jilin Ji'an Maxiangou yihao bihuamu" [Maxiangou Tomb 1 with wall paintings in Ji'an, Jilin] 吉林集安蔴線溝一號壁畫墓. *Kaogu*, no. 10, pp. 520–528.

Feng Bingqi 馮秉其 and Shen Tian 申天. 1960. "Xin faxian de Liaodai jianzhu—Laiyuan, Geyuansi, Wenshudian" [Newly discovered Liao architecture—Wenshu Hall of Geyuan Monastery in Laiyuan] 新發現的遼代建築—淶源閣院寺文殊殿. *Wenwu*, nos. 8–9, pp. 66–67.

Feng Jiren 馮繼仁. 1992. "Gongxian Songling xiandian de fuyuan gouxiang" [Reconstruction of the offering halls from Song imperial tombs at Gongxian] 鞏縣宋陵獻殿的復原構想. *Wenwu*, no. 6, pp. 63–71.

Feng Yongqian 馮永謙. 1960. "Liaoningsheng Jianping, Xinmin de sanzuo Liaomu" [Three Liao tombs in Jianping or Xinmin, Liaoning] 遼寧省建平、新民的三座遼墓. *Kaogu*, no. 2, pp. 15–23.

——. 1983. "Liaoning Faku Qianshan Liao Xiao Paolu mu" [The tomb of Liao Xiao Paolu in Qianshan, Faku, Liaoning] 遼寧法庫前山遼蕭袍魯墓. *Kaogu*, no. 7, pp. 624–635.

——. 1987. "Jianguo yilai Liaodai kaogu de zhongyao faxian" [Important discoveries in Liao archaeology since Liberation] 建國以來遼代考古的重要發現. In *Liao-Jin shi lunji*, vol. 1, ed. Chen Shu. Shanghai: Shumu wenxian chubanshe, pp. 295–334.

——. 1988. "Liaodai Yuanzhou, Fuzhou kao" [Investigation of Yuanzhou and Fuzhou in the Liao period] 遼代原州、福州考. *Beifang wenwu*, no. 2, pp. 41–45.

Fogongsi Shijiata he Chongfusi Liao, Jin bihua [Liao- and Jin-period wall paintings at Śākyamuni Pagoda of Fogong Monastery and at Chongfu Monastery] 佛宮寺釋迦塔和崇福寺遼金壁畫. 1983. Beijing: Wenwu chubanshe.

Foguangsi he Dayunyuan Tang, Wudai bihua [Tang- and Five Dynasties-period wall paintings at Foguang Monastery and Dayunyuan] 佛光寺和大雲院唐、五代壁畫. 1983. Beijing: Wenwu chubanshe.

Fu Lehuan 傅樂煥. 1984. *Liaoshi congkao* [Miscellaneous research on the Liao dynastic history] 遼史叢考. Beijing: Zhonghua shuju.

Fu Weiguang 傅惟光 and Jin Zhu 金鑄. 1989. "Heilongjiangsheng Longjiangxian Heshanxiang de Liaodai shishimu" [A Liao-period stone tomb at Heshanxiang, Longjiangxian, Heilongjiang] 黑龍江省龍江縣合山鄉的遼代石室墓. *Beifang wenwu*, no. 4, pp. 32–35.

Fu Xinian 傅熹年. 1973. "Tang Chang'an Daminggong Hanyuandian yuanzhuang de tantao" [Research on the original appearance of Hanyuan Hall of Daming palace complex from Tang Chang'an] 唐長安大明宮含元殿原狀的探討. *Wenwu*, no. 7, pp. 30–48.

——. 1977. "Tang Chang'an Daminggong Xuanwumen ji Chongxuanmen fuyuan yanjiu" [Research on the reconstruction of Xuanwu Gate and Chongxuan Gate from Daming palace complex at Tang Chang'an] 唐長安大明宮玄武門及重玄門復原研究. *Kaogu xuebao*, no. 2, pp. 131–158.

——. 1981a. "Shaanxi Qishan Fengchu Xi Zhou jianzhu yizhi chutan" [Preliminary discussion of the Western Zhou architectural remains at Fengchu, Qishan, Shaanxi] 陝西岐山鳳雛西周建築遺址初談. *Wenwu*, no. 1, pp. 35–45.

——. 1981b. "Fujian de jizuo Songdai jianzhu ji qi yu Riben Liancang 'Da Foyang' jianzhu de guanxi" [The relation between Japanese "Great Buddha Style" architecture of the Kamakura period and several Song buildings in Fujian] 福建的幾座宋代建築及其與日本鎌倉大佛樣建築的關係. *Jianzhu xuebao*, no. 4, pp. 68–77.

——. 1982. "Shanxisheng Fanshixian Yanshansi Nandian Jindai bihuazhong suohui jianzhu de chubu fenxi" [Preliminary analysis of architecture in Jin-period wall paintings in the South Hall of Yanshansi, Fanshi, Shanxi] 山西省繁峙縣巖山寺南殿金代壁畫中所繪建築的初步分析. *Jianzhu lishi yanjiu*, vol. 1, pp. 119–151.

———. 1986. "Tangdai suidao xingmu de xingzhi gouzao he suofanying de dishang gongshi" [Form and structure in Tang paths to underground tombs and architectural influences above ground] 唐代隧道型墓的形制構造和所反映的地上宮室. In Wenwu yu kaogu lunji [Collected essays on cultural relics and archaeology] 文物與考古論集. Beijing: Wenwu chubanshe, pp. 322–343.

Fu Zhanku 富占軍. 1990. "Nei Menggu Shangduxian Qianhaizicun Liaomu" [A Liao tomb in Qianhaizicun, Shangduxian, Inner Mongolia] 內蒙古商都縣前海子村遼墓. Beifang wenwu, no. 2, pp. 49–51.

Fukuyama Toshio 福山敏男 and Akiyama Terukazu 秋山光和. 1950. Eizanji Hakkakudō [The octagonal hall of Eizanji] 栄山寺八角堂. Kyōto: Kyōtō Benrido.

Fuzhou Nan Song Huang Sheng mu [The Southern Song tomb of Huang Sheng in Fuzhou] 福州南宋黃昇墓. 1982. Beijing: Wenwu chubanshe.

Gai Shanlin 蓋山林. 1978. Helinge'er Hanmu bihua [A Han tomb with wall paintings from Helinge'er] 和林格爾漢墓壁畫. Huhehaote: Nei Menggu Renmin chubanshe.

"Gansu Wuwei faxian yipi Xi Xia yiwu" [Xi Xia relics uncovered at Wuwei, Gansu] 甘肅武威發現一批西夏遺物. 1974. Kaogu, no. 3, pp. 200–204.

Gongxian [Gongxian] 鞏縣. 1985. Beijing: Wenwu chubanshe.

Gu Qiyi 辜其一. 1990. "Leshan, Pengshan he Neijiang Dong Han yamu jianzhu chutan" [Preliminary investigation of the architecture of Eastern Han tombs carved into cliffs at Leshan, Pengshan, and Neijiang] 樂山、彭山和內江東漢崖墓建築初探. In Zhonghua gujianzhu, eds. Zhang Yuhuan and Guo Husheng. Beijing: Zhongguo kexue jishu chubanshe, pp. 165–192.

Gu Tiefu 雇鐵符. "Xi'an dongjiao Tangmu bihuazhong de dougong" [Bracket sets in wall paintings from Tang tombs in the eastern suburbs of Xi'an] 西安東郊唐墓壁畫中的斗栱. 1956. Wenwu cankao ziliao, no. 11, pp. 44–45.

Gu Yanwu [1613–1682] 顧炎武. 1960 reprint. Lidai diwang zhaijing ji [Record of imperial residences and capitals through history] 歷代帝王宅京記. Taipei: Guangwen shuju.

Guo Daiheng 郭黛姮. 1988. "Dulesi Guanyinge zai Zhongguo jianzhushi de diwei" [The place of Guanyin Pavilion of Dule Monastery in Chinese architectural history] 獨樂寺觀音閣在中國建築史的地位. Jianzhushi lunwen ji 9, pp. 33–37.

Guo Daiheng 郭黛姮 and Xu Bo'an 徐伯安. 1979. "Zhongguo gudai mugou jianzhu" [Ancient Chinese timber-frame architecture] 中國古代木構建築. Jianzhushi lunwen ji 3, pp.16–71.

———. 1984. "Yingzao fashi damuzuo zhidu xiaoyi" [Brief discussion of the system of 'greater carpentry' in Yingzao fashi] 營造法法式大木作制度小議. Kejishi wenji 11, pp. 104–125.

Guo Husheng 郭湖生 et al. 1964. "Henan Gongxian Songling diaocha" [Excavation at the Song tombs in Gongxian, Henan] 河南鞏縣宋陵調查. Kaogu, no. 11, pp. 564–577.

Guo Yifu 郭義孚. 1963. "Hanyuandian waiguan fuyuan" [Reconstruction of the exterior appearance of Hanyuan Hall] 含元殿外觀復原. Kaogu, no. 10, pp. 567–572.

Guo Zhizhong 郭治中 and Li Yiyou 李逸友. 1987. "Nei Menggu Heicheng kaogu fajue jiyao" [Notes on the excavation of Heicheng in Inner Mongolia] 內蒙古黑城考古發掘紀要. Wenwu, no. 7, pp. 1–23.

Guyuan Bei Weimu qiguanhua [A Northern Wei tomb with a lacquer-painted coffin] 固原北魏墓漆棺畫. 1988. Yinchuan: Ningxia Renmin chubanshe.

Han Baode 漢寶德. 1973. Dougong de qiyuan yu fazhan [The origin and development of the bracket set] 斗栱的起源與發展. Taizhong: Jingyuxiang chubanshe.

Han Duling lingyuan yizhi [Remains of the imperial Han tomb Duling] 漢杜陵陵園遺址. 1993. Beijing: Kexue chubanshe.

Han Jiagu 韓嘉谷. 1986. "Dulesi shiji kao" [Research on the historical remains at Dule Monastery] 獨樂寺史跡考. Beifang wenwu 2, pp. 50–56.

Han Kongle 韓孔樂 and Luo Feng 羅丰. 1984. "Guyuan Bei Wei mu qiguan de faxian" [The excavation of a Northern Wei lacquer-painted coffin from Guyuan] 固原北魏墓漆棺的發現. *Meishu yanjiu*, no. 2, pp. 3–11.

"Han-Wei Luoyangcheng chubu kancha" [Early stages in the excavation of Han-Wei Luoyang] 漢魏洛陽城初步勘察. 1973. *Kaogu*, no. 4, pp. 198–208.

Harada Yoshito 原田淑卜. 1930. *Lelang* [Lelang] 樂浪. Tokyo: Tōa kōko gakkai.

Harada Yoshito 原田淑卜 and Komai Kazuchika. 駒井和愛. 1939. *Tung-ching ch'eng* [Dongjingcheng (The Bohai capital Shangjing)] 東京城. *Archaeologia Orientalis*. Vol. 5. Tokyo: Tōa kōko gakkai.

He Yeju 賀業鉅, ed. 1992. *Jianzhu lishi yanjiu* [Researches in architectural history] 建築歷史研究. Beijing: Zhongguo jianzhu gongye chubanshe.

He Zicheng 賀梓城. 1980. "'Guanzhong Tang shiba-ling' diaocha" [Investigation of the "Eighteen Tang Tombs in Guanzhong"] 關中唐十八陵調查. *Wenwu ziliao congkan*, no. 3, pp. 139–153.

"Hebei Cixian Dong Wei Ruru gongzhu mu fajue jianbao" [Brief report on the excavation of the tomb of the Ruru princess of the Eastern Wei in Cixian, Hebei] 河北磁縣東魏蠕蠕公主墓發掘簡報. 1984. *Wenwu*, no. 4, pp. 1–9.

"Hebei Luanping Liaodai Bohai yetie yizhi jianbao" [Brief report on Bohai smelting of iron from Liao-period Luanping, Hebei province] 河北灤平遼代渤海冶鐵遺址簡報. 1989. *Beifang wenwu*, no. 4, pp. 36–40.

"Hebei Qian'an Shanglucun Liao Han Xiang mu" [The tomb of Han Xiang of the Liao in Shanglu-cun, Qian'an, Hebei] 河北遷安上盧村遼韓相墓. 1973. *Kaogu*, no. 5, pp. 276–278.

"Hebei Zhengding Longxingsi Monidian faxian Song *huangyou* sinian tiji" [An inscription dated *huangyou* 4 found at Moni Hall of Longxing Monastery in Zhengding, Hebei] 河北正定隆興寺摩尼殿發現宋皇祐四年題記. 1980. *Wenwu*, no. 3, p. 94.

Helinge'er Hanmu bihua [A Han tomb with wall paintings at Helinge'er] 和林格爾漢墓壁畫. 1978. Beijing: Wenwu chubanshe.

Hong Feng 洪蜂 and Zhi Li 志立. 1988. "Jilin Hai-longzhen jiao Liao-Jin shidai jianzhu yizhi de fajue" [Discovery of architectural remains of the Liao-Jin period in the suburbs of Hailongzhen, Jilin] 吉林海龍鎮郊遼金時代建築遺的發掘. *Beifang wenwu*, no. 1, pp. 43–46.

Hong Jianmin 洪劍民. 1959. "Lüetan Chengdu jin-jiao Wudai zhi Nan Song de muzang xingzhi" [The form of tombs from the Five Dynasties to Southern Song in the near suburbs of Chengdu] 略談成都近郊五代至南宋的墓葬形制. *Kaogu*, no. 1, pp. 36–39.

Hong Qingyu 洪晴玉. 1959. "Guanyu Dong Shou de faxian he yanjiu" [Excavation and research on the tomb of Dong Shou] 關於冬壽的發現和研究. *Kaogu*, no. 1, pp. 27–35.

Hou Renzhi 侯仁之. 1959. "Guanyu gudai Beijing de jige wenti" [Several questions concerning Beijing in former times] 關於古代北京的幾個問題. *Wenwu*, no. 9: 1–7.

——. 1962. "Lishishang de Beijingcheng" [Beijing through history] 歷史上的北京城. Beijing: Zhongguo Qingnian Press.

——. 1982. "Beijingcheng: lishi fazhan de tedian ji qigaizao" [Beijing: Special features of its historical development and transformation] 北京城：歷史發展的特點及其改造. *Lishi dili* 2: 12–20.

——. 1984. "Beijingcheng de yange" [The evolution of Beijing] 北京城的沿革. In *Bufang ji*. Beijing: Beijing Press, pp. 1–12.

Huang Baoyu 黃寶瑜. 1975. *Jianzhu, zaojing, jihua* [Architecture, landscaping, planning] 建築、造景、際畫. Taipei: Dalu shudian.

Huang Xiuchun 黃秀純 and Fu Gongyue 傅公鉞. 1984. "Liao Han Yi mu fajue baogao" [Excavation report on the Liao tomb of Han Yi] 遼韓佚墓發掘報告. *Kaogu xuebao*, no. 3, pp. 361–380.

Huang Yongquan 黃湧泉. 1956. "Zhejiangsheng de jinianxing jianzhu diaocha gaikuang" [Investigative survey of noteworthy architecture in Zhejiang province] 浙江省的紀念性建築調查概況. *Wenwu cankao ziliao*, no. 4, pp. 59–65.

Ishida Hisatoyo 石田尚豊. *Mandara no kenkyū* [Research on mandala] 曼荼羅の研究. 2 vols. Tokyo: Tōkyō Bijutsu.

———. 1984. *Mandara no mikata: patan ninshiki* [A look at mandala—recognizing patterns] 曼荼羅のミカタ：パターン認識. Tokyo: Iwanami shoten.

Ji Chengkai 季承凱 and Ji Jialong 季嘉龍. 1993. *Guta* [Ancient pagodas] 古塔. Shanghai: Shanghai guji chubanshe.

Ji Chengzhang 吉成章. 1983. "Haoqianying diliuhao Liaomu ruogan wenti de yanjiu" [Research on some questions about Liao Tomb 6 at Haoqianying] 豪欠營第六號遼墓若干問題的研究. *Wenwu*, no. 9, pp. 9–14.

Ji Ping 吉平. 1991. "Liao Zhongjing Data jizuo futu fajue jianbao" [Excavation report of what was uncovered at the base of the Great Pagoda of Liao Zhongjing] 遼中京大塔基座覆土發掘簡報. *Nei Menggu wenwu kaogu*, no. 1, pp. 58–63.

Ji Xunjie 嵇訓杰. 1987. "'Yelü Yanning muzhiming' kaoshi" [Investigation of the funerary inscription of Yelü Yanning] 耶律延寧墓誌銘考釋. *Beifang wenwu*, no. 4, pp. 31–32.

Jiajing Ningxia xinzhi [New record of Ningxia of the *jiajing* period] 嘉靖寧夏新志. 16th century. 1982 printing of 1963 reprint. Shanghai: Shanghai guji shudian.

Jiang Huachang 姜華昌. 1988. "Bohai Shangjing Longquanfu yu Tang Chang'ancheng jianzhu buju de bijiao" [A comparison of the distribution of architecture in the Bohai upper capital at Longquanfu and Tang Chang'an] 渤海上京龍泉府與唐長安城建築布局的比較. *Beifang wenwu*, no. 2, pp. 29–32.

Jiang Huaiying 姜懷英. 1984. "Dali Chongshengsi santa kance baogao" [Investigative report on the three pagodas of Chongsheng Monastery in Dali] 大理崇聖寺三塔勘測報告. *Kejishi wenji* 11, pp. 71–79.

Jiang Huaiying 姜懷英, Yang Yuzhu 楊玉祝, and Yu Gengyin 于庚寅 1985. "Liao Zhongjingta de niandai ji qi jiegou" [The Liao pagoda in Zhongjing and its date and structure] 遼中京塔的年代及其結構. *Gujian yuanlin jishu*, no. 2, pp. 32–37.

Jiayuguan bihuamu fajue baogao [Excavation report on the tombs at Jiayuguan with wall paintings] 嘉峪關壁畫墓發掘報告. 1985. Beijing: Wenwu chubanshe.

"Jilin Tongyuxian Tuanjietun Liaomu" [Liao tombs in Tuanjietun, Tongyu county, Jilin] 吉林通榆縣團結屯遼墓. 1984. *Wenwu*, no. 9, pp. 859–861.

"Jin dongnan Lu'an, Pingshun, Gaoping he Jincheng sixian de gujianzhu" [Ancient architecture in the four counties Lu'an, Pingshun, Gaoping, and Jincheng of southeastern Jin (Shanxi)] 晉東南潞安、平順、高平和晉城四縣的古建築. 1958. *Wenwu cankao ziliao*, no. 3, pp. 26–42.

Jin Fengyi 靳楓毅. 1980. "Liaoning Chaoyang Qianchuanghucun Liaomu" [A Liao tomb in Qianchuanghucun, Chaoyang, Liaoning] 遼寧朝陽前窗戶村遼墓. *Wenwu*, no. 12, pp. 17–29.

Jin Fengyi 靳楓毅 and Xu Ji 徐基. 1985. "Liaoning Jianchang Guishan yihao Liaomu" [Liao Tomb 1 at Guishan, Jianchang, Liaoning] 遼寧建昌龜山一號遼墓. *Wenwu*, no. 3, pp. 48–55.

Jin Shen 金申. 1982. "Kulunqi liuhao Liaomu bihua lingzheng" [On the wall paintings in the Liao tomb Kulunqi 6] 庫倫旗六號遼墓壁畫零證. *Nei Menggu wenwu kaogu*, 2, pp. 51–53.

Jin Weinuo 金維諾, ed. 1988. *Zhongguo meishu quanji* [Comprehensive history of Chinese art] 中國美術全集. *Huihuabian* [Painting series] 繪畫編. Vol. 13: *Siguan bihua* [Monastery wall painting] 寺觀壁畫. Beijing: Wenwu chubanshe.

Jin Yongtian 金永田. 1984. "Liao Shangjing chengzhi fujin Fosi yizhi ji huozangmu" [Cremation tombs and Buddhist monastery remains in the vicinity of the city of Liao Shangjing] 遼上京城址附近佛寺遺址及火葬墓. *Nei Menggu wenwu kaogu* 3, pp. 94–97.

Jinci [The Jin Shrines] 晉祠. 1978. Beijing: Wenwu chubanshe.

Jing Ai 景愛. 1982. "Liao-Jin shidai de huozangmu" [Liao-Jin-period cremation burials] 遼金時代的火葬墓. *Dongbei kaogu yu lishi* 1, pp. 104–115.

"Jinian Dulesi Guanyinge chongjian yiqian zhounian" [Commemorating the 1000th year after the rebuilding of Guanyin Pavilion at Dule Monastery] 紀念獨樂寺觀音閣重建一千周年. 1984. Unpublished conference papers.

"Jin'nianlai Beijing faxian de jizuo Liaomu" [Several Liao tombs excavated in Beijing in recent years] 近

年來北京發現的幾座遼墓. 1980. *Kaogu*, no. 3, pp. 35–40.

Jiu Guanwu 酒冠五. 1958. "Dayunyuan" [Dayunyuan] 大雲院. *Wenwu cankao ziliao*, no. 3, pp. 43–44.

Jiuquan Shiliuguomu bihua [Wall paintings from the Sixteen Kingdoms–period tomb in Jiuquan] 酒泉十六國墓壁畫. 1989. Beijing: Wenwu chubanshe.

Kaihuasi Songdai bihua [Song-period wall paintings at Kaihua Monastery] 開化寺宋代壁畫. 1983. Beijing: Wenwu chubanshe.

Komai Kazuchika 駒井和愛. 1977. *Chūgoku tojō, Bokkai kenkyū* [Chinese cities, Bohai researches] 中國都城—渤海研究. Tokyo: Yōzan-kaku.

———. 1992. "Bohai Dongjing Longquanfu gongcheng-zhi kao" [Research on the palatial and city remains of the Bohai eastern capital at Longquanfu] 渤海東京龍泉府宮城址考. Translated by Ning Bo 寧波. *Beifang wenwu*, no. 4, pp. 106–109.

"Kulunqi diwu-, liuhao Liaomu" [Liao Tombs 5 and 6 at Kulunqi] 庫倫旗第五六號遼墓. 1982. *Nei Menggu wenwu kaogu* 2, pp. 35–46.

Kuno Takeshi 久野健 and Suzuki Kakichi 鈴木嘉吉. 1966. *Gensoku Nihon no bijutsu* [Japanese art "in color"] 原色日本の美術. Vol.2: Hōryū-ji [Hōryū-ji] 法隆寺. Tokyo: Shōgakkan.

Li Baiyao [565–648] 李百藥 et al., eds. 1972 edition. *Bei Qi shu* [Standard history of the Northern Qi] 北齊書. Beijing: Zhonghua shuju.

Li Dianfu 李殿福. 1983. "Ji'an Tongguo sanzuo bihuamu" [Three tombs with wall paintings in Tonggou, Ji'an] 集安通溝三座壁畫墓. *Kaogu*, no. 4, pp. 308–314.

———. 1988. "Bohai Shangjing Yongxingdian kao" [Research on Yongxing palace complex from Bohai Shanjing] 渤海上京永興殿考. *Beifang wenwu*, no. 4, pp. 33–35.

Li Fang 李放. 1912. *Zhongguo yishujia zhenglüe* [Collected material on Chinese artisans] 中國藝術家徵略. n.p.

Li Fengshan 李奉山. 1985. "Shanxi Zhangzixian shizhe Jindai bihua mu" [A stone tomb with wall paintings from the Jin period in Zhangzi, Shanxi] 山西長子縣石哲金代壁畫墓. *Wenwu*, no. 6, pp. 45–54.

Li Haowen 李好文. Yuan. *Chang'anzhi tu* [Illustrated record of Chang'an] 長安志圖. Edited by Bi Yuan (1730–1797) 畢沅. 1978 reprint. *Qianqingtang cong-shu* 千頃堂叢書, no. 24. (*Siku quanshu zhenben* 四庫全書珍本, ser. 9, vol. 162). Taipei: Shangwu yin-shuguan.

Li Jiafu 李甲孚. 1977. *Zhongguo gudai jianzhu yishu* [Ancient Chinese architecture and art] 中國古代建築藝術. Taipei: Beiya gongsi.

Li Jiancai 李健才. 1982. "Ji, Hei liangsheng xibu diqu sizuo Liao-Jin gucheng kao" [Investigation of four ancient Liao-Jin cities in the western districts of Jilin and Heilongjiang] 吉、黑兩省西部地區四座遼金古城考. *Lishi dili* 2, pp. 94–103.

Li Jie 李誡. 1103. 1974 edition *Yingzao fashi* [Building standards] 營造法式. Taipei: Shangwu yinshuguan.

Li Liangjiao 李良姣. 1959. "Shanxi Shuoxian Chong-fusi Mituodian jianzhu chubu fenxi" [Preliminary analysis of the architecture of Mituo Hall of Chong-fu Monastery in Shuoxian, Shanxi] 山西朔縣崇福寺彌陀殿建築初步分析. *Lishi jianzhu*, no. 1.

Li Qingyou 李慶友. 1988a. "Liaoyang Longchang liangzuo Liao-Jin mu" [Two Liao-Jin tombs in Longchang, Liaoyang] 遼陽隆昌兩座遼金墓. *Beifang wenwu*, no. 1, pp. 53–56.

———. 1988b. "Jianping Xiyaocun Liaomu" [A Liao tomb in Xiyaocun, Jianping] 建平西窯村遼墓. *Beifang wenwu*, no. 1, pp. 120–123.

Li Shaobing 李少兵. 1988. "Ningchengxian Xiaotang-shigou Liaomu" [A Liao tomb at Xiaotangshigou, Ningcheng county] 寧城縣小塘士溝遼墓. *Beifang wenwu*, no. 1, pp. 68–71.

———. 1991. "Ningchengxian Xiaotangshigou Liao-mu" [A Liao tomb at Xiaotangshigou, Ningcheng-xian] 寧城縣小塘士溝遼墓. *Nei Menggu wenwu kaogu* 5, no. 1, pp. 68–71.

Li Wei 李蔚. 1989. *Xi Xia shi yanjiu* [Research on the history of the Xi Xia] 西夏史研究. Yinchuan: Ningxia Renmin chubanshe.

Li Wenxin 李文信. 1954. "Yixian Qinghemen Liao-mu fajue baogao" [Excavation report on the Liao tombs at Qinghemen in Yixian] 義縣清河門遼墓發掘報告. *Kaogu xuebao*, no. 8, pp. 163–202.

Li Xihou 李錫厚. 1985. "Shilun Liaodai Yutian Han-shi jiazu de lishi diwei" [On the historical position of the Han family of Yutian in the Liao period] 試論遼代玉田韓氏家族的歷史地位. *Song, Liao, Jin shi luncong*, 1, pp. 251–266.

Li Yanshou 李延壽, ca. 629. 1974 edition. *Beishi* [Standard history of the Northern Dynasties (368–618)] 北史. Beijing: Zhonghua shuju.

Li Yiyou 李逸友. 1958. "Aluke'erqinqi Shuiquangou de Liaodai bihuamu" [A Liao-period wall-painted tomb at Shuiquangou, Aluke'erqinqi] 阿魯科爾沁旗水泉溝的遼代壁畫墓. *Wenwu cankao ziliao*, no. 4, pp. 72–73.

———. 1961a. "Liao Zhongjing xichengwai de gumu-zang" [Ancient tombs in the suburbs of Liao Zhong-jing] 遼中京西城外的古墓葬. *Wenwu*, no. 9, pp. 40–44.

———. 1961b. "Zhaowudameng Ningchengxian Xiaoliu-zhangzi Liaomu fajue jianbao" [Excavation report on Liao tombs at Xiaoliuzhangzi, Ningcheng, Zhao-wudameng] 昭烏達盟寧城縣小劉仗子遼墓發掘簡報. *Wenwu*, no. 9, pp. 44–49.

———. 1981. "Liao Li Zhishun muzhiming ba" [Post-script to the funerary inscription of Liao Li Zhi-shun] 遼李知順墓誌銘跋. *Nei Menggu wenwu kaogu* 1, pp. 84–85.

———. 1982. "Liao Yelü Cong mu shike ji shendao beiming" [Stelae and inscriptions along the spirit path and stone carvings at the Liao tomb of Yelü Cong] 遼耶律琮墓石刻及神道碑銘. *Dongbei kaogu yu lishi* 1, pp. 174–183.

———. 1983. "Qidan de kunfa xisu" [The Qidan cus-tom of hair on the temples] 契丹的髡髮習俗. *Wenwu*, no. 9, pp. 15–18.

———. 1987a. "Lielun Liaodai Qidan yu Hanren mu-zang de tezheng he fenxi" [Special features and analysis of Qidan vs. Han burials in the Liao period] 列論遼代契丹與漢人墓葬的特徵和分析. In *Zhongguo kaogu xuehui diliuci nianhui lunwen ji*. Beijing: Wenwu chubanshe, pp. 187–195.

———. 1987b. "Liaodai chengguo yingjian zhidu chu-tan" [Preliminary investigation of the construction system of Liao cities] 遼代城郭營建制度初探. In *Liao-Jin shi lun ji*, vol. 3, edited by Chen Shu. Bei-jing: Shumu wenxian chubanshe, pp. 45–94.

———. 1987c. "Liaodai daishi kaoshi—cong Liao Chen-guo gongzhu fuma hezangmu chutu de yaodai tanqi" [Investigation of Liao-period belts—based on belts excavated at the joint burial of the Liao Prin-cess of Chenguo and her husband] 遼代帶飾考釋—從遼陳國公主駙馬合葬墓出土的腰帶談起. *Wenwu*, no. 11, pp. 29–35.

———. 1991. "Liaodai Qidanren muzang zhidu gaishuo" [Introductory remarks on the burial system of Qidan in the Liao period] 遼代契丹人墓葬制度概說. In *Nei Menggu Dongbuqu kaoguxue wenhua yanjiu wen ji*. Beijing: Haiyang chubanshe, pp. 80–102.

———. 1992. "Lun Liaomu huaxiangshi de ticai he neirong" [On the contents and inscribed relief sculpture of a Liao tomb] 論遼墓畫像石的體裁和內容. *Liaohai wenwu xuekan*, no. 2, pp. 85–101.

Li Yufeng 李宇峰. 1988. "Fuxin Hailiban Liaomu" [A Liao tomb in Hailiban, Fuxin] 阜新海力板遼墓. *Beifang wenwu*, no. 1, pp. 106–119 and 123.

Li Yufeng 李宇峰 and Yuan Haibo 袁海波. 1988. "Liaoning Fuxin Liao Xiao Jin mu" [The Liao tomb of Xiao Jin in Fuxin, Liaoning] 遼寧阜新遼蕭儔墓. *Beifang wenwu*, no. 2, pp. 33–36. Reprinted in *Fuxin Liao-Jinshi yanjiu* [Research on Liao-Jin his-tory in Fuxin] 阜新遼金史研究, 1992, pp. 195–198.

Li Yuming 李玉明, ed. 1986. *Shanxi gujianzhu tong-lan* [Panorama of ancient architecture in Shanxi] 山西古建築通覽. Taiyuan: Shanxi renmin chu-banshe.

Li Zhengzhi 李征執. 1973. "Tulufanxian Asitana-Halahezhuo gumuqun fajue jianbao (1963–1965)" [Excavation report on the tomb of Alahezhuo in Astana and Khara-Khoja, Turfan (1963–1965)] 吐魯番縣阿斯塔那—哈拉和卓古墓群發掘簡報. *Wenwu*, no. 10, pp. 7–27.

Li Zhujun 李竹君. 1986. "Ruhe jinxing gujianzhu kance gongzuo" [Investigation of questions con-cerning ancient Chinese architecture] 如何進行古建築勘測工作. In *Zhongguo gujianzhu xueshu jiangzuo wenji*. Beijing: Zhongguotang chubanshe, pp. 353–364.

Li Zuozhi 李作智. 1985. "Lun Liao Shangjingcheng de xingzhi" [On the form of Liao Shangjing] 論遼上京城的形制. In *Zhongguo kaogu xuehui di wuci nianhui lunwen ji* 中國考古學會第五次年會論文集. Beijing: Wenwu chubanshe, pp. 128–134.

Liang Sicheng 梁思成. 1932a. "Jixian Dulesi Guanyinge, Shanmen kao" [Research on Guanyin Pavilion and the front gate of Dule Monastery in Ji county] 薊縣獨樂寺觀音閣山門考. *Zhongguo yingzao xueshe huikan* 3, no. 2, pp. 1–92.

———. 1932b. "Jixian Guanyinsi Baita ji" [Notes on the White Pagoda of Guanyin Monastery in Jixian] 薊縣觀音寺白塔記. *Zhongguo yingzao xueshe huikan* 3, no. 2, pp. 93–99.

———. 1932c. "Baodixian Guangjisi Sandashidian" [Sandashi Hall of Guangji Monastery in Baodi county] 寶坻縣廣濟寺三大士殿. *Zhongguo yingzao xueshe huikan* 3, no. 4, pp. 1–50.

———. 1932d. "Women suozhidaode Tangdai Fosi yu gongdian" [Tang Buddhist monasteries and palatial halls that we know about] 我們所知道的唐代佛寺與宮殿. *Zhongguo yingzao xueshe huikan* 3, no. 1, pp. 74–114.

———. 1933a. "Zhengding diaocha jilüe" [Notes on the investigation of Zhengding] 正定調查紀略. *Zhongguo yingzao xueshe huikan* 4, no. 2, pp. 1–41.

———, trans. 1933b. "Fuqing er shita" [Two stone pagodas in Fuzhou] 福清二石塔. Translation of article by Gustav Ecke. *Zhongguo yingzao xueshe huikan* 4, no. 1, pp. 15–21.

———. 1953. "Wutaishan Foguangsi de jianzhu" [Architecture of Foguang Monastery at Mt. Wutai] 五台山佛光寺的建築. *Wenwu cankao ziliao*, nos. 5 and 6, pp. 80–123.

———. 1954. "Zhongguo jianzhu shi" [History of Chinese architecture] 中國建築史. Reprinted in *Liang Sicheng wenji*. 1985, vol. 3, pp. 1–272.

———. 1979 [posthumous paper based on his notes]. "Song *Yingzao fashi* zhushi xuanlu" [Initial announcement of "Explanatory notes to the Song *Yingzao fashi*"] 宋營造法式注釋選錄. *Kejishi wenji* 2, pp. 1–7.

———. 1983a. "'Song *Yingzao Fashi* zhushi' xu" [Preface to "Explanatory notes to the Song *Yingzao fashi*"] 宋營造法式注釋序. *Jianzhushi lunwen ji* 1, pp. 1–9.

———, ed. 1983b. *Yingzao fashi zhushi* [Explanatory notes to *Yingzao fashi*] 營造法式注釋. Vol. 1. Beijing: Zhongguo jianzhugongye chubanshe.

——— et al. n.d. *Zhongguo jianzhu ziliao jicheng* [Selected essays on Chinese architecture] 中國建築資料集成. Taipei compilation.

Liang Sicheng 梁思成 and Liu Dunzhen 劉敦楨. 1934. "Datong gujianzhu diaocha baogao" [Report on the investigation of ancient architecture in Datong] 大同古建築調查報告. *Zhongguo yingzao xueshe huikan* 4, nos. 3 and 4, pp. 1–168.

Liang Sicheng wenji [Collected essays of Liang Sicheng] 梁思成文集. 1982. Vol. 1. Beijing: Zhongguo jianzhu gongye chubanshe.

———. 1984. Vol. 2. Beijing: Zhongguo jianzhu gongye chubanshe.

———. 1985. Vol. 3. Beijing: Zhongguo jianzhu gongye chubanshe.

———. 1986. Vol. 4. Beijing: Zhongguo jianzhu gongye chubanshe.

Liang Sicheng xiansheng danchen bashiwu zhounian jihui wenji [Collected essays on the occasion of the eighty-fifth birthday of Liang Sicheng] 梁思成先生誕辰八十五周年機會文集. 1986. Beijing: Qinghua Daxue chubanshe.

"Liaoning Beipiao Shuiquan yihao Liaomu fajue jianbao" [Excavation report on Liao Tomb 1 at Shuiquan, Beipiao, Liaoning] 遼寧北票水泉一號遼墓發掘簡報. 1977. *Wenwu*, no. 12, pp. 44–51.

"Liao Chenguo gongzhu fuma hezangmu fajue jianbao" [Brief report on the excavation of the joint burial of the Liao Princess of Chenguo and her husband] 遼陳國公主駙馬合葬墓發掘簡報. 1987. *Wenwu*, no. 11, pp. 4–24.

Liao Chenguo gongzhu mu [The tomb of the Liao Princess of Chenguo] 遼陳國公主墓. 1993. Beijing: Wenwu chubanshe.

"Liao Chenguo gongzhu mu chutu wenwu xunli" [A tour of cultural relics excavated at the tomb of Liao Princess of Chenguo] 遼陳國公主墓出土文物巡禮. 1992. *Wenhua yishubao* 4, no. 18, p. 2.

Liao Chenguo gongzhu mu wenwuzhan [An exhibition of the Tomb of the Princess of Chenguo of the Liao] 遼陳國公主墓文物展. n.d. Huhehaote: Nei Mengguo Bowuguan.

Liao Shangjing yizhi jianjie [Brief introduction to the remains of Liao Shangjing] 遼上京遺址簡介. 1983. Balinzuoqi: Balinzuoqi wenhuaguan.

Liao Zhongjing jianjie [Brief introduction to the Liao central capital] 遼中京簡介. 1985. Ningcheng: Wenwu guanlisuo.

"Liaodai Yelü Yanning mu fajue jianbao" [Excavation report on the tomb of Yelü Yanning] 遼代耶律延寧墓發掘簡報. 1980. *Wenwu*, no. 7, pp. 18–22.

"Liaoning Fuxinxian Liao Xuwang mu qingli jianbao" [Report on the tomb of Prince Xu of Liao in Fuxin county, Liaoning] 遼寧阜新縣遼許王墓清理簡報. 1977. *Wenwu ziliao congkan* 1, pp. 84–85.

Lin Huiyin 林徽因 and Liang Sicheng 梁思成. 1935. "Jinfen gujianzhu yucha jilüe" [Notes on the preliminary investigation of old architecture in the Upper Fen River Valley] 晉汾古建築預查記略. *Zhongguo yingzao xueshe huikan* 5, no. 3, pp. 12–67.

Lin Shimin 林士民. 1980. "Baoguosi" [Baoguo Monastery] 保國寺. *Wenwu*, no. 2, pp. 90–91.

Lin Shuzhong 林樹中. 1984. *Nan Chao lingmu diaoke* [Funerary sculpture from the Southern Dynasties] 南朝陵墓雕刻. Beijing: Renmin yishu chubanshe.

Lin Xuechuan 林雪川. 1992. "Ningchengxian Shanzuizi Liaomu Qidanzu touxiang de fuyuan" [Reconstructing the hairstyles of the Qidan based on a Liao tomb at Shanzuizi, Ningcheng county] 寧城縣山嘴子遼墓契丹族頭相的復原. *Nei Menggu wenwu kaogu*, nos. 1–2, pp. 124–129.

Lin Zhao 林釗. 1956. "Fuzhou Hualinsi Daxiongbaodian diaocha jianbao" [Brief report on the excavation of Daxiongbaodian of Hualin Monastery in Fuzhou] 福州華林寺大雄寶殿調查簡報. *Wenwu cankao ziliao*, no. 7, pp. 45–48 and 59.

——. 1957. "Putian Xuanmiaoguan Sanqingdian diaocha ji" [Record of the investigation of Sanqing Hall of Xuanmiaoguan in Putian] 莆田玄妙觀三清殿調查記. *Wenwu*, no. 11, pp. 52–53.

Linhuang shiji [Historical remains of Linhuang] 臨潢史跡. 1988. Balinzuoqi: Neibu ziliao.

Liu Cheng 劉成. Liao. "Chongxiu Dulesi bei" [Stele of the repair of Dule Monastery] 重修獨樂寺碑. Reprinted in *Quan Liaowen* 全遼文, ed. Chen Shu 陳述. 1982. Beijing: Zhonghua shuju, p. 101.

Liu Dunzhen 劉敦楨. 1935. "Hebeisheng xibu gujianzhu diaocha jilüe" [Notes on the investigation of ancient architecture in western Hebei] 河北省西部古建築調查記略. *Zhongguo yingzao xueshe huikan* 5, no. 4, pp. 1–55.

——. 1937. "Henansheng beibu gujianzhu diaocha ji" [Record of the investigation of ancient architecture in northern Henan] 河南省北部古建築調查記. *Zhongguo yingzao xueshe huikan* 6, no. 4, pp. 33–129.

——. 1979 [paper based on posthumous notes]. "Gugongben *Yingzao fashi* chaoben jiaokan ji" [A note on the collated edition of the Palace Museum *Yingzao fashi*] 故宮本營造法式鈔本校勘記. *Kejishi wenji* 2, p. 8.

——. 1982. *Liu Dunzhen wenji* [Collected essays of Liu Dunzhen] 劉敦楨文集. Vol. 1. Beijing: Zhongguo jianzhu gongye chubanshe.

——. 1984a. *Zhongguo gudai jianzhu shi* [History of Chinese architecture] 中國古代建築史. 2nd ed. Beijing: Zhongguo jianzhu gongye chubanshe.

——. 1984b. *Liu Dunzhen wenji* [Collected essays of Liu Dunzhen] 劉敦楨文集. Vol. 2. Beijing: Zhongguo jianzhu gongye chubanshe.

——. 1987. *Liu Dunzhen wenji* [Collected essays of Liu Dunzhen] 劉敦楨文集. Vol. 3. Beijing: Zhongguo jianzhu gongye chubanshe.

Liu Fengzhu 劉鳳翥 and Ma Junshan 馬俊山. 1983. "Qidan dazi Beidawang muzhi kaoshi" [The funerary inscription in the tomb of Qidan Beidawang] 契丹大字北大王墓誌考釋. *Wenwu*, no. 9, pp. 23–29 and p. 50.

Liu Haiwen 劉海文 et al. 1992. "Hebei Xuanhua Xiabali Liao Han Shixun mu" [The Liad tomb of Han Shixun at Xiabali, Xuanhua, Hebei] 河北宣化下八里遼韓師訓墓. *Wenwu*, no. 6, pp. 1–11.

Liu Keli 劉珂理, ed. 1990. *Zhongguo simiao daguan*

[Panoramic view of Chinese temple complexes] 中國寺廟大觀. Beijing: Beijing Yanshan chubanshe.

Liu Qian 劉謙. 1984. "Jinzhou, Zhangkangcun Liaomu fajue baogao" [Excavation report on Liao tombs at Zhangkangcun, Jinzhou] 錦州張扛村遼墓發掘報告. *Kaogu*, no. 11, pp. 990–1002.

Liu Qingzhu 劉慶柱 and Li Yufang 李毓芳. 1987. *Xi Han shiyi ling* [The eleven imperial tombs of Western Han] 西漢十一陵. Xi'an: Shaanxi Renmin chubanshe.

Liu Xiaodong 劉曉東 and Wei Cuncheng 魏存成. 1987. "Bohai Shangjingcheng yingzhu shixu yu xingzhi yuanyuan yanjiu" [Research on the periodization, form, and origins of the city and buildings of Bohai Shangjing] 渤海上京城營築時序與形制淵源研究. In *Zhongguo kaogu xuehui diliuci nianhui lunwen ji*. Beijing: Wenwu chubanshe, pp. 171–186.

Liu Xu 劉昫 [887–947] et al. 1971 edition. *Jiu Tangshu* [Old standard history of the Tang] 舊唐書. Taipei reprint of Sibu beiyao edition.

Liu Yuquan 劉玉權. 1982. "Gua-, Shanishūno Sai Ka jidai no sekkutsu" [Xi Xia period caves in Guazhou and Shazhou] 瓜沙二州の西夏時代の石窟. In *Tōnkō Bakukō kutsu* 敦煌莫高窟. Vol. 5, pp. 164–177.

Liu Zhiping 劉致平. 1957a. *Zhongguo jianzhu leixing ji jiegou* [Typology and structures of Chinese architecture] 中國建築類型及結構. Beijing: Zhongguo jianzhu gongye chubanshe.

——. 1957b. "Xi'an xijiao gudai jianzhu yizhi kancha chuji" [Preliminary report on excavated remains of ancient architecture from the western suburbs of Xi'an] 西安西郊古代建築遺址勘察初記. *Wenwu cankao ziliao*, no. 3, pp. 5–10.

Liu Zhiping 劉致平 and Fu Xinian 傅熹年. 1963. "Lindedian fuyuan de chubu yanjiu" [Preliminary research on the reconstruction of Linde Hall] 麟德殿復原的初步研究. *Kaogu*, no. 7, pp. 385–402.

Long Feiliao 龍非了. 1990. "Zhongguo gudai jianzhu de jiegou chengjiu" [The achievements of the structure of ancient Chinese architecture] 中國古代建築的結構成就. In *Zhonghua gujianzhu*, eds.

Zhang Yuhuan and Guo Husheng. Beijing: Zhongguo kexue jishu chubanshe, pp. 37–40.

Lü Jiang 呂江. 1988. "Tang-Song louge jianzhu yanjiu" [Research on pavilion architecture of the Tang and Song] 唐宋樓閣建築研究. *Jianzhushi lunwen ji* 10, pp. 22–56.

Lu Minghui 盧明輝 et al. 1987. *Nei Menggu wenwu guji sanji* [Collected essays on ancient cultural relics in Inner Mongolia] 內蒙古文物古跡散記. Huhehaote: Nei Menggu renmin chubanshe.

Lu Qi 魯琪 and Zhao Fusheng 趙福生. 1980. "Beijingshi Zhaitang Liao bihuamu fajue jianbao" [Brief report on the excavation of a Liao tomb with wall paintings at Zhaitang, Beijing] 北京市齋堂遼壁畫墓發掘簡報. *Wenwu*, no. 7, pp. 23–27.

Lu Sixian 陸思賢. 1987. "Xianbei kaoguzhong de xin keti" [New questions about Xianbei archaeology] 鮮卑考古中的新課題. In *Nei Menggu wenwu guji sanji* 內蒙古文物古跡散記, ed. Lu Minghui 盧明輝 et al. Huhehaote: Nei Menggu renmin chubanshe, pp. 90–94.

Lu Sixian 陸思賢 and Du Chengwu 杜承武. 1983. "Chayouqianqi, Haoqianying diliuhao Liaomu qingli jianbao" [Excavation report on Liao Tomb 6 at Haoqianying, Chayouqianqi] 察右前旗豪欠營第六號遼墓清理簡報. *Wenwu*, no. 9, pp. 1–8.

Lu Zhaoyin 盧兆蔭. 1964. "Tang Qinglongsi yizhi tacha jilüe" [Notes on the process of examining the remains of Tang Qinglongsi] 唐青龍寺遺址踏查記略. *Kaogu*, no. 7, pp. 346–354.

Luo Feng 羅豐. 1985. "Li Xian fufu muzhi kaolüe" [Research on the tomb of Li Xian and his wife] 李賢夫婦墓誌考略. *Meishu yanjiu*, no. 11, pp. 59–60.

Luo Jiang 羅將. 1956. "Hebei Zhengding Longxingsi Zhuanlunzangdian xiushan wangong" [The completion of repairs of the Hall of the Revolving Sutra Cabinet at Longxing Monastery in Zhengding, Hebei] 河北正定隆興寺轉輪藏殿修繕完工. *Wenwu cankao ziliao*, no. 1, pp. 56–67.

Luo Jizu 羅繼祖, ed. 1958. *Liaoshi jiaokan ji* [Corrections and collations of the Liao history] 遼史校勘記. Shanghai: Shanghai Renmin chubanshe.

Luo Zhewen 羅哲文. 1953. "Yanbei gujianzhu de diao-cha" [Investigation of ancient Chinese architecture in the North] 燕北古建築的調查. *Wenwu cankao ziliao*, no. 3, pp. 35–56.

———. 1976. "Tan Dulesi Guanyinge jianzhu de kang-zhen xingneng wenti" [On the question of the earth-quake resistance of the structure of Guanyin Pavilion of Dule Monastery] 談獨樂寺觀音閣建築的抗震性能問題. *Wenwu*, no. 10, pp. 71–73.

———. 1986. "Zhongguo guta" [Ancient Chinese pago-das] 中國古塔. In *Zhongguo gujianzhu xueshu jiangzuo wenji*. Beijing: Zhongguotang chubanshe, pp. 141–161.

———. 1993. *Zhongguo lidai huangdi lingmu* [Chinese imperial tombs through the ages] 中國歷代皇帝陵墓. Beijing: Waiwen chubanshe.

———, chief ed. 1994. *Zhongguo gudai jianzhu* [An-cient Chinese architecture] 中國古代建築. Taipei: Nantian shuju youxian gongsi.

Luo Zhewen 羅哲文 and Wang Shiren 王世仁. 1986. "Fojiao siyuan" [Buddhist monasteries] 佛教寺院. In *Zhongguo gujianzhu xueshu jiangzuo wenji*. Bei-jing: Zhongguotang chubanshe, pp. 123–130.

Luoyangshi zhi [Record of the city of Luoyang] 洛陽市志. 1995. Zhengzhou: Zhongguo guji chubanshe.

Ma Dezhi 馬得志. 1959a. *Tang Chang'an Daminggong* [Daming palace complex of Tang Chang'an] 唐長安大明宮. Beijing: Zhongguo kexue chubanshe.

———. 1959b. "Tang Daminggong fajue jianbao" [Brief report on the excavation of Tang Daming palace complex] 唐大明宮發掘簡報. *Kaogu*, no. 6, pp. 296–301.

———. 1961. "Yijiuwushijiu-Yijiuliushi-nian Tang Da-minggong fajue jianbao" [Brief excavation report on the 1959–1960 season at Tang Daming palace complex] 一九五十九一一九六十一年唐大明宮發掘簡報. *Kaogu*, no. 7, pp. 341–344.

———. 1986. "Tang Chang'an Qinglongsi jianzhu gui-mo ji duiwai yingxiang" [On the architecture of Qinglong Monastery of Tang Chang'an and its ex-ternal influences] 唐長安青龍寺建築規模及對外影響. In *Zhongguo kaoguxue yanjiu*. Beijing: Wenwu chubanshe, pp. 277–285.

———. 1989. "Tang Chang'an Qinglongsi yizhi" [Re-mains of Qinglong Monastery from Tang Chang'an] 唐長安青龍寺遺址. *Kaogu xuebao*, no. 2, pp. 231–262.

Ma Ruitian 馬瑞田. 1983. "Dingxian Kaiyuansi Liao-dita taji caihua" [Base-level painting on "Liaodi Pa-goda" of Kaiyuan Monastery in Dingxian] 定縣開元寺料敵塔塔基彩畫. *Wenwu*, no. 5, pp. 78–79.

Mancheng Hanmu fajue baogao [Excavation report on the Han tombs at Mancheng] 滿城漢墓發掘報告. 1980. Beijing: Wenwu chubanshe.

Mei Niansi 美念思. 1991. "Kaiyuan Chongshousita jian yu Liaodai kao" [Research on the Liao-period pagoda at Chongshousi in Kaiyuan] 開原崇壽寺塔建於遼代考. *Liaohai wenwu xuekan*, no. 2, pp. 110–112.

Meng Guangyao 孟廣曜. 1987. "Liaodai Shangjing yizhi zhaji" [Notes on the remains of Liao Shang-jing] 遼代上京遺址札記. In *Nei Menggu wenwu guji sanji*, ed. Lu Minghui et al. Huhehaote: Nei Menggu Renmin chubanshe, pp. 100–105.

Meng Yuanlao 孟元老. Song. 1972 reprint. *Dongjing menghua lu* [Record of dreaming of *hua* in the east-ern capital] 東京夢華錄. Taipei: Shijie shuju.

Miao Quansun 繆荃孫, chief ed. (Completed under Zhang Zhidong 張之洞 et al. 1885 and 1889.) *Shuntianfu zhi* [Record of Shuntian district] 順天府志. Facsimile reproduction of Guangxu edition (1884–1886).

Miao Runhua 苗潤華. 1988. "Nei Menggu Balinyouqi Hutulu Liaomu" [A Liao tomb at Hutulu, Balin-youqi, Inner Mongolia] 內蒙古巴林右旗虎吐路遼墓. *Beifang wenwu*, no. 3, pp. 36–37 and 29.

Miyazaki Ichisada 宮崎市定. 1976. "Chūgoku kasō kō" [Research on Chinese cremation burial] 中國火葬考. *Ajiashi ronk1* 3, pp. 63–84.

Mizuno Seiichi 水野清一. 1938a, b. "Daitō tsushin" [Communication from Datong] 大同通信. *Kōko-gaku* 9, no. 8, pp. 410–415; *Kōkogaku* 9, no. 9, pp. 434–437.

Mizuno Seiichi 水野清一 and Nagahiro Toshio 長広敏雄. 1951–1956. *Unkō sekkutsu* [Yungang, the Bud-dhist cave temples of the fifth century A.D. in North

China] 雲崗石窟. 16 vols. Kyōto: Kyōto Daigaku Jimbun Kagaku Kenkyū-jo.

Mo Zongjiang 莫宗江. 1945. "Shanxi Yuci Yongshousi Yuhuagong" [Yuhuagong of Yongshou Monastery in Yuci, Shanxi] 山西榆次永壽寺雨花宮. *Zhongguo yingzao xueshe huikan* 7, no. 2, pp. 1–24.

——. 1979. "Laiyuan, Geyuansi, Wenshudian" [Wenshu Hall of Geyuan Monastery in Laiyuan] 淶源閣院寺文殊殿. *Jianzhu shi lunwen ji*, 2, pp. 51–71.

Mochizuki Shinkō 望月信享. 1954–1967. *Mochizuki Bukkyō daijiten* [Mochizuki's Buddhist dictionary] 望月佛教大辭典. 10 vols. Kyōto: Sekai seitan kanko kyōkai.

Mori Ōsamu 森蘊 and Naitō Hiroshi 入藤寬. 1934. *Ying-ch'eng-tzu* [Yingchengzi] 營城子. *Archaeologia Orientalis*, vol. 4. Tokyo and Kyōto: Tōa-Tōkogaku-kai.

Murata Jiro 村田治郎. 1981. *Chūgoku no teito* [Chinese imperial cities] 中国の帝都. Kyōto: Sōgeisha.

Naitō Torajirō 內藤虎次郎. 1922. "Gaikatsuteki Tō-Sō jidai kan" [A general view of the Tang and Song periods] 概括的唐宋時代権. *Rekishi to chiri* 歷史と地理 9, no. 5, pp. 1–12.

Nalan Chengde 納蘭成德, ed. 1676. *Sanli tu* [Illustrated "three ritual classics"] 三禮圖.

Nan Song Yu Gongzhu fufu hezangmu [On the joint burial of Southern Song Prince Yu and his wife] 南宋虞公主夫婦合葬墓. 1985. *Kaogu xuebao*, no. 3, pp. 383–402.

"Nei Menggu Shanzuizi 'Gu Yelüshi' mu fajue baogao" [Excavation report on the tomb of "Elder Yelü" from Shanzuizi, Inner Mongolia] 內蒙古山嘴子故耶律氏墓發掘報告. 1981. *Wenwu ziliao congkan*, 5, pp. 167–171.

Ning Duxue 寧篤學 and Zhong Zhangfa 鍾長發. 1980. "Gansu Wuwei xijiao Linchang Xi Xia mu qingli jianbao" [Brief report on the material from the Xi Xia tomb at Linchang in the western suburbs of Wuwei, Gansu] 甘肅武威西郊林場西夏墓清理簡報. *Kaogu yu wenwu*, no. 3, pp. 63–66.

"Ningxia Guyuan Bei Weimu qingli jianbao" [Brief report on the excavation of the Northern Wei tomb in Guyuan, Ningxia] 寧夏固原北魏墓清理簡報. 1984. *Wenwu*, no. 6, pp. 46–56.

"Ningxia Guyuan Bei Zhou Li Xian fufu mu fajue jianbao" [Brief report on the excavation of the Northern Zhou tomb of Li Xian and his wife in Ningxia] 寧夏固原北周李賢夫婦墓發掘簡報. 1985. *Wenwu*, no. 11, pp. 1–20.

"Ningxia Shijushanshi, Xi Xia chengzhi shijue" [Investigation of the remains of a Xi Xia city at Shijushan, Ningxia] 寧夏石咀山市西夏城址試掘. 1981. *Kaogu*, no. 1, pp. 91–92 and 83.

Niu Dasheng 牛達生. 1986. "Shilun Xi Xia ducheng Xingqingfu" [Discussion of the Xi Xia capital Xingqingfu] 試論西夏都城興慶府. *Ningxia wenwu* 1, pp. 32–38.

Otagi Matsuo 愛宕松男. *Kittan kodai shi no kenkyū* [Research on the early history of the Qidan] 契丹古代史の研究. *Tōyōshi kenkyū sōkan* 6. Kyōto: Tōyōshi kenkyū-kai.

Ouyang Xiu [1007–1072] 歐陽修, comp. 1974 edition. *Xin Wudai shi* [New standard history of the Five Dynasties] 新五代史. Beijing: Zhonghua shuju.

Ouyang Xiu [1007–1072] 歐陽修 and Song Qi [998–1061] 宋祁, comps. 1975 edition. *Xin Tang shu* [New standard history of Tang] 新唐書. Beijing: Zhonghua shuju.

Pan Guxi 潘谷西. 1986. "Zhongguo gudai gongdian, tanmiao, lingmu jianzhu" [On the architecture of Chinese palatial halls, altars, temples, and tombs] 中國古代宮殿、壇廟、陵墓建築. In *Zhongguo gujianzhu xueshu jiangzuo wenji*. Beijing: Zhongguo zhanwang chubanshe, pp. 63–106.

Pan Jiezi 潘絜兹. 1979. "Lingyan caibi dongxinpo-Yanshan[g]si Jindai bihua xiaoji" [Brief notes on the artistic value of Jin-period wall paintings at Yanshan(g) Monastery] 靈巖彩壁動心魄一巖山[上]寺金代壁畫小記. *Wenwu*, no. 2, pp. 3–10.

Pan Yushan 潘玉閃 and Ma Shichang 馬世長. 1985. *Mogaoku kuqian diantang yizhi* [Remains of frontal buildings added to Mogao Caves] 莫高窟窟前殿堂遺址. Beijing: Wenwu chubanshe.

Qi Xiaoguang 齊曉光. 1987. "Nei Menggu Kulunqi qi-, bahao Liaomu" [Tombs 7 and 8 at Kulunqi, Inner Mongolia] 內蒙古庫倫旗七八號遼墓. *Wenwu*, no. 7, pp. 74–84.

Qi Xin 齊心 and Liu Jingyi 劉精義. 1980. "Beijingshi Fangshanxian Beizhengcun Liaota qingli ji" [Report of the investigation of the Liao pagoda at Beizheng village, Fangshan county, Beijing] 北京市房山縣北鄭村遼塔清理記. *Kaogu*, no. 2, pp. 147–158.

Qi Yingtao 祁英濤. 1957. "Hebeisheng Xinchengxian Kaishansi Dadian" [The Main Hall of Kaishan Monastery in Xincheng county, Hebei] 河北省新城縣開善寺大殿. *Wenwu cankao ziliao*, no. 10, pp. 23–29.

——. 1979. "Dui Shaolinsi Chuzu'an Dadian de chubu fenxi" [Preliminary analysis of the Main Hall of Chuzu'an of Shaolin Monastery] 對少林寺初祖庵大殿的初步分析. *Kejishi wenji*, no. 2, pp. 61–70.

——. 1981. *Zenyang jianding gujianzhu* [How to identify Chinese architecture] 怎樣鑑定古建築. Beijing: Wenwu chubanshe.

——. 1983. "Zhongguo zaoqi mujiegou jianzhu de shidai tezheng" [Notes on the epochal features of early Chinese timber-frame architecture] 中国早期木結構建築的時代特徵. *Wenwu*, no. 4, pp. 60–74.

——. 1986. "Jianding gudai jianzhu niandai de jige wenti" [Some questions concerning the determination of date of old Chinese buildings] 鑑定古代建築年代的幾個問題. In *Zhongguo gujianzhu xueshu jiangzuo wenji*. Beijing: Zhongguotang chubanshe, pp. 299–307.

——. 1990. "Zhongguo gudai jianzhuzhong de jinshu goujian" [Metal components of ancient Chinese architecture] 中國古代建築中的金屬構件. In *Zhonghua gujianzhu*, eds. Zhang Yuhuan and Guo Husheng. Beijing: Zhongguo kexue jishe chubanshe, pp. 71–90.

——. 1992a. "Zhengding Longxingsi Cishige fuyuan gongcheng yifang'an ji shuoming" [First reconstruction drawing and explanation of Cishi Pavilion, Longxingsi, Zhengding] 正定隆興寺慈氏閣復原工程一方案及說明. In *Qi Yingtao gujian lunwen ji*. Beijing: Huaxia chubanshe, pp. 9–10.

——. 1992b. "Zhengding Longxingsi Cishige fuyuan gongcheng erfang'an ji shuoming" [Second reconstruction drawing and explanation of Cishi Pavilion, Longxingsi, Zhengding] 正定隆興寺慈氏閣復原工程二方案及說明. In *Qi Yingtao gujian lunwen ji*. Beijing: Huaxia chubanshe, pp. 11–13.

——. 1992c. "Zhongguo gudai mujiegou jianzhu de baoyang yu weixiu" [Conservation and repair of ancient Chinese timber-frame architecture] 中國古代木結構建築的保養與維修. In *Qi Yingtao gujian lunwen ji*. Beijing: Huaxia chubanshe, pp. 28–105.

——. 1992d. "Monidian xinfaxian de tiji de yanjiu" [Research on newly discovered inscriptions at Moni Hall] 摩尼殿新發現的題記的研究. In *Qi Yingtao gujian lunwen ji*. Beijing: Huaxia chubanshe, pp. 106–113.

——. 1992e. "Zhongguo gudai jianzhu de weixiu yuanze he shili" [Principles and examples of repair of traditional Chinese architecture] 中國古代建築的維修原則和實例. In *Qi Yingtao gujian lunwen ji*. Beijing: Huaxia chubanshe, pp. 124–132.

——. 1992f "Yingxian Muta jixiang tan-shisi niandai ceding" [Some determinations based on carbon-14 dating at Yingxian Timber Pagoda] 應縣木塔幾項碳十四年代測定. In *Qi Yingtao gujian lunwen ji*. Beijing: Huaxia chubanshe, pp. 133–136.

——. 1992g. "Zhengding Longxingsi jianjie" [Introduction to Longxingsi, Zhengding] 正定隆興寺簡介. In *Qi Yingtao gujian lunwen ji*. Beijing: Huaxia chubanshe, pp. 155–156.

——. 1992h. "Shanxi Wutai de liangzuo Tangdai mugou dadian" [Two Tang-period timber-frame main halls from Wutai, Shanxi] 山西五台的兩座唐代木構大殿. In *Qi Yingtao gujian lunwen ji*. Beijing: Huaxia chubanshe, pp. 157–158.

——. 1992i. "Gaodu fangzhen xingneng de Tianjin Dulesi Guanyinge" [The high level of earthquake-proof resistance of Guanyin Pavilion of Dule Monastery, Tianjin] 高度防震性能的天津獨樂寺觀音閣. In *Qi Yingtao gujian lunwen ji*. Beijing: Huaxia chubanshe, pp. 159–160.

——. 1992j. "Zhongguo gudai jianzhu geshidai tezheng gailun" [Discussion of special features of Chinese ancient architecture of each time period]

中國古代建築各時代特徵概論. In *Qi Yingtao gujian lunwen ji*. Beijing: Huaxia chubanshe, pp. 237–295.

———. 1992k. "Longxingsi Monidian xiushan gongcheng jianjie" [Notes on repair work at Moni Hall of Longxingsi] 隆興寺摩尼殿修繕工程簡介. In *Qi Yingtao gujian lunwen ji*. Beijing: Huaxia chubanshe, p. 304.

———. 1992l. "Nanchansi Dadian fuyuan gongcheng jianjie" [Notes on the restoration of the Main Hall of Nanchansi] 南禪寺大殿復原工程簡介. In *Qi Yingtao gujian lunwen ji*. Beijing: Huaxia chubanshe, p. 305.

———. 1992m. "Zhongguo gudai jianzhu de tezheng ji jiazhi" [Special features and value of ancient Chinese architecture] 中國古代建築的特徵及價值. In *Qi Yingtao gujian lunwen ji*. Beijing: Huaxia chubanshe, pp. 313–318.

Qi Yingtao 祁英濤 and Chai Zejun 柴澤俊. 1980. "Nanchansi Dadian xiufu" [The restoration of the Main Hall of Nanchansi] 南禪寺大殿修復. *Wenwu*, no. 11, pp. 61–75.

———. 1982. "Wutai Nanchansi Dadian xiufu gongcheng baogao" [Report on the restoration work of the Main Hall of Nanchansi, Wutai] 五台南禪寺大殿修復工程報告. *Jianzhu lishi yanjiu*, no. 1, pp. 152–170.

Qi Yingtao 祁英濤, Du Xianzhou 杜仙洲, and Chen Mingda 陳明達. 1954. "Liangnianlai Shanxisheng xinfaxian de gujianzhu" [Ancient architecture discovered in Shanxi two years ago] 兩年來山西省新發現的古建築. *Wenwu cankao ziliao*, no. 11, pp. 49–54.

Qi Yingtao gujian lunwen ji [Collected essays on ancient architecture by Qi Yingtao] 祁英濤古建論文集. 1992. Beijing: Huaxia chubanshe.

"Qidan kaogu xueshu huiyi jiyao" [Minutes from the meeting on Qidan archaeology] 契丹考古學術會議紀要. 1984. *Nei Menggu wenwu kaogu* 3, pp. 1–6 and p. 12.

Qiu Xiting 仇錫廷, ed. *Jixian zhi* [Record of Ji prefecture] 薊縣志. 1969 reprint. Taipei: Chengwen chubanshe.

Qu Haoran 屈浩然. 1991. *Zhongguo gudai gao jianzhu* [High buildings of ancient China] 中國古代高建築. Tianjin: Tianjin kexue jishu chubanshe.

Ren Changtai 任常泰, ed. 1995. *Zhongguo lingqin shi* [History of Chinese royal tombs] 中國陵寢史. Taipei: Wenjin chubanshe.

Saitō Tadashi 斎藤忠. 1976. *Kofun no hekiga* [Wall paintings in *kofun*] 古墳の壁画. Tokyo: Shibundō, 1976.

2*Sanshanzhi* [Record of the "three mountains" (Fuzhou)] 三山志. In *Song-Yuan difangzhi congshu* 宋元地方志叢書, vol. 12, *juan* 33.

Sekiguchi Masayuki 関口正之, ed. 1988. *Nihon no Bukkyō* [Japanese Buddhism] 日本の佛教. Vol. 2: *Mikkyō* [Esotericism] 密教. Tokyo: Shinchosha.

Sekino Tadashi 關野貞. 1932. "Kei-ken Dokurakuji" [Dule Monastery in Ji county] 薊縣獨樂寺. *Bijutsu kenkyū* 8, pp. 271–278.

———. 1933. "Manshū Gi-ken Hōkoku-ji Daiyūhōden" [Daxiongbao Hall of Fengguo Monastery in Yi county, Manchuria] 滿洲義縣奉國寺大雄寶殿. *Bijutsu kenkyū* 14, pp. 37–49.

———. 1938. *Shina no kenchiku to geijutsu* [Chinese architecture and art] 支那の建築と藝術. Tokyo: Iwanami shoten.

Sekino Tadashi 關野貞 and Itō Chūta 伊東忠太. 1925. *Tōyō kenchiku* [East Asian architecture] 東洋建築. Tokyo: Kenchiku kōgei shuppansha.

Sekino Tadashi 關野貞 and Takeshima Takuichi 竹島卓一. 1925. *Ryō Kin jidai no kenchiku to sono Butsuzō* [Liao-Jin architecture and its Buddhist sculpture] 遼金時代の建築と其佛像. 2 vols. Tokyo: Tōhō bunka gakuin Tōkyō kenkyūjo.

Sekino Tadashi 關野貞 et al. 1929. *Kokuri jidai no iseki* [Remains of the Koguryŏ period] 高句麗時代の遺跡. 2 vols. Tokyo: Chōsen sōtokufu.

Shang Xiaobo 尙曉波. 1989. "Liaoningsheng Chaoyangshi faxian Liaodai Gongxiangmu" [The Liao-period Gongxiang Tomb excavated in Chaoyang, Liaoning] 遼寧省朝陽市發現遼代龔祥墓. *Beifang wenwu*, no. 4, pp. 28–31.

Shanhuasi [Shanhua Monastery] 善化寺. 1987. Beijing: Wenwu chubanshe.

"Shanxi Datong nanjiao chutu Bei Wei jin tong qi" [Gold and bronze objects from the Northern Wei period unearthed in the southern suburbs of Datong] 山西大同南郊出土北魏金銅器. 1983. *Kaogu*, no. 11, pp. 997–999.

"Shanxi Datong Shijiazhai Bei Wei Sima Jinlong mu" [The tomb of Sima Jinlong of the Northern Wei from Shijiazhai, Datong, Shanxi] 山西大同石家寨北魏司馬金龍墓. 1972. *Wenwu*, no. 3, pp. 20–33.

"Shanxi Datong Wohuwan sizuo Liaodai bihua mu" [Four Liao tombs with wall paintings in Wohuwan, Datong, Shanxi] 山西大同臥虎灣四座遼代壁畫墓. 1963. *Kaogu*, no. 8, pp. 432–433.

"Shanxi Yingxian Fogongsi Mutanei faxian Liaodai zhengui wenwu" [Precious cultural relics found in the Liao-period Timber Pagoda of Fogong Monastery in Yingxian, Shanxi] 山西應縣佛宮寺木塔內發現遼代珍貴文物. 1982. *Wenwu*, no. 6, pp. 1–8.

Shao Fuyu 邵福玉. 1980. "Fengguosi" [Fengguo Monastery] 奉國寺. *Wenwu*, no. 12, pp. 86–87.

Shao Guotian 邵國田. 1978. "Aohanqi Baitazi Liaomu" [A Liao tomb at Baitazi, Aohanqi] 敖漢旗白塔子遼墓. *Kaogu*, no. 2, pp. 119–121.

——. 1984. "Nei Menggu Zhaowudameng Aohanqi Beisanjia Liaomu" [Liao tombs in Beisanjia, Aohanqi, Zhaowudameng, Inner Mongolia] 內蒙古昭烏達盟敖漢旗北三家遼墓. *Kaogu*, no. 11, pp. 1003–1011.

——. 1987. "Neimenggu Aohanqi Shazigou, Dahenggou Liaomu" [Liao tombs at Shazigou and Dahenggou in Aohanqi, Inner Mongolia] 內蒙古敖漢旗沙子溝、大橫溝遼墓. *Kaogu*, no. 10, pp. 889–904.

Shen Rui 沈銳, comp. 1831. 1968 reprint. *Jizhou zhi* [Record of Ji prefecture] 薊州志. 3 vols. Taipei: Xuesheng shuju.

Shi Guiping 石圭平. 1987. "Liaodai Qidan nüshi chutu sanji" [Miscellaneous notes on Liao-period Qidan female corpses] 遼代契丹女屍出土散記. *Nei Menggu wenwu guji sanji*, ed. Lu Minghui et al. Huhehaote: Nei Menggu Renmin chubanshe.

Shi Jinbo 史金波. 1986. *Xi Xia wenhua* [Xi Xia culture] 西夏文化. Changchun: Jilin jiaoyu chubanshe.

Shi Jinbo 史金波, Bai Bin 白濱, and Wu Fengyun 吳峰雲. 1988. *Xi Xia wenwu* [Xi Xia cultural relics] 西夏文物. Beijing: Wenwu chubanshe.

Shimada Masao 島田正郎. 1952. *Ryō no shakai shi kenkyū* [Research on the history of Liao society] 遼社会史研究. Kyōto: Sanwa shobō.

——. 1955. *So-shū jō* [Zuzhou] 祖州城. Tokyo: Bunkodō shoten.

——. 1956. *Ryō no shakai to bunka* [Liao society and culture] 遼の社会と文化. Tokyo: Kōbundō.

——. *Ryōchō shi no kenkyū* [Research on history of the Liao dynasty] 遼朝史の研究. Tokyo: Sobunsha.

Shu Fen 舒焚. 1984. *Liao shi gao* [A history of Liao] 遼史稿. Wuhan: Hubei Renmin chubanshe.

Sima Tan 司馬談 and Sima Qian 司馬遷. Han dynasty. 1959 edition. *Shi ji* [Record of the Grand Historian] 史記. Beijing: Zhonghua shuju.

Song Dejin 宋德金. 1987. "Qidan Hanhua lisu shulüe" [Brief discussion of sinicization of Liao rituals and customs] 契丹漢化禮俗述略. In *Liao-Jin shi lun ji*, vol. 1, ed. Chen Shu. Shanghai: Shanghai guji chubanshe, pp. 129–139.

Song Huanju 宋煥居. 1958. "Fengjun, Chezhoushan, Shoufengsi" [Shoufeng Monastery in Chezhushan, Fengjun] 豐潤車軸山壽豐寺. *Wenwu cankao ziliao*, no. 3, pp. 52–53.

Song Lian [1310–1381] 宋濂 et al., eds. 1976 edition. *Yuanshi* [Standard history of the Yuan] 元史. 5 vols. Beijing: Zhonghua shuju.

Song Minqiu 宋敏求. 1075. *Chang'an zhi* [Record of Chang'an] 長安志. Reprint. *Siku quanshu zhenben* 四庫全書珍本, ser. 9, vol. 162. Taipei: Shangwu yinshuguan.

Song Yuntao 宋云濤 and Tian Jianzhong 慕建中. 1992. "Luoyang Mangshan Songdai bihua mu" [A Song tomb with wall paintings in Mangshan, Luoyang] 洛陽邙山宋代壁畫墓. *Wenwu*, no. 12, pp. 37–51.

Su Bai 宿白. 1952. "Chaoxian Anyue suofaxian de Dong Shou mu" [The tomb of Dong Shou excavated in Anak, Korea] 朝鮮安嶽所發現的多壽墓. *Wenwu cankao ziliao*, no. 1, pp. 101–104.

———. 1957. *Baisha Songmu* [Song tombs at Baisha] 白沙宋墓. Beijing: Wenwu chubanshe.

———. 1977. "Dong Bei, Nei Menggu diqu de Xianbei yiji" [Xianbei remains in the northeastern provinces and Inner Mongolia] 東北、內蒙古地區的鮮卑遺跡. *Wenwu*, no. 5, pp. 42–54.

———. 1978. "Bei Wei Luoyangcheng he Bei Mang lingmu" [Northern Wei Luoyang and tombs at the North Mang Mountains] 北魏洛陽城和北邙陵墓. *Wenwu*, no. 7, pp. 42–52.

———. 1982. "Xi'an diqu Tangmu bihua de buju he neirong" [The distribution and contents of Tang tombs with wall paintings in Xi'an] 西安地區唐墓壁畫的布局和內容. *Kaogu xuebao*, no. 2, pp. 137–153.

———. 1985. "Dulesi Guanyinge yu Jizhou Yutian Hanjia" [Guanyin Pavilion of Dule Monastery and the Han family of Yutian, Ji prefecture] 獨樂寺觀音閣與薊州玉田韓家. *Wenwu*, no. 7, pp. 32–48.

—— et al. 1983. "Bitan Taiyuan Bei Qi Lou Rui mu" [Discussion of the tomb of Lou Rui of the Northern Qi period in Taiyuan] 筆談太原北齊婁叡墓. *Wenwu*, no. 10, pp. 24–39.

———, ed. 1989. *Zhongguo meishu quanji* [Comprehensive history of Chinese art] 中國美術全集. *Huihuabian* [Painting series] 繪畫編. Vol. 12: *Mushi bihua* [Tombs with wall paintings] 墓室壁畫. Beijing: Wenwu chubanshe.

Su Ritai 蘇日泰. 1982. "Keyouzhongqi Bazhalaga Liaomu" [A Liao tomb at Bazhalaga, Keyouzhongqi] 科右中旗巴扎拉嘎遼墓. *Nei Menggu wenwu kaogu* 2, pp. 64–68.

Su Tianjun 蘇天鈞. 1962. "Beijing Nanjiao Liao Zhao Dejun mu" [The Liao tomb of Zhao Dejun in the southern suburbs of Beijing] 北京南郊遼趙德鈞墓. *Kaogu*, no. 5, pp. 246–253.

———. 1963. "Beijing xijiao Baiwanzhuang Liaomu fajue jianbao" [Excavation report on Liao tombs in Baiwanzhuang, western suburb of Beijing] 北京西郊百萬莊遼墓發掘簡報. *Kaogu*, no. 3, pp. 145–146.

Sun Binggen 孫秉根. 1994. "Bohai muzang de leixing yu fenqi" [Typology and periodization of Bohai tombs] 渤海墓葬的類型與分期. *Han-Tang yu bianjiang kaogu yanjiu* 漢唐與邊疆考古研究. Vol. 1. Beijing: Kexue chubanshe, pp. 188–224.

Sun Dazhang 孫大章 and Yu Weiguo 喻唯國, chief eds. 1991. *Zhongguo meishu quanji* [Comprehensive history of Chinese art] 中國美術全集. *Jianzhu yishubian* [Architecture series] 建築藝術編. Vol. 4: *Zongmiao jianzhu* [Religious architecture] 宗廟建築. Beijing: Zhongguo jianzhu gongye chubanshe.

Sun Guoping 孫國平, Du Shouchang 杜守昌, and Zhang Lidan 張麗丹. 1992. "Liaoning Chaoyang Sunjiawan Liaomu" [A Liao tomb at Sunjiawan, Chaoyang, Liaoning] 遼寧朝陽孫家灣遼墓. *Wenwu*, no. 6, pp. 12–16.

Sun Ji 孫機. 1989. "Guyuan Bei Wei qiguanhua yanjiu" [Research on a Northern Wei painted lacquer coffin from Guyuan] 固原北魏漆棺畫研究. *Wenwu*, no. 9, pp. 38–44 and 12.

Sun Yuliang 孫玉良, ed. 1992. *Bohai shiliao quanbian* [Commentaries on Bohai history] 渤海史料全編. Changchun: Jilin wenshi chubanshe.

Sun Zhongjia 孫忠家. *Zhongguo lidai lingqin jilüe* [Chinese tombs through the ages] 中國歷代陵寢記略. Ha'erbin: Heilongjiang Renmin chubanshe.

—— et al. 1987. *Zhongguo diwang lingqin* [Chinese imperial tombs] 中國帝王陵寢. Ha'erbin: Heilongjiang Renmin chubanshe.

Ta La 塔拉 and Yi You 一友. 1984. "Aohanqi Fanzhangzi Liaomu" [A Liao tomb in Fanzhangzi, Aohanqi] 敖漢旗范仗子遼墓. *Nei Menggu wenwu kaogu* 3, pp. 75–79.

"Taiyuanshi Bei Qi Lou Rui mu" [The tomb of Lou Rui of the Northern Qi in Taiyuan] 太原市北齊婁叡墓. 1983. *Wenwu*, no. 10, pp. 1–23.

Takeshima Takuichi 竹島卓一. 1944. *Ryō-Kin jidai no kenchiku to sono Butsuzō* [Liao-Jin architecture and its Buddhist sculpture] 遼金時代の建築と其佛像. Tokyo: Ryūbun shokyoku.

———. 1972. *Eizō hōshiki no kenkyū* [Research on the Yingzao fashi] 營造法式の研究. 3 vols. Tokyo: Chūō-koron bijutsu shuppan.

Tamura Jitsuzō 田村實造. 1964–1986. *Chūgoku sei-fuku ōchō no kenkyū* [Research on the Chinese conquest dynasties] 中国征服王朝の研究. 3 vols. Kyōto: Tōyōshi kenkyūkai.

———. 1977. *Keiryō no hekiga* [Wall paintings from Qingling] 庆陵の壁画. Kyōto: Dōhōsha.

Tamura Jitsuzō 田村實造 and Kobayashi Yukio 小林行雄. 1953. *Keiryō [Qingling]* 庆陵. 2 vols. Kyōto: Kyōto daigaku bungakubu.

Tan Qixiang 譚其驤. 1982–1987. *Zhongguo lishi ditu ji* [Historical atlas of China] 中國歷史地圖集. 8 vols. Beijing: Xinhua shudian.

Tanaka Tan 田中淡. 1975. "Chōgen to Dai Butsu zaiken" [Chōgen and the reconstruction of the Great Buddha] 重源と大佛再建. *Genkkan bunkazai* 75, no. 5, pp. 12–21.

———. 1977a. "Chūsei shinyōshini okeru kōzō no kaikakuni kansuru shiteki kosatsu" [Historical consideration of structural changes in new medieval styles] 中世新樣式における構造の改革に関する史的考察. In *Nihon kenchiku no tokushitsu—Ōta Hirotarō Hakase kanreki kinen rombunshū* 日本建築の特質——太田博太郎博士還暦紀念論文集. Tokyo: Chūei kōron bijutsu shuppan.

———. 1977b. "Chōgen no eizō katsudo" [Chōgen's construction activities] 重源の造營活動. *Bukkyō geijutsu*, no. 105, pp. 20–50.

———, ed. and trans. 1981. *Chūgoku kenchiku no rekishi* [History of Chinese architecture] 中国建築の歷史. Tokyo: Heibonsha.

———. 1983. "Jujiro ni tatsu hoji rokaku" [Towers for keeping time at the crossroads] 十字路に立つ報時樓閣. *Chyamus*, no. 5, pp. 20–22.

———. 1990. "Zhongguo bihuazhong de jianzhutu ji Tang chuqi de jianzhu yangshi" [Illustrations of architecture in Chinese wall painting and architectural styles of the early Tang] 中國壁畫中的建築圖及唐初期的建築樣式. Translated by Dong Li 冬籬 and Cheng Guoqing 程國慶. In *Zhonghua gujianzhu*, eds. Zhang Yuhuan and Guo Husheng. Beijing: Zhongguo kexue jishu chubanshe, pp. 144–164.

"Tang Qianling kancha ji" [Notes on the investigation of Tang Qianling] 唐乾陵勘察記. 1960. *Wenwu*, no. 4, pp. 53–60.

"Tang Qinglongsi yizhi fajue jianbao" [Brief excavation report on the remains of Tang Qinglongsi] 唐青龍寺遺址發掘簡報. 1974. *Kaogu*, no. 5, pp. 322–327 and 321.

Tang Yin 唐音. 1992. "Jilinsheng Yongjixian Liao-Jin yizhi shulüe" [Brief discussion of Liao-Jin remains in Yongji county, Jilin] 吉林省永吉縣遼遺址述略. *Beifang wenwu*, no. 2, pp. 31–37.

Tang Yunming 唐雲明. 1973. "Hebei Qian'an Shanglucun Liao Han Xiang mu" [The tomb of Han Xiang of the Liao in Shanglucun, Qian'an, Hebei] 河北遷安上蘆村遼韓相墓. *Kaogu*, no. 5, pp. 276–278.

Tao Fuhai 陶富海 and Jie Xigong 解希恭. 1986. "Shanxi Xiangfenxian Qulicun Jin-Yuan mu qingli jianbao" [Excavation report on a Jin-Yuan period tomb in Qulicun, Xiangfen county, Shanxi] 山西襄汾縣曲里村金元墓清理簡報. *Wenwu*, no. 12, pp. 47–52.

Tao Zongyi 陶宗儀. 1368. 1959 edition. *Nancun zhuogeng lu* [Record upon resting from the plow] 南村輟耕錄. Shanghai: Zhonghua shuju.

———, comp. 14th century. 1972 edition. *Shuo fu* [Writings] 說郛. Taipei: Shangwu yinshuguan.

Tao Zongzhi 陶宗治, Liu Zhongyu 劉宗羽, and Zhao Xin 趙欣. 1990. "Hebei Xuanhua Xiabali Liao-Jin bihua mu" [Liao-Jin period tombs with wall paintings in Xiabali, Xuanhua, Hebei] 河北宣化下八里遼金壁畫墓. *Wenwu*, no. 10, pp. 1–19.

Tian Guanglin 田廣林 and Zhang Jianhua 張建華. 1992. "Qidan zangsu yanjiu" [Research on Qidan burial customs] 契丹葬俗研究. In *Beifang minzu wenhua. Zhaowuda Mengzu shizhuan xuebao*, no. 13, pp. 1–14.

"Tianjin Jixian Dulesi ta" [The pagoda of Dule Monastery in Jixian, Tianjin] 天津薊縣獨樂寺塔. 1989. *Kaogu xuebao*, no. 1, pp. 83–119.

Toganoo Shōun 梅尾祥雲. 1927. *Mandara no kenkyū* [Research on mandala] 曼荼羅の研究. Koya-san: Koya-san Daigaku shuppansha.

Tokiwa Daijō 常盤大定 and Sekino Tadashi 關野貞. 1928–29. *Shina Bukkyō shiseki* [Buddhist remains in

China] 支那佛教史蹟. 5 vols. Tokyo: Bukkyō shi-seki kenkyū kai.

Tonkō Bakukō kutsu [Dunhuang Mogao caves] 敦煌莫高窟. 1980–1982. 5 vols. Tokyo: Heibonsha.

Torii Ryūzō 鳥居竜蔵. 1931. "Ryōdai no hekiga ni tsuite" [On Liao wall painting] 遼代の壁画について. *Kokka* 490, pp. 272–280; 491, pp. 283–289; 492, pp. 313–317; 493, pp. 343–350.

——. 1936. *Kōkogakujō yori mitaru Ryō no bunka: Zufu* [Liao culture seen from archaeology: Illustrations] 考古学上より見たる遼の文化：図譜. 4 vols. Tokyo: Tōhōbunka gakuin, Tōkyō kenkyūsho.

——. 1937. *Ryō no bunka o saguru* [On Liao culture] 遼の文化を探る. Tokyo: Shokasha.

Tuotuo [1313–1355] 脫脫 et al., eds. 1975 edition. *Jinshi* [Standard history of the Jin] 金史. 8 vols. Beijing: Zhonghua shuju.

—— et al., eds. 1974 edition. *Liaoshi* [Standard history of the Liao] 遼史. 5 vols. Beijing: Zhonghua shuju.

—— et al., eds. 1977 edition. *Songshi* [Standard history of the Song] 宋史. 40 vols. Beijing: Zhonghua shuju.

Umehara Kaoru 梅原郁 and Kinugawa Tsuyoshi 衣川強. 1972. *Ryō Kin Gejin denki sakuin* [Index to biographies of Liao, Jin, and Yuan] 遼金元人伝記索引. Kyōto: Kyōto daigaku jimbun kagaku ken-kyūjo.

Umehara Sueji 梅原末治. 1938–1940. *Tonggou* 通溝. 2 vols. Tokyo: Nichiman bunka kyokai.

——. 1947–1966. *Chōsen kodai no bosei* [The tomb systems of ancient Korea] 朝鮮古代の墓制. Tokyo: Zauho kankokai.

Umehara Sueji 梅原末治 and Fujita Ryōsaku 藤田亮策. 1947–1966. *Chōsen kobunka sōkan* [Catalog of archaeological objects of ancient Korea] 朝鮮古文化綜鑑. 4 vols. Tokyo: Yotokusha.

Umehara Sueji 梅原末治 and Kobayashi Yukio 小林行雄. *Chikuzen-kuni Jumyo-gun Ōtsuka soshoku kofun* [The ornamented tomb Ōtsuka in Jumyo prefecture, Chikuzen-kuni] 筑前国嘉穂郡王塚装飾古墳. Kyōto: Kyōto Teikoku daigaku.

Wang Chengguo 王成國. "Liaodai kexue jishu jian-shu" [Notes on Liao science and technology] 遼代科学技術簡述. *Dongbei difangshi yanjiu*, no. 4, pp. 28–32.

Wang Chengli 王承禮. 1990. *Liao-Jin Qidan-Nüzhen shi yiwenji* [Selected essays on Liao-Jin Qidan-Nüzhen history] 遼金契丹女眞史譯文集. Changchun: Jilin wenshi chubanshe.

Wang Feizao 王飛藻 and Wu Fuhong 吳輔宏. 1776. *Datongfu zhi* [Record of Datong prefecture] 大同府志.

Wang Guixiang 王貴祥. 1982–1983. "√2 yu Tang-Song jianzhu zhuyan guanxi" [The relation between pillars and eaves and the √2 in Tang-Song architecture] √2與唐宋建築柱檐關係. *Jianzhu lishi yu lilun* 3–4, pp. 137–144.

Wang Hanfeng 王寒楓. 1992. *Quanzhou Dong, Xi ta* [The East and West pagodas of Quanzhou] 泉州東西塔. Fuzhou: Fujian Renmin chubanshe.

Wang Huguo 王護國. n.d. *Datong lansheng* [Taking in the sites in Datong] 大同攬勝. Datong: Shanxi Renmin chubanshe.

Wang Jian 王建. 1983. "Jilin Shuangliaoxian faxian liangzuo Liaomu" [Two Liao tombs excavated in Shuangliaoxian, Jilin] 吉林雙遼縣發現兩座遼墓. *Kaogu*, no. 8, pp. 753–754.

Wang Jianqun 王健群. 1978. "Kulunqi erhao Liaomu fajue sanji" [Record of the excavation of Liao Tomb 2 at Kulunqi] 庫倫旗二號遼墓發掘散記. *Shehui kexue zhanxian* 1, pp. 209–213.

Wang Jianqun 王健群 and Chen Xiangwei 陳相偉. 1989. *Kulun Liaodai bihuamu* [A tomb with wall paintings in Kulun] 庫倫遼代壁畫墓. Beijing: Wenwu chubanshe.

Wang Jingru 王靜如. 1980. "Dunhuang Mogaoku he Anxi Yulinkuzhong de Xi Xia bihua" [Wall paintings of the Xi Xia in the Yulin Caves at Anxi and the Mogao Caves at Dunhuang] 敦煌莫高窟和安西榆林窟中的西夏壁畫. *Wenwu*, no. 9, pp. 49–55.

Wang Ju'er 王菊耳. 1988. "Liaodai Wugoujingguang Shelita digong sitianwang bihua chutan" [Initial investigation of the wall paintings of Four Heavenly Kings buried in the Liao-period Wugoujingguang Pagoda] 遼代無垢淨光舍利塔地宮四天王壁畫初探. *Beifang wenwu*, no. 4, pp. 46–52.

Wang Long 王瀧. 1984. "Guyuan qiguan caihua" [A painted lacquer coffin from Guyuan] 固原漆棺彩畫. *Meishu yanjiu*, no. 2, pp. 12–16.

Wang Pingge 王平格, comp. 1864.1968 facsimile reproduction. *Yucixian zhi* [Record of Yuci prefecture] 榆次縣志. Taipei: Xuesheng shuju.

Wang Pinglu 王平魯. 1988. "Fushunshi Guangmingjie Liaomu fajue jianbao" [Excavation report on a Liao tomb on Guangming Street in Fushun] 撫順市光明街遼墓發掘簡報. *Beifang wenwu*, no. 1, pp. 76–78.

Wang Puzi 王璞子. 1984. "Liao-Jin Yanjing chengfang gongdian shulüe" [Discussion of city districts and palatial halls of Liao-Jin Yanjing] 遼金燕京城坊宮殿述略. *Kejishi wenji* 11, pp. 20–43.

Wang Shiren 王世仁. 1963 "Ji Houtucimiao mao bei" [A note on the stele of the Temple to the Earth God] 記后土祠廟貌碑. *Kaogu*, no. 5, pp. 273–277.

Wang Shuang 王瀧. 1984. "Guyuan qiguan caihua" [A lacquer-painted coffin from Guyuan] 固原漆棺彩畫. *Meishu yanjiu*, no. 2, pp. 12–16.

Wang Wenlin 王文林 et al. 1957. *Nan Tang erling* [Two Southern Tang tombs] 南唐二陵. Beijing: Wenwu chubanshe.

Wang Wuyu 王武鈺 and Qi Qingguo 祁慶國. 1992. "Beijing Shunyi Anxinzhuang Liaomu fajue jianbao" [Excavation report on a Liao tomb at Anxinzhuang, Shunyi, Beijing] 北京順義安辛莊遼墓發掘簡報. *Wenwu*, no. 6, pp. 17–23.

Wang Xuan 王選 et al., comps. 1892. 1968 reprint. *Shanxi tongzhi* [Record of Shanxi province] 山西通志. Taipei: Huawen shuju.

Wang Yong 王庸. 1958. *Zhongguo ditu shigang* [Brief history of Chinese cartography] 中國地圖史綱. Beijing: Sanlian shudian.

Wang Yuping 汪宇平. 1955. "Nei Menggu Wenhuaju diaocha Liaodai Zuzhoucheng Liao Taizumu" [The Inner Mongolia Wenhuaju's excavation of the tomb of Liao Taizu at Zuzhou] 內蒙古文化局調查遼代祖州城遼太祖墓. *Wenwu cankao ziliao*, no. 5, pp. 109–110.

Wang Zengxin 王增新. 1960. "Liaoning Liaoyangxian Jinchang Liaohuaxiangshimu" [A Liao tomb with paintings and relief sculpture in Jinchang, Liaoyang, Liaoning] 遼寧遼陽縣金廠遼畫像石墓. *Kaogu*, no. 2, pp. 25–27.

Wang Zeqing 王澤慶. 1973. "Kulunqi yihaomu bihua chutan" [Preliminary discussion of the wall paintings in Liao Tomb 1 at Kulunqi] 庫倫旗一號墓壁畫初探. *Wenwu*, no. 8, pp. 30–35.

Wang Zhenzhong 王震中, Sha Zhenyu 沙振宇, and Dan Huasha 丹化沙. 1957. "Heilongjiangsheng de jichu wenwu yizhi" [Some archaeological remains in Heilongjiang] 黑龍江省的幾處文物遺址. *Wenwu*, no. 11, pp. 59–60.

Wang Zhili 汪之力. 1984. "Lüelun Zhongguo gudai jianzhu" [Discussion of traditional Chinese architecture] 略論中國古代建築. *Kejishi wenji* 11, pp. 1–13.

Wangdu Hanmu bihua [A tomb with wall paintings at Wangdu] 望都漢墓壁畫. 1955. Beijing: Zhongguo gudian yishu chubanshe.

Wei Changyou 魏昌友. 1989. "Liaodai Zuzhou yu Zuling" [Liao Zuzhou and Zuling] 遼代祖州與祖陵. *Dongbei difangshi yanjiu* 4, pp. 143–144.

Wei Cuncheng 魏存成. 1982. "Bohai chengzhi de faxian yu fenqi" [Excavation and stages of Bohai city remains] 渤海城址的發現與分期. *Dongbei kaogu yu lishi* 1, pp. 89–94.

Wei Kejing 魏克晶. 1993. *Yingzao ji* [Collected buildings] 營造集. Tianjin: Yangliujinghua chubanshe.

Wei Shou [506–572] 魏收. 1977 edition. *Weishu* [Standard history of the Wei (386–550)] 魏書. Beijing: Zhonghua shuju.

Wei Shu 韋述, comp. 1736. 1965 reprint. *(Qinding) Shengjing tongzhi* [Record of Shengjing (of the Jinding period)] (欽定) 盛京通志. Taipei: Wenhai chubanshe.

Wei Zheng [580–643] 魏徵 et al. 1973 edition. *Suishu* [Standard history of Sui] 隋書. Beijing: Zhonghua chubanshe.

Wen Lihe 溫麗和. 1989. "Liaoning Fakuxian Yemaotai Liao Xiao Yi mu" [The Liao tomb of Xiao Yi at Yemaotai, Faku county, Liaoning] 遼寧法庫縣葉茂臺遼蕭義墓. *Kaogu*, no. 4, pp. 324-330.

Wen Weijian 文惟簡, comp. Southern Song. *Luting shishi* 虜廷事實. In *Shuofu*, comp. Tao Zongyi.

Wenwu kaogu gongzuo sanshinian 1949–1979 [Thirty years of work in cultural relics and archaeology] 文物考古工作三十年 1949–1979. 1979. Beijing: Wenwu chubanshe.

Wenwu kaogu gongzuo shinian 1979–1989 [Ten years of work in cultural relics and archaeology] 文物考古工作十年 1979–1989. 1990. Beijing: Wenwu chubanshe.

Wu Fengyun 吳峰雲. 1986. "Xi Xia lingyuan ji qi jianzhu tedian" [Special features of the Xi Xia royal tombs and their architecture] 西夏陵園及其建築特點. *Ningxia wenwu* 1, pp. 26–31 and 9.

Wu Fengyun 吳峰雲 and Li Fanwen 李范文. 1978. "Xi Xia lingqu yibaiba-hao mu fajue jianbao" [Brief excavation report on Tomb 108 at the Xi Xia royal cemetery] 西夏陵區一百八號墓發掘簡報. *Wenwu*, no. 8, pp. 71–78.

Wu Qilao 鄔啓佬. 1982. "Zhelimumeng Naimanqi, Kulunqi kaogu diaocha ji" [Record of the archaeological investigation at Kulunqi, Naimanqi, Zhelimumeng] 哲里木盟奈曼旗、庫倫旗考古調查記. *Nei Menggu wenwu kaogu* 2, pp. 78–86.

Wu Zhuo 吳焯. 1987. "Bei Zhou Li Xian mu chutu liujin yinhu kao" [Investigation of the silver ewer excavated in the tomb of Li Xian of the Northern Zhou] 北周李賢墓出土鎏金銀壺考. *Wenwu*, no. 5, pp. 66–76.

Wutaishan [Mt. Wutai] 五臺山. Beijing: Wenwu chubanshe.

Xi Mude 希木德. 1988. "Nei Meng Tongliaoxian Yuliangbao Liaomu" [A Liao tomb at Yuliangbao, Tongliao, Inner Mongolia] 內蒙通遼縣餘糧堡遼墓. *Beifang wenwu*, no. 1, pp. 41–42.

"Xi Xia bahaoling fajue jianbao" [Brief excavation report on Xi Xia Tomb 8] 西夏八號陵發掘簡報. 1978. *Wenwu*, no. 8, pp. 60–68.

"Xi Xia lingyuan beiduan jianzhu yizhi fajue jianbao" [Brief report on the excavation of architectural remains in the northern corner of the Xi Xia royal cemetery] 西夏陵園北端建築遺址發掘簡報. 1988. *Wenwu*, no. 9, pp. 57–66 and 77.

Xia Nai 夏鼐. 1976. "Cong Xuanhua Liaomu de xingtu lun ershiba xiu he huangdao shi'er gong" [Discussion of the twenty-eight lunar lodges and the twenty palaces based on a star map in a Liao tomb at Xuanhua] 從宣化遼墓的星圖論二十八宿和黃道十二宮. *Kaogu xuebao*, no. 2, pp. 35–58.

Xiang Chunsong 項春松. "Zhaomeng diqu de Liaodai muzang" [Liao-period tombs in "Zhaomeng"] 昭盟地區的遼代墓葬. *Nei Mengu wenwu kaogu* 1, pp. 73–79.

———. 1982. "Shangyaoguo Liaomuqun" [A Liao tomb group at Shangyaoguo] 上燒鍋遼墓群. *Nei Menggu wenwu kaogu* 2, pp. 56–68.

———. 1984a. *Liaodaibihua xuan* [Selected Liao wall paintings] 遼代壁畫選. Shanghai: Shanghai Renmin meishu chubanshe.

———. 1984b. "Keshiketengqi Erbadi yi-, er-hao Liao mu" [Liao Tombs 1 and 2 at Erbadi, Keshiketengqi] 克什克騰旗二八地一二號遼墓. *Nei Menggu wenwu kaogu* 3, pp. 80–90.

———. 1989. "Nei Menggu Wengniuteqi Liaodai Guang Degong mu" [The Tomb of Guang Degong in Wengniuteqi, Inner Mongolia] 內蒙古翁牛特旗遼代廣德公墓. *Beifang wenwu*, no. 4, pp. 41–44.

———. 1990. "Nei Menggu Chifengjiaoqu xinde Liaomu" [A new Liao tomb in the suburbs of Chifeng, Inner Mongolia] 內蒙古赤峰郊區新的遼墓. *Beifang wenwu*, no. 4, pp. 38–41.

———. 1991. "Chifengshi jiaoqu faxiande Liaomu" [Liao tombs discovered in the suburbs of Chifeng] 赤峰市郊區發現的遼墓. *Beifang wenwu*, no. 3, pp. 33–39 and 49.

Xiao Dengfu 蕭登福. 1993. *Daojiao yu mizong* [Daoism and esoteric Buddhism] 道教與密宗. Taipei: Xinwenfeng.

Xiao Mo 蕭默. *Dunhuang jianzhu yanjiu* [Research on architecture at Dunhuang] 敦煌建築研究. Beijing: Wenwu chubanshe.

Xiao Xun 蕭洵. 1398. 1963 edition. *Gugong yilu* [Record of the remains of imperial palaces] 故宮遺錄. Taipei: Shijie shuju.

Xie Guoxiang 謝國祥, chief comp. 1989. *Tianjin gudai jianzhu* [Premodern architecture in Tianjin] 天津古代建築. Tianjin: Tianjin kexue jishu chubanshe.

Xie Mincong 謝敏聰. 1976. *Zhongguo lidai diwang lingqin kaolüe* [Research on Chinese imperial tombs through the ages] 中國歷代帝王陵寢考略. Taipei: Zhengzhong shuju.

Xin Yan 辛岩 and Hua Yubing 華玉冰. 1991. "Liaoning Jianpingxian liangchu Liaomu qingli jianbao" [Brief report on two Liao tombs in Jianping, Liaoning] 遼寧建平縣兩處遼墓清理簡報. *Beifang wenwu*, no. 3, pp. 40–47.

Xin Zhongguo de kaogu faxian he yanjiu [Archaeological discoveries and research in New China] 新中國的考古發現和研究. 1984. Beijing: Wenwu chubanshe.

Xinchengxian zhi [Record of Xincheng county] 新城縣志. 1934 reprint. Taipei: Chengwen chubanshe.

Xinjiang Weiwu'er Zizhiqu Bowuguan [Xinjiang Uygher Autonomous Region Museum] 新疆維吾兒自治區博物館. 1996. Taipei: Dadi dili chubanshiye fufen youxian gongsi.

Xu Bo'an 徐伯安. 1985. "*Yingzao fashi* dougong xingzhi jieyi, tanwei" [Investigation and explanation of bracket sets according to *Yingzao fashi*] 營造法式斗栱型制解疑探微. *Jianzhushi lunwen ji* 7, pp. 1–35.

Xu Bo'an 徐伯安 and Guo Daiheng 郭黛姮. 1981. "*Yingzao fashi* de diaojuan zhidu yu Zhongguo gudai jianzhu zhuangshi de diaoke" [The systems of sculpture in the *Yingzao fashi* and in Chinese architectural decoration] 營造法式的雕鐫制度與中國古代建築裝飾的雕刻. *Kejishi wenji* 7, pp. 34–42.

———. 1984. "Song *Yingzao fashi* shuyu huishi—haozhai, shizuo, damuzuo zhidu bufen" [Collected comments on terminology in the Song *Yingzao fashi*—from the "greater carpentry" section on moats and fortifications and stonework] 宋營造法式術語匯釋一壕寨、石作、大木作制度部分. *Jianzhushi lunwenji* 6, pp. 1–79.

Xu Pingfang 徐苹芳. "Song-Yuan shidai de huozang" [Song-Yuan period cremation burials] 宋元時代的火葬. *Wenwu cankao ziliao*, no. 9, pp. 21–26.

———. 1981. "Zhongguo Qin, Han, Wei, Jin, Nan-Bei Chao shidai lingyuan he yingyu" [Tombs and graves of the ten periods from Qin through the Northern and Southern dynasties] 中國秦漢魏晉南北朝時代陵園和塋域. *Kaogu* 6, pp. 521–530.

———. 1984a. "Song, Liao, Jin, Yuan" [Song, Liao, Jin, and Yuan dynasties] 宋遼金元. In *Xin Zhongguo de kaogu faxian yu yanjiu* 新中國的考古發現與研究. Beijing: Wenwu chubanshe, pp. 599–616.

———. 1984b. "Gudai Beijing de chengshi guihua" [The city plan of ancient Beijing] 古代北京的城市規劃. *Huanjing bianqian yanjiu* 1, pp. 115–121.

———. 1987. "Bei Song Kaifeng Da Xiangguosi pingmian fuyuan tushuo" [Illustrations and notes on the reconstruction of the plan of Great Xiangguo Monastery from Northern Song Kaifeng] 北宋開封大相國寺平面復原圖說. In *Wenwu yu kaogu lun ji* 文物與考古論集. Beijing: Wenwu chubanshe.

Xu Yulin 許玉林. 1977. "Liaoning Beipiao Shuiquan yihao Liaomu fajue jianbao" [Excavation report on Liao Tomb 1 at Shuiquan, Beipiao, Liaoning] 遼寧北票水泉一號遼墓發掘簡報. *Wenwu*, no. 12, pp. 44–51.

Xu Zhen 徐鎮 and Zhang Rongqing 張榮慶, eds. 1990. "Tengwangge" [Prince Teng's pavilion] 滕王閣. In *Zhonghua gujianzhu*, eds. Zhang Yuhuan and Guo Husheng. Beijing: Zhongguo kexue jishu chubanshe, pp. 269–274.

Xue Juzheng [912–981] 薛居正 et al., eds. 1976 edition. *Jiu Wudai shi* [Old standard history of the Five Dynasties] 舊五代史. Beijing: Zhonghua shuju.

Yan Wenru 閻文儒, Fu Zhenlun 傅振倫, and Zheng Enhuai 鄭恩淮. 1982. "Shanxi Yingxian Fogongsi Shijiata faxian de 'Qidanzang' he Liaodai kejing" [The "Qidan Sutra" and other Liao-period sutras found in the Śākyamni Pagoda at Fogongsi in Yingxian, Shanxi] 山西應縣佛宮寺釋迦塔發現的『契丹藏』和遼代刻經. *Wenwu*, no. 6, pp. 9–19.

Yan Yu 雁羽. 1960a. "Jinxi Dawopu Liao-Jin shidai huaxiang shimu" [A Liao-Jin stone tomb with paintings from Jinxi Dawopu] 錦西大臥鋪遼金時代畫像石墓. *Kaogu*, no. 2, pp. 29–33.

———. 1960b. "Jinxi Xigushan Xiao Xiaozhong mu qingli jianbao" [Excavation report on the tomb of Xiao Xiaozhong at Xigushan, Jinxi] 錦西西孤山蕭孝忠墓清理簡報. *Kaogu*, no. 2, pp. 34–35.

Yang Aizhen 楊愛珍. 1987. "Datong Liaodai Huayansi dongxiang de yuanyin jiqi tiji he zaoxiang" [Reasons for the eastward orientation of Huayan Monastery in Datong and its inscriptions and sculptures] 大同遼代華嚴寺東向的原因及其題記和造像. In *Liao-Jin shi lunwen ji*, vol. 1, ed. Chen Shu. Shanghai: Shumu wenxian chubanshe, pp. 260–270.

Yang Binglun 楊秉倫, Wang Guixiang 王貴祥, and Zhong Xiaoqing 鍾曉青. 1988. "Fuzhou Hualinsi Dadian" [The Main Hall of Hualin Monastery in Fuzhou] 福州華林寺大殿. *Jianzhushi lunwen ji* 9, pp. 1–32.

Yang Cuntian 楊存田 and Chen Jinsong 陳勁松. 1983. "Woguo gudai de huozang zhidu" [The Chinese system of cremation burial] 我國古代的火葬制度. *Kaogu yu wenwu*, no. 3, pp. 88–95.

Yang Daoming 楊道明, ed. 1991. *Zhongguo meishu quanji* [Comprehensive history of Chinese art] 中國美術全集. *Jianzhu yishubian* [Architecture series] 建築藝術編. Vol. 2: *Lingmu jianzhu* [Funerary architecture] 陵墓建築. Beijing: Zhongguo jianzhu gongye chubanshe.

Yang Hongxun 楊鴻勛. 1976. "Cong Panlongcheng Shangdai gongdian yizhi tan Zhongguo gongdian jianzhu fazhan de jige wenti" [Several questions concerning the development of Chinese palatial architecture in the light of Shang palace remains from Panlongcheng] 從盤龍城商代宮殿遺址談中國宮殿建築發展的幾個問題. *Wenwu*, no. 2, pp. 16–25.

———. 1981. "Xi Zhou Qiyi jianzhu yizhi chubu kaocha" [Early stages of the investigation of architectural remains at Qiyi of the Western Zhou] 西周岐邑建築遺址初步考察. *Wenwu*, no. 3, pp. 23–33.

———. 1987a. *Jianzhu kaoguxue lunwen ji* [Collected essays in Chinese archaeology] 建築考古學論文集. Beijing: Wenwu chubanshe.

———. 1987b. "Zhanguo Zhongshanwangling ji *zhaoyutu* yanjiu" [Research on the tomb of the Zhongshan kings and *zhaoyutu*] 戰國中山王陵及兆域圖研究. In *Jianzhu kaoguxue lunwen ji*. Beijing: Wenwu chubanshe, pp. 120–142.

———. 1987c. "Guanyu Qindai yiqian mushang jianzhu de wenti" [Some questions concerning buildings on top of tombs in the pre-Qin period] 關于秦代以前墓上建築的問題. In *Jianzhu kaoguxue lunwen ji*. Beijing: Wenwu chubanshe, pp. 143–149.

———. 1987d. "Guanyu Qindai yiqian mushang jianzhu de wenti jiadian de zhongshen" [Reiteration of important points in "Some questions concerning buildings on top of tombs in the pre-Qin period"] 關於秦代以前墓上建築的問題幾點的重申. In *Jianzhu kaoguxue lunwen ji*. Beijing: Wenwu chubanshe, pp. 150–152.

———. 1987e. "Qin Xianyanggong diyihao yizhi fuyuan wenti de chubu tantao" [Notes on the restoration of Palace 1 at Qin Xianyang] 秦咸陽宮第一號遺址復原問題的初步探討. In *Jianzhu kaoguxue lunwen ji*. Beijing: Wenwu chubanshe, pp. 153–168.

———. 1987f. "Cong yizhi kan Xi Han Chang'an mingtang (biyong) xingzhi" [Looking at the forms of ritual halls in Western Han Chang'an based on remains] 從遺址看西漢長安明堂 (辟雍) 形制. In *Jianzhu kaoguxue lunwen ji*. Beijing: Wenwu chubanshe, pp. 169–200.

———. 1987g. "Tang Chang'an Qinglongsi Zhenyan mizong diantang (yizhi 4) fuyuan yanjiu" [Research on the reconstruction of an esoteric hall (remains no. 4) of the Zhenyan sect at Qinglong Monastery in Tang Chang'an] 唐長安青龍寺眞言密宗殿堂 (遺址 4) 復原研究. In *Jianzhu kaoguxue lunwen ji*. Beijing: Wenwu chubanshe, pp. 210–233.

———. 1987h. "Tang Daminggong Lindedian fuyuan yanjiu jieduan baogao" [Brief report on the reconstruction of Linde Hall of Tang Daming palace-complex] 唐大明宮麟德殿復原研究階段報告. In *Jianzhu kaoguxue lunwen ji*. Beijing: Wenwu chubanshe, pp. 234–252.

———. 1987i. "Dougong qiyuan kaocha" [Examination of the origins of the bracket set] 斗栱起源考察. In *Jianzhu kaoguxue lunwen ji*. Beijing: Wenwu chubanshe, pp. 253–267.

Yang Jialuo 楊家駱, ed. 1973. *Liaoshi huibian* [Collected writings on Liao history] 遼史彙編. Taipei: Dingwen shuju.

Yang Jing 楊晶. 1987. "Liaodai huozangmu" [Liao-period cremation tombs] 遼代火葬墓. In *Liao-Jin shi lunji*, vol. 3, ed. Chen Shu. Beijing: Shumu wenxian chubanshe, pp. 213–219.

Yang Kuan 楊寬. 1985. *Zhongguo gudai lingqin zhidushi yanjiu* [The history of the ancient Chinese imperial tomb system] 中國古代陵寢制度史研究. Shanghai: Shanghai guji chubanshe.

Yang Lie 楊烈. 1962. "Shanxi Pingshunxian gujianzhu kancha ji" [Notes on the investigation of ancient architecture in Pingshun county, Shanxi] 山西平順縣古建築勘察記. *Wenwu*, no. 2, pp. 40–49.

Yang Lin 楊林 and Li Zhongfu 黎中輔. 1830. *Datongxian zhi* [Record of Datong county] 大同縣志.

Yang Renkai 楊仁凱. 1975. "Yemaotai Liaomu chutu guhua de shidai ji qita" [On the date and other aspects of paintings excavated in a Liao tomb at Yemaotai] 葉茂臺遼墓出土古畫的時代及其他. *Wenwu*, no. 12, pp. 37–39.

———. "Liaodai huihua yishu zongshu" [Summarizing the art of Liao painting] 遼代繪畫藝術綜述. *Ajiani okeru sansui hyōgenni tsuite* アジアにおける山水表現について. Kokusai kōryū bijutsu kenkyūkai. Kyōto: Kyōto Kokuritsu Hakubutsukan.

———. 1984. *Yemaotai diqihao Liaomu chutu guhuakao* [Research on Liao paintings excavated in Yemaotai Liao Tomb 7] 葉茂臺第七號遼墓出土古畫考. Shanghai: Shanghai Renmin meishu chubanshe.

Yang Yutan 楊玉潭 et al. 1985. *Wutaishan simiao daguan* 五臺山寺廟大觀. Taiyuan: Shanxi Renmin chubanshe.

Yanshansi Jindai bihua [Jin-period wall paintings at Yanshan Monastery] 巖山寺金代壁畫. 1983. Beijing: Wenwu chubanshe.

Yao Congwu 姚從吾. 1959. *Dongbeishi luncong* [Essays on the history of the Northeast] 東北史論叢. 2 vols. Taipei: Zhengzhong shuju.

Yao Qian 姚謙 and Gu Bing 古兵. 1981. *Nanchao lingmu shike* [Stone funerary sculpture of the Southern Dynasties] 南朝陵墓石刻. Beijing: Wenwu chubanshe.

Ye Dasong 葉大松. 1971. *Zhongguo jianzhu shi* [History of Chinese architecture] 中國建築史. Vol. 1. Taipei: Xinming chubanshe.

———. 1976. *Zhongguo jianzhu shi* [History of Chinese architecture] 中國建築史. Vol. 2. Taipei: Zhongguo dianji jishu chubanshe.

Ye Longli 葉隆禮, comp. 1968 edition. *Qidanguo zhi* [Record of the Qidan state] 契丹國志. Taipei: Taiwan shangwu yinshuguan.

Yi Qing'an 易青安. 1956. "Liaoyangshi Dalinzicun faxian Liao *shouchang* ernian shiguan" [A Liao stone coffin dated to the year *shouchang* 2 excavated at Dalinzicun, Liaoyang] 遼陽市大林子村發現遼壽昌二年石棺. *Wenwu cankao ziliao*, no. 3, pp. 79–80.

Yi Shitong 伊世同. 1990. "Hebei Xuanhua Liao-Jin mu tianwentu jianxi" [Brief analysis of the star map in Liao-Jin tombs in Xuanhua, Hebei] 河北宣化遼金墓天文圖簡析. *Wenwu*, no. 10, pp. 20–24 and 71.

Yingxian Muta Liaodai mizang [A Liao-period esoteric sutra from the Timber Pagoda in Yingxian] 應縣木塔遼代秘藏. 1991. Beijing; Wenwu chubanshe.

Yongle dadian [Encyclopedia of the Yongle reign] 永樂大典. 1408.

Yu Haiyan 于海燕. 1992. "Chifengshi Hongshanqu Xishuidi faxian yizuo Liaomu" [A Liao tomb uncovered in Xishuidi, Hongshan district, Chifeng] 赤峰市紅山區西水地一座遼墓. *Nei Menggu wenwu kaogu*, nos. 1–2, pp. 153–156.

Yu Wuqian 余鳴謙. 1958. "Hebei Zhengding Longxingsi Zhuanlunzangdian jianzhu de chubu fenxi" [Early stages of analysis of the architecture of the Hall of the Revolving Sutra Cabinet at Longxing Monastery in Zhengding, Hebei] 河北正定隆興寺轉輪藏殿建築的初步分析. *Lishi jianzhu*, no. 12, pp. 67–79.

Yu Zhuoyun 于倬雲 and Lou Qingxi 樓慶西, eds. 1991. *Zhongguo meishu quanji* [Comprehensive history of Chinese art] 中國美術全集. *Jianzhu yishubian* [Architecture series] 建築藝術編. Vol. 1: *Gongdian jianzhu* [Palace architecture] 宮殿建築. Beijing: Zhongguo jianzhu gongye chubanshe.

Yuan Hairui 員海瑞 and Tang Yunjun 唐雲俊. 1982. "Huayansi" [Huayan Monastery] 華嚴寺. *Wenwu*, no. 9, pp. 78–91.

Yun Yao 雲瑤 and Ri Ping 日平. 1991. "Heilongjiangsheng Daqingshi Shajiayao faxian de Liaodai muzang" [A Liao tomb excavated at Shajiayao, Daqingshi, Heilongjiang] 黑龍江省大慶市沙家窰發現的遼代墓葬. *Beifang wenwu*, no. 2, pp. 32–33.

Yun'gang shiku [Rock-cut caves at Yun'gang] 雲崗石窟. 1977. Beijing: Wenwu chubanshe.

Zhan Libo 詹立波. 1976. "Mawangdui Hanmu chutu de shoubeitu tantao" [Investigation of the military map excavated in a Han tomb at Mawangdui] 馬王堆漢墓出土的守備圖探討. *Wenwu*, no. 1, pp. 24–27.

Zhang Bozhong 張柏忠. 1985. "Nei Menggu Tongliaoxian Erlinyang Liaomu" [A Liao tomb at Erlinyang, Tongliao, Inner Mongolia] 內蒙古通遼縣二林場遼墓. *Wenwu*, no. 3, pp. 56–62.

———. 1992. "Chenguo gongzhu yu fuma Xiao Shaoju de jiashi" [On the generations of the Princess of Chenguo and her husband, the emperor's son-in-law Xiao Shaoju] 陳國公主與駙馬蕭紹矩的家世. *Nei Menggu wenwu kaogu* 1, no. 2, pp. 39–50 and 38.

Zhang Buqian 張步騫. 1958. "Fuzhou Hualinsi Dadian" [The Main Hall of Hualin Monastery in Fuzhou] 福州華林寺大殿. Unpublished paper.

Zhang Hanjun 張漢君. 1994. "Liao Qingzhou Shijiafo Shelita yingzao lishi jiqi jianzhu gouzhi" [The architectural structure and construction history of the Śākyamuni pagoda in Qingzhou of the Liao dynasty] 遼慶州釋迦佛舍利塔營造歷史及其建築構制. *Wenwu*, no. 12, pp. 65–72.

Zhang Hongbo 張洪波 and Li Zhi 李智. 1990. "Beipiao Quanjuyong Liaomu faxian jianbao" [Excavation report of a Liao tomb in Quanjuyong, Beipiao] 北票泉巨涌遼墓發現簡報. *Liaohai wenwu xuekan*, no. 2, pp. 24–28.

Zhang Hongbo 張洪波 and Lin Xiangxian 林象賢. 1992. "Chaoyang santa kao" [Investigation of three pagodas in Chaoyang] 朝陽三塔考. *Beifang wenwu*, no. 2, pp. 48–50.

Zhang Jingxian 張靜嫻. 1979a. "Dougong de yunyong, anzhuang ji sunmao" [On the use, positioning, and tenoning of bracket sets] 斗栱的運用、安裝及榫卯. *Jianzhushi lunwen ji* 2, pp. 149–160.

———. 1979b. "Feiyan yijiao (shang)" [Roof eaves with turned-up corners (pt. 1)] 飛檐翼角 (上). *Jianzhushi lunwen ji* 3, pp. 72–92.

———. 1980. "Feiyan yijiao (xia)" [Roof eaves with turned-up corners (pt. 2)] 飛檐翼角 (下). *Jianzhushi lunwen ji* 4, pp. 67–84.

Zhang Shaoqing 張少青. 1988. "Liaoning Kangping faxian de Qidan, Liaomu gaishu" [General discussion of Qidan and Liao tombs excavated in Kangping, Liaoning] 遼寧康平發現的契丹遼墓概述. *Beifang wenwu*, no. 4, pp. 36–42.

Zhang Shunmin 張舜民. 14th century. 1972 edition. "Huaman lu" 畫墁錄. *Shuofu* 說郛, comp. Tao Zongyi 陶宗儀. Taipei: Shangwu yinshuguan.

Zhang Songbo 張松柏. 1984. "Liao Huaizhou Huailing diaocha ji" [Notes on the excavation of Liao Huaizhou and Huailing] 遼懷州懷陵調查記. *Nei Menggu wenwu kaogu* 3, pp. 67–71.

Zhang Songbo 張松柏 and Feng Lei 馮雷. "Zuzhou Shishi tansuo" [Investigation of the Stone House in Zuzhou] 祖州石室探索. In *Nei Menggu dongbuqu kaoguxue wenhua yanjiu wenji*. Beijing: Haiyang chubanshe, pp. 127–134.

Zhang Songbo 張松柏 and Ren Xuejun 任學軍. "Liao Gaozhou diaocha ji" [Report on excavation at Liao-period Gaozhou] 遼高州調查記. *Nei Menggu wenwu kaogu*, nos. 1–2, pp. 106–112.

Zhang Xiande 張先得. 1980. "Beijingshi Daxingxian Liaodai Ma Zhiwen fuqi hezangmu" [The joint burial of Ma Zhiwen and his wife in Daxingxian, Beijing] 北京市大興縣遼代馬直溫夫妻合葬墓. *Wenwu*, no. 12, pp. 30–37.

Zhang Xiufu 張秀夫 et al. 1982. "Hebei Pingquanxian Xiaojigou Liaomu" [A Liao tomb at Xiaoqigou, Pingquanxian, Hebei] 河北平泉縣小吉溝遼墓. *Wenwu*, no. 7, pp. 50–53.

Zhang Yaping 張亞平 and Zhao Jinzhang 趙晉樟. 1979. "Shanxi Fanshi Yanshan[g]si de Jindai bihua" [Jin-period wall paintings at Yanshan Monastery in Fanshi, Shanxi] 山西繁峙巖山 [上] 寺的金代壁畫. *Wenwu*, no. 2, pp. 1–2.

Zhang Yu 張郁. 1984. "Huhehaote Xi Baita gucheng" [The old city of the West White Pagoda in Huhehaote] 呼和浩特西白塔故城. *Nei Menggu wenwu kaogu* 3, pp. 98–102.

———. 1987a. "Liao Chenguo gongzhu fufu binzang fushi xiaoji" [Notes on the funeral, interment, and burial clothing of the Liao Princess of Chenguo and her husband] 遼陳國公主夫婦殯葬服飾小記. *Wenwu*, no. 11, pp. 25–28.

———. 1987b. "Liaodai xishi zhi zhen—Chenguo gongzhu mu" [A rare treasure of the Liao—the tomb of Princess of Chenguo] 遼代稀世之珍——陳國公主墓. In *Nei Menggu wenwu guji sanji*, ed. Lu Minghui et al. Huhehaote: Nei Menggu Renmin chubanshe, pp. 95–99.

———. 1991. "Huhehaote jiaoqu Liaodai Fosi fajueji" [Notes on excavation of Liao-period Buddhist monasteries in the vicinity of Huhehaote] 呼和浩特郊區遼代佛寺發掘記. *Nei Menggu wenwu kaogu*, no. 1, pp. 72–81.

Zhang Yuhuan 張馭寰. "Nanfang guta gaiguan" [General survey of old pagodas in South China] 南方古塔概觀. *Kejishi wenji* 11, pp. 51–70.

———. 1985. *Zhongguo gudai jianzhu jishu shi* [History and development of ancient Chinese architecture] 中國古代建築技術史. Beijing: Kexue shuku.

———. 1990. "Shanxi Fosi chuxi" [Preliminary analysis of Buddhist monasteries in Shanxi] 山西佛寺初析. In *Zhonghua gujianzhu*, eds. Zhang Yuhuan and Guo Husheng. Beijing: Zhongguo kexue jishu chubanshe.

Zhang Yuhuan 張馭寰 and Guo Husheng 郭湖生, eds. 1990. *Zhonghua gujianzhu* [Traditional Chinese architecture] 中華古建築. Beijing: Zhongguo keji-shu chubanshe.

Zhang Yuhuan 張馭寰 and Luo Zhewen 羅哲文. 1988. *Zhongguo guta jingcui* [The cream of Chinese pagodas] 中國古塔精粹. Beijing: Kexue chubanshe.

Zhang Zhengming 張正明. 1979. *Qidan shilüe* 契丹史略. Beijing: Zhonghua shuju.

Zhao Hongguang 趙虹光. 1988. "Bohai Shangjing Longquanfu chengzhi diaocha fajue gongzuo de huigu" [Looking back on the excavation of the remains of the Bohai upper capital Longquanfu] 渤海上京龍泉府城址調查發掘工作的回顧. *Beifang wenwu*, no. 2, pp. 26–28.

Zhao Pingchun 趙評春. "Liaodai Muyeshan kao" [Investigation of Liao-period Muyeshan] 遼代木葉山考. *Beifang wenwu*, no. 1, pp. 93–95.

Zhao Runxing 趙潤星 and Yang Baosheng 楊寶生. 1986a. *Tanzhesi* [Tanzhe Monastery] 潭柘寺. Beijing: Beijing Yanshan chubanshe.

———. 1986b. *Jietaisi* [Jietai Monastery] 戒臺寺. Beijing: Beijing Yanshan chubanshe.

Zhao Wengang 趙文剛. 1992. "Tianjinshi Jixian Yingfangcun Liaomu" [A Liao tomb in Yingfangcun, Jixian, Tianjin] 天津市薊縣營房村遼墓. *Beifang wenwu*, no. 3, pp. 36–41.

Zhao Zhengzhi 趙正之. 1983. "Zhongguo gujianzhu gongcheng jishu" [Building technology of ancient Chinese architecture] 中國古建築工程技術. *Jianzhushi lunwen ji* 1, pp. 10–33.

Zheng Dajin 鄭大進 et al. 1762. 1968 facsimile reproduction. *Zhengdingfu zhi* [Record of Zhengding county] 正定府志. Taipei.

Zheng Long 鄭隆. 1961. "Zhaowudameng Liao Shang Weifu mu qingli jianbao" [Report on the investigation of the tomb of Liao Shang Weifu in Zhaowudameng] 昭烏達盟遼尚暐符墓清理簡報. *Wenwu*, no. 9, pp. 50–51.

———. 1982. "Kulunqi Liaomu bihua qiantan" [Simple notes on the Liao tomb wall paintings at Kulunqi] 庫倫旗遼墓壁畫淺談. *Nei Menggu wenwu kaogu* 2, pp. 47–50.

Zheng Shaozong 鄭紹宗. 1956. "Chifengxian Dayingzi Liaomu fajue baogao" [Excavation report on a Liao tomb at Dayingzi, Chifeng county] 赤峰縣大營子遼墓發掘報告. *Kaogu xuebao*, no. 3, pp. 1–26.

———. 1962. "Qidan Qinjinguo Dazhang gongzhu muzhiming" [The funerary inscription from the tomb of the official and princess of Qinjinguo of the Qidan] 契丹秦晉國大長公主墓誌銘. *Kaogu*, no. 8, pp. 429–435 and 403.

——. 1975a. "Hebei Xuanhua Liao bihuamu fajue jianbao" [Excavation report on a Liao tomb with wall paintings in Xuanhua, Hebei] 河北宣化遼壁畫墓發掘簡報. *Wenwu*, no. 8, pp. 31–39.

——. 1975b. "Liaodai caihui xingtu shi woguo tianwenshishang de zhongyao faxian" A Liao-period painting of a star map—an important discovery in Chinese astronomy] 遼代彩繪星圖是我國天文史上的重要發現. *Wenwu*, no. 8, pp. 40–44.

——. 1981. "Yelü Jiayili fei muzhiming" [The funerary inscription of Yelü Jiayili's concubine] 耶律加乙里妃墓誌銘. *Kaogu*, no. 5, pp. 469–470.

——. 1993. "Zhangjiakou qingli Liao bihuamu qun" [Sorting out a group of Liao tombs in Zhangjiakou] 張家口清理遼壁畫墓群. *Zhongguo wenwu bao* 8, no. 8.

Zhong Kan 鍾侃. 1978. "Ningxia Huizu Zizhiqu wenwu kaogu gongzuo de zhuyao shouhuo" [Important achievements in archaeological work in the Ningxia Hui Autonomous Region] 寧夏回族自治區文物考古工作的主要收穫. *Wenwu*, no. 8, pp. 54–59 and 11.

Zhongguo gudai tianwen wenwu tuji [Illustrations of cultural relics of early Chinese astronomy] 中國古代天文文物圖集. 1978. Beijing: Wenwu chubanshe.

Zhongguo gujianzhu xueshu jiangzuo wen ji [Collected lectures in ancient Chinese architecture] 中國古建築學術講座文集. Beijing: Zhongguotang chubanshe.

Zhongguo jianzhu jianshi [Short history of Chinese architecture] 中國建築簡史. 1962. Beijing: Zhongguo gongye chubanshe.

Zhongguo kaoguxue tonglun [Essays in Chinese archaeology] 中國考古學通論. 1991. Nanjing: Nanjing Daxue chubanshe.

Zhongguo kaoguxue wenxian mulu 1900–1949 [Index of articles on Chinese archaeology 1900–1949] 中國考古學文獻目錄 1900–1949. 1991. Beijing: Wenwu chubanshe.

Zhongguo mingsheng cidian [Dictionary of famous places in China] 中國名勝詞典. 2nd ed. Shanghai: Shanghai cishu chubanshe.

Zhongguo mingta [Famous Chinese pagodas] 中國名塔. 1993. Guangdong: Guangdong Renmin chubanshe.

Zhongguo wenwu ditu ji: Jilin [Atlas of Chinese cultural relics: Jilin province] 中國文物地圖集: 吉林. 1993. Beijing: Zhongguo ditu chubanshe.

Zhou Jie 洲杰. 1966. "Nei Menggu Zhaomeng Liao Taizuling diaocha sanji" [Notes on the excavation of the tomb of Liao Taizu in "Zhaomeng," Inner Mongolia] 內蒙古昭盟遼太祖陵調查散記. *Kaogu*, no. 5, pp. 263–266.

Zhou Yangsheng 周陽生, Li Xiaozhong 李曉鐘, and Liu Huanmin 劉煥珉. 1986. "Shenyang Wanwugoujingguang Shelita tagong qingli baogao" [Report on the contents of the Wanwugoujingguang Śarīra pagoda in Shenyang] 瀋陽灣無垢淨光舍利塔塔宮清理報告. *Beifang wenwu*, no. 2, pp. 30–52.

Zhu Qiqian 朱啓鈐. 1936. "Liao-Jin Yanjing chengguo gongyuan tukao" [Plans and research on the palace halls and gardens of Liao-Jin Yanjing] 遼金燕京城郭宮苑圖考. *Wenzhe jikan* 6, no. 1, pp. 49–81.

Zhu Xie 朱偰. 1936a. *Jinling guji mingsheng yingji* [Collection of notable spots that remain in Jinling] 金陵古蹟名勝影記. Shanghai: Shangwu yinshuguan.

——. 1936b. *Jinling guji tukao* [Pictures and research on ancient remains at Jinling] 金陵古蹟圖考. Shanghai: Shangwu yinshuguan.

Zhu Xiyuan 朱希元. 1984. "Bei Song 'Liaodi' yongde Dingxian Kaiyuansi ta" [The Northern Song pagoda for "spying on the enemy" of Kaiyuan Monastery in Dingxian] 北宋料敵用的定縣開元寺塔. *Wenwu*, no. 3, pp. 83–84.

——. 1985. "Taiyuan Jinci" [The Jin Shrines at Taiyuan] 太原晉祠. *Gujian yuanlin jishu*, no. 2, pp. 38–42.

Zhu Yizun 朱彝尊. 1688 (with later additions). 1968 facsimile reproduction. *Rixia jiuwen (kao)* [(Research into) Record of life day by day] 日下舊聞 (考). Taipei: Guangwen shuju.

WESTERN LANGUAGES

Abe, Stanley Kenji. 1989. *Mogao Cave 254: A Case Study in Early Chinese Buddhist Art.* Ph.D. dissertation, University of California, Berkeley.

——. 1990. "Art and Practice in a Fifth-Century Chinese Buddhist Cave Temple." *Ars Orientalis* 20:1–31.

Adams, Edward B. 1986. *Korea's Kyongju: Cultural Spirit of Silla in Korea.* Seoul: Seoul International Publishing House.

Akiyama Terukazu and Matsubara Saburo. 1969. *Buddhist Cave Temples: New Researches.* Vol. 2 of *Arts of China.* Translated by Alexander C. Soper. Tokyo and Palo Alto: Kodansha International.

Ancient Chinese Architecture. 1982. Beijing and Hong Kong: China Building Industry Press and Joint Publishing Company.

Balzer, Marjorie Mandelstam, ed. 1990. *Shamanism: Soviet Studies of Traditional Religion in Siberia and Central Asia.* Armonk, N.Y.: M. E. Sharpe.

Barfield, Thomas J. 1981. "The Hsiung-nu Imperial Confederation: Organization and Foreign Policy." *Journal of Asian Studies* 41:45–61.

——. 1989. *The Perilous Frontier: Nomadic Empires and China.* Edited by Charles Tilly. Oxford: Basil Blackwell.

Barnes, Gina L. 1993. *China, Korea and Japan: The Rise of Civilization in East Asia.* London: Thames & Hudson.

Bartol'd, Vasilii V. 1968. *Turkestan Down to the Mongol Invasion.* Translated by T. Minorsky. 3rd ed. E. J. Gibb Memorial Series, n.s., no. 5. London: Luzac.

Boerschmann, Ernst. 1911. *Die Baukunst und religiöse Kultur der Chinesen.* Berlin: G. Reimer.

——. 1923. *Baukunst und Landschaft in China: Eine Reise durch zwölf Provinzen.* Berlin: E. Wasmuth.

——. 1925. *Chinesische Architektur.* Berlin: E. Wasmuth.

——. 1931. *Chinesische Pagoden.* Berlin: W. de Gruyter.

Boyd, Andrew. 1962. *Chinese Architecture and Town Planning.* London: Tiranti.

Cahill, James. 1958. "Ch'ien Hsüan and His Figure Paintings." *Archives of the Chinese Art Society of America* 12:11–29.

——. 1980a. *An Index of Early Chinese Painters and Paintings.* Berkeley: University of California Press.

——. 1980b. "Some Aspects of Tenth-Century Painting as Seen in Three Recently-Published Works." Paper for International Conference on Sinology, Academia Sinica, Taipei.

——. 1988. *Three Alternative Histories of Chinese Painting.* Franklin D. Murphy Lectures IX. Lawrence: Spencer Museum of Art, University of Kansas.

Cahill, Suzanne, trans. 1979. "An Analysis of the Western Han Murals in the Luoyang Tomb of Bo Qianqiu." *Chinese Studies in Archeology* 2(2):44–78.

Cammann, Schuyler. 1960. "Magic Squares: The Evolution of the Magic Square in China." *Journal of the American Oriental Society* 80(2):116–119.

——. 1962. "Old Chinese Magic Squares." *Sinologica* 7(1):14–53.

Capon, Edmund, and William MacQuitty. 1973. *Princes of Jade.* New York: Dutton.

Castell, Wulf Diether, Graf zu. 1938. *Chinaflug.* Berlin: Atlantis-Verlag.

Caswell, James O. 1988. *Written and Unwritten: A New History of the Buddhist Caves at Yungang.* Vancouver: University of British Columbia Press.

Chan Hok-lam. 1970. *The Historiography of the Chin Dynasty (1115–1234): Three Studies.* Münchener Ostasiatische Studien, no. 4. Wiesbaden: Steiner.

——. 1981. "Chinese Official Historiography at the Yüan Court: The Composition of the Liao, Chin, and Sung Histories." In *China Under Mongol Rule,* ed. John D. Langlois, Jr. Princeton, N.J.: Princeton University Press.

——. 1984. *Legitimation in Imperial China: Discussions Under the Jurchen-Chin Dynasty (1115–1234).* Seattle: University of Washington Press.

Chang Kwang-chih. 1980. *Shang Civilization.* New Haven: Yale University Press.

——. 1986. *The Archaeology of Ancient China.* 4th ed. New Haven: Yale University Press.

Chavannes, Édouard. 1893. *La sculpture sur pierre en Chine au temps des deux dynasties Han.* Paris: E. Leroux.

——. 1897. "Voyageurs Chinois chez les Khitan et les Joutchen." Pt. 1. *Journal Asiatique,* 9th series, no. 9:377–442.

——. 1898. "Voyageurs Chinois chez les Khitan et les Joutchen." Pt. 2. *Journal Asiatique,* 9th series, no. 11:361–439.

——. 1909–1915. *Mission archéologique dans la Chine septentrionale.* 3 vols. Paris: E. Leroux.

Chaves, Jonathan. 1968. "A Han Painted Tomb at Lo-yang." *Artibus Asiae* 30(1):5–27.

Cheng Te-k'un. 1945. "The Royal Tomb of Wang Chien." *Harvard Journal of Asiatic Studies* 8:235–240.

——. 1982a. "The Excavation of T'ang Dynasty Tombs at Chüan-chou, Southern Fukien." In *Studies in Chinese Archaeology,* ed. Cheng Te-k'un. Hong Kong: Chinese University Press.

——. 1982b. "The Royal Tomb of Wang Chien, Szechwan." In *Studies in Chinese Archaeology,* ed. Cheng Te-k'un. Hong Kong: Chinese University Press.

——. 1982c. *Studies in Chinese Archaeology.* Hong Kong: Chinese University Press.

——. 1982d. "Sketches of a Trip of Archaeological Investigation in Hopei, Honan and Shantung." In *Studies in Chinese Archaeology,* ed. Cheng Te-k'un. Hong Kong: Chinese University Press.

Chung Saehyang P. 1990. "A Study of the Daming Palace: Documentary Sources and Recent Excavations." *Artibus Asiae* 50(1/2):23–72.

——. 1991. "Hsing-ch'ing Kung: Some New Findings on the Plan of Emperor Hsüan-tsung's Private Palace." *Archives of Asian Art* 44:51–67.

"Clay Figures in the Huayan Temple, Liao Dynasty." n.d. 12-slide set. Beijing Slides Studio.

Colvin, Howard. 1991. *Architecture and the After-Life.* New Haven: Yale University Press.

Creswell, K.A.C. 1932 and 1940. *Early Muslim Architecture.* 2 vols. Oxford: Oxford University Press.

Dallapiccola, Anna Libera, and Stephanie Zingle-avé Lallemant, eds. 1980. *The Stūpa: Its Religious, Histori-cal and Architectural Significance.* Wiesbaden: Steiner.

De Bary, Theodore, et al. 1964. *Sources of Chinese Tradition.* Vol. 1. New York: Columbia University Press.

Demiéville, Paul. 1925a. "Che-yin Song Li Ming-tchong Ying tsao fa che: Édition photolithographique de la méthode d'architecture de Li Ming-chong des Song. 8 fasc." *Bulletin de l'École Française d'Extrême-Orient* 25:213–264.

——. 1925b. "Les tombeaux des Song méridionaux." *Bulletin de l'École Française d'Extrême-Orient* 25:458–567.

——. 1973. *Choix d'études sinologiques (1921–1970).* Edited by Yves Hervouet. Leiden: Brill.

Deydier, Christian. 1990. *Imperial Gold from Ancient China.* Pt. 1. London: Oriental Bronzes Ltd.

——. 1991. *Imperial Gold from Ancient China.* Pt. 2. London: Oriental Bronzes Ltd.

Di Cosmo, Nicola. 1994. "Ancient Inner Asian Nomads: Their Economic Basis and Its Significance in Chinese History." *Journal of Asian Studies* 53(4):1092–1126.

Dien, Albert. 1991. "A New Look at the Xianbei." In *Ancient Mortuary Traditions of China: Papers on Chinese Ceramic Funerary Sculptures,* ed. George Kuwayama. Los Angeles: Los Angeles County Museum of Art.

Dien, Albert, and Jeffrey Riegel. 1985. *A Decade of Chinese Archaeology: Abstracts from Chinese Archaeological Journals Published Between 1972 and 1981.* Los Angeles: Institute of Archaeology, University of California.

Dunnell, Ruth W. 1981. "Tanguts and the Tangut State of Ta Hsia." Ph.D. diss., Princeton University.

——. 1984. "Who Are the Tanguts? Remarks on Tangut Ethnogenesis and the Ethnonym Tangut." *Journal of Asian Studies* 18:78–89.

——. 1988. "Tanguts." In *Encyclopedia of Asian History,* ed. Ainslee Embree. New York: Columbia University Press.

——. 1996a. *The Great State of White and High: Bud-*

dhism and State Formation in Eleventh-Century Xia. Honolulu: University of Hawaiʻi Press.

——. 1996b. "The Recovery of Tangut History." *Orientations* 27(4):28–31.

Durkheim, Emile. 1915. *The Elementary Forms of Religious Life*. Translated by Joseph Ward Swain. London: Allen & Unwin.

Eberhard, Wolfram. 1949. *Das Toba-Reich Nordchina: Eine soziologische Untersuchung*. Leiden: Brill.

——. 1952. *Conquerors and Rulers: Social Forces in Medieval China*. Stanford: Stanford University Press.

——. 1964. "Temple-Building Activities in Medieval and Modern China." *Monumenta Serica* 23:264–318.

Ebner von Eschenbach, Silvia Freiin. 1994. "Public Graveyards of the Song Dynasty." In *Burial in Song China*, ed. Dieter Kuhn. Heidelberg: Edition Forum.

Ebrey, Patricia. 1990. "Cremation in Sung China." *American Historical Review* 95(2):406–428.

Ecke, Gustav. 1935–1936. "Structural Features of the Stone-Built 'T'ing Pagoda.'" *Monumenta Serica* 1(pt. 1):253–273.

——. 1936–1937. "The Institute for Research in Chinese Architecture: A Short Summary of the Field Work Carried on from Spring 1932 to Spring 1937." *Monumenta Serica* 2:448–474.

——. 1942. "Contributions to the Study of Sculpture and Architecture: Once More Shen-t'ung ssu and Ling-yen ssu." *Monumenta Serica* 7(1/2):295–311.

——. 1948. "Structural Features of the Stone-Built 'T'ing Pagoda.'" *Monumenta Serica* 13(pt. 2):331–365.

Ecke, Gustav, and Paul Demiéville. 1935. *The Twin Pagodas of Zayton*. Cambridge: Harvard University Press.

Eisenstadt, Shmuel. 1963. *The Political Systems of Empires*. New York: Free Press of Glencoe.

Eliade, Mircea. 1959. *The Sacred and the Profane: The Nature of Religion*. Translated by Willard R. Trask. New York: Harper & Row.

——. 1961. *Images and Symbols: Studies in Religious Symbolism*. Translated by Philip Mairet. New York: Sheed & Ward.

——. 1964. *Shamanism*. New York: Bollingen Foundation.

——. 1985. *Symbolism, the Sacred and the Arts*. New York: Crossroad.

Elisseeff, Danielle. 1994. "A propos d'un cimitière Liao. Les belles dames de Xiabali." *Arts Asiatiques* 49:70–81.

Ettinghausen, Richard, and Oleg Grabar. 1987. *The Art and Architecture of Islam, 650–1250*. Harmondsworth: Penguin.

Fairbank, Wilma. 1972. *Adventures in Retrieval*. Cambridge: Harvard University Press.

——. 1994. *Liang and Lin: Partners in Exploring China's Architectural Past*. Philadelphia: University of Pennsylvania Press.

Fairbank, Wilma, with Kitano Masao. 1954. "Han Mural Paintings in the Pei-yuan Tomb at Liao-yang, South Manchuria." *Artibus Asiae* 17(3/4):238–264.

Feng Han-yi. 1947. "Discovery and Excavation of the Yong-ling Royal Tomb of Wang Chien (847–918)." *Archives of the Chinese Art Society of America* 2:11–19.

Five Thousand Years of Korean Art. 1979. San Francisco: Asian Art Museum.

Fong, Mary. 1991. "Antecedents of Sui-Tang Burial Practices in Shaanxi." *Artibus Asiae* 51(3/4):147–198.

Fong Wen. 1980. *The Great Bronze Age of China*. New York: Metropolitan Museum of Art.

Fontein, Jan, and Wu Tung. 1973. *Unearthing China's Past*. Boston: Museum of Fine Arts.

Forte, Antonino. 1988. *Mingtang and Buddhist Utopias in the History of the Astronomical Clock*. Rome: Istituto Italiano per il Medio ed Estremo Oriente.

Franke, Herbert. 1990. "The Forest Peoples of Manchuria: Kitans and Jurchens." In *The Cambridge History of Early Inner Asia*, ed. Denis Sinor. Cambridge: Cambridge University Press.

Franke, Herbert, and Denis Twitchett, eds. 1994. *Alien Regimes and Border States, 907–1368*. Vol. 6 of *The Cambridge History of China*. Cambridge: Cambridge University Press.

Franz, Heinrich G. 1978. *Pagode, Turmtempel, Stupa*. Graz: Akademische Drucke Verlagsanstalt.

Friedley, David, trans. and intro. 1979. "Xianbei Remains in Manchuria and Inner Mongolia." *Chinese Studies in Archaeology* 2(2):44–78.

Fu Tian-chou. 1981. "The Clay Sculptures of Pingyao." *Chinese Literature* (March):111–115.

Fukuyama Toshio. 1976. *Heian Temples.* Vol. 9 of *The Heibonsha Survey of Japanese Art.* Translated by Ronald K. Jones. New York and Tokyo: Weatherhill.

Fussman, Gérard. 1986. "Symbolisms of the Buddhist Stūpa." *Journal of the International Association of Buddhist Studies* 9(2):37–53.

Futagawa Yukio. 1964. "The Hall of the Great Buddha at the Tōdai-ji." *Japan Architect* 6:47.

Geertz, Clifford. 1965. *The Impact of the Concept of Culture on the Concept of Man.* Chicago: University of Chicago Press.

——, ed. 1971. *Myth, Symbol, and Culture.* New York: Norton.

——. 1973. *The Interpretation of Cultures: Selected Essays.* New York: Basic Books.

Getty, Alice. 1962. *The Gods of Northern Buddhism.* Rutland: Tuttle.

Gibert, Lucien. 1934. *Dictionnaire historique et géographique de la Mandchourie.* Hong Kong: Imprimerie de la Société des missions-étrangères.

Giedion, Sigfried. 1967. *Space, Time and Architecture.* Cambridge: Harvard University Press.

——. 1971. *Architecture and the Phenomena of Transition.* Cambridge: Harvard University Press.

Glahn, Else. 1975. "On the Transmission of the *Yingzao fashi.*" *T'oung Pao* 61:232–265.

——. 1981. "Chinese Building Standards in the 12th Century." *Scientific American* 144(10):162–173.

Goepper, Roger, intro., and Roderick Whitfield, ed. 1984. *Treasures from Korea: Art Through 5000 Years.* London: British Museum Publications.

Goodrich, L. Carrington. 1942. "The Revolving Book-Case in China." *Harvard Journal of Asiatic Studies* 7:130–161.

Granet, Marcel. 1934. *La pensée chinoise.* Paris: La Rénaissance du livre.

Gridley, Marilyn L. 1992. "Historical Implications of the Colossal Sculpture of Guanyin at Liao Shangjing." *Proceedings of the International Academic Conference of Archaeological Cultures of the Northern Chinese Ancient Nations.* Huhehaote: Nei Menggu wenwu kaogu yanjiusuo.

——. 1993a. "Protecting the Kingdom with Sumeru at Fansghan." Paper presented at Mountains and the Cultures of Landscape in China conference, Santa Barbara, University of California.

——. 1993b. *Chinese Buddhist Sculpture Under the Liao.* New Delhi: International Academy of Indian Culture and Aditya Prakashan.

——. 1995–1996. "Three Buddhist Sculptures from Longquanfu and the Luohans from Yi Xian." *Oriental Art* 41(4):20–29.

Grootaers, Willem A. 1945. "Les temples villageois de la region au sudest de Tat'ong (Chansi nord), leurs inscriptions et leur histoire." *Folklore Studies* 4:161–212.

Grousset, René. 1970. *The Empire of the Steppes.* Translated by Naomi Walford. New Brunswick: Rutgers University Press.

Guo Qinghua. 1995. "The Structure of Chinese Timber Architecture." Ph.D. dissertation, Chalmers University of Technology.

Han, Woo-kuen. 1971. *The History of Korea.* Translated by Kyung-shik Lee, edited by Grafton K. Mintz. Honolulu: University of Hawai'i Press.

Harle, John. 1986. *The Art and Architecture of the Indian Subcontinent.* Pelican History of Art series. Harmondsworth: Penguin.

Harley, J. B., and David Woodward, eds. 1994. *The History of Cartography.* Vol. 2, Bk. 2: *Cartography in the Traditional East and Southeast Asian Societies.* Chicago: University of Chicago Press.

Harper, Prudence. 1990. "An Iranian Silver Vessel from the Tomb of Feng Hetu." *Bulletin of the Asia Institute* 4:51–59.

Hertz, Robert. 1960. *The Death of the Right Hand.* Translated by Rodney and Claudia Needham. Glencoe: Free Press.

Hesselgren, Sven. 1972. *The Language of Architecture.* London: Applied Science.

Ho, Judy Chungwa. 1991. "The Twelve Calendrical Animals in Tang Tombs." In *Ancient Mortuary Traditions* of China: Papers on Chinese Funerary Ceramic Sculpture, ed. George Kuwayama. Los Angeles: Los Angeles County Museum.

Hodder, Ian. 1986. *Reading the Past.* Cambridge: Cambridge University Press.

———, ed. 1989. *The Meanings of Things: Material Culture and Symbolic Expression.* London: Unwin Hyman.

Hodder, Ian, and Clive Orton, 1976. *Spatial Analysis in Archaeology.* Cambridge: Cambridge University Press.

Holmgren, Jennifer. 1986a. "Marriage, Kinship and Succession Under the Ch'i-tan Rulers of the Liao Dynasty (907–1125)." *T'oung Pao* 72:44–91.

———. 1986b. "Yeh-lü, Yao-lien and Ta-ho: Views of the Hereditary Prerogative in Early Khitan Leadership." *Papers on Far Eastern History* 34:37–81.

Honey, David. 1992. "Stripping Off Fur: An Essay on Nomadic Sinification." *Papers on Inner Asia*, no. 21. Bloomington: Indiana University Research Institute for Inner Asian Studies.

Hoppal, Mihaly, ed. 1984. *Shamanism in Eurasia.* 2 vols. Gottingen: Édition Herodot.

Hoppal, Mihaly, and V. Diozegi, eds. 1978. *Shamanism in Siberia.* Budapest: Akadensai Kiado.

Howard, Angela F. 1983. "Planetary Worship: Some Evidence, Mainly Textual, in Chinese Esoteric Buddhism." *Asiatische Studien* 37(1):104–119.

———. 1984. "Buddhist Sculptures of the Liao Dynasty." *Bulletin of the Museum of Far Eastern Antiquities* 56:1–95.

Howorth, Sir Henry Hoyle. 1881. "The Northern Frontagers of China. Pt. V: The Khitai or Khitans." *Journal of the Royal Asiatic Society*, n.s., 13:121–182.

Hsu Cho-yun and Katheryn M. Lindhuff, 1988. *Western Chou Civilization.* New Haven: Yale University Press.

"The Huayen Temple." n.d. 12-slide set. Beijing Slides Studio.

Hucker, Charles O. 1985. *A Dictionary of Official Titles in Imperial China.* Stanford: Stanford University Press.

Huntington, John. 1986. "The Iconography and Iconology of the 'Tan Yao' Caves at Yungang." *Oriental Art* 32(2):142–160.

Huntington, Richard, and Peter Metcalf. 1979. *Celebrations of Death.* Cambridge: Cambridge University Press.

Imperial Tombs of China. 1995. Memphis International Cultural Series. Memphis: Wonders.

Irwin, John. 1980. "The Axial Symbolism of the Early Stūpa: An Exegesis." in *The Stūpa, Its Religious, Historical and Architectural Significance,* eds. A. L. Dallapiccola and S. Z. Lallemant. Wiesbaden: Steiner.

Ishida Hisatoyo. 1987. *Esoteric Buddhist Painting.* Translated by E. Dale Saunders. Tokyo: Kodansha International.

Itō Nobuo. 1957. "The Nandaimon of the Tōdai-ji Monastery." *Japan Architect* 5:43–50.

Jagchid, Sechin. 1981. "The Kitans and Their Cities." *Central Asiatic Journal* 25:70–88.

———. 1982. "Kitan Struggles Against Jürchen Oppression: Nomadism Versus Sinicization." *Zentralasiatische Studien* 16:165–185.

Jagchid, Sechin, and Van Jay Simons. 1989. *Peace, War and Trade Along the Great Wall: Nomadic-Chinese Interaction Through Two Millennia.* Bloomington: Indiana University Press.

Jenner, W.J.F., trans. 1981. *Memories of Lo-yang, 495–534.* New York: Oxford University Press.

Jettmar, Karl. 1967. *The Art of the Steppes.* Translated by Ann E. Keep. New York: Greystone Press.

Johnson, Linda Cooke. 1983. "The Wedding Ceremony for an Imperial Liao Princess: Wall Paintings from a Liao Dynasty Tomb in Jilin." *Artibus Asiae* 44:107–136.

Karetsky, Patricia Eichenbaum. 1980. "The Recently Discovered Chin Dynasty Murals Illustrating the Life of the Buddha at Yen-shan[g]-ssu, Shansi." *Artibus Asiae* 42:245–260.

Karetsky, Patricia Eichenbaum, and Alexander C. Soper. 1991. "A Northern Wei Painted Coffin." *Artibus Asiae* 51(1/2):5–20.

Kazin, V. N. 1961. "K istorii Khara-Khoto." *Trudy Gosudarstvennogo Ermitazh* 5:273–285.

Ker, L. 1923. "Le tombeau de l'empereur Tao-tsong des Leao et les premières inscriptions connues en écriture K'itan." *T'oung Pao* 22:292–301.

Kessler, Adam T. 1993. *Empires Beyond the Great Wall: The Heritage of Genghis Khan*. Los Angeles: Natural History Museum.

Kidder, J. Edward. 1972. *Early Buddhist Japan*. New York: Praeger.

——. 1973. "The Newly Discovered Takamatsuzuka Tomb." *Monumenta Nipponica* 27(3):245–251.

Kim Won-yong. 1983. *Recent Archaeological Discoveries in the Republic of Korea*. Paris: UNESCO; Tokyo: Centre for East Asian Cultural Studies.

——. 1986. *The Art and Archaeology of Ancient Korea*. Seoul: Taekwang.

Kim Won-yong, Choi Sun-u, and Im Chang-soon. 1979. *The Arts of Korea*. Vol. 2: *Paintings*. Seoul: Dong Hwa.

Kiselev, Sergei. 1965. *Drevnemongol'skie goroda*. Moscow: Nauka.

Koslov, Piotr K. 1923. *Mongoliīā Amdo i mertvyĭ gorod Khara-khoto*. St. Petersburg: State Press.

Kottkamp, Heino. 1992. *Der Stupa als Repräsentation des buddhistische Heilsweges: Untersuchen zur Entstehung und Entwicklung architektonischer Symbolik*. Wiesbaden: Harrassowitz.

Kozloff, P. K. [Piotr K. Koslov]. 1909. "The Mongolia–Sze-chuan Expedition of the Imperial Russian Geographical Society." *Geographical Journal* 34(10): 384–408.

——. 1910. "The Mongolia–Sze-chuan Expedition of the Imperial Russian Geographical Society." *Geographical Journal* 36(9):288–310.

Kuhn, Dieter. 1987. *Die Song-Dynastie: Eine neue Gesellschaft im Spiegel ihrer Kultur*. Wienheim: Acta Humaniora.

——. 1990. *Die stummen Zeugen (The Mute Witnesses)*. Heidelberg: Edition Forum.

——, ed. 1992. *Arbeitsmaterialien aus chinesischen Ausgrabungsberichten (1988–1991) zu Gräbern aus der Han bis Tang-Zeit*. Würzburger Sinologische Schriften. Institut für Sinologie. Heidelberg: Edition Forum.

——. 1994. *Burial in Song China*. Heidelberg: Edition Forum.

——. 1996. *A Place for the Dead: An Archaeological Documentary on Graves and Tombs of the Song Dynasty (960–1279)*. Heidelberg: Edition Forum.

Kuwayama, George, ed. 1991. *Ancient Mortuary Traditions of China: Papers on Chinese Funerary Ceramic Sculpture*. Los Angeles: Los Angeles County Museum.

Laing, Ellen Johnston. 1978. "Patterns and Problems in Later Chinese Tomb Decoration." *Journal of Oriental Studies* 16:3–20.

——. 1992. "Liao Dynasty (A.D. 907–1125) Bird-and-Flower Painting." In *Proceedings of the International Conference of Archaeological Cultures of the Northern Chinese Ancient Nations*. Huhehaote: Nei Menggu wenwu kaogu yanjiusu.

——. 1994. "A Survey of Liao Dynasty Bird-and-Flower Painting." *Journal of Sung-Yuan Studies* 24:57–99.

Ledderöse, Lothar. 1980. "Chinese Prototypes of the Pagoda in the stūpa." In *The Stūpa, Its Religious, Historical and Architectural Significance*, eds. A. L. Dallapiccola and S. Z. Lallemant. Wiesbaden: Steiner.

——. 1990. "Massenproduktion angesichts der Katastropie." *Asiatische Studien/Études Asiatiques* 44(2):217–233.

——. 1992. "Mass Production of Sutra Stones Under Liao." Unpublished paper.

Lee, Ki-baik. 1984. *A New History of Korea*. Translated by Edward W. Wagner with Edward J. Shultz. Cambridge: Harvard University Press.

Lei Runze. 1996. "The Structural Character and Tradition of Ningxia's Tangut Stupas." *Orientations* 27(4):55–62.

Li Chi. 1977. *Anyang: A Chronicle of the Discovery, Excavation, and Reconstruction of the Ancient Capital of the Shang Dynasty*. Seattle: University of Washington Press.

Li Xueqin. *Eastern Zhou and Qin Civilizations*. New Haven: Yale University Press.

Liang Ssu-ch'eng [Sicheng]. 1984. *A Pictorial History of Chinese Architecture*. Edited by Wilma Fairbank. Cambridge: MIT Press.

Lim, Lucy, ed. 1987. *Stories from China's Past: Han Dynasty Pictorial Tomb Reliefs and Archaeological Objects from Sichuan Province, People's Republic of China.* San Francisco: Chinese Culture Center.

Lindner, Rudi P. 1982. "What Was a Nomadic Tribe?" *Comparative Studies in Society and History* 24:689–711.

Liu, Cary. 1996. "Sung Dynasty Painting of the T'ai-ch'ing-lou Library Hall: From Historical Commemoration to Architectural Renewal." Paper presented to Arts of the Sung and Yuan symposium, May 1996, Princeton University.

Loewe, Michael. 1979. *Ways to Paradise: The Chinese Quest for Immortality.* London: Allen & Unwin.

——. 1982. *Chinese Ideas of Life and Death.* London: Allen & Unwin.

Lubo-Lesnichenko, E. I. 1968. "Istoriko-arkheologicheskoe izuchenie g. Khara-khoto." *Strany i narody Vostoke* 6:115–124.

Lubo-Lesnichenko, E. I., and T. K. Safronovskaia. 1968. *Mertvyĭ gorod Khara-khoto.* Moscow: Nauka.

Luo Feng. 1990. "Lacquer Painting on a Northern Wei Coffin." *Orientations* 21(7):18–29.

Marra, Michele. 1988. "The Development of Mappō Thought in Japan." *Japanese Journal of Religious Studies* 1:25–54; 4:287–305.

McCune, Evelyn. 1962. *The Arts of Korea.* Rutland: Tuttle.

McNair, Amy. 1988–1989. "On the Date of the Shengmudian Sculptures at Jinci." *Artibus Asiae* 49:238–253.

Mino Yutaka. 1973. *Ceramics in the Liao Dynasty.* New York: China House Gallery.

——, exhibition organizer. 1986. *The Great Eastern Temple: Treasures of Japanese Buddhist Art from Tōdai-ji.* Chicago: Art Institute of Chicago.

Mitra, Debala. 1971. *Buddhist Monuments.* Calcutta: Sahitya Samsad.

Miyakawa Hisayuki. 1955. "An Outline of the Naitō Hypothesis and Its Effects on Japanese Studies of China." *Far Eastern Quarterly* 14(4):533–552.

Mizuno Seiichi. 1950. "Archaeological Survey of the Yün-kang Grottoes." *Archives of the Chinese Art Society of America* 4:39–60.

Moses, Larry. 1974. "A Theoretical Approach to the Process of Inner Asian Confederation." *Études Mongoles* 5:113–122.

Mote, F. n.d. "Late Imperial China." Unpublished manuscript.

Moule, Arthur C., and Paul Pelliot. 1938. *Marco Polo: The Description of the World.* 2 vols. London: Routledge.

Mullie, Joseph L. 1922. "Les anciennes villes de l'empire des grands Leao au royaume mongol de Bārin." *T'oung Pao* 21:105–231.

——. 1933. "Les sepulchres de K'ing des Leao." *T'oung Pao* 30:1–25.

Murata Jirō. 1957. "Hōoh-dō of Byōdō-in." *Japan Architect* 12:40–41.

——. 1962. "The Phoenix Hall at the Byōdō-in." *Japan Architect* 1/2:122–127; 3:82–89; 4:81–87.

——. 1963. "The Main Hall of Tōshōdai-ji." *Japan Architect* 2:93–99.

Nelson, Sarah Milledge. 1993. *The Archaeology of Korea.* Cambridge: Cambridge University Press.

Ōkura Saburō. 1956. "The Amitabha Hall, Hōkai-ji Monastery." *Japan Architect* 9:27–32.

Ol'denburg, Sergeĭ F. 1914. *Materialy po Buddiiskoi ikonografii Khara-khoto.* St. Petersburg: Akademiaya nauk.

Ōmori Kenji. 1964. "The Main Hall of Jōruri-ji." *Japan Architect* 1:91–99.

——. 1965. "The Great South Gate of Tōdai-ji." *Japan Architect* 5:80–89.

Ooka Minoru. 1973. *Temples of Nara and Their Art.* Vol. 7 of *The Heibonsha Survey of Japanese Art.* Translated by Dennis Lishka. New York and Tokyo: Weatherhill/Heibonsha.

Owen, Elizabeth. 1993. "Case Study in Xianbei Funerary Painting: Examination of the *Guyuan sarcophagus* in the Light of the Chinese Funerary Painting Tradition." M.A. thesis, University of Pennsylvania.

Paine, Robert Treat. n.d. *Figure Compositions of China and Japan.* Boston: Museum of Fine Arts.

Paine, Robert Treat, and Alexander C. Soper. 1981. *The Art and Architecture of Japan.* Pelican History of Art series. 3rd ed. with revisions and updated notes and bibliography to pt. 1 by D. B. Waterhouse. Harmondsworth: Penguin.

Pak, Youngsook. 1978. "Buddhist Themes in Koguryo Murals." *Asiatische Studien/Études Asiatiques* 44(2):177–204.

Paludan, Ann. 1988. "The Chinese Spirit Road." Pt. 1. *Orientations* 9:56–65.

———. 1989. "The Chinese Spirit Road." Pt. 2. *Orientations* 4:64–73.

———. 1990. "The Chinese Spirit Road." Pt. 3. *Orientations* 3:56–66.

———. 1991. *The Chinese Spirit Road: The Classical Tradition of Stone Tomb Statuary.* New Haven: Yale University Press.

Pelliot, Paul. 1914. "Les documents chinois trouvé par la mission à Khara-Khoto." *Journal Asiatique* 3:503–518.

Perlstein, Elinor. 1984. "Pictorial Stones from Chinese Tombs." *Bulletin of the Cleveland Museum of Art* 11:302–331.

Perzyński, Friedrich. 1913. "Jagd auf Götter." *Neue rundschau* 2:1427–1446.

———. 1920. *Von Chinas Göttern.* Munich: Kurt Wolff Verlag.

Piotrovsky, Mikhail, ed. 1993. *Lost Empire of the Silk Road: Buddhist Art from Khara Khoto (X–XIIIth Century).* Milan: Thyssen-Bornemisza Foundation.

Pirazzoli-T'Serstevens, Michèle. 1971. *Living Architecture: Chinese.* Translated by Robert Allen. New York: Grosset & Dunlap.

———. 1982. *The Han Civilization of China.* Translated by Janet Seligman. Oxford: Phaidon.

———. 1994. "Pour une archéologie des échanges. Apports étrangers en China—transmission, réception, assimilation." *Arts Asiatiques* 49:21–33.

Poo, Mu-chou. 1990. "Ideas Concerning Death and Burial in Pre-Han and Han China." *Asia Major* 3(2):25–62.

Pozdneyev, A. M. 1971. *Mongolia and the Mongols.* Edited by John R. Krueger. Bloomington: Indiana University Press.

Prip-Moller, Johannes. 1967. *Chinese Buddhist Monasteries.* 1937. Reprint, Hong Kong: Hong Kong University Press.

Pulleyblank, E. G. 1983. "The Chinese and Their Neighbors in Prehistoric and Early Historic Times." In *The Origins of Chinese Civilization*, ed. David N. Keightley. Berkeley: University of California Press.

The Quest for Eternity. 1987. Los Angeles: Los Angeles County Museum of Art.

Rachewiltz, Igor de. 1974. "Some Remarks on the Khitan Clan Name Yeh-lü—I-la." *Papers on Far Eastern History* 9:187–204.

Redfield, Robert, Ralph Linton, and Melville Herskovits. 1936. "Memorandum for the Study of Acculturation." *American Anthropologist*, n.s., 38:149–152.

Rhie, Marilyn. 1977a. *The Fo-kuang ssu: Literary Evidence and Buddhist Images.* New York: Garland.

———. 1977b. "Two Eleventh-Century Chinese Buddhist Sculptures." *Honolulu Academy of Arts Journal* 2:23–35.

Rorex, Robert A. 1984. "Some Liao Tomb Murals and Images of Nomads in Chinese Paintings of the Wenchi Story." *Artibus Asiae* 45:174–198.

Rossabi, Morris, ed. 1983. *China Among Equals: The Middle Kingdom and Its Neighbors, 10th–14th Centuries.* Berkeley: University of California Press.

Ruitenbeek, Klaas. 1993. *Carpentry and Building in Late Imperial China.* Leiden: Brill.

Sawa Takaaki. 1972. *Art in Japanese Esoteric Buddhism.* Vol. 8 of *The Heibonsha Survey of Japanese Art.* Translated by Richard L. Gage. New York: Weatherhill.

Schafer, Edward. 1963. "The T'ang Imperial Icon." *Sinologica* 7:156–160.

———. 1977. *Pacing the Void.* Berkeley: University of California Press.

Schwartz-Schilling, Christian. 1959. *Der Friede von Shan-yüan.* Vol. 1 of *Asiatische Forschungen.* Wiesbaden: Harassowitz.

Seckel, Dietrich. 1968. *The Art of Buddhism.* Translated by Ann E. Keep. Rev. ed. New York: Greystone Press.

———. 1980. "Stūpa Elements Surviving in East Asian Pagodas." In *The Stūpa, Its Religious, Historical, and Architectural Significance*, eds. A. L. Dallapiccola and S. Lallement. Wiesbaden: Steiner.

———. 1989. *Buddhist Art of East Asia.* Translated by

Ulrich Mammitzsch. Center for East Asian Studies. Bellingham: Western Washington University.

Segalen, Victor. 1978. *The Great Statuary of China*. Translated by Eleanor Levieux. Chicago: University of Chicago Press.

"Shanhua Temple: A Historic Site in Shanxi." n.d. 12-slide set. Beijing Slides Studio.

Shih Hsio-yen. 1959. "I-nan and Related Tombs." *Artibus Asiae* 22:277–312.

Shinohara Kazuo. 1964. "Jōdō-dō at the Jōdō-ji." *Japan Architect* 6:48.

Sickman, Laurence, and Alexander Soper. 1971. *The Art and Architecture of China*. Pelican History of Art series. First integrated edition (based on third hardback edition). Harmondsworth: Penguin.

Sinor, Denis, ed. 1990. *The Cambridge History of Early Inner Asia*. Cambridge: Cambridge University Press.

Sirén, Osvald. 1924. *The Walls and Gates of Peking*. 3 vols. London: John Lane.

———. 1926. *The Imperial Palaces of Peking*. 3 vols. Paris and Brussels: G. Van Oest.

———. 1930. *A History of Chinese Art*. Vol. 4: *Architecture*. London: Ernest Benn.

———. 1932. "A Chinese Temple and Its Plastic Decoration of the Twelfth Century." *Études d'orientalisme, publiée par Le Musée Guimet à la memoire de Raymonde Linossier*, 2.

———. 1942. "Chinese Sculpture of the Sung, Liao and Chin Dynasties." *Bulletin of the Museum of Far Eastern Antiquities* 14:45–64.

———. 1956. *Chinese Painting: Masters and Principles*. 7 vols. New York: Ronald.

Smithies, Richard. 1984. "The Search for the Lohans of I-chou (Yixian)." *Oriental Art* 20(3):260–274.

Snellgrove, David, ed. 1978. *The Image of the Buddha*. Paris: Kodansha International.

Snodgrass, Adrian. 1985. *The Symbolism of the Stupa*. Ithaca: Cornell University Press.

Soothill, William E. 1951. *The Hall of Light: A Study of Early Chinese Kingship*. London: Lutterworth.

Soothill, William E., and Hodous, Lewis. 1937. *A Dictionary of Chinese Buddhist Terms*. London: Kegan Paul, Trench, Trubner.

Soper, Alexander C. 1939–1940. "Contributions to the Study of Sculpture and Architecture III: Japanese Evidence for the History of the Architecture and Iconography of Chinese Buddhism." *Monumenta Serica* 4:638–679.

———. 1942. *The Evolution of Buddhist Architecture in Japan*. Princeton: Princeton University Press.

———. 1947. "The 'Dome of Heaven' in Asian Art." *Art Bulletin* 29:225–248.

———. 1948. "Hisang-kuo ssu, an Imperial Temple of the Northern Sung." *Journal of the American Oriental Society* 68(1):19–45.

———. 1959. *Literary Evidence for Early Buddhist Art in China*. Ascona: Artibus Asiae.

———. 1990. "Whose Body?" *Asiatische Studien/Études Asiatiques* 44(2):205–216.

Stein, Sir Aurel. 1928. *Innermost Asia*. 2 vols. Oxford: Oxford University Press.

Stein, Rolf. 1940. "Leao-tche." *T'oung Pao* 35:1–154.

Steinhardt, Nancy S. 1981a. "Imperial Architecture Under Mongolian Patronage: Khubilai's Imperial City of Daidu." Ph.D. diss., Harvard University.

———. 1981b. "Chinese Ladies in the Istanbul Albums." In *Between China and Iran: Paintings from Four Istanbul Albums*. Colloquies on Art and Archaeology in Asia, no. 10. London: Percival David Foundation of Chinese Art. (Reprinted in *Islamic Art* 1:77–84.)

———. 1983. "The Plan of Khubilai Khan's Imperial City." *Artibus Asiae* 44:137–158.

———. 1984. *Chinese Traditional Architecture*. New York: China Institute in America.

———. 1986. "Why Were Chang'an and Beijing So Different?" *Journal of the Society of Architectural Historians* 45(4):339–357.

———. 1987. "Siyah Qalem and Gong Kai." *Muqarnas* 4:59–71.

———. 1988. "Toward the Definition of a Yuan Dynasty Hall." *Journal of the Society of Architectural Historians* 47(1):57–73.

———. 1989. "Imperial Architecture Along the Mongolian Road to Dadu." *Ars Orientalis* 18:59–95.

———. 1990. *Chinese Imperial City Planning*. Honolulu: University of Hawai'i Press.

——. 1990–1991. "Yuan Period Tombs and Their Decoration: Cases at Chifeng." *Oriental Art* 36(4):198–221.

——. 1991. "The Mizong Hall of Qinglong Si: Space, Ritual, and Classicism in Chinese Architecture." *Archives of Asian Art* 44:27–50.

——. 1992. "Symbolism in Liao Architecture." *Proceedings of the International Academic Conference of Archaeological Cultures of the Northern Chinese Ancient Nations.* Huhehaote: Nei Menggu kaogu wenwu yanjiusuo.

——. 1993. "The Tangut Royal Tombs near Yinchuan." *Muqarnas* 10:369–381.

——. 1994. "Liao: An Architectural Tradition in the Making." *Artibus Asiae* 44(1/2):5–39.

——. 1995. "Chinese Architecture, 963–966." *Orientations* 26(2):46–52.

Stone, Jackie. 1985. "Seeking Enlightenment in the Last Age." *Far Eastern Buddhist*, n.s., 1:28–59; 2:35–64.

Sui An-der. 1992. "The Construction Bureau and Its Officials in the Song Dynasty." M.A. thesis, University of Pennsylvania.

Suzuki Kakichi. 1980. *Early Buddhist Architecture in Japan.* Vol. 9 in *Japanese Arts Library.* Translated by Mary N. Parent and Nancy S. Steinhardt. Tokyo, New York, and San Francisco: Kodansha International.

Tabbaa, Yasser. 1985. "The Muqarnas Dome: Its Origin and Meaning." *Muqarnas* 3:61–74.

Tao Jing-shen. 1976. *The Jurchen in Twelfth-Century China: A Study of Sinicization.* Seattle: University of Washington Press.

——. 1983. "Barbarians or Northerners: Northern Sung Images of the Khitan." In *China Among Equals: The Middle Kingdom and Its Neighbors, 10th–14th Centuries,* ed. Morris Rossabi. Berkeley: University of California Press.

——. 1988. *Two Sons of Heaven: Studies in Sung-Liao Relations.* Tucson: University of Arizona Press.

Thorp, Robert. 1981–1982. "The Sui Xian Tomb: Re-thinking the Fifth Century." *Artibus Asiae* 43(1–2):67–92.

——. 1983: "An Archeological Reconstruction of the Lishan Necropolis." In *The Great Bronze Age of China: A Symposium,* ed. George Kuwayama. Los Angeles County Museum Symposium. Seattle: University of Washington Press.

——. 1991. "Mountain Tombs and Jade Burial Suits: Preparations for Eternity in the Western Han." In *Ancient Mortuary Traditions of China,* ed. George Kuwayama. Los Angeles: Los Angeles County Museum of Art.

Tietze, Klaus. 1979. "The Liao-Sung Border Conflict of 1074–76." In *Studia Sino-Mongolica: Festschrift für Herbert Franke,* ed. Wolfgang Bauer. Wiesbaden: Steiner.

Till, Barry. 1986. "The Imperial Xi Xia Tombs at Yinchuan, Ningxia." *Orientations* 17(11):48–54.

Till, Barry, and Paula Swart. 1982. *In Search of Old Nanking.* Hong Kong: Joint Publishing Company.

Tillman, Hoyt C., and Stephen H. West. 1995. *China Under Jurchen Rule: Essays on Chin Intellectual and Cultural History.* Albany: SUNY Press.

Torii, Ryūzō. 1942. *Sculpted Stone Tombs of the Liao.* Beiping: Harvard Yenching Institute.

Twitchett, Denis C., and John K. Fairbank, eds. 1979. *Sui and T'ang China, 589–906, pt. 1.* Vol. 3 of *The Cambridge History of China.* Cambridge: Cambridge University Press.

Vaudescal, Le Commandant. 1914. "Le Chê kīng chān et le Yūn kiū sséu." *Journal asiatique,* ser. 11, 3:375–459.

Vinograd, Richard. 1981. "New Light on Tenth-Century Sources for Landscape Painting Styles of the Late Yüan Period." *Chūgoku kaiga-shi ronshū.* (Festschrift for Professor Suzuki Kei.) Tokyo: Yoshikawa Kōbunkan.

Wang Gung-wu. 1963. *The Structure of Power in North China During the Five Dynasties.* Kuala Lumpur: University of Malaya Press.

——. 1983. "The Rhetoric of a Lesser Empire." In *China Among Equals: The Middle Kingdom and Its Neighbors, 10th–14th Centuries,* ed. Morris Rossabi. Berkeley: University of California Press.

Wang Tianyi. 1989. *Underground Art Gallery: China's Brick Paintings 1,700 Years Old.* Beijing: New World Press.

Wang Yi-t'ung, trans. 1984. *A Record of Buddhist Monasteries in Lo-yang.* Princeton: Princeton University Press.

Wang Zhongshu. 1982. *Han Civilization.* New Haven: Yale University Press.

Watson, William. 1974. *Style in the Arts of China.* Harmondsworth: Penguin.

———. 1981. "Chinese Style in the Paintings of the Istanbul Albums." In *Between China and Iran: Paintings from Four Istanbul Albums. Colloquies on Art and Archaeology in Asia*, no. 10. London: Percival David Foundation of Chinese Art. (Reprinted in *Islamic Art* 1:69–76.)

Weber, Charles. 1978. "The Spirit Road in Chinese Funerary Practice." *Oriental Art*, n.s., 24(2):168–178.

Wilkinson, Endymion. 1975. *The History of Imperial China: A Research Guide.* East Asian Research Center. Cambridge: Harvard University Press.

Willetts, William. 1958. *Foundations of Chinese Art, from Neolithic Pottery to Modern Architecture.* 2 vols. in 1. New York: Braziller.

Wittfogel, Karl A., and Feng Chia-sheng. 1949. *History of Chinese Society: Liao (907–1125). Transactions of the American Philosophical Society*, n.s., vol. 36. Philadelphia: American Philosophical Society.

Wolf, Marion. 1969. "The Lohans from I-chou." *Oriental Art* 15(1):51–57.

Wright, Arthur, and Denis Twitchett, eds. 1973. *Perspectives on the Tang.* New Haven: Yale University Press.

Wright, David C. 1993. "Sung-Liao Diplomatic Practices." Ph.D. diss., Princeton University.

Wu Hung. 1986. "Buddhist Elements in Early Chinese Art (2nd and 3rd Centuries A.D.)." *Artibus Asiae* 47(2/3):263–352.

———. 1989. *The Wu Liang Shrine: The Ideology of Early Chinese Pictorial Art.* Stanford: Stanford University Press.

Wu Liangyong. 1986. *A Brief History of Ancient Chinese City Planning. Urbs et Regio*, special issue 38. Kassel: Gesamthochschulebibliothek.

Wu Zhuo. 1989. "Notes on the Silver Ewer from the Tomb of Li Xian." *Bulletin of the Asia Institute*, n.s., 3:61–70.

Yang Jidong. 1995. "Return to Righteousness: Zhang Yichao and His *guiyi jun*." Unpublished paper.

Yang Renkai. 1981. "Yeh-mao-t'ai." Paper presented at the Symposium on the Eight Dynasties Exhibition, Cleveland, Ohio.

Yetts, Percival W. 1926–1928. "A Chinese Treatise on Architecture." *Bulletin of the School of Oriental Studies* 4(3):473–492.

———. 1930. "A Note on the 'Ying tsao fa shih.'" *Bulletin of the School of Oriental Studies* 5(4):855–860.

"Yunju Temple." n.d. 12-slide set. Beijing Slides Studio.

Zhang Yuhuan et al. 1986. *History and Development of Ancient Chinese Architecture.* Beijing: Science Press.

Index

Foxiang Pavilion, **175**, **176**, **182**, 193, 194–195, 197, 203, 222, 223, 224
Front Hall (Youxiansi). *See* Youxian Monastery
Fu Xi (6th century), 198
Fujiwara: no Michinaga, 119; no Yorimichi, 119
Fuma, 285, 286
Funerary bed. *See* Coffin beds
Furen, 258
Fuxin, 3
Fuzhou: Pagodas, 25. *See also* Hualin Monastery

Ganggangmiao (village), 254
Gate-tower, 385. See also *Que*
Ge, 42–43, **69**, 75, 96, 126, 147, 156–157, 185, 197, 206, 208, 210, 212, 222, 229, 411 n. 35
Geertz, Clifford, 243
Geyuan Monastery, 15, 17, 27, **81**, **82**, **83**, 83–86, 96, 98, 101, 140, 147, 164, **164**, 169, 170, 184, 222, 225
Glahn, Else, 183
Gong, **38**, 47, 48, 79, 174, 178, 183. *See also* Bracket sets; *Puzuo*
Gong dianban, 174
Gong scheme, **230**, 246
Gongbu gongcheng zuofa zeli, 40, 169
Gongxian (Song tombs), **257**, 276
Gongyan bi, 68, 73
Great Wild Goose Pagoda, **357**, 386, 393
"Greater carpentry." See *Damuzuo*
Ground plans (Liao), 169–173
Gualunzhuang, 213
Guan, 310
Guanchuang, 313
Guandi, 154
Guandi Temple (Hebei), 162
Guangji Monastery (Baodi), 18, 24, **149**, **150**, **151**, **152**, **153**, 153–159, 224; history, 154–157. *See also* Sandashi Hall
Guangji Monastery (Jizhou), 96, **96**, **97**, 98–99, 139, 224
Guanyin Hall (Kaiyuan Monastery), **158**, 161–162, **164**, 169, 170

Guanyin Monastery (Jizhou). *See* White Pagoda, Jizhou
Guanyin Pagoda (Jizhou). *See* White Pagoda, Jizhou
Guanyin Pavilion (Dulesi), **6**, **23**, 24, **31**, **32**, **33**, 34, **34**, 35, **35**, **37**, **38**, **39**, 40–54, **40**, **41**, **42**, **45**, **46**, 64, 67, 68, 73, 75, 78, 83, 86, 92, 93, 107, 108, 119, 127, 129, 130, 131, 147, 148, 153, 158, 164, **164**, 169, 173–174, 184, 185, 192, 194, 195, 197, 198, 199, 205, 206, 209, 222, 223, 234, 236, 247, 265, 370, 373, 379, 398, 403, 404; bracket sets, 36–49, **37**, **38**, **39**, 175–179; ceiling, 49; compared with Timber Pagoda, 116–120
Guazi gong, **38**, 68, **122**, **137**, **166**, 175, 177, 178. See also *Gong*
Gujin tushu jicheng, 111
Guyuan tomb, 270
Güyug (Khan), 126

Haihui Hall, **118**, 126, **130**, **131**, **132**, 132–134, **133**, 161, 164, 169, 187; bracket sets, 134; timber-frame style, **171**, 181
Hailingwang, 229
Half bracket-arm, **85**
Han (family, of Jizhou), 119
Han architecture, 60, 160, 379. *See also* Tombs, Han
Han Derang, 17
Han Kuangsi, 17, 34–35, 55, 291
Han Xiang tomb, **308**, 334
Han Yanhui, 338
Han Yi and wife tomb, **313**, 337–338, 343
Han Zhibai, 55
Han Zhigu, 17, 314
Hangtu, 253, 254
Hanyuan Hall, **54**, **56**, 64
Haoqianying tomb, 7, 9, **288**, **289**, **290**, **291**, 318–321
Harmikā, 362, 391, 395
Hemudu, 60
Herodotus, 321
Hertz, Robert, 243
Hip-gable roof, **294**, 323
Holy Mother Hall. *See* Shengmu Hall

Hōnen, 93
Hong Taiji, 398, 400
Hongji (Liao Daozong), 20, 55, 117, 121, 125, 126, 156, 250, 256, 257, 263, 307, 310, 315, 346
Hongyan, 155
Hōryū-ji, 191, 347
Hu Jiao, 251
Hua gong, 38, 39, 68, 73, **122**, **137**, 139, 145, 161, **166**, 174, 177, 178, **196**, **203**, 208, 213, 217, 231, 330. *See also* Bracket sets; *Gong*
Huailing, 15, **235**, 254, 258
Huaizhou, 15, **235**, **236**, 253–256, 257, 398
Hualin Monastery, 76, 84, **92**, 95, **170**, **172**, **173**, **174**, 181, 188–193, 195, 203, 213, 214, 217, 222, 225, 237; bracket sets, 192; history, 188
Huang Huashan, 35
Huang Sheng tomb, 279
Huangchengdi, 154
Huayan Monastery, **118**, 123, 124–140, 147, 151, 270; history, 125–127; orientation, 139–140. *See also* Daxiongbao Hall; Haihui Hall; Sutra Library
Huimeng, 126
Humen yazi, 138, 145
Huntington and Metcalf, 253

Ideology (Qidan), 351
"Imperial dried meat," 10, 242
Interior pillars, **142**, 173. See also *Jin zhu*; *Nei zhu*
Inverted V-shaped strut/brace, 64, 75. See also *Chashou*
Ito Chuta, 141

Jade Emperor Hall. *See* Yuhuangmiao
Japanese architecture, 177, 222
Ji tuan, 49, 68. See also *Tuan*
Jiafu Monastery, 97, 98–99
Jiajing Ningxia xinzhi, 354
Jian, 38–39. See also *Ci jian*; *Cishao jian*; *Dangxin jian*; *Jin jian*; *Shao jian*
Jiao Xiyun, 88

Written By:
Jillian Krueger & Dennis Terdy

Illustrations By:
Kara Baichtal

Jillian Krueger is a full time mommy. She loves spending time with her family, traveling, and reading. She's a former teacher and reading specialist. She has instilled her love of reading in her children. You can never have too many books!

Dennis Terdy is Jillian's father. Raising three daughters and a son over a 14 year period, he has spent hours reading bedtime stories. With a career learning and teaching about languages, he enjoys watching his children pass on their own passions about language and reading.

Kara Baichtal is studying Economics at the University of Denver and is the babysitter of the kiddos that inspired this book! She enjoys cooking, reading, and playing with her dog, Mabel! She has had a passion for art throughout her entire life, and is excited to share this book with you!

Acknowledgements:

With gratitude to our family and friends for helping us create timeless scenarios around the bedtime ritual.

Ollie and Ellie are ready for bed. They have their jammies on and their teeth are brushed.

As mom tucks Ollie in, she says,
"Now, we've read our books and
sung our songs. Time for bed.
Good night sleepy head."

In Ellie's room, Dad is tucking her into bed and says, "Now, we've read our books and sung our songs. Time for bed. Good night sleepy head."

"Finally...
What a long day!" Mom says to
Dad as they settle in on the couch.

Mom quickly runs up to
Ollie's bedroom. "A meteor?
Really?"

"Good Night!"

"We've already said our prayers!" Dad says.

"Good Night!!"

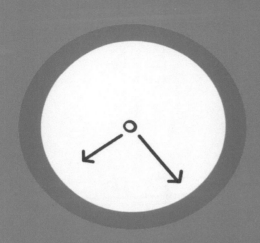

Dad sinks down in the couch next to Mom and sighs, "What a long day! This could go on forever…"

"Mom! Mom! I just heard a coyote!" screams Ollie.

"Dad! Dad! There's sand in my bed!" screams Ellie.

CPSIA information can be obtained
at www.ICGtesting.com
Printed in the USA
BVHW052330200720
584153BV00002B/12